C000128762

Cohabitation
Law, Practice and Precedents

Cohabitation
Law, Practice and Precedents

Sixth Edition

Helen Wood MA
District Judge

John Eames BA (Hons)
Barrister, Judge of the First-tier Tribunal (Social Entitlement and Immigration & Asylum Chambers) and Judge of the Court of Protection

Mark Harrop MA
Senior Associate, Collyer Bristow LLP

Ashley Murray LLB (Hons)
Barrister and Recorder

Angharad Palin, LLB (Hons), TEP, NP
Solicitor (non-practising) and Notary Public

David Salter MA, LLM
Joint National Head of Family Law, Mills & Reeve LLP, Deputy High Court Judge and Recorder

Family Law

Published by Family Law
A publishing imprint of Jordan Publishing Limited
21 St Thomas Street
Bristol BS1 6JS

Whilst the publishers and the author have taken every care in preparing the material included in this work, any statements made as to the legal or other implications of particular transactions are made in good faith purely for general guidance and cannot be regarded as a substitute for professional advice. Consequently, no liability can be accepted for loss or expense incurred as a result of relying in particular circumstances on statements made in this work.

© Jordan Publishing Limited 2015

All rights reserved. No part of this publication may be reproduced, stored in a retrieval system, or transmitted in any way or by any means, including photocopying or recording, without the written permission of the copyright holder, application for which should be addressed to the publisher.

Crown Copyright material is reproduced with kind permission of the Controller of Her Majesty's Stationery Office.

British Library Cataloguing-in-Publication Data

A catalogue record for this book is available from the British Library.

ISBN 978 1 84661 987 8

Typeset by Letterpart Limited, Caterham on the Hill, Surrey CR3 5XL

Printed in Great Britain by Hobbs the Printers Limited, Totton, Hampshire SO40 3WX

ACKNOWLEDGMENTS

The authors wish to thank David Burrows for his contribution to the child support and enforcement section of Chapter 5, and to acknowledge his help and advice along with Nick Wikeley, Desmond Rutledge, Andy King, Jane Gordois and Carole Broadwith.

They are also indebted to Professor Rebecca Probert for providing the much needed Introduction, and to Professor Chris Barton whose idea this was.

FOREWORD TO THE FIFTH EDITION

The ease with which a couple can opt for cohabitation, consciously or by default, belies the complexity that often attends the termination of their relationship.

In many respects legislation has provided safeguards and remedies that place cohabitants in a similar if not identical position to those who are married or in a civil partnership. In other important respects, notably property and financial provision, there has been a reluctance to do so. There are public policy arguments about the importance of marriage and the family for society, and counter arguments that point out that nearly half of all children are born outside marriage and the law should reflect the realities of family life in the 21st century.

Further attempts to legislate for inclusivity for cohabitants have been abandoned. As far as rights over property are concerned, these remain rooted in land law, equity and trusts. There is little or no discretion and the end result can often appear unfair.

The outcome of litigation can never be certain, and in disputes between cohabitants this is especially so. Many expensive arguments could be avoided if only cohabitants could be persuaded to take appropriate advice at the outset, whether as to beneficial interests on the purchase of the shared home or by the formalisation of agreed terms in a properly drafted cohabitation agreement.

The advice that cohabitants need reaches into all aspects of legal practice. This book provides a clear and authoritative exposition of the law, both contentious and non-contentious, with guidance on practice and procedure, precedents and checklists. It will be an invaluable reference for all those advising at every stage of a cohabitation relationship.

Eleanor King
High Court Judge, Family Division

PREFACE

The aim of this book is to assist practitioners when dealing with the particular requirements of those who are neither married nor in a civil partnership.

A lawyer will usually only be consulted when a relationship is either in difficulties or at an end. It is at this stage that myths as to entitlement to property and financial provision may have to be exploded. This is so especially in relation to property where there remains very little statutory protection for cohabitants and uncertainty abounds.

The approach of this book is that 'prevention is better than cure'. It is divided into ten sections. Each sets out the substantive law and, where appropriate, precedents and procedural guides. As such it is multi-disciplinary, enabling practitioners to advise clients fully at all stages of a cohabitation relationship, and on every aspect.

The law is as stated at 1 February 2015.

Helen Wood
February 2015

CONTENTS

TABLE OF CASES

References are to paragraph numbers.

TABLE OF STATUTES

References are to paragraph numbers.

TABLE OF STATUTORY INSTRUMENTS

References are to paragraph numbers.

TABLE OF INTERNATIONAL MATERIALS

References are to paragraph numbers.

TABLE OF ABBREVIATIONS

AA 1976	Adoption Act 1976
ACA 2002	Adoption and Children Act 2002
ASP	Additional State Pension
BDRA 1953	Births and Deaths Registration Act 1953
CA 1989	Children Act 1989
CCR	County Court Rules
CPA 2004	Civil Partnership Act 2004
CPR 1998	Civil Procedure Rules 1998
CSA 1991	Child Support Act 1991
CSPSSA 2002	Child Support, Pensions and Social Security Act 2002
CTC	Child tax credit
DVMPA 1976	Domestic Violence and Matrimonial Proceedings Act 1976
DVCVA 2004	Domestic Violence, Crime and Victims Act 2004
FA	Finance Act
FLA 1996	Family Law Act 1996
FLRA 1969	Family Law Reform Act 1969
FPFO 2008	Family Proceedings Fees Order 2008
FPR 2010	Family Procedure Rules 2010
HA	Housing Act
IA 1986	Insolvency Act 1986
IHTA 1984	Inheritance Tax Act 1984
I(PFD)A 1975	Inheritance (Provision for Family and Dependants) Act 1975
ITPA 2014	Inheritance and Trustees' Powers Act 2014
LPA	Lasting power of attorney
LPA 1925	Law of Property Act 1925
LRA 2002	Land Registration Act 2002
LR(MP)A 1970	Law Reform (Miscellaneous Provisions) Act 1970
LRR 2003	Land Registration Rules 2003
LTA 1927	Landlord and Tenant Act 1927
MCA 1973	Matrimonial Causes Act 1973
MPPA 1970	Matrimonial Proceedings and Property Act 1970
MWPA 1882	Married Women's Property Act 1882
PACE	Police and Criminal Evidence Act 1984
PHA 1997	Protection from Harassment Act 1997
PRAR 1991	Parental Responsibility Agreement Regulations 1991

RA 1977   Rent Act 1977
RSC   Rules of the Supreme Court
S2P   State Second Pension
SDLT   Stamp duty land tax
SERPS   State Earnings Related Pensions
SSCBA 1992   Social Security Contributions and Benefits Act 1992
TCA 2002   Tax Credits Act 2002
TLATA 1996   Trusts of Land and Appointment of Trustees Act 1996
UC   Universal credit
WTC   Working tax credit

INTRODUCTION

The need for a work that deals with the legal position of unmarried couples is greater today than ever before: the latest figures show that the number of cohabiting couples has reached 2.9 million,[1] and it has been predicted that by 2033 that number will have risen to 3.8 million, or one-quarter of all couples.[2] Cohabitation has become the norm for first partnerships, and while many will go on to marry their partner, many others will not.[3] While the availability of first civil partnerships and then same sex marriage has enabled thousands of couples to formalise their relationships who would not otherwise have been able to do so,[4] – and marriage is still the most popular family form, the number of couples living in unformalised relationships is clearly too significant for the law to ignore.

Yet the law has not as yet developed a comprehensive approach to cohabiting couples: in some contexts cohabitants are treated as if they were married, in others they are accorded lesser rights, and in yet others they have no rights at all, or at least none that are specific to their status as cohabitants. It is clear that many cohabitants, particularly women, experience disadvantage upon relationship breakdown.[5] Proposals for reform have proliferated in recent years, but as yet no action has been taken. Nor has there been any review of the totality of laws applicable to cohabiting couples in order to evaluate the coherence of the current approach.

In order to understand the current position – and in particular to understand how we got to where we are and why more progress has not been made – it is essential to understand something of the background. This introductory

---

[1] ONS, *Families and Households, 2013* (2013).

[2] ONS, *Marital Status population projections* (2010).

[3] B Wilson and R Stuchbury, 'Do partnerships last? Comparing marriage and cohabitation using longitudinal census data' (2010) 139 *Population Trends* 37 found that two-fifths of their 1991 sample of cohabiting adults had married their partner by 2001, while two-fifths had split up and the remaining one-fifth were still living together.

[4] By the end of 2012, 60,454 couples had entered into a civil partnership (ONS, *Civil Partnerships in the UK, 2012* (October 2013)), while in the first three months after the Marriage (Same Sex Couples) Act 2013 came into force on 29 March there were 1,409 marriages between persons of the same sex (ONS, *How many marriages of same sex couples have been formed in England and Wales so far?* (August 2014)).

[5] See eg J Miles and R Probert (eds) *Sharing Lives, Dividing Assets* (2009), chs 7 and 8.

chapter sets out a brief history of the extent and legal treatment of cohabitation, and then considers the challenges facing those responsible for advising modern cohabitants.

A BRIEF HISTORY OF COHABITATION

There is a widespread but erroneous belief that cohabitation was popular in earlier centuries, in particular the late-eighteenth and early-nineteenth centuries,[6] and that we are today seeing the revival of 'social marriage'.[7] In fact, rates of cohabitation were very low in this earlier period: the proportion of children born outside marriage barely edged above 5 per cent until the mid-nineteenth century,[8] and only a very small proportion of such children were born within cohabiting relationships.[9] Marriage in church was almost universal even before Lord Hardwicke's Clandestine Marriages Act of 1753 put the rules governing the formation of marriage on a statutory basis for the first time.[10]

Nor did the supposed strictness of the 1753 Act encourage couples to eschew legally-binding rites. The Act merely put the long-established canonical requirements for the formation of marriage on a statutory footing and gave them teeth by stipulating that a failure to comply with certain formalities would render the marriage void. Although observance of Anglican rites was therefore mandatory for all (save Jews and Quakers, who were exempted from the Act), there is little evidence that other Protestant dissenting sects had married according to their own rites before 1754, and ample evidence that they complied with the law after that date.[11] Similarly, although Catholics had shown a greater tendency to marry according to their own rites before the 1753 Act, in its wake the vast majority accepted the need to supplement the Catholic ceremony with a legally-binding Anglican marriage.[12] For the vast majority, religious nonconformity was not seen as a reason for refusing to formalise a relationship.

---

[6]   See eg J Gillis *For Better, For Worse: British Marriages 1600 to the Present* (1985); K O'Donovan, *Sexual Divisions in Law* (1985), p 46; S Parker *Informal Marriage, Cohabitation and the Law, 1754—1989* (1990), pp 14—27; A Diduck and F Kaganas *Family Law, Gender and the State: Text, Cases and Materials* (2nd edn, 2005), pp 58—60.

[7]   See eg S McRae *Cohabiting Mothers* (1993); A Barlow, S Duncan, G James and A Park *Cohabitation, Marriage and the Law: Social Change and Legal Reform in the 21st Century* (2005), p 53.

[8]   P Laslett 'Introduction: comparing illegitimacy over time and between cultures', ch 1 in P Laslett, K Oosterveen and R Smith *Bastardy and its Comparative History* (1980).

[9]   R Probert *Marriage Law and Practice in the Long Eighteenth Century: A Reassessment* (2009), ch 3.

[10] R Probert and L D'Arcy Brown 'The Impact of the Clandestine Marriages Act: Three Case-studies in Conformity' (2008) 23 Continuity and Change 309.

[11] See generally R Probert *Marriage Law and Practice in the Long Eighteenth Century: A Reassessment* (2009).

[12] R Probert and L D'Arcy Brown 'Catholics and the Clandestine Marriages Act of 1753' (2008) Local Population Studies 78.

Of course, there were always *some* couples who flouted the conventions of the time and who lived together unmarried. And the number of such couples undoubtedly increased during the nineteenth century, as more of the population moved to or grew up in an urban setting and as traditional controls and structures weakened. The very fact that such controls were weakening led some contemporary commentators to fulminate against the perceived immorality of the times: cohabitation was seen as characteristic of 'outcast London'.[13] The journalist Henry Mayhew, writing in the 1850s, certainly discovered a number of unmarried couples during his investigation of the lives of the London poor,[14] although some street sellers were so incensed by his claim that only one-tenth of them were formally married that they held a public meeting to protest.[15]

Even when marriage and the family came under increasing criticism towards the end of the nineteenth century, with radical intellectuals proposing new alternatives to formal, permanent marriage, few actually put such ideas into practice. The nascent feminist movement did not champion 'free unions': most believed that the preferable way forward was to reform the law of marriage and that cohabitation offered too little protection to women.[16]

Given the stigma that continued to attach to cohabiting relationships well into the 1950s,[17] it is unsurprising that cohabitation remained rare during this period. Indeed, it was not until the 1970s that cohabitation emerged as a statistically significant family form;[18] prior to this, as Mike Murphy has noted, 'under 1 per cent of women aged 18–49 were cohabiting'.[19] Since then, both pre-marital[20] and non-marital cohabitation have increased, as has the proportion of children born to cohabiting parents.[21]

What this tells us is that the current popularity of cohabitation is unprecedented, and that the English legal system has never had to deal with unformalised relationships on such a scale before. But how has English law reacted to the existence of such relationships?

---

[13] A Mearns *The Bitter Cry of Outcast London* (1883).

[14] H Mayhew *London Labour and the London Poor* (1851).

[15] R Probert *The Changing Legal Regulation of Cohabitation: From Fornicators to Family, 1600—2010* (2012).

[16] L Bland *Banishing the Beast: English Feminism and Sexual Morality 1885—1914* (1995).

[17] See R Probert 'Looking back on the overlooked: cohabitants and the law 1857—2007', in N Lowe and G Douglas (ed) *Family Law: Legacies and Prospects* (2009).

[18] See eg K Kiernan, H Land and J Lewis *Lone Motherhood in Twentieth Century Britain* (1998), p 40; J Haskey 'Cohabitational and marital histories of adults in Great Britain' (1999) 96 Population Trends 13.

[19] M Murphy 'The evolution of cohabitation in Britain, 1960-95' (2000) 54 Population Studies 43.

[20] J Haskey 'Spouses with identical residential addresses before marriage: an indicator of pre-marital cohabitation' (1997) 89 Population Trends 13.

[21] S Smallwood 'Characteristics of sole registered births and the mothers who register them' (2004) 117 Population Trends 20, table 1.

A BRIEF HISTORY OF COHABITATION LAW

Just as there are misunderstandings about the prevalence of cohabitation in times past, so too there is an equally widespread – and equally erroneous – belief that cohabiting couples would have enjoyed legal protection by means of a 'common-law marriage' prior to 1754. This rests on the double assumption that it was possible to marry by a simple exchange of consent before the Clandestine Marriages Act and that a cohabiting couple would be presumed to have exchanged such consent. However, given that a bare exchange of consent carried no legal rights – other than that of insisting that the marriage be solemnised in church – such a presumption would have conferred no legal protection on cohabitants.[22] There *was* a presumption that couples who had cohabited and were reputed to have married had in fact gone through a legally binding ceremony of marriage, but several points need to be noted. First, it should be borne in mind that the presumption operated against a background in which cohabitation was punishable as fornication: cohabitation gave rise to a presumption that the parties were married precisely because it was assumed that no one would cohabit unless they were married. Similarly, couples would not enjoy the reputation of married couples within the community unless there was reason to believe that they had married. At a time when the community was responsible, through the poor law, for the support of those settled in the parish, and when children born outside marriage obtained a legal settlement in the parish of their birth, neighbours had good reason to check the marital status of any newcomers. Secondly, and vitally, the presumption only operated in certain contexts, where a child or remoter issue of the supposed marriage was claiming an interest and was unable to provide precise details. Given the unsatisfactory state of registration and record-keeping at the time, there would have been many formally-celebrated marriages of which no documentary evidence existed. The presumption was therefore an evidentiary tool to allow other means of proving a legal marriage rather than a mechanism for equating the married and the unmarried. Finally, it should be noted that the presumption does, in theory, still exist – although given the very different conditions of modern society it will rarely be appropriate for the courts to presume that a marriage has taken place where there is no formal evidence.[23]

So, how *did* the law treat cohabiting couples? The practice of presenting and punishing cohabiting couples for fornication had died out almost everywhere by the late eighteenth century, and over the course of the following century the law rarely engaged with cohabitants save when they obtruded themselves on its notice.[24] There were of course a few cases in which cohabitants were involved in disputes over contracts, trusts, and wills (with varying degrees of success), but the family law of the time – known then as the law of domestic relations – was exclusively concerned with marriage.

---

[22]   See R Probert 'Common law marriage: myths and misunderstandings' [2008] CFLQ 1.

[23]   See eg *Martin v Myers* [2004] EWHC 1947 (Ch).

[24]   See eg G Frost *Living in Sin* (2008), for examples of cases in which cohabiting couples were involved.

As the state began to intervene more directly in family life, however, there was some limited recognition of cohabiting relationships. Section 17 of the Prevention of Cruelty to Children (Amendment) Act 1894 provided that rules designed to protect children against their parents should apply to step-parents and 'to any person cohabiting with the parent of the child', while under the Workman's Compensation Act of 1906 children born outside marriage could claim compensation on the same footing as legitimate children.

But it took a national emergency for rights to be extended to unmarried partners: the outbreak of the First World War saw separation allowances being extended to all dependants of soldiers – including the so-called 'unmarried wives' – and provision was also made for such women to receive a pension in the case of the soldier's death or injury.[25] Such provision was, however, less generous than that conferred on legal wives. Post-war unemployment was similarly seen as a national, short-term emergency, leading to the provision of dependants' allowances for women living with unemployed workers.[26] But there was concern about the explicit recognition of unmarried relationships, and in 1927 the law was changed to limit such allowances to women who had care of the unemployed worker's children. Of course, such a woman might well be the mother of those children, but the change in terminology allowed a veneer of respectability to be preserved. Had the original wording remained on the statute book, it might have provided a precedent for further reform, but this was not to be.

In the meantime, a more durable principle had been introduced by the Widows' Orphans' and Old Age Contributory Pensions Act, which stipulated that widows who remarried or cohabited would not be entitled to receive a pension. The application of the 'cohabitation rule' was extended to new contexts in the wake of the Second World War, as the state assumed greater responsibility for the welfare of its citizens.[27] But the growing financial burden of such provision – and increasing suspicion that women were obtaining benefits fraudulently by failing to disclose a cohabiting relationship – led to a renewed scrutiny of cohabiting relationships. After 1964, the undisclosed presence of a man in the household of a woman who was in receipt of national assistance was sufficient ground to prosecute her for fraud: it was no longer necessary to establish that he was actually supporting her.

And of course women had no legal means of securing support from cohabiting partners. It was not until the 1970s that the law began to make positive provision for cohabitants – but then, as we have seen, it was not until the 1970s that couples began to cohabit in significant numbers. The Inheritance (Provision for Family and Dependants) Act 1975 allowed a wider range of 'dependants' to claim provision from the estate of a deceased individual, the Domestic Violence and Matrimonial Proceedings Act 1976 enabled the courts to grant an injunction to protect cohabitants against domestic violence, and

---

[25] R Probert '"Unmarried Wives" in War and Peace' [2005] CFLQ 1.

[26] Unemployed Workers' Dependants (Temporary Provision) Act 1921, s 1(2).

[27] See eg National Insurance (Industrial Injuries) Act 1946, s 88(3).

'reputed' spouses were included as dependants under the Pneumoconiosis (Workers' Compensation) Act 1979. Cohabitants also benefited from reforms to the general law: the rejection of the 'family assets' doctrine in *Pettitt v Pettitt*[28] and *Gissing v Gissing*,[29] and the reiteration that interests in the family home were to be determined by principles of trusts law, did have one benefit for cohabiting couples, in that judicial creativity was refocused on the boundaries of the constructive trust, which, unlike the earlier family assets doctrine, applied outside marital relationships.[30] Such changes were both a product of, and encouraged, a greater social acceptance of cohabitation.[31]

Yet there was clearly no coherent policy of extending rights to cohabiting couples, as is evident from the fact that they were excluded from other contemporary pieces of legislation dealing with family issues.[32] The Law Commission did consider carrying out a review of the legal position of unmarried couples at this time, but decided against it on the grounds that the topic was one 'largely governed by considerations of social and financial policy.'[33] And in the 1980s there was a shift in social policy that led to limits being placed on a number of the doctrines developed in the previous decade.[34] The few reforms benefiting cohabiting couples to be passed by the Conservative administration of the time focused on the established categories of the bereaved cohabitant[35] and the victim of domestic violence (and even this was controversial, as evidenced by the reaction to the Family Homes and Domestic Violence Bill in 1995[36]). By contrast, those living with a bankrupt were – contrary to the recommendations of the Cork Report[37] – not included within the scope of new rules protecting the family home.[38] Moreover, same sex relationships were specifically stigmatised as 'pretended family relationships' by s 28 of the Local Government Act 1988.

The 1980s did, however, witness a number of developments affecting cohabitants in their role as parents. The Family Law Reform Act 1987 removed most of the negative legal consequences of being born outside marriage, while the Children Act 1989 marked a decisive shift away from marriage to

---

[28] [1970] AC 777.

[29] [1971] AC 886.

[30] See eg *Cooke v Head* [1972] 2 All ER 38.

[31] See eg R Probert 'Common law marriage: myths and misunderstandings' [2008] CFLQ 1.

[32] For example, the Fatal Accidents Act 1976 and the Domestic Proceedings and Magistrates' Courts Act 1978.

[33] Law Commission *Fourteenth Annual Report, 1978—79* Law Com No 97 (1980), para 2.32.

[34] R Probert, 'Cohabitation in Twentieth Century England and Wales: Law and Policy' (2004) 26 Law and Policy 13.

[35] See eg the Administration of Justice Act 1982, defining cohabitants as dependants for the purposes of the Fatal Accidents Act 1976; Law Reform (Succession) Act 1995, amending the Inheritance (Provision for Family and Dependants) Act and obviating the need for cohabitants to bring themselves within the concept of 'dependant'.

[36] S Doughty 'Anger at Bill to "sabotage" marriage' (1995); W Oddie, 'How could MPs fail to spot this blow to marriage?' *Daily Mail* 23 October 1995.

[37] Cork Report, *Insolvency Law and Practice: Report of the Review Committee* Cmnd 8558 (London: HMSO, 1982).

[38] R Probert 'The security of the home and the home as security' in R Probert (ed) *Family Life and the Law: Under One Roof* (Ashgate, 2007).

parenthood as the basis for rights and responsibilities. The desirability of assisting cohabiting couples to have children was, however, a much more contested issue. The appropriate status of the male partner of a woman receiving fertility treatment was not even considered in the original draft of the Human Fertilisation and Embryology Bill, and when a clause dealing with the issue was introduced it was with the grudging message that it 'should not be seen as encouraging unmarried people to use infertility treatments'.[39]

At the start of the twenty-first century the focus shifted to those who could not marry: same sex couples were accepted as members of each other's family in *Fitzpatrick v Sterling Housing Association*,[40] while in *Ghaidan v Mendoza* the House of Lords was willing to accept that such couples could be described as living together 'as husband and wife'. More significantly, the passage of the Civil Partnership Act 2004 provided same sex couples with a means of formalising their relationship and thereby acquiring virtually the same rights and responsibilities as married couples; it also equated the legal position of same sex and opposite-sex cohabitants.

Yet although this was a significant improvement in the legal position of same sex cohabitants, the legal regime to which they were now subject was far from comprehensive. The lack of any substantial progress in the treatment of cohabiting couples more generally was in part due to the fact that the equality agenda of the Labour government that had led to the 2004 Act (and which is evident in the recent Human Fertilisation and Embryology Act 2008) was combined with a clear preference for marriage over cohabitation.[41] However, the fact that no provision was made for heterosexual cohabitants – in contrast to an earlier bill introduced by Lord Lester, which had sought to address both formal and unformalised relationships – provoked new calls for reform, and in 2005 the Law Commission began a project examining the legal consequences of relationship breakdown for cohabiting couples.

A substantial consultation paper was produced with impressive swiftness and thoroughness,[42] and in 2007 the Law Commission set out its recommendations.[43] The key features of the recommended scheme were that cohabiting couples who had satisfied certain eligibility criteria (basically, having had a child together or having lived together for a certain period) should be able to apply for financial relief on separation unless they had specifically opted out of the scheme. The applicant would also have to prove that he or she had experienced economic disadvantage and/or that the respondent had a retained benefit as a result of the applicant's 'qualifying' contributions – these being defined as 'any contribution arising from the cohabiting relationship which is made to the parties' shared lives or to the

---

[39] Hansard (HL) 20/3/90, vol 517, col 209.
[40] [2000] 1 FLR 271.
[41] See eg Home Office *Supporting Families* (1998), para 4.3.
[42] *Cohabitation: the financial consequences of relationship breakdown – A Consultation Paper* Law Com CP No 179 (2006).
[43] *Cohabitation: the financial consequences of relationship breakdown* Law Com No 307 (2007).

welfare of members of their families'.[44] The level of financial relief would then be determined by the court first reversing the retained benefit and then sharing any remaining economic disadvantage, but in both cases only in so far as it deemed this 'reasonable and practicable', having regard to a list of discretionary factors (including the welfare of any minor children, the financial needs, obligations and resources of both parties, and their conduct).

In March 2008, the then Government indicated that it would examine the operation of similar principles in Scotland before deciding whether the scheme should be introduced in England and Wales,[45] and in 2011, the coalition Government that had been elected in 2011 announced that it did not intend to take forward the Law Commission's recommendations for reform during its existing term in office.[46]

In the meantime, Lord Lester, in conjunction with Resolution, then announced his intention to introduce a bill to reform the rights of cohabiting couples.[47] The Cohabitation Bill introduced into the House of Lords on 11 December 2008 adopted a more discretionary approach, while incorporating the concepts of economic advantage and disadvantage within the list of factors to be taken into account. The Bill received a second reading in the House of Lords,[48] but failed to proceed any further.

Subsequently, in a review of the law relating to intestacy and family provision claims, the Law Commission further recommended that a surviving cohabitant should automatically be entitled to receive a share of the deceased's estate under the intestacy rules.[49] It was proposed that a cohabitant of five years' standing should receive the same as a spouse. Where the cohabiting relationship had lasted between two and five years, the survivor would receive 50 per cent of what a spouse would have received. However, if the couple had had a child together, the surviving cohabitant should automatically receive the same as a spouse would have done, regardless of the duration of the relationship. The Cohabitants (Inheritance) Bill 2012 sought to give effect to these proposals, but like its predecessors failed to proceed beyond a second reading.[50]

At present, therefore, legislative reform seems unlikely.

---

[44] Above, para 4.34.
[45] Ministerial Statement to Parliament, Hansard HC vol 472 col 22WS (6 March 2008). For information on the operation of the scheme in Scotland, see the briefing paper issued by the Centre for Research on Families and Relationships, 'No longer living together: how does Scots cohabitation law work in practice?' (2010).
[46] Hansard HL, vol 730, col 118; HC, vol 532, cols 15—16WS (6 September 2011).
[47] *Reforming the law for people who live together: A consultation paper* (2008).
[48] Hansard HL, vol 708, col 1413 (13 March 2009).
[49] Law Commission, *Intestacy and Family Provision Claims on Death*, Consultation Paper No 191.
[50] See http://services.parliament.uk/bills/2012-13/inheritancecohabitants.html.

THE COHABITANT AS CLIENT

In the meantime, one challenge for the lawyer in this context may be the very basic one of disabusing their clients of the belief that cohabitation already entails certain legal rights and responsibilities. A survey carried out in 2000 found that 56 per cent of the general population, and 59 per cent of cohabiting couples, believed that cohabiting couples had a 'common-law marriage', which conferred the same rights as if they were married.[51] The Living Together Campaign (funded by the then Department of Constitutional Affairs) was subsequently launched to inform cohabitants of their (lack of) rights. That it enjoyed only modest success in dispelling the common law marriage myth is clear from a subsequent study. This found that the numbers believing in the existence of common law marriage fell slightly (to 51 per cent of the general population and 53 per cent of cohabitants), but that belief was being replaced by uncertainty rather than by knowledge of the correct legal position, the percentage who were unsure of the legal position having risen from 6 per cent in the earlier study to 10 per cent in the later one.[52] More recent research has confirmed 'substantial and ongoing public misunderstanding of cohabitation law'.[53]

Such uncertainty – and the persisting belief in common law marriage – may in part be due to the way in which cohabitation is discussed in the media. It was during the late 1970s – when discussions of the new legal rights being conferred on cohabitants regularly overstated the extent of legal protection – that the common law marriage myth emerged.[54] And today, for every article highlighting the fact that there is no such thing as common law marriage, there are many more using terms such as 'common law wife' or 'common law husband' to refer to cohabiting individuals.[55] And the modern tendency to present proposals for reform as presaging imminent change may well lead couples to believe that, even if they do not yet enjoy legal rights, they soon will.[56]

Couples who believe that they already enjoy legal rights are by definition unlikely to seek advice as to how to acquire them. But even those who do *not* believe that they are protected by a common law marriage do not always take steps to put matters on a legal footing by making contracts, declarations of

---

[51] A Barlow, S Duncan, G James and A Park 'Just a piece of paper? Marriage and cohabitation in Britain' in A Park, J Curtice, K Thomson, L Jarvis and C Bromley (eds) *British social attitudes: the 18th report* (2001).

[52] A Barlow, C Burgoyne, E Clery and J Smithson 'Cohabitation and the law: myths, money and the media' in A Park, J Curtice, K Thompson, M Phillips and E Clery (eds) *British social attitudes – the 24th report* (2008).

[53] P Pleasence and N J Balmer, 'Ignorance in Bliss: Modelling Knowledge of Rights in Marriage and Cohabitation' (2012) *Law & Society Review* 297, p 321.

[54] R Probert, 'The evolution of the common law marriage myth' [2011] Fam Law 283.

[55] R Probert 'Why do couples still believe in common law marriage?' [2007] Fam Law 403.

[56] See eg C Dyer 'Unmarried couples to get new rights: Reforms will cover gay relationships', *The Guardian*, 31 May 2006; M Kite 'Unmarried couples to get rights on property: Harriet Harman announced plans to bring forward legislation', *The Sunday Telegraph*, 15 October 2006.

trust, or wills. Many are put off by the perceived cost of legal advice; others fall prey to an 'optimism bias', believing that their relationship will endure.[57] Even those who are involved in a legal transaction – for example the purchase of a home in joint names – often misunderstand the advice that they are given or are not made aware of its potential implications for their future relationship.[58]

It should also be noted that the fact that an individual does *not* believe in common law marriage does not necessarily mean that they have a correct understanding of the law. Here, again, the presentation of the issue in the media may play a part. Articles debunking the common law marriage myth tend to emphasise cohabitants' lack of legal rights and rarely draw attention to the rights that they do enjoy.[59] This may go some way to explaining why cohabitants are far less likely than married couples to seek legal advice upon relationship breakdown:[60] if they believe that they have *no* legal rights then there will be no reason for them to consult a solicitor.

For those that do make it through the doors of a solicitor's office, it is clearly essential that they obtain accurate and comprehensive advice as to the legal options that *are* available to them. It is the aim of the chapters that follow to assist in the task of providing such advice.

Rebecca Probert
Professor of Law, University of Warwick

---

[57] A Barlow, C Burgoyne and J Smithson *The Living Together Campaign – an investigation of its impact on legally aware cohabitants* (2007).

[58] See eg G Douglas, J Pearce and H Woodward 'Cohabitation and conveyancing practice: problems and solutions' [2008] Conv 365; M Pawlowski and J Brown, 'Joint Purchasers and the presumption of joint beneficial ownership – a matter of informed choice?' (2013) Tru L I 3.

[59] See eg J Husband 'Your money: not marrying is a rights thing to do', *Mirror*, 11 October 2008.

[60] S Arthur, J Lewis, M Maclean, S Finch and R Fitzgerald *Settling Up: Making Financial Arrangements After Separation* (National Centre for Social Research, 2002).

CHAPTER 1

PROPERTY

PART A   LAW AND PRACTICE

SECTION 1   OWNERSHIP OF THE HOME

1.1   Introduction

As many cohabitants discover to their surprise, and often to their cost, living together does not in itself found an interest in the shared home.

When a relationship of cohabitation breaks down the court does not have the power to make orders in relation to property on the same discretionary basis as if the parties were married to one another or in a civil partnership and making application for a financial remedy.[1] Instead, cohabitants are reliant on the principles of land and trust law to determine any dispute regarding the ownership of property.

Mindful of the rise in the number of people living together without getting married or entering a civil partnership, in 2002, the Law Commission published a discussion paper 'Sharing Homes'. This concluded that:

> 'It is not possible however to devise a statutory scheme for the ascertainment and quantification of beneficial interests in the shared home which can operate fairly and evenly across the diversity of domestic circumstances which are now to be encountered.'[2]

However, in a subsequent report, *Cohabitation: The Financial Consequences of Relationship Breakdown*[3] the Law Commission recommended the provision of a new statutory scheme of financial relief for cohabitants who fulfil specific eligibility criteria, having either had a child together or lived together for a minimum period. The provision proposed was analogous to that provided to those on breakdown of a marriage or civil partnership. The recommendations met with a lukewarm response from government and it has been made clear that reforms will not be made during the current parliamentary term.

---

[1]   Matrimonial Causes Act 1973 (MCA 1973), s 25; CPA 2004.
[2]   Law Com No 278 (November 2002).
[3]   Law Com No 307 (July 2007).

1.2   The duty of the solicitor on the purchase of a shared home

If a solicitor is instructed in the purchase of a property by an unmarried couple, or others who intend to share the occupation of the property, the following duties arise:[4]

–   to explain the differences between beneficial joint tenancies and tenancies in common;[5]

–   to assess and explain the advantages and disadvantages of holding the beneficial title as joint tenants as against holding as tenants in common;[6]

–   to assist the prospective purchasers to reach a decision as to how to deal with the beneficial interest and, if necessary, to advise one or more of the parties to obtain independent legal advice;[7]

–   to record how the beneficial interests are to be held.[8]

A large number of cohabitants will by-pass the opportunity to have legal advice either because they move into a property which has already been acquired by the other cohabitant, or because they are simply not involved in the purchase. In the latter case, a solicitor will have a duty nonetheless to enquire whether any other person is to contribute to the purchase price or is otherwise likely to be beneficially interested in the property.[9] This duty applies even where the solicitor is not also acting for a mortgagee.

Despite a number of stern judicial warnings as to the culpability of solicitors who fail to make pertinent enquiries and give appropriate advice to prospective purchasers, there still appears to be a reticence about declaring the beneficial interests.[10] There are a number of possible explanations for this.

---

4   In *Carlton v Goodman* [2000] 2 FLR 259 Ward LJ wearily reminded conveyancers 'that they would save their clients a great deal of later difficulty if only they would sit the purchasers down, explain the difference between a joint tenancy and a tenancy in common, ascertain what they want and then expressly declare in the conveyance or transfer how the beneficial interest is to be held because that will be conclusive and save all argument'.

5   *Taylor and Harman v Warners* (unreported) 21 July 1987, summarised in *The Law Society's Gazette* 29 June 1988 at pp 26 and 27. Warner J said that merely to inform the purchasers of the survivorship right in a beneficial joint tenancy is 'perfunctory'.

6   See *Taylor and Harman v Warners* (above): it is not sufficient simply to explain the difference between the two.

7   The SRA Code of Conduct 2011, chapter 3.

8   See **1.3** below.

9   *City of London Building Society v Flegg* [1988] AC 54; *Walker v Hall* [1984] FLR 126.

10   'I ask in despair how often this court has to remind conveyancers that they would save their clients a great deal of later difficulty if only they would sit the purchasers down, explain the difference between a joint tenancy and a tenancy in common, ascertain what they want and then expressly declare in the conveyance or transfer how the beneficial interest is to be held because that will be conclusive and save all argument. When are conveyancers going to do this as a matter of invariable standard practice? This court has urged that time after time. Perhaps conveyancers do not read the law reports. I will try one more time: ALWAYS TRY TO AGREE ON AND THEN RECORD HOW THE BENEFICIAL INTEREST IS TO BE HELD. It is not very difficult to do.' Lord Justice Ward in *Carlton v Goodman* [2002] 2 FLR 259.

– In most cases the purchasers themselves give no consideration to the question of beneficial ownership when they acquire the property.[11]

– To declare the trusts might well be construed as demonstrating a lack of optimism that the relationship will succeed. It could be taken as an assumption that the relationship will fail, sooner or later, and there may be a fear that to insist on declaring the trusts could precipitate this.

– It is necessary to ask probing personal questions. To ask them can be embarrassing for the practitioner; to answer them can be embarrassing for the clients.

– Some practitioners may feel that the exercise serves little useful purpose where the couple intends eventually to marry or become civil partners, because the court will have the power to adjust the beneficial interests in the event that the marriage or civil partnership breaks down.

– There are various ways of calculating the beneficial interests.[12] It may be difficult to decide, when a couple purchases, which method of calculation will produce the fairest result when they come to sell.

– Family finances are often pooled, which can make it difficult to pinpoint the exact contributions made by either party towards the mortgage payments.

– There have been one or two judicial statements to the effect that shares can only be assessed arithmetically when the property is bought outright, and that there is no place for mathematical calculations where generally the property is purchased with the aid of a mortgage.[13]

– The potential immutability of a declaration of trust is often an inhibiting factor. Having 'fixed' the beneficial interests on acquisition, what happens if the co-owners' circumstances change? In theory, another declaration of trust should be executed to record the variation, but in practice it is unlikely to happen. It may be thought to be preferable to rely upon the principles of implied trusts in the absence of an express declaration.

– There is competition between conveyancers to cut purchase costs to a minimum, particularly in the first-time buyers' market. Proper advice and documentation concerning the beneficial interests can add substantially to the costs.[14]

---

[11] 'When two people are about to be married and are negotiating for a matrimonial home it does not naturally enter the head of either to enquire carefully, still less to agree, what should happen to the house if the marriage comes to grief' (*Re Rogers' Question* [1948] 1 All ER 328, per Evershed LJ). 'In a great many cases, perhaps in the vast majority, no consideration will have been given by the parties ... to the question of beneficial ownership of the home at the time that is being acquired' (*Gissing v Gissing* [1970] 2 All ER 780 at 785, per Viscount Dilhorne).

[12] See **1.7–1.13** below.

[13] 'Where the house is bought outright and not on mortgage, the extent of their respective shares will depend upon a more-or-less precise arithmetical calculation of the extent of their contributions to the purchase price. Where, on the other hand, and as is more usual nowadays, the house is bought with the aid of a mortgage, then the court has to assess each of the parties' respective contributions in a broad sense' (*Burns v Burns* [1984] FLR 216 at 241G, per May LJ).

[14] Compare: 'The additional costs would be insignificant' (*Cowcher v Cowcher* [1972] 1 All ER 943 at 959h, per Bagnall J).

–   Sometimes there is a conflict, or a potential conflict of interests between the buyers. The need to obtain independent legal advice would further increase the costs.

–   Declarations of trust do not fall completely or comfortably within the province of a conveyancer, a trust lawyer or a family lawyer. It is sometimes difficult to establish who is best suited to advise on, negotiate or draft a declaration. Having to refer to several people in the same firm could increase the costs.

–   There is a mistaken belief amongst lawyers that failing to enquire about and declare the beneficial interests is not negligent.

1.3 Declaring the beneficial interests on acquisition

It will always be preferable to have a clear statement of the cohabitants' intentions with regard to the ownership of property that is recorded at the time of acquisition, than to have to rely on the courts to determine the position at a later date in the event of a dispute.

To be effective as a declaration of the beneficial interests, all the formalities must be complied with.

1.4 Express declaration of trust

An express declaration of trust in respect of land is an instrument in writing, which is signed by the person or persons competent to declare the trust and which records the beneficial interests of those who are entitled to the land, its net proceeds of sale and its net income until sale.[15]

Even if the declaration of trust is not signed a draft may be evidence of intention and be upheld by the court.[16]

In the absence of an express declaration of trust, it is open to anyone claiming a beneficial interest in the land to rely on the doctrines of implied trusts, resulting trusts and constructive trusts, which are exempt from the written formalities.[17] An interest could also be claimed on the basis of proprietory estoppel[18] or contract.[19]

1.5 Effects of an express declaration of trust

Section 53(1)(b) of the LPA 1925 states that:

---

[15]   Law of Property Act 1925 (LPA 1925), s 53(1)(b) (see **1.5** below).
[16]   *Williamson v Sheikh* [2008] EWCA Civ 990.
[17]   Law of Property Act 1925 (LPA 1925), s 53(2).
[18]   As in *Pascoe v Turner* [1979] 1 WLR 431.
[19]   As in *Tanner v Tanner* [1975] 1 WLR 1346.

'a declaration of trust respecting any land or any interest therein must be manifested and proved by some writing signed by some person who is able to declare such trust or by his will.'

The trust does not need to be declared in writing at the time of its creation. A subsequent declaration will suffice, provided that it is in existence before any action is brought.[20]

Although there is no legal requirement that there should be more than one deed, it is considered better practice to keep the trusts off the title.[21] So, generally, there will be two deeds: one (the transfer) vesting the legal estate in a sole owner or in the trustees of land; and the other (the declaration of trust) setting out the beneficial interests.

An express declaration of trust which comprehensively declares the beneficial interests in the property and its proceeds of sale is conclusive unless and until it is varied by those who are competent to vary it, or it is rectified or set aside on the grounds of fraud or mistake.[22] However, such a declaration is only conclusive as to the position at the time when the trust is declared.[23] Subsequent events may cause the beneficial interests to vary.

An express declaration of trust can be varied provided that the variation is manifested and proved by an instrument in writing signed by the person or persons able to vary the original trusts.[24] The new trusts will then operate by virtue of the new instrument.[25] The beneficial interests may in certain circumstances also be varied by an order of the court.[26]

1.6 Land Registry Forms; restrictions and cautions[27]

Since 1 December 1990 every district in England and Wales has been an area of compulsory registration of title.[28]

---

[20] *Rochefoucauld v Boustead* [1897] 1 Ch 196 at 206.

[21] 'The declaration of beneficial trusts could perfectly well have been contained in a separate document altogether off the face of the title to the land, and many conveyancers would regard that as the more proper method of proceeding' (*Wilson v Wilson* [1969] 3 All ER 945 at 948H, per Buckley J).

[22] *Goodman v Gallant* [1986] 1 FLR 513 at 517C.

[23] 'If that document declares not merely in whom the legal title is to vest but in whom the beneficial title is to vest, that necessarily concludes the question of title as between the (co-owners) for all time, and in the absence of fraud or mistake at the time of the transaction the parties cannot go behind it at any time thereafter even on death or the break-up of the marriage' (*Pettitt v Pettitt* [1970] AC 777 at 813E, per Lord Upjohn).

[24] 'The trust and the equitable interests arising under it cannot be changed except with the consent of all interested parties' (*Cowcher v Cowcher* [1972] 1 All ER 943 at 950f, per Bagnall J).

[25] *Re Holmden's Settlement Trusts* [1968] AC 685 at 713D, per Lord Wilberforce.

[26] For example: Matrimonial Causes Act 1973 (MCA 1973), s 24; Inheritance (Provision for Family and Dependants) Act 1975 (I(PFD)A 1975), s 9; Insolvency Act 1986 (IA 1986), s 339; Children Act 1989 (CA 1989), Sch 1.

[27] See, generally, Ruoff and Roper *Registered Conveyancing* (Sweet & Maxwell, Looseleaf).

[28] Land Registration Act 2002 (LRA 2002), s 4. Registration of title to land was introduced in Scotland by the Land Registration (Scotland) Act 1979.

The Land Registry is not interested in trusts and, as far as possible, any reference to a trust must be excluded from the registers.[29]

Except where joint proprietors are beneficial joint tenants, in order to give effect to the concurrent or successive interests in the land they hold, joint proprietors should apply for the entry of the appropriate restriction on the register.[30]

The standard restriction that is inserted by the Land Registry is as follows:

RESTRICTION: No disposition by a sole proprietor of the registered estate (except a trust corporation) under which capital money arises is to be registered unless authorised by an order of the court.

When official copies of the entries are obtained, the presence of this restriction on the register means that the property is not held as joint tenants so that the surviving registered proprietor cannot sell the property without appointing a second trustee. It will either be held as tenants in common by the registered proprietors or on some other trusts under which the registered proprietors hold as trustees and which may also include other persons as beneficiaries. It is not possible to establish the trusts on which the property is held from the register and other documentation will have to be investigated.

The standard forms of transfers (Land Registry Forms TR1 (Transfer of Whole) (see **1.193** below) TP1 (Transfer of Part) and FR1 (on first registration) give three boxes to tick, depending on whether the property is to be held as joint tenants, tenants in common in equal shares or as otherwise specified by the joint proprietors. The third box can be used to indicate that the property is held as tenants in common in unequal shares, although this will not appear on the register. It can also be used to refer to another document, eg a declaration of trust or will. The transfer should also be executed by the transferees. Often it is not, particularly where no indemnity covenant is given.

In the case of a beneficial joint tenancy, it is only necessary to tick the relevant box on the transfer. In the case of a beneficial tenancy in common, it is considered best practice to declare the beneficial interests in an instrument entirely separate from the transfer itself.[31] In any event, the transfer is usually retained by the Land Registry and it may be difficult to obtain a copy.

---

[29]   Land Registration Act 2002, s 78.

[30]   The form to be used for a standard Form A restriction on severance of a joint tenancy is Form SEV and it must be signed by the applicants or their solicitors. Unless the applicants are the registered proprietors, their signed consent is required or other evidence that the applicant has sufficient interest to have a restriction registered (Land Registration Rules 2003 (LRR 2003), rr 91–95). Modifications of restrictions are made using Form RX2, cancellations Form RX3 and withdrawals RX4 in accordance with LRR 2003, rr 96–99. See generally Ruoff and Roper (above).

[31]   *Wilson v Wilson* [1969] 3 All ER 945 at 948.

It may be necessary for a person who is not on the Land Registry Title as a proprietor, but who believes that he or she has a beneficial interest in the property, to take steps to prevent a disposition of the property. A restriction may be registered on the Title by a non-owner to prevent a contravention of s 6(6) or (8) of the TLATA 1996 (see footnote 32 to this paragraph). Alternatively, a person claiming a beneficial interest in the land may register a caution. A Caution Against First Registration will be appropriate where the land is unregistered. This gives the person entering the caution the right to receive notice of any transaction affecting the property, and 14 days in which to make an objection. Cautions Against Dealings were abolished from 13 October 2003 by the Land Registration Act 2002. Rights previously protected by a Caution Against Dealings must now be protected by a notice or restriction. An interest under a trust of land or settlement cannot be protected by a notice and so the only method of protection now available is a restriction.[32]

Expressing the shares

1.7   *Fixed shares and floating shares*

Usually, the co-owners' shares of the net proceeds of sale are ascertained or fixed at the time of purchase.[33] In this book, such shares are referred to as *fixed shares*.

In the absence of any deed or variation executed by those who are competent to vary the original trusts, and in the absence of any court order, fixed shares remain static throughout the duration of the trust of land.[34]

Alternatively, and more unusually in practice, the ascertainment of the shares can be deferred until the property is sold, and then determined in the light of the actual contributions made by either party while the trust of land subsisted.[35] In this book, such shares are referred to as *floating shares*.[36]

The effect of executing a declaration of trust which creates floating shares is much the same as expressly creating a resulting trust and a constructive trust at the outset.

---

32   Land Registration Act 2002, s 33(a).
33   'In the absence of any special circumstances ... the time at which the beneficial interest crystallises is the time of the acquisition' (*Bernard v Josephs* (1983) 4 FLR 178 at 188F, per Griffiths LJ).
34   *Pettitt v Pettitt* [1970] AC 777 at 813E.
35   'There is nothing inherently improbable in their acting on the understanding that the wife should be entitled to a share which was not quantified immediately on the acquisition of the home, but should be left to be determined when the mortgage was repaid or the property disposed of, on the basis of what would be fair having regard to the total contributions, direct or indirect, which each spouse had made by that date' (*Gissing v Gissing* [1970] 2 All ER 780 at 793d, per Lord Diplock).
36   The expression 'floating shares' is not a technical term. They could be referred to as, say, 'deferred shares'. When floating shares crystallise, they become fixed.

1.8   The advantages of fixed shares

Ascertaining or 'fixing' the co-owners' shares of the net proceeds of sale when they purchase the property has a number of advantages.[37] They include the following.

–   Certainty. The position is clear from the start.

–   At any given time each co-owner can work out approximately how much he or she would be entitled to receive if the property were sold.

–   Simplicity. All that is needed to work out 'who gets what' is a completion statement when the property is sold or – during the subsistence of the trust – a current valuation of the property and a mortgage redemption statement or a statement of the surrender value of any mortgage-linked insurance policy.

–   Convenience. There is less paperwork needed than for floating shares. There is no need for the co-owners to keep receipts and accounts as evidence of their respective contributions.

–   If the co-owners' circumstances change (eg if their contributions towards the mortgage payments vary, or if they contribute disproportionately towards the cost of any repairs and improvements to the property) the imbalance can be rectified by means of a supplemental declaration of trust.

–   The fixed share system enables one co-owner to confer a gratuitous benefit on the other – if that is the intention.[38]

1.9   The disadvantages of fixed shares

The fixed share system is not without its disadvantages.[39]

–   Fixed shares are potentially immutable. They conclude the question of title between the co-owners for all time 'and in the absence of fraud or mistake at the time of the transaction the parties cannot go behind the declaration of trust at any time thereafter, even on death or the breakdown of their relationship'.[40]

–   Circumstances change. What seemed fair and reasonable when the property was purchased may be quite unconscionable when the time comes to sell it.

–   Often it requires each co-owner to commit himself to paying a specified share of the mortgage payments. For various reasons such as pregnancy or unemployment, one or other co-owner may be unable or unwilling to keep up those payments.

---

[37]   For the distinction between fixed shares and floating shares, see **1.7** above. For a discussion of the disadvantages of fixed shares, see **1.9** below.

[38]   For example, where the co-owners declare themselves to be beneficial joint tenants or beneficial tenants in common in equal shares, and one co-owner has contributed substantially more than the other towards the purchase price or the mortgage payments.

[39]   For the distinction between fixed shares and floating shares, see **1.7** above.

[40]   *Pettitt v Pettitt* [1970] AC 777 at 813E, per Lord Upjohn.

- It may be necessary to keep the fixed shares under constant review. In practical terms such a review may be forgotten, producing an unfair result when the property is sold.

- In practice, it is unlikely that the co-owners will execute a supplemental declaration of trust if their contributions vary. Inviting one's partner to enter into a further declaration could create difficulties within the relationship. It may involve some expenditure on valuation fees. It will almost certainly involve legal fees.

- There are several ways of calculating fixed shares. It is not easy to decide at the outset which method will produce the fairest result when the property is sold. One method of calculation might favour one partner, while another method might favour the other. Occasionally, the differences between the various formulae can produce perverse results.[41]

- Problems arise over post-separation contributions, particularly where one co-owner has abandoned the property and stopped making contributions towards the mortgage payments.

- It is not entirely clear when the fixed shares should 'crystallise' if the couple separate. Should they crystallise on the date of separation or on the date when the property is eventually sold? The Court of Appeal has experienced difficulties in answering these questions.[42]

1.10 The advantages of floating shares

Floating shares may be considered preferable to fixed shares for the following reasons.[43]

- The concept is more equitable, in theory at least because 'who gets what?' depends on 'who paid what?'.

- There should be no need to keep floating shares under constant review.

- Any variations in the co-owners' contributions will automatically be taken into account. There is no need to execute a supplemental declaration of trust.

- The contributions made by each party will be examined retrospectively from the date on which the property was sold or from the date on which the co-owners separated, in much the same way that a court is able to look back with the benefit of hindsight on all the relevant facts.[44]

---

[41] See Precedents **1.131** and **1.136** below and the footnotes thereto.

[42] In *Hall v Hall* (1982) 3 FLR 379, the court held that the plaintiff was entitled to a share of the equity valued at the date on which the relationship ended. This decision was explained and distinguished in *Gordon v Douce* [1983] 1 WLR 563. In *Turton v Turton* [1988] 1 FLR 23, it was held that 'unless there is some express declaration or agreement to the effect that the parties' respective beneficial shares are to be valued at the time of their separation ... the parties' beneficial interests would always have to be regarded in the normal way under a trust for sale, with the effect that they would endure until such time as the property is sold, and that they then attach to the proceeds of sale' (at 34A, per Kerr LJ).

[43] For the distinction between fixed shares and floating shares, see **1.7** above. For a discussion of some of the disadvantages of floating shares, see **1.11** below.

[44] *Gissing v Gissing* [1970] 2 All ER 780 at 793.

–   There should be less difficulty over post-separation contributions.[45]

–   Any possible need to apply to the court for a declaration of trust to be rectified or set aside on the grounds of fraud or mistake is virtually eliminated.

–   There should be less likelihood of one co-owner inadvertently conferring a gratuitous benefit on the other.

–   Although it may appear that the mathematics of calculating floating shares are complex, in reality – given all the relevant information and a reliable calculator – the exercise should not take very much longer than the calculation of fixed shares.[46]

1.11   The disadvantages of floating shares

Floating shares have their drawbacks.[47]

–   There is less certainty. A co-owner may find it difficult to quantify his or her entitlement at any time.

–   Co-owners must keep accounts, receipts and statements, showing who paid what and when. In many cases it is unlikely that they will do so.

–   Even if they do keep accounts, the co-owners could still disagree about the contributions made, especially if they came from a joint account.

–   The calculations may be more complicated than the calculation of fixed shares.

–   It is difficult to know where to draw the line with repairs and improvements, for example what repairs should affect the beneficial interests, and what repairs are so minor as to be irrelevant.

–   Although floating shares reflect the direct cash contributions made by each co-owner, inflation can play havoc with the equities. For example, payment of £1,000 by co-owner A when the property was purchased in 1974 would probably, in real terms, be worth five times as much as a payment of £1,000 made by co-owner B towards improvements to the property in 1993.[48]

–   Cash contributions towards repairs and improvements are not always identical to the enhancement value; the co-owners might disagree about the extent to which the value of the property has been enhanced.[49]

–   Floating shares can only exist in the context of a beneficial tenancy in common. Accordingly, they are subject to any perceived disadvantages to which tenancies in common are themselves subject.

---

[45]   For the difficulties over post-separation contributions, see **1.9** above.
[46]   See Precedents **1.136–1.139** below.
[47]   For the distinction between fixed shares and floating shares, see **1.7** above. For a discussion of some of the advantages of floating shares, see **1.10** above.
[48]   Alluded to by Nicholls LJ in *Passee v Passee* [1988] 1 FLR 263 at 271.
[49]   In *Pettitt v Pettitt* [1970] AC 777 at 780, the wife was not prepared to concede that her husband's expenditure of £723.17s had increased the value of Tinker's Cottage by £1,000.

– There is less scope for mutual dependence. For example, floating shares would prejudice a co-owner who had left work in order to have a baby or to look after children, and who was therefore unable to make any financial contribution towards the mortgage payments or any repairs or improvements to the property.

– Two methods of calculating floating shares are described in this book. One is the simple addition of each co-owner's contributions, and an apportionment of the net proceeds of sale pro rata.[50] The other identifies the extent to which any change in the value of the property is attributable to a co-owner's lump-sum contributions and his or her mortgage-related contributions.[51] These methods will produce different (sometimes substantially different) results.[52]

– An injustice might occur if one co-owner pays the mortgage (which will affect his or her beneficial interest) and the other co-owner pays other outgoings which may not affect any beneficial interests.

1.12 Fractions, percentages and ratios

Fixed shares are usually expressed as fractions or percentages of the sale price or the net proceeds of sale. Occasionally, they appear as ratios. When quoting fractions there is a tendency to reduce them to the lowest common denominator, but this could diminish the understanding of the document for the sake of visual amenity. In the final analysis, how the shares are expressed will be a compromise between strict accuracy and ease of understanding. This is best illustrated by examples:

Example: A and B buy a bungalow for £56,000. B pays £40,000, and A pays £16,000. A declaration of trust which states that B is entitled to 71.4286 per cent of the net proceeds of sale and that A is entitled to 28.5714 per cent would be entirely accurate, but rather bizarre. A declaration which states that B is entitled to 40/56ths and A 16/56ths, would be much easier to reconcile with the original contributions: probably easier to reconcile than reducing the fractions to the lowest common denominator – B 5/7ths and A 2/7ths.

Example: A and B buy a house for £73,850. A contributes £47,264, and B contributes £26,586. A declaration of trust, which provides that A is entitled to receive 47,264/73,850ths and B 26,586/73,850ths of the net proceeds of sale would be precise but a little clumsy. It would be much better to say that A will receive 64 per cent and B 36 per cent.

1.13 Shares of the sale price and shares of the net proceeds of sale

The sale or disposal of a property usually comprises four cash elements:

(1) the sale price itself;

(2) the amount required to redeem the mortgage;

---

[50] See Precedent 1.137 below.
[51] See Precedent 1.139 below.
[52] See Precedent 1.139.

(3)   the incidental costs of the sale; and

(4)   the net proceeds of the sale.

A statement in a declaration of trust to the effect that one co-owner will receive 75 per cent of the sale price and the other co-owner will receive 25 per cent of the sale price is, on its own, deficient, because it fails to take into account the co-owners' liability for the payment of the sale costs or for the redemption of the mortgage, if there is one. So, any reference to the sale price should be followed by some indication as to how the deductions are to be apportioned between the co-owners.

'The net proceeds of sale', on the other hand, generally refers to the balance of the sale price remaining after all the deductions have been made. So, in principle, the expression 'net proceeds of sale' should be preceded by some indication as to how the deductions were apportioned between the co-owners. In isolation, a statement that one co-owner will receive three-quarters, and the other co-owner one-quarter, of the net proceeds of sale, assumes that the sale costs and the amount required to redeem the mortgage have already been deducted from the sale price in those proportions.

The acquisition of a property also usually consists of four distinct cash elements:

(1)   the purchase price;

(2)   the mortgage advance;

(3)   the incidental purchase costs; and

(4)   the co-owners' down payments or cash contributions.

A common mistake is to correlate the co-owners' down payments – their cash contributions towards the purchase price – and their eventual shares of the net proceeds of sale. It is only safe to correlate the co-owners' original contributions to their shares of the net proceeds of sale where:

–   there is no mortgage; or

–   there is a mortgage, but the co-owners intend to contribute towards the mortgage payments in exactly the same proportions as their down payments bear to each other; and

–   they also intend to pay the sale costs in exactly the same proportions as their down payments bear to each other.

It is recommended that wherever there is a mortgage, the shares of the co-owners should be expressed as a fraction or percentage of the sale price, *less* a fraction or percentage of the amount required to redeem the mortgage, *less* a fraction or percentage of the incidental costs of selling the property.

It is important to remember both the purchase costs and the sale costs. Often they are overlooked.

1.14 Who owns what if there is a dispute?

The starting point for determining who owns what in any dispute over property will be the title deeds and documents.

If the property was bought at the outset with the purpose of providing a home for the cohabitants, the solicitors acting at the time should have ensured that the parties' intentions were clearly recorded (see **1.1** above). In practice, this does not always happen.

There are two aspects to the ownership of property: the legal title to the property and the beneficial interests in it. Both may be vested in the same people, but this is not necessarily the case.

On the face of it, if the title deeds show a person to be the legal owner, there is a presumption that he or she will also own the beneficial interest. This presumption can be rebutted by showing that the legal owner holds the beneficial interest on trust for another, whether jointly or in common with him, or absolutely.

A trust can be shown to exist either by producing a document in writing in which it is expressly set out, or where no such document exists, by asking the court to infer the existence of a trust, relying upon principles of equity.

1.15 Express declaration of beneficial interests

If there is a declaration in the conveyance or transfer of the property to the legal owner(s) as to those in whom the beneficial title will vest, then in the absence of fraud, mistake or undue influence, or the operation of proprietory estoppel that declaration will be conclusive.

This was the position in *Goodman v Gallant*.[53] In that case, Mr Goodman transferred the former matrimonial home into the names of Mrs Goodman and her cohabitant, Mr Gallant. There was an express declaration that they held the property as beneficial joint tenants. Before long, the relationship turned sour and Mrs Goodman severed the joint tenancy. In the litigation which followed she contended that the beneficial interests in the property should be 75/25 per cent in her favour on the basis of contribution. The court held that it could not disturb the express declaration that the parties were to hold the proceeds of sale as joint tenants, and following the severance of the joint tenancy, in equal shares. The equitable doctrine of implied trusts could not be invoked where there was an express declaration.[54] This was confirmed by the important decision of the House of Lords in *Stack v Dowden*.[55]

---

[53] [1986] 1 FLR 513.
[54] See **1.5** above.
[55] [2007] UKHL 17.

1.16   Beneficial joint tenants

The express declaration as to the beneficial interests may provide that the parties are beneficial joint tenants. This means that unless or until the joint tenancy is severed[56] each joint tenant has an equal and identical interest in the entire property, or the net proceeds of sale thereof. Where property is held by beneficial joint tenants, on the death of a joint tenant his or her interest passes to the remaining joint tenants in equal shares by operation of the right of survivorship. A beneficial joint tenant of property cannot leave his or her share by will, nor can it be distributed on an intestacy because it will not form part of the estate for succession purposes.[57]

1.17   Tenants in common

If the beneficial interests are held as tenants in common, the interest of each will be expressly specified. For example, the beneficial interests may be expressed to be held by the parties as tenants in common in equal shares or such other proportion as may be agreed. This will mean that each will own a specified share of the property which will form part of his or her estate on death, rather than passing to the surviving tenant(s) as would be the case if they had been joint tenants.

1.18   Severing the joint tenancy

If a joint tenancy is severed, the nature of the parties' interests in the property changes to that of tenants in common in equal shares. The severed shares will then form part of each owner's estate for succession purposes.

A joint tenancy can be severed by the tenant who wishes to sever the joint tenancy serving[58] a notice of severance on the other joint tenant(s) (s 36(2) of the LPA 1925). There will be good service of the notice of severance if it is either left at or sent by registered post to the last known home address or business of the person to be served.[59]

For registered land a restriction should be entered.[60]

---

[56]   See **1.18** below.

[57]   However, see **6.11** and the court's powers under s 9 of the I(PFD)A 1975 to treat a severable share as part of the net estate for the purposes of an application under that Act.

[58]   See *Kinch v Bullard* [1999] 1 FLR 66, in which a notice was deemed served once it arrived at the address of the addressee, even if it never came to his notice, and even though the sender had decided to withdraw it and so had destroyed it on arrival.

[59]   LPA 1925, s 199.

[60]   See **1.6**.

A severance can be brought about in other ways. For example in *Burgess v Rawnsley*[61] it was suggested that a common intention or agreement between joint tenants that the tenancy should be severed may be sufficient, even if there was nothing in writing.[62]

The effect of one joint tenant making an application for an order for sale or becoming bankrupt can be to sever the joint tenancy, as can one joint tenant dealing with his interest as if it were held as a tenant in common, for example by selling, assigning or charging it.[63] In *Perkins v Borden*[64] a brother and sister owned a house as joint tenants but both gave instructions to a solicitor to prepare wills leaving each other a life interest in their share with the remainder to go to other relatives. It was held that the element of agreement present in their instructions was sufficient to sever the joint tenancy and that the pre-1926 methods of severance were still applicable; 'it is not a case of one of them acting behind the back of the other. The reference in the will to a half share makes it clear that they were treating their share as disposed by their wills.' It would not of course have amounted to severance if only one had made a will disposing of that share.

In *Wallbank and Wallbank v Price*,[65] Mr and Mrs Wallbank owned their matrimonial home as joint beneficial owners. The marriage came to an end and Mrs Wallbank signed a declaration in the following terms:

'I ... have voluntarily agreed to vacate [the former matrimonial home] and also to forfeit any moneys or profit in anyway connected with this property, and by signing this declaration I revoke any rights in the disposal of the ... property.'

She alleged that Mr Wallbank had exerted undue influence upon her to obtain her signature to the declaration. This was not made out, and the court held that the declaration was not only sufficient to sever the joint tenancy but also to dispose of her own beneficial interest in the property.

In *Davis v Smith*[66] the Court of Appeal upheld the decision of the judge at first instance that the joint tenancy had been severed even though there was no formal notice given. In that case there were divorce proceedings, and negotiations were in progress for the resolution of financial matters. The division of the assets was broadly accepted as being equal. To that end an endowment policy had been surrendered, and an unequal division made in favour of the husband to enable him to proceed on the purchase of a house. The intention was that the inequality would be addressed in the division of the proceeds of sale of the family home. The family home was already on the market and an offer had been received. Before contracts could be exchanged, an

---

[61] [1975] Ch 429. See also *Perkins v Borden re Woolnough deceased* [2002] WRLT 595.
[62] See also *Quigley v Masterson* [2011] EWHC 2529 (Ch).
[63] *Ahmed v Kendrick* [1988] 2 FLR 22; *Re Drapers Conveyance* [1969] 1 Ch 486; *First National Securities v Hegerty* [1984] 1 All ER 139.
[64] *Perkins v Borden re Woolnough deceased* LSG 2002 (99) 24, [2002] WTLR 595.
[65] [2008] 2 FLR 501.
[66] [2012] 1 FLR 1177.

accident befell the wife, who died. The court held that whilst a joint tenancy could survive even the sale of a jointly owned property, in this case it was apparent that the parties had already expressed an intention and an expectation that the proceeds would be shared equally.

Where the relationship between joint tenants has broken down, consideration should always be given to severing the joint tenancy and appropriate advice given. Such advice was given to both parties in *Davis v Smith* but not acted upon.

1.19   No express declaration of beneficial interests

If the title deeds and documents do not disclose an express declaration as to the ownership of the beneficial interests in the property, it may be possible to establish an intention that a person not on the legal title would nonetheless have a beneficial interest, and that the legal owner holds the property on trust for them both beneficially, or indeed for the non-owner absolutely.

A beneficial interest may be established in the absence of express declaration by relying upon an implied trust, either a resulting or a constructive trust. The non-owner may alternatively be able to rely upon the equitable doctrine of proprietary estoppel to found a beneficial interest.

1.20   Sole legal ownership or joint legal ownership?

In the absence of an express declaration as to beneficial ownership, for example by a tick in the appropriate box of the TR1 or FR1, or a separate trust deed, the route to ascertaining the beneficial interests will depend upon whether the legal title in the property is held in the sole name of one of them, or jointly.

If the property is held in the sole name of one of the parties, the presumption is that on the basis that 'equity follows the law' the legal owner is also entitled to the entire beneficial interest. The onus is upon the non-owner to persuade the court, first that he or she has a beneficial interest, and secondly as to the extent of it.

If the legal title to the property is held in the parties' joint names, there will be a presumption that the beneficial interests will be held in the same way as the legal title, ie equally. The burden of proof will be upon the joint owner who asserts that the beneficial interests should be held in different proportions to show why they should be other than equal. However, the joint owner will not usually have to persuade the court as to the fact of the sharing of the beneficial interests as this is presumed by the registration of the title in joint names.

1.21 Implied trusts

Using the principle of implied trusts, the court is able to determine whether and if so how the beneficial interests are to be shared in cases where either the property is held in one party's sole name, or if in joint names, no express declaration of the beneficial interests has been made.

Implied trusts can take the form of either a resulting trust, or a constructive trust. The significance of the distinction is in quantification. Where there is a resulting trust, quantification of shares is on the basis of contributions to the purchase price. Where the court finds a constructive trust, the court is able to use a broader brush in order to ascertain the extent of each party's beneficial share.

The two approaches can often produce quite different monetary outcomes.[67]

Until *Stack v Dowden,* it was not always clear from the authorities which of the two applied in any given set of circumstances. That case provided much needed clarification. The majority view of the House of Lords was that where there is a dispute about the beneficial ownership of a shared home in the *domestic context*,[68] whether between cohabitants or family members, constructive trust principles should be applied. However, in relation to other property that may be owned by the same parties, but on a more commercial rather than domestic footing, the principles of resulting trusts will generally apply.

1.22 Resulting trusts

A resulting trust will arise where a person whose name may not be on the legal title to the property has nonetheless provided all or part of the purchase price. In the absence of evidence as to how they should share the beneficial interests, they would be entitled in direct proportion to their financial contribution.

The presumption that the financial contributions of a non-owner were intended to be recognised by a beneficial interest in the property may be rebutted by evidence that the money was a gift or a loan, or even payment of rent. In *Sekhon v Alissa*[69] it was held that there was a resulting trust in favour of a mother who had contributed £22,500 towards her daughter's purchase of a house. The daughter could not rebut the presumption that in contributing to the purchase price it was the intention that her mother would have an interest in the house, as she could not show either that the money was intended as a gift or as a loan to her.

Equity will presume an intention to make a gift where the donor is under an equitable obligation to make provision for or support another, for example parent and child, and husband and wife, and it will apply to gifts made by the

---

[67] See *Drake v Whipp* [1996] 1 FLR 826.
[68] Baroness Hale at para 69.
[69] [1989] 2 FLR 94.

man where a man and woman are engaged to be married. However, the presumption of advancement, or gift, does not apply as between cohabitants.[70]

The situation may arise where there is a dispute between the parties as to their respective intentions regarding the contributions. Generally speaking, it will be the intention of the person making the contribution that will be determinative, regardless of whether that intention was communicated to the legal owner, as long as there was no question of fraud or deceit. Very often no clear intention will be discernible. In such cases, the lack of a positive intention, either to have a share of the property or for the contribution to be a gift or a loan, will operate either positively to rebut the presumption of advancement if the presumption of resulting trust applies, or negatively if the presumption of advancement applies when it will be insufficient to dislodge that presumption.

The relevance of resulting trusts in the context of the shared home of cohabitants has been eroding gradually. In *Oxley v Hiscock* [71] the Court of Appeal said the principle of resulting trusts was likely to be largely overridden by constructive trusts in those cases in which the parties could bring themselves within one of the two categories identified by Lord Bridge in *Lloyds Bank Plc v Rosset*.[72] In other words, where the party seeking to establish a beneficial interest can rely upon a common intention that the beneficial ownership was to be shared, either expressly agreed or understood, or to be inferred from the parties' conduct. This was considered by the House of Lords in *Stack v Dowden*. Baroness Hale endorsed the suggestion of the Law Commission in the Discussion Paper, *Sharing Homes*, that an 'holistic approach to quantification, undertaking a survey of the whole course of dealing between the parties and taking account of all conduct which throws light on the question which shares were intended',[73] was preferable to a strict arithmetical approach to financial contributions to the purchase price. This was the approach that would be more likely to produce the outcome that the parties intended. It is clear from the Supreme Court decision *Jones v Kernott*[74] that the court is concerned to ascertain the parties' common intention as to the sharing of the beneficial interests and not to embark upon an accounting exercise.[75]

However, resulting trusts may still be relevant as between cohabitants where, for example, they have both contributed to the purchase of property other than the home they share and where the context is more commercial than domestic. In *Laskar v Laskar*[76] a mother and daughter bought the mother's council house with the benefit of the 'Right to Buy' discount that accrued to the mother through her secure tenancy. There was a mortgage in joint names, and each contributed a small amount of cash to make up the balance of the purchase price. The property was conveyed into their joint names without a declaration

---

[70]   *Lowson v Coombes* [1999] 1 FLR 799; *Cantor v Cox* [1975] 239 EG 121.
[71]   [2004] 2 FLR 669.
[72]   [1990] 2 FLR 155; see **1.25** below.
[73]   At para 61.
[74]   [2011] UKSC 53.
[75]   See para 24.
[76]   [2008] 2 FLR 589.

as to the beneficial ownership. It had always been the plan that the mother would live with another daughter and that the property would be let to tenants. The mother managed the lettings and saw to repairs and the rent was applied to discharge the mortgage repayments. After a family disagreement the daughter sought to realise her interest in the property and claimed that after *Stack v Dowden* there was a presumption that as a joint legal owner she owned the beneficial interests in equal shares with her mother.

The Court of Appeal held that the presumption applied to a family home occupied by cohabitants, but not as in that case to a property that had been purchased as an investment with a view to obtaining rental income and capital appreciation. The doctrine of resulting trusts would therefore apply and in the absence of any relevant discussions between the parties the beneficial shares would reflect the contributions to the purchase price. On this basis the daughter's share was assessed at 33 per cent taking into account the right to buy discount that was a contribution entirely from the mother.

The court went on to say that even if the presumption of joint beneficial ownership had applied, it would have been rebutted by the following factors:
- their financial affairs were always kept separate;
- the property had not been bought as a home for either or both of them;
- the property had been bought primarily as an investment;
- there was a wide disparity in contribution and it could not presumed that the mother would intend to make a gift of such a size to only one of her children;
- the daughter had joined in the purchase because otherwise the mother could not afford to exercise the right to buy.

1.23 Quantification and resulting trusts

Where one or more parties contribute cash to the purchase of a property, and there is no mortgage advance, their respective contributions will be easily ascertained, and thus the shares arising under the resulting trust.

Quite often a party will assert a beneficial interest by virtue of other contributions made, not necessarily at the time of purchase.

Expenses connected with the purchase, for example legal fees and stamp duty land tax (SDLT), have generally been treated as part of the purchase price.[77]

However, furniture, soft furnishings, fittings and even improvement work have not been regarded as contributions to the purchase price.[78]

---

[77] See *Re Densham* [1975] 1 WLR 1519; *Walker v Hall* [1984] FLR 126; *Huntingford v Hobbs* [1993] 1 FLR 736.
[78] *Pettitt v Pettitt* [1970] AC 777.

Since the 'Right to Buy' was introduced by the Housing Act 1985 (HA 1985), public sector tenants have been able to buy their homes at a discount. The question of whether this discount, accrued over the period of the tenancy, can amount to a contribution to the purchase price of the property has been considered in a number of cases. In *Springette v Defoe*, it was held that the discount should be treated as a cash contribution. This was confirmed as good authority in *Laskar v Laskar*.[79]

Most purchases are made with the assistance of a mortgage advance. This can complicate quantification under the doctrine of resulting trusts as taking responsibility for a loan is not necessarily the same as contributing cash. Generally speaking however, moneys raised by way of a loan and applied to the purchase price of a property have been regarded as a contribution by the person who obtained the loan.

Mr Huntingford's interest in the home bought jointly with Mrs Hobbs was quantified by reference to the sum borrowed on mortgage, rather than the sum of the mortgage repayments actually made, the parties having agreed at the time of the purchase that he would be solely responsible for the repayments.

In both *Stack v Dowden* and *Laskar v Laskar* Lord Neuberger was dubious about the principle of treating liability under a mortgage as the equivalent of a cash contribution when assessing beneficial shares under a resulting trust. However, in *Laskar* he said, 'there was a strong case for apportioning the mortgage equally between the parties when it comes to assessing their respective contributions to the purchase price'.[80] In that case the parties had assumed joint responsibility for the mortgage, and the repayments were made from the rental income on the property.

1.24   Constructive trusts

The restrictions upon and uncertainty about what can properly be called contributions to the purchase price for the purposes of establishing a resulting trust, as well as the strictly arithmetical approach to quantification, have given way to the constructive trust in the domestic context of cohabitants and other home sharers as it more properly reflects the realities of the give and take, in financial and other terms, of close personal relationships.

A constructive trust may arise where two (or more) people acquire property with the common intention that it is to be shared, although the property is conveyed into the name of one (or some) of them only. To establish a beneficial interest, the non-owner also has to show that in reliance upon a common intention that the beneficial interests in the property were to be shared, he or she acted to his or her detriment. The basis for the trust is that it would be

---

[79]   However the resulting trust approach taken in *Springette v Defoe* was disapproved in *Oxley v Hiscock* as it concerned co-ownership in a domestic context and to that extent it should not be followed.

[80]   At para 29.

inequitable for the non-owner to be denied the share that it was the common intention that he or she should have. The same principles can be applied where a joint legal owner wishes to show that he or she is beneficially entitled to more than the half share that would otherwise be presumed from joint legal ownership.

1.25 Establishing a constructive trust

The jurisprudence in this area can be traced back to *Pettitt v Pettitt*[81] and *Gissing v Gissing*[82] and on through a succession of cases culminating in *Lloyds Bank Plc v Rosset*,[83] and thereafter *Oxley v Hiscock*,[84] the important decision of the House of Lords in *Stack v Dowden*[85] followed by that of the Supreme Court in *Jones v Kernott*.[86]

In *Gissing v Gissing* the basic principles were set out. In order to establish a beneficial interest, a non-owner would have to persuade the court that it would be inequitable for the legal owner to claim sole beneficial ownership. To achieve this, it would be necessary to demonstrate that there was a common intention to share the beneficial interests, and that the non-owner had acted to his or her detriment in reliance upon that common intention.

The common intention could be proved by direct evidence of an agreement to this effect, or this could be inferred by the court by the parties' conduct.

This was developed further in *Lloyds Bank Plc v Rosset*[87] with Lord Bridge's helpful analysis of the approach that the court should take in a case involving a dispute between cohabitants or co-owners over their interest in property.

Lord Bridge identified a 'two-stage enquiry' for the court. The court should first establish whether there was a common intention that the beneficial interests in the property were to be shared. If not, the matter ended there. If a common intention to share the beneficial interests was established, the court would go on to consider in what proportions the beneficial interests would be shared.

In a case in which the legal title is vested in joint names this will usually suffice to satisfy the court as to a common intention to share the beneficial ownership and the enquiry moves on to one of quantification.

However, where the title is registered in the sole name of one of two cohabitants, further evidence will be necessary for the court to consider whether there was a common intention that the beneficial ownership was to be

---

[81]   [1970] AC 777.
[82]   [1971] AC 886.
[83]   [1990] 2 FLR 155.
[84]   [2004] 2 FLR 669.
[85]   [2007] 1 FLR 1858.
[86]   [2011] UKSC 53.
[87]   [1990] 2 FLR 155.

shared. The court will begin by looking to see if there was an express agreement, arrangement or understanding reached between the parties as to the sharing of the beneficial ownership. This will be a question of fact, 'based on evidence of express discussions between the parties however imperfectly remembered or however imprecise'.[88] This highlights the importance of taking very detailed instructions at the outset in order to give reliable advice, and to form the basis of a full witness statement if it is considered that an arguable case is made out.

In the absence of anything express, the court will then look at the conduct of the parties to see if an intention to share the beneficial ownership can be inferred.[89] Again, the taking of full and detailed instructions at an early stage is of vital importance.

The conduct that might give rise to a constructive trust in these circumstances was considered in detail by Lord Bridge in *Lloyds Bank Plc v Rosset*. He said that 'direct contributions to the purchase price by the partner who is not the legal owner, whether initially or by payment of mortgage instalments, will readily justify the inference necessary to the creation of a constructive trust. But, as I read the authorities, it is at least extremely doubtful whether anything less will do'. In that case the wife's fairly heavy involvement in the renovation and redecoration of a property purchased in her husband's sole name with funds inherited by him but used as the matrimonial home was insufficient to found a beneficial interest, in the absence of either evidence of contributions to the purchase price or of an intention to share the ownership of the property beneficially.

Although not directly concerned with the issues that arise in cases where only one party is legally entitled to property, there was support from the House of Lords in *Stack v Dowden*[90] for the proposition that the words of Lord Bridge in *Rosset* set the first hurdle, of contribution from which a common intention may be inferred, '... rather too high in certain respects ...'[91] suggesting that when dealing with this issue courts should take a broader approach. There is encouragement for the view that the court will not be restricted to direct financial contributions, but will be able to look at the parties' whole course of conduct in order to ascertain their shared intentions. The majority in the House of Lords was of the opinion that the law had moved on since *Rosset* and that the court could and should take 'a wide view of what is capable of counting as a contribution towards the acquisition of a residence, while remaining sceptical of the value of alleged improvements that are really insignificant, or elaborate arguments (suggestive of creative accounting) as to how the family finances

---

[88]	[1990] 2 FLR 155. *Rosset No 1*.
[89]	*Rosset No 2*.
[90]	For a full discussion see **1.28** below.
[91]	Baroness Hale of Richmond at para 63.

were arranged'.[92] Lord Walker went on to say that he 'would include contributions in kind by way of manual labour, provided that they are significant'.[93]

This reflects the views put forward in the Law Commission's Discussion Paper *Sharing Homes*.[94] Although the Law Commissioners found it impossible to devise a statutory scheme for the determination of shares in the shared home that would work fairly, they suggested that there were measures that the courts could take to assist. For example, the courts could take a broader approach both to the kinds of contribution from which a common intention may be inferred, as well as to the quantification of the share.

1.26 Conduct from which a common intention to share the beneficial interests may be inferred in sole name cases

Cases decided before *Stack v Dowden* will still have some relevance to the question of which contributions may be sufficient to enable the court to infer an intention to share the beneficial interest. Apart from direct financial contribution to the purchase price at the time the property was acquired, for example by paying the deposit,[95] financial contribution by paying the mortgage instalments, particularly if combined with expenditure of money and effort on repairs may be conduct sufficient to demonstrate an intention to share the beneficial ownership in the absence of any evidence that there was an express agreement or understanding that this would be the case. It seems clear from *Grant v Edwards*[96] that the expenditure must be referable to the acquisition of the home. In that case the court gave a 50 per cent beneficial interest to a cohabitant, Miss Grant, who made regular and substantial contributions to the outgoings. Mr Edwards had made an excuse for leaving Miss Grant's name off the legal title from which she could reasonably have concluded that she was intended to have a share, and furthermore, without her contributions to the household expenses he would not have been able to afford the mortgage repayments.

In *Le Foe v Le Foe and Woolwich plc; Woolwich plc v Le Foe and Le Foe*,[97] a deputy High Court judge considered that Lord Bridge in *Rosset* was not saying in absolute terms that there were no circumstances in which indirect contributions may suffice in cases where there is no express agreement to share the beneficial ownership, simply that such cases will be the exception. In

---

92 Lord Walker at para 34.
93 At para 36.
94 Published on 18 July 2002.
95 In *McHardy & Sons (A Firm) v Warren* [1994] 2 FLR 338, a wedding gift of £650 from the husband's parents used to pay the deposit on the purchase of the first matrimonial home was held to be sufficient to establish a joint intention that they should share the beneficial interest in the property. See also *Midland Bank v Cooke* [1995] 2 FLR 915 in which the wife's notional half share of the gift by the husband's parents of the deposit for the couple's first home amounted to the wife's financial contribution to the purchase price.
96 [1987] 1 FLR 87.
97 [2001] 2 FLR 970.

determining the extent of Mrs Le Foe's beneficial interest in the former matrimonial home, held in the sole name of Mr Le Foe and subject to a mortgage, direct repayments of which were made by him, the deputy judge concluded that indirect contributions made by Mrs Le Foe to the mortgage were sufficient for him to infer a common intention that she should have a beneficial interest in the former matrimonial home. The court found that although Mr Le Foe earned more than his wife there was 'no doubt that the family economy depended for its functions on [Mrs Le Foe's] earnings. It was an arbitrary allocation of responsibility that [Mr Le Foe] paid the mortgage, service charge and outgoings, whereas [Mrs Le Foe] paid for day-to-day domestic expenditure'.

In *Cooke v Head*[98] a small contribution to the mortgage repayments and a significant practical contribution to the construction of the property was found to amount to conduct from which a common intention to share the beneficial ownership could be inferred.

In *Thomas v Fuller-Brown*[99] the fact that Mr Fuller-Brown had carried out substantial improvement works to the property in which he was living with Mrs Thomas, and which was in her sole name, did not of itself entitle him to an interest in the property, in the absence of an express agreement, or a common intention to be inferred from their conduct. As Lord Justice Slade put it, 'a man who does work by way of improvement to his cohabitee's property without a clear understanding as to the financial basis on which the work is to be done does so at his own risk'.[100]

In *Eves v Eves*[101] it was said that in the absence of a common intention to share the beneficial ownership, which was in fact found in that case, the female cohabitant's contribution by way of assistance with decoration and improvements to the home would have been insufficient as conduct from which the court could have inferred such an intention.[102]

In *Windeler v Whitehall*[103] contributions by way of keeping the house, and business entertaining, albeit with flair and to a high standard, were insufficient to entitle Miss Windeler to a beneficial interest in the home she had shared with Mr Whitehall.[104]

There have been a number of cases on the question of common intention, decided after *Stack v Dowden*. In *James v Thomas*,[105] the Court of Appeal considered a case in which the shared home was in the sole name of

---

[98] [1972] 1 WLR 518.
[99] [1988] 1 FLR 237.
[100] At 247B.
[101] [1975] 3 All ER 768.
[102] See also *Hammond v Mitchell (Property: Beneficial Interest)* [1992] 1 FLR 229.
[103] [1990] 2 FLR 505.
[104] See also *Lloyds Bank plc v Rosset* [1990] 2 FLR 155; *McFarlane v McFarlane* [1972] NI 59; *Ivin v Blake (Property: Beneficial Interest)* [1995] 1 FLR 70.
[105] [2008] 1 FLR 1598.

Mr Thomas. He had acquired the property some time before he met Miss James and she later moved in with him. Miss James relied upon her contributions to Mr Thomas' agricultural contracting business in which she worked hard, and until they went into partnership together, for no remuneration. It was her case that Mr Thomas had told her that she would benefit from the success of the business and would be well provided for in the event of his death, and it was on this basis that she put all her energies into the business. Other than the contribution she made to the business through her hard work she made no direct financial contributions. Mr Thomas paid all the outgoings on the property from the profits of the business, later the partnership. The relationship broke down after four years and Miss James sought a declaration that she had a beneficial interest in the shared home on constructive trust principles. She was unsuccessful both at first instance and in the Court of Appeal.

In order to establish a constructive trust she had first to establish that there was either an express agreement between them that she would have a beneficial share in the house, or that such an agreement could be inferred from their conduct during the whole course of dealings in relation to the property, and that she had acted to her detriment in reliance upon that agreement.

Although the Court of Appeal acknowledged that in *Stack v Dowden* it had been made clear that it was possible for an agreement to share the beneficial interests to be made or inferred at any point after the property had been acquired, in this case it was held that where there was no evidence of an express agreement to share the beneficial interests, the court would be reluctant to infer an agreement simply from the parties' conduct. The highest Miss James could put her case was that the profits of the business, later the partnership, had been enhanced by her efforts, and those moneys had been applied to the payment of the mortgage instalments. The Court of Appeal was unable to infer an agreement that she should have a beneficial interest in the property on that basis, whilst making the point that there may be circumstances in which contributions to capital repayments by a non-owning cohabitant may evidence an agreement that the beneficial interests were to be shared.

Holman v Howes[106] concerned a couple who had formerly been married and then reconciled. They bought a house to live in together, the legal title to which was registered in Mr Howes' sole name. They each contributed roughly the same amount to the purchase price. They separated and after a brief reconciliation the parties again split up and Miss Holman remained in the house with their child for over 20 years. She took on all the responsibilities connected with the property and sought a declaration that she was entitled to the entire beneficial interest. Adopting the approach set out in the judgment of Baroness Hale in *Stack v Dowden* to find what was intended between the parties the Court of Appeal upheld the finding of the judge at first instance that the intention of the parties at the time of purchase was that it would be a joint venture. The fact that Miss Holman had taken on all the financial responsibility for the upkeep of the property after the separation could not be evidence of a

---

[106] [2008] 1 FLR 1217.

common intention that she was to have the entire beneficial interest in the absence of any discussions between the parties about this either at the time of acquisition or since. What the evidence pointed to was a joint enterprise and the beneficial shares would therefore be equal.

Abbott v Abbott[107] was a decision of the Privy Council relating to a married couple and their property in Antigua. There is no legislation in Antigua equivalent to the Matrimonial Causes Act 1973 and so property disputes fall to be dealt with on the same basis as that applying to unmarried couples in England and Wales.

The matrimonial home was in the sole name of the husband, having been built on land conveyed to him by his mother shortly after the marriage. The building costs were met in part by gifts from the husband's mother, and in part by secured borrowing for which the husband and wife were jointly and severally liable. They operated a joint bank account and pooled their resources. When the marriage broke down the wife claimed half the property. At first instance the judge adopted constructive trust principles and determined that the husband held the matrimonial home on trust for himself and his wife in equal shares. The husband appealed to the East Caribbean Court of Appeal and was successful. Reinstating the decision of the judge at first instance on the wife's appeal, the Privy Council said that the Court of Appeal had been in error in concluding from the famous words of Lord Bridge in *Rosset* that a common intention to share the beneficial ownership could not be inferred in the absence of direct financial contributions to the purchase price by the wife. Baroness Hale said that the law had moved on since then and that the approach now was to look at the entire course of dealings between the parties in relation to the property and from that ascertain their common intention as to the beneficial ownership. In the present case the factors that lent weight to a common intention to share the beneficial ownership equally were these:

– the inference to be drawn from the gifts of land and cash from the husband's mother was that it was a gift to them both, not just to the husband;[108]

– the parties organised their finances jointly;

– they were jointly liable for the secured borrowing;

– the husband accepted that the wife had a beneficial share, although he disputed the extent of it.

In *Thompson v Humphrey*[109] Warren J conducted a helpful review of the authorities on contribution. In that case the subject property was in the sole name of Mr Humphrey. His cohabitant, Mrs Thompson, claimed a beneficial interest in Church Farm, the property in which they had lived together along with the children of her former husband. Her case was put on the basis that it was intended between them that they would share the beneficial ownership

---

[107] [2008] 1 FLR 1451.
[108] *Warren v McHardy*; *Midland Bank v Cooke*.
[109] [2010] 2 FLR 107.

equally. There was a paucity of detailed evidence about any express discussions the parties had, but at its highest the applicant could establish only that there had been a common intention that Church Farm would be a home for them and her children, and that the respondent had said that he would always look after her financially. This was insufficient for Warren J to find that there was a common intention that the applicant should have a beneficial share in the property.

Walsh v Singh[110] was a reminder that contributions alone will not establish a beneficial share in the absence of a common intention or specific representations as to beneficial ownership by the legal owner to support detrimental reliance. In that case the property had been bought by Mr Singh in his sole name two years after the parties commenced cohabitation. The mortgage was in the sole name of Mr Singh and no financial contribution was made to the purchase by the applicant. The parties became engaged to be married but they separated without marrying some four years later. In the meantime the applicant had assisted in the development of the property and adjoining land purchased subsequently as an equestrian centre. The land had been placed in Mr Singh's SIPP. Miss Walsh provided financial assistance for the purchase of the land but this was held by the judge to be a loan rather than a contribution to the purchase price.

In support of her claim for a beneficial half share in the property Miss Walsh relied upon the fact that she had given up a promising career at the Bar in order to focus on the equestrian business. It was her case that she would not have done this unless she had been told that 'half of everything we were doing was mine' and that this amounted to detrimental reliance. HHJ Purle QC found that the motivation for this was not a promised half share, but her commitment to Mr Singh whom she was intending to marry. The decision to give up the Bar was essentially a joint decision that suited them both, for different reasons.

In conclusion, whilst accepting that Miss Walsh had made significant contributions to the equestrian business that would have been sufficient to found a beneficial interest, the necessary common intention coupled with detrimental reliance were missing and her claim in this regard therefore failed. He identified the specific factors from the evidence that informed his decision:

- the property was purchased in Mr Singh's name and he bore all the expense of renovation and development;
- the applicant was not in a financial position at that time to make any monetary contribution;
- the applicant retained her own property which she let out, and when sold she retained the proceeds;
- the parties did not pool their finances;

---

[110] [2010] 1 FLR 1658.

–   there was never any record in writing of the alleged beneficial half share – this was surprising in view of Miss Walsh's high intelligence and legal training;

–   there was evidence that at the time the property was purchased the applicant told Mr Singh's bank manager that she knew that she would not have any interest in the property;

–   there was evidence that subsequently the applicant had told a third party that if she and Mr Singh ever split up she would only have a few horses, the dog and the horse box;

–   Mr Singh was too financially astute to promise a beneficial share when it was he putting all the money in to the project;

–   an agreement drawn up after separation did not make any reference to a sharing of the beneficial interests, rather it was predicated on the express basis that Mr Singh was sole owner;

–   Miss Walsh's contributions were referable to her commitment to the relationship rather than a belief in a beneficial interest;

–   although significant, her contributions were small compared with the financial and other contributions of Mr Singh.

The judge also found it 'likely that Mr Singh would have told Miss Walsh also that she could live at [the property] with him indefinitely, that he would support her, and that she should have no fears for the future, as they were to be married. This was consistent with the protestations of love and long-term commitment he expressed from an early stage of their relationship. It was in this context that he probably also told Miss Walsh from time to time that her financial future was secure. He may well have said something to that effect also at the time of the purchase of [the property] but I do not think that this was understood by Miss Walsh or could reasonably have been understood by her as promising her a beneficial interest in [the property]. She knew Mr Singh was buying that property for them both to live in, but in his own name, as he was paying both the cash element of the purchase price and the mortgage. She understood that this meant that he would be the sole owner, and went ahead because she hoped to marry him and spend the rest of her life with him. She knew that there was a risk that things would go wrong, but took that risk willingly.'[111]

Geary v Rankine[112] was one of the first reported decisions on establishing a common intention constructive trust after *Jones v Kernott*.[113] The property in question, a guest house in Hastings, had been bought by Mr Rankine in his sole name and with his own funds as an investment. He employed a manager to run the guest house as he and Mrs Geary were living together in London. The manager proved less than satisfactory and first Mr Rankine and then Mrs Geary went to Hastings to work in the business. This state of affairs

---

[111]   At para 43.
[112]   [2012] 2 FLR 1409.
[113]   [2012] 1 FLR 45.

continued for around 13 years until the couple separated. Mrs Geary claimed a beneficial interest in the guest house which was rejected both at first instance and on appeal to the Court of Appeal.

Following the principles in *Jones v Kernott* and *Stack v Dowden*[114] the starting point for ascertaining beneficial entitlement was the legal title. This was in Mr Rankine's sole name giving rise to a presumption that the beneficial interest was also intended for him. The burden was upon Mrs Geary to establish that there was a different common intention.

It was conceded on behalf of Mrs Geary that a common intention at the time of purchase could not be sustained. She therefore had to satisfy the court that the position changed subsequently, either by express statement or by inference from the parties' conduct. The trial judge had found that there was no such change in Mr Rankine's intention so far as the beneficial interests were concerned. He found also that Mrs. Geary had not acted to her detriment in reliance upon any assertion that she was to have a beneficial interest in the property.

It was emphasised that the court could not at the first stage, when the legal title was in a party's sole name and the court had to ascertain whether or not there was a common intention constructive trust, *impute*[115] a common intention to the parties. It was only at the second stage, when a common intention had been established, that the court was able to impute to them, from the whole course of dealings between the parties, what their intention was as to their respective beneficial shares.[116]

In *Thompson v Hurst* [117] Ms Hurst bought the council house of which she had been the tenant for a little under twenty years. She contributed the purchase price by way of the right to buy discount and a mortgage advance that was serviced by her earnings. Mr Thompson had lived with her there for all but the first two years and had made some contributions to the housekeeping.

The parties' relationship broke down four years after the purchase and Mr Thompson asked the court to determine their beneficial interests. At first instance the court found that there was a common intention constructive trust, and that in the absence of anything express as to sharing, the court finding that they did not address their minds to this, a fair division 10%/90% in favour of Ms Hurst would be fair on the basis of the whole history of the parties' relationship.

Mr Thompson appealed. The argument was advanced on his behalf that the fact that the parties had set out to own the house jointly, but were prevented from this by the mortgage lender's refusal to consider Mr Thompson suitable as

---

[114] [2007] 1 FLR 1858.
[115] Cf *infer*.
[116] Further on this point see the commentary of Rebecca Bailey-Harris on *Bhura v Bhura* [2014] EWHC 727 (Fam) reported in August [2014] Fam Law 1116.
[117] [2014] 1 FLR 238.

a party to a mortgage deed, was sufficient for the court to find that there was an intention that they should share the beneficial interests jointly. This was roundly rejected by the Court of Appeal:[118]

> '... [this] argument amounts to a submission that there should be a legal presumption of joint beneficial ownership, not merely where the parties are indeed the joint legal owners, but where there is evidence that they would have liked to be joint legal owners but for one reason or another that was not practical or desirable. Neither *Stack* nor *Jones* nor any other case, is authority for such a proposition. Indeed, the proposition is not consistent with principle nor sound policy.'

The court's task in sole name cases was succinctly set out:[119]

> 'In the case of a single legal owner ... where there is no express declaration of trust, the claimant has first to establish some sort of implied trust, normally what is now termed a common intention constructive trust ... The claimant must show that it was intended that he or she was to have a beneficial interest at all. That can only be achieved by evidence of the parties' actual intentions, express or inferred, objectively ascertained. If such evidence does show a common intention to share beneficial ownership, but does not show what shares were intended, then each of them is to have that share which the court considers fair, having regard to the whole of dealing in relation to the property.'

Aspden v Elvy[120] was an unusual case with substantial disputes of fact. Mr Aspden claimed a beneficial interest in a converted barn that in 2006, before its conversion, he had transferred to Ms Elvy. The barn had formed part of a farmhouse and associated land and buildings that he had bought in his sole name in 1986. He and Ms Elvy had commenced cohabitation shortly afterwards, by then having had a relationship for a little under a year. They went on to have two children.

In 2006 Mr Aspden had a reversal of fortunes in that he was unsuccessful in unrelated litigation. The parties had already separated, although they saw each other most days because Ms Elvy continued to run a business from the outbuildings at the farm. Mr Aspden realised that he would have to sell the farm to meet the costs of the litigation, and when in a very low state he told Ms Elvy that he proposed to divide the property, and transfer the barn and some land to her. The transfer was effected within a very short space of time. The farmhouse was sold later the same year. Mr Aspden paid his creditors from the proceeds and set up home in a static caravan on part of the land that had been transferred to Ms Elvy.

Between 2006 and 2009, the barn was converted to a dwellinghouse that was then occupied by Ms Elvy and the parties' children. The cost of conversion was in the region of £90,000. Both parties contributed financially and by assisting

---

[118] Etherton LJ at para 20.
[119] Etherton LJ at para 22.
[120] [2012] EWHC 1387 (Ch).

with the manual labour, although to what extent was in dispute. In 2009 Ms Elvy announced that she had formed a new relationship and would be selling the barn.

HHJ Behrens had to determine whether Mr Aspden had a beneficial interest, and if so, how this should be quantified.

His finding was that when the barn was purchased in 1986, as part of the larger property, Mr Aspden was the sole legal and beneficial owner. He found also that when Mr Aspden transferred his interest in the barn to Ms Elvy in 2006 there was nothing in his words or conduct at that time that would give rise to an inference that he was to retain any interest in the barn.

However, the judge accepted that Mr Aspden had contributed between £65,000 and £70,000 to the conversion costs. This represented a substantial part of his remaining assets. In the light of this he rejected Ms Elvy's assertion that his financial contributions were intended as gifts, preferring Mr Aspden's account that he hoped and expected that he would be able to move into the barn with Ms Elvy when the work was completed, and that she was aware of this.

In concluding that it was possible for there to be a change in the parties' intentions he relied upon the words of Griffiths LJ in *Bernard v Joseph*:[121]

> 'It might in exceptional circumstances be inferred that the parties agreed to alter their beneficial interests after the house was bought; an example would be if the man bought the house in the first place and the woman years later used a legacy to build an extra floor to make more room for the children. In such circumstances the obvious inference would be that the parties agreed that the woman should acquire a share in the greatly increased value of the house produced by her money ....'

As there were no express discussions between the parties as to quantification, the judge approached this by inputing an intention by reference to what he considered fair having regard to the whole course of dealings between the parties. This resulted in a 25% share for Mr Aspden on the basis of what the judge considered to be a fair return on the money he had put into the conversion, given the eventual value of the barn.

1.27 Detrimental reliance

As well as establishing a common intention to share the property beneficially, a non-owner who wishes to persuade the court to impose a constructive trust must also show detrimental reliance in the belief of the shared ownership.

If a common intention has been established by inference from the non-owner's financial contributions to the property, then the same contributions can be used as evidence of detriment.

---

[121] [1982] 3 All ER 162, at para 171.

1.28   Quantification and constructive trusts

Once the court is satisfied that a beneficial interest has been established it is necessary to quantify that beneficial share.

The beneficial interest may arise by the presumption in joint names cases, or in sole name cases by evidence either of express discussions at the time of purchase or by inference from conduct, including contributions, whether directly to the purchase price or by other contributions (financial or otherwise) together with in either case the non-owner having acted to his or her detriment.

The starting point, however, is different depending upon whether the legal title to the property is held in joint names or in one party's sole name.

In a joint names case the court starts with the presumption that the beneficial interests are held in the same way as the legal estate, that is in equal shares, and it is for the party contending for sharing in some other proportion to rebut that presumption. In other words the question for the court is whether the parties intended their beneficial interests to be different from their legal interests, and if so to what extent. The fact that the parties may have made unequal contributions to the purchase of the home will not usually be sufficient to displace the presumption.

In a sole name case the court is looking to ascertain the parties' common intention as to the sharing of the benefical interests and there is no presumption that they will be shared equally.

This exercise where a constructive trust is concerned is to be contrasted with the position where there is a resulting trust, when quantification will very largely be an accounting exercise, the beneficial interests being determined pro rata to the respective contributions to the purchase price. It will depend upon the facts of each particular case whether a resulting trust or a constructive trust analysis will provide the better outcome for the applicant, but on the basis of the decision of the majority in *Stack v Dowden* the constructive trust approach is the one that should be followed in the context of cohabitants and other home sharers.

The approach of the court to quantification of beneficial interests where there is a constructive trust in a sole name case was considered by the decision of the Court of Appeal in *Oxley v Hiscock*.[122] That decision confirmed that in the absence of express agreement at the time of purchase as to how the beneficial interests were to be shared, the court should look at the entire history of the financial dealings between the parties in relation to the property from the date of purchase onwards. This is reflected in what Baroness Hale identified in *Stack v Dowden* as 'The search ... to ascertain the parties' shared intentions, actual, inferred or imputed, with respect to the property in the light of their whole course of conduct in relation to it'. However, she cautioned that, '... it does not

---

[122] [2004] 2 FLR 669.

enable the court to abandon that search in favour of the result which the court itself considers fair ...' and to that extent it is suggested that the Court of Appeal went too far in *Oxley v Hiscock*.

The facts of *Oxley v Hiscock* were as follows. Mr Hiscock and Mrs Oxley had met in the mid-1980s. Mr Hiscock worked abroad, but when he was in the UK they lived together at Mrs Oxley's property, in Page Close, Bean, Dartford, of which she was a secure tenant. When she had the opportunity to become the owner of that property under the 'Right to Buy' at a discount of £20,000 she did so, and Mr Hiscock provided the £25,200 needed to complete the purchase. That property was sold in 1991 and the property in dispute, in Dickens Close, Hartley, Kent, was purchased as a home for them both, and Mrs Oxley's children. The purchase was funded by the net proceeds of sale of Page Close, £61,500, borrowing of £30,000 and £35,500 from Mr Hiscock's own funds. The property was conveyed into the sole name of Mr Hiscock.

The solicitors advised Mrs Oxley that she ought to record the beneficial interests in view of the contribution she was making to the purchase of Dickens Close. Her reply was:

> '... I am quite satisfied with the present arrangements, and feel I know Mr Hiscock well enough not to need written legal protection in this matter.'

In due course, the relationship came to an end and Dickens Close was put on the market in 2001. The proceeds were divided by Mr Hiscock, substantially in his favour.

At first instance, the court found that there had been discussions between the parties at the time of purchase as to whose name should appear on the legal title in the context of a possible claim by Mrs Oxley's former husband. On this basis, the judge concluded that there was an intention that they should share the beneficial interests and there was therefore a constructive trust. In reaching a decision on quantification, she determined that on an examination of the whole course of dealings between the parties, all the evidence pointed to '... an intention to share the benefit and the burden ... jointly and equally'.

Mr Hiscock appealed on the basis that in the absence of any express agreement as to how the beneficial interests were to be shared the court had to follow resulting trust principles, as in *Springette v Defoe*.

The Court of Appeal endorsed the general approach of the judge at first instance to quantification but held that on the evidence there was no basis for a finding that the parties had agreed on an equal division. Indeed, there appeared to be no agreement about the proportions in which they were to share:

> 'This must ... be seen as a case where there is no evidence of any discussion between the parties as to the amount of the share which each was to have. And on that basis, the judge asked herself the wrong question. She should not have sought, by reference to the conduct of the parties while they were living together at ...

Dickens Close, to determine what intention both were then "evincing" – unless, by that, she was able to find a common intention, communicated to each other, to determine, definitively, the shares which had been left undetermined at the time of acquisition. She might have asked herself whether their subsequent conduct, while living together at ... Dickens Close, was consistent only with a common intention, at the time of acquisition, that their shares should be equal; but she did not. The right question, in the circumstances of this case, was "what would be a fair share for each party having regard to the whole course of dealing between them in relation to the property?"'[123]

The Court of Appeal considered that to give Mrs Oxley 50 per cent failed to take into account the substantially greater cash contribution by Mr Hiscock to the purchase price of Dickens Close, £60,700 as against £36,300, but was prepared to accept that the balance of the purchase price funded by mortgage advance was provided equally through the pooling of their resources whilst they were living together. On this basis, the beneficial interests were held to be shared 60/40 in favour of Mr Hiscock.

This decision confirmed that the broad brush approach of the court in *Midland Bank v Cooke* to quantification of beneficial interests where a constructive trust is found is to be preferred to the restrictive resulting trust approach adopted in *Springette v Defoe* at least in the domestic context.

In *Stack v Dowden,* the majority of the House of Lords agreed that the constructive trust approach was the appropriate approach to quantification. However, it was a unanimous view that in considering the whole course of dealings between the parties the object was to determine what their intention had been as to the share each would have, not to impose what the court might consider to be a fair apportionment.

Stack v Dowden concerned the quantification of beneficial interests where the legal title was registered in the parties' joint names. The fact of joint legal ownership meant that the court was not troubled by the issue of whether there was an intention to share the beneficial interest. This was to be presumed. Baroness Hale identified the question for the court in joint names cases to be this: '... did the parties intend their beneficial interests to be different from their legal interest ... and if they did, in what way and to what extent?'[124]

The burden of proof will be on the party who asserts that the beneficial interests are held differently from the legal interests. In determining the question on the particular facts of each case, Baroness Hale set out[125] a non-exhaustive list of factors that may be relevant:

'Many more factors than financial contributions may be relevant 'to divining the parties' true intentions. These include: any advice or discussions at the time of the transfer which cast light upon their intentions then; the reasons why the home was

---

[123] Chadwick LJ at para 44.
[124] At para 66.
[125] At para 69.

acquired in their joint names; the reasons why (if it be the case) the survivor was authorised to give a receipt for the capital moneys; the purpose for which the home was acquired; the nature of the parties' relationship; whether they had children for whom they both had responsibility to provide a home; how the purchase was financed, both initially and subsequently; how the parties arranged their finances, whether separately or together or a bit of both; how they discharged the outgoings on the property and their other household expenses. When a couple are joint owners of the home and jointly liable for the mortgage, the inferences to be drawn from who pays for what may be very different from the inferences to be drawn when only one is owner of the home. The arithmetical calculation of how much was paid by each is also likely to be less important. It will be easier to draw the inference that they intended that each should contribute as much to the household as they reasonably could and that they would share the eventual benefit or burden equally. The parties' individual characters and personalities may also be a factor in deciding where their true intentions lay. In the cohabitation context, mercenary considerations may be more to the fore than they would be in marriage, but it should not be assumed that they always take pride of place over natural love and affection.'

She concluded that 'At the end of the day, having taken all this into account, cases in which the joint legal owners are to be taken to have intended that their beneficial interest should be different from their legal interests will be very unusual'.

Notwithstanding this, the majority decision of the House of Lords was that the position in *Stack v Dowden* was unusual and that the presumption of joint beneficial interests was rebutted.

In that case the parties had been together for around 30 years, and had four children. They had never married. They lived together in rented accommodation until 1983 when Ms Dowden took the opportunity to buy the house of her late Uncle Sidney at a favourable price. The property was conveyed into her sole name. The deposit came from a building society account in her sole name into which some payments had been made by Mr Stack. The balance was borrowed by way of mortgage advance for which she alone was contractually liable. Ms Dowden made the mortgage repayments and paid all the household bills. Ten years later that property was sold and the parties bought a property in Chatsworth Road, London NW2. The legal title was registered in the parties' joint names. There was no express declaration as to the beneficial interests, although there was a statement on the standard form of transfer then current to the effect that the survivor of them could give a valid receipt for the purchase money. Although this would ordinarily point to joint beneficial interests, it was held that in the absence of any evidence that the parties understood the effect of this declaration, it was ineffective to determine the beneficial ownership.

The purchase price of Chatsworth Road was found from the net sale proceeds of the first house in Ms Dowden's sole name, savings also in her sole name, and a mortgage in joint names linked to two endowment policies, one in the name of each of them. Mr Stack made the mortgage repayments and paid the premium on the policy in his name. Ms Dowden paid most of the other outgoings on the house and paid the premium on the policy in her name. Throughout their relationship the parties kept their financial arrangements quite separate and made payments referable to the property from their respective resources. This included reducing the sum outstanding on the mortgage by making capital repayments from time to time. It was accepted that Ms Dowden contributed more in this way than did Mr Stack.

A little under 10 years after the purchase of Chatsworth Road the parties separated. Ms Dowden remained in the property with the children. Mr Stack made a claim for an order for sale and an equal division of the net proceeds. At first instance he was successful and Ms Dowden appealed. The Court of Appeal substituted an apportionment of 65 per cent/35 per cent in her favour. Mr Stack appealed to the House of Lords and the appeal was dismissed.

Baroness Hale identified that the onus was upon Ms Dowden to show that the parties' common intention when the legal title to the property was put into their joint names was that they would hold the property otherwise than as beneficial joint tenants. It was her view that Ms Dowden made out her case. She identified the following factors as relevant in rebutting the presumption of joint beneficial ownership:

–   Ms Dowden had contributed far more to the acquisition of Chatsworth Road.
–   Ms Dowden had contributed far more to the capital reduction of the outstanding mortgage.
–   Although Mr Stack paid the mortgage interest and the premium on the joint endowment policy Ms Dowden was responsible for all the other regular expenditure, negating any suggestion that they had each agreed to contribute to their joint needs according to their means.
–   The parties kept their financial affairs separate.

Since *Stack v Dowden* there have been a number of decisions in which the principles emerging from that case have been applied.

Fowler v Barron[126] underlined the severe burden of proof upon the party seeking to displace the presumption that the beneficial interests are shared differently from the legal title. In that case the family home was in the joint names of Mr Barron and Miss Fowler. Theirs was a 23-year relationship and they had two children. There was no express declaration as to the beneficial interests. There was a mortgage in joint names and the balance of the purchase price came from Mr Barron's resources. The mortgage repayments and all other outgoings including the weekly shop were paid by Mr Barron. Ms Fowler spent her earnings on herself and the children and paid for holidays and occasional treats. When the parties separated, Mr Barron claimed that he was sole beneficial owner and that he had agreed to the property being in joint names

---

[126] [2008] 2 FLR 831.

with the intention only that Miss Fowler would succeed to his share in the event that he pre-deceased her. He did not intend her to benefit in any other circumstances.

At first instance the case was heard before the decision in *Stack v Dowden* and the judge applied resulting trust principles to find in Mr Barron's favour. Miss Fowler appealed. The Court of Appeal had the benefit of the decision in *Stack v Dowden*. Applying constructive trust principles as required following that case, the onus was on Mr Barron to satisfy the court that the beneficial interests should be held other than in equal shares. The court said that in the absence of any express discussions between the parties it was a question of searching for the common intention to be inferred from 'the whole of the parties' relationship so far as it illumined their shared intentions'.

In that case it was held that it was relevant to 'consider whether the facts were inconsistent with the inference of a common intention to share the property in equal shares, to an extent to discharge the civil standard of proof on the person seeking to displace the presumption. The emphasis was on the parties' shared intentions'.[127] The factors that led the court to a conclusion that the presumption had not been rebutted and that Ms Fowler was entitled to an equal share were these. First, Mr Barron's evidence that he intended that Ms Fowler should benefit from the property only in the event of his death did not evince a common intention as he had not disclosed this to Ms Fowler. Secondly, the fact that the mortgage was joint was not inconsistent with a shared intention to share the beneficial interests equally. In relation to Ms Fowler's financial contributions the court held as follows:[128]

> 'The proper inference as to the way in which the woman had spent her income was that, with the exception of clothing for herself, her payments for gifts, school clubs and trips, holidays and special occasions, were her contributions to household expenses for which they were both responsible. The further inferences to be drawn were that the parties intended that who paid what should make no difference to their interests, and that the parties simply did not care about the respective size of each other's contributions; [they] had largely treated their incomes and asset as one pool from which household expenses would be paid.'

Adekunle v Ritchie[129] concerned joint ownership of a property by a mother and her son. They had been living in a council property of which the mother was a secure tenant. The mother decided to exercise her right to buy but could not do this without the help of the son. They took out a joint mortgage for 100 per cent of the purchase price. The property was conveyed into their joint names but without an express declaration of the beneficial interests. Two years later the son moved out but returned after 12 years. Two years later the mother died intestate and an issue arose between the son and his nine siblings as to beneficial ownership of the property.

---

[127] At p 831.
[128] At p 832.
[129] Unreported, 17 August 2007, Leeds County Court.

The approach of the judge was to apply constructive trust principles following *Stack v Dowden* and this was referred to and approved by Lord Neuberger in *Laskar v Laskar*. Although both *Laskar* and the present case concerned the purchase of a council house by a parent and child, the distinguishing features of this case were that the the house had been bought as a home for the mother and the parties had enjoyed a domestic relationship. In these circumstances a resulting trust would not be appropriate.

The judge found that the mother and son had made roughly similar contributions to the mortgage and other outgoings but that it was unlikely that the mother had intended that one son should benefit so disproportionately from her estate when she had ten children altogether. Taking an holistic approach to the situation he concluded that the son was entitled to a one-third interest.

The decision of the Supreme Court in *Jones v Kernott*[130] provided long awaited clarity in this area of the law. Ms Jones and Mr Kernott met in 1980. They had two children together but never married. In 1985 they bought a property together in their joint names. There was no express declaration of the beneficial interests. Ms Jones paid a deposit of 5 per cent of the purchase price, the balance of which was funded on an interest-only mortgage. A year later Mr Kernott built an extension which he funded almost exclusively, and also worked on himself, which increased the value of the property by about 50 per cent. They lived in the property together for around eight years during which time they had two children. Both parties worked. From her earnings and £100 a week housekeeping money from Mr Kernott, Ms Jones paid all the household bills including the mortgage.

When the relationship broke down Ms Jones stayed at the property with the children. Using his half share of a joint endowment policy that by agreement the parties surrendered, Mr Kernott was able to put down a deposit on a house of his own.

About 12 years after the separation, by which time house price inflation had brought about an increase in the value of both properties, Mr Kernott served notice to sever the joint tenancy. Ms Jones countered this with an application under the Trusts of Land and Appointment of Trustees Act 1996 (TLATA) for a declaration that she owned the entire beneficial interest in the property in joint names or a beneficial interest in the house in Mr Kernott's sole name. In the years of their separation Ms Jones alone had maintained the joint property and Mr Kernott his own property. He had made little contribution to the upkeep of the children.

The judge at first instance found that up until Mr Kernott's purchase of his own house using the endowment moneys there was no evidence to displace the presumption that equity followed the law. However, the judge also found that 'whilst the intentions of the parties may well have been at the outset to provide them as a couple with a home for themselves and their progeny, those

---

[130] [2011] UKSC 53.

intentions have altered significantly over the years to the extent that [Mr Kernott] demonstrated that he had no intention until recently of availing himself of the beneficial ownership in this property, having ignored it completely by way of an investment in it or attempt to maintain or repair it whilst he had his own property on which he concentrated'.

Having made this crucial finding of fact, that the parties' intentions had changed significantly from what they had been when the property was acquired, he concluded that in the absence of any indication by words or conduct as to how they intended that the beneficial interests were thereafter to be shared, the appropriate criterion was what he considered to be fair and just. Accordingly he apportioned the beneficial interests 90/10 in Ms Jones' favour.

Ms Jones' claim for a beneficial interest in Mr Kernott's property was dismissed.

Mr Kernott appealed to the High Court arguing that the judge was wrong to infer or impute an intention that the parties' beneficial interests should change after their separation and to quantify these in a way which he considered fair. The deputy High Court Judge concluded that the change in intention could readily be inferred or imputed from the parties' conduct. Mr Kernott appealed again. The Court of Appeal held that the beneficial interests in the joint property were held in equal shares. The 'ambulatory' constructive trust that the court below had invoked in order to increase Ms Jones' share from 50 per cent over the passage of time was roundly rejected. Giving the judgment of the court, Wall LJ as he then was, applied *Oxley v Hiscock*[131] and *Stack v Dowden*[132] and found that there was no basis for varying the shares in which the property was held. The presumption from the legal title was that the beneficial interests were in equal shares. The court could not depart from this unless there was evidence that the parties had expressly, or could by their conduct be inferred to have agreed or intended something other than this.

The court said that there was no evidence about what the parties intended. They did not appear to have given the matter any thought, much less discussed it. The only indicator was that in serving notice to sever the joint tenancy, Mr Kernott must have believed that he had a half share. The court felt unable to infer from the parties' conduct since separation a joint intention that over the passage of time the shares would be varied to the 90/10 split determined by the court below.

Permission was given to Ms Jones to appeal to the Supreme Court and the decision of that court was handed down on 9 November 2011. The appeal was allowed and the decision of the trial judge that the beneficial interests were held 90/10 in Ms Jones' favour restored.

---

[131] [2004] 2 FLR 669.
[132] [2007] 1 FLR 1858.

The essential difference between the Court of Appeal and the Supreme Court was in the approach to inferences to be drawn from the parties' conduct and the extent to which their intentions as to the sharing of the beneficial interests might change over time.

The Supreme Court said that the logical inference to be drawn from the finding of the county court judge that the parties' intentions had changed significantly from what they had been when the property was acquired was that the parties intended that Mr Kernott's interest in the shared home should crystallise at the point at which he bought his own home using the endowment moneys, leaving him to benefit from any capital gain in his own home, and Ms Jones to benefit from any further capital gain in the shared home. A rough calculation on that basis produced a result so close to that achieved by the trial judge that the Supreme Court considered that it would be wrong to interfere in that decision.

The lead judgment of Lord Walker and Baroness Hale sets out a clear summary of the principles that will apply in a case between cohabiting couples where the legal title is vested in their joint names, but without any express declaration of their beneficial interests, and where both are liable for any mortgage:

(1) The starting point is that equity follows the law and they are joint tenants both in law and equity.

(2) That presumption can be displaced by showing: (a) that the parties had a different common intention at the time when they acquired the home, or (b) that they later formed the common intention that their respective shares would change.

(3) Their common intention is to be deduced objectively from their conduct: 'the relevant intention of each party is the intention which was reasonably understood by the other party to be manifested by that party's words and conduct notwithstanding that he did not consciously formulate that intention in his own mind or even acted with some different intention which he did not communicate to the other party' (Lord Diplock in *Gissing v Gissing*). Examples of the sort of evidence which might be relevant to drawing such inferences are given in *Stack v Dowden*, at para 69.

(4) In those cases where it is clear either: (a) that the parties did not intend joint tenancy at the outset, or (b) had changed their original intention, but it is not possible to ascertain by direct evidence or by inference what their actual intention was as to the shares in which they would own the property, 'the answer is that each is entitled to that share which the court considers fair having regard to the whole course of dealing between them in relation to the property': Chadwick J in *Oxley v Hiscock*, para 69. In our judgment, 'the whole course of dealing … in relation to the property' should be given a broad meaning, enabling a similar range of factors to be taken into account as may be relevant to ascertaining the parties' actual intentions.

(5) Each case will turn on its own facts. Financial contributions are relevant but there are many other factors which may enable the court to decide what shares were either intended (as in case (3)) or fair (as in case (4)).

Thus in joint names cases such as *Jones v Kernott* the search is to ascertain the shares in which the beneficial interests are held. This will be a question of evidence and the court is not free to impose a solution upon the parties that is different from what the evidence shows their intention to have been. However, in the absence of any evidence as to what the parties' intentions were, the court has to reach a conclusion and it will do so by posing the hypothetical question as to what their intentions as reasonable and just people would have been had they thought about it at the time.[133]

In other words, the court is entitled in those circumstances to impute an intention as to the beneficial interests and give each that share which the court considers fair having regard to the whole course of dealing between them in relation to the property.[134] The 'whole course of dealing ... in relation to the property' should be given a broad meaning, enabling a similar range of factors to be taken into account as may be relevant to ascertaining the parties' actual intentions.[135]

In this case there was no need for the court to impute an intention that the parties' beneficial interests in the property would change at the point at which Mr Kernott used the joint endowment policy to fund the purchase of his own home, since the trial judge had already made that finding. However, in view of the blurring of the distinction between inference and imputation evident in the earlier authorities, notably *Pettitt v Pettit* and *Gissing v Gissing*, and the misgivings expressed by Lord Neuberger in *Stack v Dowden* as to the propriety of imputing to the parties an intention that could not be deduced objectively from their actions and statements, it was necessary for the Supreme Court to clarify the position.

---

[133] At para 47.
[134] At para 51(4) quoting from Chadwick LJ in *Oxley v Hiscock*, para 69.
[135] At para 51(4).

JOINT NAMES	JOINT NAMES	SOLE NAME
+ Express declaration of trust in TR1/FR1 or separate trust deed	No express declaration of trust	
Conclusive as to beneficial interests in the absence of fraud or mistake	'Equity follows the law' ie there is a presumption that the registered proprietors are joint tenants in law and equity in equal shares	'Equity follows the law' ie there is a presumption that the sole legal owner is also the sole beneficial owner
		Two stage enquiry for the court[136]
Goodman v Gallant[137]	Burden of proof is on the owner seeking to show otherwise. Not to be 'lightly embarked upon' *Stack v Dowden*[138]	(1) Was there a common intention that the beneficial interests in the property were to be shared?
	Applicant has to establish *either*: that they had a different common intention than equal shares when the home was acquired, *or*	Was there an express agreement, arrangement or understanding reached between the parties?
	that they subsequently formed a common intention that their shares would change	This is a question of fact 'based on evidence of express discussions between the parties however imperfectly remembered or however imprecise' *(Rosset No 1)*
	The parties' common intention is to be deduced (inferred) objectively from the conduct and dealings between the parties	In the absence of anything express can an intention to share the beneficial ownership be inferred?
	See *Stack v Dowden* para 69 for examples of the sort of evidence that might be relevant to drawing inferences	'direct contributions to the purchase price by the partner who is not the legal owner, whether initially or by payment of mortgage
	Where it is clear either that the parties did not intend joint tenancy at the outset, or had changed their original intention, but it is not possible to ascertain by direct	instalments, will readily justify the inference necessary ... it is at least extremely doubtful whether anything less will do' *(Rosset No 2)*

---

[136] *Lloyds Bank v Rosset* [1990] 2 FLR 155.
[137] [1986] 1 FLR 513.
[138] [2007] 1 FLR 1858.

JOINT NAMES	JOINT NAMES	SOLE NAME
+ Express declaration of trust in TR1/FR1 or separate trust deed	No express declaration of trust	
	evidence what their actual intention was, the court can impute[139] an intention to share in the way the court considers fair having regard to the whole course of dealing between them in relation to the property[140]	Since *Lloyds Bank v Rosset* judicial encouragement to lower the hurdle for contributions from which an inference can be drawn:
		The court should 'take a wide view of what is capable of counting as a contribution ... while remaining sceptical of the value of alleged improvements that are reallyinsignificant, or elaborate arguments (suggestive of creative
		accounting) as to how the family finances were arranged ... would include contributions in kind by way of manual labour, provided that they are significant' *Stack v Dowden*[141]
		If the answer to (1) is 'no' no beneficial interest If the answer to (1) is 'yes' establish detrimental reliance and proceed to (2) quantification – in the absence of any discussion between the parties what would be a fair share for each party having regard to the whole course of dealing between them in relation to the property?[142]

1.29 Proprietary estoppel

Similar principles to those relied upon in constructive trusts are evident when the court is asked to invoke its equitable jurisdiction to prevent one party from asserting his or her strict legal rights against another where a promise has been made to the other party, and that party has acted to his or her detriment in reliance upon the promise. However, in *Stack v Dowden*, Lord Walker

---

[139] *Jones v Kernott* [2011] UKSC 53.
[140] *Oxley v Hiscock* [2004] 2 FLR 669.
[141] [2007] 1 FLR 1858.
[142] *Oxley v Hiscock* [2004] 2 FLR 669.

cautioned against the merging of the two doctrines and specifically disapproved the suggestion in *Oxley v Hiscock* that there was little or no difference between them:[143]

> 'Proprietary estoppel typically consists of asserting an equitable claim against the conscience of the "true" owner. The claim is a "mere equity". It is to be satisfied by the minimum award necessary to do justice ... which may sometimes lead to no more than a monetary award. A "common intention" constructive trust, by contrast, is identifying the true beneficial owner or owners, and the size of their beneficial interests.'

In *Q v Q*[144] Black J, as she then was, considered the law on proprietary estoppel and constructive trusts and the distinctions between them, particularly in relation to remedy. With proprietary estoppel the court has a discretion to do the minimum required by equity in order to effect a just outcome.

Proprietary estoppel may arise in cases where there has been no financial contribution to the purchase price by the non-owner and so no question of finding a resulting trust, and as between cohabitants and others in the domestic context where there is no common intention to share the beneficial interests. In the context of cohabitants this may have relevance where the property is acquired by one party before the commencement of the cohabitation and contributions are made against the background of assurances of provision.

In *Wayling v Jones*[145] the court found that the claimant had been promised the hotel in which he had worked for the deceased unstintingly and for nominal payment, and when the deceased failed to leave it to him in his will it was held that he was entitled to it under the doctrine of estoppel.

There was a similar outcome in *Pascoe v Turner*.[146] At the end of their cohabitation, Mr Pascoe told Mrs Turner that she need not trouble to move out of what had been their shared home, a property paid for by him and in his sole name, it was all hers. There was no formal transfer of the property, but Mr Pascoe was well aware that Mrs Turner subsequently spent a quarter of her modest savings on repairs, improvements and redecoration to the house. Some time later, Mr Pascoe sought unsuccessfully to determine Mrs Turner's occupation of the house. The court held that whilst there was no evidence from which the court could infer a constructive trust, there had been a clear statement by Mr Pascoe that he had given the property to her as a gift, and she had acted to her detriment in reliance upon this by spending money on the fabric of the property. Mr Pascoe was held to his promise and was ordered to transfer the house to Mrs Turner outright.

---

[143] At para 37.
[144] [2008] EWHC 1874 (Fam).
[145] [1995] 2 FLR 1029.
[146] [1979] 1 WLR 431.

In *Yaxley v Gotts and Gotts*[147] the defendants owned several properties that they rented out. The claimant was a friend of the defendants and a self-employed builder who had worked for them from time to time. The claimant had seen a property which he thought would be a suitable investment for the defendants. They bought it, and it was agreed that in return for the claimant carrying out unpaid building work to convert the property into flats, he would become the owner of one of them. There was no formal agreement in writing. The parties fell out and the defendants denied the claimant's interest in the property. The Court of Appeal held that the defendants should be held to the agreement that the claimant was entitled to one of the flats, the claimant having fulfilled his side of the agreement and carried out the building work without payment.

In *Lissimore v Downing*[148] a former cohabitant sought to rely upon proprietary estoppel to salvage something from the eight-year relationship she enjoyed with a member of a rock band. Miss Lissimore's claim was that Mr Downing had made 'representations and/or promises ... which she relied upon to her detriment, such that it would be inequitable for the defendant to resile from the said representations and/or promises'.

At their highest, the representations amounted to statements to the effect, 'I bet you never thought all of this [the estate] would be yours in a million years' and references to the claimant as the 'Lady of the Manor'. There were also general statements that Miss Lissimore would never want for anything, and that Mr Downing always looked after his girlfriends.

In terms of detriment, Miss Lissimore's case was that she had given up her job, turned down an offer of a better job, and had become financially dependant upon Mr Downing and so had not invested the modest capital she had received on her divorce. She also claimed that she invested considerable time and effort in the running of the estate.

The findings of the judge were that although Mr Downing had supported Miss Lissimore financially throughout their relationship to a high standard, and that she had taken a full part in the activities of the estate, she had voluntarily given up her modest employment to enjoy life with Mr Downing. He did not induce her with promises for the future, and she did not sacrifice anything in terms of her career. She willingly helped out on the estate but not out of any belief that she had ownership of any part of it. In any event, the statements made by Mr Downing were not sufficiently specific to enable the court to assess what was promised.

This decision has been regarded in some quarters as an unduly restrictive approach to both the nature of the representation necessary, and detriment.[149]

---

[147] [1999] 2 FLR 941.
[148] [2003] 2 FLR 308.
[149] See [2003] Fam Law 567, Professor Rebecca Bailey-Harris.

However, what all these cases highlight is that where the court is concerned essentially to make findings about the party's usually differing accounts of events and conversations, possibly many years before, the court's assessment of the reliability of each party's evidence, and the entire history of their relationship will have considerable bearing upon the outcome.

Thorner v Majors[150] was a case in point. The claimant had worked unpaid on his cousin's farm for approaching 30 years. They were both what Lord Walker called 'taciturn and undemonstrative men committed to a life of hard and unrelenting physical work'. The context for what few oblique indications there were of an assurance given by the deceased to the claimant that the farm would one day be his was therefore of critical importance.

After about 14 years of helping on the farm, the deceased handed to the claimant a Prudential Bonus Notice relating to two policies on his life saying that they were to cover his death duties. The claimant had understood this, reasonably so the court found, as confirmation of what he had privately hoped would be the case, namely that it was his cousin's intention that he would inherit the farm. Thereafter there were occasional remarks made by the deceased that reinforced the claimant's expectation. For example, the deceased pointed out to the claimant a water trough that he said would never freeze up in the cold weather. The claimant understood this, and similar casually made observations, as being intended to give him information that he would need as his successor on the farm.

That case also raised the issue of certainty in relation to the property in question. The House of Lords said that it was sufficiently clear that what the deceased had intended the claimant to have was the farm, whatever it comprised, at the date of his death. It was irrelevant that during the years since the claimant was given the Prudential Bond Notice the farm was made up of different land holdings, the deceased having bought and sold land in the intervening period.

In another farming case, *Davies & Anor v Davies*[151] the principles of proprietary estoppel were summarised by Floyd LJ. He quoted from Lord Walker in *Thorner v Major*:[152]

> '... the doctrine is based on three main elements ... a representation or assurance made to the claimant; reliance on it by the claimant; and detriment to the claimant in consequence of his (reasonable) reliance ...'

He suggested that:[153]

---

[150] [2009] 2 FLR 405.
[151] [2014] EWCA Civ 568.
[152] At para 29.
[153] At para 30.

'Whilst these three elements are useful for the purposes of analysis and structured decision-making, they are not to be treated as watertight compartments. He quoted from Robert Walker LJ, as he then was, in *Gillett v Holt* ... although the judgment is, for convenience divided into several sections with headings which give a rough indication of the subject-matter, it is important to note at the outset that the doctrine of proprietary estoppel cannot be treated as subdivided into three or four watertight compartments ... the quality of the relevant assurances may influence the issue of reliance, that reliance and detriment are often intertwined, and that whether there is a distinct need for a "mutual understanding" may depend on how the other elements are formulated and understood. Moreover the fundamental principle that equity is concerned to prevent unconscionable conduct permeates all the elements of the doctrine. in the end the court must look at the matter in the round ... the detriment need not consist of the expenditure of money or other quantifiable financial detriment, so long as it is something substantial. The requirement must be approached as part of a broad inquiry as to whether repudiation of an assurance is or is not unconscionable in all the circumstances.'

He added that:[154]

'Two further principles emerge clearly from [*Gillet v Holt*]. Firstly, whether the claimant has suffered detriment must be judged at the point where the person who gave the assurance seeks to go back on it. Secondly, whether the detriment is sufficiently substantial must be judged by whether it would be unjust or inequitable to allow the assurance to be disregarded.

Whether there is detrimental reliance in any given case is an evaluative judgment on the facts, which normally lies within the exclusive province of the trial judge.'

Applying those principles, Floyd LJ refused to interfere with the finding of the trial judge that the claimant had given up her career in reliance upon an assurance from her parents that if she returned to work on the family farm it would one day be hers, and that in so doing there was a net detriment to her.

More recently in *Southwell v Blackburn*[155] the Court of Appeal considered the claim by Mrs Blackburn to an interest in the property she had shared with Mr Southwell. The decision of the judge at first instance to award a sum of £28,500 to Mrs Blackburn under the principles of proprietary estoppel was upheld on appeal. In that case Mrs Blackburn had left the rented home that she had established for herself and her daughters following her divorce to set up home with Mr Southwell. The property that they lived in had been bought in Mr Southwell's sole name to be their family home and they lived together there for about nine years. Although the parties had jointly chosen the property, the purchase had been financed entirely by Mr Southwell and he paid the mortgage and most of the household outgoings. He had been scrupulous in ensuring that Mrs Blackburn was not involved in the legal and financial side of the property because, as the judge found, he was mindful of the risk that she may try to establish a beneficial interest.

---

[154] At para 32.
[155] [2014] EWCA Civ 1347.

It was clear however that in leaving the security of her own property to move to live with Mr Southwell, Mrs Blackburn was taking a risk. She had invested the bulk of the £25,000 that she received in her divorce settlement in fitting out and furnishing that house. Against this background the judge found that Mr Southwell had reassured her that she would always have a home and be secure, and that in making such promises as were necessary to persuade her to move to live with him, he knew that she would rely upon them.

On that basis the judge concluded, and the Court of Appeal agreed, that it would be unconscionable for him to go back on his promise. In terms of quantification, the judge considered that the appropriate figure was one that, allowing for inflation, would put Mrs Blackburn back in the position she had been in before she moved to live with Mr Southwell.

Although the elements necessary to establish a constructive trust were not present in that case since there had been no clear promise that Mrs Blackburn would have any legal ownership of the property, the court was satisfied that Mr Southwell's promise that she would, 'always have a home and be secure in this one' was sufficient to amount to a commitment to her beyond the end of their relationship.

In relation to the necessary detrimental reliance upon the promise, whilst Mrs Blackburn had benefitted from the arrangement in terms of living rent free and additional financial support provided by Mr Southwell, so too had Mr Southwell, who had the support of Mrs Blackburn at home whilst he was furthering his career. The court concluded that making an assessment of detriment, particularly in the context of cohabitants, was not necessarily a strict accounting exercise, and should be viewed over the entire course of the relationship. In this case the direct consequence to Mrs Blackburn of the reliance upon Mr Southwell's promise was the loss of her investment in the home she left to move in with him, and this was the basis of the assessment of the sum that Mr Southwell was ordered to pay.

1.30 Accounting for occupation rent

When cohabitants separate and one remains in a property in which it is agreed or determined that the other has a beneficial interest, there may have to be an account taken of occupation rent. Following *Stack v Dowden* it is clear that the statutory principles contained in TLATA[156] must be applied. In simple terms, these enable the court to order the beneficial owner in occupation to pay compensation to a beneficial owner who is out of occupation. The court must have regard to the following factors when making such an order:

–   the intentions of the person(s) who created the trust;

–   the purpose for which the property subject to the trust is held;

–   the welfare of any minor who occupies or might reasonably be expected to occupy the property as his home; and

---

[156] Sections 12–15.

– the interest of any secured creditor of any beneficiary.

In *Stack v Dowden,* Mr Stack had asked the court for an order that Ms Dowden account to him for an occupation rent as she was living in the property and he had to provide separate accommodation for himself at his own expense. Applying the statutory criteria, the majority of the House of Lords considered that there should be no compensation. Lord Neuberger dissented from this view for the following reasons:

'First, both parties had the right in principle to occupy [the house], Ms Dowden was living there on her own as she wanted, she had excluded Mr. Stack against his will, and he was incurring the cost of alternative accommodation: accordingly such a payment seems appropriate in the absence of any good reason to the contrary. Secondly, the parties plainly thought it was right, when agreeing [that he should leave] that, as a quid pro quo for his exclusion from the house, Mr. Stack should be paid (or credited) at the rate of £900 per month. The circumstances of the parties do not appear to have changed [by or at the date] when they effectively accepted that Mr. Stack would remain excluded from the house.

Thirdly ... the four specific matters set out in s 15(1) ... either favour ordering a payment in favour of Mr. Stack, or they are neutral or irrelevant. Thus, ... the purpose for which the house was bought and the purpose for which it was held, favour the conclusion, as the house was bought as a home for Mr. Stack (as well as Ms Dowden and the children) ... the welfare of minors residing in the house ... is neutral as there is no suggestion of prejudice to the four children whether or not he was paid ... the interest of any secured creditor ... is irrelevant for present purposes.'

The Court of Appeal looked at the issue of compensation in *Murphy v Gooch.*[157] In that case the property was held by Ms Murphy and Mr Gooch as tenants in common in equal shares. On the breakdown of their relationship Ms Murphy left and commenced proceedings in order to realise her beneficial share. During the period that Mr Murphy was in sole occupation he paid the mortgage and the rent, this being a property bought under a shared ownership scheme. It was not in issue that he should be credited with Ms Gooch's share of those payments, but he resisted the suggestion that he should pay compensation to Ms Gooch by way of occupation rent. Lightman J reviewed the statutory principles[158] and concluded that the payments made by Mr Murphy on behalf of Ms Gooch cancelled out the payments that she should receive as an occupation rent. In the context of this case the relevant factors were that the parties had bought the property as a home for them both, but that since Ms Gooch was constrained to leave at the end of their relationship Mr Murphy alone had been enjoying this.[159]

---

[157] [2007] EWCA Civ 603, [2007] 3 FCR 96, [2007] 2 FLR 934.
[158] At para 19.
[159] The reasoning was not challenged but as to the net result see Elizabeth Cooke 'Accounting Payments: Please can we get the Maths Right?' [2007] Fam Law 1024.

1.31   Illegality of purpose

Many cohabitants may have to rely upon equity to resolve their property disputes. Will equity intervene if there is evidence of illegality in the arrangements between them?

In *Tinsley v Milligan*[160] a property was acquired jointly by two women, but was conveyed into the name of only one of them to enable the other to make fraudulent claims for State benefits. When they fell out, the legal owner tried to persuade the court that the other could not assert her beneficial interest as her name was not on the title in order that she could perpetrate a fraud. The court was not so persuaded and held that the non-owner could rely on the resulting trust that arose by virtue of her contribution to the purchase price. This case was followed in *Lowson v Coombes*.[161]

The judgment of Black J, as she then was, in the case of *Q v Q*[162] provides an authoritative review of the law in this area.

1.32   Applications for declaration of interest in trust property and order for sale

Sections 14 and 15 of the Trusts of Land and Appointment of Trustees Act 1996 (TLATA 1996) make provision for the court to order the sale of property held on trust and replaced s 30 of the LPA 1925 with effect from 1 January 1997.

Property held on trust will include all land held on either an express trust, for example where there are joint owners, or where there is a resulting or constructive trust.[163]

Trust property will include the proceeds of sale of trust property, and any other property acquired with the proceeds of sale.

A trust of land can include a mixed trust of land and personalty.

1.33   What relief is available?

The court's powers under ss 14 and 15 of the TLATA 1996 are more comprehensive than those under s 30 of the LPA 1925. In addition to ordering or preventing the sale of trust property the court may declare the nature or extent of a person's interest in the trust property, and may make orders relating to the exercise of the trustees' functions. The court may also give directions as to the application of the right to occupy provisions under ss 12 and 13 of TLATA 1996 and order the payment of an occupation rent.

---

[160] [1993] 2 FLR 963.
[161] [1999] 1 FLR 799. See also *Tribe v Tribe* [1995] 2 FLR 966.
[162] [2008] EWHC 1874 (Fam).
[163] See **1.20** and **1.22** above.

1.34 *Who may apply?*

An application under s 14 of the TLATA 1996 may be made by any person who is a trustee of land, or has an interest in trust property.[164] This includes a secured creditor, or a creditor who has a charging order, and a trustee in bankruptcy.

1.35 *Which court?*

The county court has unlimited jurisdiction in applications under s 14 of the TLATA 1996.[165]

In the High Court, application may be made to either the Chancery Division or the Family Division. In any event, there is power to transfer between Divisions, and between the county court and High Court and vice versa.

1.36 *Issuing the application*

In the county court, the application must be made to the court for the district in which the respondent resides or carries on business or the district in which the property is situated.[166]

In the High Court, the application may be made to the Central Office in London or any District Registry.

1.37 *Procedure*

The procedure is the same in the High Court and county court. CPR 1998 apply, and application should be made by claim form in Form N208 under Part 8.[167] The claim form must state:

- that Part 8 applies to the claim;
- the remedy the claimant is seeking and the legal basis for the claim;
- that the claim is brought under the TLATA 1996; and
- if any party is acting in a representative capacity, what that capacity is.

The claim form must contain a statement of truth.[168]

At the time of issue of the claim the claimant is required to file evidence in support of the claim. It may be contained within the claim form, but except for

---

[164] Section 14(1) of the TLATA 1996.
[165] Section 23(3) of the TLATA 1996, and the High Court and County Court Jurisdiction Order 1991 (SI 1991/724).
[166] CPR 1998 Sch 2, CCR Ord 4, r 3; High Court and County Courts Jurisdiction (Amendment) Order 1996 (SI 1996/3141).
[167] See CPR 1998, Part 22.
[168] 1.115, 1.197 and 1.198. For further reading see Da Costa and Garrod 'Procedural Aspects of Cohabitation Claims' [2003] Fam Law 270.

the most straightforward case it will generally be preferable for there to be a separate witness statement. A defendant to the claim is also required to file any evidence relied upon at the same time as returning the acknowledgement form, and what follows in relation to the preparation of witness statements applies to all parties.

The reported decisions in this area underline the importance that is often attached to the minutiae of the parties' financial and other history. It is worth setting out in full the closing words of the judgment of Waite J, as he then was, in *H v M (Beneficial Interest)* [1992] 1 FLR 229:

> 'The primary emphasis accorded by the law in cases of this kind to express discussions between the parties ("however imperfectly remembered and however imprecise their terms") means that the tenderest exchanges of a common law courtship may assume an unforeseen significance many years later when they are brought under equity's microscope and subjected to an analysis under which many thousands of pounds of value may be liable to turn on fine questions as to whether the relevant words were spoken in earnest or in dalliance and with or without representational intent. This requires that the express discussions to which the court's initial inquiries will be addressed should be pleaded in the greatest detail, both as to language and as to circumstance. In the Family Division, where there is no procedure for pleadings or particulars, the degree of particularity with which the relevant discussions are asserted in the claimant's initial affidavit will be of prime importance for both sides. From the claimant's point of view, failure to achieve particularity at that stage may cause the claim to founder for vagueness at the trial, where the affidavit will stand as her evidence-in-chief, on which she will be unlikely to be allowed to enlarge orally before she is cross-examined on it. From the respondent's point of view, he must be entitled, in an area of law where the nuances of language are all-important, to know exactly what case he has to meet.
>
> Particularity will have the further advantage to both sides of enabling the strength of the claim to be assessed by the parties' advisers at an early stage, with sufficient definition to provide a fair basis for reasonable compromise. That will be an especially desirable objective in the case of separating unmarried couples, whose distress or bitterness is often found, paradoxically, to have been increased rather than diminished by their decision not to undertake a commitment to each other in marriage.'

It is of vital importance therefore that full and detailed instructions are taken at the outset in order that a party's case is set out clearly from the start, and is focused on the issues that the court will have to determine.[169]

The claim form and evidence in support, together with as many copies as there are defendants should be filed at court with the fee payable. On receipt, the court will issue the claim and return copies for service together with a response pack in Form N208C for service on each defendant. The claimant will receive Notice of Issue in Form N209.

---

[169] If an application is to be made under Sch 1 CA 1989 consideration should be given to conjoining the applications. See *W v W (Joinder of Trusts of Land Act and Children Act Applications)* [2004] 2 FLR 321.

Each defendant is required within 14 days of service of the claim form to return the acknowledgement form that will be in the response pack indicating whether the claim is contested together with any written evidence relied upon. On receipt of the acknowledgement form, or after 16 days, the court will put the papers before the district judge. The district judge will give directions which will usually include listing a hearing date for a case management conference.

At the case management conference, directions will be given. These may include provision for each defendant to file a statement of case, disclosure of documents, filing of witness statements and obtaining evidence of valuation. If the claim is disputed, as will usually be the case, the district judge will direct that it proceed under CPR 1998, Part 7.

In terms of disclosure, in any dispute as to the beneficial ownership, it will be essential to obtain the conveyancing file, mortgage application form and any documents filed at the Land Registry.

In all cases the court, and the parties, should consider Alternative Dispute Resolution (ADR) and in an appropriate case the district judge may stay the claim to enable the parties to mediate. Some judges may direct a dispute resolution hearing similar to the Financial Dispute Resolution appointment (FDR) in applications under the Matrimonial Causes Act 1973 for a financial order.

Directions will be subject to a strict timetable which should include provision for a further case management conference so that the district judge can ensure that the case will be ready for hearing.

In the event that any defendant fails to attend the case management conference, the claimant will have to prove service of the claim.[170]

1.38 The exercise of the court's discretion

In deciding whether to make an order for sale, or declaration of a person's interest in the trust property under s 14 of the TLATA 1996 the court must take into account all relevant matters, including those set out in s 15(1) and (3), namely:

– s 15(1):
- (a) the intentions of the person or persons (if any) who created the trust;
- (b) the purposes for which the property subject to the trust is held (ie the current purpose rather than the original purpose);
- (c) the welfare of any minor who occupies or might reasonably be expected to occupy any land subject to the trust as his home; and
- (d) the interests of any secured creditor of any beneficiary; and

---

[170] CPR 1998, Part 6.

– s 15(3): the circumstances and wishes of any beneficiaries of full age and entitled to an interest in possession in property subject to the trust or (in case of dispute) of the majority (according to the value of their combined interests).

The factors set out in s 15 are not exhaustive and the court may consider any other matters that it considers relevant. *Mortgage Corporation v Shaire*[171] is an example of the court exercising its discretion in favour of families and against banks and other chargees, and is of interest also because it summarises the court's approach to the question of who owns what when there is a dispute.

The story began in 1980 with the breakdown of the marriage of Mr and Mrs Shaire. Mr Shaire moved out of the jointly-owned matrimonial home leaving Mrs Shaire in the house with their child. In 1986, Mrs Shaire began a relationship with a Mr Fox, and he moved in with her in 1987.

There were then divorce proceedings between Mr and Mrs Shaire. It was agreed as part of the divorce settlement that the house would be transferred into the joint names of Mrs Shaire and Mr Fox in exchange for a lump sum payment to Mr Shaire. This was raised by Mrs Shaire and Mr Fox by way of a mortgage advance.

The couple lived in the house with the child. Mrs Shaire worked part-time and had only modest earnings. Mr Fox paid the mortgage and the household expenses.

In 1992, Mr Fox died from a heart attack. After his death it came to light that he had forged Mrs Shaire's signature on several documents, including a mortgage to First National Bank and a charge to The Mortgage Corporation to secure a substantial sum which he had used to pay off the earlier borrowings.

In 1994, The Mortgage Corporation brought possession proceedings. Mrs Shaire was still living in the house with her son, although by this time he was an adult.

The issues raised by the possession proceedings included how the beneficial interests in the property had been shared between Mr Fox and Mrs Shaire, and whether there should be an order for sale so that The Mortgage Corporation could enforce their charge.

In relation to the beneficial share, those representing the bank said it was 50/50.

Those representing Mrs Shaire said it was a minimum of 75/25 in her favour.

The court decided that Mrs Shaire was beneficially entitled to a 75 per cent interest in the house.

---

[171] [2000] 1 FLR 973.

The approach taken was first to decide the shares in which Mr and Mrs Shaire had owned the property. The court agreed with counsel for both sides that it was 50/50 but set out the following factors that it was to take into account:

- there was an equal contribution to the purchase price by means of a wedding present of £2,000 to them both, and the balance by mortgage in joint names;
- the house was held in joint names;
- the house was intended as a family home and the parties lived there until the marriage breakdown;
- Mrs Shaire believed that joint names meant equal shares;
- the fall back presumption is that equality is equity.

It did not affect the court's decision that it was Mr Shaire who had made the mortgage repayments and paid all household outgoings.

The question then for the court was whether Mr Fox took over Mr Shaire's share so that they held in equal shares or whether Mr Shaire's share was divided between Mr Fox and Mrs Shaire so that they held as a minimum 75/25 in Mrs Shaire's favour.

The documents of title transferring the property to Mr Fox and Mrs Shaire did not set out the shares in which they were beneficially entitled, and the court was not prepared to accept that the standard wording in the old form of HM Land Registry Transfer Form providing that the survivor could give a valid receipt for the purchase money meant that they held the property as joint tenants in equal shares. The judge said that people who were not lawyers could not possibly intend that such a clause would mean that they shared equally.

There was nothing else in writing, and so the judge concluded that there was not an express agreement between them as to how they should share the beneficial interests that would cast any light on what they had agreed, if anything.

The court therefore had to look at the parties' conduct and in so doing the court set out a number of factors that it said made the arguments in favour of 75 per cent for Mrs Shaire compelling:

- they took on equal liability for the mortgage raised to buy out Mr Shaire;
- Mr Shaire was bought out for less than the value of his interest – the element of gift should be regarded as a gift to Mrs Shaire not Mr Fox;
- Mrs Shaire gave up capital claims against Mr Shaire in the divorce settlement;
- 25 per cent was Mr Fox's contribution in terms of his shared liability for the mortgage;
- the wording of agreement on the divorce was that Mr Fox and Mrs Shaire were together buying out Mr Shaire's half share, Mr Fox therefore had a one-quarter share.

The next question was whether there should be an order for sale.

It was argued on behalf of The Mortgage Corporation that a sale should be ordered unless there were exceptional circumstances. The court rejected that argument and said that it was able to exercise its discretion on the basis of the matters set out in s 15(1).

On the facts of this case the following matters were held to be relevant to the exercise of the court's discretion:
- Mrs Shaire had a 75 per cent interest in the house, the bank only 25 per cent;
- the house had been Mrs Shaire's home since 1976;
- she still lived there and wanted to stay there;
- for her to leave would be a real and significant hardship, but not an enormous one;
- the bank was in the business of lending money and they could be compensated for failing to realise their interest by payments of interest which Mrs Shaire could afford to pay.

There would therefore be no order for sale on condition that Mrs Shaire paid either interest to the bank for the use of its share of the property, or one-quarter of what would be the fair rent for the property.

The criteria upon which an order will be made under s 14 of the TLATA 1996 are much clearer than under s 30 of the LPA 1925. Furthermore, as the TLATA 1996 removes the concept of the trust for sale, and the power of the trustees by agreement to postpone sale, the court is no longer approaching the dispute from the standpoint that there is a presumption in favour of sale.

Note, however, that where an application is made by a trustee in bankruptcy the factors set out in s 15 do not apply.[172] The more restrictive matters to which the court must have regard in those circumstances recognise the interests of a spouse or former spouse, or a child for the 12 months after the bankruptcy order, but not the interests of a cohabitant.

1.39   The order

As well as making an order for the sale of the trust property, the court may prevent the sale in order to allow one party to occupy the property. In those circumstances there is power to order compensation to the party who is thereby unable to realise his or her interest in the trust property.[173] If it is not appropriate to make an order for immediate sale, the application should be dismissed leaving the parties to come back to court should circumstances change. Conditional orders should be avoided.

---

[172] Section 15(4) of the TLATA 1996.
[173] Section 13(6) of the TLATA 1996.

Where there is also a dispute about the ownership of the beneficial interest, the court may make a declaration as to the nature or extent of a party's interest in the trust property.

1.40 Injunctions

The court has the power to make an order restraining the disposal of trust property pending the final hearing. Application will be made on notice (exceptionally without notice) to the judge with an affidavit in support. The affidavit will set out fully and frankly all the circumstances, and the applicant's grounds for believing that the trust property is to be disposed of or otherwise dealt with.

1.41 Applications under the Married Women's Property Act 1882

Some cohabitants may be able to use the procedure contained in s 17 of the MWPA 1882. This will only apply to those who were engaged to be married, provided that no more than three years has elapsed since the engagement was broken off.

1.42 What relief is available?

The court has the power to resolve any dispute over the title to or possession of property but it cannot adjust the interests in property.

Property will include personal property, and the net proceeds of sale of property, or any other property bought with the net proceeds.

1.43 Who may apply?

Apart from spouses and former spouses, s 17 of the MWPA 1882 is only available to couples who were formerly engaged to be married within three years of the termination of the engagement.

1.44 Which court?

Application must be made to the Family Court.

1.45 Procedure

Applications under s 17 of the MWPA 1882 are family proceedings and so the Family Procedure Rules 2010 (FPR 2010) will apply. Application is made in Form D50 or D50B if the application is for a transfer of tenancy. The application must state what order is sought and have annexed to it a draft order.

Where the application relates to the title to or possession of land, the application must contain details of any mortgage, and state whether the title to the land is registered or unregistered, and if registered, the Title Number.

1.46   Service of the application

The application and any written evidence in support must be served on the respondent together with a form of acknowledgement of service in Form D50A. Where there is a mortgage, the mortgagee must be served with the application.

1.47   The hearing

The district judge has jurisdiction to make interim or final orders in applications under s 17 of the MWPA 1882. The hearing is in private.

1.48   The court's approach

When resolving a dispute as to the ownership of property, the usual trust principles will apply as laid down in *Pettitt v Pettitt*[174] and *Gissing v Gissing*[175] and restated in *Lloyds Bank plc v Rosset*.[176]

In determining the size of a party's share in property, the same principles will apply.[177]

When deciding whether or not to order the sale of property in dispute the court has an unfettered discretion, but one of the factors that will be relevant in relation to a dwelling house is whether the house provides a home for any relevant children.

1.49   The order

The court may make an order that is merely declaratory of a party's beneficial interest in property, real and/or personal, and it may order the sale of property.

1.50   Injunctions

The district judge may make an injunction restraining the disposal of property which is the subject of the application pending the final hearing. Application will be made on notice (in exceptional circumstances without notice), with an affidavit in support.

---

[174] [1970] AC 777.
[175] [1971] AC 886.
[176] [1990] 2 FLR 155. See **1.25** above.
[177] See **1.28** above.

1.51 Applications under Matrimonial Proceedings and Property Act 1970

Like the MWPA 1882, whilst primarily of relevance to married people, s 37 of the MPPA 1970 is available to those who are or were engaged to be married. This section can be invoked where an entitled applicant has made a substantial contribution to the improvement of property (real or personal), whether or not that person has a beneficial interest in the property. If successful, the applicant is treated as acquiring a share, or increasing an existing share, by reference to the contribution.

If an application is also to be made under the MWPA 1882, the proceedings should be consolidated.

SECTION 2   OCCUPATION OF THE HOME

The owner-occupied home

1.52   Rights of occupation

If a cohabitant can establish a beneficial interest in the family home, either by being a joint owner, or by virtue of a resulting or constructive trust,[178] the right to occupy the property will be undeniable, unless it has been prohibited, suspended or restricted by an order under Part IV of the Family Law Act 1996 (FLA 1996), or by the court's powers under s 13 TLATA.

Difficulties often arise where both cohabitants have rights of occupation as a result of their beneficial interests, and both choose to exercise those rights. In those cases, it may be appropriate to make application under Part IV of the FLA 1996 for an order prohibiting, suspending or restricting the exercise of the right by the other cohabitant, or for an exclusion order under s13 TLATA.

It is possible for a cohabitant who does not have rights of occupation to acquire them by making application under Part IV of the FLA 1996. If all the relevant criteria for making an order are satisfied, rights of occupation may be granted, but only in cases in which the cohabitant who is the respondent to the application is 'entitled' to occupy.[179]

Problems can arise where there is mortgage default, particularly where the party in possession is not a party to the mortgage. The provisions of s 54(5) of the Family Law Act 1996 enable a 'connected person' to make the mortgage repayments in respect of the home and to seek to be joined to any possession proceedings. For these purposes a connected person, in relation to the mortgagee, includes that person's cohabitant or former cohabitant.

---

[178] See **1.22** above.
[179] See **4.17** below.

1.53   Licences

If a cohabitant cannot establish or acquire rights of occupation, it may be possible to remain in occupation of the family home by relying on a licence to occupy.

During the subsistence of the relationship, the cohabitant with rights of occupation will have either expressly or by implication granted a licence to the other cohabitant to occupy the property. Ordinarily, a bare licence will be determinable upon reasonable notice and in these circumstances there will be no answer to a claim for possession.

However, the licence may have some contractual basis and will be enforceable if all the requirements for a valid contract are present. For example, in *Tanner v Tanner*[180] the court found that by giving up her secure rented accommodation to live in a property owned by the father of her two children a woman had given good consideration for an implied contractual licence to remain in the property until the children had finished their education.

Similarly, if an owner of property has led a person with a licence to occupy to believe that such occupation will continue, and in reliance upon that the licensee acts to his or her detriment, then the court may prevent or estop the owner from denying the right of occupation. This was the position in *Greasley v Cooke*.[181]

1.54   Orders under Sch 1 to the Children Act 1989

A cohabitant may be able to occupy property by virtue of looking after a child of the relationship where a transfer of property order has been made under Sch 1 to the CA 1989.[182]

The rented home

1.55   Rights of occupation

The law relating to landlord and tenant is a complex area and the following is intended as no more than a very basic outline.

Where cohabitants are living in rented property (as their only or principal residence), the right to remain in occupation if the cohabitation ceases for any reason will be the primary concern.

The position will vary according to whether the tenancy is held in joint names or in the sole name of one of the cohabitants, and will also depend upon the

---

[180] [1975] 3 All ER 776.
[181] [1980] 3 All ER 710.
[182] See 5.49.

nature of the tenancy under which the property is held. Different provisions apply to the different types of tenancy, for example in relation to security of tenure, rent control, assignment and succession on death.

1.56 Rights of occupation under Part IV of the Family Law Act 1996

An order giving a non-tenant cohabitant rights of occupation under Part IV of the FLA 1996 is not capable of affecting the rights of third parties. Accordingly, such an order will not in itself provide a defence to possession proceedings by the landlord.[183]

1.57 Private sector tenancies[184]

Tenancies of dwelling-houses created before 15 January 1989 are known as protected tenancies (contractual or statutory) and are governed by the Rent Act 1977 (RA 1977).

Most tenancies created after 15 January 1989 will either be assured or assured shorthold tenancies, and the provisions of the Housing Act 1988 (HA 1988) will apply. Following the HA 1996, most tenancies created after 28 February 1997 will be assured shorthold tenancies unless the landlord expressly provides otherwise.

Assured shorthold tenancies are a species of tenancy lacking long-term security of tenure. Rent control and ease of recovering possession are essentially geared to commercial considerations.

1.58 Housing associations and other registered social landlords

Tenancies granted by housing associations after 15 January 1989 are governed by Part 1 of the HA 1988 and may be either assured or assured shorthold tenancies. The provisions that apply are set out at **1.59** below.

Tenancies in existence before 15 January 1989 will almost certainly be secure tenancies which are effectively the same as those granted by local authorities.[185]

Assured tenancies

1.59 Security

Assured tenancies afford greater protection to the tenant than assured shorthold tenancies. However, it should be noted that in order for a tenancy to be or remain as an assured tenancy, the tenant, or at least one of the joint

---

[183] See also **1.72** below.
[184] Ie those outside the local authority sector.
[185] Housing Act 1988.

tenants, must be living in the property. Thus, if cohabitants are joint tenants, the removal of one of them from the property will not of itself affect the tenancy.[186] However, if the tenancy is in the sole name of one of the cohabitants, and that cohabitant leaves the property, the tenancy will cease to be an assured tenancy, and the landlord will be able to obtain possession.[187]

A fixed-term assured tenancy cannot be brought to an end by one joint tenant unilaterally as long as the fixed term has not expired. When a fixed-term assured tenancy comes to an end, for example by effluxion of time, it is replaced by a periodic tenancy on more or less the same terms as the fixed-term tenancy. Although the periodic tenancy will also be a joint tenancy, one tenant will be able to bring the tenancy to an end by serving a notice to quit. The situation could arise in which one cohabitant leaves during the currency of the periodic tenancy and serves notice to quit. This will determine the joint periodic tenancy leaving the tenant in occupation to deal with any possession proceedings brought by the landlord. There will be no answer to the landlord's claim as the court has no power to revive the tenancy.[188] However, the tenancy itself is property for as long as it remains in existence, ie before termination by notice to quit, and in *Bater v Greenwich London Borough Council and Another*[189] Thorpe LJ confirmed that the court has both statutory and inherent powers to prevent unilateral termination of a tenancy in certain circumstances.[190]

1.60   Assignment

An assured tenancy will either be for a fixed term, or a periodic tenancy determinable upon giving notice to quit. Whereas an assured tenancy for a fixed term may be assigned as long as the terms of the individual tenancy agreement do not prohibit assignment, a periodic tenancy may not be assigned without the landlord's consent unless the tenancy agreement expressly provides otherwise. There is no requirement that the landlord must not unreasonably withhold his consent.[191]

1.61   Succession

On the death of one joint tenant of an assured tenancy, the tenancy will automatically vest in the survivor.

An assured tenancy in the name of one person only is an interest in land and can be left by will, and in the absence of a valid will, it will be subject to the

---

[186] Section 1(1)(b) of the HA 1988.
[187] Section 5(1)(b) of the HA 1988. Compare with the situation as between husband and wife in *Griffiths v Renfree* [1989] 2 FLR 167.
[188] *Hammersmith and Fulham London Borough Council v Monk* [1992] 1 FLR 465.
[189] [1999] 2 FLR 993.
[190] See **1.74** below.
[191] Section 15 of the HA 1988 implies a covenant against assignment without the landlord's consent in the absence of any provision in the tenancy agreement.

intestacy rules.[192] If the surviving cohabitant is specified in the deceased tenant's will as the beneficiary of the deceased's interest in the tenancy, there will be no short-term difficulty. However, Ground 7 in Sch 2 to the HA 1988 is a mandatory ground that will enable a landlord to recover possession of property subject to a periodic tenancy that has devolved under the former tenant's will, provided that the proceedings for possession are started within 12 months of the tenant's death, or if the court directs, 12 months after the landlord became aware of the death.

If there is no will, a cohabitant cannot benefit under the intestacy rules. However, where there is a periodic assured tenancy, a cohabitant can succeed to the tenancy in the sole name of the other cohabitant if they were living together as husband and wife immediately before the death, the survivor was occupying the property as his or her only or principal home and the deceased had not acquired the tenancy by succession. In these circumstances, the periodic assured tenancy will not form part of the deceased's estate.[193]

The effect of this in practice is that if a person went to live with the survivor to a joint tenancy, on the death of the surviving tenant, the surviving cohabitant would have no right to succeed to the tenancy, no rights of occupation, and the landlord would be able to apply for an order for possession without having to satisfy the court as to the usual grounds for possession set out in Sch 2.

In *Harrogate Borough Council v Simpson*[194] the court held that same-sex cohabitants could not live together as 'husband and wife' for these purposes. This was confirmed in *Fitzpatrick v Sterling Housing Association Ltd* [2000] 1 FLR 271. However, these decisions pre-dated the implementation of the Human Rights Act 1998 (HRA 1998). The decision in *Mendoza v Ghaidan* [2004] 2 FLR 600 removed the inherent discrimination on the basis of sexual orientation by adopting an interpretation of the domestic statute that is compatible with the Convention.

CPA 2004 extended succession rights to civil partners and those living together as civil partners.

1.62 Protected tenancies

Slightly different considerations apply to tenancies created before 15 January 1989 to which the provisions of the RA 1977 apply. These tenancies will either be protected contractual tenancies or statutory tenancies. A contractual tenancy is a tenancy agreement to which the provisions of the RA 1977 apply. A statutory tenancy will arise by the operation of the provisions of the RA 1977 where a contractual tenancy comes to an end by effluxion of time or service of a notice to quit, or where the tenancy is acquired by succession.

---

[192] See **6.11**.
[193] Section 17(1) and (4) of the HA 1988.
[194] [1986] 2 FLR 91.

1.63   Security

One of the cohabiting parties can serve a notice to quit on the landlord which will terminate that party's obligations under the tenancy but will not jeopardise the tenancy for the remaining cohabitant as long as he or she continues to use the property as a residence.[195] The remaining cohabitant will then be a statutory tenant.[196] However, if the tenancy is in the sole name of the cohabitant who has left, the cohabitant in occupation has no rights in respect of the tenancy and no rights of occupation.

1.64   Assignment

Unless the tenancy agreement contains a covenant against assignment, protected contractual tenancies can be assigned with the landlord's consent, which is not to be unreasonably withheld.[197]

A statutory tenancy cannot be assigned.

1.65   Succession

If a protected contractual or a statutory tenancy is in joint names, on the death of one of the joint tenants the survivor will automatically succeed to the tenancy. A surviving cohabitant will succeed to a protected tenancy in respect of which the deceased was the original sole tenant if the surviving cohabitant was living at the property as the husband or wife of the deceased immediately before the death and if, and for so long as, he or she occupies the property as his or her residence. In these circumstances, the surviving cohabitant will become entitled to an assured tenancy (or statutory tenancy if the succession was before 15 January 1989) of the property on the same terms as under the contractual tenancy.

Following *Ghaidan v Godin Mendoza,*[198] 'living with the original tenant as his or her wife or husband' means 'as if they were his or her wife or husband'. The House of Lords upheld the decision of the Court of Appeal that sought to address the breach of the Convention found in the provisions of para 2(2) of Sch 1 to the Rent Act 1977. In this, the Court of Appeal had gone far beyond what at the time had seemed to be the liberal decision of the House of Lords in *Fitzpatrick v Sterling Housing Association Ltd.*[199] In that case it was decided that although a cohabitant of the same sex could not succeed to a statutory tenancy on the death of the other cohabitant, it was possible to succeed to a lesser form of tenancy as a member of the deceased tenant's family. It was then

---

[195] This is subject to the discretionary ground for possession in Case 5 of Sch 15 to the RA 1977 – where the tenant has given notice to quit and, in consequence of that notice, the landlord has contracted to sell or let the dwelling-house or has taken any other steps as the result of which he would, in the opinion of the court, be seriously prejudiced if he could not obtain possession.

[196] *Lloyd v Sadler* [1978] 2 All ER 529.

[197] Section 19 of the Landlord and Tenant Act 1927 (LTA 1927).

[198] [2004] 2 FLR 600.

[199] [2000] 1 FLR 271.

a question of fact as to whether or not the survivor could satisfy the court as to the necessary elements of the relationship.

At first instance the trial judge had applied *Fitzpatrick v Sterling Housing Association Ltd* and found that the same-sex partner of the deceased tenant was entitled to succeed only to an assured tenancy, as a member of the tenant's family, not to the secure tenancy that a spouse of a deceased tenant would have succeeded to.

The surviving partner appealed that decision on the basis of Art 14 of the European Convention for the Protection of Human Rights and Fundamental Freedoms 1950, which provides:

> 'The enjoyment of the rights and freedoms set forth in this Convention shall be secured without discrimination on any ground such as sex, race, colour, language, religion, political or other opinion, national or social origin, association with a national minority, birth or other status.'

The facts were very similar to those in *Fitzpatrick v Sterling Housing Association Ltd*. Two men had lived together for many years in an intimate and loving relationship. The property in which they lived was subject to a secure tenancy of which the deceased partner was the sole tenant.

The issue raised in both cases was the interest in the tenancy of the surviving partner on the death of the tenant.

Before the implementation of the Human Rights Act 1998, the House of Lords felt unable to construe para 2(2) of Sch 1 to the Rent Act 1977 as including same-sex relationships. The Court of Appeal in *Mendoza v Ghaidan*, unable to find any objective and reasonable justification for the exclusion of same-sex relationships from the relevant Schedule, concluded that such an interpretation was an infringement of Art 14:

> '… to afford a statutory tenancy to the survivor of a heterosexual relationship when the survivor of an equivalent homosexual relationship was limited to the less beneficial assured tenancy constituted discrimination on grounds of sexual orientation.'

In order to remedy the breach of the Convention, the court reinterpreted the Schedule to include those living as if they were the husband or wife of the deceased tenant, so as not to discriminate on grounds of sexual orientation, and so as to render the domestic legislation compatible with the Convention. This was upheld by the House of Lords, dismissing the defendant's appeal.

If the deceased tenant was the sole tenant of an assured tenancy (or statutory tenancy pre-15 January 1989) acquired by succession, a cohabitant will not automatically qualify to succeed. Instead, the surviving cohabitant will have to establish that he or she was a member of the family of both the original tenant and the successor to the tenancy immediately before their respective deaths, and that he or she was living with the tenant who succeeded to the original tenancy at the time of death and for the two years immediately before the death of the successor to the tenancy. Whilst this provision may be relevant to sons and daughters and other close family members, it is difficult to imagine the sort of ménage to which it could apply!

CPA 2004 extends succession rights to civil partners and those living together as civil partners.

1.66 Local authority housing

Tenancies granted by local authorities are known as secure tenancies and the HA 1985 applies. Tenancies granted by housing associations before 15 January 1989 will also be secure tenancies.

1.67 *Security*

If the tenancy is in joint names, whilst the removal of one joint tenant from the property will not affect the security of tenure of the other, if either of the tenants serves a valid notice this will defeat the other tenant's interest if the tenancy is a periodic tenancy.[200]

Neither tenant can unilaterally bring a fixed-term tenancy to an end by serving a notice to quit or surrendering the lease.

If the tenancy is in the sole name of the cohabitant who leaves the property, the remaining cohabitant has no interest in the tenancy and no rights of occupation unless an order is obtained under Part IV of the FLA 1996.[201]

1.68 *Assignment*

A secure tenancy cannot be assigned except in the specific cases mentioned in s 91(3) of the HA 1985. These include assignments pursuant to an order made under Sch 1 to the CA 1989 and the assignment of secure tenancies to a person who would have qualified to succeed on the death of the tenant. If the tenancy is in joint names, the other joint tenant will qualify. If the property is in the sole name of the cohabitant who wishes to assign the tenancy, the other cohabitant must satisfy two criteria. First, the assignee must have lived with the assignor for the entire 12-month period immediately before the assignment. Secondly, the assignee must come within the definition of 'a member of the [assignor's] family'.[202]

---

[200] *Hammersmith and Fulham London Borough Council v Monk* [1992] 1 FLR 465.
[201] *Gay v Sheeran* [1999] 2 FLR 519, CA.
[202] See s 113 of the HA 1985 for definition of members of a person's family.

1.69 Succession

If the tenancy is in the joint names of cohabitants, the surviving cohabitant will succeed to the tenancy automatically. If the tenancy was in the sole name of the deceased cohabitant, the survivor may succeed if he or she can satisfy two criteria. First, the survivor must have lived with the deceased for the entire 12-month period immediately before the death of the tenant. Secondly, the survivor must come within the definition of 'a member of the tenant's family'.[203]

There can only be one succession to a secure tenancy. Accordingly, the survivor of joint tenants, or a person who himself succeeded to a secure tenancy, cannot pass on a tenancy.

CPA 2004 extends succession rights to civil partners and those living together as civil partners.

1.70 Tenancy in joint names

If a tenancy is in joint names, both parties will be jointly and severally liable to pay the rent and perform all the other obligations of the tenancy, but they will both have the right to occupy and enjoy the property and cannot lawfully exclude the other except where an exclusion order is in force, for example pursuant to Part IV of the FLA 1996.

The survivor of joint tenants will automatically succeed to the tenancy, and in view of the restrictions on succession by cohabitants that apply to some forms of tenancy, if a tenancy can be taken in joint names, or assigned into joint names by agreement, this will usually be preferable.

A joint tenant will be in a better position than a cohabitant who is not a tenant when it comes to applying for an order under Part IV of the FLA 1996. As a joint tenant, he or she will be able to apply under s 33 and orders made under that section may last for longer than orders made in favour of a cohabitant who is not a tenant.[204]

The provisions of Sch 7 to the FLA 1996 in relation to orders for the transfer of tenancies may also operate in favour of joint tenants as the criteria to be considered in the case of a cohabitant who is not a tenant (and is without rights of occupation given by the FLA 1996) are wider ranging and more discriminatory. They include, for example, the length of the cohabitation and the fact that the parties have not committed themselves to marriage or civil partnership.

---

[203] See s 113 of the HA 1985.
[204] See **4.26** above.

It is important to be aware that although one of two joint tenants cannot determine a fixed-date tenancy or surrender a lease before the end of the term, the service of a valid notice to quit on the landlord by one tenant of a periodic tenancy can bring the tenancy to an end regardless of the other tenant's wish to remain in the property.[205] Furthermore, following the decision of the Supreme Court in *Sims v Dacorum Borough Council,* any challenge to this either as a violation of Art 8 ECHR rights[206] or under Art 1 of the First Protocol to the Convention[207] is likely to be unsuccessful.

The action that can be taken to prevent the termination of a joint tenancy in this way is set out at **1.74** below.

1.71 Tenancy in sole name

Whilst a cohabitant who is not the tenant of a shared property has no obligation to pay rent or other charges, neither will that person have any right to occupy the property beyond the licence impliedly or expressly granted by the cohabitant who is the tenant.[208]

If that licence is terminated on the breakdown of a cohabitation relationship, a cohabitant may only acquire rights of occupation by obtaining an order under Part IV of the FLA 1996. This is a discretionary remedy and is likely to be available for interim protection only.[209]

Even if the cohabitant who is not the tenant remains in occupation after the tenant has left, the tenant may terminate the tenancy by serving a notice to quit on the landlord or surrendering the tenancy to the landlord. Clearly, he or she will be anxious to be relieved of the responsibilities imposed by the tenancy, regardless of any other motive there may be. In these circumstances, in the absence of an order giving the non-tenant cohabitant rights of occupation, there will be no defence to possession proceedings brought by the landlord unless, exceptionally, the remaining cohabitant could establish that a new tenancy had been granted.

If the tenant has not brought the tenancy to an end and the non-tenant cohabitant remains at the property, he or she may be able to apply for an order transferring the tenancy.[210]

---

[205] *Hammersmith and Fulham London Borough Council v Monk* [1992] 1 FLR 465.
[206] Right to respect for one's home.
[207] Right to peaceful enjoyment of possessions.
[208] See **1.2**.
[209] See **4.35**.
[210] See further below.

1.72 Protecting the cohabitant in occupation

Whether the tenancy is in the sole name of the departing cohabitant, or in joint names, urgent action may be necessary to preserve the property for the remaining cohabitant.

Once a tenancy has been brought to an end it cannot be revived for any purposes,[211] although if the landlord is co-operative a new tenancy could be granted.

The fact that a tenancy may be in joint names does not prevent one tenant from serving a notice to quit and thereby defeating the other tenant's interest in the tenancy.[212]

This will not apply in the case of protected tenancies under the RA 1977.

1.73 Notice to quit

To be valid to terminate the tenancy, a notice to quit must fulfil two basic requirements. First, it must be in writing and secondly, it must give four weeks' notice. Whether acting for the tenant giving notice to quit, or the unfortunate tenant or cohabitant remaining at the property, it will be as well to check that the formalities have been complied with before concluding that the notice to quit is effective.[213]

Service of a notice to quit is not a 'disposition of property' that can be set aside by the court[214] and, therefore, it is of prime importance to keep the tenancy alive by preventing service of a notice to quit.

1.74 Injunction to prevent termination of tenancy

The only remedy open to the cohabitant remaining in the shared home who is faced with the prospect of the other cohabitant serving a notice to quit is to apply to the court for an order to prevent such service. The basis for the court's jurisdiction is the power given by Sch 7 to the FLA 1996 to transfer tenancies between cohabitants. Clearly any disposal of the tenancy before the court had determined an application to transfer would pre-empt the court's decision.[215]

---

[211] *Newlon Housing Trust v Alsulaimen* [1998] 2 FLR 690.

[212] *Hammersmith and Fulham London Borough Council v Monk* [1992] 1 FLR 465; *Harrow London Borough Council v Johnstone* [1997] 1 FLR 887.

[213] Section 5(1) of the Protection from Eviction Act 1977.

[214] In *Harrow London Borough Council v Johnstone* [1997] 1 FLR 887, the concession made in *Newlon Housing Trust v Alsulaimen* [1998] 2 FLR 690 that notice of termination could be set aside as a reviewable disposition under MCA 1973, s 37(2)(b) if no injunction had been granted before service of the notice was called into question.

[215] *Bater v Greenwich London Borough Council and Another* [1999] 2 FLR 993, CA.

Any application for an injunction should ideally be within an existing application for a transfer of tenancy, but in cases of urgency, the court will generally accept an undertaking to issue the substantive application within a short timescale.

If a notice to quit is served after an application has been made for a transfer of the tenancy, this will not affect the court's powers to transfer the tenancy.[216]

1.75 Applying to transfer the tenancy

In common with married parties, or those in a civil partnership, who separate, it will usually be prudent to ensure a cohabitant's continued security of tenure by making application for a transfer of the tenancy of the former shared home, whether the tenancy is in joint names or the sole name of the cohabitant who has left.

Until Sch 1 to the CA 1989 came into force, there was no jurisdiction to entertain such an application, and then application could be made only by a parent with the care of a child, with the primary intention of benefitting the child.

However, Part IV of the FLA 1996 now gives the court wide powers to order the transfer of tenancies between cohabitants, and this will generally be the preferred route.

In the case of a secure tenancy under the HA 1985, if the remaining cohabitant is not a tenant, and the tenancy has not been brought to an end by a valid notice to quit, the remaining tenant will have to acquire rights of occupation under s 36 of the FLA 1996 before the court will have power to order a transfer of tenancy under s 53 and Sch 7. This was the position in *Gay v Sheeran*.[217] In that case, the tenancy was in the joint names of the departing cohabitant and his previous cohabitant. It was agreed that neither the landlord nor either of the joint tenants had brought the tenancy to an end, but it was a fact that the tenant condition was not satisfied. Section 79(1) of the HA 1985 provides that for a tenancy to be a secure tenancy, the tenant condition in s 81 has to be satisfied. In this case, that condition was not satisfied because none of the tenants was in occupation. In order to satisfy the condition, the remaining cohabitant had to acquire rights of occupation by way of an occupation order under s 36 of the FLA 1996 in order for her occupation to be treated as occupation by the departing cohabitant pursuant to s 30(4) of the FLA 1996.

The court held that even if the occupation order was sought partly with a view to obtaining a transfer order, this was not outside the scope of s 36 of the FLA 1996, although the requirements for an order under that section would have to be satisfied.

---

[216] *Hammersmith and Fulham London Borough Council v Monk* [1992] 1 FLR 465; *Lewis v Lewis and Another* [1984] FLR 492.

[217] [1999] 2 FLR 519.

Even though the remaining cohabitant was able to put herself in a position to apply for the transfer of the tenancy, in her case the court expressed doubts as to whether there was power under Sch 7 to the FLA 1996 to transfer a tenancy that was in the name of a third party as well as the cohabitant who had left. It was considered that the words in the Schedule effectively limited a relevant tenancy to one held in a tenant's 'own right or jointly with the other spouse or cohabitant', in other words, not held jointly with a person other than the spouse or cohabitant.

Application to transfer a tenancy under Part IV of the Family Law Act 1996

1.76   Which court?

Application should be made to the Family Court, noting that the Lay Justices have no jurisdiction in these applications. If there are other family proceedings in a particular court it will generally be good practice to make an application to transfer the tenancy to that court.

1.77   Who may apply?

As well as a spouse or former spouse and following implementation of CPA 2004 civil partners and former civil partners, there is provision for applications to be made by a cohabitant who is no longer living with the other cohabitant.

1.78   Which tenancies may be transferred?

Not all tenancies may be the subject of an order for transfer. For example, assured shorthold tenancies are excluded.

Only a 'relevant tenancy' may be transferred. This will include:
(1)   a protected tenancy or statutory tenancy to which the RA 1977 applies;
(2)   a statutory tenancy under the Rent (Agriculture) Act 1976;
(3)   a secure tenancy under s 79 of the HA 1985;
(4)   an assured tenancy or assured agricultural occupancy to which Part I of the HA 1988 applies.

The court may make an order only in relation to a property that was the home in which the cohabitants lived together, and only if one of the parties is entitled to occupy the home by virtue of one of the relevant tenancies.

The court can only transfer the interest that the transferor had in the tenancy immediately before the order for transfer.

1.79   Time for the application

There is no prescribed time for an application by a former cohabitant, simply a requirement that the parties are no longer living together, and the applicant's marriage or new relationship will not prevent an application being made. Having said that, the lapse of time since cohabitation, and marriage or a new relationship, whilst not a bar to relief, may be considered by the court on the exercise of its discretion.

1.80   The exercise of the court's discretion

In deciding whether or not to make what is known as a Part II order in favour of a former cohabitant, the court is to have regard to all the circumstances of the case, including:

(1)   the circumstances in which the tenancy was granted, or the circumstances in which one or both of the cohabitants became tenants;

(2)   the matters set out in s 33(6) of the FLA 1996, namely:
    –   the housing needs and housing resources of the parties and any relevant child,
    –   the financial resources of the parties, and
    –   the likely effect of any order, or the refusal of an order, on the health, safety or well-being or the parties or any relevant child;

(3)   if only one of the cohabitants is entitled to occupy under a relevant tenancy the matters set out in s 36(6) of the FLA 1996, namely:
    –   the nature of the parties' relationship,
    –   the duration of the cohabitation,
    –   whether there are or have been any children who are children of both parties or for whom both parties have or have had parental responsibility, and
    –   the length of time since the parties lived together; and

(4)   the suitability of the parties as tenants.

1.81   Issuing the application

The application should be made on Form D50B. It is effectively treated as if it were an application for an occupation order. A sworn statement in support should be filed. The statement should confirm the applicant's eligibility to apply, that the tenancy is a relevant tenancy, and that one or both of the parties, as the case may be, is entitled to occupy the property by reason of the tenancy. The criteria upon which the court will exercise its discretion should also be addressed.

To issue the application, the applicant's solicitor will attend at the court office with sufficient copies of the Form D50B and supporting statement. A fee is payable unless exemption/remission is claimed. The court will seal all documents and return copies for service on the respondent and the landlord.

1.82 Service

The application and statement in support, will be served by post on the other cohabitant and the landlord by the court unless the court directs otherwise.

1.83 What the respondent should do

The respondent will receive with the application a Notice of Proceedings and acknowledgement of service in Form D50A. This must be completed and returned to the court within 14 days of receipt. If the application is contested it will be usual for a statement setting out the reasons for this to be sent to the court and to the applicant within a further 14 days.

1.84 The hearing

Unless the court is able to make an order on the papers, a short hearing will be fixed when the parties will be required to attend.

The hearing will be in private unless the court directs otherwise.

If the court has sufficient information to make an order transferring the tenancy, or if the respondent consents, a final order can be made. Otherwise, directions will be given.

1.85 The order

Part II of Sch 7 to the FLA 1996 sets out the types of order that the court may make. These vary according to the type of tenancy, but essentially they provide for a transfer of the tenancy without the requirement for any further documentation, and confirm that the transferor takes the tenancy subject to all existing rights and obligations. This has been held to extend to the terms of a suspended order for possession of a property.[218] However, the court can mitigate the effect of this by directing that the parties are to be jointly and severally liable to discharge or perform all or any of the liabilities and obligations in respect of the property which otherwise only one of them would be liable to deal with. This power extends to liabilities and obligations in respect of the property that arise apart from the tenancy, for example payment for services, decoration and repair. If the court makes such a direction, the order may also provide for one party to indemnify the other against any such liability.[219]

In addition, when the court makes an order under Part II, there is power to award compensation to be paid by the transferee to the transferor. In deciding whether to exercise that power, the court must have regard to all the circumstances, including:

---

[218] *Church Commissioners for England v Emarah and Another* [1996] 2 FLR 544.
[219] Part III, para 11.

(1)　whether the transfer of the tenancy will result in a financial loss to the transferor;

(2)　the financial needs and resources of the parties;

(3)　the financial needs and obligations which the parties have, or are likely to have in the foreseeable future, including financial obligations to each other and to any relevant child.

The court may either at the time the order is made, or at any time before the payment is due to be made in full, direct that any compensation payment may be deferred to a specified date or event, or paid by instalments, unless to do so would cause the transferee greater financial hardship than the transferor.[220]

1.86　*Application under Sch 1 to the Children Act 1989*

Paragraph 1(2) of CA 1989, Sch 1 enables the court to make a number of financial and property provisions in respect of children, including the transfer of property which will include the transfer of a tenancy.

1.87　*Which court?*

Application should be made to the Family Court, noting that the Lay Justices have no jurisdiction in these applications.

1.88　*Who may apply?*

Paragraph 1(1) of CA 1989, Sch 1 provides that applications for the transfer of property, which will include a tenancy, may be made by the following:

–　the parent of a child ('parent' includes a step-parent);

–　the guardian of a child; or

–　any person who has a residence order with respect to a child.

1.89　*Procedure*

The application is for a financial remedy and FPR 2010 apply as for any other application under Schedule 1, CA 1989 for a financial remedy for a child. Where there is also to be an application under TLATA generally speaking it will be preferable for the applications to be conjoined and heard at the same time.[221]

1.90　*Service*

Service of the application need not be personal service, but 14 days' notice must be given.

---

[220]　Part III, para 10(2), (3) and (5).
[221]　*W v W (Joinder of Trusts of Land Act and Children Act Applications)* [2004] 2 FLR 321.

There is no requirement to serve the landlord of the property, but it may be prudent for the applicant to obtain his consent to what is proposed, and to provide the court with evidence of that consent.

1.91   The exercise of the court's discretion

The matters to which the court must have regard when deciding whether or not to order a transfer of tenancy are broadly speaking the same as when the court is exercising its discretion under s 25(3) of the MCA 1973. However, there is no specific requirement that the child's welfare is to be either the court's 'first consideration'[222] or the 'paramount consideration'.[223]

The court must have regard to all the circumstances, which will include:
- the financial needs of the child;
- the income, earning capacity (if any), property and other financial resources of the child;
- any physical or mental disability of the child; and
- the manner in which the child was being, or was expected to be, educated or trained.

In addition, the court will look at the income, earning capacity, property and other financial resources, and financial needs, obligations and responsibilities, at the time of the hearing and in the foreseeable future, of the child's parents, which will include a step-parent or former step-parent, and that of the applicant and any other person in whose favour the court proposes to make the order.

1.92   The court's approach

Although the matters to which the court must have regard when making orders under Sch 1 to the CA 1989 are effectively the same as those in s 25 of the MCA 1973, the approach is slightly different.

The court takes the view that the provision is to be for the child during his minority, and only exceptionally will provision be carried beyond a child's 18th birthday or the completion of full-time tertiary education.

In practice, this means that any property which is transferred for the benefit of a child will usually revert to the transferor when the child reaches the age of 18, or ceases full-time education, whichever occurs first.

In the context of a tenancy, it may be unnecessary for there to be provision for the tenancy to revert to the transferor as in most cases, unlike owner-occupied property, a tenancy will have no value other than as a place in which to live. However, the position can be complicated if the transferor has the right to buy

---

[222] Section 25(1) of the MCA 1973.
[223] Section 1(1) of the CA 1989.

the property under the HA 1980, and will lose that right if a transfer is effected. In *K v K (Minors: Property Transfer)*[224] a transfer of tenancy was ordered despite the fact that the transferor would thereby lose benefits under the HA 1980 right to buy scheme.

There is no provision in the CA 1989 for the court to award compensation as there is in Part IV of the FLA 1996.[225]

1.93   The homeless cohabitant

If a cohabitant is without accommodation, for example on the breakdown of the relationship, or if the family home is repossessed, there are certain limited steps that can be taken to assist. What follows is intended to be a broad outline of the position and if more detail is required a specialist text should be consulted.[226]

1.94   *Application to the local authority*

Local housing authorities have a statutory duty to rehouse homeless persons. This duty is limited and applied strictly.

HA 1996, Part VII as amended by the Homelessness Act 2002 and the regulations which supplement it[227] set out the statutory duties of the local authorities towards homeless persons. The local authorities must also have regard to the guidance issued by the Department for Communities and Local Government.[228] The basic objective of the statutory duty is to require the local housing authorities to provide accommodation for certain limited categories of homeless applicants.

To be eligible, four criteria must be satisfied. The applicant must:

(1)   be eligible for assistance – this requirement effectively excludes refugees and asylum seekers;

(2)   be homeless or threatened with homelessness – this will include a 28-day possession order and homelessness as a result of domestic violence;

(3)   have a priority need, for example be pregnant, live with a pregnant woman, have dependent children,[229] be vulnerable because of old age,

---

[224] [1992] 2 FLR 220.

[225] See also S Bridge *Transferring Tenancies of the Family Home* [1998] Fam Law 26.

[226] For example, Arden and Hunter *Homelessness and Allocations*, 9th edn (Legal Action Group, 2012).

[227] Allocation of Housing (England) Regulations 2000 (SI 2000/702); Allocation of Housing (Wales) Regulations 2000 (SI 2000/1080); Homeless Persons (Priority Need) (Wales) Order 2001 (SI 2001/607); Homelessness (Priority Need for Accommodation) (England) Order 2002 (SI 2002/2051).

[228] *Homelessness prevention: a guide to good practice*, DCLG June 2006.

[229] A shared residence order under Children Act 1989 will not necessarily influence the decision of the housing authority: *Holmes-Moorhouse v Richmond-upon-Thames LBC* [2009] UKHL 7.

mental illness, physical disability or fall within one of the categories contained in the statutory instruments,[230] or be a victim of a disaster such as a fire or flood; and

(4) not be intentionally homeless – a stringent test is laid down by s 191 of the HA 1996 and is strictly interpreted by the local housing authorities.

If a homeless applicant is dissatisfied with the decision of a local housing authority, the HA 1996 makes provision for a review of the decision, and if a point of law is involved, a right of appeal to the county court. However, there are strict time-limits which cannot be extended by the court.[231]

1.95 Request to local authority under s 20 of the Children Act 1989

The harsh effects of the operation of the homelessness provisions of the HA 1996 are mitigated at least as far as children are concerned by s 20 of the CA 1989. This places a duty on local authorities to provide accommodation for children in need. The definition of a child in need includes a child whose carer has been prevented from providing him with suitable accommodation. However, the duty does not extend to providing accommodation for the carer as well as the child, and the reality will almost certainly be that the child will be separated from the adult members of the family.

---

[230] The statutory instruments add the following additional categories. It should be noted that the situation differs between England and Wales. In Wales, the categories are:
• a person who is 18 or older but under 21 and at any time while still a child was, but no longer is, looked after, accommodated or fostered or is at particular risk of sexual or financial exploitation (it should be noted that there is no restriction in time or duration on the fostering and so a child accommodated with the parent's agreement at the age of three for six months will qualify as priority need);
• a person who is 16 or 17 years old;
• a person without dependent children who has been subject to domestic violence or is at risk of such violence, if he or she returns to their home;
• a person serving in the armed forces who has been homeless since leaving those forces;
• a former prisoner who has been homeless since leaving custody and who has a local connection within the area of the local housing authority.
The English provisions are more restrictive, being:
• a person aged 16 or 17 who is not either a relevant child for the purposes of s 23A of the Children Act 1989 and to whom a local authority do not owe duty to provide accommodation under s 20 of the Children Act 1989;
• a person (other than a relevant student) who is under 21 and, at any time after reaching 16, but while still under 18, was, but is no longer, looked after, accommodated or fostered;
• a person (other than a relevant student) who has reached the age of 21 and who is vulnerable as a result of having been fostered, accommodated or looked after;
• a person who is vulnerable as a result of having been a member of the armed forces;
• a person who is vulnerable as a result of having served a custodial sentence, having been committed for contempt of court or any kindred offence;
• a person who is vulnerable as a result of ceasing to occupy accommodation by reason of violence from another person or threats of violence from another person which are likely to be carried out.

[231] See ss 202 and 204 of the HA 1996.

1.96   Request to the social services department under s 17 of the Children Act 1989

It is arguable that it is within the general duty imposed upon social services departments by s 17 of the CA 1989 to provide services for children in need and their families to make cash available for a deposit for private rented accommodation to avoid homelessness. Although the circumstances have to be exceptional for cash to be made available, in practice it will largely be a question of resources.

1.97   Application for a loan from the social fund

For those in receipt of income support, there is the prospect of obtaining a loan from the social fund for the deposit on private rented accommodation.[232] Such payments are discretionary and there are strict criteria for eligibility. Although no interest is payable, the loan does have to be repaid.

SECTION 3   OWNERSHIP AND USE OF CHATTELS

1.98   Introduction

Disputes over chattels are notorious for the ill feeling and expense that they engender, usually to a wholly disproportionate degree.

Although the courts are reluctant to determine the ownership of chattels,[233] there will be occasions when litigation will be the only way to resolve a dispute.

However, the procedures are generally more cumbersome than for married parties or civil partners, when the court can be invited to divide chattels on the basis of the wide discretion exercisable under s 25 of the MCA 1973 or CPA 2004.

1.99   Ownership of chattels

The basis for division of the personal property of cohabitants is that of ownership, not need. The principles determining ownership are broadly the same as those applying to disputes over real property, that is trust principles.[234] This will mean that certain contributions, for example by way of housekeeping and bringing up children, will have limited if any relevance.

What will be relevant, in the case of a resulting trust, will be any contribution to the purchase price, in the case of a constructive trust, the existence of any

---

[232] Social Fund Directions issued by Secretary of State for Social Security.
[233] See *H v M (Property: Beneficial Interest)* [1992] 1 FLR 229 at 240, and District Judge Gerlis, *Divorce and the Counting of Spoons* [1998] Fam Law 47.
[234] See **1.14** et seq.

agreement between the parties as to the ownership of a chattel, or the parties' intentions (express or implied), regardless of contribution to the purchase price.

Unlike the position where there is a disagreement about the ownership of real property, with personal property it is possible to establish an express trust without having to show that the terms were in writing. If an express trust is established, this will avoid the need for a claimant to pursue the perhaps less straightforward argument that there was a constructive trust. This was the position in *Rowe v Prance*.[235] In that case, a man and a woman had a close relationship for 14 years. They planned to buy a boat and sail around the world. The man bought a boat from the net proceeds of sale of his matrimonial home and told the woman that they would live together on the boat. He referred to the boat as 'ours' and said that the woman had an interest in it. He had not at that stage even permanently separated from his wife. The woman gave up her rented house and put her furniture into storage. The couple's plans never came to fruition, and the woman successfully claimed an interest in the boat. On the basis that equality is equity, she was held to have an equal share with the man.

The 'Up Yaws'[236] concerned two boats. The parties, Miss Parrott and Mr Parkin, bought the first boat using credit in Miss Parrott's name, although the boat was registered to Mr Parkin. He did any maintenance that was necessary and Miss Parrott paid for materials and the mooring fees. They sold the first boat and bought the second, 'Up Yaws'. They traded in the first boat and the balance of the purchase price came from a loan secured on their shared home of which Miss Parrott was the legal owner, and a small amount of cash, the bulk of which was provided by Miss Parrott. When their relationship came to an end, Miss Parrott sought to realise her interest in the second boat. This required the court to look back and consider the beneficial interests in the house and the first boat. The court held that in relation to the property a common intention to share the beneficial ownership could be inferred and that Mr. Parkin had acted to his detriment in reliance upon that common intention. In relation to the first boat, the court found that the parties had agreed that in raising a loan against the security of the house in order to buy the boat she was buying out Mr. Parkin's interest in the house with the intent that thereafter she would own the house and he would own the boat. However, the significant contribution by Miss Parrott to the purchase of the second boat raised the presumption of a resulting trust in her favour quantified in accordance with her contribution to the purchase price.

If goods are bought on credit terms, contribution by way of payment of the deposit and the instalments will be relevant. Such a situation was considered by Walton J in *Richards v Dove*[237] who concluded that certain principles could be derived from the authorities:

---

[235] [1999] 2 FLR 787.
[236] [2007] 2 FLR 444.
[237] [1974] 1 All ER 888.

(1) as it is extremely tricky to define ownership by reference to disputed evidence on who paid most of the hire-purchase instalments on particular items, a broad approach is justifiable;

(2) merely paying one or two instalments on a particular item may not entitle the payer to any share; but

(3) on the other hand, it is unrealistic to suppose that substantial or regular contributions were not intended by the parties to be reflected in some corresponding beneficial interest.

1.100   Bank accounts

There is a presumption that funds in a bank or building society account held in joint names and intended to be used as a common pool will be divided in equal shares, regardless of the source of the credits to the account, and any items bought with funds from the account will be regarded as jointly owned property. Of course, the presumption can be rebutted by evidence showing a contrary intention, either express or implied, and in those circumstances the funds will be held in proportion to the contributions made.

Conversely, trust principles may be applied to establish that the funds held in an account in the name of one of the cohabitants belong to both jointly.[238]

It may be necessary to take action as soon as there is a breakdown in a cohabitation relationship to ensure that the funds in a joint account are not removed unilaterally. If the bank in question is alerted, the account will generally be frozen so that neither party may withdraw funds without the consent of the other. This may create practical difficulties in the short term if the account is the only source of living expenses, or if direct debits and standing orders are paid from it.

1.101   Existing property

It will generally be the case that items owned by either party before the cohabitation began, or bought by one party from his or her own resources during the currency of the relationship, will remain the property of that party.

1.102   Gifts

Gifts will remain the property of the donee. It will not be uncommon for one party to give sums of money to, or pay for goods or services on behalf of, the

---

[238] In *Paul v Constance* [1977] 1 All ER 195 an account in the sole name of the deceased cohabitant was held to belong to the survivor absolutely rather than to form part of the deceased's estate. The funds had chiefly comprised the deceased's damages from a personal injury claim, but they had in addition paid in joint bingo winnings, and had on one occasion withdrawn monies which were shared between them equally. The deceased had told the surviving cohabitant that the money in the account was as much hers as it was his. The court held that it was the parties' intention to create an express trust for themselves in equal shares.

other during the course of the relationship. The fact that the relationship subsequently comes to an end does not give the donor the automatic right to reclaim those monies from the other party. In the absence of clear evidence that the monies were a loan, any payments made will be deemed to be a gift and, therefore, not recoverable.

If it is the donee who is seeking to establish that certain items were intended as gifts, it will be necessary to show that there was an intention to transfer ownership, and that there was actual delivery.

Mere usage of items will not be sufficient to satisfy the court as to ownership. For example, in *Windeler v Whitehall*,[239] Mr Whitehall had bought a dressing table for use by his cohabitant, Miss Windeler. When she moved out of Mr Whitehall's home at the end of their relationship she took the dressing table with her. Mr Whitehall claimed its return. The court drew a distinction between items bought exclusively for Miss Windeler's use, consumables such as perfume and toiletries, and items of furniture. Whilst the dressing table was bought by Mr Whitehall for Miss Windeler's exclusive use, the court required more evidence than this to find that it was a gift. Against the background of the parties' relationship in this case the court formed the view that Mr Whitehall would expect Miss Windeler to leave the dressing table in the house if she left, and accordingly ordered its return.

In the event of a dispute over ownership of an engagement ring, s 3(2) of the Law Reform (Miscellaneous Provisions) Act 1970 governs the position. The gift of an engagement ring is presumed to be an absolute gift. The presumption can be rebutted by evidence to show that the gift was expressly or by implication conditional upon the marriage taking place. In *Cox v Jones*[240] the judge rejected the evidence of Mr Jones that he had given an engagement ring to Miss Cox on the express understanding that if the engagement were broken off for any reason the ring would have to be returned. Having heard all the evidence the judge considered that this was implausible.

1.103 Cohabitation agreement

If there is an enforceable cohabitation agreement,[241] there may be provision in the agreement for the ownership and/or division of chattels at the end of the cohabitation. At the very least, the agreement should be evidence of the parties' intention at the outset.

---

[239] [1990] 2 FLR 505.
[240] [2004] 2 FLR 1010.
[241] See **2.146**.

1.104 Applications for declarations of ownership and orders for sale

If there is really no alternative but to invite the court to decide the ownership of disputed chattels, the correct procedure is to apply for a declaration or enquiry as to the beneficial interest.

1.105 Which court?

The High Court and any county court have jurisdiction.

1.106 The court's approach

When resolving a dispute as to the ownership of property, the usual trust principles will apply as laid down in *Pettit v Pettitt*[242] and *Gissing v Gissing*[243] down through *Lloyds Bank plc v Rosset*[244] to the recent cases of *Oxley v Hiscock*[245] and *Stack v Dowden*.[246]

The role of the judge is to decide, on the basis of the oral evidence, and any relevant documentary evidence, whether the court's equitable jurisdiction can be invoked to assist the applicant. In practice, this may well come down to which of the two versions of events that are presented in the parties' evidence is the more plausible. It is rare for a couple's intentions as to their home to be recorded in writing, much less the contents. The nature of the parties' relationship may play a part in the judge's decision as to what is more likely to have been the intention with regard to a particular item of personal property.

The courts can be expected to take a more 'broad-brush' approach when dealing with an inventory of furniture and personal effects, than say a small number of valuable items.

In relation to determining the size of the beneficial interest, in the absence of any conclusive evidence on the point, the court will resort to the maxim, 'equality is equity'.

1.107 The order

The court may make an order that is merely declaratory of a party's beneficial interest in property, and it may order the sale of the property, or for one party to account to the other to the value of that beneficial interest.

---

[242] [1970] AC 777.
[243] [1971] AC 886.
[244] [1990] 2 WLR 867.
[245] [2004] 2 FLR 669.
[246] [2007] 1 FLR 1858.

1.108   Injunctions

Any judge may make an injunction restraining the disposal of property which is the subject of the application pending the final hearing. In practice, the application will generally be made to the district judge. The application will usually be made on notice, but in certain circumstances there may be merit in an application without notice. The application must be supported by a witness statement. In the case of an application without notice, the witness statement must set out exactly why the applicant wishes the court to consider the application without giving notice to the respondent.

1.109   Engaged couples

Some cohabitants will also be engaged to be married. If their relationship breaks down, the fact of their engagement will enable them to make application to the court under the MWPA 1882 for a declaration as to beneficial ownership of real or personal property. The application must be made within three years of the termination of the engagement. Although this procedure is analogous to the procedure available to cohabitants who have not been engaged to apply under the court's equitable jurisdiction for such a declaration, applications made under the MWPA 1882 benefit from the provisions of s 37 of the MPPA 1970. This will enable the court to take into account a substantial contribution in money or money's worth to the improvement of real and personal property when assessing that party's beneficial interest, unless there was an express agreement between the parties that such contributions were purely gratuitous. The total contribution must be substantial and the court must find that the only explanation for the size of the contribution must be that the applicant believed that it was founding an interest in the property.

The use of chattels

1.110   *Part IV of the Family Law Act 1996*

When the court makes an occupation order under ss 33, 35 or 36 (only ss 33 and 36 will apply to cohabitants), it can grant either party possession or use of furniture or other contents of the shared home.[247]

In deciding whether to make such provision, the court will have regard to all the circumstances of the case, including:
– the financial needs and resources of the parties; and
– the financial obligations which they have or are likely to have in the foreseeable future, including financial obligations to each other and to any relevant child.

---

[247] Section 40(1)(c).

The court may also order either party to take reasonable care of any furniture or other contents, and to keep them secure.[248]

An order made under s 40 will cease to have effect when the occupation order ceases to have effect.

---

[248] Section 40(1)(d) and (e).

PART B PROCEDURAL GUIDES

Order under Trusts of Land and Appointment of Trustees Act 1996, s 14

1.111 Legal background

TLATA 1996, s 14 entitles a trustee or a beneficiary of the proceeds of sale of land to apply for any order relating to the exercise by the trustees of any of their functions (including the power of exclusion and the power of sale), or declaring the nature and extent of a person's interest in a trust of land. Applications may be made by former cohabitants, family members or third parties such as trustees in bankruptcy wishing to establish a beneficial interest. By virtue of the HCCCJO 1991 (as amended), the county court's jurisdiction is unlimited. Section 14 of the 1996 Act is to be read together with ss 13 and 15. An application under TLATA 1996 is governed by CPR 1998, Pt 7 or 8. See also CPR PD7A and CPR PD8A.

1.112 Procedure

Who may apply	A trustee, a joint legal or beneficial owner, or a judgment creditor holding a charging order	*Midland Bank v Pike* [1988] 2 All ER 434
Property	Legal title owned jointly by co-owners	
Application	For an order 'declaring the nature or extent of a person's interest in [the] property'	TLATA 1996, s 14(2)(*b*)
Court	High Court: Chancery Division County court: if issued in a county court the claim form must be marked 'Chancery Business'	CPR PD7A, para 2.5
Fee	For recovery of land: in High Court: £465 in county court: £175	CPFO 2008, fee 1.4
Procedure	CPR 1998, Pt 7 – normally claims will be more appropriate for issue under this procedure	

	CPR 1998, Pt 8 – traditionally claims have often been issued under the Pt 8 procedure (formerly originating summons). Pt 8 only applies where there is 'unlikely [to be] a dispute of fact'. By definition most s 14 claims involve disputed questions of fact	CPR 1998, r 8.1(2)(*a*)
Issue of claim: Pt 7	Issue claim in Form N1 with particulars of claim (in the form or separately)	CPR 1998, r 7.1; r 7.4(1)(*a*)
Particulars of claim: served separately	Particulars of claim are likely to include the following: (1) the background facts; (2) reference to the facts which define the form of trust or equity claimed: (*a*) contributions; (*b*) any agreement with terms defined (if possible) and description of when formed; (*c*) detrimental reliance; (3) aspects of the claim that come within s 15(1); (4) aspects of the claim relevant to the check list at para [69] of *Stack*	TLATA 1996, s 15; *Stack v Dowden* [2007] 1 FLR 1858 at para [69]
Defendant	Other owner of the property	
Pt 8 claim: issue of claim	If there is little 'dispute of fact' this procedure can be used Claim issued in Form 208 with specific requirements, eg: (1) statement that Pt 8 applies; (2) remedy sought by the claimant and the 'legal basis' for it; (3) enactment for claim: ie, TLATA 1996 (shown in the heading to the claim)	CPR 1998, r 8.1(2)(*a*); CPR PD8A; CPR 1998, r 8.2
Pt 8 claim: evidence	(1) Claimant's evidence: served with claim form	CPR 1998, r 8.5(2)

	(2) Any 'written evidence': filed with claim form	CPR 1998, r 8.5(1)
	(3) Any other written evidence: only with permission	CPR 1998, r 8.6(1)(*b*)
Defence	(1) Acknowledgement of service	CPR 1998, r 8.3
	(2) Service of defendant's evidence on claimant with acknowledgement of service	CPR 1998, r 8.5(3), (4)
Case management	Pt 8: treated as allocated to the multi-track	CPR 1998, r 8.9(*c*)
	Definition of issues:	
	(1) What are the issues of fact?	CPR 1998, r 1.4(2)(*b*)
	(2) Are there any issues of law?	r 3.1(2)(*i*), (*l*)
Order	Declaration as to the parties' respective holding of the beneficial interests	TLATA 1996, s 14(2)(*b*)
	Under TLATA 1996 the court may then go on to deal with other matters, such as sale of the property, provision for an occupation rent, etc	TLATA 1996, TLATA 1996, s 14(2)(*a*) (see, for example, *Mortgage Corporation v Shaire* [2000] 1 FLR 973)

Transfer of a Tenancy under Family Law Act 1996, Pt IV, s 53 and Sch 7

1.113 Legal background

Since the coming into force of FLA 1996, Pt IV on 1 October 1997, the court is empowered to transfer tenancies, both contractual and statutory, between cohabitants who no longer live together as husband and wife, as well as between spouses and former spouses. As set out in FLA 1996, Sch 7, para 10, the person to whom the tenancy is transferred can be ordered to pay compensation to the other party. The power to transfer the tenancy to a former spouse arises on decree nisi; the order becomes effective on decree absolute; and there is a prohibition on applying if that former spouse has remarried. If there is a decree of judicial separation, the power to transfer arises after the decree is pronounced. A tenancy in the other spouse's name, or in joint names, can be destroyed by the unilateral surrender or giving of notice to quit by one tenant without consultation with the other (*Hammersmith and Fulham London Borough Council v Monk* [1992] 1 FLR 465). A party should ask for an undertaking that the tenancy will not be surrendered and then serve that undertaking on the landlord. If the undertaking is not given the applicant should apply for an injunction and serve the order on the landlord (*Bater v Greenwich London Borough Council* [1999] 2 FLR 993).

An application under FLA 1996, s 53 and Sch 7 is governed by the procedure in FPR 2010, rr 8.29–8.34.

1.114 Procedure

Who may apply	Either spouse, but a decree of judicial separation must be granted before the order is made	FLA 1996, Sch 7, para 2(2)
	Either former spouse, but a decree nisi must be granted before the order is made and the applicant must not have remarried; if application is for the transfer of a statutory tenancy or contractual tenancy containing a prohibition on assignment, it must be made before decree absolute	FLA 1996, Sch 7, para 13
	A cohabitant who is no longer living with the other cohabitant as husband and wife	FLA 1996, Sch 7, para 3
Application	To the Family Court or the same court as existing matrimonial/civil partnership proceedings	FLA 1996, Sch 7, para 2(2); FPR 2010, r 8.30; PD 8A, para 1.1(a)
Fee	£75	FPFO 2008, fee 1.4
Service	The court will serve the respondent and the landlord unless the applicant is directed to serve	FPR 2010, r 8.31
	A landlord may be made a party to proceedings	FPR 2010, r 8.32

Respondent	The other spouse or cohabitant	
Interlocutory injunction	The court may grant an injunction if ancillary or incidental to the assistance sought; an application for an injunction must be in accordance with procedure under FPR 2010, r 20.4	FPR 2010, r 8.34
Orders for disclosure	Any party may apply to the court under r 21.2 for any person to attend a production appointment to produce documents specified or described in the order	FPR 2010, r 8.33
Order	Transfer of tenancy or statutory tenancy	FLA 1996, Sch 7, paras 7–9
	Payment by the spouse or cohabitant to whom the tenancy is transferred, to the other; deferment of payment or payment by instalments if transferee's financial hardship greater than transferor's	FLA 1996, Sch 7, para 10
	Order that both liable to discharge obligations prior to date of transfer and indemnity	FLA 1996, Sch 7, para 11

PART C   CHECKLISTS

1.115   Essential information where the dispute is over owner-occupied property

A   About the property

(1)   address;

(2)   date of acquisition;

(3)   solicitors who acted on acquisition (obtain file?);

(4)   what information and advice was given by the solicitors about ownership of the legal and beneficial interests (negligence claim?);

(5)   ownership of legal title (Index Map Search/apply for office copy entries/register restriction or caution? (see **1.6**)/advise on possible severance of joint tenancy? (see **1.18**));

(6)   any declaration of beneficial interests (trust deed);

(7)   purchase price and contributions to it (deposit/mortgage advance/gifts or loans from third parties/contribution to costs and disbursements);

(8)   contributions since purchase (mortgage repayments/repairs and renovations/other payments/non-financial contributions);

(9)   any agreement or understanding as to the beneficial ownership and status of financial or other contributions;

(10) valuation; and

(11) details of mortgagee and redemption figure.

B   About the cohabitation

(1)   dates of cohabitation;

(2)   dates of any agreement to marry (have three years elapsed since termination?);

(3)   details of any children of the relationship/other children;

(4)   arrangements for payment of shared outgoings;

(5)   any agreement or understanding as to the ownership of the property and the status of contributions, financial or otherwise; and

(6)   details of any acts of detriment and/or reliance pursuant to the agreement.

C   Evidence

(1)   file of papers from solicitors acting on the acquisition of the property;

(2)   title deeds and documents and any express declarations of trust;

(3)   documentary evidence of contributions made; and

(4)   oral or written evidence of any agreements or understandings as to the ownership of the legal and/or beneficial interests and the status of any contributions financial or otherwise.

1.116   Essential information where the dispute is over rented property

(1) Address.

(2) Landlord's name and address/landlord's agent's name and address.

(3) Copy of tenancy agreement.

(4) Date of agreement.

(5) Parties to the agreement.

(6) Type of tenancy.

(7) Rent payable/arrears?

(8) Has the tenancy been determined by a valid notice to quit?

(9) Should urgent steps be taken to prevent termination of the tenancy by the other party?

(10) Who is living at the property?

1.117   Acting for a cohabiting couple on the acquisition of property

(1) Who is to live at the property?

(2) How are the purchase price, costs and disbursements to be funded?

(3) In whose name(s) is the title to be registered?

(4) If in one name only, consider whether the other party/parties should be advised to take independent legal advice.

(5) If in joint names, advise on the difference between holding as tenants in common/joint tenants, and if necessary advise the parties to take independent legal advice.

(6) Consider any potential for a conflict of interest.

(7) If in joint names, consider how the beneficial interests are to be declared.

(8) Advise on the importance of making a will.

(9) Invite the parties to consider entering into a cohabitation agreement.

PART D PRECEDENTS

1.118   How to use these precedents

The following section contains a considerable number of individual clauses and comparatively few complete precedents. The individual clauses can be pieced together to form a complete declaration of trust which, when completed will assume the following structure, or something similar:

(1)   commencement and date;[249]

(2)   recitals (both of fact and intention);[250]

(3)   trusts;[251]

(4)   shares (either fixed shares[252] or floating shares[253]);

(5)   a clause introducing the contingencies,[254] or in other words, 'What happens if ...?' – it is recommended that the provisions for each contingency are set out in a separate Schedule at the end of the declaration;

(6)   general, miscellaneous clauses;[255]

(7)   Schedules;[256] and

(8)   attestation clause.[257]

There are two types of complete precedent: the short form and the long form. The short forms tend to combine the recitals, trusts and shares in the context of the co-owners jointly and each co-owner separately. In addition, the short forms do not provide for any contingencies, although Schedules setting them out could be appended to any of the short-form precedents. The long-form precedents are essentially illustrations of the effect of combining any number of individual clauses.

---

[249] **1.119** below.
[250] **1.120–1.125** below.
[251] **1.126–1.130** below.
[252] **1.131–1.135** below.
[253] **1.136–1.142** below.
[254] **1.143** below.
[255] **1.144–1.165** below.
[256] **1.167** below.
[257] **1.166** below.

Section 1   Non-contentious precedents

Clauses: Commencement and recitals

1.119   Commencement and date[258]

THIS DECLARATION OF TRUST is made on (*date*)

BETWEEN 'the co-owners' (1) (*name 1*) of (*address*) ('*name*') and (2) (*name 2*) (also) of (*address*) ('*name 2*').

IT IS AGREED AND DECLARED as follows:

Recitals of fact

1.120   Purchase of property[259]

RECITALS

- The co-owners are the proprietors of (address) ('the property').
- Title to the property is registered at the Land Registry under title number (number).
- The co-owners purchased the property on (completion date).[260]
- The co-owners purchased the property for £
- The incidental costs of purchasing the property came to £
- (Name 1) paid £   towards the purchase price and purchase costs.
- (Name 2) paid £   towards the purchase price and purchase costs.
- The co-owners obtained an advance of £   from and have mortgaged the property to (lender) ('the mortgage').[261]

1.121   Mortgage of property[262]

- The mortgage is a repayment mortgage.

---

[258] LPA 1925, s 53(1)(b) states that 'a declaration of trust respecting any land or any interest therein must be manifested and proved by some writing signed by some person who is able to declare such trust or by his will'.

Although it is imperative that the declaration of trust be in writing, it is not essential that it should be a deed.

Stamp Duty Land Tax (SDLT) applies to land transactions and is a tax on the transaction rather than the document. A declaration of trust is not substantively registrable at HM Land Registry. It is no longer necessary to complete an SDLT 60 self-certificate if you don't need to notify HMRC about a Stamp Duty Land Tax transaction

[259] For the effect of recitals on the construction of an instrument, see, generally, *Halsbury's Laws of England*, Vol 32 (2012, 5th edn) at para 418.

[260] The completion date is probably preferable to the date on which contracts were exchanged.

[261] For separate recitals relating to the mortgage, see **1.121**.

[262] There are so many possible variables that only a small selection has been included here. Perhaps the facts relating to the mortgage are less important than the co-owners' intentions regarding the mortgage payments (see **1.124** below).

- The mortgage is an endowment mortgage.
- (*Name 1*) has taken out an endowment policy on their life with (*insurance company*) numbered (*number*).
- The endowment policy is (assigned to)/(deposited with)/(neither assigned to nor deposited with) (*lender*).
- The co-owners entered into a mortgage indemnity policy for a single premium of £   (which will be added to the mortgage and repaid over the mortgage term) [*OR*] (of which (*name 1*) paid £   and (*name 2*) paid £   ).

1.122   The underlying purpose of the trust[263]

- The co-owners purchased the property for their joint occupation.[264]
- The co-owners purchased the property in order to provide a home for themselves and their (respective) children.[265]
- The co-owners purchased the property as an investment.

1.123   Recitals of fact and intention: third party contributions[266]

- (*Name 3*) paid £   towards the purchase price and purchase costs with the intention of acquiring a beneficial interest in the property.
- (*The co-owners*) [*OR*] (*Name 1* and *name 2*) acknowledge that the payment of £   made by (*name 3*) towards the purchase price and purchase costs was neither a loan nor a gift to them but was made with the express intention that (*name 3*) would acquire a beneficial interest in the property.

Recitals of intention

1.124   Mortgage payments[267]

- The co-owners intend to contribute equally towards the mortgage payments.

---

[263] The underlying purpose of the trust for sale could be an important consideration in any possible future application to the court for an order under TLATA 1996, s 14(1). The courts have progressively developed this theme since *Re Buchanan-Wollaston's Conveyance* [1939] Ch 738.

[264] The court is more likely to order a sale where no children are involved and the parties have simply purchased the property for their joint occupation (*Smith v Smith* (1976) 120 SJ 100).

[265] 'If there were young children, the position would be different. One of the purposes of the trust would no doubt have been to provide a home for them, and while that purpose still existed a sale would not generally be ordered' (*Rawlings v Rawlings* [1964] P 398 at 419, per Salmon LJ). See also *Re Evers' Trust* [1980] 1 WLR 1327.

[266] The law presumes a resulting trust in favour of the third party unless that presumption is rebutted by evidence that the third party intended to make a gift or a loan without acquiring any beneficial interest (*Sekhon v Alissa* [1989] 2 FLR 94).

[267] It is very important to ascertain the co-owners' intentions regarding the mortgage payments. Without any clear instructions in this respect, it would be unwise to channel them into holding fixed shares of the net proceeds of sale, but see **1.135** below. For a definition of 'the mortgage payments', see **1.161** below.

[OR]

- The co-owners intend that their contributions towards the mortgage payments will be treated as equal, regardless of any inequality that may exist at any time.

[OR]

- (*Name 1*) intends to pay   per cent of the mortgage payments.
- (*Name 2*) intends to pay   per cent of the mortgage payments.

[OR]

- The co-owners intend to contribute towards the mortgage payments in the proportions that their respective incomes bear to each other, or in such other proportions as they may from time to time agree.

1.125 Co-owners intend to marry/enter into a registered civil partnership with each other: provisions of this declaration to apply despite marriage/civil partnership

- The co-owners are engaged to be married to each other/intend to enter into a registered civil partnership together.[268]

[OR]

- The co-owners expect to marry each other/enter into a registered civil partnership together.

[AND]

- The co-owners intend that the provisions of this Declaration of Trust will apply regardless of their marriage/civil partnership and its possible dissolution.[269]

Warning

The effect of this clause is to turn the declaration of trust into a form of pre-nuptial agreement. See, generally, Chapter 8 below.

---

[268] For provisions relating to the property of engaged couples, or couples who have been engaged to each other within the last three years, see LR(MP)A 1970, s 2.

[269] For property adjustment orders in connection with dissolution of marriage or civil partnership, see MCA 1973, s 24 and CPA 2004.

Clauses: Trusts

1.126 The standard trusts[270]

Trusts

The co-owners (declare that they):

(1) hold the property on a trust of land;[271]

(2) hold the property and its net proceeds of sale (and its net income until sale)[272] in trust for themselves (*and any third party, if appropriate*)[273] as beneficial (joint tenants)[274]/(tenants in common)[275]/(regardless of their actual contributions towards acquiring, financing and improving the property).[276]

1.127 Co-owners to be joint tenants until severance and tenants in common in unequal shares after severance[277]

Trusts[278]

The co-owners (declare that they):

(1) hold the property on a trust of land;

(2) hold the property and its net proceeds of sale and its net income until sale in trust for themselves as beneficial joint tenants until the beneficial joint

---

[270] This precedent sets out the standard trust of land. It also states whether the co-owners hold as beneficial joint tenants or beneficial tenants in common.

[271] Under the TLATA 1996 a trust of land now applies to any trust of property, including land (s 1). Trustees of land have in relation to the land all the powers of an absolute owner (s 6(1)), unless there is any provision to the contrary (s 8). The trustees therefore have both a power of sale and a power to postpone the sale.

[272] The phrase 'the net income until sale' should be deleted if the net proceeds of sale and the net income until sale are enjoyed in differing shares. See **1.129** below.

[273] The name of anyone else who is beneficially interested should be inserted, for example someone who has contributed to the purchase price with the intention of acquiring a beneficial interest, rather than with the intention of making a gift or a loan.

[274] 'Joint tenants' and 'tenants in common' are alternatives. One must be deleted. See *Joyce v Barker Bros* (1980) *The Times*, February 26, where a conveyance stated that the purchasers were joint tenants and tenants in common.

[275] This precedent assumes that in the case of a beneficial tenancy in common the shares will be set out in a separate clause. Sometimes the method of calculating the shares is lengthy and complex, and in such cases it may be preferable to separate the clauses relating to the shares and the trusts. However, if the shares are simple and straightforward (for example 'in equal shares') they could be dealt with in this clause, without the need for a separate clause.

[276] The words 'regardless of their actual contributions ... etc' are not essential. They are unnecessary if the co-owners hold floating shares. Their inclusion may be considered useful for clarity where one co-owner is likely to confer a gratuitous benefit on the other.

[277] This is, presumably, the sort of declaration of trust Slade LJ had in mind when he said that 'it would no doubt be possible for a trust in terms to provide that the beneficial interests of two parties should be equivalent to those of joint tenants unless and until severance occurred, but that in the event of severance their interests should be otherwise than in equal shares' (*Goodman v Gallant* [1986] 1 FLR 513 at 525C).

[278] See, generally, the footnotes to **1.126** above.

tenancy is severed (regardless of their actual contributions towards acquiring, financing and improving the property);[279]

(3)   will hold the property and its net proceeds of sale (and its net income until sale[280] in trust for themselves as beneficial tenants in common in the shares set out below[281] after the beneficial joint tenancy has been severed.

1.128   Co-owners to be tenants in common until their marriage/civil partnership and subsequently joint tenants[282]

Trusts[283]

The co-owners (declare that they):

(1)   hold the property on a trust of land);

(2)   hold the property and its net proceeds of sale (and its net income until sale)[284] in trust for themselves as beneficial tenants in common (in the shares set out below)[285] until the solemnisation of their intended marriage/the registration of their civil partnership;

(3)   will hold the property and its net proceeds of sale and its net income until sale in trust for themselves as beneficial joint tenants after their intended marriage/civil partnership has been solemnised/registered(regardless of their actual contributions towards acquiring, financing and improving the property).[286]

1.129   Shares of the net proceeds of sale differ from those of the net income until sale

Trusts[287]

The co-owners (declare that they):

(1)   hold the property on a trust of land;

(2)   hold the net proceeds of sale in trust for themselves as beneficial tenants in common (in the shares set out in Clause   ) (regardless of their actual contributions towards acquiring, financing and improving the property);

---

[279]   See **1.126**.

[280]   See **1.126**.

[281]   These shares could be fixed or floating.

[282]   The effect of the inheritance tax exemptions must be considered, ie transfers between spouses/civil partners (Inheritance Tax Act 1984, s 18), and gifts in consideration of marriage/registration of civil partnership (ibid, s 22). Note also the effect of IA 1986, s 339, in respect of transactions at an undervalue.

[283]   See, generally, the footnotes to **1.126** above.

[284]   See the comments in **1.126**.

[285]   The shares could be fixed or floating. If the co-owners hold 'in equal shares', it would be preferable to insert those words here instead of 'in the shares set out below', thus avoiding the need for an additional clause.

[286]   See **1.126**.

[287]   See, generally, the footnotes to **1.126** above.

(3) hold the net income until sale in trust for themselves as beneficial tenants in common (in the shares set out in Clause   )[288] regardless of the manner in which the net proceeds of sale will be divided between them.

1.130   Deferred trust of land: 'Mesher' and 'Martin'-type trusts[289]

Trusts

The co-owners (declare that they):

(1)   hold the property on a trust of land;

(2)   will postpone the sale of the property, unless they agree otherwise or unless the court orders otherwise, until the first of these events occurs:

    (2.1)   (*child's name*) [*OR*] (the youngest child of the family) attains the age of 18 or completes full-time secondary education, whichever is later; or

    (2.2)   the co-owner with whom (*child's name*) [*OR*] (the youngest child of the family) lives in the property marries or cohabits;[290]

(3)   hold the property and its net proceeds of sale (and its net income until sale) in trust for themselves as beneficial tenants in common in the shares set out below.

Clauses: Shares

1.131   Fixed shares: expressed as fractions or percentages of the net proceeds of sale

Shares

When the property is sold (*name 1*) will receive (*fraction or percentage*)[291] of the net proceeds of sale and (*name 2*) will receive (*fraction or percentage*) of the net proceeds of sale.[292]

---

[288] See Precedent **1.144** below.

[289] An order of the court whereby the sale of a family home is postponed until the youngest child of the family is aged 18, or some other age, is usually known as a '*Mesher* order' (*Mesher v Mesher* [1980] 1 All ER 126). Although it was not reported until 1980, the case was, in fact, heard by the Court of Appeal on 12 February 1973. An order of the court whereby the sale is postponed until the wife dies, remarries or cohabits, is usually known as a '*Martin* order' (*Martin v Martin* [1978] Fam 12). *Mesher* orders have experienced variable popularity over the years since the case and, for example, found favour after the 2007—8 global financial crisis. For a historical discussion of the rise and fall of the *Mesher* order see *Clutton v Clutton* [1991] 1 All ER 340 at 345, per Lloyd LJ.

[290] The word 'cohabits' tends to defy definition.

[291] In the case of fractions, the combined total of the numerators must be the same as the denominator. In the case of percentages, the combined total must be 100.

[292] It may be considered prudent to define 'net proceeds of sale' (see **1.159** below).

Warning

Care should be taken when expressing the co-owners' shares as fractions or percentages of the net proceeds of sale. It is only safe to do so if: (a) there is no mortgage; or (b) they contribute to the mortgage payments in fractions or percentages which are identical to their respective entitlements out of the net proceeds of sale; and (c) they intend to pay the sale costs in the same fractions or percentages. *See Example.*

Example

A and B bought a house for £88,500. The purchase costs amounted to £1,500. A contributed £30,000, B contributed £10,000. They obtained a mortgage advance of £50,000 and contributed equally to the mortgage payments. They intended to share the sale costs equally. Five years later they sold the house for £130,000. The sale costs amounted to £4,000. The amount required to redeem the mortgage was £46,000. The net proceeds of sale came to £80,000. Who got what?

Wrong solution

A and B had executed a declaration of trust which said that A would receive 75 per cent of the net proceeds of sale and B would receive 25 per cent. These percentages reflected their original contributions to the purchase price (A £30,000 and B £10,000). It was a mistake to correlate their contributions to their entitlements from the net proceeds of sale because these percentages fail to take into account the shared responsibility for the mortgage payments and the sale costs. A ended up with £60,000, and B £20,000.

Wrong solution

A and B executed a declaration of trust which stated that A would receive 55/90^{ths} of the net proceeds of sale and B would receive 35/90^{ths}. In each case the denominator (90) represents £90,000 (the purchase price of £88,500 plus the purchase costs of £1,500). In A's case the numerator (55) represents £55,000 (her original contribution of £30,000 plus £25,000, half of the mortgage advance). In B's case, the numerator (35) represents £10,000 plus £25,000. On this basis, A ended up with £48,889 and B with £31,111.

This formula will only work if the mortgage debt is repaid over its full term. Say, for example, A and B had split up shortly after they bought the house, and had sold it for £93,000. The sale costs came to £3,000, and the amount required to redeem the mortgage was the same as the original advance, £50,000. The net proceeds of sale would have been £40,000 and, in effect, the couple would be back to square one in terms of the combined total of their original contributions. The application of this formula would mean that A would receive £24,444 and B £15,556.

Suggested solution

It would have been better if A and B had executed a declaration of trust which stated that A would receive 55/90^{ths} of the sale price, *less* half of the amount required to redeem the mortgage, *less* half of the sale costs. B would receive

35/90[ths] of the sale price *less* half of the amount required to redeem the mortgage, *less* half of the sale costs. On this basis A would receive (£79,444—£23,000—£2,000) = £54,444. B would receive (£50,556—£23,000-£2,000) = £25,556.

Even this solution is not perfect. Problems would arise if the couple failed to pay the mortgage in equal shares, or if only one of them contributed towards repairs and improvements to the property.

1.132   Fixed shares: expressed as a fixed share of the sale price, less a fixed share of the amount required to redeem the mortgage, less a fixed share of the sale costs[293]

Shares

When the property is sold:

(1)   (*name 1*) will receive (*fraction or percentage*)[294] of the sale price[295] less:
   (1.1)   (*fraction or percentage*)[296] of the amount required to redeem the mortgage;[297] and
   (1.2)   (*fraction or percentage*)[298] of the incidental costs of selling the property;

(2)   (*name 2*) will receive (*fraction or percentage*)[299] of the sale price[300] less:
   (2.1)   (*fraction or percentage*)[301] of the amount required to redeem the mortgage;[302] and
   (2.2)   (*fraction or percentage*)[303] of the incidental costs of selling the property;

---

[293] For an illustration of how this formula works, see the suggested solution at **1.131** above.

[294] The denominator will, presumably, represent the purchase price plus the purchase costs. The numerator will represent the co-owner's original contribution, plus the share of the mortgage debt for which he or she is assuming responsibility.

[295] For a definition of 'the sale price', see **1.156** below.

[296] The denominator will, presumably, represent the mortgage advance itself; and the numerator will represent the extent to which the co-owner assumes responsibility for the mortgage payments.

[297] For a definition of 'the amount required to redeem the mortgage', see **1.157** below.

[298] If the co-owners intend to share the sale costs equally, insert one-half or 50 per cent, as the case may be.

[299] The denominator will, presumably, represent the purchase price plus the purchase costs. The numerator will represent the co-owner's original contribution, plus the share of the mortgage debt for which he or she is assuming responsibility.

[300] For a definition of 'the sale price', see **1.156** below.

[301] The denominator will, presumably, represent the mortgage advance itself; and the numerator will represent the extent to which the co-owner assumes responsibility for the mortgage payments.

[302] For a definition of 'the amount required to redeem the mortgage', see **1.157** below.

[303] If the co-owners intend to share the sale costs equally, insert one half or 50 per cent, as the case may be.

(3) if the total amount to be deducted from one co-owner's share of the sale price exceeds the value of that share then the excess will be paid from the other co-owner's share.[304]

Example

A and B bought a house for £57,000. The purchase costs came to £1,000. A contributed £4,000 and B contributed £10,000. They took out a mortgage of £44,000. A assumed responsibility for three-quarters of the mortgage payments and B assumed responsibility for one-quarter of the mortgage payments. Two years later they sold the house for £48,000. The amount required to redeem the mortgage was £43,500. The sale costs came to £1,500 and the net proceeds of sale were £3,000. Who got what?

They had signed a declaration of trust that said that A would receive 37/58[ths] of the sale price *less* three-quarters of the amount required to redeem the mortgage, *less* one half of the sale costs. It said that B would receive 21/58[ths] of the sale price, *less* one quarter of the amount required to redeem the mortgage, *less* one half of the sale costs.

On that basis, A would receive (£30,620—£32,625—£750). The result is a minus sum: —£2,755. B would receive (£17,380—£10,875—£750)=£5,755.

Their declaration of trust also stated that if the total amount to be deducted from one co-owner's share of the sale price exceeded the value of that share, then the excess would be paid from the other co-owner's share. So B paid A's shortfall of £2,755, and was entitled to retain all of the net proceeds of sale (£3,000).

1.133 Fixed shares: refund of original contributions: provision for abatement: fixed shares of the balance of the net proceeds of sale[305]

Shares

When the property is sold:

(1) (*name 1*) will receive a refund of (*name 1's*) original contribution of £   towards the purchase price and the purchase costs;

(2) (*name 2*) will receive a refund of (*name 2's*) original contribution of £   towards the purchase price and the purchase costs;

(3) if the net proceeds of sale are insufficient to refund the co-owners' original contributions fully, the contributions will abate (in the proportions that they bear to each other)[306] [OR] (equally);

---

[304] This subclause provides for the possibility that the property has gone down in value, or the mortgage debt exceeds the market value. One co-owner will be liable for the excess of the other co-owner's debt. *See Example.*

[305] For a variation of this formula, see **1.134** below. *See Example 1.*

[306] A provision for abatement is necessary to cover any downturn in property values. *See Example 2.*

(4)   when the original contributions have been refunded the remaining balance of the net proceeds of sale will be divided as to (*fraction or percentage*) for (*name 1*) and (*fraction or percentage*)[307] for (*name 2*).

Example 1

A and B bought a house for £88,500. The purchase costs amounted to £1,500. A contributed £30,000 and B contributed £10,000. They obtained a mortgage advance of £50,000 and contributed equally to the mortgage payments. They agreed to share the sale costs equally. Five years later they sold the house for £130,000. The sale costs totalled £4,000. The amount required to redeem the mortgage was £46,000. The net proceeds of sale were £80,000. Who got what?

When they bought the house, A and B executed a declaration of trust which said that each of them would get back his or her original contribution, and that the balance of the net proceeds of sale would be divided equally between them. Therefore, A was refunded her £30,000. B was refunded his £10,000. The balance of the net proceeds (£40,000) was divided equally between them. A received, in total, £50,000 and B received £30,000.

The problem with applying this formula is more noticeable in A's case. Her original contribution has remained stationary, or stagnated. The value of the property has increased by about 47 per cent, and in real terms her original contribution of £30,000 should have grown to roughly £44,000.

Compare the suggested solution at **1.131** where the facts are identical and the example in the footnote at **1.134** below, where the original contribution is credited with interest.

Example 2

The facts are similar to those in footnote 1 above, except that the property was sold for £76,000. The amount required to redeem the mortgage was £46,000. The sale costs came to £2,000 and the net proceeds of sale were £28,000, representing an overall loss of £12,000.

The declaration of trust provided that the original contributions would abate in the proportions that they bear to each other. So, A's original contribution of £30,000 was reduced to £21,000; and B's original contribution of £10,000 was reduced to £7,000.

If the declaration of trust had stated that their original contributions would abate equally, A would have received £24,000, and B would have ended up with £4,000. In other words, their net loss of £12,000 would have been shared by them equally.

---

[307] The denominator will, presumably, represent the mortgage debt and the sale costs. The numerator will reflect the extent to which each co-owner assumes responsibility for the mortgage and the sale costs.

1.134 Fixed shares: refund of original contributions plus interest: provision for abatement: fixed shares of the balance of the net proceeds of sale[308]

Shares

When the property is sold:

(1) (*name 1*) will receive a refund of (*name 1's*) original contribution of £   towards the purchase price and the purchase costs *plus* (simple) interest at a rate of (7) per cent per year from the date (on which the purchase of the property was completed) [*OR*] (of this Declaration of Trust) to the date on which the refund of the contribution is made;

(2) (*name 2*) will receive a refund of (*name 2's*) original contribution of £   towards the purchase price and the purchase costs *plus* (simple) interest at a rate of (7) per cent per year from the date (on which the purchase of the property was completed) [*OR*] (of this Declaration of Trust) to the date on which the refund of the contribution is made;

(3) if the net proceeds of sale are insufficient to refund the co-owners' original contributions plus interest, the original contributions and the interest on them will abate (in the proportions that they bear to each other) [*OR*] (equally);

(4) subject to the above, the remaining balance of the net proceeds of sale will be divided as to (*fraction or percentage*) for (*name 1*) and (*fraction or percentage*) for (*name 2*).

Example

The facts are identical to those in the example given at **1.133** above, except that A and B's declaration of trust said that they would be entitled to simple interest at 7 per cent a year. A receives her original contribution of £30,000, plus £10,500 in interest, plus £13,000 (half of the remaining balance): a total of £53,500. B receives a total of £26,500 (his contribution of £10,000, plus £3,500 in interest, plus £13,000 (half of the remaining balance)).

---

[308] See the footnotes to **1.133** above. *See Example.*

1.135   Fixed shares: refund of original contributions expressed as a fraction or percentage of the sale price: alternative provisions for the division of the balance of the net proceeds of sale[309]

Shares

When the property is sold:

(1)   (*name 1*) will receive (*fraction or percentage*)[310] of the sale price, representing the return on (*name 1's*) original contribution of £   towards the purchase price and purchase costs;

(2)   (*name 2*) will receive (*fraction or percentage*)[311] of the sale price, representing the return on (*name 2's*) original contribution of £   towards the purchase price and purchase costs;

(3)   the amount required to redeem the mortgage will be paid from the remaining (*fraction or percentage*)[312] of the sale price ('the mortgage share');

(4)   if the amount required to redeem the mortgage exceeds the mortgage share, the excess will be paid by the co-owners (in equal shares) [*OR*] (as to   per cent by (*name 1*) and   per cent by (*name 2*)) [*OR*] (in the proportions that each of them has contributed towards the mortgage payments);[313]

(5)   subject to the above, the remaining balance of the mortgage share will be divided between the co-owners (in equal shares) [*OR*] (as to   per cent for (*name 1*) and   per cent for (*name 2*)) [*OR*] (in the proportions that each of them has contributed towards the mortgage payments);[314]

(6)   the co-owners will pay the incidental costs of selling the property (in equal shares) [*OR*] (as to   per cent by (*name 1*) and   per cent by (*name 2*)) [*OR*] (in the proportions that their respective shares of the rest of the net proceeds of sale bear to each other).

---

[309]   This is probably the most satisfactory formula for expressing fixed shares. In principle, it is the same as the formula at **1.132** above. However, it is more flexible than in that case because it addresses the possibility that, when they purchase, the co-owners may have no definite plans as to the extent to which each of them will assume responsibility for the mortgage payments.

[310]   The numerator should represent the co-owner's contribution; the denominator should represent the purchase price plus the purchase costs.

[311]   The numerator should represent the co-owner's contribution; the denominator should represent the purchase price plus the purchase costs.

[312]   The numerator should represent the mortgage advance; the denominator should represent the purchase price plus the purchase costs. The fractions or percentages in subclauses 1, 2 and 3 should come to 100 per cent of the purchase price and purchase costs.

[313]   The words 'in the proportions that each of them has contributed towards the mortgage payments' creates floating shares. In other words, those proportions will not be finally ascertained until the trust for sale comes to an end.

[314]   The words 'in the proportions that each of them has contributed towards the mortgage payments' creates floating shares. In other words, those proportions will not be finally ascertained until the trust for sale comes to an end.

1.136   Floating shares: in proportion to the contributions made by each co-owner throughout the duration of the trust[315]

Shares

When the property is sold, the net proceeds of sale[316] will be divided between the co-owners in proportion to (the extent to which the change in the value of the property is attributable to)[317] the contributions made by each of them towards the:

(1)   purchase price;

(2)   incidental costs of the purchase;

(3)   payment of mortgage interest;

(4)   payment of mortgage endowment policy premiums;

(5)   repayment of mortgage capital;

(6)   cost of repairs and improvements to the property;

(7)   payment of interest and repayment of capital on further advances and loans taken out for repairs and improvements to the property; (and

(8)   incidental costs of selling the property).[318]

1.137   Floating shares: calculation of the shares: addition of contributions and apportionment of net proceeds of sale pro rata[319]

Calculation of shares

The share of the net proceeds of sale to which each co-owner is entitled will be calculated by:

---

[315] For the distinction between fixed shares and floating shares, see **1.7** above. For a discussion of some of the advantages and disadvantages of floating shares, see **1.8–1.11** above.

[316] For a definition of 'the net proceeds of sale', see **1.159** below.

[317] The words in brackets should be deleted if the shares are to be calculated by the addition of the contributions and the apportionment of the net proceeds of sale pro rata (see **1.137** below). The words in brackets must be included if the shares are to be calculated in accordance with the formulae set out in **1.139** (narrative form) and **1.140** (tabular form) below.

[318] For a definition of 'the incidental costs of selling the property', see **1.158** below. The sale costs should only be included here if the co-owners intend to pay the sale costs in the proportions that their respective shares bear to each other. If the co-owners intend to pay the sale costs in equal shares, or in some other fixed proportions, there should be included a separate clause to this effect (see **1.154** below).

Other items could be included in this list, for example mortgage guarantee premiums, mortgage protection policy premiums, buildings insurance premiums, rent, rentcharge, ground rent, service charges, etc.

[319] As there is more than one method of calculating floating shares, it is sensible to set out clearly the manner in which the shares will be calculated. The method of calculating A's share is as follows:

(a) A's individual contribution is £104,000; (b) the combined contributions are £139,500; (c) the net proceeds of sale (£124,500) are divided by the combined contributions to produce a dividend of 0.89247; (d) A's individual contribution is multiplied by the dividend to produce his

(1) adding together his or her contributions to produce 'the individual contribution'; and then

(2) adding together (both)/(all) of the co-owners' individual contributions to produce 'the combined contributions'; and then

(3) dividing the net proceeds of sale (plus the incidental costs of selling the property)[320] by the combined contributions to produce 'the dividend'; and finally

(4) multiplying the individual contribution by the dividend to produce the share.

Warning

This method of calculating floating shares does not take into account the extent to which the change in the value of the property can be attributed to each co-owner's lump sum contributions and mortgage-related contributions. If the change in value is to be taken into account, Precedents **1.139** and **1.140** can be used instead.

Although this method of calculating the shares is far simpler than the formulae, in certain circumstances it can produce a perverse result. For an illustration, see the example in Precedent **1.140** below.

Example

A and B bought a bungalow for £165,000. The purchase costs came to £2,500. A paid £87,500 and B paid £18,000. They took out a mortgage for £62,000. They lived together for three years. A paid £15,000 towards the mortgage. B paid £5,000 towards the mortgage. They carried out improvements which cost £20,000. B paid £12,000 in cash towards the improvements but A paid nothing in cash towards the improvements. They obtained a loan of £8,000 for the improvements. A paid £1,500 on the loan and B paid £500. They sold the bungalow for £197,000. The amount required to redeem the mortgage was £60,000. The amount required to repay the loan was £7,500. The sale costs came to £5,000 and the net proceeds of sale were £124,500. Who got what?

---

share, which is £92,817. Applying the same method, B's share is £31,683. Incidentally, had the formulae in Precedents **1.139** and **1.140** below been used on this occasion, A would have been better off by £74.

[320] The sale costs should only be included if their payment is to be borne pro rata to the shares of the rest of the net proceeds of sale.

Suggested solution

A and B's individual contributions were:

	A	B
Purchase price and costs	87,500	18,000
Mortgage payments	15,000	5,000
Improvements: cash	0	12,000
Loan payments	1,500	500
	£104,000	£35,500

The method of calculating A's share is as follows:

(a)   his individual contribution is £104,000;

(b)   the combined contributions are £139,500;

(c)   the net proceeds of sale (£124,500) are divided by the combined contributions to produce a dividend of 0.89247;

(d)   A's individual contribution is multiplied by the dividend to produce his share, which is £92,817.

Applying the same method, B's share is £31,683. Incidentally, had the formulae in Precedents **1.139** and **1.140** below been used on this occasion, A would have been better off by £74.

1.138   Floating shares: calculation of the shares:[321] introductory clause to the formulae[322]

Calculation of shares

The share of the net proceeds of sale to which each co-owner is entitled will be calculated in accordance with the provisions of Schedule (*number*).

Floating shares: formulae for calculating floating shares[323]

1.139   Narrative form

SCHEDULE (*number*)

(1)   The share of the net proceeds of sale to which each co-owner is entitled ('share') before the deduction of his or her share of the incidental costs of

---

[321]   It is assumed that this clause would be immediately preceded by wording identical or similar to that contained in Precedent **1.136** above.

[322]   The formulae contained in Precedents **1.139** and **1.140** below are quite complicated. It may be considered preferable to set them out in a separate schedule, rather than include them in the main body of the declaration of trust.

[323]   The formulae set out in this precedent are identical to those set out in **1.140** below. The only difference is the style. Here they are described in narrative form; in **1.140** they appear in tabular form.

The formulae seek to identify and isolate the extent to which any change in the value of the property can be attributed to the lump sums provided by each co-owner and to the lump sum

selling the property will be calculated by adding together his or her lump sum contributions and his or her mortgage-related contributions.

LUMP SUM CONTRIBUTIONS

(2)   Each co-owner's lump sum contributions ('lump sum') will be calculated by applying the following formula.

$$\frac{\text{Individual payments}}{\text{purchase price} + \text{improvements}} \times \text{sale price} = \text{lump sum}$$

WHERE:

(2.1)   *Individual payments* is the total of the individual co-owner's lump sum payments towards:
   (a)   the purchase price; and
   (b)   the incidental costs of purchasing the property; and
   (c)   repairs and improvements to the property.

(2.2)   *Purchase price* is the total of:
   (a)   (both)/(all) of the co-owners' lump sum payments towards the purchase price; and
   (b)   (both)/(all) of the co-owners' lump sum payments towards the incidental costs of purchasing the property; and
   (c)   the mortgage advance.

(2.3)   *Improvements* is the total of:
   (a)   (both)/(all) of the co-owners' lump sum payments towards repairs and improvements to the property; and
   (b)   all further mortgage advances and all loans, whether secured or unsecured, taken out for the purpose of carrying out repairs and improvements to the property.

(2.4)   *Sale price* is the gross sale price of the property before any deductions.

MORTGAGE-RELATED CONTRIBUTIONS

(3)   Each co-owner's mortgage-related contributions ('mortgage related contribution') will be calculated by applying the following formulae.
   (3.1)   *First*[324]
      WHERE:
      (3.1.1)   *Loans* is the total of:
         (a)   the mortgage advance; and
         (b)   all further mortgage advances; and

---

which they have borrowed on a mortgage. The change in value of the share purchased by the mortgage is then apportioned between the co-owners according to the sums which each has paid towards the mortgage.

In most cases, the application of these formulae will produce a more equitable result than the other method of calculating floating shares: namely the simple addition of the contributions, followed by an apportionment of the net proceeds of sale pro rata (**1.137** above). The example is an illustration.

[324] To double-check the accuracy of the calculations at this stage the co-owners' combined lump sum contributions plus the gross mortgage share should be the same as the sale price. *Note:* A calculator is necessary. The formulae require exact figures. Approximate figures will not do.

$$\frac{\text{loans}}{\text{purchase price} + \text{improvements}} \times \text{sale price} = \text{gross mortgage share}$$

> (c) all loans taken out for the purpose of carrying out repairs and improvements to the property; and
>
> (d) all improvement grants.

(3.1.2) *Purchase price* has the same meaning as it has in para (2.2) above.

(3.1.3) *Improvements* has the same meaning as it has in para (2.3) above.

(3.1.4) *Sale price* has the same meaning as it has in para (2.4) above.

(3.1.5) *Gross mortgage share* represents the extent to which the change in the value of the property can be attributed to the sums of money provided by way of mortgages, loans and grants.

(3.2) *Second*

gross mortgage share — redemption = net mortgage share

WHERE:

(3.2.1) *Redemption* is the total amount required to redeem or repay:

> (a) the mortgage advance; and
>
> (b) all further mortgage advances; and
>
> (c) all loans taken out for the purpose of carrying out repairs and improvements to the property; and
>
> (d) all improvement grants.

(3.3) *Third*[325]

$$\frac{\text{individual mortgage payments}}{\text{combined mortgage payments}} \times \text{net mortgage share} = \text{mortgage related contribution}$$

WHERE:

(3.3.1) *Individual mortgage payments* is the total of each individual co-owner's contributions towards the repayment or payment of capital, interest and premiums on:

> (a) the mortgage advance; and
>
> (b) all mortgage-linked insurance policies; and
>
> (c) all further mortgage advances; and
>
> (d) all loans taken out for the purpose of carrying out repairs and improvements to the property; and
>
> (e) all improvement grants.

---

[325] To double-check the accuracy of the calculations at this stage the co-owners' combined mortgage-related contributions should be the same as the net mortgage share in para (3.2) above. *Note:* A calculator is necessary. The formulae require exact figures. Approximate figures will not do.

(3.3.2)   *Combined mortgage payments* is the total of (both)/(all) of the co-owners' individual mortgage payments.

THE SHARE[326]

(4)   Lump sum + mortgage related contribution = share

SALE COSTS

(5)   The incidental costs of selling the property will be paid by the co-owners (in equal shares) [OR] (in the proportions that each share bears to the other share or shares).

Example

A and B bought a flat for £44,000. The purchase costs came to £1,000. B paid £4,000. A paid £1,000. They took out a mortgage for £40,000. B paid £2,000 in mortgage payments. They sold the flat for £50,000. The amount required to redeem the mortgage was £39,000. The sale costs were £2,000 and the net proceeds of sale were £9,000. Who got what?

Addition of contributions: apportionment of net proceeds pro rata (wrong solution)

If A and B had executed a declaration of trust which contained the method of calculating floating shares set out in Precedent **1.137** above, the result would have been as follows.

A's contributions came to £12,000 overall — £1,000 towards the purchase and £11,000 towards the mortgage.

B's contributions came to £6,000 overall — £4,000 towards the purchase and £2,000 towards the mortgage.

The net proceeds of sale (£9,000) would be divided between them in the ratio 12:6.

A would get £6,000. B would get £3,000. A would receive twice as much as B. Even though the property has increased in value, B seems to have lost £1,000 on the original contribution of £4,000.

Suggested solution: applying the formulae

The result would have been totally different if these formulae had been applied, because they would have separated A's and B's lump sum contributions from their mortgage-related contributions.

The property went up in value, by roughly 11 per cent, from £45,000 (including purchase costs) to £50,000.

---

[326] To double-check the accuracy of the calculations at this stage the combined total of both or all shares should be the same as the net proceeds of sale plus the sale costs. *Note:* A calculator is necessary. The formulae require exact figures. Approximate figures will not do.

Tim's lump sum contribution of £1,000 increased by the same percentage to £1,111. B's lump sum contribution of £4,000 increased to £4,444.

The share of the property bought by the mortgage advance of £40,000 increased in value to £44,445. This is called the 'gross mortgage share'. By deducting from the gross mortgage share the amount required to redeem the mortgage (£39,000), we arrive at the 'net mortgage share' of £5,445. By virtue of A's mortgage-related contributions, A is entitled to 11/13ths of the net mortgage share (£4,607). B is entitled to 2/13ths of the net mortgage share (£838). A's lump sum contribution (£1,111) and mortgage-related contribution (£4,607) are added to produce £5,718. B's lump sum contribution (£4,444) and mortgage-related contribution (£838) are added to produce £5,282. The sale costs (£2,000) are paid pro rata. A £1,040, B £960. A ends up with £4,678. B ends up with £4,322.

Warning

The application of these formulae could cause hardship if:

(a)   a large share of the property is bought by the mortgage; and
(b)   one co-owner contributes substantially more than the other towards the mortgage payments; and
(c)   the property goes down in value.

1.140   Tabular form[327]

CALCULATION OF SHARES

The share of the net proceeds of sale to which each co-owner is entitled will be calculated by:

(1)   completing the record of contributions set out in the (first) Schedule; and then

(2)   applying the formulae set out in the (second) Schedule.

---

[327] For the two Schedules containing the record of contributions and the formulae, see below. The formulae are the same as those expressed in narrative form in **1.139** above. They identify the extent to which each co-owner's lump sum contributions and mortgage-related contributions affect the value of the property.

FIRST SCHEDULE

RECORD OF CONTRIBUTIONS

PURCHASE		£	
NAME 1	Contribution to purchase price and costs		A
NAME 2	Contribution to purchase price and costs		B
Mortgage advance			C
Gross purchase price	[A + B + C]		D

IMPROVEMENT		£	
NAME 1	Contributions		E
NAME 2	Contributions		F
Improvement grant(s) and further mortgage advance(s) and loan(s) taken out for improvements			G
Combined cost of improvements	[E + F + G]		H

MORTGAGE PAYMENTS		£	
NAME 1	Contributions		I
NAME 2	Contributions		J
Combined contributions	[I + J]		K

SALE		£	
Sale price (or, if one co-owner is selling his/her share in the property to the other, the agreed current market value of the whole property)			L
Mortgage redemption and repayment of any improvement grant and loan taken out for improvements			M

Sale costs: estate agency/legal fees/apportionments of outgoings			N
Net proceeds of sale	$[L - (M + N)]$		O

SECOND SCHEDULE

CALCULATION OF SHARES

STAGE ONE: In which the change in the value of the property is apportioned between the contributions towards the purchase and improvement of the property made by the co-owners individually and by virtue of the mortgage advance(s)			
NAME 1	$\dfrac{A + E}{D + H} \times L =$		P
NAME 2	$\dfrac{B + F}{D + H} \times L =$		Q
Mortgage(s)	$\dfrac{C + G}{D + H} \times L =$		R
Sale price	$[P + Q + R]$		L

STAGE TWO: In which the increase or reduction in the value of the property attributable to the amount(s) provided by way of the mortgage(s) is apportioned between the co-owners according to their respective contribution towards repayment of the mortgage(s)			
	$R - M$		S
NAME 1	$\dfrac{I}{K} \times S =$		T
NAME 2	$\dfrac{J}{K} \times S =$		U

STAGE THREE: In which the co-owner's entitlements from stages one and two are added together			
NAME 1	$P + T$		V
NAME 2	$Q + U$		W
Net proceeds of sale + sale costs	$[O + N]$		X

STAGE FOUR: In which the sale costs are apportioned between the co-owners in accordance with their entitlements in stage three			
NAME 1	$\dfrac{V}{X \times N}$		Y
NAME 2	$\dfrac{W}{X \times N}$		Z
Sale costs			N

STAGE FIVE: In which the co-owner's shares of the net proceeds of sale are ascertained			
NAME 1	V – Y		
NAME 2	W – Z		
Net proceeds of sale			O

Fixed shares or floating shares

1.141   The average of two or more methods of calculating the shares[328]

SHARES

When the property is sold:

(1) (*name 1*) will receive the *average* of the sums to which (*name 1*) is entitled in Schedules (*number*) and (*number*) to this Declaration of Trust;

(2) (*name 2*) will receive the *average* of the sums to which (*name 2*) is entitled in Schedules (*number*) and (*number*) to this Declaration of Trust.

1.142   Supplemental clause providing for the gradual equalisation of the shares[329]

GRADUAL EQUALISATION OF SHARES[330]

(1) The co-owners intend that on the (seventh)[331] anniversary of the date (on which the purchase of the property was completed) [OR] (of this

---

[328] If the average of two or more methods of calculating the shares is to be used, it is probably better to set out the different methods of calculation in separate Schedules. A single clause that attempted to describe various different methods would, almost certainly, be difficult to understand and would probably be very lengthy.

[329] This clause could apply equally to fixed shares and floating shares. It is recommended that this Clause should immediately follow the Clause setting out the respective shares.

[330] The concept is quite simple. The co-owners 'split the difference' over a given period. Inheritance tax implications should be considered. There is certainly a transfer of value, but it is not entirely clear whether there is one transfer of value, or a series of transfers. The provisions of IA 1986, s 339, which relate to transactions at an undervalue, should also be considered.

[331] Insert the appropriate anniversary.

Declaration of Trust) their respective shares of the net proceeds of sale will become and remain equal, and to that intent the following provisions will apply.

(2) In this Clause:

    (2.1) 'the larger share' means the share of the co-owner who is entitled to the larger share of the net proceeds of sale;[332]

    (2.2) 'the smaller share' means the share of the co-owner who is entitled to the smaller share of the net proceeds of sale; and

    (2.3) 'the difference' means the difference between the larger share and the smaller share on the date when the property is sold or either share is realised.

(3) For each complete year that has elapsed since the date (on which the purchase of the property was completed) [OR] (of this Declaration of Trust) the larger share will decrease by ($1/14^{th}$)[333] of the difference and the smaller share will increase by ($1/14^{th}$)[334] of the difference.

(4) For the avoidance of doubt:

    (4.1) no apportionment will be made in respect of any period of less than a year (*see Example*);

    (4.2) the calculations in this Clause will cease to have effect immediately after the (seventh)[335] anniversary of the date (on which the purchase of the property was completed) [OR] (of this Declaration of Trust); and

    (4.3) if the co-owners separate, the calculations in this Clause will apply only in respect of each complete year that has elapsed since the date (on which the purchase of the property was completed) [OR] (of this Declaration of Trust) and the date on which the co-owners separated (see Example).

Example

A and B purchased a house and executed a declaration of trust on 20 January 1989. On 9 October 1991 they separated. On 16 March 1992 they sold the property. The net proceeds of sale came to £150,000, of which A was entitled to the 'larger share' of £110,000 and B was entitled to the 'smaller share' of £40,000. The declaration of trust provided that their respective shares should be equalised over a seven-year period. Who gets what?

The 'difference' between the larger share and the smaller share on the date when the property is sold is £70,000. A's share will decrease by $2/14^{ths}$ of the difference and B's share will increase by $2/14^{ths}$ of the difference. The numerator represents the two complete years from 20 January 1989 to 20 January 1991, during which

---

[332] This clause only envisages a gradual equalisation of the shares of two co-owners.

[333] The denominator should be double the number of years. So, for a five-year period it would be 1/10th; for six years, 1/12th; for 10 years, 1/20th, etc. In most cases the fraction will be more intelligible than a percentage.

[334] The denominator should be double the number of years. So, for a five-year period it would be 1/10th; for six years, 1/12th; for 10 years, 1/20th, etc. In most cases the fraction will be more intelligible than a percentage.

[335] Insert the appropriate anniversary.

time they were living together. No apportionment is made in respect of the period from 21 January 1991. So, A gets £100,000 and B gets £50,000.

General clauses

1.143   Contingencies: introductory clause[336]

Contingencies

- If one of the co-owners fails to pay their share of the mortgage payments, the provisions of Schedule (*number*) will apply.[337]
- If one of the co-owners wishes to sell the property and the other co-owner refuses to sell it, the provisions of Schedule (*number*) will apply.[338]
- If one of the co-owners dies and the other co-owner does not become solely and beneficially entitled to the property, the provisions of Schedule (*number*) will apply.[339]
- If one of the co-owners is declared bankrupt, the provisions of Schedule (*number*) will apply.[340]
- If one of the co-owners ceases permanently to reside in the property and the other co-owner continues to reside in it, the provisions of Schedule (*number*) will apply.[341]

---

[336] A declaration of trust may need to address a number of contingencies, uncertainties or risks. It is recommended that these are briefly introduced by a single sentence in the main body of the declaration, and that the substantive provisions are, in each case, incorporated in a separate Schedule at the end of the declaration.

The contingencies included in these precedents are typical of many of the problems that arise, but are not exhaustive. They serve a variety of purposes.

In some cases they are included primarily for information purposes, for example **1.171** and **1.167**.

Some of the contingencies provide that payments made by one co-owner on the other's behalf will be treated as a loan, and that their respective beneficial interests will not be affected. Examples include the precedents at **1.168**, **1.173** and **1.175** below.

In the case of the precedent at **1.174**, the payments made by the other co-owner are treated as a gift. To a lesser degree, other precedents may contain a gift element, but generally such contingencies are designed to deal only with a temporary state of affairs.

Where there is likely to be a long-term imbalance, the contingencies provide that fixed shares will be converted into floating shares. Illustrations can be found at **1.172** and **1.176** below.

Some of the contingencies give a co-owner the opportunity to 'buy out' the other co-owner's share on favourable terms, but usually subject to a strict time limit. Examples include the precedents at **1.170** and **1.180** below.

There are also contingencies which might best be described as dispute resolution contingencies. Illustrations are the precedents at **1.177** and **1.178** below, which try to get to grips with the problem that could arise if both co-owners wish to keep the property.

Note: If more than one contingency Schedule is being used, care must be taken to ensure that they are not inconsistent with each other.

[337] See **1.168** below.
[338] See **1.169** below.
[339] See **1.170** below.
[340] See **1.171** below.
[341] See **1.179** below.

- If one of the co-owners is unemployed or incapable of working, the provisions of Schedule (*number*) will apply.[342]

- If one of the co-owners is unemployed or incapable of working because she is pregnant, or he or she is looking after a child or children, the provisions of Schedule (*number*) will apply.[343]

- If one of the co-owners attends a full-time course of education which lasts for less than (one year), the provisions of Schedule (*number*) will apply.[344]

- If one of the co-owners attends a full-time course of education which lasts for more than (one year), the provisions of Schedule (*number*) will apply.[345]

- If the co-owners permit any other person to reside with them in the property, the provisions of Schedule (*number*) will apply.[346]

- If the co-owners separate within a period of (12 months) after purchasing the property, the provisions of Schedule (*number*) will apply.[347]

- If the co-owners are about to separate, or have recently separated, and both of them wish to keep the property, the provisions of Schedule (*number*) will apply.[348]

- If the co-owners carry out building works and contribute towards the cost of the building works disproportionately to their respective shares of the net proceeds of sale, the provisions of Schedule (*number*) will apply.[349]

- If one of the co-owners wishes to realise his or her share of the property, the provisions of Schedule (*number*) will apply.[350]

Net income until sale[351]

1.144   General

Regardless of the manner in which the net proceeds of sale of the property are to be divided between the co-owners (in equal shares) [*OR*] (as to   per cent for (*name 1*) and as to   per cent for (*name 2*)).

1.145   Payments from lodgers

Regardless of the manner in which the net proceeds of sale of the property are to be divided between them, any payment made to one or both of the

---

[342] See **1.173** below.
[343] See **1.174** below.
[344] See **1.175** below.
[345] See **1.176** below.
[346] See **1.167** below.
[347] See **1.180** below.
[348] See **1.177** and **1.178** below.
[349] See **1.172** below.
[350] See **1.181** below.
[351] Note that in the case of a husband and wife who are living together, special rules relate to the apportionment of income arising from property held in their joint names. These rules are contained in the Income Tax Act 2007, ss 836 and 837.

co-owners by anyone who normally resides with them as a contribution towards his or her living and accommodation expenses will be divided between the co-owners (in equal shares) [*OR*] (as to   per cent for (*name 1*) and as to   per cent for (*name 2*)).

1.146   Payments from grown-up children

Regardless of the manner in which the net proceeds of sale of the property are to be divided between the co-owners, any payments received by (*name 2*) from any of (*name 2's*) children who normally reside in the property as a contribution towards his or her living and accommodation expenses will belong to (*name 2*) [*OR*] (the co-owners in equal shares).

Circumstances in which an application can be made to the court for an order to sell the property

1.147   Separation[352]

Either co-owner can apply to the court for an order that the property be sold[353] if the co-owners have lived apart for a continuous period of at least (three) months immediately preceding the presentation of the application.

1.148   A co-owner's death[354]

After the end of a period of (6) months from the date of the death of a co-owner, his or her personal representatives, or any person who is entitled under the deceased co-owner's will or the law relating to intestacy to his or her beneficial interest in the property, can apply to the court for an order that the property be sold.

1.149   Contributions towards repairs and improvements not to affect the co-owners' fixed shares[355]

No contribution in money or money's worth which either co-owner may make towards repairs and improvements to the property will affect the size of their respective shares of the net proceeds of sale.

---

[352] If this Clause is being used in conjunction with any of the contingency schedules, there must be no inconsistency between the time-limits.

[353] LPA 1925, s 30, giving power to apply to the court where trustees for sale refuse to sell, has been replaced by ss 14 and 15 of the TLATA 1996.

[354] If this Clause is used in conjunction with the contingency schedule at **1.170** below, there must be no inconsistency between the timespans.

It may be preferable to specify a period commencing on the death rather than on the date on which a grant of representation is first taken out, because the issue of the grant could be delayed for various reasons.

[355] If a definition of 'repairs and improvements' is considered necessary, see **1.162**. Compare MPPA 1970, s 37.

Covenants

1.150 Prohibited acts

Neither co-owner will do or attempt to do any of the following things without the other co-owner's consent, and if they are living apart that consent must be in writing:

(1) carry out or take out a loan for the purpose of carrying out any structural alterations or major repairs or improvements to the property;

(2) grant any tenancy or licence or allow anyone else to occupy the property;

(3) transfer his or her beneficial interest in the property other than by Will or Codicil;

(4) charge or incumber the property or any part of it or any interest in it.

1.151 Positive acts

Each co-owner will:

(1) Obligations

Always comply with the obligations imposed on the co-owners jointly and individually in:

(1.1) the registers kept at the Land Registry;

(1.2) this Declaration of Trust;

(1.3) the mortgage;

(1.4) any insurance policy that is linked to the mortgage;

(1.5) any insurance policy that affects the building or its contents;

(1.6) any order affecting the property that has been issued by a body acting on statutory authority;

(1.7) the Lease;

(1.8) the Memorandum and Articles of Association of the Management Company.

(2) Payments

Promptly pay his or her share of the mortgage payments, insurance premiums, and all other outgoings on the property.

(3) Repair

Keep and contribute towards the cost of keeping the property in reasonable repair, condition and decoration.

(4) Insure

Keep and contribute towards the cost of keeping the property adequately insured under comprehensive cover to its full re-instatement value.

(5) Keep accounts

Keep proper accounts, receipts and statements recording all the contributions made by each and both of the co-owners towards the mortgage payments and the costs of all repairs and improvements to the property.

(6) Execute further assurances

Complete, sign and execute any form, document and deed which may be required in order to transfer the legal estate and beneficial interest in the property or otherwise to implement the provisions of this Declaration of Trust.

(7) Allow access

Let any valuer have access to the property and any information about the property which may be relevant in assessing its open market value.

(8) Indemnity

Indemnify the other co-owner from and against the consequences of the failure of the co-owner giving this indemnity to comply with any of the obligations imposed on him or her.

1.152   Legal advice[356]

Each of the co-owners has received independent legal advice on the provisions and implications of this Declaration of Trust.

1.153   Costs of this declaration

(*Name 1*) will pay all the legal costs relating to the preparation and execution of this Declaration of Trust.

[OR]

The co-owners will pay the legal costs relating to the preparation and execution of this Declaration of Trust (in equal shares).

---

[356] See, generally, **1.2** and **2.2**.
Note that the effect of acting for clients with different interests is that the solicitor must act with caution as hemay suddenly find that he is in the position of having a duty to one client, the effect of which if carried out will be contrary to the interest of the other client. A solicitor that continues to act for both clients in these circumstances risks proceedings for negligence being brought against him by one client or the other.

[OR]

Each of the co-owners will pay the costs incurred by him or her in obtaining independent legal advice on the provisions and implications of this Declaration of Trust.

1.154   Sale costs[357]

The co-owners will pay the incidental costs of selling the property (in equal shares) [OR] (in the proportions that their respective shares of the rest of the net proceeds of sale of the property bear to each other).

1.155   Costs of transfer of beneficial interest

Unless the co-owners agree otherwise, if one of them transfers all his or her legal estate and beneficial interest in the property to the other (or the other's nominee), the valuation fees, legal fees and other costs incurred by the transferor will be paid by the transferor, and the valuation fees, legal fees and other costs incurred by the transferee will be paid by the transferee.

Definitions

1.156   Sale price

'The sale price' means:

(1)   the price for which the property is sold; and

(2)   the price paid by the buyer of the property for any chattels jointly owned by the co-owners, whether or not a separate price is paid for those chattels.

1.157   Amount required to redeem the mortgage[358]

'The amount required to redeem the mortgage' means the sums of money required by the lenders to enable the co-owners to repay all mortgages, charges and loans to which the property is subject (other than a charge created by one of the co-owners affecting his or her beneficial interest alone) and to enable the co-owners to be completely released and discharged from the performance of all their obligations under such mortgages, charges and loans, and includes:

(1)   all legal and administrative fees incurred or charged by any lender in connection with the repayment; and

---

[357] It is important that the co-owners clearly agree in advance how the incidental costs of selling the property will be borne between them. These costs usually include estate agents' commissions as well as legal fees, and are sometimes substantial.

There is no need to include this Clause if the method of calculating the co-owners' shares already takes the sale costs into account.

[358] In the case of an endowment mortgage or insurance-linked mortgage it may be considered desirable to add the words 'less the surrender values of all insurance policies linked to the mortgage, whether or not those policies have been assigned to or deposited with the lenders'.

(2)   any financial penalty imposed by any lender for each repayment.

1.158   Incidental costs of selling the property[359]

'The incidental costs of selling the property' means the total sum of money (including VAT) to be paid in respect of:

(1)   estate agent's commission; and

(2)   legal costs and disbursements; and

(3)   apportionments of rates, taxes, insurance, and other outgoings on the property; and

(4)   any other costs incurred in connection with the sale or transfer of the property or any interest in it.

1.159   Net proceeds of sale

'The net proceeds of sale' means the sale price,[360] less:

(1)   the amount required to redeem the mortgage;[361] and

(2)   the incidental costs of selling the property.[362]

1.160   Open market value

'The open market value' means the best price for the property that the co-owners could reasonably be expected to obtain if they sold the property on the date of the valuation, assuming that:

(1)   the property is being sold with vacant possession; and

(2)   there is no discount in respect of the joint ownership of the property; and

(3)   a buyer, who is not connected with (either)/(any) of the co-owners, is ready, willing and able to complete the purchase of the property immediately for cash; and

(4)   all carpets, curtains, fixtures and fittings which are jointly owned by the co-owners are included in the sale.

1.161   Mortgage payments

'The mortgage payments' means the sums of money paid or payable from time to time to the lender(s) in respect of all mortgages, charges and loans to which the property is subject, and includes:

(1)   the payment of interest; and

(2)   the repayment of capital; and

(3)   the payment of insurance premiums; and

---

[359] Note that in the 'short form' complete precedents, 'the incidental costs of selling the property' has been abbreviated to 'the sale costs'.
[360] For a definition of 'the sale price', see **1.156** above.
[361] For a definition of 'the amount required to redeem the mortgage', see **1.157** above.
[362] For a definition of 'the incidental costs of selling the property', see **1.158** above.

(4) the payment of penalties imposed by the lender(s); and

(5) the payment of interest and the repayment of capital on all loans taken out, with or without security, for the purpose of carrying out repairs and improvements to the property.

1.162 Repairs and improvements[363]

'Repairs and improvements' means major repairs necessary to maintain the fabric of the property, and any of the following measures undertaken with a view to improving its fitness for occupation:

(1) installation of a fixed bath, shower, wash basin, sink or lavatory, and any necessary associated plumbing;

(2) damp proofing measures;

(3) provision or improvement of ventilation and natural lighting;

(4) provision of electric lighting and sockets;

(5) provision or improvement of drainage facilities;

(6) improvements to the structural condition of the property;

(7) improvements to the facilities for storing, preparing and cooking food;

(8) provision of heating, including central heating;

(9) provision of storage facilities for fuel and refuse;

(10) improvements to the insulation of the property; and

(11) any other major repairs analogous to those listed above.[364]

1.163 Co-owners

'The co-owners' means (*name 1*) and (*name 2*) and the trustees for the time being of the property.

1.164 The nature of this declaration

This Declaration of Trust:

(1) is a deed[365] and is executed as a deed[366] by the (co-owners) [*OR*] (parties to it);

---

[363] It is submitted that the definition of 'repairs and improvements' will depend on the age and condition of the property, and perhaps also the socio-economic backgrounds of the co-owners. For an alternative definition, see the definition of 'building works' at **1.172** below.

[364] When a couple buy a property with the intention of carrying out substantial repairs and improvements, it may be preferable to express their shares of the net proceeds of sale as floating, rather than fixed. For the distinction between fixed shares and floating shares, see **1.6** above.

[365] LPA 1925, s 53(1)(b) requires that 'a declaration of trust respecting any land or any interest therein must be manifested and proved by some writing signed by some person who is able to declare such trust or by his will'. Although the declaration must be in writing, it is not essential that it be executed as a deed, unless there are covenants in it.

[366] Law of Property (Miscellaneous Provisions) Act 1989, s 1.

(2)   can be varied by a subsequent Declaration of Trust executed by all the persons who are able to vary the original trusts;[367]

(3)   will be legally binding on the (co-owners) [OR] (parties to it) unless and until it is varied or set aside by an order of the court;[368]

(4)   contains the entire understanding of the (co-owners) [OR] (parties to it) and supersedes any previous agreements, representations and promises made by them in respect of the property.[369]

1.165   Execution in duplicate[370]

This Declaration of Trust has been executed in (duplicate)/(triplicate)/ (quadruplicate) so that each (co-owner) [OR] (person who has a beneficial interest in the property) may possess a copy of it, and (both)/(all) copies will be regarded as one deed, and each copy will be as efficacious as the other(s).

1.166   Attestation clause[371]

SIGNED as a Deed by (*name 1*) in the presence of:

SIGNED as a Deed by (*name 2*) in the presence of:

Contingencies

1.167   If the co-owners permit any other person to reside with them in the property[372]

SCHEDULE (*number*)

(1)   This Schedule applies if:

(1.1)   the co-owners permit any other person to reside with them in the property; and

(1.2)   there is no alternative agreement between the co-owners.

---

[367] For a form of deed of variation, see **1.191** below.

[368] For example, the court could set the declaration of trust aside on the grounds of fraud or mistake (*City of London Building Society v Flegg* [1988] AC 54; *Wilson v Wilson* [1969] 1 WLR 1470). The beneficial interests may also be affected by orders under, for example the IA 1986, the CA 1989, the I(PFD)A 1975.

[369] *Lloyds Bank Plc v Rosset* [1990] 1 All ER 1111 at 1118.

[370] For the effect of multiple execution of deeds see, generally, Co Litt 229a, and *Burchell v Clark* (1876) 2 CPD 88 at 96.

[371] It is usual, but not essential, for a declaration of trust to be executed as a deed. For provisions relating to deeds and their execution, see the Law of Property (Miscellaneous Provisions) Act 1989, s 1.

[372] The co-owners may permit other occupants to reside with them in a variety of circumstances: for example lodgers, the grown-up child of one of the co-owners or the boyfriend or girlfriend of a co-owner. This Schedule provides that, in the absence of any contrary agreement between the co-owners, the other occupant will be a bare licensee. In many cases where the occupation of premises is shared on an informal basis, particularly if the parties are related, the non-owner will have a bare licence. If, however, an intention to create legal relations can be found together with some form of consideration, there may be a contractual licence.

(2) In this Schedule:

    (2.1) 'the licensee' means any person (aged 18 or over) who normally resides with the co-owners, whether or not he or she is related to or dependent on either of them,[373] and

    (2.2) 'the licence' means the terms and conditions on which the co-owners permit the licensee to occupy the property.

(3) The co-owners permit the licensee to occupy the property as a bare licensee.[374]

(4) The licensee will have no right to exclusive possession of the property or any part of it.[375]

(5) The licensee will not acquire any tenancy or beneficial interest in the property despite:

    (5.1) any payment the licensee makes to either or both of the co-owners as a contribution towards his or her living and accommodation expenses; and

    (5.2) any repairs or improvements to the property which the licensee carries out with or without the consent of the co-owners.

(6) The licence can be terminated by the licensee at any time.[376]

(7) The licence can be revoked by either of the co-owners at any time.[377]

(8) The licence is personal to the licensee and cannot be transferred by him or her to any other person.

(9) The co-owners will take whatever steps are necessary to ensure that the licensee clearly understands the terms and conditions on which he or she is permitted to occupy the property.

1.168 *If a co-owner fails to pay his or her share of the mortgage payments*[378]

SCHEDULE (*number*)

(1) This Schedule applies if:

---

[373] Although, in general, a bare licence can be revoked at any time, the licence of a child (even an adult child) to remain in the home will only be revocable in exceptional circumstances (*Egan v Egan* [1975] Ch 218).

[374] Anyone sharing residential accommodation with the consent of the owners is, at the very least, a bare licensee. The owners' consent to the sharing of accommodation prevents the licensee from being a trespasser.

[375] Without exclusive possession there cannot be a tenancy. A lodger will always be a licensee and never a tenant. 'The occupier is a lodger if the landlord provides attendance or services which require the landlord or his servants to exercise unrestricted access to and use of the premises. A lodger is entitled to live in the premises but cannot call the place his own' (*Street v Mountford* [1985] AC 809 at 818, per Lord Templeman).

[376] *Australian Blue Metal v Hughes* [1963] AC 74 at 98.

[377] The licence can be revoked by either co-owner at will and without notice (*Crane v Morris* [1965] 1 WLR 1104 at 1108). The licence can also be revoked by one co-owner without reference to the other (*Annen v Rattee* (1984) 273 EG 503, CA).

[378] 'Where ... a fund is being distributed, a party cannot take anything out of the fund until he has made good what he owes to the fund' (*Re Rhodesia Goldfields Ltd* [1910] 1 Ch 239 at 247, per Swinfen Eady J). Anyone who discharges another's secured obligation, wholly or in part, is

(1.1)   there is no alternative agreement between the co-owners; and

(1.2)   one of the co-owners ('the debtor') is unable or unwilling or otherwise fails to pay his or her share of the mortgage payments when it is due; and

(1.3)   the other co-owner ('the creditor') pays all or part of the debtor's share of the mortgage payments on the debtor's behalf. (; and

(1.4)   the provisions of Schedule(s)   do not apply).[379]

(2)   The payment made by the creditor on the debtor's behalf ('the loan') will be treated as a loan from the creditor to the debtor.

(3)   The loan is made on the condition that:

(3.1)   it must be repaid as soon as possible; and

(3.2)   if it has not been repaid within (3) months from the date on which it was made, the loan, or so much of it as remains outstanding, will bear interest at a rate of (one) per cent a year above the rate of interest payable from time to time in respect of the mortgage (before)/(after) the deduction of basic rate income tax.

1.169   *If one co-owner wishes to sell the property and the other co-owner refuses to sell it*

SCHEDULE (*number*)*

(1)   This Schedule applies if:**

(1.1)   there is no alternative agreement between the co-owners; and

(1.2)   one of the co-owners ('the applicant') wishes to sell the property; and

(1.3)   the other co-owner ('the objector') refuses to sell it.

(2)   The applicant will give written notice to the objector of the applicant's wish to sell the property.

(3)   The date on which the objector receives that notice is 'the application date'.

(4)   After the end of a period of (12) weeks beginning on the application date the applicant can apply to the court for an order that the property be sold if:***

(4.1)   the objector has not contractually agreed to purchase the applicant's estate and interest in the property; and

(4.2)   the objector refuses to sell the property.

*   This precedent could be used in conjunction with the precedent at **1.147**. If both precedents are used, it is essential to ensure that the dates on which an application can be made to the court coincide.

---

entitled to be repaid, out of the security, the amount of the sum or sums paid by him (*Pitt v Pitt* (1823) Turn & R 180; *Outram v Hyde* [1875] 24 WR 268; *Cowcher v Cowcher* [1972] 1 All ER 943 at 951).

[379]   For example if a co-owner is unemployed or incapable of working (see **1.173** below), if a co-owner is unemployed or incapable of working because of pregnancy or childcare (see **1.174** below), or if a co-owner attends a full-time course of education (see **1.175** below).

** The rule that it was the prime duty of trustees for sale to sell the property was abolished by the TLATA 1996.

*** The application shall be made under the TLATA 1996.

1.170 *If one co-owner dies and the other does not become solely and beneficially entitled to the property*

SCHEDULE (*number*)

(1) This Schedule applies if:

    (1.1) one of the co-owners ('the deceased') dies; and

    (1.2) the other co-owner ('the survivor') does not become solely and beneficially entitled to the property.[380]

(2) This Schedule applies subject to and without prejudice to all rights that the survivor may have under the deceased's will[381] and generally in law.[382]

(3) The survivor will be primarily liable for:

    (3.1) the payment of the mortgage;

    (3.2) the payment of all outgoings on the property;

    (3.3) keeping the property adequately insured; and

    (3.4) keeping the property in reasonable repair and condition.

(4) In this Schedule:

    (4.1) 'the death' means the date on which the deceased died;

    (4.2) 'the share' means the deceased's beneficial interest in the property; and

    (4.3) 'the estate' may mean either the deceased's personal representative(s) or the person(s) entitled to the share under the deceased's will or the law relating to intestacy.[383]

(5) If the survivor is asked to do so, he or she will, as soon as practicable after the death, appoint the estate to be a new trustee of the property and will register the new trustee as a joint proprietor of the property, and the costs of effecting such appointment and registration will be paid by the estate.[384]

(6) When the property or the share is sold the estate will be credited with a lump sum payment by way of reimbursement of all (if any) mortgage payments it has made in respect of the property since the death.

(7) Part 1 of this Schedule applies during the period of (6) months beginning with the death ('the concessionary period').[385]

---

[380] This Schedule would not apply if the co-owners were beneficial joint tenants, or if the deceased had, by will, made an absolute gift of his or her share to the survivor.

[381] For example a life or lesser interest, or an option to purchase.

[382] For example, under the I(PFD)A 1975.

[383] The definition of 'the estate' is inevitably vague. Much will depend on the circumstances of each individual case.

[384] For the recommended procedures where registered land is held on a trust of land and it is necessary to appoint a new trustee, see Ruoff and Roper *Registered Conveyancing* (Sweet & Maxwell, Looseleaf) at para 32–18.

[385] The concessionary period is designed to safeguard the survivor's rights of occupation for a reasonable time, and to encourage the survivor to purchase the deceased's share.

(8)   Part 2 of this Schedule applies after the end of the concessionary period.

Part 1

(9)   During the concessionary period the survivor can reside in the property rent-free.

(10) During the concessionary period the value of the share can be discounted by   per cent, by virtue of the fact that the property is jointly owned.[386]

(11) During the concessionary period the survivor's nominee can purchase the share for its value immediately after the death.[387]

Part 2

(12) After the concessionary period the estate can apply to the court for an order that the property be sold.[388]

(13) After the concessionary period the value of the share will not be discounted even though the property is jointly owned.[389]

(14) After the concessionary period the survivor will pay an occupation rent to the estate.[390]

(15) The occupation rent will be such proportion of the fair rent as the value of the share bears to the value of the whole of the net proceeds of sale of the property.

(16) The fair rent is the market rent that would be payable for the property between a willing landlord and willing tenant.[391]

1.171   If a co-owner is declared bankrupt[392]

SCHEDULE (*number*)

(1)   This Schedule applies if one of the co-owners ('the bankrupt') is declared bankrupt.

(2)   The provisions of this Schedule are:

(2.1)   not a matter for agreement or negotiation between the co-owners;

(2.2)   an abbreviated summary of the law;

(2.3)   included in this Declaration of Trust for information purposes only.

---

[386] In *Wight and Another v IRC* (1982) 264 ERG 935, Lands Tribunal, it was held that, because it was unlikely that a purchaser would be able to obtain an order for sale under LPA 1925, s 30, the discount in the value of a half share for capital transfer tax purposes should be 15 per cent.

[387] The words 'immediately after the death' should cover the effect of the payments of any mortgage-linked insurance policy proceeds, and the valuation discount which applies during the concessionary period.

[388] The application would be made under the TLATA 1996. See, **1.32** above.

[389] See footnote above.

[390] For 'occupation rent', see generally: *Leake v Bruzzi* [1974] 1 WLR 1528; *Suttill v Graham* [1977] 1 WLR 819; and *Dennis v McDonald* (1982) 3 FLR 398. Since the introduction of shorthold tenancies a market rent may be more appropriate.

[391] See the dicta of Sir John Arnold P in *Dennis v McDonald* (1982) 3 FLR 398 at 409.

[392] Note para 2. This Schedule is purely for information purposes.

(3) The bankrupt's beneficial interest in the property will automatically vest in his or her trustee in bankruptcy ('the trustee').[393]

(4) The trustee has a statutory duty to get in, realise and distribute the bankrupt's estate[394] and in the exercise of that duty the trustee may apply to the court for an order that the property be sold.[395]

(5) The bankrupt's rights of occupation will depend on whether a child under 18 was living with the bankrupt at:
(5.1)   the time when the bankruptcy petition was presented; and
(5.2)   the commencement of the bankruptcy.[396]

(6) If the bankrupt has entered into a transaction at an undervalue with anyone else in respect of his or her share of the property, the trustee may apply to the court for an order restoring the position to what it would have been if the bankrupt had not entered into that transaction.[397]

1.172   If the co-owners extend, alter, improve or repair the property

(Conversion from fixed shares to floating shares)[398]

SCHEDULE *(number)*

(1) This Schedule applies if the co-owners:
(1.1)   carry out building works (as defined below); and
(1.2)   contribute towards the cost of the building works disproportionately to their respective shares of the net proceeds of sale; and
(1.3)   fail to execute a further Declaration of Trust to reflect the change in circumstances.

(2) This Schedule also applies if the co-owners:
(2.1)   carry out building works; and
(2.2)   take out a loan or further mortgage for that purpose; and
(2.3)   repay or are in the process of repaying that loan or further mortgage disproportionately to the shares in which they had been making the mortgage payments before the building works commenced; and
(2.4)   fail to execute a further Declaration of Trust to reflect the change in circumstances.

(3) In this Schedule 'building works' means any works of a major nature which enhance or are intended to enhance the value of the property, and includes, but is not restricted to:
(3.1)   the building of an extension to the property;
(3.2)   major alterations to the exterior or interior of the property;
(3.3)   the conversion of the property into separate flats or units;

---

[393] IA 1986, s 306.
[394] IA 1986, s 305(2) and Ch IV.
[395] An order under TLATA 1996, s 14.
[396] IA 1986, ss 336 and 337. See *Re Gorman (A Bankrupt), ex parte Trustee of the Bankrupt v The Bankrupt* [1990] 1 WLR 616.
[397] IA 1986, s 339. For the 'relevant time' limits, see ibid, s 341.
[398] For the distinction between fixed shares and floating shares and a discussion of their advantages and disadvantages, see **1.7** above. *See Example.*

(3.4)   major works undertaken with a view to improving the fitness of the property for occupation;

(3.5)   the purchase of additional land to be enjoyed with the property;

(3.6)   the construction of a garage or outbuildings;

(3.7)   major works affecting the landscape of the garden;

(3.8)   major works to the boundaries;

(3.9)   major works connected with the access to or exit from the property;

(3.10)   all works analogous to those listed above.

(4)   Immediately before the building works commence the property will be valued or will be treated as having been valued ('the unimproved value').

(5)   The unimproved value will be assessed:

(5.1)   by the co-owners themselves at such figure as they agree; or

(5.2)   by a professionally qualified property valuer instructed by the co-owners; or

(5.3)   if the co-owners fail to agree the unimproved value or on instructing a valuer, by a valuer appointed by the President of the Royal Institution of Chartered Surveyors.

(6)   Immediately before the building works commence there will be a deemed sale of the property by the co-owners as if:

(6.1)   it were being sold at the unimproved value; and

(6.2)   each co-owner were able to realise his or her share ('the fixed share') of the net proceeds of sale calculated in accordance with the provisions of Clause (*number*) of this Declaration of Trust.

(7)   Immediately after the deemed sale of the property there will be a deemed re-acquisition of it by the co-owners as if:

(7.1)   they were acquiring it at the unimproved value; and

(7.2)   the fixed share of each co-owner were his or her cash contribution towards the acquisition price.

(8)   Immediately after the deemed re-acquisition of the property the provisions of Clause (*number*) of this Declaration of Trust relating to the calculation of the co-owners' shares of the net proceeds of sale will cease to have effect and the following provisions will apply.

(9)   After the deemed re-acquisition of the property the co-owners will hold the property and its net proceeds of sale in trust for themselves as beneficial tenants in common in shares which are proportionate to the contributions made by each of them towards the deemed re-acquisition of the property and the payments made by each of them after the deemed re-acquisition towards:

(9.1)   the building works;

(9.2)   any subsequent building works;

(9.3)   mortgage interest;

(9.4)   mortgage capital;

(9.5)   mortgage-linked insurance premiums;

(9.6)   interest and capital on loans taken out for the purpose of carrying out the building works and any subsequent building works; and

(9.7)   the incidental costs of selling the property.

(10) (Formulae for calculating floating shares.)[399]

Example

A and B decided to 'improve' their house. In its unimproved state it is worth £88,000. The amount required to redeem their mortgage is £48,000. When they bought the house they executed a declaration of trust which stated that A would receive 75 per cent of the net proceeds of sale, and B would receive 25 per cent.

The building works take exactly a year to complete. During that time B pays £21,000 towards the works and £1,000 towards the mortgage payments. During that time A pays £5,000 towards the works and £3,000 towards the mortgage payments.

As soon as the building works have been completed, A and B decide to move house. They sell the house for £128,000. The amount required to redeem their mortgage is still £48,000. The net proceeds of sale come to £80,000. Who gets what?

If their declaration of trust had not incorporated this Schedule, A would still be entitled to 75 per cent of the net proceeds, and B 25 per cent. On that basis A would receive £60,000 and B would receive £20,000.

The effect of this Schedule is to create a deemed sale and re-acquisition of the property when the building works begin, and to convert A's and B's shares from fixed shares to floating shares.

Since the deemed re-acquisition, A's contributions have been £30,000 (A's original 75 per cent fixed share treated as downpayment on the re-acquisition) plus £5,000 (towards the building works) plus £3,000 (A's mortgage payments). So, A's total contribution has been £38,000.

Since the deemed re-acquisition, B's contributions have been £10,000 (B's original 25 per cent fixed share treated as downpayment on the re-acquisition) plus £21,000 (towards the bulding works) plus £1,000 (B's share of the mortgage). So, B's total contribution has been £32,000.

The net proceeds of sale (£80,000) are divided between A and B in the proportions 38:52. A receives £43,429 and B receives £39,571. The incidental costs of selling the property are paid by them in the same proportions.

1.173 If a co-owner is unemployed or incapable of working[400]

SCHEDULE (*number*)

(1) This Schedule applies if:

---

[399] See Precedents **1.136–1.140** above.

[400] '... the judge must look at the contributions of each to the "family" finances and determine as best he may what contribution each was making towards the purchase of the house. This is not to be carried out as a strictly mathematical exercise; for instance, if the man was ill for a time and out of work so that the woman temporarily contributed more, that temporary state of

(1.1)   the co-owners are living together;[401] and

(1.2)   one of the co-owners ('the unemployed co-owner') is unemployed or incapable of working; and

(1.3)   because of a reduction in his or her income the unemployed co-owner has difficulty in maintaining his or her share of the mortgage payments; and

(1.4)   the co-owners do not execute a further Declaration of Trust to reflect the change in circumstances; and

(1.5)   the provisions of Schedule (*number*) do not apply.[402]

(2)   The unemployed co-owner will do all he or she can to contribute towards the mortgage payments from whatever resources are available to him or her.[403]

(3)   Subject to the above, the other co-owner will be responsible for all the mortgage payments from the date on which the unemployed co-owner ceased to be employed or his or her incapacity to work began ('the commencement date').[404]

(4)   The mortgage payments made by the other co-owner on behalf of the unemployed co-owner:

(4.1)   during the period of (6) months[405] starting on the commencement date will not affect the beneficial interests of either co-owner in the property;

(4.2)   after the end of the period of (6) months starting on the commencement date will be treated as a loan from the other co-owner to the unemployed co-owner.[406]

(5)   The loan is made on the basis that:

(5.1)   it must be repaid as soon as possible; and

(5.2)   if it has not been repaid before the property is sold it, or so much of it as remains outstanding, will be repaid to the other co-owner out of the unemployed co-owner's share of the net proceeds of sale.

---

affairs should not increase her share, nor should her share be decreased if she was temporarily unable to work whilst having a baby. The contributions must be viewed broadly by the judge to guide him to the parties' unexpressed, and probably unconsidered, intentions as to the beneficial ownership of the house' (*Bernard v Josephs* (1983) 4 FLR 178 at 188, per Griffiths LJ).

[401] If the parties were not living together the temporary support obligation contained in para 4.1 of this Schedule might be considered inappropriate.

[402] For example, **1.174** and **1.175** below.

[403] For example, savings or any redundancy payment.

[404] Alternatively, the commencement date could be the date on which the unemployed co-owner is no longer able to keep up his or her agreed share of the mortgage payments.

[405] The timespan which the co-owners consider appropriate in the circumstances shold be inserted here. Note that in the passage from *Bernard v Josephs* (above), Griffiths LJ merely envisaged a 'temporary state of affairs' which should not affect the beneficial interests.

[406] If the co-owners wish to penalise 'fault', a further paragraph should be added to the effect that: 'Despite the provisions of paragraph 4 of this Schedule all mortgage payments made by the other co-owner on behalf of the unemployed co-owner will be treated as a loan (a) from the commencement date itself if the unemployed co-owner lost employment through misconduct or voluntarily left employment without good cause; or (b) from the date on which the unemployed co-owner, without good cause, refused or failed to take a reasonable opportunity to secure employment'.

1.174 *If a co-owner is unemployed or incapable of working because she is pregnant or he or she is looking after a child or children*[407]

SCHEDULE (*number*)

(1)   This Schedule applies if:

    (1.1)   the co-owners are living together;[408] and

    (1.2)   (*name 2*) is unemployed or incapable of working because she is pregnant; and

    (1.3)   either of the co-owners is unemployed or incapable of working because he or she is looking after his, her or their child or children; and

    (1.4)   that co-owner who is unemployed or incapable of working has difficulty in maintaining his or her share of the mortgage payments because of a reduction in his or her income; and

    (1.5)   the co-owners fail to execute a further Declaration of Trust to reflect the change in circumstances.

(2)   The co-owner who is unemployed or incapable of working will do all he or she can to contribute towards the mortgage payments from whatever resources are available.[409]

(3)   Subject to the above, the other co-owner will be responsible for all the mortgage payments, and the mortgage payments that he or she makes will not affect the beneficial interests of either co-owner in the property.

If a co-owner attends a full-time course of education

1.175 *Mortgage payments made by the other co-owner to be treated as a loan*[410]

SCHEDULE (*number*)

(1)   This Schedule applies if:

---

[407] Note the dicta of Griffiths LJ in *Bernard v Josephs* (1983) 4 FLR 178 at 188 (see footnote 381 to Precedent **1.173** above). In his view the woman's share should not be decreased 'if she was temporarily unable to work whilst having a baby' (ibid, at 188B). The word 'temporarily' is significant. The implication is that if the state of affairs is anything other than 'temporary', the beneficial interests should be affected.

[408] The support obligation might be considered inappropriate if the co-owners are not living together.

[409] For example, enhanced maternity pay from an employer, statutory maternity pay or savings.

[410] This precedent is intended to cover 'a temporary state of affairs' which should not materially affect the beneficial interests of either co-owner (*Bernard v Josephs* (1983) 4 FLR 178 at 188). It assumes that the course is of comparatively short duration and will last no longer than, say, one academic year. If the course is of a longer duration, perhaps the beneficial interests should be affected: in which case Precedent **1.176** may be preferred, or used in addition to this precedent. This precedent establishes that the payments made on the student's behalf by the other co-owner are to be treated as a loan, and not a gift.

Query: If the student is not living in the property during term-time, should the other co-owner be paying the student an 'occupation rent'? (*Dennis v McDonald* (1982) 3 FLR 398).

(1.1)   one of the co-owners ('the student') attends a full-time course of education ('the course'); and

(1.2)   the course does not last for more than (one year); and

(1.3)   the student has difficulty in maintaining his or her share of the mortgage payments because of a reduction in his or her income; and

(1.4)   the co-owners do not execute a further Declaration of Trust to reflect the change in circumstances.

(2)   The student will do all that he or she can to contribute towards the mortgage payments from whatever resources are available.[411]

(3)   Subject to the above, the other co-owner will be responsible for the mortgage payments from the date on which the student begins the course.

(4)   The mortgage payments made by the other co-owner on the student's behalf will be treated as a loan to the student from the other co-owner.

(5)   The loan is made on the basis that:

(5.1)   it is interest free; and

(5.2)   the student will repay the loan as soon as he or she can; and

(5.3)   if it has not been repaid before the property is sold, the loan, or so much of it as remains outstanding, will be repaid to the other co-owner out of the student's share of the net proceeds of sale.

1.176   Conversion of fixed shares into floating shares[412]

SCHEDULE (*number*)

(1)   This Schedule applies if:

(1.1)   one of the co-owners ('the student') attends a full-time course of education ('the course'); and

(1.2)   the course lasts or is expected to last for more than (one year); and

(1.3)   while the student is on the course the other co-owner pays a larger share of the mortgage payments than he or she had originally agreed to pay (in Clause   of this Declaration of Trust); and

(1.4)   the co-owners do not execute a further Declaration of Trust to reflect the change in circumstances.

(2)   Immediately before the student begins the course:

(2.1)   the property will be valued or treated as having been valued ('the pre-course value'); and

(2.2)   a statement of the amount required to redeem the mortgage will be obtained or treated as having been obtained.

(3)   Immediately before the student begins the course there will be a deemed sale of the property as if:

---

[411] For example from savings, scholarship income, a student loan or a grant.

[412] For the distinction between fixed shares and floating shares, see **1.7** above. For a discussion of the relative advantages and disadvantages of each type of shareholding, see **1.8–1.11** above. This precedent is intended to cover the situation where one of the co-owners embarks on a comparatively lengthy course of further education, ie one which will last for more than, say, one year. In this case the beneficial interets of the co-owners are affected. By contrast **1.175** above is designed to deal with a more temporary state of affairs, where the course lasts for no longer than, say, one year, and the beneficial interests are not materially affected. *See Example.*

(3.1)   it were being sold by the co-owners at the pre-course value; and

(3.2)   each co-owner could then realise his or her fixed share of the net proceeds of sale ('the fixed share') calculated in accordance with the provisions of Clause   of this Declaration of Trust.

(4)   Immediately after this deemed sale of the property there will be a deemed re-acquisition of it by the co-owners as if:

(4.1)   they were acquiring it at the pre-course value; and

(4.2)   each co-owner's fixed share were his or her cash contribution towards the acquisition price.

(5)   Immediately after the deemed re-acquisition of the property the provisions of Clause   of this Declaration of Trust relating to the calculation of the fixed share of each co-owner will cease to have effect and the following provisions will apply instead.

(6)   After the deemed re-acquisition of the property the co-owners will hold the property and its net proceeds of sale in trust for themselves as beneficial tenants in common in shares which are proportionate to the contributions made by each of them towards the deemed re-acquisition of the property and the payments made by each of them after the deemed re-acquisition towards:

(6.1)   mortgage interest;

(6.2)   mortgage capital;

(6.3)   mortgage-linked insurance premiums;

(6.4)   repairs and improvements to the property;

(6.5)   interest and capital on loans taken out for the purpose of carrying out repairs and improvements to the property; and

(6.6)   the incidental costs of selling the property.

(7)   The share of the net proceeds of sale to which each co-owner will be entitled will be calculated in accordance with the provisions of Schedule (*number*).[413]

Example

In July 1988, A and B bought a terraced house. They contributed more or less the same amount towards the purchase price, and agreed to share the mortgage payments equally. They executed a declaration of trust stating that they were beneficial tenants in common in equal shares. In October 1990, A began a three-year course leading to a degree in computer studies. At that time the house was worth £45,000, and the amount required to redeem their mortgage was £30,000. While A was away studying, B remained in the house and made all the mortgage payments herself. Christmas 1991 was not a happy time for them. Each, quite rightly, suspected that the other had found a new partner. So, they decided to go their own separate ways.

In June 1992, the house was sold for £40,000. The amount required to redeem the mortgage was still £30,000. The net proceeds of sale came to £10,000. Who got what?

---

[413] For the formulae for calculating floating shares, see **1.136–1.140** above.

If they followed the 50:50 shareout in their declaration of trust, B and A would have received £5,000 each.

However, the effect of the incorporation of this Schedule into their declaration of trust meant that their fixed shares (50:50) were converted into floating shares when A began his computer studies course.

B paid the mortgage on her own for 20 months, while A paid nothing. The total mortgage payments she made came to £5,500. So, B's 'floating share' was worth a basic £13,000, which represented her cash contribution to the deemed re-acquisition of the property in October 1990 (£7,500) plus the £5,500 which B contributed towards the mortgage payments. A's 'floating share' remained stationary at £7,500, being A's cash contribution to the deemed re-acquisition.

The net proceeds of sale (£10,000) were divided between them in the ratio 13,000:7,500. B was entitled to £6,341, and A was entitled to £3,659. The incidental costs of selling the property came to £1,250. These were paid in the same ratios: B paid £793 and A £457.

If both co-owners wish to keep the property

1.177   One co-owner to have prior rights

SCHEDULE (*number*)

(1)   This schedule applies if:
- (1.1)   the co-owners are about to separate or have recently separated;[414] and
- (1.2)   both of them wish to keep the property; and
- (1.3)   neither of them is willing to relinquish the property to the other; and
- (1.4)   each of them is able to purchase the other's share.

(2)   (*Name 2*) will have the right to remain in the property and to purchase (*name 1's*) share in it (because) (*state reasons, if considered appropriate*).

(3)   This Schedule will not apply if:
- (3.1)   the co-owners have been living apart for a continuous period of at least (2) months; and
- (3.2)   (*name 1*) has been living in the property during the whole of that period.

1.178   Rules for determining who has prior rights

SCHEDULE (*number*)

(1.1)   The co-owners are about to separate or have recently separated; and

(1.2)   both of them wish to keep the property; and

---

[414] The words 'or have recently separated' are intended to cover the possibility of constructive desertion.

(1.3)   neither of them is willing to relinquish the property to the other; and

(1.4)   each of them is able to purchase the other's share.

(2)   The co-owner who has the superior right to remain in the property and to purchase the other's share in it will be determined in accordance with the following order of priority, and the co-owner who is first described in this list will be preferred to the other co-owner;

(2.1)   the co-owner with whom a child under the age of 18 will live after the co-owners have separated;

(2.2)   if the preceding category applies equally to both of the co-owners, the co-owner with whom the greater number of children under 18 will live after the co-owners have separated;

(2.3)   if both of the preceding categories apply equally to both of the co-owners, the co-owner with whom the children whose school is nearest to the property will live after the co-owners have separated;

(2.4)   the co-owner whose only or principal place of business is at the property;

(2.5)   the co-owner whose only or principal place of business or employment is nearer to the property;

(2.6)   the co-owner who is entitled to the larger share of the net proceeds of sale of the property.

(3)   This Schedule will not apply if:

(3.1)   the co-owners have been living apart for a continuous period of at least (2) months; and

(3.2)   the co-owner who does not have the superior right to remain in the property has been living in the property during the whole of that period.

1.179   If a co-owner moves out before the property is sold

SCHEDULE (*number*)

(1)   Applicability

This Schedule applies if:

(1.1)   one of the co-owners ('the non-resident') ceases permanently to reside in the property;[415] and

(1.2)   the other co-owner ('the occupier') continues to reside in the property; and

(1.3)   there is no alternative agreement between the co-owners. [; and

(1.4)   the provisions of Schedule (*number*) do not apply.][416]

(2)   Crystallisation of shares

The co-owners' respective shares of the net proceeds of sale of the property will be quantified and will crystallise on the date on which the

---

[415] For a discussion of the meanings of expressions such as 'ceases permanently to reside', see *Re Coxen* [1948] 2 All ER 492 at 500.

[416] For example the schedule in 1.180 below.

non-resident leaves the property with the intention of never resuming residence in it with the occupier ('the separation date').[417]

(3) The settlement date

In this Schedule 'the settlement date' means the date on which the non-resident:

(3.1) receives his or her share of the net proceeds of sale of the property together with the additions but subject to the deductions mentioned below; or

(3.2) receives such sum as he or she has agreed to accept in full and final settlement in consideration of the transfer of his or her legal estate and beneficial interest in the property; or

(3.3) pays to the occupier such sum as the occupier has agreed to accept in full and final settlement in consideration of the transfer of the occupier's legal estate and beneficial interest in the property to the non-resident or to such other person(s) as the non-resident directs.

(4) Election

If the settlement date is more than (6) months after the separation date the non-resident can elect to have the value of his or her share on the settlement date substituted for its value on the separation date.[418]

(5) Occupier's post-separation contributions

Before the net proceeds of sale are divided, the occupier will be credited with a lump sum payment equal to all the payments that he or she has made during the period between the separation date and the settlement date towards:

(5.1) the mortgage; and

(5.2) repairs and improvements to the property.

(6) Non-resident's post-separation contributions

Before the net proceeds of sale are divided, the non-resident will be credited with a lump sum payment equal to all the payments (if any) that he or she has made during the period between the separation date and the settlement date towards:

(6.1) the mortgage; and

(6.2) repairs and improvements to the property.

(7) Occupation rent

(7.1) Before the net proceeds of sale are divided, the non-resident will be credited with a lump sum payment representing an occupation rent in

---

[417] Note that in *Hall v Hall* (1982) 3 FLR 379, the Court of Appeal held that the equity was to be valued when the parties separated. This decision was not followed by the same court in *Turton v Turton* [1988] 1 FLR 23 at 34A, where Kerr LJ stated that:

'... unless there is some express declaration or agreement to the effect that the parties' respective beneficial shares are to be valued at the time of their separation if and when this should occur, there could never be any sufficient ground for attributing any such intention to them merely by implication from the circumstances. In the result, therefore, the parties' beneficial interests would always have to be regarded in the normal way under a trust for sale, with the effect that they would until such time as the property is sold, and that they will then attach to the proceeds of sale.'

[418] It may be sensible to include a clause to this effect in order to cover fluctuations in value during inflationary and deflationary periods.

respect of the occupier's occupation of the property during the period from the separation date to the settlement date or during such shorter period as the non-resident agrees;

(7.2) the occupation rent will be such proportion of the fair rent as the value of the non-resident's share bears to the value of the whole of the net proceeds of sale on the separation date;

(7.3) the fair rent is the market rent that would be payable for the property between a willing landlord and a willing tenant.[419]

1.180 *If the co-owners separate shortly after they purchase the property*[420]

SCHEDULE (*number*)

(1) This Schedule applies if:

(1.1) the co-owners separate within a period of (12) months from the date (on which they completed the purchase of the property) [OR] (of this Declaration of Trust); and

(1.2) it is possible to procure the release of the non-resident (as defined below) from his or her obligations under the mortgage; and

(1.3) there is no alternative agreement between the co-owners.

(2) In this Schedule:

(2.1) 'the occupier' means the co-owner who continues to occupy the property;

(2.2) 'the non-resident' means the co-owner who has ceased to reside in the property;

(2.3) 'the non-resident's share' means all the legal estate and beneficial interest of the non-resident in the property freed and discharged from his or her obligations under the mortgage;

(2.4) 'the separation date' means the date on which the non-resident left the property with the intention of never resuming residence in it with the occupier, being a date within a period of (12) months from the date (of completion of the purchase of the property) [OR] (of this Declaration of Trust).

(3) Within a period of (3) months beginning on the separation date the occupier can purchase the non-resident's share for the amount that the non-resident paid towards the purchase price of the property (and the incidental costs of purchasing it), disregarding the amounts which the non-resident has paid towards:

(3.1) the mortgage interest;

(3.2) the mortgage capital;

---

[419] For consideration of the proper way in which an 'occupation rent' should be assessed, see *Dennis v McDonald* (1982) 3 FLR 398. Since the introduction of shorthold tenancies a market rent may be more appropriate.

[420] This Schedule is designed to cover the practical problems arising if the co-owners separate within, say, 12 months of completing the purchase of the property. The party remaining in occupation is given an opportunity to buy out the share of the partner who has left the property for the leaver's original cash contribution towards the purchase price, or such lesser sum as the leaver agrees.

    (3.3)   mortgage-linked insurange premiums;

    (3.4)   repairs and improvements to the property; and

    (3.5)   the incidental costs of purchasing the property.[421]

(4)   If at the end of a period of (3) months beginning on the separation date, the occupier has not purchased the non-resident's share for the amount stated above or for such lesser amount as the non-resident has agreed, the non-resident can apply to the court for an order that the property be sold.

(5)   The non-resident can elect that the provisions of this Schedule will not apply, but only if:

    (5.1)   their application would result in an unconscionable gain for the occupier; and

    (5.2)   the circumstances are such that the occupier has effectively ousted the non-resident from the property.[422]

1.181 *If a co-owner wishes to realise his or her share in the property*[423]

SCHEDULE (*number*)

(1)   This Schedule applies if:

    (1.1)   one of the co-owners ('the seller') wishes to realise his or her beneficial interest in the property ('the share'); and

    (1.2)   there is no alternative agreement between the co-owners.

(2)   At his or her own expense the seller will obtain the following information ('the relevant information'):

    (2.1)   a valuation of the open market value of the property prepared by a professionally qualified property valuer who is familiar with the locality of the property;

    (2.2)   an up-to-date statement of the amount required to redeem the mortgage and every other charge to which the property is subject;

    (2.3)   an up-to-date statement of the surrender value of all mortgage-linked insurance policies; and

    (2.4)   all other information which may be relevant to the valuation of the co-owners' respective shares.

(3)   The seller will give to the other co-owner ('the buyer'):

    (3.1)   the relevant information; and

    (3.2)   a written offer to sell the share ('the offer').

---

[421] The incidental costs of the purchase must be included either in the amount for which the occupier is able to purchase the leaver's share, or as one of the payments made by the leaver which can be disregarded. Other disregards might include the price paid towards any fitted carpets and curtains.

[422] This clause is intended to avoid inequity in a case of constructive desertion. Its application is not necessarily limited to a period of inflationary property prices. The leaver might have been paying the lion's share of the mortgage payments; or could have paid a substantial amount towards repairs and improvements to the property.

[423] With some minor adaptations to reflect their respective bargaining positions, this Schedule could be applied *mutatis mutandis* if one co-owner wishes to 'buy out' the other.

(4) The date on which the buyer receives the relevant information and the offer is 'the offer date'.

(5) The offer will state:

    (5.1) the price at which the seller is willing to sell the share to the buyer or the buyer's nominee;

    (5.2) the date on which the seller wishes to complete the transaction, being a date at least (8) weeks after the offer date; and

    (5.3) all the other terms and conditions (if any) on which the seller is willing to sell the share.

(6) At his or her own expense the buyer can obtain any further information which may be relevant to the valuation of the co-owners' respective shares.

(7) Within a period of (4) weeks beginning on the offer date the buyer can either:

    (7.1) accept the offer in writing and comunicate such acceptance to the seller; or

    (7.2) give to the seller a written counter-offer ('the counter-offer').

(8) The counter-offer will state:

    (8.1) all the terms and conditions (including the price and completion date) on which the buyer or the buyer's nominee is willing to buy the share; or

    (8.2) all the terms and conditions (including the price and completion date) on which the buyer is willing to sell the buyer's share in the property to the seller or the seller's nominee.

(9) All negotiations between the co-owners should be concluded within a period of (8) weeks beginning on the offer date.

(10) After the end of a period of (12) weeks beginning on the offer date either co-owner can apply to the court for an order that the property be sold if:

    (10.1) neither co-owner has agreed to buy the other's share; and

    (10.2) the other co-owner refuses to sell the property.[424]

Forms

Declaration of trust by co-owners

Fixed shares

1.182   Short form

THIS DECLARATION OF TRUST is made on (*date*)

BETWEEN 'the co-owners' (1) (*name 1*) of (*address*) ('*name 1*') and (2) (*name 2*) also of (*address*) ('*name 2*').

IT IS AGREED AND DECLARED that:

(1) The co-owners:

---

[424] The application would be made under TLATA 1996, s 14. See **1.32** above.

(1.1)   are the proprietors of (*address*) title to which is registered at the Land Registry under title number (*number*) ('the property');

(1.2)   purchased the property on (*completion date*);

(1.3)   purchased the property for £ (*purchase price*);

(1.4)   paid incidental purchase costs of £ (*costs*);

(1.5)   obtained in advance of £   from and mortgaged the property to (*lender*) ('the mortgage');

(1.6)   are beneficial tenants in common.

(2)   (*Name 1*):

(2.1)   paid £   towards the purchase price;

(2.2)   paid £   towards the incidental purchase costs;

(2.3)   will pay   per cent of the mortgage payments;

(2.4)   will receive   per cent of the sale price,[425] less:

(a)   per cent of the amount required to redeem the mortgage;[426] and

(b)   per cent of the incidental costs of selling the property.

(3)   (*Name 2*):

(3.1)   paid £   towards the purchase price;

(3.2)   paid £   towards the incidental purchase costs;

(3.3)   will pay   per cent of the mortgage payments;

(3.4)   will receive   per cent of the sale price,[427] less:

(a)   per cent of the amount required to redeem the mortgage;[428] and

(b)   per cent of the incidental costs of selling the property.

SIGNED as a Deed by (*name 1*) in the presence of:

SIGNED as a Deed by (*name 2*) in the presence of:

1.183   LONG FORM

THIS DECLARATION OF TRUST is made on (*date*)

BETWEEN 'the co-owners' (1) (*name 1*) of (*address*) ('*name 1*') and (2) (*name 2*) also of (*address*) ('*name 2*').

IT IS AGREED AND DECLARED that:

(1)   Recitals

(1.1)   The co-owners are the proprietors of (*address*) title to which is registered at the Land Registry under title number (*number*) ('the property').

(1.2)   The co-owners purchased the property on (*completion date*).

---

[425] Presumably (2.1 + 2.2 + (2.3 x 1.5))/(1.4 + 1.4) expressed as a percentage.

[426] Presumably the same percentage as in (2.3).

[427] Presumably (3.1 + 3.2 + (3.3 x 1.5))/(1.3 + 1.4) expressed as a percentage.

[428] Presumably the same percentage as in (3.3).

(1.3) The co-owners purchased the property for £   ('the purchase price').

(1.4) The incidental costs of the purchase totalled £   ('the purchase costs').

(1.5) (*Name 1*) paid £   towards the purchase price and the purchase costs.

(1.6) (*Name 2*) paid £   towards the purchase price and the purchase costs.

(1.7) The co-owners obtained in advance of £   from and have mortgaged the property to (*lender*) ('the mortgage').

(1.8) (*Name 1*) will pay   per cent of the mortgage payments.

(1.9) (*Name 2*) will pay   per cent of the mortgage payments.

(1.10) The co-owners will pay the incidental costs of selling the property in equal shares ('the sale costs').

(1.11) The co-owners will pay the costs incurred in connection with the preparation and execution of this Declaration in equal shares.

(1.12) In the absence of any agreement to the contrary, if one of the co-owners transfers all his or her legal estate and equitable interest in the property to the other co-owner, the legal costs incurred by the transferor will be paid by the transferor and the legal costs incurred by the transferee will be paid by the transferee.

(2) Trusts

The co-owners:

(2.1) hold the property on a trust of land;

(2.2) hold the property and its net proceeds of sale and its net income until sale in trust for themselves as beneficial tenants in common.

(3) Shares

When the property is sold:

(3.1) (*Name 1*) will receive   per cent of the sale price, less:

    (a) per cent of the amount required to redeem the mortgage; and

    (b) 50 per cent of the sale costs;

(3.2) (*Name 2*) will receive   per cent of the sale price less:

    (a) per cent of the amount required to redeem the mortgage; and

    (b) 50 per cent of the sale costs.

(3.3) If the deductions from one co-owner's share exceed the value of the percentage of the sale price to which he or she is entitled the excess will be paid out of the other co-owner's share.

(4) Contingencies

(4.1) If one co-owner fails to pay his or her share of the mortgage payments when it is due, the provisions of Schedule 1 will apply.

(4.2) If one or both of the co-owners pay(s) for extensions, alterations, repairs or improvements to the property, the provisions of Schedule 2 will apply.

(4.3) If one co-owner is unemployed or incapable of working, the provisions of Schedule 3 will apply.

(4.4)   If anyone else normally resides with the co-owners, the provisions of Schedule 4 will apply.

(5)   The nature of this declaration
This Declaration of Trust:
(5.1)   is a deed and is executed as a deed by the co-owners;
(5.2)   can be varied by a subsequent Declaration of Trust executed by both of the co-owners or those who are able to vary the trusts contained in it;
(5.3)   can be set aside or varied by the court.

SCHEDULE 1

(If a co-owner fails to pay his or her share of the mortgage payments when it is due.[429])

SCHEDULE 2

(If the co-owners pay for extensions, alterations, repairs or improvements to the property.[430])

SCHEDULE 3

(If a co-owner is unemployed or incapable of working.[431])

SCHEDULE 4

(If anyone else normally resides in the property with the co-owners.[432])

SIGNED as a Deed by (*name 1*) in the presence of:

SIGNED as a Deed by (*name 2*) in the presence of:

1.184   ONE CO-OWNER ALONE TO BE RESPONSIBLE FOR THE MORTGAGE PAYMENTS

THIS DECLARATION OF TRUST is made on (*date*)

BETWEEN 'the co-owners' (1) (*name 1*) of (*address*) ('*name 1*') and (2) (*name 2*) also of (*address*) ('*name 2*').

IT IS AGREED AND DECLARED that:
(1)   Recitals
(1.1)   The co-owners are the proprietors of (*address*) ('the property').
(1.2)   Title to the property is registered under title number (*number*).
(1.3)   The property is mortgaged to (*lender*) ('the mortgage').

---

[429] See **1.168** above.
[430] See **1.172** above.
[431] See **1.173** above.
[432] See **1.167** above.

(1.4)   The co-owners purchased the property on (*date*).

(1.5)   The purchase price was £   .

(1.6)   The incidental costs of the purchase came to £   .

(1.7)   (*Name 1*) contributed £   towards the purchase price and purchase costs.

(1.8)   (*Name 2*) contributed £   towards the purchase price and purchase costs.

(1.9)   The mortgage advance was £   .

(1.10)   Although the mortgage is in the co-owners' joint names (*name 1*) will be primarily responsible for the mortgage payments.

(2)   Trusts

The co-owners declare that they:

(2.1)   hold the property on a trust of land;

(2.2)   hold the property and its net proceeds of sale and its net income until sale in trust for themselves as beneficial tenants in common.

(3)   Shares

When the property is sold:

(3.1)   (*name 1*) will receive   per cent of the sale price, less:

    (a)   100 per cent of the amount required to redeem the mortgage; and

    (b)   50 per cent of the incidental costs of selling the property;

(3.2)   (*name 2*) will receive   per cent of the sale price, less:

    (a)   0 per cent of the amount required to redeem the mortgage; and

    (b)   50 per cent of the incidental costs of selling the property;

(3.3)   if the amounts to be deducted from (*name 1's*) share of the sale price exceed the value of that share, then the excess will be paid from (*name 2's*) share.

(4)   Definitions

(4.1)   'The sale price' means:

    (a)   the price for which the property is sold; and

    (b)   the price paid by the buyer of the property for any chattels jointly owned by the co-owners, whether or not a separate price is paid for those chattels.

(4.2)   'The amount required to redeem the mortgage' means the sum of money required by the lender to enable the co-owners to repay the mortgage and be completely released and discharged from all obligations under it.

(4.3)   'The incidental costs of selling the property' means the total sum of money (including VAT) to be paid in respect of:

    (a)   estate agents' commission;

    (b)   legal costs and disbursements;

    (c)   apportionments of rates, taxes, insurance, and other outgoings on the property.

SIGNED as a Deed by (*name 1*) in the presence of:

SIGNED as a Deed by (*name 2*) in the presence of:

Floating shares

1.185   Tabular form

THIS DECLARATION OF TRUST is made on (*date*)

BETWEEN 'the co-owners' (1) (*name 1*) of (*address*) ('*name 1*') and (2) (*name 2*) also of (*address*) ('*name 2*').

IT IS AGREED AND DECLARED that:

(1)   Recitals
  (1.1)   The co-owners are the proprietors of (*address*) ('the property').
  (1.2)   Title to the property is registered at the Land Registry under title number (*number*).
  (1.3)   The co-owners purchased the property on (*completion date*).
  (1.4)   The purchase price was £   ('the purchase price').
  (1.5)   The purchase costs came to £   ('the purchase costs').
  (1.6)   (*Name 1*) paid £   towards the purchase price and the purchase costs.
  (1.7)   (*Name 2*) paid £   towards the purchase price and the purchase costs.
  (1.8)   The co-owners obtained an advance of £   from and have mortgaged the property to (*lender*).
  (1.9)   The co-owners intend to contribute towards the mortgage payments in the proportions that their respective incomes bear to each other, or in such other proportions as they may from time to time agree.

(2)   Trusts
The co-owners:
  (2.1)   hold the property on a trust of land;
  (2.2)   hold the property and its net proceeds of sale and its net income until sale in trust for themselves as beneficial tenants in common.

(3)   Shares
When the property is sold the net proceeds of sale will be divided between the co-owners in proportion to the extent to which the change in value of the property can be attributed to the contributions made by each of them towards the:
  (3.1)   purchase price;
  (3.2)   purchase costs;
  (3.3)   mortgage payments;
  (3.4)   cost of repairs and improvements to the property; and
  (3.5)   the incidental costs of selling the property will be borne pro rata.

(4)   Calculation of shares
The share of the net proceeds of sale to which each co-owner is entitled will be calculated by:
  (4.1)   completing the record of contributions set out in the First Schedule; and then

(4.2) applying the formulae set out in the Second Schedule.

FIRST SCHEDULE (Record of contributions).[433]

SECOND SCHEDULE (The formulae).[434]

SIGNED as a Deed by (*name 1*) in the presence of:

SIGNED as a Deed by (*name 2*) in the presence of:

1.186   LONG FORM

THIS DECLARATION OF TRUST is made on (*date*)

BETWEEN 'the co-owners' (1) (*name 1*) of (*address*) ('*name 1*') and (2) (*name 2*) also of (*address*) ('*name 2*').

IT IS AGREED AND DECLARED as follows:

(1)   **Recitals**
  (1.1)   The co-owners are the proprietors of (*address*) title to which is registered at the Land Registry under title number (*number*) ('the property').
  (1.2)   The co-owners purchased the property on (*completion date*).
  (1.3)   The co-owners purchased the property for £   ('the purchase price').
  (1.4)   The incidental costs of the purchase totalled £   ('the purchase costs').
  (1.5)   (*Name 1*) paid £   towards the purchase price and the purchase costs.
  (1.6)   (*Name 2*) paid £   towards the purchase price and the purchase costs.
  (1.7)   The co-owners obtained an advance of £   from and have mortgaged the property to (*lender*) ('the mortgage').
  (1.8)   The co-owners intend to contribute to the mortgage payments (whether they are repayments of capital or payments of interest or insurance premiums) in the proportions that their incomes bear to each other or in such other proportions as they may from time to time agree.
  (1.9)   Each of the co-owners has received independent legal advice on the provisions and implications of this Declaration.
  (1.10)   The legal costs incurred in connection with the preparation and execution of this Declaration (including the costs of obtaining independent legal advice) will be paid by the co-owners in equal shares.

---

[433] See **1.140** above.
[434] See **1.140** above.

(2) Trusts
The co-owners:
(2.1)   hold the property on a trust of land;
(2.2)   hold the property and its net proceeds of sale and its net income until sale in trust for themselves as beneficial tenants in common.

(3) Shares
When the property is sold its net proceeds of sale will be divided between the co-owners in proportion to the contributions made by each of them towards the:
(3.1)   purchase price;
(3.2)   purchase costs;
(3.3)   mortgage payments;
(3.4)   cost of repairs and improvements to the property; and
(3.5)   other payments (if any) analogous to those above.

(4) Calculation of shares
The share of the net proceeds of sale to which each co-owner is entitled will be calculated by:
(4.1)   adding together his or her contributions to produce 'the individual contribution'; and then
(4.2)   adding together both of the co-owners' individual contributions to produce 'the combined contributions'; and then
(4.3)   dividing the net proceeds of sale plus the incidental costs of selling the property by the combined contributions to produce 'the dividend'; and finally
(4.4)   multiplying the individual contribution by the dividend to produce the share.

(5) Sale and transfer costs
(5.1)   When the property is sold the incidental costs of selling it will be paid by the co-owners in the proportions that their respective shares bear to each other.
(5.2)   In the absence of any agreement to the contrary, if one of the co-owners transfers all his or her legal estate and equitable interest in the property to the other co-owner or to a third party at the direction of the other co-owner, the valuation fees, legal fees and other costs incurred by the transferor will be paid by the transferor, and the valuation fees, legal fees and other costs incurred by the transferee will be paid by the transferee.

(6) Contingencies
(6.1)   If one of the co-owners dies and the other does not become solely and beneficially entitled to the property, the provisions of Schedule 1 will apply.
(6.2)   If one of the co-owners wishes to sell the property and the other refuses to sell it, the provisions of Schedule 2 will apply.
(6.3)   If the co-owners decide to separate and both of them wish to keep the property, the provisions of Schedule 3 will apply.
(6.4)   If one of the co-owners moves out of the property before it is sold, the provisions of Schedule 4 will apply.

(7) This declaration
This Declaration of Trust:
(7.1) contains the whole agreement between the co-owners and supersedes any earlier agreements, representations or promises made by either co-owner in respect of the property;
(7.2) can be varied by a subsequent Declaration of Trust executed by all the persons who are able to vary the original trusts;
(7.3) has been executed in duplicate so that each of the co-owners may possess a copy of it, and both copies will be regarded as one deed, and each copy will be as efficacious as the other.

SCHEDULE 1.[435]

SCHEDULE 2.[436]

SCHEDULE 3.[437]

SCHEDULE 4.[438]

SIGNED as a Deed by (*name 1*) in the presence of:

SIGNED as a Deed by (*name 2*) in the presence of:

The person who 'moves in'

1.187   *Deed of surrender of any potential right to claim a beneficial interest in the property*

THIS DEED made on (*date*)

BETWEEN (1) (*name 1*) of (*address*) ('*name 1*') and (2) (*name 2*) also of (*address*) ('*name 2*') WITNESS that:
(1) Recitals
(1.1) (*Name 1*) is the registered proprietor of (*address*) ('the property').
(1.2) (*Name 2*) has lived in the property with (*name 1*) since (*date*).
(2) Surrender
In consideration of (*name 1*) continuing to provide (him)/(her) with accommodation (*name 2*) releases, renounces and surrenders to (*name 1*) all if any rights that (he)/(she) may have at any time to claim a beneficial interest in the property, regardless of any contributions (he)/(she) may make towards:
(2.1) (his)/(her) living and accommodation expenses; and
(2.2) the payment of any mortgage on the property; and

---

[435] See **1.170** above.
[436] See **1.169** above.
[437] See **1.177** above.
[438] See **1.178** above.

(2.3)   any repairs and improvements to the property.

(3)   Reservation of right
Nothing in this Deed deprives (*name 1*) of the right at any time during (his)/(her) life or by Will to transfer all or any part of (his)/(her) legal estate and beneficial interest in the property to (*name 2*).

(4)   Procedural safeguards
(*Name 2*) acknowledges that (he)/(she) understands the nature and effect of this Deed and is entering into it:
(4.1)   freely and voluntarily;
(4.2)   without any form of pressure or coercion from (*name 1*) or anyone else; and
(4.3)   after receiving independent legal advice on its provisions and implications.

SIGNED as a Deed by (*name 1*) in the presence of:

SIGNED as a Deed by (*name 2*) in the presence of:

1.188   Declaration of trust by sole owner acknowledging that the partner has acquired a beneficial interest

THIS DECLARATION OF TRUST is made on (*date*)

BETWEEN 'the parties' (1) (*name 1*) of (*address*) ('*name 1*') and (2) (*name 2*) also of (*address*) ('*name 2*).

IT IS AGREED AND DECLARED that:
(1)   Recitals
(1.1)   (*Name 1*) is the sole proprietor of (*address*) ('the property').
(1.2)   Title to the property is registered at the Land Registry under title number (*number*).
(1.3)   The property is mortgaged to (*lender*) ('the mortgage').
(1.4)   (*Name 2*) moved into the property on (*date*) and has lived there with (*name 1*) ever since.
(1.5)   (*Name 2*) has been contributing towards the mortgage payments (and has paid for repairs and improvements to the property).
(1.6)   The parties intend to continue living together for an indefinite length of time.

(2)   Acknowledgment, declaration and covenants
(*Name 1*):
(2.1)   acknowledges that (*name 2*) has acquired a beneficial interest in the property by virtue of (*name 2's*) contributions towards the mortgage payments (and repairs and improvements);
(2.2)   declares that (*name 1*) holds the property and its net proceeds of sale and its net income until sale in trust for (*name 2*) and (*name 2*) as beneficial tenants in common;

(2.3) will apply to the Land Registry for a restriction to be entered in the register in order to protect (*name 2's*) beneficial interest in the property; and

(2.4) will do all that (*name 1*) can to transfer the property and the mortgage into the parties' joint names, if (*name 2*) wishes.

(3) Valuation of prior share

When (*name 2*) moved into the property:

(3.1) its open market value was £ ;

(3.2) the amount required to redeem the mortgage was £ ; and

(3.3) the equity to which (*name 1*) was then entitled was £ ('the prior share').

(4) Calculation of shares

When the property is sold:

(4.1) (*name 1*) will receive (*fraction or percentage*) of the sale price representing the return on the prior share;

(4.2) the remainder of the net proceeds of sale will be divided between the parties in equal shares;

(4.3) if the incidental costs of selling the property and the amount required to redeem the mortgage exceed the remainder of the net proceeds of sale, the excess will be paid from (*name 1's*) share of the sale price representing the return on the prior share.

(5) Contingency

Unless the parties agree otherwise, if they separate or are about to separate:

(5.1) (*name 1*) will have the right to remain in the property and to purchase (*name 2's*) share in it;

(5.2) (*name 1*) will complete the purchase of (*name 2's*) share within a period of (8) weeks beginning on the date on which (*name 2*) moves out of the property;

(5.3) if at the end of that period of (8) weeks (*name 1*) has not completed the purchase of (*name 2's*) share, (*name 2*) can apply to the court for an order that the property be sold;

(5.4) (*name 1*) will pay the valuation fees, legal fees and other costs which (*name 1*) incurs; and

(5.5) (*name 2*) will pay the valuation fees, legal fees and other costs wich (*name 2*) incurs.

SIGNED as a Deed by (*name 1*) in the presence of:

SIGNED as a Deed by (*name 2*) in the presence of:

Declaration of trust by sole owner

1.189   Another person has contributed to the purchase price[439]

THIS DECLARATION OF TRUST is made on (*date*)

BETWEEN (1) (*name 1*) of (*address*) ('*name 1*') and (2) (*name 2*) of (*address*) ('*name 2*').

IT IS AGREED AND DECLARED that:

(1) (**Name 1**):

    (1.1)   is the proprietor of (*address*) title to which is registered at the Land Registry under title number (*number*) ('the property');

    (1.2)   purchased the property on (*completion date*);

    (1.3)   purchased the property for £   ('purchase price');

    (1.4)   paid £   towards the purchase price;

    (1.5)   paid £   towards the incidental purchase costs which amounted in total to £   ('the purchase costs');

    (1.6)   obtained an advance of £   from and mortgaged the property to (*lender*) ('the mortgage').

(2) (**Name 2**):[440]

    (2.1)   paid £   towards the purchase price (and the purchase costs);

    (2.2)   made that payment with the intention of acquiring a beneficial interest in the property;[441]

    (2.3)   is not a registered proprietor of the property.

(3) (**Name 1**):

    (3.1)   acknowledges that the payment made by (*name 2*) towards the purchase price (and the purchase costs) was neither a gift nor a loan to (*name 1*);[442]

    (3.2)   declares that (*name 1*) holds the property and its net proceeds of sale in trust for (*name 1*) and (*name 2*) as beneficial tenants in common;

    (3.3)   will apply to the Land Registry for the entry of the appropriate restriction in order to protect the beneficial interest of (*name 2*).[443]

---

[439] 'A resulting trust arises where a person acquires a legal estate but has not provided the consideration or the whole of the consideration for its acquisition, unless a contrary intention is proved' (*Cowcher v Cowcher* [1972] 1 All ER 943 at 949e, per Bagnall J).

[440] If necessary, the parties' relationship could be stated at this point. For example: '(*name 2*): is the (mother)/(father) of (*name 1*)'.

[441] *Sekhon v Alissa* [1989] 2 FLR 94.

[442] 'The next question is whether the mother's contribution was to be an unsecured loan or to give her a beneficial interest. In my judgment the law presumes a resulting trust in her favour and that presumption has to be rebutted by evidence that she intended a personal loan without acquiring any interest in the property' (*Sekhon v Alissa* [1989] 2 FLR 94 at 99D, per Hoffmann J).

[443] An interest behind a trust of land is an excluded interest. It should be protected by a restriction on the register (LRA 2002, ss 40–47; LRA2002 s 33(a)(i)).

(4)   When the property is sold:
>   (4.1)   (*name 1*) will receive   per cent of the sale price from which
>   will be deducted:
>>   (a)   the amount required to redeem the mortgage; and
>>   (b)   the incidental costs of selling the property;
>   (4.2)   (*name 2*) will receive   per cent of the sale price.[444]

SIGNED as a Deed by (*name 1*) in the presence of:

SIGNED as a Deed by (*name 2*) in the presence of:

*1.190   Elderly person buys his or her council house with financial assistance
from his or her children*[445]

THIS DECLARATION OF TRUST is made on (*date*)

BETWEEN (1) (*name 1*) of (*address*) ('*name 1*') and (2) (*name 2*) of (*address*)
('*name 2*').

IT IS AGREED AND DECLARED that:

(1)   Recitals
>   (1.1)   (*Name 1*) is the sole proprietor of (*address*) title to which is
>   registered at the Land Registry under title number (*number*) ('the
>   property').
>   (1.2)   The property formerly belonged to (*Borough/City/County/District*)
>   Council ('the Council').
>   (1.3)   (*Name 1*) purchased the property from the Council on (*date*)
>   ('completion date').
>   (1.4)   On completion date the value of the property was £   .

---

[444] Presumably (*name 2's* contribution)/(purchase price + purchase costs) expressed as a
percentage.

[445] The purchase of a council house by a tenant with financial assistance from his or her children
is, potentially, fraught with difficulties and raises important policy issues. The former tenant
and his or her children should receive independent legal advice. Among the questions to be
asked are as follows.
(a) Who is to have the benefit of the discount?
(b) Who will be liable for the repayment of the discount if there is a disposal of the property
within the relevant period?
(c) To what extent should the children be allowed to benefit at the expense of their parent and,
indirectly, the ratepayer and taxpayer?
(d) How can the children be protected from losing out on the transaction?
(e) What is the underlying purpose of the children's involvement?
(f) What are the parties' intentions regarding the former tenant's continued occupation of the
property?
(g) Does the former tenant have other children who might reasonably be expected to benefit
from his or her estate?
(h) To what extent is securing entitlement to or increasing the amount of any income-related
benefits a 'significant operative purpose' behind any value-shifting exercise? See, generally, the
Income Support (General) Regulations 1987 (SI 1987/1967), reg 51, and the Commissioner's
decision in *R (SB) 40/85*.

(1.5) The value of the property was discounted by £   ('the discount') because (*name 1*) had occupied the property as a Council tenant for (*number*) of years.

(1.6) In the transfer to (*name 1*) it was stated that (*name 1*) had paid the Council £   for the property ('the purchase price').

(1.7) The incidental costs of purchasing the property came to £   ('the purchase costs').

(1.8) (*Name 1*) paid £   towards the purchase price and the purchase costs.

(1.9) (*Name 2*), who is (*name 1's*) (son)/(daughter), paid £   towards the purchase price and the purchase costs.

(1.10) (*Name 2*) contributed to the purchase partly as an investment and partly to enable (*name 1*) to live in (*name 1's*) own home.

(1.11) (*Name 2*) intends that (*name 1*) should continue to live in the property for as long as (*name 1*) wishes, rent-free.

(1.12) (*Name 2*) acknowledges that the discount should primarily enure for the benefit of (*name 1*).

(1.13) (*Name 1*) acknowledges that (*name 1*) would have been unable to purchase the property without financial assistance from (*name 2*).

(2) Trusts

(*Name 1*) declares that (*name 1*) holds the net proceeds of sale of the property in trust for (*name 1*) and (*name 2*) as beneficial tenants in common.

(3) Shares

When the property is sold:

(3.1) (*name 1*) will receive   per cent of the sale price, representing the return on the discount and (*name 1's*) contribution towards the purchase price and the purchase costs, *less* (50) per cent of the incidental costs of selling the property ('*name 1's* share');

(3.2) (*name 2*) will receive   per cent of the sale price, representing the return on (*name 2's*) contribution towards the purchase price and the purchase costs, *less* (50) per cent of the incidental costs of selling the property ('*name 2's* share');

(3.3) if all or any part of the discount has to be repaid to the Council, it will be paid from (*name 1's*) share;

(3.4) if (*name 2's*) share is less than (*name 2's*) original contribution towards the purchase price and the purchase costs, the shortfall will be paid from (*name 1's*) share.

(4) Gradual diminution of (name 1's) share

(4.1) In consideration of the fact that (*name 1*) would have been unable to purchase the property without financial assistance from (*name 2*), and in consideration of the assurance from (*name 2*) that (*name 1*) can continue to live in the property rent-free for as long as (*name 1*) wishes, (*name 1*) agrees that the value of (*name 1's*) share will gradually decrease and that the value of (*name 2's*) share will proportionately increase, and to that intent the following provisions will apply.

(4.2)   When the property is sold or when either party realises their share in it ('the disposal') (*name 1's*) share will be reduced by (10) per cent for each complete year that has elapsed between the (1st) anniversary of completion date and the disposal.

(4.3)   The amount by which (*name 1's*) share is reduced will be added to (*name 2's*) share.

(4.4)   For the avoidance of doubt:

(a)   there will be no reduction of (*name 1's*) share before the (1st) anniversary of completion date because of the provisions relating to the repayment of the discount to the Council; and

(b)   there will be no reduction of (*name 1's*) share in respect of any period of less than a complete year.

(5)   Terms of continued occupation

(*Name 2*) agrees that (*name 1*) can continue to live in the property rent-free for as long as (*name 1*) wishes on the terms that (*name 1*):

(5.1)   pays all the outgoings on the property;

(5.2)   keeps it in reasonable repair and condition;

(5.3)   keeps it insured to its full reinstatement value; and

(5.4)   complies with all the covenants and conditions to which it is subject.

SIGNED as a Deed by (*name 1*) in the presence of:

SIGNED as a Deed by (*name 2*) in the presence of:

1.191   Variation of a Declaration of Trust[446]

THIS VARIATION is made on (*date*)

BETWEEN 'the co-owners'[447] (1) (*name 1*) of (*address*) ('*name 1*') and (2) (*name 2*) (also) of (*address*) ('*name 2*').

IT IS AGREED AND DECLARED that:

(1)   Recitals

(1.1)   This deed is supplemental[448] to the Declaration of Trust ('the Declaration') made between the co-owners on (*date*).

(1.2)   The co-owners wish to vary the Declaration as follows.

---

[446]   'If all the beneficiaries are *sui iuris* they can join together with the trustees and declare different trusts which supersede those contained in the original declaration. These new trusts operate *proprio vigore* by virtue of a self-contained instrument, namely the deed of arrangement or variation. The original declaration will have lost any force or relevance' (*Re Holmden's Settlement Trusts* [1968] AC 685 at 713C, per Lord Wilberforce).

[447]   This precedent assumes that the original co-owners are the parties able to vary the trusts. If the variation is being made by, say, the personal representatives of one of the co-owners, the wording should be adapted accordingly.

[448]   LPA 1925, s 58: 'any instrument ... expressed to be supplemental to a previous instrument, shall, as far as may be, be read and have effect as if the supplemental instrument contained a full recital of the previous instrument'. It would be sensible to endorse a memorandum of the variation on the original declaration of trust.

(2) Revocation

The co-owners revoke Clause(s) (*number(s)*) [AND/OR] Schedule(s) (*number(s)*) of the Declaration.

(3) Shares

From now onwards the co-owners will hold the property (as defined in the Declaration)[449] and its net proceeds of sale in trust for themselves as beneficial tenants in common in the following shares:

(set out the shares)

(4) Confirmation

The co-owners confirm the Declaration in all other respects.

SIGNED as a Deed by (*name 1*) in the presence of:

SIGNED as a Deed by (*name 2*) in the presence of:

1.192   Checklist for ownership of the home

(1) Names and addresses of parties

(2) Address of property

(3) Has the property already been bought, if so:
  (3.1) Whose name(s) is it in?
  (3.2) Obtain copy of Land Registry Official Entries
  (3.3) Is there a mortgage and who pays it?
  (3.4) Is there a life policy to pay off the mortgage. Will it benefit survivor?
  (3.5) Does the title reflect what the parties want?

(4) If property is being bought
  (4.1) In whose name will the purchase be?
  (4.2) Will there be a mortgage and who will pay it?
  (4.3) Is there to be a life policy to pay off the mortgage. Will it benefit survivor?
  (4.4) Is the property to be bought in joint names?
  (4.5) If not how will the other party's share be protected.
  (4.6) If in joint names is it to be bought equally as joint tenants or as tenants in common and in what shares?

(5) Is there a conflict of interest and should parties be separately represented?

(6) Can the arrangement be reflected in the transfer to the parties or will a declaration of trust be required?

(7) Terms of Declaration of Trust
  (7.1) Contributions
  (7.2) Costs
  (7.3) Fixed shares – proportions
  (7.4) Floating shares – recording contributions
  (7.5) Provisions for contingencies
    (7.5.1) Other person residing

---

[449] The words in brackets 'as defined in the Declaration' are not, strictly speaking, necessary.

1.193   HM Land Registry Form TR1

Transfer of whole
of registered title(s)

Land Registry

TR1

If you need more room than is provided for in a panel, use continuation sheet CS and attach to this form.

1.   Stamp Duty

Place "X" in the appropriate box or boxes and complete the appropriate certificate.

☐   It is certified that this instrument falls within category ☐ in the Schedule to the Stamp Duty (Exempt Instruments) Regulations 1987 ·

☐   It is certified that the transaction effected does not form part of a larger transaction or of a series of transactions in respect of which the amount or value or the aggregate amount or value of the consideration exceeds the sum of   **£**

☐   It is certified that this is an instrument on which stamp duty is not chargeable by virtue of the provisions of section 92 of the Finance Act 2001

2.   Title Number(s) of the Property *Leave blank if not yet registered.*

3.   Property

4.   Date

5.   Transferor *Give full names and company's registered number if any.*

6.   Transferee for entry on the register *Give full name(s) and company's registered number, if any. For Scottish companies use an SC prefix and for limited liability partnerships use an OC prefix before the registered number, if any. For foreign companies give territory in which incorporated.*
Unless otherwise arranged with Land Registry headquarters, a certified copy of the Transferee's constitution (in English or Welsh) will be required if it is a body corporate but is not a company registered in England and Wales or Scotland under the Companies Acts.

7.   Transferee's intended address(es) for service (including postcode) for entry on the register *You may give up to three addresses for service **one** of which **must** be a postal address but does not have to be within the UK. The other addresses can be any combination of a postal address, a box number at a UK document exchange or an electronic address.*

8.   The Transferor transfers the Property to the Transferee

9.   Consideration *Place "X" in the appropriate box. State clearly the currency unit if other than sterling. If none of the boxes applies, insert an appropriate memorandum in the additional provisions panel.*

☐   The Transferor has received from the Transferee for the Property the sum of *In words and figures.*

☐   *Insert other receipt as appropriate.*

☐   The transfer is not for money or anything which has a monetary value

---

10. The Transferor transfers with *Place "X" in the appropriate box and add any modifications.*

   ☐ full title guarantee   ☐ limited title guarantee

---

11. Declaration of trust *Where there is more than one Transferee, place "X" in the appropriate box.*

   ☐ The Transferees are to hold the Property on trust for themselves as joint tenants

   ☐ The Transferees are to hold the Property on trust for themselves as tenants in common in equal shares

   ☐ The Transferees are to hold the Property *Complete as necessary.*

---

12. Additional provisions *Insert here any required or permitted statements, certificates or applications and any agreed covenants, declarations, etc.*

---

13. Execution *The Transferor must execute this transfer as a deed using the space below. If there is more than one Transferor, all must execute. Forms of execution are given in Schedule 9 to the Land Registration Rules 2003. If the transfer contains Transferee's covenants or declarations or contains an application by the Transferee (e.g. for a restriction), it must also be executed by the Transferee (all of them, if there is more than one).*

1.194   HM Land Registry Form SEV

Land Registry
Application to enter Form A restriction on
severance of joint tenancy by agreement
or notice

	LAND REGISTRY USE ONLY

Form RX1 should be used for an application following severance in other circumstances.

If you need more room than is provided for in a panel, and your software allows, you can expand any panel in the form. Alternatively use continuation sheet CS and attach it to this form.

Land Registry is unable to give legal advice but our website www1.landregistry.gov.uk provides guidance on Land Registry applications. This includes public guides and practice guides (aimed at conveyancers) that can also be obtained from any Land Registry office. Public Guide 18 deals specifically with joint property ownership.

See www1.landregistry.gov.uk/regional if you are unsure which Land Registry office to send this application to.

'Conveyancer' is a term used in this form. It is defined in rule 217(1) of the Land Registration Rules 2003 and includes, among others, solicitor, licensed conveyancer and fellow of the Institute of Legal Executives.

LAND REGISTRY USE ONLY
Record of fees paid

Particulars of under/over payments

Reference number
Fees debited £

Where there is more than one local authority serving an area, enter the one to which council tax or business rates are normally paid.	1	Local authority serving the property:
You must enter the title number(s) relating to the property otherwise we cannot accept the application.	2	Title number(s) of the property:
Insert address including postcode (if any) or other description of the property, for example 'land adjoining 2 Acacia Avenue'.	3	Property:

Currently no fee is payable for the entry of a Form A restriction.	4	Application and fee

Application	Fee paid (£)
Entry of Form A restriction	

Fee payment method

☐ cheque made payable to 'Land Registry'

☐ direct debit, under an agreement with Land Registry

Provide the full name(s) of the person(s) applying to enter the restriction. Where a conveyancer lodges the application, this must be the name(s) of the client(s), not the conveyancer.	5	The applicant:

	6	This application is sent to Land Registry by
If you are paying by direct debit, this will be the account charged.		Key number (if applicable):
This is the address to which we will normally send requisitions and return documents. However if you insert an email address, we will use this whenever possible.		Name: Address or UK DX box number:

Email address:
Reference:

Phone no:	Fax no:

You must place 'X' in only one box in this panel.

If option (A) is chosen, all joint proprietors or their conveyancers must sign panel 9.

Although you do not need to lodge evidence of severance when all the registered proprietors are applying, the joint tenancy must have been severed before the Form A restriction is entered.

If you supply the original document and a certified copy, we shall assume that you request the return of the original; if a certified copy is not supplied, we may retain the original document and it may be destroyed.

Section 36(2) of the Law of Property Act 1925 allows one joint owner to serve a written notice on the other joint owners, severing their joint tenancy in equity. Section 196 of that Act, as modified by section 1 of the Recorded Delivery Service Act 1962, says how such a notice must be served.

| 7 | Evidence of severance |

(A) Application is by all the registered proprietors

☐ All registered proprietors of the title number referred to in panel 2 are applying (no further evidence required).

(B) Application is not by all the registered proprietors – severance is by document signed by all the registered proprietors

☐ The original or a certified copy of the document is enclosed.

☐ I am the applicant's conveyancer and I certify that I hold the original or a certified copy of the document.

(C) Application is not by all the registered proprietors – notice of severance has been served

☐ The original or certified copy of the notice of severance and a signed acknowledgement of receipt by the other registered proprietors is enclosed.

☐ The original or certified copy of the notice of severance and my certificate is enclosed, confirming that the notice was given to the other registered proprietor(s), left at their last known place of abode or business in the UK or sent by registered post or recorded delivery service to them at their last known place of abode or business and not returned undelivered.

☐ I am the applicant's conveyancer and I certify that I hold the original [or certified copy of] notice of severance with an acknowledgement of receipt signed by the other registered proprietors.

☐ I am the applicant's conveyancer and I certify that I hold the original [or certified copy of] notice of severance, and that it was served on the other registered proprietors in accordance with sections 36(2) and 196 of the Law of Property Act 1925.

| 8 | Application |

The applicant applies for the following restriction to be entered in the register of the above title(s):

No disposition by a sole proprietor of the registered estate (except a trust corporation) under which capital money arises is to be registered unless authorised by an order of the court.

| 9 | |

If a conveyancer is acting for the applicant, that conveyancer must sign. If no conveyancer is acting, the applicant (and if more than one person then each of them) must sign.

Signature of applicant or their conveyancer: ------------------------------------

Date:

WARNING
If you dishonestly enter information or make a statement that you know is, or might be, untrue or misleading, and intend by doing so to make a gain for yourself or another person, or to cause loss or the risk of loss to another person, you may commit the offence of fraud under section 1 of the Fraud Act 2006, the maximum penalty for which is 10 years' imprisonment or an unlimited fine, or both.

Failure to complete this form with proper care may result in a loss of protection under the Land Registration Act 2002 if, as a result, a mistake is made in the register.

Under section 66 of the Land Registration Act 2002 most documents (including this form) kept by the registrar relating to an application to the registrar or referred to in the register are open to public inspection and copying. If you believe a document contains prejudicial information, you may apply for that part of the document to be made exempt using Form EX1, under rule 136 of the Land Registration Rules 2003.

© Crown copyright (ref: LR/HO) 07/08

1.195　HM Land Registry Form RX1

Application to enter a restriction	Land Registry

If you need more room than is provided for in a panel, use continuation sheet CS and attach to this form.

1.　Administrative area and postcode if known

2.　Title number(s)

3.　If you have already made this application by **outline application**, insert reference number:

4.　Property *Insert address or other description.*

The restriction applied for is to affect *Place "X" in the appropriate box and complete as necessary.*

☐　the whole of each registered estate

☐　the part(s) of the registered estate(s) shown on the attached plan by *State reference e.g. "edged red".*

☐　the registered charge(s) dated　　　　　　　　　in favour of
　　　　　　　　　　　　　　　　referred to in the Charges Register

5.　Application and fee *A fee calculator for all types of applications can be found on Land Registry's website at www.landregistry.gov.uk/fees*

Restriction　　　　　　　　　Fee paid £

Fee payment method: *Place "X" in the appropriate box.*
I wish to pay the appropriate fee payable under the current Land Registration Fee Order:

☐　by cheque or postal order, amount £ _____ made payable to "Land Registry".

☐　by Direct Debit under an authorised agreement with Land Registry.

FOR OFFICIAL USE ONLY
Record of fee paid

Particulars of under/over payment

Fees debited £

Reference number

6.　Documents lodged with this application *If this application is accompanied by either Form AP1 or FR1 please only complete the corresponding panel on Form AP1 or DL. Number the documents in sequence; copies should also be numbered and listed as separate documents, alternatively you may prefer to use Form DL. If you supply the original document and a certified copy, we shall assume that you request the return of the original; if a certified copy is not supplied, we may retain the original document and it may be destroyed.*

7.　The applicant is: *Please provide the full name of the person applying for the restriction.*

The application has been lodged by:
Land Registry Key No. (if appropriate)
Name (if different from the applicant)
Address/DX No.

Reference
E-mail

Telephone No.	Fax No.

FOR OFFICIAL USE ONLY
Codes
Dealing

Status

8. Where you would like us to deal with someone else *We shall deal only with the applicant, or the person lodging the application if different, unless you place "X" against one or more of the statements below and give the necessary details.*

   ☐ Send title information document to the person shown below

   ☐ Raise any requisitions or queries with the person shown below

   ☐ Return original documents lodged with this form (see note in panel 6) to the person shown below
     If this applies only to certain documents, please specify.

Name
Address/DX No.

Reference
E-mail

Telephone No.	Fax No.

9. Entitlement to apply for a restriction *Place "X" in the appropriate box.*

   ☐ The applicant is the registered proprietor of the registered estate/charge referred to in panel 4.

   ☐ The applicant is the person **entitled** to be registered as proprietor of the registered estate/charge referred to in panel 4. **Complete panel 12.**

   ☐ The consent of the registered proprietor of the registered estate/charge referred to in panel 4 accompanies this application or the applicant's conveyancer certifies that he holds this consent. **Complete panel 11.**

   ☐ The consent of the person **entitled** to be registered as proprietor of the registered estate/charge referred to in panel 4 accompanies this application or the applicant's conveyancer certifies that he holds this consent. **Complete panels 11 and 12.**

   ☐ Evidence that the applicant has sufficient interest in the making of the entry of the restriction applied for in panel 10 accompanies this application. **Complete panel 13.**

10. The applicant applies to enter the following restriction against the registered estate/charge referred to in panel 4: *Please set out the form of restriction required. Schedule 4 to the Land Registration Rules 2003 contains standard forms of restrictions. Use this form to apply for a standard form of restriction (as set out in Schedule 4 to the Land Registration Rules 2003) or, where appropriate, a restriction in another form. If the restriction is not a standard form of restriction, the registrar must be satisfied that the terms of the proposed restriction are reasonable and that applying the proposed restriction would be straightforward and not place an unreasonable burden on him. If the restriction requires notice to be given to a person, requires a person's consent or certificate or is a standard form restriction that refers to a named person, **include that person's address for service**.*

11. Evidence of consent *Please complete this panel if instructed to do so in panel 9. Place "X" in the appropriate box.*

☐ The [registered proprietor of][person entitled to be registered as the proprietor of] the registered estate/charge referred to in panel 4 consents to the entry of the restriction and that person or their conveyancer has completed panel 15.

☐ I am the applicant's conveyancer and certify that I hold the consent referred to in panel 9.

☐ The consent referred to in panel 9 is contained on page ____ of the document numbered ____ referred to in [panel 6][Form AP1][Form DL].

12. Evidence of entitlement to be registered as proprietor *Please complete this panel if instructed to do so in panel 9. Place "X" in the appropriate box.*

☐ I am the applicant's conveyancer and certify that I am satisfied that the applicant/person consenting to this application is entitled to be registered as proprietor and that I hold the originals of the documents that contain evidence of that person's entitlement, or an application for registration of that person as proprietor is pending at Land Registry.

☐ Evidence that the applicant/person consenting to this application is entitled to be registered as proprietor is contained in the document(s) numbered ____ referred to in [panel 6][Form AP1][Form DL].

13. Evidence that the applicant has sufficient interest *Please complete this panel if instructed to do so in panel 9.*

☐ State brief details of the applicant's interest in the making of the entry of the restriction applied for in panel 10.

☐ Evidence of this interest is contained in the document(s) numbered ____ referred to in [panel 6] [Form AP1][Form DL].

14. Signature of applicant
or their conveyancer _____ Date _____

15. Consent

Consent to the entry of the restriction specified in panel 10 is given by:

Names *BLOCK CAPITALS*	**Signatures**
1.	1.
2.	2.
3.	3.

© Crown copyright (ref: LR/HQ/CD-ROM) 6/03

Section 2   Contentious precedents

1.196   Claim form for a declaration of a beneficial interest in property and an order for sale under the Trusts of Land and Appointment of Trustees Act 1996

Claim Form (CPR Part 8)	In the OAKWOOD COUNTY COURT
	Claim No. OK 12345

Claimant

JANE PLANE
66a Sycamore Road
Oakwood
Elmshire

SEAL

Defendant(s)

RICHARD HORNBEAM
6 Firs Avenue
Oakwood
Elmshire

Details of claim (see also overleaf)

In the matter of the Trusts of Land and Appointment of Trustees Act 1996

In relation to 6 Firs Avenue Oakwood: registered at HM Land Registry under Title No OAK 5432
1. An order for the sale of the property
2. A declaration that the property and the net proceeds of sale thereof belong to the Claimant and Defendant in equal shares or such other shares as the Court may decide
3. Further or other relief
4. Costs

Defendant's name and address   £

RICHARD HORNBEAM 6 Firs Avenue Oakwood Elmshire	Court fee	
	Solicitor's costs	
	Issue date	

The court office at

is open between 10 am and 4 pm Monday to Friday. When corresponding with the court, please address forms or letters to the Court Manager and quote the case number.

N208 Claim form (CPR Part 8) (4.99)   *Printed on behalf of The Court Service*

	Claim No.	

Details of claim (continued)

See witness statement attached.

Statement of Truth
*~~I believe~~ (The Claimant believes) that the facts stated in these
particulars of claim are true.
*~~I am duly authorised by the claimant to sign this statement~~

Full name ____JANE PLANE_____

Name of claimant's solicitor's firm_____

signed _____   position or office held _____
*(Claimant)(~~Litigation friend~~)   (~~if signing on behalf of firm or company~~)
(~~Claimant's solicitor~~)

delete as appropriate

Claimant's or claimant's solicitor's address
to which documents should be sent if
different from overleaf. If you are prepared
to accept service by DX, fax or e-mail,
please add details.

1.197 Claimant's witness statement in support of application for declaration/order for sale

(1) I, [name] of [address] make this statement in support of my application for a declaration that I have a beneficial interest in [the property] and for an order for the sale of the property.

(2) In [date] I began living with the defendant at [address]. This property was in his sole name. We lived there together until [date] when [the property] was purchased. That property was also purchased in the defendant's sole name.

(3) During the time that we lived together at [address] we each put part of our earnings into a savings account in our joint names. The account was held at the High Street branch of [bank]. These savings were intended to be used for any items of joint expenditure such as holidays, replacement of furniture and appliances in the property, decoration and repair and ultimately for use in the purchase of our next house.

(4) I was not in a position to put as much as the defendant into this joint account as my earnings were about half of what he earned. As a general rule I would pay in about a third of what the defendant paid in. However, I also paid for any extras for the house, for example I would often buy food apart from the food we bought together on the shared weekly shop, and I would buy household linen and oddments for the kitchen if I saw anything that I particularly liked. I am aware that the defendant had other savings that he kept apart from the joint savings account.

(5) In [date] we started to look for another house. The defendant said that it would be better for us financially if we bought a better house as that was how people made money. We looked around for quite a long time and eventually decided to buy [the property]. We were able to sell [address] for £ . I understand that about £ was used to redeem the mortgage. We paid £ for [the property] and as far as I am aware £ from the joint account went towards the purchase price. The balance was raised by way of mortgage advance but as I was not directly involved in the financial dealings I do not know how much was borrowed, nor how much of the equity from [address] was applied to the purchase of [the property]. I have had a valuation of [the property] a copy of which is annexed to this statement. The valuation is £ .

(6) I was not involved in the financial side of the purchase of [the property]. The defendant told me that there was no need for me to be involved with the mortgage because he could raise what was needed on the strength of his own earnings. I did not think anything about this at the time, and as I remember going to see the solicitors to sign something I presumed that my name was on the deeds. As far as I was concerned the purchase of [the property] was a joint venture. Nothing that the defendant did or said ever made me think otherwise.

When we bought [the property] he said that it would help secure our financial future and he would encourage me to save in the joint account rather than spend my money on clothes, or a holiday for us, saying that we would reap the benefits.

(7) After we moved in to [the property], we started again to build up the savings in the joint account. The defendant made the mortgage repayments and paid the bills as he had done at [address], but after about six months he said that he would like me to contribute to the bills as the mortgage repayments were more expensive than the old house and he was finding it difficult. I agreed of course, and took over responsibility for payment of the telephone and water bills, and one half of the council tax. These payments amounted to about £ per month. We continued to share the cost of the weekly shop.

(8) In [date] we decided that we would like to have the house decorated throughout and have beech flooring on the ground floor. The cost of this, approximately £ , was paid from the joint account.

(9) In [date] my relationship with the defendant began to deteriorate and by the end of that year we decided to separate. I suggested that he buy out my interest, or alternatively that the house be sold. It was at this stage that the defendant informed me that the house was in his sole name and that because we were not married I had no claim to it. He would not leave the house, and because of his attitude towards me I could not continue to live there and so I left and I am currently in a rented flat.

(10) I would like to realise what I believe to be my interest in [the property] and I ask the court to make a declaration as to my beneficial entitlement by virtue of my direct financial contribution to the purchase price, and my contributions to the household expenditure generally. These contributions were made in the belief that I would have an interest in the property and not be left after six years with nothing. If I had thought that only the defendant was entitled to the house I would not have done as he suggested and save in the joint account for expenditure to improve the house, nor would I have made contributions to the outgoings. I have acted to my detriment in this regard.

(11) I ask the court to declare that I have a beneficial interest in [the property] on the basis of the understanding that I believed the defendant and that the property was a joint venture and that I was to have an interest in it. Although I knew that only the defendant was bound by the mortgage he led me to believe that my name was on the title deeds and this is the reason he gave me for my having to go to the solicitor's office to sign a document. I have acted to my detriment in reliance upon the understanding that I believed that we shared and I ask the court to find that the defendant holds [the property] on a constructive trust for both of us in equal shares, and that if the defendant will not buy out my share that there be a sale of the property and a division of the net proceeds.

Dated this   day of

I believe that the facts stated in this witness statement are true.

. . . .

1.198 Claimant's witness statement in support of application for sale of land under the Trusts of Land and Appointment of Trustees Act 1996

(1) I, [name] of [address] make this statement in support of my application for the sale of [the property].

(2) I lived with [name] at [the property] from [date] until [date] when I left. I had formed a relationship with another woman who I have now married. The defendant still lives at [the property] and I believe that she has her boyfriend living there on a more or less permanent basis.

(3) I had known the defendant for about three years before we started to live together. At first we lived in a rented place but after a short time we decided to buy [the property]. The property was put into our joint names. We were both working in good jobs and as much as anything else regarded the purchase as an investment. We paid equal amounts towards the deposit and the property was put into joint names. We shared the mortgage repayments and other household outgoings. Generally speaking, if repairs needed to be done I would do them as I am good at DIY, but if there was anything major we would contribute to the cost equally. As far as I am concerned [the property] belongs to us jointly.

(4) When I first left, the defendant indicated that she would buy me out. She is now dragging her feet and refusing to communicate with me. I know of no good reason why if she is not prepared to buy out my interest [the property] should not be sold.

(5) Accordingly, I ask for an order for sale, and for me to receive one half of the net proceeds. I also ask the court to order that the defendant pays me an occupation rent for the period since I left until the date of sale.

Dated this   day of

I believe that the facts stated in this witness statement are true.

. . . .

1.199 Order for sale of property under the Trusts of Land and Appointment of Trustees Act 1996

IN THE [ ] COUNTY COURT   CASE NUMBER

BETWEEN:

A	Claimant

and

B	Defendant

ORDER

UPON hearing counsel for the claimant and counsel for the respondent (AND BY CONSENT)

[IT IS DECLARED THAT the defendant holds the property described in the schedule hereto on trust for the claimant and the defendant as tenants in common in equal shares (or as the case may be)]

IT IS ORDERED THAT:

(1) The property described in the schedule hereto shall be sold forthwith by agents to be agreed between the parties and at a price to be agreed between the parties and in the event of disagreement to be determined by the court.

(2) The claimant's/defendant's solicitors shall have the conduct of the sale.

(3) The claimant's costs shall be the subject of a detailed assessment if not agreed and shall be paid by the defendant and charged against his share of the net proceeds of sale of the property.

THE SCHEDULE

The freehold/leasehold property known as [address] and registered at HM Land Registry under Title Number   .

1.200   Applicant's sworn statement in support of injunction to prevent service of Notice to Quit

IN THE [ ] COUNTY COURT   CASE NUMBER

In the Matter of the Family Law Act 1996,
Part IV

BETWEEN:

A	Applicant

and

B	Respondent

SWORN STATEMENT OF APPLICANT

I, [name], of [address] MAKE OATH and say as follows:

(1) I make this statement in support of my application for an order that the respondent be restrained from serving a Notice to Quit of the house in which we live together, [the property].

(2) The respondent is the sole tenant [we are joint tenants] of the property, the landlords being the [landlord]. I moved into the property six years ago with my two children from a previous relationship aged 9 and 11. The respondent and I have two children who are aged 2 and 4.

(3) Our relationship was always a turbulent one, and the respondent would often leave the property and go and stay with friends, sometimes for days on end. The respondent's behaviour became such that a month ago after an incident that caused the respondent to leave the property again I applied for a non-molestation order and an occupation order. The respondent did not attend the hearing and so the judge made a non-molestation order, and an order that the respondent should not return. The order will remain in force for a further five months.

(4) After the order was served on him, the respondent came to the house and tried to persuade me into a reconciliation. I said that I would think about it. However there was a recent incident of violence following which I told the respondent that I did not want him back. He turned nasty and said that if that was the case I should find somewhere else to live because it was his house, and that if he couldn't live there then he didn't see why I should.

(5) The respondent is so unpredictable and vindictive that I am sure he will tell the landlords that he no longer wants the tenancy of the property. It is for this reason also that I ask the court to make an order without giving notice to the respondent. If he has not already thought of doing so, this application will certainly give him the idea and I do not want anything to jeopardise my application for a transfer of the tenancy.

SWORN etc.

1.201 Application for transfer of tenancy under Part IV of the Family Law Act 1996

See Form FL401 at **4.89**.

1.202 Sworn statement in support of application for transfer of tenancy under Part IV of the Family Law Act 1996

I, [name] of [address] MAKE OATH and say as follows:

(1) I am the applicant and I make this statement in support of my application for the transfer of the tenancy of [the property] from the sole name of the respondent into my sole name.

(2) The respondent and I have lived together at the property since [date]. The respondent moved out two months ago after I obtained a non-molestation injunction against him. He now lives at his mother's. I remain at the property with our two children, Jack who is five, and Emma who is three. My eight-year-old daughter from a previous relationship also lives with us.

(3) The property is a three-bedroomed semi-detached house rented from [landlord]. The respondent is the sole tenant as he was already living at the property when I met him. We never bothered to have the tenancy changed into joint names. I gave up my own council flat when I moved in with the respondent.

(4) As the tenancy is in the respondent's sole name, I assumed that he would continue to make the rent payments after he left. However, I discovered that he had not been making the payments when I had a visit from the [landlord's] housing officer. I have been paying what I can aford, which is effectively the weekly rent payments, but the [landlords] say that unless the arrears are cleared they may not allow the transfer of the tenancy to my name.

(5) As far as I am aware, the respondent is under no pressure to move from his mother's and only the two of them live in her two-bedroomed bungalow, but the respondent says he will not give up the tenancy because he says he doesn't see why I should have the benefit of it.

(6) I have a greater need for the house with three young children to care for, and the house has been their home for as long as they can remember. I could not aford to pay a deposit for private rented accommodation, whereas the respondent is in a position to save money for that purpose if he wanted to.

(7) In all the circumstances I ask the court to make an order for the transfer of the tenancy into my name, and for the respondent to pay the accrued rent arrears.

SWORN etc.

1.203   Order for transfer of protected or secure tenancy under Part IV of the Family Law Act 1996

IN THE [ ] COUNTY COURT   CASE NUMBER

BETWEEN:

| A | Applicant |

and

| B | Respondent |

ORDER

UPON hearing the solicitor for the applicant and the respondent appearing in person (AND BY CONSENT)

IT IS ORDERED THAT:

Pursuant to the Family Law Act, s 53, with the effect from the   day of   the estate or interest which the respondent has in [the property] shall be transferred to and vested in the applicant by virtue of this order and without further assurance.

Dated this   day of

1.204   Order for transfer of statutory tenancy under Part IV of the Family Law Act 1996

IN THE [ ] COUNTY COURT   CASE NUMBER

BETWEEN:

A

Applicant

and

B

Respondent

ORDER

UPON hearing the solicitor for the applicant and the respondent appearing in person

IT IS ORDERED THAT:

Pursuant to the Family Law Act, s 53, the respondent shall with effect from the   day of   cease by virtue of his statutory tenancy of [the property], to be entitled to occupy the property and the applicant shall be deemed to be the sole tenant of the property under the said statutory tenancy.

Dated this   day of

1.205   Tomlin order on compromise of dispute over property

IN THE [ ] COUNTY COURT   CASE NUMBER

BETWEEN:

A

Claimant

and

B

Defendant

The parties having agreed terms of settlement as set out in the Schedule

BY CONSENT IT IS ORDERED THAT:

(1) All further proceedings in this action be stayed except for the purpose of implementing the agreed terms for which purpose the parties have permission to apply to the court.

(2) The defendant shall pay the claimant's costs of the action to be the subject of a detailed assessment if not agreed.

SCHEDULE

(A) The defendant will on or before the   day of
           pay or cause to be paid to the claimant the sum of £X,000.

(B) If the defendant fails to pay all or any part of the sum of £X,000 by the due date the following provisions shall apply:
   (a) the sum outstanding shall carry interest at 4 per cent above the base rate for the time being of [bank];
   (b) the property [address] shall be sold forthwith by public auction, the claimant's solicitors to have the conduct of the sale;
   (c) the net proceeds of sale shall be applied as follows:
       (i)   to redeem the mortgage outstanding to [lender];
       (ii) to pay the solicitors' and estate agents' costs of sale;
       (iii) to pay the outstanding sum due to the claimant with accrued interest;
       (iv) in satisfying any outstanding liability of the defendant for the costs ordered to be paid in paragraph 2 above;
       (v)   in payment of the balance to the defendant.

Dated this   day of

1.206   *Declaration of ownership of chattels*

IN THE [ ] COUNTY COURT   CASE NUMBER

BETWEEN:

                                A   Claimant

and

                                B   Defendant

UPON HEARING the solicitors for the parties

IT IS ADJUDGED AND DECLARED THAT:

(1) The items listed in Schedule A to this order are the property of the claimant.

(2) The items listed in Schedule B to this order are the property of the defendant.

(3) The items listed in Schedule C to this order are the property of the claimant and defendant in equal shares.

IT IS ORDERED THAT:

(4) The defendant shall by 4 pm on   and at his own expense deliver up to the claimant all the items listed in Schedule A to this order.

(5) The claimant and defendant shall by 4 pm on   agree the division between them of the items listed in Schedule C to this order. In default of agreement all the items listed in Schedule C shall forthwith be sold by public auction and the net proceeds of sale after deducting the costs of removal and sale shall be divided by the claimant and defendant in equal shares.

(6) The defendant shall pay the claimant's costs assessed at £   by 4 pm on   .

Dated this   day of   .

CHAPTER 2

COHABITATION AGREEMENTS

PART A   LAW AND PRACTICE

2.1   Introduction

Despite the prevalence of couples living together in England and Wales, agreements regulating cohabitation, and more particularly its aftermath, are rarely found in practice. This is consistent with the general lack of attention to the possible consequences of transactions entered into between cohabitants. This reluctance to transform the deliberately informal into a formal arrangement is understandable. Furthermore, at the outset of a relationship, the possibility that it may come to an end is generally not given any thought.

2.2   Advising clients

Those who are cohabiting, or intending to cohabit, will rarely see a solicitor for the express purpose of entering into a cohabitation agreement. They are more likely to present themselves as prospective purchasers of a property. Clearly, the duty of the solicitor in these circumstances is to give advice about the legal implications of buying the property together, and if there is likely to be a conflict of interest, to advise one or both parties to seek separate representation.[1] Although there is no duty to give advice about cohabitation agreements, many solicitors take this opportunity to introduce the subject and to suggest how it may help to prevent difficulties in the future, should the relationship terminate for whatever reason. Although the solicitor may explain the process and implications to both parties in general terms, he or she will not be able to represent both parties if instructions are given to proceed. In order to avoid a conflict of interest it will be necessary to refer one or both parties for independent legal advice. If the parties are established clients, the solicitor may act for one of them if the other agrees.

The case of *Sutton v Mishcon de Reya and Gawor and Co*[2] went some way to clarifying the court's approach to cohabitation agreements. It is now clear that as long as the parties can establish an intention to create legal relations, that there is no express or implied provision for payment for sexual relations and the agreement complies with the necessary requirements for a valid contract,

---

[1]   See **1.2, 1.152** above.
[2]   [2004] 1 FLR 837.

the agreement may be valid and enforceable. Even so, there can be no guarantee and it is vital that any agreement is in writing.

Those advising couples proposing to enter into an agreement should emphasise that in an imperfect world they are the best that is currently available to cohabitants to record what they have agreed and to attempt to regulate their relationship whilst it is subsisting and to make provision in the event that it breaks down. It should also be emphasised that a cohabitation agreement is no substitute for properly recording the shares in which property is owned,[3] and making provision by will and/or nomination to receive benefits under a policy or pension in the event of separation by death.[4]

What follows in relation to the contents and drafting of cohabitation agreements must therefore be viewed against this background.

2.3   Validity of cohabitation agreements

Those in this jurisdiction wishing to enter into a cohabitation agreement may do so, but in the absence of any specifically applicable legislation, they have to rely upon the law of contract if they wish to take enforcement steps. This presupposes that their agreement is a valid one.

At one time, an agreement that was founded on the premise that the contracting parties would be living together in a union other than marriage would have been declared void as a matter of public policy, being sexually immoral and likely to prejudice the status of marriage.[5]

Social attitudes have changed sufficiently so that today it is unlikely that a cohabitation agreement would be considered invalid on either of these grounds. Care should nonetheless be taken to ensure that the agreement is not expressed in such a way as to suggest that the cohabitation itself, or more particularly the provision of sexual services, is the consideration for entering into the agreement.

In *Sutton v Mishcon de Reya and Gawor and Co*[6] a distinction was drawn between a cohabitation agreement regulating the property and financial arrangements of a couple who were enjoying a sexual relationship and were cohabiting or intending to cohabit, and an agreement such as the one in that case the primary purpose of which was to regulate the parties' sexual relationship. The former would not be contrary to public policy, the latter would, and would therefore be invalid.

---

3   See **1.3** above.
4   See **6.6** below.
5   'The law will not enforce an immoral promise, such as a promise between a man and a woman to live together without being married ...' per Lord Wright in *Fender v St John-Mildmay* [1938] AC 1 at 42.
6   [2004] 1 FLR 837.

The facts of *Sutton* were unusual. Two men had agreed to enter into a cohabitation agreement. They took legal advice from the first defendants and a written agreement was concluded.

The basis of their relationship and the proposed cohabitation was the enactment of a sexual fantasy of master and slave. The agreement contained details about provision of property and income, by the 'slave' for the 'master' both during the cohabitation and in the event that the relationship came to an end. There was also a separate Statement of Trust, referred to in the cohabitation agreement, in which the details of the master/slave relationship were recorded.

Property and other assets were transferred from the claimant, the 'slave', to the 'master' pursuant to the agreement and in anticipation of the cohabitation. However, the relationship soon came to an end and the parties never cohabited. The 'slave' sought the return of property and other assets that he had transferred to the 'master'. This was resisted, and on the advice of the second defendants the 'slave' entered into a deed of separation which required the 'master' to transfer back the property, but enabled him to retain the benefit of cash and other gifts given to him during the relationship.

The claimant brought a claim in negligence against both firms of solicitors. They applied to strike out the claim and succeeded, the judge finding that the claim had no prospects of success as the solicitors had given appropriate advice.

Central to the decision to strike out the claim was the non-enforceability of the cohabitation agreement. The main reason was the public policy consideration, the judge concluding that this '… was not a property contract between two people whose sexual relationship involved them in cohabitation. It was itself an attempt to express the sexual relationship in the property relations contained in the contract … It was an attempt to reify an unlawful ideal.'

The judgment also touched upon the question of misrepresentation, the 'master' having failed to inform the claimant that he was HIV positive, and the domination of the one by the other in the playing out of the fantasy clearly raised the issue of undue influence.[7]

2.4 Enforceability of cohabitation agreements

Even if a cohabitation agreement were valid, it could nonetheless be unenforceable if it failed to comply with the essential requirements of contract law.

---

[7] For further reading see Mark Pawlowski 'Cohabitation Contracts The Sutton Case' [2004] Fam Law 199 and Gerald Wilson 'Sutton in Practice' [2004] Fam Law 202.

2.5   The intention to create legal relations

As between those in a close personal relationship, there is a marked reluctance for courts to find that there was an intention to create a legally binding contract.[8] Entering into a formal, written agreement may have the effect of rebutting the presumption that the parties do not intend their domestic arrangements to be legally binding.[9] However, factors such as whether the parties took independent legal advice and whether there was full and frank disclosure before entering into the agreement will be relevant to this question. Similarly, the court is more likely to find that there was an intention that the agreement would be legally binding if it is confined to matters concerning property and money, rather than simply the minutiae of domestic life.

2.6   Consideration

If the agreement is in the form of a deed, no consideration is necessary. This avoids the risk of inadvertently overlooking the requirement for there to be consideration, or of making the consideration the cohabitation itself, which may render the contract void for illegality.

2.7   Uncertainty

If the terms of any contract are uncertain or vague so as to be incapable of being enforced, they may jeopardise the entire agreement. The same applies to cohabitation agreements. This is a matter for the draftsman. There should be no scope for uncertainty in the interpretation of the terms of the contract, but for safety a severance clause should be included.[10]

2.8   Duress or coercion; inequality of bargaining power

There is no presumption of undue influence as between cohabiting couples as there is in other close relationships, such as those between engaged couples,[11] or uncle and nephew.[12] However, there is clearly the potential for one party to exploit the emotional involvement and trust of the other. It is important therefore that both parties to the agreement are separately advised and represented, and that there is full and frank disclosure of the financial position of each party.

---

[8]   For contractual intention in social and domestic arrangements generally, see G H Treitel *The Law of Contract* (Sweet & Maxwell, 8th edn), at pp 151—153; see also *Balfour v Balfour* [1919] 2 KB 571.

[9]   See *Jones v Padavatton* [1969] 1 WLR 328.

[10]   See **2.116** below.

[11]   *Re Lloyds Bank Ltd, Bomze and Lederman v Bomze* [1931] 1 Ch 289; *RBS v Etridge (No 2)* [2002] 2 AC 773.

[12]   *Cheese v Thomas* [1994] 1 All ER 35.

2.9   *Ousting the court's jurisdiction*

Provisions in the agreement that purport to oust the jurisdiction of the court will be void on public policy grounds.

2.10   Contents of a cohabitation agreement

In the interests of enforceability it will generally be preferable to confine the contents of any agreement that is intended to be legally binding to matters of land, property and money. Provisions relating to the day-to-day regulation of the relationship are better contained in a separate document, essentially for reference purposes. Checklists of matters which should be contained in every cohabitation agreement and additional matters which may be contained in agreements intended to regulate property and financial matters may be found at **2.12** and **2.13**.

PART B　CHECKLISTS

2.11　Checklist – points to consider when advising on and drafting a cohabitation agreement

The initial interview

(1)　Clearly explain to the couple that, if as a result of their discussions they decide to go ahead with a cohabitation agreement, you will be able to act for only one of them, and will recommend the other to obtain independent legal advice.

(2)　Advise generally on the common law, equitable, and statutory rights and obligations of cohabiting partners.

(3)　If necessary, explain how these rights and obligations differ from those which apply to an engaged or married couple.

(4)　Discover whether their needs could be met more readily and effectively by other deeds and documents instead of, or in addition to, a cohabitation agreement.

(5)　Advise on the present status of a cohabitation agreement in English law.

(6)　Discuss the remedies that are available for breach of contract.

(7)　Establish whether, in the light of the advice given, there is consensus that they both wish to enter into a cohabitation agreement.

(8)　Clarify the extent to which they wish the agreement to be legally binding on them.

(9)　Establish exactly which partner if either, you will be able to represent.

(10)　Give the other party the name, address and telephone number of at least one legal practitioner who can give competent, independent advice.

(11)　Extract from the client all the information required to prepare a preliminary draft contract.

(12)　Find out which partner will pay your costs.

Drafting

The usual drafting rules apply to a cohabitation agreement with, perhaps, the following modifications.

(1)　It may be necessary to state a lot of facts and intentions, with the result that the recitals may be lengthier than in most documents.

(2)　The parties will be setting down the ground rules for a relationship which may be entirely unique to them: it is not a marriage, and it may be difficult simply to compartmentalise this relationship into a pre-existing formula, or precedent.

(3)　Four copies of the draft should be prepared (for the file, the client, the client's partner, and the remaining copy for the partner's legal adviser).

Submitting the Draft to the Client

When discussing the draft contract with the client, either in correspondence or at a further meeting, you should:

(1) inform the client once again about his or her rights and obligations in the absence of the agreement;

(2) state how those rights and obligations are or may be affected by the draft agreement;

(3) advise the client whether the draft is fair and reasonable in the circumstances;

(4) advise the client whether or not it is in his or her best interests, financially or otherwise, to enter into the agreement;

(5) establish that nothing has been erroneously omitted or admitted, and that the draft reflects the whole agreement between the parties;

(6) reiterate the advice given before, that the client's partner should seek independent legal advice;

(7) warn the client that under no circumstances should he or she:
    (a) try to 'explain' the draft agreement to his or her partner;
    (b) make any verbal promises that are not expressly included in the draft agreement; and
    (c) pressurise his or her partner into agreeing the draft and signing the agreement.

2.12 Checklist of matters to be contained in every cohabitation agreement

(1) an acknowledgement that each party has received independent legal advice;

(2) an expression of the intention to be legally bound by the agreement;

(3) confirmation that the agreement is freely entered into;

(4) a commencement date;

(5) the proposed duration of the agreement;

(6) any determining events;

(7) a schedule setting out the parties' respective financial positions;

(8) clarification of the status of after-acquired property;

(9) provision for variation of the agreement;

(10) a severance clause;

(11) a jurisdiction clause;

(12) provision for the document to be executed as a deed;

(13) agreement as to payment of the costs of the agreement;

(14) ADR clause.

2.13   Checklist of matters that may be contained in agreement intended to regulate property and financial matters

Land and property

(1) purchase and beneficial interests (in addition to trust deed);

(2) liability for repayment of mortgage or other loan for purchase;

(3) liability for any negative equity;

(4) payment for repairs and improvements;

(5) payment of outgoings;

(6) non-monetary contributions;

(7) sale of property;

(8) purchase of replacement home;

(9) application of proceeds of sale.

Insurance policies

(10) legal ownership and beneficial interests;

(11) payment of premiums;

(12) surrender;

(13) distribution on maturity;

(14) distribution of any windfalls;

(15) provision on death.

Stock exchange and other investments

(16) ownership;

(17) sale and distribution of proceeds.

Joint bank/building society accounts

(18) contributions to the account;

(19) withdrawals from the account;

(20) distribution of account on any separation.

Pension

(21) nominations for death benefits.

House contents

(22) those in sole name only;

(23) those in joint names;

(24) provision for division on separation;

(25) car purchase and running expenses;

(26) items subject to credit.

PART C   PRECEDENTS

Clauses

2.14   Acknowledgment of advice received

Each party acknowledges that he or she has been separately advised by a qualified lawyer and is aware of the rights and obligations of cohabitants generally and the manner in which those rights and obligations are or may be affected by this agreement.

After-acquired property

2.15   Separate

Any property that is subsequently owned by one party alone (whether created by its owner, or acquired by purchase, gift, inheritance or otherwise), and any income derived from it, and any increase in its value, will remain the separate property of the party who owns it.

2.16   Shared

Any property that is subsequently acquired by either party (whether by purchase, gift, inheritance or otherwise), and any income derived from it, and any increase in its value will belong to both parties equally, unless they expressly agree otherwise in writing.

2.17   Aims and expectations

The parties' aims and expectations are:

(1)   to build and maintain a relationship which is based on mutual friendship, love, loyalty, respect and trust; and

(2)   to support each other not only financially but also emotionally.

Amendments (*see* **2.141** and **2.142** below).

Arbitration (*see* **2.49–2.51** below).

2.18   Attestation clause incorporating legal adviser's certificate[13]

SIGNED as a Deed[14] by (*name 1*) in my presence after I had given (him)/(her) independent legal advice on the effects and implications of this Agreement.

---

[13]   See footnote to **2.80** below.

[14]   Execution as a deed may overcome any difficulties arising from the lack of consideration.

Bank accounts

2.19   Separate

(1)   Each party will maintain separate bank or building society accounts and the money in each such account will remain his or her separate property.

(2)   The parties do not intend to open any joint account.

2.20   Shared

(1)   The parties will (open and) maintain an account in their joint names ('the joint account') at (*name and address of bank or building society branch*).

(2)   The joint account and any interest credited to it will, at all times, belong to the parties in equal shares, regardless of the actual sums which either of them may have paid into or withdrawn from the joint account.

(3)   Each party may draw cheques on and withdraw cash from the joint account (up to a limit of £   , but any cheque or withdrawal exceeding that sum must be signed or made by both parties).

(4)   If either party purchases goods or makes an investment in his or her sole name out of funds held in the joint account then, in the absence of any contrary agreement between the parties, the goods or the investment will belong to the person making the purchase or investment.

2.21   Beneficial interests: separate

Neither party will acquire, or seek to acquire, or claim to have acquired a beneficial interest in any present or future property owned solely by the other party.

2.22   Binding effect of agreement

This agreement is legally binding on the parties and their respective executors and administrators, estates and assigns.

2.23   Birth control

(*Name*) will be primarily responsible for birth control arrangements.

2.24   Business interests: separate

(1)   The present and future business interests of (*name*) and any income derived from them, and any increase in their value are, will be and will remain (his)/(her) separate property.

(2)   (*Name's*) 'business interests' include (but are not restricted to (*set out details*)) [OR] (any asset, interest, share, rights and obligations in any business, trade, profession or vocation, or any firm, partnership, company or organisation in which (he)/(she) may be engaged, employed or concerned or to which (he)/(she) may render services now or in the future).

(3)   (*Name*) warrants that (his)/(her) business interests are currently worth approximately £ .

2.25   *Cancellation of cohabitation agreement*

THIS AGREEMENT made on (*date*)

BETWEEN (1) (*name 1*) of (*address*) and (2) (*name 2*) of (*address*).

WITNESSES that the parties now cancel and rescind in all respects and for all purposes the Cohabitation Agreement made by them on (*date*) on which this Agreement is endorsed.

SIGNED as a Deed by (*name 1*) in the presence of:

SIGNED as a Deed by (*name 2*) in the presence of:

Cars

2.26   *Separate*
(1)   The car that each party owns now and any vehicle that may be acquired to replace it is and will remain the separate property of that party.
(2)   Each party is solely responsible for the costs of acquiring, insuring, maintaining and running his or her car.
(3)   Each party will permit and effect proper insurance cover to enable the other party to drive his or her car.

2.27   *Shared*
(1)   The (*description of car*) registration number (*number*) that the parties own at present ('the car') belongs to the parties in equal shares, regardless of whose name actually appears on the vehicle registration document, and regardless of the contributions made by either party towards its acquisition.
(2)   Unless the parties agree otherwise in writing, any vehicle which is subsequently acquired to replace the car will also belong to the parties in equal shares, regardless of whose name actually appears on the vehicle registration document, and regardless of the contributions made by either party towards its acquisition.

2.28   *One party to provide a car for the other*
(1)   Until the termination of this agreement (*name 1*) will provide (*name 2*) with a car for (his)/(her) own use and enjoyment.
(2)   (*Name 1*) will pay all the running expenses of the car, including vehicle excise duty, insurance, maintenance, repairs, (membership of the AA/RAC) and petrol.

(3) The car will be replaced every (3) years with another car, and each replacement will be no more than (one year) old when it is acquired, and will have an engine capacity of not less than (1600) cc.

(4) (*Name 1*) will retain ownership of the car.

(5) On the termination of this agreement (*name 2*) will deliver up possession of the car to (*name 1*).

2.29   Careers

The parties consider that (*name 1's*) career is of greater social and economic importance to them than (*name 2's*) career and (*name 2*) agrees that if (*name 1*) is required to move elsewhere to further (his)/(her) career (*name 2*) will transfer (his)/(her) own job to the new location.

Child care

2.30   Allocation of responsibility[15]

The parties intend to share the responsibility of looking after their children and so far as practicable will take turns in staying home from work whenever a child is unwell or the children are on holiday.

2.31   Support of carer[16]

If one party temporarily stops working in order to stay at home to look after the children, the other party will pay him or her (one half) of his or her disposable income until the youngest child is placed in a nursery or primary school.

2.32   Children: statement of intentions

The parties have been advised and understand that any provision in this agreement which affects their child or children may be unenforceable in law or varied by the Court. Nevertheless, if the parties have a child or children, they intend:

(1) jointly to register the child's birth;[17] or

(2) that the child's surname will be (*surname*);[18]

---

[15] See also **2.32** below, to which this clause could, if considered appropriate, be added as a sub-clause.

[16] See **2.32** below, to which this clause could, if considered appropriate, be added as a sub-clause.

[17] Births and Deaths Registration Act 1953, ss 10 and 10A (as amended); a father who jointly registers the child's birth with the child's mother will automatically acquire parental responsibility (CA 1989, s 4(1)(a)).

[18] The right to determine the child's name is vested in the parent who has parental responsibility except where a residence order or care order is in force (see **5.21**). For the position where the child's father and mother were not married to each other at the time of the child's birth, see Children Act 1989, s 2(2).

(3) that the child's forename(s) will be chosen by the parties jointly;[19]

(4) by means of a Parental Responsibility Agreement to provide for (*name 1*) to have parental responsibility for the child;[20]

(5) that any major decision about the child's health and welfare, education and upbringing will be made by the parties jointly;

(6) to contribute financially towards the child's upbringing for as long as is necessary on the basis of their respective abilities to pay;[21] and

(7) that if they separate, the parent with whom the child is living will use his or her best endeavours to ensure that the child maintains contact with the parent with whom he or she is no longer living.[22]

2.33 Commencement

THIS COHABITATION AGREEMENT is made on (*date*)

BETWEEN 'the parties': (1) (*name 1*) of (*address*) ('*name 1*') and (2) (*name 2*) (also) of (*address*) ('*name 2*').

IT IS AGREED that:

2.34 Commencement date

This Agreement will come into force on (*date*).

2.35 Confidentiality

Each party promises never to use, disclose or divulge to the detriment or disadvantage of the other any confidential information about the other's private life, family life or business affairs which may have come to his or her knowledge during the course of their relationship.

2.36 Consideration: specific

In consideration of (*name 2*) giving up (his)/(her) present job in order to live with (*name 1*), (*name 1*) will (*set out details*).

---

[19] The right to determine the child's name is vested in the parent who has parental responsibility except where a residence order or care order is in force (see **5.21**). For the position where the child's father and mother were not married to each other at the time of the child's birth, see Children Act 1989, s 2(2).

[20] Children Act 1989, s 4(1)(b). For the prescribed form of parental responsibility agreement, see **5.84** below.

[21] See, generally, Children Act 1989, Sch 1, and Child Support Act 1991.

[22] For 'contact orders' see Children Act 1989, s 8(1).

2.37   Consideration: general

This Agreement is made in consideration of the mutual promises (and releases) it contains and for other good and valuable consideration the sufficiency of which each of the parties acknowledges.

Cooling-off clause

2.38   Counselling

If either party is seriously thinking of ending the relationship, both parties will attend at least (2) counselling session(s) before making any final decision.

2.39   Trial separation

If either party is seriously thinking of ending the relationship, both parties will spend at least (7) days apart before making any final decision.

Costs

2.40   Shared equally

The legal costs relating to the preparation (negotiation) and execution of this Agreement (including the combined total of the costs incurred by each of the parties in obtaining independent advice) will be paid by the parties in equal shares.

2.41   One party to pay all the costs

(*Name 1*) will pay all the legal costs relating to the preparation (negotiation) and execution of this Agreement (including the costs incurred by (*name 2*) in obtaining independent advice and assistance).

2.42   One party to pay for independent advice

(1)   (*Name 1*) will pay the legal costs relating to the preparation (negotiation) and execution of this Agreement.

(2)   (*Name 2*) will pay the costs incurred by (him)/(her) in obtaining independent legal advice on the provisions and implications of this Agreement.

2.43   Covenants relating to residential property[23]

Each party promises:

(1)   at all times to comply with the covenants and conditions affecting (*address*) ('the property');

(2)   at all times to keep the property in good repair and condition and insured to its full reinstatement value;

(3)   not to create or attempt to create any mortgage or charge over the property or any part of it or any interest in it without the other's consent; and

(4)   not to create or attempt to create any tenancy, licence, agreement or any other right affecting the property without the other's consent.

Credit cards

2.44   Separate

Each party will maintain separate credit accounts and neither party will use the other's credit.

2.45   Shared[24]

(1)   (*Name 1*) will nominate (*name 2*) to use a credit card on (his)/(her) (*credit company*) account number (*account number*).

(2)   Between the parties themselves (*name 2*) will be responsible for the payment for all purchases made by (him)/(her) on the account and for any interest attributable to those purchases.

(3)   (*Name 2*) promises at all times to use the card with care and consideration and to indemnify (*name 1*) against any loss incurred as a result of (his)/(her) use, misuse or abuse of the card.

2.46   Debts

(1)   Each of the parties will remain personally liable for any current and future debts incurred in his or her sole name.

(2)   The payment by one party of any part of the other's personal debts will in no way render the payer liable for or obliged to make any further payment in respect of those debts.

---

[23]   It may be sensible to include these covenants in a cohabitation agreement if they are not already incorporated in, for example, a declaration of trust.

[24]   Usually a principal cardholder can nominate one other person to be an authorised user of a credit card. The authorised user generally has to sign an acknowledgment accepting and agreeing to be bound by the conditions of use imposed by the bank or credit company. The card itself is usually the company's property. The principal cardholder is usually liable for repayment. It may be worthwhile checking each individual agreement and the terms and conditions of use.

2.47 Declaration of trust[25]

The rights and interests of the parties in the property known as (*address*) and its net proceeds of sale are set out in a Declaration of Trust dated (*date*) and are not in any way varied or affected by this Agreement.

2.48 Deed[26]

This Agreement is a deed and is executed by the parties as a deed.

Dispute resolution[27]

2.49 Arbitration

(If any attempt at conciliation or mediation is unsuccessful) any difference, disagreement or dispute arising out of or in connection with this Agreement will be referred to an Arbitrator nominated at the request of either party by the (President) of the (Area) District Law Society.

2.50 Conciliation

Any difference, disagreement or dispute arising out of or in connection with this Agreement will be referred in the first instance to (the local family mediation service) without prejudice to the right of either party to apply subsequently to the Court for adjudication.

2.51 Named mediator[28]

(1) Any difference, disagreement or dispute which arises out of or in connection with this Agreement will be referred in the first instance to (*name*) who will act as a mediator.

(2) If (*name*) is unwilling or unable to act as mediator the problem will be referred to (*name B*) instead.

---

[25] It may be considered preferable to deal with the beneficial interests in jointly owned property in a completely separate declaration of trust rather than to include, possibly lengthy, additional clauses in the cohabitation agreement. The execution of a declaration of trust by an unmarried couple who jointly own property is now virtually a mandatory requirement.

[26] One of the grounds on which it is argued that a cohabitation agreement may be unenforceable at law is lack of consideration. This problem can be overcome by executing the cohabitation agreement as a deed. To take effect as a deed the instrument must make it clear on its face that it is intended to be a deed (whether by describing itself as a deed or expressing itself to be executed as a deed) and it must be validly executed as a deed by the parties to it (Law of Property (Miscellaneous Provisions) Act 1989, s 1(2)).

[27] For clauses referring the dispute to a conciliator or mediator, see **2.50** and **2.51**.

[28] In certain circumstances a named mediator may be preferred to, for example, the local family mediation service. Selecting a personal friend might place that friend in a difficult position. It is probably wiser to choose someone who is known to and respected by both parties but who is not a close, personal friend of either. As a courtesy to the proposed mediator, and to avoid any potential problems about acceptance of that role, the parties should obtain the consent of the proposed mediator before making such an appointment.

Duration

2.52   Indefinite

The parties plan to live together indefinitely.

2.53   Fixed term

Unless it terminates earlier in accordance with the provisions of Clause (*number*), this Agreement will terminate on (*date*).

Dwelling

2.54   Joint tenancy[29]

The parties own (*address*) as beneficial joint tenants, regardless of the actual contributions made by either party towards its acquisition.

2.55   Tenancy in common[30]

The parties own (*address*) as beneficial tenants in common as to   per cent of the net proceeds of sale for (*name 1*) and as to   per cent for (*name 2*), regardless of the actual contributions made by either party towards its acquisition.

2.56   One party is sole owner

(*Name 1*) owns (*address*) and (*name 2*) acknowledges that (he)/(she) has not acquired, will not acquire and will not claim to have acquired any beneficial interest in that property.

2.57   Estate rights[31]

(1)   Neither party is under any obligation to make financial provision for or to confer any other benefit on the surviving party on death.

(2)   Neither party has agreed, promised or represented to the other that he or she will execute a will or sign any other instrument which will make financial provision for or confer any other benefit on the surviving party.[32]

(3)   Each party releases, renounces and surrenders to the other party and the other party's estate any right which he or she may have as a cohabitee to

---

[29]   See, generally, Chapter 1 'Property'.
[30]   See, generally, Chapter 1 'Property'.
[31]   See Chapter 7.
[32]   See *Synge v Synge* [1894] 1 QB 466, CA, where the man made an antenuptial promise in writing to leave the woman a life interest, and the woman was entitled to enforce the promise. See also *Re Basham (Deceased)* [1986] 1 WLR 1498 – deceased giving assurances as to a stepdaughter's future rights to his estate.

apply to the court for an order under section 2 of the Inheritance (Provision for Family and Dependants) Act 1975 or any statutory modification or re-enactment of it.[33]

(4)   Nothing in this Agreement constitutes a renunciation of the right of the surviving party (if entitled) to obtain a grant of representation to the estate of the deceased party or a disclaimer by the surviving party of any financial provision, benefit or right conferred by the deceased party in his or her will or arising otherwise as a result of his or her death.

2.58   Execution of this agreement[34]

This Agreement has been executed in duplicate and each copy will be deemed an original and will constitute one and the same agreement between the parties.

2.59   Fiduciary duty

Each party promises to show the utmost good faith and to deal fairly with the other in implementing the provisions of this Agreement.

Financial disclosure

2.60   By one party only[35]

(1)   (*Name 1*) has disclosed to (*name 2*) details of the income, earning capacity, property and other financial resources, and the financial needs, obligations and responsibilities which (he)/(she) has now and is likely to have in the foreseeable future.

(2)   (*Name 1*) has neither asked for, nor received, nor wishes to receive similar information from (*name 2*).

2.61   By both cohabitants

(1)   (*Name 1*) estimates that (his)/(her) net capital resources are currently worth about £   and that (his)/(her) net annual income from all sources is approximately £   .

(2)   (*Name 2*) estimates that (his)/(her) net capital resources are currently worth about £   and that (his)/(her) net annual income from all sources is approximately £   .

---

[33]   See **2.108** below.

[34]   For multiple execution of deeds, see generally, Co Litt 229a; *Burchell v Clark* (1876) 2 CPD 88 at 96, CA.

[35]   As a general rule, a person who is about to enter into a contract is under no duty to disclose material facts known to him but not known to the other party. A contract 'uberrimae fidei' is an exception to such general rule. It is not clear whether a cohabitation agreement would be classified as a contract 'uberrimae fidei', akin to a family arrangement. In *Wales v Wadham* [1977] 1 WLR 199 at 218, it was held that although there might be cases where there was a duty to make full and frank disclosure before there was a duty to do so by affidavit, when the jurisdiction of the court had been invoked, no such duty arose in this case because the parties had made a bargain at arm's length. On contracts 'uberrimae fidei' see, generally G H Treitel *The Law of Contract* (Sweet & Maxwell, 8th edn) at pp 349—362.

(3) Both parties acknowledge that each of them has been given the opportunity to examine the other's financial records.

2.62 Further assurances

When required to do so, each party will complete, sign and execute any deed, document or form which may be needed in order to implement the provisions of this Agreement.

Gifts between cohabitants

2.63 Presumption that the gift is absolute

Any gift from one party to the other will be presumed to be an absolute gift unless it is expressly given on the condition that it will be returned to the giver on the termination of the parties' relationship.

2.64 Reservation of rights

Nothing in this Agreement regarding the separate property and assets of the parties deprives either party of the right to give to or receive from the other property and assets of any description by way of gift, transfer or legacy.

2.65 Gifts received: separate

Any gift, inheritance or unexpected good fortune received by either party will be and will remain the separate property of that party.

2.66 Guests

Neither party will, without first obtaining the other party's consent, invite any friend, relative or guest to stay (for longer than (*24 hours*)).

2.67 Headings

The headings in this Agreement have been inserted for convenience and reference and must not be interpreted as defining, limiting or extending the substance and scope of the provisions above which they appear.

2.68 Housekeeping allowance: fixed sum

(1) For as long as the parties are living together (*name 1*) will pay to (*name 2*) a housekeeping allowance of £   a (week)/(month).

(2) The allowance will be adjusted at least once a year in line with the Retail Prices Index.

(3) Any property purchased by (*name 2*) from any surplus or accumulations of the allowance will belong to (*name 2*) absolutely.

2.69   Housework

The parties will share the housework equally.

[OR]

The parties will take turns in doing the housework.

[OR]
(1)   (*Name 1*) will be primarily responsible for the following household tasks:
(2)   (*Name 2*) will be primarily responsible for the following household tasks:

Illness or incapacity

2.70   Attorneyship[36]

Each party will as soon as practicable execute an instrument appointing the other party to be his or her attorney for the purpose of the Mental Capacity Act 2005.

2.71   Next of kin

So far as it is legally possible to do so each party will nominate and appoint the other to be his or her 'next of kin' or 'nearest relative' (for contact, emergency, visiting, advocacy and representation purposes).[37]

2.72   Support

For as long as the parties are living together each will be responsible for supporting the other.

Income

2.73   Separate

Each party's income from all sources and all accumulations of that income will be and will remain his or her separate property and will not be subject to division between the parties on the termination of their relationship.

---

[36]   If either party should become seriously ill or incapacitated the other party could be treated by various authorities as a 'legal stranger'. If the cohabitee has been appointed as an attorney, he or she will have authority to act on behalf of the incapacitated party. If the parties separate, a lasting power of attorney ('LPA') can easily be revoked. If, however, the EPA has been registered in the Court of Protection, revocation must be confirmed by the court.
[37]   See generally **6.88–6.94**.

2.74   Shared

The parties will pool and commingle their respective incomes from all sources (and will share equally all accumulations of and property acquired from their pooled incomes, regardless of the actual income earned or received by either party).

2.75   Intention to create legal relations

(1)   (Part I) [OR] (Clauses   to   inclusive) of this Contract contain(s) agreements that will be legally binding on the parties and their personal representatives and estates.

(2)   (Part II) [OR] (Clauses   to   inclusive) of this Contract contain(s) agreements to which the parties are bound in honour only and which give rise to no legal rights and for the breach of which no legal action will lie.

(3)   (Part III) [OR] (Clauses   to   inclusive) of this Contract contain(s) provisions of general application.

2.76   Interpretation of this agreement[38]

No provision in this Agreement will be construed against one party merely because it was drafted or inserted by his or her legal adviser.

Joint property

2.77   Joint tenancy[39]

Any property or asset acquired jointly by the parties while they are living together will belong to them as beneficial joint tenants, regardless of their respective contributions towards its acquisition, unless they provide otherwise in writing[40] and clearly identify their respective shares or interests in the property or asset in question.

2.78   Tenancy in common[41]

Any property or asset acquired jointly by the parties while they are living together will belong to them as beneficial tenants in common in shares corresponding to the actual contributions made by each of them towards the acquisition of the property or asset, unless they provide otherwise in writing.

---

[38]   This clause is designed to negate the effects of the 'contra proferentem' rule of construction, whereby the wording of a document is construed more strongly against the party putting it forward. This rule of construction is applied in cases of ambiguity, where other rules of construction fail.

[39]   This clause relates to any jointly acquired assets, and could include investments, a dwelling and personal chattels.

[40]   This clause envisages that all joint property will be held as beneficial joint tenants unless the contrary is provided in a separate declaration of trust in writing. In the case of pure personalty, an oral declaration suffices, but is hardly satisfactory.

[41]   See footnotes to **2.77** above.

2.79   Joint use: separate ownership

The use by one party of any property which belongs to the other party will not give rise to the joint ownership of that property.

2.80   Legal adviser's certificate[42]

I (*legal adviser's name*) of (*professional address*), (a solicitor of the Supreme Court) [OR] (a Fellow of the Institute of Legal Executives) [OR] (*as the case may be*), CERTIFY that before (he)/(she) signed this Agreement I advised (*name 1*) independently of (*name 2*) on:

(1)   (his)/(her) rights and responsibilities in the absence of this Agreement; and

(2)   the manner in which those rights and responsibilities are or may be affected by this Agreement; and

(3)   whether or not it was prudent or advantageous, financially or otherwise, to enter into this Agreement; and

(4)   whether or not at that time and in the light of such circumstances as were then reasonably foreseeable the provisions of this Agreement were fair and reasonable.

Dated:

Signed:

2.81   Life insurance: agreement to take out and maintain a policy[43]

(*Name 1*) will take out a policy of insurance on (his)/(her) life in the sum of £   for the benefit of (*name 2*) and for as long as (he)/(she) has an obligation to do so under this Agreement will maintain that policy in full force and effect[44] (and will authorise the insurer to disclose to (*name 2*) any information regarding that policy that (he)/(she) may ask for).

---

[42]   This certificate is based on the wording of the De Facto Relationships Act 1984 (New South Wales), s 47(d), which requires that the certificates be endorsed on, or annexed to, or should otherwise accompany the agreement (ibid, s 47(e)).
For a briefer certificate incorporated as part of the attestation clause, see **2.18**.

[43]   Other provisions could be added. For example: increasing the cover periodically; an undertaking not to charge or assign the policy; remedies available if the insured fails to pay the premiums, etc.

[44]   This envisages that the obligation will cease on termination of the agreement or shortly afterwards. The legal adviser should ensure that there are provisions to this effect in the clauses relating to the consequences of termination.

Living expenses

2.82   To be paid from joint account[45]

The following living expenses will be paid out of the parties' joint account: mortgage payments; rent; buildings insurance; contents insurance; water; gas; electricity; telephone; groceries; cleaning materials; general toiletries; television licence; holidays; joint recreation; car insurance; car maintenance ...[46]

2.83   To be paid in proportion to the parties' respective incomes

Except for any expenses that are solely attributable to one or the other of them, the parties agree to share all living expenses[47] in proportion to their respective incomes or in such other proportions as they may from time to time agree.

2.84   Fixed percentages

(*Name 1*) will pay   per cent of the parties' living expenses[48] and (*name 2*) will pay the other   per cent.

2.85   One party pays all

(1)   For as long as the parties are living together (*name 1*) will pay all their living expenses.

(2)   'Living expenses' include, but are not restricted to: mortgage payments; rent; building insurance; contents insurance; water; gas; electricity; telephone; groceries; cleaning materials; toiletries; holidays; joint recreation (etc).

2.86   Defined areas of responsibility

(1)   (*Name 1*) will be primarily responsible for paying the following living expenses: (*set out details*).

(2)   (*Name 2*) will be primarily responsible for paying the following living expenses: (*set out details*).

(3)   Both parties will contribute equally towards the payment of the following living expenses: (*set out details*).

Marriage

2.87   Agreement to continue on marriage

(1)   The parties intend that their respective rights and responsibilities contained in this Agreement will not be varied or affected in any way if they marry each other.

---

[45]   This clause assumes that reference is made elsewhere in the agreement to a joint bank or building society account. See **2.20** above.

[46]   Delete and add as appropriate.

[47]   It would be wise to define 'living expenses'. See **2.85** below.

[48]   It may be sensible to define 'living expenses'. See **2.85** below.

(2) The parties also intend that, if their marriage is subsequently dissolved or annulled, the provisions of this Agreement should be one of the matters to which the court should have regard in deciding whether and how to exercise its powers.[49]

(3) Despite the provisions above, nothing in this Agreement constitutes an agreement by either party to marry the other.[50]

2.88   Agreement ceases to apply on marriage[51]

This Agreement will cease to have effect if and when the parties marry each other.

2.89   Medical insurance

(1) (*Name 1*) will take out and maintain in full force and effect for as long as he has an obligation to do so under this Agreement[52] medical insurance with (*company*) for (*name 2*).

(2) (*Name 1*) will take out and maintain in full force and effect medical insurance with (*company*) for the parties' children until each child reaches the age of (*18*).

(3) Despite the above, (*name 1's*) obligation to take out and maintain medical insurance for (*name 2*) (*and the children*) will continue only for as long as such insurance is available under the scheme operated by (his)/(her) company, business or employer and will be limited to the coverage provided under that scheme.

2.90   Mortgage payments[53]

(*Name 1*) will pay   per cent and (*name 2*) will pay   per cent of the mortgage payments (and these payments will not affect the parties' respective beneficial interests in the property).[54]

---

[49] In exercising its powers under ss 23, 24 and 24A of the Matrimonial Causes Act 1973, the court should have regard to, inter alia, all the circumstances of the case which might include entering into such an agreement.

[50] Law Reform (Miscellaneous Provisions) Act 1970, s 1, provides that an agreement between two persons to marry one another does not have effect as a contract giving rise to legal rights.

[51] See footnotes to **2.87** above.

[52] If this obligation is to cease on the termination of the agreement, words to that effect should be included in the clause relating to consequences of termination.

[53] For other permutations, see **2.82–2.86** relating to living expenses and adapt accordingly. For example: where payments are to be made from a joint account or where they paid in proportion to the parties' respective incomes or when one party pays all the mortgage payments.

[54] Include or exclude the words in brackets as appropriate.

2.91 *Non-disclosure of agreement to third parties*

Neither party will disclose any part of this Agreement to any third party unless compelled to do so by legal process, or unless disclosure is necessary in order to protect or enforce the terms of this Agreement.

2.92 *Pensions and death-in-service benefits*[55]

Each party will:

(1) nominate the other to receive (per cent of) the pension and death-in-service benefits payable under any pension scheme of which he or she may from time to time be a member;

(2) at the other's request provide written evidence that such nomination has been received and recorded by the trustees of the pension scheme to which it relates.

2.93 *Present property: separate*

(1) The property listed in Schedule (*number*) belongs to (*name 1*) and will at all times remain (his)/(her) separate property.

(2) The property listed in Schedule (*number*) belongs to (*name 2*) and will at all times remain (his)/(her) separate property.

(3) Neither party will acquire any right or title to or interest in the other's separate property simply by virtue of the parties' cohabitation.[56]

2.94 *Present property and debts: separate*[57]

(1) The property listed in Part 1 of Schedule (*number*) belongs to (*name 1*) and will at all times remain (his)/(her) separate property.

(2) The debts listed in Part 2 of Schedule (*number*) have been incurred by (*name 1*) and (he)/(she) will at all times remain solely liable for their repayment.

(3) [As in 1 above, but in respect of name 2.]

(4) [As in 2 above, but in respect of name 2.]

2.95 *Proper law*

This Agreement will be governed and interpreted in accordance with the law of (England and Wales).

---

[55] See **6.6** below.
[56] See **2.107** below.
[57] See also **2.46** above and **2.140** below.

Recitals

2.96   Cohabitation

The parties (intend to) live together.

[OR]

The parties have been living together since (*date*).

2.97   Intention to create legal relations[58]

The parties intend that this Agreement will be legally binding on them and their respective personal representatives and estates.

2.98   Intention not to create legal relations

The parties intend that this Agreement will give rise to no legal rights and that no legal action will lie for its breach.

2.99   Purpose of this agreement

The purpose of this Agreement is to define and regulate the respective rights and responsibilities of the parties both during and after their cohabitation.

2.100   No duress or undue influence[59]

Each party is entering into this Agreement freely and voluntarily and without coercion or pressure from the other party or anyone else.

2.101   Cohabitant under 18[60]

(*Name*) is a minor and understands that this Agreement will be legally binding on (him)/(her) unless and until (he)/(she) repudiates it during (his)/(her) minority or within a reasonable time after (his)/(her) eighteenth birthday.

---

[58] 'As a rule when arrangements are made between close relations ... there is a presumption against an intention of creating any legal relationship. This is not a presumption of law, but of fact' (*Jones v Padavatton* [1969] 1 WLR 328 at 332, per Salmon LJ). In the absence of any statement to the contrary, a formal written contract should in itself rebut such presumption of fact. For a clause expressly stating that no legal relationship is created, see **2.98** below.

[59] A contract is voidable at common law if it was made under duress. Equity will also give relief against unconscionable bargains if one party has taken advantage of the fact that there is a marked inequality of bargaining power between the parties.
'The English Law gives relief to one who, without independent advice, enters into a contract upon terms which are unfair or transfers property for a consideration which is grossly inadequate, where his bargaining power is grievously impaired by reason of his own needs or desires, or by his own ignorance or infirmity, coupled with undue influence or pressures brought to bear on him by or for the benefit of the other' (*Lloyds Bank Ltd v Bundy* [1975] QB 326 at 339, per Lord Denning MR).

[60] The status, in English law, of a cohabitation agreement, is uncertain (see **2.3**). A fortiori, the

2.102   Recitals to be legally binding

The parties warrant that these recitals are true and accurate and intend that they will be legally binding on them.

2.103   Independent legal advice[61]

Before signing this Agreement each party received independent legal advice on its provisions and implications.

2.104   Understanding the nature and effect of the agreement

Each party warrants that he or she understands the nature and effect of this Agreement and is entering into it after careful consideration of all the facts, circumstances and implications.

2.105   Recitals: personal information about the parties

(1)   (*Name*) was born on (*date*).

(2)   (*Name*) is employed as a (*job description*). [OR] (*Name*) is a self-employed (*job description*). [OR] (*Name*) is unemployed. [OR] (*Name*) is a retired (*former job description*).

(3)   (*Name*) is (single)/(separate)/(divorced)/(a widow/widower).

(4)   Details of (*name's*) current assets, liabilities and income are recorded in Schedule (*number*).

2.106   Recitals relating to the child(ren)

(1)   The parties are the mother and father of (*child's name*) who was born on (*date*); (*child's name*) who was born on (*date*).

(2)   By a Parental Responsibility Agreement made between the parties and recorded in the Principal Registry of the Family Division on (*date*)[62] (*name 1*) has parental responsibility for (*child's or children's name(s)*) in addition to (his)/(her)/(their) mother or the parties jointly registered the birth and both have parental responsibility, and no order has been made by the court under CA 1989, s 4(2A).

(3)   (*Name 2*) is also the mother of (*number*) child(ren) by her (former marriage(s))/relationship(s)) namely: (*child's name*) who was born on (*date*); (*child's name*) who was born on (*date*).

---

status of a cohabitation agreement made by a minor is highly uncertain. It is assumed that such an agreement would be voidable at the minor's option before attaining 18 or within a reasonable time after attaining 18.

61   See, generally, **1.2**, **1.152**, and **2.2** above.

62   A parental responsibility agreement will not take effect until the prescribed form, duly completed and signed, has been filed in the Principal Registry of the Family Division (Parental Responsibility Agreement Regulations 1991 (SI 1991/1478)). For the prescribed form, see **5.84**.

(4)   (*Name 1*) is also the father of (*number*) child(ren) by his (former marriage(s))/(relationship(s)) namely: (*child's name*) who was born on (*date*); (*child's name*) who was born on (*date*).

(5)   (*Child's or children's name(s)*) live with the parties.

2.107   Release of rights (if any) over the other's separate property

Each party releases, renounces and surrenders all (if any) rights that he or she may now or subsequently have to claim any right or title to or any share or interest in any property or income now or subsequently owned or acquired by the other party alone.

2.108   Release of right to apply to the court for an order under the Inheritance (Provision for Family and Dependants) Act 1975[63]

Each of the parties releases, renounces and surrenders to the other and the other's estate any right which he or she may have as a cohabitant[64] to apply to the court for an order under section 2 of the Inheritance (Provision for Family and Dependants) Act 1975 or any statutory modification or re-enactment of it.

2.109   Religious upbringing of child(ren)

If the parties have a child or children, he, she or they will be brought up as members of (the Roman Catholic Church; the Jewish faith; the Church of England; the Methodist Church; *or as the case may be*).

2.110   Remedies for breach of agreement[65]

If either party breaches or fails to comply with any promise or provision contained in this Agreement the other may be entitled to apply to the Court for an order awarding:

(1)   damages;

(2)   specific performance;

(3)   an injunction;

(4)   costs.

---

63   Whether it is actually possible to 'contract out' in this way was left an open question in *Zamet v Hyman* [1961] 1 WLR 1442, CA, where a similar release was entered into for monetary consideration by an elderly woman who was shortly to be married. In any event, strict proof would be required to establish that when the parties signed the contract they 'fully understood its significance and after full, free and informed (and particularly informed) thought about it' (at 1450, per Lord Evershed MR). Compare s 15 of the Act which applies only in divorce proceedings, etc.

64   See, generally, the Inheritance (Provision for Family and Dependants) Act 1975, ss 1(1)(e), (3) and 3(4). See also **6.35**.

65   The inclusion of a clause of this nature puts the parties on notice as to the possible consequences of their failure to comply with any of the specific provisions of the contract.

2.111   Rent

Each party will pay one half of the rent.

[OR] (*Name 1*) will pay   per cent of the rent and (*name 2*) will pay
     per cent of the rent.

[OR] (*Name*) will pay the rent.

2.112   Review: ad hoc review

If for any reason either party is unhappy about any provision in this Agreement
he or she may request an ad hoc review of that provision after giving the other
party at least (7) days' notice.

2.113   Review of agreement

(1) The parties will review the provisions of this Agreement:
     (a) at least once every year (on or about the anniversary of the date of
          this Agreement); and
     (b) whenever there is a major change in the personal circumstances of
          either or both of them.

(2) Events giving rise to a major change in the personal circumstances of
     either or both of the parties include, but are not restricted to:
     (a) engagement or marriage;
     (b) childbirth;
     (c) illness, injury or accident;
     (d) unemployment, re-employment or retirement;
     (e) inheritance or unexpected good fortune;
     (f) bankruptcy.

(3) The purpose of a review is to decide whether, in the light of the
     information available and the circumstances reasonably foreseeable at the
     time:
     (a) any provision of this Agreement should be deleted;
     (b) any provision of this Agreement should be varied;
     (c) any provision should be added to this Agreement;
     (d) this Agreement should be cancelled; or
     (e) this Agreement should be superseded by a new contract.

(4) If as a result of a review any deletions, variations or additions are
     necessary or this Agreement is to be cancelled or superseded such change
     must be recorded in an instrument in writing executed (as a deed) by both
     parties.

2.114   Revocation clause

This Agreement revokes and replaces any previous written or oral agreement
between the parties.

2.115 *Separation*

After the termination of this Agreement neither party will:

(a)   without invitation enter or occupy any premises owned or occupied by the other party;

(b)   annoy, embarrass, or interfere with the other party and his or her relatives, friends, acquaintances, and business colleagues and contacts.

2.116 *Severance*[66]

If the court finds that any provision of this Agreement is illegal, invalid, or otherwise unenforceable, such provision may be severed from this Agreement without affecting its other provisions which will continue to have full force and effect.

(The inclusion of this clause does not imply that the parties or their legal advisers believe that any provision of this Agreement may be illegal, invalid, or otherwise unenforceable.)

2.117 *Sexual relations*[67]

Nothing in this Agreement is to be interpreted as imposing an obligation on either party to have sexual relations with the other (or to abstain from having sexual relations with anyone else).

Support

2.118   *Mutual support*

For as long as the parties are living together each will be responsible for supporting the other.

---

[66]   'The general rule is that, where you cannot sever the illegal from the legal part of a covenant, the contract is altogether void; but where you can sever them, whether the illegality be created by statute or by the common law, you may reject the bad part and retain the good' (*Pickering v Ilfracombe Railway Co* (1868) LR 3 CP 235 at 250, per Willes J)).
The illegal term must be capable of being separate from the remainder of the contract under what is generally known as 'the blue pencil rule'.

[67]   This is a clause for the ultra cautious. One of the grounds on which it is considered that cohabitation agreements generally may be illegal is that they promote sexual immorality and are, accordingly, contrary to public policy. Principles decided in 18th and 19th century case-law are still binding precedents. It is unlikely, however, that a court would now strike down a typical cohabitation agreement as immoral. 'The court's function is to apply the law, not personal prejudice. Only in a case where there is still a generally accepted moral code can the court refuse to enforce rights in such a way as to offend that generally accepted code' (*Stephens v Avery* [1988] 2 All ER 477 at 481, per Sir Nicolas Browne-Wilkinson V-C). See *Sutton* **2.2** above.

2.119 No obligation

Neither party is under any obligation to maintain, support or make any form of financial provision to or for the benefit of the other at any time during or after their cohabitation.

2.120 No promises made

Neither party has agreed, promised or represented to the other that he or she will maintain, support or make any form of financial provision to or for the benefit of the other at any time during or after their cohabitation.

2.121 Reservation of right

Nothing in this Agreement deprives either party of the right voluntarily to maintain, support or make any other form of financial provision to or for the benefit of the other.

2.122 Waiver of rights

Each party waives, releases and surrenders any right which he or she may now or subsequently have to claim or receive maintenance, support or any other form of financial provision from the other party at any time during or after their cohabitation.

Surname

2.123 Each to retain their own surname

Each party will retain his or her own surname.

2.124 Both to be known by the same surname

Both parties will use the surname (*surname*).

2.125 End of relationship[68]

Either party can terminate this Agreement at any time simply by ceasing to live with the other party.

2.126 Notice

Either party can terminate this Agreement by giving the other party at least (2) weeks' notice in writing.

---

[68] There is no fixed or uniform approach as to what constitutes a termination of cohabitation. For a more comprehensive list of terminating events, see **2.127** below.

2.127   Terminating events

Without prejudice to any provisions of this Agreement that come into force on or remain in force after its termination, this Agreement will terminate when the earliest of these events occurs:

(1)   The death of a party.

(2)   The marriage of the parties to each other.[69]

(3)   The parties mutually agree on its termination and sign a written instrument cancelling this Agreement.[70]

(4)   The expiration of a period of (4) weeks beginning on the date when one party gives to the other written notice of his or her wish to terminate this Agreement.

(5)   If the parties have lived apart for a continuous period of at least (4) weeks and one party gives to the other written notice that this Agreement is terminated.

(6)   If the Court grants an injunction under Part IV of the Family Law Act 1996 or the Protection from Harassment Act 1997 or any statutory modification or re-enactment of either and (either party) [OR] (the party who applies for the injunction) gives to the other party written notice that this Agreement is terminated.

(7)   If one party excludes the other from (the property) without reasonable cause and the excluded party gives written notice to the excluding party that this Agreement is terminated.

(8)   The Court or an Arbitrator orders that this Agreement is terminated.

Termination consequences

2.128   General introductory clause

If this Agreement is terminated for any reason other than the death of a party or the marriage of the parties to each other, the provisions of Schedule (*number*) will apply.

2.129   Bank and building society accounts

(If this Agreement is terminated (for any reason other than the death of a party or the marriage of the parties to each other)) the parties will:

(1)   immediately close all bank accounts and building society accounts held in their joint names;

(2)   immediately destroy all plastic or other cards relating to the joint account(s) and return the pieces to the bank or building society;

(3)   immediately destroy all unused cheques;

---

[69]   For a clause providing that the contract will continue on marriage, see **2.87** above; for the consequences of termination on marriage, see **2.139** below.

[70]   See **2.25** above.

(4) immediately take whatever steps are necessary to ensure that their earnings and other income are no longer credited to any joint account;

(5) on receiving the closing statements, divide the balances on all joint accounts equally between themselves;

(6) continue to be jointly and severally liable for the repayment of all overdrafts, debts and interest payable in respect of the joint account(s);

(7) punctually pay their respective share of all overdrafts, debts and interest, and each party indemnifies the other from and against all actions, demands, proceedings and losses arising from his or her failure to do so.

2.130   Credit and charge cards

(If this Agreement is terminated (for any reason other than the death of a party or the marriage of the parties to each other)) the parties will:

(1) immediately close all joint credit and charge card accounts;

(2) immediately close all credit and charge card accounts in the name of one party alone where the other party is an additional cardholder or authorised user;

(3) immediately destroy all plastic or other cards relating to such accounts and return the destroyed cards to the creditor;

(4) when they receive the closing statements, allocate the debts between themselves on the basis of who will retain each specific item obtained on credit or, where an item obtained on credit has been consumed, who consumed it or who ordered it;

(5) punctually pay their respective share of all debts and interest payable on such accounts, and each party indemnifies against any consequences of his or her failure to do so.

2.131   The dwelling: option to 'buy out' the other's share

(If the Agreement is terminated (for any reason other than the death of a party or the marriage of the parties to each other)):

(1) (*Name 1*) will have the option to purchase (*name 2's*) share of (*address*) or failing which any other principal residence jointly owned by the parties ('the property').

(2) The property will be valued by the parties themselves at such figures as they agree.

(3) If the parties are unable to agree a valuation of the property, it will be formally valued by a professionally qualified valuer, and if more than one formal valuation is obtained the average of the valuations will prevail.

(4) The property will be valued on the basis that:
   (a) it is being sold with vacant possession at arm's length on the open market;
   (b) all fixtures, fittings, carpets and curtains which do not belong to (*name 2*) alone are included in the sale;

(c)   there is no discount for joint ownership.

(5)   The price that (*name 2*) will receive for (his)/(her) estate and interest in the property will be (his)/(her) share of the value of the property less (his)/(her) share of all mortgages and charges to which the property is subject.

(6)   In the absence of any alternative agreement between them, the parties will observe the following time limits:

(a)   within (2) weeks of the termination of this Agreement the property will be valued and a redemption statement will be obtained in respect of every mortgage and charge to which the property is subject;

(b)   within (4) weeks of the termination of this Agreement (*name 1*) will give (*name 2*) written notice of (his)/(her) intention to exercise this option;

(c)   within (8) weeks of the termination of this Agreement (*name 1*) will complete (his)/(her) purchase of (*name 2's*) share.

(7)   If (*name 1*) is unable or unwilling to exercise this option within (4) weeks of the termination of this Agreement or within such other time limit as (*name 2*) has agreed:

(a)   (his)/(her) option to purchase (*name 2's*) share will lapse;

(b)   (*name 2*) will have the option to purchase (*name 1's*) share of the property on the same terms mutatis mutandis and the following time-limits will apply in the absence of any alternative agreement between the parties;

(c)   within (2) weeks of the date on which (*name 1's*) option lapsed (*name 2*) will give (*name 1*) written notice of (his)/(her) intention to exercise this option;

(d)   within (4) weeks of the date on which (*name 1's*) option lapsed (*name 2*) will complete the purchase of (*name 1's*) share.

2.132   *Separate property*

(If this Agreement is terminated (for any reason other than the death of a party or the marriage of the parties to each other)) each party will keep his or her separate property (and each party will remain personally liable for his or her separate debts.)

2.133   *Jointly owned goods and chattels*[71]

If this Agreement is terminated (for any reason other than the death of a party or the marriage of the parties to each other) all goods and chattels which the parties jointly own will be divided between them as they agree, and where they fail to agree on division those goods and chattels will be sold and the proceeds of sale will be divided equally between them.

---

[71]   For more comprehensive provisions relating to the division of chattels, see **2.150** below.

2.134 Support

(If this Agreement is terminated (for any reason other than the death of a party or the marriage of the parties to each other)) neither party will be under any continuing obligation to support or maintain the other party.

2.135 Lump sum payment

(If this Agreement is terminated (for any reason other than the death of a party or the marriage of the parties to each other)) within (4) weeks of the termination of this Agreement (*name 1*) will pay to (*name 2*) the sum of £ to enable (him)/(her) (to establish a separate household) [OR] (in full and final settlement of any possible claim for support that may have arisen while the parties were living together.)

2.136 Miscellaneous cancellations

(If this Agreement is terminated (for any reason other than the death of a party or the marriage of the parties to each other)) either party may:

(1) cancel any nomination that names the other party as a potential recipient of any pension or other benefits arising on the nominator's death;

(2) cancel any nomination that names the other party as the recipient of the benefits payable under any policy of insurance on the nominator's life;

(3) revoke any (enduring) power of attorney which appoints the other party to be his or her attorney;

(4) disclaim any appointment as the other party's attorney by giving the other party written notice of such disclaimer.

2.137 Children

(If this Agreement is terminated (for any reason other than the death of a party or the marriage of the parties to each other)) subject always to the ascertainable wishes and feelings of any child concerned considered in the light of his or her age and understanding:

(1) the children of the parties' relationship ('the children') will live with (*name 2*);

(2) the children can have contact with (*name 1*) and (his)/(her) family;

(3) both parties will maintain the children according to their respective abilities to pay;

(4) neither party will cause any of the children to be known by a new surname without the written consent of the other party or the leave of the court.

2.138   The other's child(ren)[72]

If this Agreement is terminated (for any reason other than the death of a party or the marriage of the parties to each other) neither party will be under any continuing obligation to support or maintain the other party's child or children.

2.139   Termination of agreement on marriage: consequences[73]

If this Agreement is terminated on the marriage of the parties to each other:

(1)   the separate property and debts of each party will continue to be his or her separate property and debts;

(2)   any property that is jointly owned by the parties will continue to be jointly owned by them in the proportions or shares existing at the time of their marriage;

(3)   any debts for which the parties are jointly liable will continue to be their joint liability in the proportions or shares existing at the time of their marriage.

2.140   Transfers between cohabitants

(1)   Either party can at any time transfer his or her own separate property to the other party solely or jointly, conditionally or unconditionally.

(2)   Any such transfer must comply with the legal formalities governing the transfer of property of that nature.

(3)   If the nature of the property is such that no specific legal formalities govern its transfer then for the avoidance of doubt such transfer will be evidenced by an instrument in writing dated and signed by the transferor and transferee.

Variation of agreement

2.141   Clause

This Agreement can only be varied by an instrument in writing executed (as a Deed)[74] by both parties.

2.142   Deed

THIS (DEED OF) VARIATION made on *(date)*

BETWEEN (1) *(name 1)* of *(address)* and (2) *(name 2)* also of *(address)*.

---

[72]   But see CA 1989, Sch 1, para 4(2).

[73]   See footnotes to **2.87**.

[74]   In *Berry v Berry* [1929] 2 KB 316, it was held that a separation agreement which had been made by deed (even though there was no legal requirement that it should be made by deed) could be varied by a subsequent agreement which was not a deed.

WITNESSES as follows.

(1) This (Deed)/(Variation) is supplemental to a Cohabitation Agreement ('the agreement') made between the parties on (*date*).

(2) The parties now cancel and rescind Clause(s) (*number(s)*) of the agreement.

(3) The parties now add to the agreement the Clauses set out in the Schedule.

THE SCHEDULE

(*insert new clauses*)

SIGNED as a Deed by (*name 1*) in the presence of:

SIGNED as a Deed by (*name 2*) in the presence of:

2.143 Waiver of breach

If either party fails to enforce any provision of this Agreement at any time such acquiescence will not constitute a waiver of that provision or of the right at any other time to enforce that provision and all the other provisions of this Agreement.

2.144 Whole agreement

(1) This Agreement contains the whole agreement between the parties and replaces any previous written or oral agreements between them.

(2) The parties confirm that neither of them has entered into this Agreement on the basis of any promises or representations which are not expressly included in this Agreement.

2.145 Wills

Each party is aware of the rights[75] of the survivor if one of them should die, and each party intends to execute a will as soon as practicable.[76]

---

[75] The surviving cohabitant *may* be entitled to:
  (a) property passing by right of survivorship;
  (b) property passing under a statutory or non-statutory nomination;
  (c) claim under the Inheritance (Provision for Family and Dependants) Act 1975, or under the Fatal Accidents Act 1976.
  The surviving cohabitant has no rights on intestacy. See, generally, Chapter 6.

[76] A will made pursuant to a contract to make a will in a particular form can be revoked, although the testator or his estate may be liable for breach of contract (*Schaefer v Schuhmann* [1972] AC 572).

Forms

Cohabitation Agreement

Sharing everything

2.146   Short form

THIS COHABITATION AGREEMENT is made on (*date*)

BETWEEN (1) (*name 1*) and (2) (*name 2*) both of (*address*).

THE PARTIES AGREE:

(1) to combine their incomes for the purpose of living together as a family unit;

(2) to support each other while they are living together;

(3) that if they separate, each party will keep his or her own separate property; and

(4) that if they separate, any property which they jointly own will be divided equally between them.

SIGNED as a Deed by (*name 1*) in the presence of:

SIGNED as a Deed by (*name 2*) in the presence of:

2.147   Longer form

THIS COHABITATION AGREEMENT is made on (*date*)

BETWEEN 'the parties' (1) (*name 1*) of (*address*) ('*name 1*') and (2) (*name 2*) (also) of (*address*) ('*name 2*').

IT IS AGREED that:

1 Recitals

1.1 (*Name 1*) was born on (*date*).

1.2 (Name 1) is a (job description).

1.3 (*Name 1*) has a current net annual income of approximately £   from all sources.

1.4 (*Name 1*) has current net capital resources worth approximately £   .

1.5 (*Name 2*) was born on (*date*).

1.6 (Name 2) is a (job description).

1.7 (*Name 2*) has a current net annual income of approximately £   from all sources.

1.8 (*Name 2*) has current net capital resources worth approximately £   .

1.9 The parties (intend to) live together.

1.10 The purpose of this Agreement is to define and regulate the respective rights and responsibilities of the parties while they are living together and if they separate.

1.11 Each party has received independent legal advice on the provisions and implications of this Agreement.

1.12 Each party has had an opportunity to examine the other party's financial records.

1.13 The parties intend that this Agreement will be legally binding on them.

2 The house

2.1 The parties (intend to) live at (*address*) ('the house').

2.2 The parties (intend to) own the house as beneficial (joint tenants) [*OR*] (tenants in common in equal shares), regardless of the actual contributions made by either party towards its acquisition.

3 Separate property

3.1 The items listed in Schedule 1 belong to (*name 1*) and will continue to be (his)/(her) separate property.

3.2 The items listed in Schedule 2 belong to (*name 2*) and will continue to be (his)/(her) separate property.

4 Gifts

4.1 Nothing in this Agreement regarding the separate property of each party deprives either party of the right to give to or receive from the other party any property and assets by way of gift transfer or legacy.

4.2 Any gift from one party to the other will be presumed to be an absolute gift unless it is expressly given on the condition that it will be returned to the giver on the termination of the parties' relationship.

4.3 Any gift, inheritance or unexpected good fortune received by either party will be and will remain the separate property of that party.

5 Income

The parties will pool their respective incomes from all sources, except for the income received from any assets which are specified as the separate property of one party, and will share equally all accumulations of and property acquired from their pooled incomes, regardless of the actual income earned or received by either party.

6 Support

For as long as parties are living together each party will support the other.

7 Termination

This Agreement will terminate:

7.1   if and when the parties marry each other, although nothing in this Agreement constitutes an agreement by either party to marry the other; or, earlier

7.2   if and when the parties cease to live together.

8 Termination: consequences

If this Agreement terminates because the parties cease to live together:

8.1   neither party will be under any continuing obligation to support the other;

8.2   the trust for sale on which the house is held may be enforced by either party;

8.3   all bank accounts, building society accounts, credit accounts and charge card accounts held in the parties' joint names will immediately be closed and the balances and debts will be divided equally between the parties;

8.4   each party will retain his or her separate property;

8.5   all goods and chattels which are jointly owned by the parties will be divided between them as they agree, and in default of agreement the goods and chattels will be sold and the proceeds of sale will be divided equally between the parties.

9 Dispute resolution

Any difference, disagreement or dispute arising out of or in connection with this Agreement will be referred in the first instance to a Conciliator, without prejudice to the right of either party to apply subsequently to the Court for adjudication.

10 Variation

This Agreement can only be varied by an instrument in writing executed as a Deed by both parties.

11 Whole agreement

This Agreement contains the whole agreement between the parties and neither of them has entered into it on the basis of any promises or representations which are not expressly included in it.

12 Severability

If the Court finds that any provision of this Agreement is illegal, invalid, or otherwise unenforceable, such provision may be severed from this Agreement without affecting any other provisions which will continue to have full force and effect.

SCHEDULE 1

((*Name 1's*) separate property.)

SCHEDULE 2

((*Name 2's*) separate property.)

SIGNED as a Deed by (*name 1*) in the presence of:

SIGNED as a Deed by (*name 2*) in the presence of:

2.148   *Keeping everything separate*

THIS COHABITATION AGREEMENT is made on (*date*)

BETWEEN (1) 'the parties' (1) (*name 1*) of (*address*) (*name 1*) and (2) (*name 2*) (also) of (*address*) (*name 2*)

IT IS AGREED that:

1 Recitals

(Similar to the recitals in **2.147** above.)

2 The house

2.1   The parties own (*address*) ('the house').

2.2   The parties bought the house on (*date*).

2.3   The purchase price of the house was (*price*).

2.4   The incidental costs of purchasing the house amounted to £ .

2.5   The house is mortgaged to (*lender*).

2.6   The mortgage advance was £ .

2.7   (*Name 1*) paid £   towards the purchase price and purchase costs.

2.8   (*Name 1*) will pay   per cent of the mortgage payments.

2.9   (*Name 1*) will pay   per cent of the sale costs.

2.10   (*Name 1*) will receive   per cent of the sale price less   per cent of the amount required to redeem the mortgage and less   per cent of the sale costs.

2.11   (*Name 2*) paid £   towards the purchase price and purchase costs.

2.12   (*Name 2*) will pay   per cent of the mortgage payments.

2.13   (*Name 2*) will pay   per cent of the sale costs.

2.14   (*Name 2*) will receive   per cent of the sale price less   per cent of the amount required to redeem the mortgage and less   per cent of the sale costs.

3 Bank accounts

3.1   Each party will maintain separate bank accounts and building society accounts and the money in each such account will remain the separate property of that party.

3.2   The parties do not intend to open a joint account.

4 Debts

4.1   Each party will remain personally liable for his or her current debts and any future debts incurred in his or her sole name.

4.2   The payment by one party of any part of the other's personal debts will in no way render the payer liable for or to make any further contribution in respect of those debts.

5 Separate property

5.1   The items listed in Schedule 1 belong to (*name 1*) and will continue to be (his)/(her) separate property.

5.2   The items listed in Schedule 2 belong to (*name 2*) and will continue to be (his)/(her) separate property.

5.3   The use by one party of any property belonging to the other party will not give rise to the joint ownership of that property.

5.4   Each party releases, renounces and surrenders all (if any) rights he or she may now or subsequently have to claim any right or title to or share or interest in any property and income which is now or subsequently owned or acquired by the other party alone.

6 Cars

Each party will permit and effect proper insurance to enable the other party to drive his or her car.

7 Gifts

(As in **2.147**, Clause 4 above.)

8 Living expenses

The parties will contribute equally towards their joint living expenses which include, but are not restricted to, payments for water, gas, electricity, telephone, food, drink, cleaning, joint recreation and holidays.

9 Support

9.1 Except for the extent to which each party is liable to contribute towards the mortgage payments and their joint living expenses, neither party is under any obligation to support or maintain the other while they are living together and after they have ceased to live together.

9.2 Each party releases, renounces and surrenders to the other and the other's estate any right which he or she may have as a cohabitee to apply to the Court for an order under section 2 of the Inheritance (Provision for Family and Dependants) Act 1975 or any statutory modification or re-enactment of it.

10 Review

The parties will review the provisions of this Agreement:

10.1 at least once every year; and

10.2 whenever there is a major change in the personal circumstances of either of them.

11 Variation

This Agreement can only be varied by an instrument in writing executed as a Deed by both parties.

12 Termination

This Agreement will terminate:

12.1 if and when the parties marry each other; or, earlier

12.2 if and when the parties cease to live together.

13 Termination consequences

If this Agreement is terminated on the marriage of the parties to each other:

13.1 the separate property and debts of each party will continue to be his or her separate property and debts;

13.2 any property that is jointly owned by the parties will continue to be owned by them in the proportions or shares existing at the time of their marriage;

13.3 any debts for which the parties are jointly liable will continue to be their joint liability in the proportions or shares existing at the time of their marriage.

14 Whole agreement

(As in **2.147**, Clause 11 above.)

15 Severability

(As in **2.147**, Clause 12 above.)

SCHEDULE 1

((*Name 1's*) separate property.)

SCHEDULE 2

((*Name 2's*) separate property.)

SIGNED as a Deed by (*name 1*) in the presence of:

SIGNED as a Deed by (*name 2*) in the presence of:

2.149   *One party supporting the other*

THIS COHABITATION AGREEMENT is made on (*date*)

BETWEEN 'the parties' (1) (*name 1*) of (*address*) ('*name 1*') and (2) (*name 2*) (also) of (*address*) ('*name 2*').

IT IS AGREED that:

1 Recitals

(The same as, or similar to, those in **2.147** above.)

2 Consideration

The promises made in this Agreement by (*name 1*) are made in consideration of:

2.1 (*name 2*) giving up (his)/(her) present (job)/(accommodation) in order to live with (*name 1*); and

2.2 the releases given by (*name 2*).

3 The house

3.1 The parties (intend to) live together at (*address*) ('the house').

3.2 (*Name 1*) owns the house.

3.3 (*Name 2*) releases, renounces and surrenders all (if any) rights (he/she) may have to claim any right or title to or any share or interest in the house and its net proceeds of sale.

4 Living expenses

While the parties are living together (*name 1*) will pay:

4.1 the costs of financing, maintaining and running the house;

4.2 the bills for the utilities;

4.3 the grocery bills;

4.4 for their joint recreation and holidays.

5 Housekeeping allowance

5.1 While they are living together (*name 1*) will pay (*name 2*) a (weekly)/(monthly) allowance of £ .

5.2 The allowance will be adjusted at least once a year in order to bring it in line with the cost of living.

5.3 Any property that (*name 2*) acquires with the allowance and any accumulations of the allowance will belong to (*name 2*) absolutely.

6 Car

6.1 While they are living together (*name 1*) will provide (*name 2*) with the use of a car.

6.2 (*Name 1*) will pay all the expenses of running the car, including vehicle excise duty, insurance, maintenance, repairs, membership of the (AA)/(RAC) and petrol.

6.3 (*Name 1*) will retain the ownership of the car.

6.4 On the termination of this Agreement (*name 2*) will deliver up possession of the car to (*name 1*).

7 Credit

7.1 (*Name 1*) will nominate (*name 2*) to be an additional cardholder on (his)/(her) (*credit company*) account.

7.2 Between themselves (*name 2*) will be responsible for paying for all purchases on that account made solely for (his)/(her) own use, enjoyment and benefit and will be accountable for any interest attributable to those purchases.

8 Separate property

8.1 The items listed in Schedule 1 belong to (*name 1*) and will continue to be (his)/(her) separate property.

8.2 The items listed in Schedule 2 belong to (*name 2*) and will continue to be (his)/(her) separate property.

8.3 The use by one party of any property belonging to the other will not give rise to the joint ownership of that property.

8.4   Each party releases, renounces and surrenders all (if any) rights he or she may now or subsequently have to claim any right or title to or any share or interest in any property and income which now or subsequently belongs to the other party alone.

9 Gifts

9.1   Nothing in this Agreement regarding the separate property of each party deprives either party of the right to give to or receive from the other party any property or assets by way of gift or transfer.

9.2   Any gift from one party to the other will be presumed to be an absolute gift unless it is expressly given on the understanding that it will be returned to the giver on the termination of the parties' relationship.

9.3   Any gift, inheritance or unexpected good fortune received by either party alone will be and will remain the separate property of that party.

10 Estate rights

10.1   (*Name 2*) acknowledges that (*name 1*) is under no obligation to make any financial provision for (him)/(her) or to confer any other benefits on (him)/(her) by Will or otherwise in the event of (his)/(her) death.

10.2   (*Name 1*) has not agreed, promised or represented to (*name 2*) that (he)/(she) will execute a Will or sign any other instrument which will make financial provision for or confer any benefit on (*name 2*) in the event of (his)/(her) death.

10.3   (*Name 2*) releases, renounces and surrenders to (*name 1*) and (his)/(her) estate any right which (he)/(she) may have as a cohabitee to apply to the Court for an order under section 2 of the Inheritance (Provision for Family and Dependants) Act 1975 or any statutory modification or re-enactment of it.

10.4   Nothing in this Agreement constitutes a renunciation of the right of (*name 2*) (if entitled) to obtain a grant of representation to (*name 1's*) estate or a disclaimer by (*name 2*) of any benefits conferred on (him)/(her) by (*name 1*) in (his)/(her) Will or arising otherwise as a result of (his)/(her) death.

11 Confidentiality

(*Name 2*) promises never to use, disclose or divulge to the detriment or disadvantage of (*name 1*) any confidential information about (his)/(her) private life, family life or business affairs which may have come to (his)/(her) knowledge or attention during the course of their relationship.

12 Termination

This Agreement will terminate when the parties cease to live together.

13 Termination: rights and obligations of (*name 1*)

When this Agreement terminates (*name 1*) will:

13.1 be entitled to stop paying the (weekly)/(monthly) allowance to (*name 2*);

13.2 pay (*name 2*) a lump sum of £   to assist (him)/(her) to establish a separate household;

13.3 pay (*name 2*) an additional lump sum of £   in respect of every complete year which has elapsed between the date of this Agreement and the date on which it terminates;

13.4 be entitled to deduct from these lump sum payments any unpaid balance on the (credit card) account which represents purchases made by (*name 2*) for (his)/(her) sole use, enjoyment or benefit together with any interest attributable to that unpaid balance;

13.5 make the above payments to (*name 2*) within a period of (4) weeks from the latest of the following dates, namely the date on which:
  (a) this Agreement terminates;
  (b) (*name 2*) ceases to live in the house;
  (c) (*name 2*) removes all (his)/(her) belongings from the house;
  (d) (*name 2*) delivers up possession of the car to (him)/(her);
  (e) (*name 2*) returns the credit card to (him)/(her).

14 Termination: rights and obligations of (*name 2*)

When this Agreement terminates (*name 2*) will:

14.1 leave the house;

14.2 remove all (his)/(her) belongings from the house;

14.3 deliver up possession of the car to (*name 1*);

14.4 return the credit card to (*name 1*);

14.5 be entitled to receive the payments less deductions mentioned in the preceding clause.

15 Separation

After this Agreement has terminated neither party will:

15.1 without invitation enter or occupy any premises that are owned or occupied by the other party;

15.2 annoy, embarrass, interfere with or molest the other party and his or her relatives, friends, acquaintances, business colleagues and contacts.

16 Remedies

If either party breaches or fails to comply with any promise or provision contained in this Agreement the other may be entitled to apply to the Court for an order awarding (inter alia):

16.1 damages;

16.2   specific performance;

16.3   an injunction;

16.4   costs.

17 Variation

This Agreement can only be varied by an instrument in writing executed as a deed by both parties.

18 Whole agreement

This Agreement contains the whole agreement between the parties and neither of them has entered into it on the basis of any promises or representations which are not expressly included in it.

19 Proper law

The Agreement will be governed and interpreted in accordance with the law of England and Wales.

20 Severability

If the Court finds that any provision of this Agreement is illegal, invalid or otherwise unenforceable, such provision may be severed from this Agreement without affecting any other provisions which will continue to have full force and effect.

SCHEDULE 1

((*Name 1's*) separate property.)

SCHEDULE 2

((*Name 2's*) separate property.)

SIGNED as a Deed by (*name 1*) in the presence of:

SIGNED as a Deed by (*name 2*) in the presence of:

2.150   *Agreement relating to personal chattels acquired jointly by cohabitants*[77]

THIS AGREEMENT is made on (*date*)

BETWEEN 'the parties' (1) (*name 1*) of (*address*) ('*name 1*') and (2) (*name 2*)

---

[77]   This Agreement could be adapted to provide for several joint purchases. It could also be incorporated into a 'cohabitation contract' proper.

(also) of (*address*) ('*name 2*').

THE PARTIES AGREE as follows:

(1)   They bought a (*description of item*) ('*the item*')[78] at/from (shop; seller; auctioneer, etc) on (*date*) for (*price*).

(2)   (*Name 1*) contributed £   and (*name 2*) contributed £   towards the purchase price.

(3)   The purpose of this Agreement is to establish what will happen to the (*item*) if one party dies or if the parties separate.

(4)   If the parties are living together and one of them dies the (*item*) will belong to the survivor absolutely.[79]

(5)   If the parties separate and neither of them wishes to keep the (*item*):
   (a)   it will be sold; and
   (b)   its net proceeds of sale will be divided between the parties (equally) [OR] (in the proportions that each of them contributed towards the purchase price).

(6)   If the parties separate and only one of them wishes to keep the (*item*):
   (a)   it will be valued; and
   (b)   the party who wishes to keep it will pay the other party (one half of its value) [OR] (the proportion of its value that the other party contributed towards the purchase price).

(7)   If the parties separate and both of them wish to keep the (*item*) and neither of them is willing to relinquish it to the other:
   (a)   the (*item*) will be valued;
   (b)   the parties will (toss a coin) [OR] (draw lots) [OR] (throw a dice);[80]
   (c)   the winner will keep the (*item*); and
   (d)   the winner will pay the loser (one half of its value) [OR] (the proportion of its value that the loser contributed towards the purchase price).

(8)   For the purposes of Clauses 6 and 7 of this Agreement:
   (a)   the (*item*) will be valued informally by the parties themselves at such sum they agree;
   (b)   in default of agreement between the parties the (*item*) will be valued formally by one or more persons whom the parties reasonably believe to be qualified to value it;
   (c)   if more than one formal valuation is obtained the average of the valuations will prevail;
   (d)   the cost of a formal valuation which is requested jointly by the parties will be paid by the parties in equal shares and the cost of obtaining any other formal valuation will be paid by the party instructing the valuer.

---

[78]   Describe the item fully and accurately, and then give it a brief but appropriate definition: eg 'the cat'; 'the DVD'; 'the Rembrandt'.

[79]   Subject to the de minimis rules, the deceased's share may have to be brought into account for inheritance tax purposes.

[80]   For King Solomon's solution, see 1 Kings 3, 24 and 25.

(9) Any difference, disagreement or dispute that arises out of or in connection with this Agreement will be referred in the first instance to (*name*), who will act as a mediator between the parties, without prejudice to the right of either party to apply subsequently to the Court for adjudication.[81]

(10) Without prejudice to (his)/(her) role as mediator (*name*) may, at the parties' request, supervise and have conduct of any of the procedures set out in this Agreement.

(11) (Other clauses).[82]

SIGNED as a Deed by (*name 1*) in the presence of:

SIGNED as a Deed by (*name 2*) in the presence of:

2.151　*Agreement setting up a joint account to pay housing costs, etc*

THIS AGREEMENT is made on (*date*)

BETWEEN 'the parties' (1) (*name 1*) of (*address*) ('*name 1*') and (2) (*name 2*) (also) of (*address*) ('*name 2*').

IT IS AGREED that:

(1) The parties (intend to) live together at (*address*) ('the property').

(2) The parties (intend to) own the property as beneficial tenants in common (in equal shares) [*OR*] (as to　　　per cent of the net proceeds of sale for (*name 1*) and　　　per cent for (*name 2*)).

(3) On the (first) day of each month (*name 1*) will pay the sum of £　　　by standing order from (his)/(her) separate bank account.

(4) On the (first) day of each month (*name 2*) will pay the sum of £　　　by standing order from (his)/(her) separate bank account.

(5) The monthly sums paid by each party will be credited to the account held in their joint names at (*name and branch of bank or building society*) ('the joint account').

(6) The monthly sums payable by each party will be revised in (September) each year and each revision will take into account:
  (a) any variation in the cost of living in the property during the preceding 12 months; and
  (b) any foreseeable variation in the cost of living in the property during the next 12 months.

(7) The revised monthly sums will become payable on the (1 October) each year and before that date each party will instruct his or her bank to amend the standing order accordingly.

---

[81] See Law of Property Act 1925, s 188(1).

[82] Other clauses might include: provisions relating to payment; further assurance to effect the transfer; assumption of responsibility for future payments where the item is being acquired on HP, etc; indemnity for the other party.

(8) The following payments will be made from the joint account:
   (a) the mortgage payments;
   (b) the mortgage endowment policy premiums;
   (c) buildings and contents insurance;
   (d) water services charges;
   (e) gas bills;
   (f) electricity bills;
   (g) telephone bills;
   (h) Council Tax;
   (i) repairs and improvements to the property;
   (j) any other payments that the parties jointly authorise.

(9) Either party can terminate this Agreement by giving the other party not less than (one month's) notice in writing.

(10) When one party gives the other written notice of his or her intention to terminate this Agreement, the parties will immediately:
   (a) close the joint account;
   (b) cut into pieces all plastic and other cards relating to the joint account and return the pieces to the bank (or building society);
   (c) destroy all unused cheques on the joint account;
   (d) cancel the standing orders relating to their respective monthly sums.

(11) When the joint account has been closed the parties will:
   (a) divide the balance on it between themselves (equally) [*OR*] (in the proportions that their respective monthly sums bear to each other);
   (b) continue to be jointly and severally liable for any overdraft, debt, interest and bank charges incurred on the joint account;
   (c) punctually pay their respective shares of any such overdraft, debt, interest and bank charges, and each party indemnifies the other against the consequences of the indemnifying party's failure to do so.

SIGNED as a Deed by (*name 1*) in the presence of:

SIGNED as a Deed by (*name 2*) in the presence of:

CHAPTER 3

TAXATION OF UNMARRIED COUPLES

LAW AND PRACTICE

3.1 Introduction

In general, cohabitants are taxed in exactly the same way as single people who do not live together. This contrasts with the treatment of married couples and civil partners where there are specific exemptions and reliefs, particularly for inheritance tax and capital gains tax (all references made to spouses and married couples in this text apply to civil partners as well). In some cases, the exemptions are dependent on the married couple living together. Over the years, and with the exception of a limited relief that will be introduced in April 2015, the income tax advantages of marriage have been whittled away with the result that for the purposes of that tax there are few incentives to couples to marry rather than to cohabit. There are also some tax benefits that apply to those with children.

3.2 Income tax

Both parties to a couple are entitled to a personal allowance for income tax. In the tax year 2014/2015 this amounts to £10,000. This represents the amount that can be earned before any tax is payable. For those who receive income of a higher figure, the personal allowance represents that part of their income on which no tax is payable, although the personal allowance is reduced or removed for incomes over £100,000. As everyone is entitled to a personal allowance, minor children (under the age of 18) can also benefit although there are anti-avoidance provisions to prevent parents channelling income through their children.[1]

3.3 *Married couples*

Married couple's allowance was abolished for most people from 6 April 2000 and was replaced in April 2001 with a new Children's Tax Credit. Therefore, there was a gap of one year when married couples with children received no additional income tax reliefs. Children's Tax Credit was in turn replaced by Child Tax Credit from 6 April 2003.

---

[1] Income Tax (Trading and Other Income) Act 2005, s 629.

In order to provide some recognition of marriage/civil partnership within the income tax system, from 6 April 2015, a spouse or civil partner who is not liable to income tax above the basic rate will be able to transfer up to £1,000 of their personal allowance to their spouse or civil partner provided that the recipient of the transfer is not liable to income tax above the basic rate.

3.4   Elderly married couples

A higher personal allowance applies to those over the age of 65 at the commencement of the tax year. For the tax year 2014/2015 this amounts to £10,500 for those over 65 and £10,660 for those over 75. The allowance is reduced in respect of income over £27,000 on a tapering basis until no higher allowance is given.

The married couples allowance was retained for elderly couples after 6 April 2000, provided that the elder of the couple had reached the age of 65 before that date. It will also apply when a person born before 6 April 1935 gets married or enters a civil partnership after 6 April 2000. The calculation is different for marriages entered into before 5 December 2005, when the allowance is paid to the husband and the calculation is based upon his income. For marriages and civil partnerships after 5 December 2005, the allowance is given to the person with the highest income and the amount is based upon his or her income.

The maximum amount of married couple's allowance is £8,165 and the minimum amount is £3,140 for the 2014/15 tax year. The eligible person receives 10% of the allowance amount – giving a tax saving (based on a full year's eligibility) of at least £314 and up to £816.50. Again, the allowance is reduced in respect of income over £27,000 on a tapering basis.

3.5   Allowances for children

The additional personal allowance aimed at single parents was abolished with effect from 6 April 2000.

3.6   Universal credit, child tax credit and working tax credit

Universal credit (UC) is replacing a number of benefits including child tax credit (CTC) and working tax credit (WTC). It is being phased in geographically and is expected to be rolled out completely by 2017.

There are no limits to the number of hours a week that a person can work whilst receiving UC. The payment will reduce gradually as the claimant earns more. The new system is designed to encourage people to seek work, to reduce dependency on benefits and to simplify the benefits system. UC is paid monthly to each eligible household and the system is managed online.

UC is subject to the benefit cap (although those eligible for WTC are excluded from the cap) which is designed to make it impossible for anyone to receive more on benefits than the average weekly wage after tax and national insurance. The cap is £500 for couples with or without children.

CTC is payable to single parents and couples, whether married or unmarried, who have responsibility for one or more children under 16 or a child over 16 but under 20 and in full-time secondary education. There is a family element of £545 per annum for all who qualify. There is also a child element for each eligible child of £2,780 with enhancements for disabled and severely disabled children.[2]

WTC is also available to cohabiting couples, whether married or in a civil partnership or not, who have dependent children, a mental or physical disability or where one of the couple is aged over 25. It is necessary to work a certain number of hours per week to qualify (30 hours for those aged 25 to 59 with no children and without a disability, 16 or 24 hours for most other people). Where available, WTC provides a 'basic' amount, a lone parent or couple element, an element for those in 30 hours' work or more, a disabled worker element, a severe disability element and, for single parents and some couples, a childcare element of 70 per cent of eligible childcare costs up to prescribed maximums.

Awards are calculated by adding together all the relevant elements of a family's CTC or WTC or both. Those on income support, income-based jobseeker's allowance, income-related employment and support allowance, or pension credit then receive this amount with no further means-test. Those not on any of these four benefits however have their total tax credits reduced by 41 per cent of their income above a specified income threshold.

Claims are usually based on the income for the preceding tax year. The calculation is complex and changed in April 2012 but entitlement is withdrawn at the rate of 41 per cent of income above £6,420 in cases that include any WTC elements (or less commonly, 41 per cent income above £16,105 in cases involving only CTC and *no* WTC elements).

3.7 Capital gains tax

Although married couples and civil partners are treated as separate individuals in relation to assessment for capital gains tax, special rules apply to transfers between spouses living together[3] which are beneficial and are unavailable to unmarried couples. Where a husband and wife are living together during any year of assessment, any disposals between them, except for stock in trade, are on the basis of a no gain, no loss situation. This effectively means that the receiving spouse takes the asset at the transferring spouse's acquisition date.

---

[2]   At 2015-2016 rates
[3]   Taxation of Chargeable Gains Act 1992 (TCGA 1992), s 58.

Despite the rules about transfers between spouses, each spouse has an annual exemption of £11,000 (for 2014/2015) of gains like any unmarried couple.

Disposals between unmarried couples or married couples who are not living together give rise to tax on any capital gains. Tax is payable at the top rate applicable to the individual making the disposal by adding the taxable gain to their income. For basic rate taxpayers the rate is 18% and for higher rate taxpayers the rate is 28%. Disposals between husband and wife who are not living together are most likely to apply on the occasion of splitting assets between them on separation or divorce and they face an additional disadvantage which an unmarried couple would not be affected by, namely that they are treated as 'connected persons' meaning that any disposal between them is treated as a transaction otherwise than by way of a bargain at arm's length. Such a disposal is deemed to be for a consideration equal to the market value of the asset and in particular any losses can only be set off against gains on other disposals to the same person and not other gains generally.

Although disposals between an unmarried couple would also be treated as being made at market value if not at arm's length, there is no automatic presumption that the transfer is not at arm's length and losses can be set against any gains.

The most common transfers between couples, whether married or not, are either those on separation or divorce or to take advantage of other tax benefits. It is common for spouses to transfer investments between themselves so that a non-working or lower earning spouse can take advantage of lower rates of tax on investment income. Likewise, a spouse may transfer assets as part of an inheritance tax planning exercise. If the transfer is of chattels, there is an exemption where the value of the consideration for each chattel does not exceed £6,000, the level that was fixed in 1989/90.[4] Special rules apply to chattels which form part of a set.

3.8   Private residence relief

Probably the most important capital gains tax relief available to couples, whether married or unmarried, is the relief available on the disposal of a private residence.[5] The exemption applies on the disposal of a dwelling-house or part of a dwelling-house or an interest in it. It must have been the person's only or main residence at any time during the period of ownership. Where the property has been the only or main residence during the whole period of ownership, the exemption applies to the whole of the gain. There is also an overlap relief, so that the whole of the gain is still exempt even if the property has not been the only or main residence during the last 18 months of ownership (prior to 5 April 2014 the final 36 months of ownership were included). If the property does not qualify for the whole of the period other than the last 18 months, the proportion of the gain taxable is calculated by dividing the gain by the fraction

---

4   TCGA 1992, s 262.
5   TCGA 1992, ss 222–224.

of the period when the property was the only or main residence over the whole period of ownership. If when the land or house is bought, either a house is built on it or alterations are required to an existing house, a delay of 12 months is permitted in taking up residence or two years where there are good reasons outside the individual's control.[6]

The rules are relatively straightforward where only one property is involved. Where there are two properties, an unmarried couple can be at an advantage in that for a husband and wife living together there can be only one main residence.[7] Therefore, they cannot claim that one house is the husband's main residence and another is the wife's. However, this option may be available to an unmarried couple if one property is owned by one and the second by the other. Although the question of which of two or more properties is a person's only or main residence is decided by the Inspector of Taxes making a determination, a taxpayer can serve a notice concluding the question within two years of the start of the period where there is ownership of two or more properties. Thus, it would be open to an unmarried couple who had two residences to qualify for two private residence exemptions, provided that each was occupied sufficiently to qualify as a residence.

Where an unmarried couple jointly own a property, they are treated as owning an undivided share in the whole provided that they have unrestricted access to the whole. This means that they can both claim private residence relief on their own share.

The private residence exemption applies to the dwelling house and land for the occupation and enjoyment with the residence as its garden or grounds up to 0.5 hectares. Where the garden and grounds exceed 0.5 hectares, a larger area may be allowed where it is required for the reasonable enjoyment of the dwelling house as a residence, having regard to the size and character of the dwelling house. A number of cases have also come before the courts where relief has been sought for part of a property occupied by domestic staff.

Periods of absence are also allowed subject to detailed rules and in particular a general period of up to three years.[8]

Inheritance tax

3.9 Introduction

In terms of the tax treatment of married as opposed to unmarried couples, inheritance tax is by far the most beneficial to married couples. It is primarily a tax payable on death, although certain transfers of value made during lifetime are either taxable at the time or on a subsequent death.

---

6   Extra-statutory concession D49.
7   TCGA 1992, s 222(6).
8   TCGA 1992, s 223(3).

Transfers between spouses are exempt whether during lifetime or on death provided that both spouses are domiciled in the United Kingdom. From 5 April 2013, if the transferor spouse is UK domiciled but the transferee spouse is not, the exemption only applies to transfers up to the prevailing nil rate band for inheritance tax purposes (£325,000 in 2014/15). Before 5 April 2013, the exemption only applied to transfers up to £55,000.

In *Holland v IRC*[9] the Special Commissioners rejected arguments that the spouse exemption should apply where a couple had lived together as husband and wife but unmarried for 31 years. Arguments under the Human Rights Act were also rejected.

In *Burden v United Kingdom*[10] the European Court of Human Rights rejected an application from two unmarried sisters living together that the liability to pay inheritance tax on the death of the first to die was in breach of the European Convention of Human Rights because it would not be faced by the survivor of a marriage or civil partnership.

In contrast, any transfers of value between an unmarried couple could end up being taxable. In broad terms, all transfers on death are liable to inheritance tax together with any potentially exempt transfers made within seven years prior to the death. Certain lifetime transfers, such as those to relevant property trusts, are also taxable during lifetime.

The rate of tax is 40 per cent on death on the amount of all transfers above the nil-rate band of £325,000 for the tax year 2014/15. The rate on taxable lifetime transfers is 20 per cent, but this rate increases to 40 per cent if the transferor dies within seven years (with taper relief if the transferor lives at least three years but less than seven).[11]

Unmarried couples are at a further disadvantage since 9 October 2007, from which date transferable nil-rate bands were introduced for spouses and civil partners. Where the survivor of spouses or civil partners dies after that date and on the death of the first to die, their nil-rate band had not been fully used, the unused proportion can be carried forward and used on the death of the survivor. The proportion unused is calculated by reference to the nil-rate band in force on the first death but then applied to the nil-rate band in force at the second death. Thus if the first spouse died in 2002/03 when the nil-rate band was £250,000, and left legacies of £50,000 which were not exempt, four fifths of the nil-rate band would be unused. If the survivor dies in 2014/15 when the nil-rate is £325,000, £260,000 transferable nil-rate band can be claimed in addition to the survivor's own nil-rate band of £325,000.[12]

---

[9]   [2003] ST1 62.
[10]   [2007] STC 252.
[11]   IHTA 1984, s 7(4).
[12]   Finance Act 2008, s 10 and Sch 4.

3.10   Lifetime gifts

The main scope for avoiding inheritance tax between persons who are not married lies in the use of lifetime gifts. As explained above, no inheritance tax is payable on a gift made more than seven years before the death of the donor. This is known as a 'potentially exempt transfer'. To qualify, however, there must be no reservation of benefit by the donor. This means that if:

'(a)   possession and enjoyment of the property is not bona fide assumed by the donee at or before the beginning of the relevant period; or

(b)   at any time in the relevant period the property is not enjoyed to the entire exclusion of the donor and of any benefit to him by contract or otherwise'

the gift will not be potentially exempt and the seven-year period will not start to run until those conditions are satisfied.[13]

3.11   Gifts of residence

The most common area where the gift with reservation provisions apply is that of gifts of houses and shares in houses. In general, if a person gives away a house or a share in a house but remains living in it, there is a reservation of benefit and the gift is ineffective for inheritance tax purposes. For example, a couple might start living together in the house owned by one of them. If the owner then wished to give a half-share in the house to his partner and to remain living there, at first sight this would constitute a reservation of benefit.

In a letter dated 18 May 1997, the Inland Revenue confirmed that the estate duty practice on the treatment of gifts involving a share in a house where the gifted property is occupied by all the joint owners including the donor will continue to apply:

'The donor's retention of a share in the property will not of itself amount to a reservation. If, and for so long as, all the joint owners remain in occupation, the donor's occupation will not be treated as a reservation provided the gift is itself unconditional and there is no collateral benefit to the donor. The payment by the donee of the donor's share of the running costs, for example, might be such a benefit. An arrangement will not necessarily be jeopardised merely because it involves a gift of an unequal share in a house.'

On the basis of this interpretation, a gift by one of an unmarried couple to the other of an undivided share in a house would not be a gift with a reservation provided that both continued to occupy the property and the donor continued to pay his fair share of the running costs.

This principle was given statutory force by the Finance Act 1999.[14]

---

[13]   Finance Act 1986, s 102.
[14]   Finance Act 1986 (FA 1986), s 102B.

In Finance Act 2004, the Government introduced legislation to counteract schemes to avoid the gift with reservation provisions by introducing an income tax charge on the use of pre-owned assets such as land and chattels from 6 April 2005. There is an exemption in the legislation for transfers between spouses and former spouses by court order.[15] The pre-owned assets charge does not catch the use of assets where the transfer is still caught by the gift with reservation provisions and is therefore still treated as part of the transferor's estate for inheritance tax purposes. A specific exemption from the pre-owned assets charge is also given to arrangements that are exempt under the shared occupation provisions described in this section.[16] Great care must be taken when there is a transfer of value of land or chattels between unmarried couples and also where there is an element of gift between a couple on the purchase of a property.

3.12 Gifts not intended to confer benefit

A disposition that is not intended to confer any gratuitous benefit is not a transfer of value and so is not liable to inheritance tax. In establishing this principle, an unmarried couple are at an advantage in that they are not connected persons and so only have to show that the transfer was made in a transaction at arm's length. A married couple (being connected persons) would also have to establish that the transfer was such as might be expected to be made at arm's length between persons who were not connected. In other words, an objective test is substituted for a subjective test.

3.13 Gifts of other property

The gift with reservation provisions cause less of a problem with money and investments provided that the donee has the benefit of the income from the asset given. Therefore, there is scope for an unmarried couple to maximise income tax reliefs by the transfer of assets to the member of the couple with no income, or with a lower income. The pre-owned assets charge does apply to cash gifts and assets derived from them, such gifts not being caught by the reservation of benefit provisions.

3.14 Business and agricultural reliefs

Generous reliefs of up to 100 per cent are available on transfers of business and agricultural property. As transfers between spouses are exempt, most tax planning involving these assets concentrates on maximising the reliefs by transfers to children or other beneficiaries. However, married couples do benefit from rules concerning successive ownership. To qualify for business property relief, there is a minimum period of ownership of two years.[17] Where business property is transferred, the transferee has to hold the property for two years

---

[15]   Finance Act 2004, Sch 15, para 10(1)(b).
[16]   Finance Act 2004, Sch 15, para 11(5).
[17]   IHTA 1984, s 106.

before qualifying and so is vulnerable to tax in the event of death during that period. However, where one spouse becomes entitled to business property on the death of the other spouse, the second spouse is attributed with the period of ownership of the first spouse and so in most cases will immediately be entitled on the death of the first spouse. In the case of the unmarried couple, however, the survivor inheriting on the death of a partner will have to wait two years before qualifying for relief on the asset inherited. Similar rules apply to agricultural property relief[18] but the problem can be greater in the case of qualification by ownership rather than occupation where the qualifying period is seven years rather than two years.

3.15 *Inheritance tax on death*

For the unmarried couple, careful planning is required to avoid inheritance tax both on property passing between the couple and where there are children, on property subsequently passing to them. If the estate of the first to die exceeds £325,000, inheritance tax would be payable on the balance passing to the survivor and, on the death of the survivor, inheritance tax would be payable on what was left of the combined estates of the couple over and above the nil-rate band level.

Whereas a married couple can utilise their transferable nil-rate bands to pass property to their children and thereby pay no inheritance tax on £650,000 (for the tax year 2014/15), an unmarried couple can only achieve this by both leaving an amount equal to the nil-rate band direct to their children. This may leave the survivor of the couple with insufficient assets, unless he or she is wealthy in his or her own right.

It makes sense in pure taxation terms for a stable unmarried couple to try to equalise their estates between them to mitigate inheritance tax, although in terms of splitting up the couple's assets on a breakdown of the relationship such a strategy could be disastrous for the richer of the two who has passed assets to the partner.

Tax planning is also essential in the common circumstance where a couple come together who have both been in previous relationships and each have children from those relationships. Both are likely to want to ensure that their own children eventually receive their parent's capital whilst ensuring that during the lifetime of the survivor, he or she is adequately provided for. Wills are vital for a couple in this situation.

Where the couple are married this situation is commonly catered for by each leaving the survivor a life interest in all or part of his or her estate with the capital going to his or her own children on the death or remarriage of the other spouse. Here there would be no inheritance tax on the first death, but on the second death the capital value of the life interest fund would be aggregable with

---

[18] IHTA 1984, s 120.

the estate of the survivor provided it was an immediate post death interest and inheritance tax would be payable on the combined total.

In the case of the unmarried couple in the same situation, inheritance tax would be payable on the first death as well.[19]

Until the introduction of transferable nil-rate bands, a well-known tax planning device for married couples used to be the nil-rate band discretionary trust set up by will. On the death of the first spouse, the amount of the nil-rate band was left on discretionary trusts of which the beneficiaries were the surviving spouse, children and a wider class. The rest of the estate was left to the surviving spouse. No inheritance tax was payable on the first death because the taxable part was covered by the nil-rate band and the remainder qualified for the spouse exemption. During the lifetime of the survivor, he or she could benefit from the income from the discretionary trust with access to the capital if needed. Unlike a life or absolute interest, however, on the second death the amount of the discretionary trust is not aggregated with the survivor's estate and can be distributed to the children or others with little or no inheritance tax being payable. Holdover relief is also available for capital gains tax purposes.

A similar solution may also save inheritance tax for an unmarried couple. If each of the couple leave the whole of their estate on discretionary trusts with the other as a potential beneficiary,[20] inheritance tax will be payable on the first death on any balance over the nil-rate band and this will establish the rate applicable to distributions from that discretionary trust for at least the first 10 years of its existence. On the death of the second of the couple, the estate of the first held on discretionary trust will not be aggregable with the estate of the second and the overall rate of tax may be lower. *See Example.*

The 'trust rate' of tax on income and gains within relevant property trusts is not favourable and this is clearly a factor that must be taken into account. It is possible to convert the discretionary trust into a life interest trust provided this is done more than two years after the death and this would have the effect of lowering the tax payable on income and capital gains to the survivor's marginal rate. If it is done within the two year period after death then the interest would be treated as an immediate post-death interest under the reading back provision in Inheritance Tax Act 1984, s 144 and aggregated with the survivor's free estate on their death.

Example

Unmarried couple A and B:

A has estate of £650,000;

B has estate of £450,000.

---

[19]   Precedents for life interests under wills are included at **6.132** and **6.133**.
[20]   Precedent at **6.136**.

A dies first leaving life interest to B.

On death of A, inheritance tax (IHT) is £130,000.

On death of B, the IHT is payable on combined estates of £450,000 plus £650,000 (less IHT on first death £130,000) = £970,000 and amounts to £258,000.

Total IHT (£130,000 + £258,000) = £388,000.

If, instead, A left whole of estate on discretionary trusts:

On death of A, IHT £130,000 as before.

On death of B, tax on B's estate would be £50,000. The tax on distribution of discretionary trust of £520,000 within 10 years would be at a maximum rate of 3.00 per cent amounting to £15,600, a total of £65,600.

Total IHT (£130,000 + £65,600) = £195,600, a saving of £192,400.

In contrast, on the same figures, the IHT on a married couple still using a nil-rate band discretionary trust would be £180,000.

3.16   Stamp duty land tax

Stamp duty land tax replaced stamp duty on transactions involving land after 1 December 2003. Stamp duty land tax is a tax on transactions. An unmarried couple buying a house pay exactly the same stamp duty land tax as a married couple. Likewise, gifts between unmarried couples are free of stamp duty land tax as transactions for no chargeable consideration in just the same way as gifts between spouses.

The only instance where married couples have an advantage for stamp duty land tax purposes is where property is transferred from one party of a marriage to another in pursuance of an order of a court made on the grant of a decree of divorce, nullity of marriage or judicial separation either on the occasion of the order or in connection with it. The exemption also applies to orders made under ss 22A, 23A or 24A of the MCA 1973 and to transfers made at any time in pursuance of an agreement made by the parties to a marriage in contemplation of the dissolution or annulment of the marriage or the judicial separation or making of a separation order.[21] This replicates the similar exemption for stamp duty.

As with stamp duty, there can be a charge to stamp duty land tax where there is an assumption of debt on a transfer of land. Thus, if one of an unmarried

---

[21]   FA 2003, Sch 3, para 3.

couple transfers a share in a house to the other subject to a mortgage, stamp duty land tax will be payable on the amount of the debt assumed by the transferee.[22]

---

[22] FA 2003, Sch 4, para 8.

CHAPTER 4

PERSONAL PROTECTION

PART A   LAW AND PRACTICE
SECTION 1   FAMILY LAW ACT 1996, PART IV

4.1   Introduction

The Family Law Act 1996 (FLA 1996), Part IV governs applications for personal protection in the Family Court. This legislation was the outcome of the recommendations in The Law Commission's Report *Domestic Violence and Occupation of the Family Home*, published in 1992 (Law Com No 207). The Law Commission was asked to produce a report as a response to the growing recognition of domestic abuse as a huge social problem. It was evident that the earlier legislation was inadequate and reform was needed. Although FLA 1996, Part IV was a significant step in the right direction, it became clear that further reform was necessary. Accordingly, in 2003 the Government introduced the Domestic Violence, Crime and Victims Bill which received royal assent on 15 November 2004. Sections 1 and 4 of the Domestic Violence, Crime and Victims Act 2004 (DVCVA 2004) came into force on 1 July 2007 and made important amendments to FLA 1996, Part IV.

The most significant amendment was by a new s 42A that made it a criminal offence, punishable by up to five years' imprisonment, to breach a non-molestation order without reasonable excuse. As a result, it is no longer permissible to attach a power of arrest to a non-molestation order although the power of arrest is retained for occupation orders. Apart from that, the existing enforcement provisions remain and the applicant may elect to pursue the civil route and an application for committal for contempt of court, rather than leave the matter to be dealt with in the criminal courts. However, the civil court will not be able to punish for contempt of court when a person has been convicted of an offence of breaching a non-molestation order, and vice versa.

The DVCVA 2004 also extended the category of associated persons eligible to apply for relief under FLA 1996, Part IV by including same-sex couples in the definition of cohabitants and those in an intimate personal relationship which is, or was, of significant duration.

4.2 The relief available

Under FLA 1996, Part IV, the court may make orders between associated persons. Associated persons include cohabitants and former cohabitants, which definition now includes those of the same sex in an equivalent relationship, and *those who have or have had an intimate personal relationship with each other which is or was of significant duration*. Orders may restrain the use and threatened use of violence, intimidation, pestering, harassment or other specified forms of molestation. There is also power to make orders relating to the occupation of a home that is, was, or was intended to be a home shared by the associated persons. When making an occupation order, the court has the power to make additional provision, which includes the imposition of terms in the order as to payment of an occupation rent, payment of outgoings, and the use and care of chattels.

A power of arrest may be attached to an occupation order, but since 1 July 2007 not to a non-molestation order. Breach of both non-molestation and occupation orders remains a contempt of court but breach of a non-molestation order without reasonable excuse is now also a criminal offence.

4.3 Which level of judiciary?

Part IV of the FLA 1996 gives the Family Court the power to make orders for protection between associated persons and relevant children and occupation orders in respect of the shared home.

All levels of judiciary in the Family Court may deal with these matters,[1] save that an application made by a child under 18 cannot be dealt with by lay justices.[2] A child under 16 requires the permission of the court to make an application. Lay Justices cannot deal with transfers of tenancies under s 53 of and Sch 7 to FLA 1996 and do not have jurisdiction where there is a dispute over a party's right to occupy the home.[3] Otherwise the powers and provision in FLA 1996, Part IV are the same for all levels of judiciary.

If an application is made within existing proceedings the court will allocate it to the same level of judge as in the existing proceedings.[4]

4.4 Applications to vary, extend or discharge an order made under Part IV

These applications must be made to the same court which made the order. Rules 10.5–10.7 FPR 2010 apply. These provide for service of the application and any order in essentially the same way as the initial order that was made.

---

[1]   FC (CDB) R 2014.
[2]   FC (CDB) R 2014, r 16.
[3]   FLA 1996, s 59.
[4]   FC (CDB) R 2014, r 17.

Non-molestation orders

4.5 Who may apply for a non-molestation order?

Part IV provides that orders may be made between persons who are associated.

For the purposes of Part IV, people are associated if:

(a) they are or have been married to each other or they are or have been civil partners of each other;

(b) they are cohabitants or former cohabitants or if of the same sex in an equivalent relationship;[5]

(c) they live or have lived in the same household, otherwise than merely by reason of one of them being the employee, tenant, lodger or boarder of the other;

(d) they are relatives;[6]

(e) they have agreed to marry one another, even if the engagement has been broken off;[7]

(ea) they have or have had an intimate personal relationship with each other which is or was of significant duration;[8]

(f) in relation to any child, they are both either parents of the child or one or both has or has had parental responsibility for the child;

(g) they are parties to the same family proceedings;

(h) in the case of an adopted child or a child freed for adoption, two people are associated with each other if one is a natural parent or grandparent of the child and the other is either an adoptive parent or a person with whom the child has at any time been placed for adoption.

For the purposes of Part IV, a relevant child is any person under the age of 18 years who is living with, or might reasonably be expected to live with, either party to the proceedings, any child who is the subject of adoption proceedings, or proceedings under the Children Act 1989, and any other child whose interests the court considers relevant.

---

[5] *G v G (Non-Molestation Order: Jurisdiction)* [2000] 2 FLR 533. FLA 1996, s 62(3) should not be narrowly construed so as to exclude borderline cases where swift and effective protection is required for the victims of domestic violence. The category of former cohabitants will not include cohabitants who cease to be cohabitants by reason of their marriage to one another. The Domestic Violence, Crime and Victims Act 2004 amends the definition of cohabitants to 'two persons who although not married to each other, are living together as husband and wife or (if not the same sex) in an equivalent relationship': DVCVA 2004, s 3.

[6] This is broadly defined to include members of earlier and later generations of the whole and half blood and, in the case of cohabitants, those who would be so related if the parties were married to one another. It now also includes first cousins: Sch 7, para 41(3)(a).

[7] The fact of the engagement must be proved by documentary evidence (eg engagement notice in the newspaper or wedding invitation) or other evidence (eg giving of an engagement ring). In the case of applications for a non-molestation order, no application may be brought after the end of the period of three years beginning on the day on which the agreement to marry was terminated (FLA 1996, s 42(4)).

[8] Additional category of associated person inserted by DVCVA 2004, s 4.

A notable omission from the definition of associated persons has now been addressed up to a point by the amendment made to s 62 that broadens the definition of 'associated persons' to include those who 'have or have had an intimate personal relationship with each other which is or was of significant duration'. There is the potential for difficulties to arise in the interpretation of *significant duration*, but it is to be expected that the court will aim to take a purposive approach where personal safety is at stake.

4.6   What is molestation?

There is no guidance in Part IV, nor indeed any statutory definition, as to what amounts to molestation. If there is any doubt about this, case-law provides examples of behaviour that the courts have restrained by making a non-molestation order.[9]

In practice, the professional adviser and the courts will use common sense, but molestation is clearly widely construed. It will include violence and threats of violence, but will also include more subtle acts of intimidation and harassment. In *Johnson v Walton*[10] the applicant was entitled to restrain the respondent from publishing intimate personal information and photographs in the national press, the court finding that it was done with the intention of causing distress to the applicant. However, in *C v C*[11] revelations by the wife in the tabloid press of her marriage to a well-known sports personality were held not to amount to molestation: 'the term implied quite deliberate conduct which was aimed at a high degree of harassment of the other party so as to justify the intervention of the court'. The Law Commission Report *Domestic Violence and Occupation of the Family Home*[12] offered the following definition of domestic violence:

> 'Domestic violence can take many forms ... In its narrower meaning it describes the use or threat of physical force against a victim in the form of assault or battery. But in the context of the family, there is also a wider meaning which extends to abuse beyond the more typical instances of physical assaults to include any form of physical, sexual or psychological molestation or harassment which has a serious detrimental effect upon the health and well-being of the victim, albeit that there is no "violence" involved in the sense of physical force. Examples of such "non-violent" harassment or molestation cover a very wide range of behaviour. Common instances include persistent pestering and intimidation through shouting, denigration, threats or arguments, nuisance telephone calls, damaging property, following the applicant about and repeatedly calling at her home or place of work

---

9   *Spindlow v Spindlow* [1979] 1 All ER 169: merely pushing the applicant onto the sofa and
      threatening to smack her child was not sufficient to amount to molestation. *Vaughan v
      Vaughan* [1973] 3 All ER 449: there was a history of violence, but the court made a
      non-molestation order on the basis of the respondent pestering the applicant and making a
      nuisance of himself. *Horner v Horner* (1983) 4 FLR 50: threatening letters and intercepting the
      applicant on the way to the station, 'the kind of conduct that makes life extremely difficult',
      was sufficient for an order.
10   [1990] 1 FLR 350.
11   [1998] 1 FLR 554.
12   Law Com No 207.

... The degree of severity of such behaviour depends less upon its intrinsic nature than upon it being part of a pattern and upon its effect upon the victim ...'

Support for an expansive definition of violence was evident in *Yemshaw v London Borough of Hounslow*.[13] Although that case concerned the definition of violence in the context of s 177(1) of the Housing Act 1996, the judgments of Baroness Hale and Lord Rodger make it clear that a proper understanding of violence, domestic or otherwise, must include threatening or intimidating behaviour and any other form of abuse which, directly or indirectly, may give rise to the risk of harm. In that case the housing authority had rejected an application for local authority accommodation on the basis that although the applicant had found it necessary to leave the family home with the two children because of her husband's behaviour, this had not included any violence or even threats of violence. The applicant appealed and the unanimous decision of the Supreme Court was that the case should be sent back to the local authority to be reconsidered.

4.7   The exercise of the court's discretion

The court has a discretion whether to make a non-molestation order. In deciding whether or not to make an order, the court is required to look at all the circumstances, including the health, safety and well-being of the applicant and any relevant child. 'Health' includes mental as well as physical health.

Procedure on an application for a non-molestation order

4.8   Issuing the application

Non-molestation orders may be made on a free-standing application, as well as in existing family proceedings. Note also that the court has the power to make a non-molestation order of its own motion in family proceedings in which the respondent is a party, if it would be for the benefit of any other party to the proceedings.

Application is made in Form FL401 whether in existing family proceedings or free-standing. The application must be fully completed and signed and must indicate the relationship between the applicant and respondent and the type of order sought. If the application is based on an agreement to marry, the date of the agreement and of the termination of the agreement must be stated.

No fee is payable.[14]

Every application must be supported by a witness statement setting out the evidence in support. The witness statement must contain a statement of truth.[15]

---

[13]   [2011] 1 FLR 1614.
[14]   Family Proceedings Fees (Amendment) Order 2014 (SI 2014/877).
[15]   FPR 2010, Pt 17.

An application may be made without notice to the respondent. In that case, the witness statement must set out the reasons why the relief sought should be granted without giving the respondent the opportunity to be heard.

To issue the application, the applicant's solicitor will attend at the court office with sufficient copies of the application in Form FL401 and the witness statement for the court and every party to be served. The court will seal all documents and issue Notice of Proceedings in Form FL402. If the application is urgent, arrangements will be made to see the judge as soon as possible.

If the application is on notice, a hearing date will be given with no less than two clear days' notice[16] unless an order has been made abridging time for service[17] by the judge.

4.9   Service

Where the application is not made without notice, an application in Form FL401, witness statement in support and the Notice of Proceedings endorsed with the return date must be served personally on the respondent not less than two clear days before the hearing date, unless the court abridges time for service or makes an order for service by an alternative method.

An application for service by an alternative method may be made where service cannot be effected by the prescribed means.[18] The application is to the judge without notice to the respondent by way of a witness statement setting out the circumstances. Service by the court is only available on request by an applicant acting in person.[19]

A Certificate of Service in Form FL415 confirming service on all relevant parties must be filed by the applicant's solicitor.

4.10   The hearing

The hearing will be in private unless the court directs otherwise and the court will keep a record of the hearing in Form FL405.

At a hearing on notice, if the respondent does not appear, the court will need to have proof of personal service of the application and supporting documents in order for the matter to proceed. In the absence of this, the hearing will usually be adjourned to another date.

If the respondent attends a hearing on notice but is not represented and the court considers that the interests of justice require that he has an opportunity to seek advice and representation, the hearing may be adjourned to another date.

---

[16]   Family Procedure Rules 2010, r 10.3(b)(i).
[17]   FPR 2010, r 10.3(b)(ii).
[18]   FPR 2010, r 6.35.
[19]   FPR 2010, r 10.3(2).

To avoid having to serve the respondent personally with notice of the new hearing date, the court has power to fix the date and time there and then, and communicate it to the respondent, or to ask the respondent if he is prepared to accept service of the notice of hearing by ordinary first-class post.

If the respondent appears at the hearing on notice and is represented but denies the allegations against him, the hearing will usually have to be adjourned and re-listed with an adequate time estimate to enable evidence to be heard from both sides. Directions will be given for filing of witness statements.

If the respondent denies the allegations but does not wish to have a fully contested hearing, in an appropriate case the court may accept an undertaking. DVCVA 2004 amended FLA 1996 s 46 in relation to the court's power to accept an undertaking in place of making a non-molestation order although the practical effect is much the same as before. The court must not accept an undertaking instead of making a non-molestation order where the respondent has used or threatened violence towards the applicant or a relevant child, and it is necessary for the protection of the applicant or child that an order is made so that any breach may be punishable under s 42A, that is as a criminal offence.

The position is unchanged when the court is considering accepting an undertaking in place of making an occupation order.

Section 46(4) of the FLA 1996 was amended by DVCVA 2004 to make provision for an application to be made for a warrant of arrest if an undertaking is alleged to have been breached.

If the court is not prepared to accept an undertaking, and the applicant does not wish to pursue his or her application to a contested hearing, he or she will have to withdraw the application or have it dismissed.

In practice, as the court's discretion in relation to non-molestation orders is so wide, unless the applicant's sworn statement is a complete fabrication it will rarely be productive for there to be a contested hearing. Courts tend to take the view that there is generally no excuse for using or threatening violence, or intimidating, harassing or pestering another person, and even if only a fraction of the allegations is made out, a non-molestation order will be made. However, where there is a concurrent dispute concerning contact to a child it may be necessary to hear evidence in order to make findings of fact for the purposes of the Children Act 1989 proceedings.

4.11 The order

Before DVCVA 2004 it was possible for the court to make one order containing both non-molestation and occupation provisions. The position now is that the provisions must be contained in separate orders. This is because breach of a non-molestation order without reasonable excuse is a criminal offence and therefore has serious consequences.

A non-molestation order will be drawn on Form FL404a. This contains a form of penal notice that sets out that breach of the order without reasonable excuse may be punishable as a criminal offence or as a contempt of court. It is not permissible to attach a power of arrest to a non-molestation order.

An occupation order, made under FLA 1996, Part IV, ss 33—38, will be drawn on Form FL404 bearing a penal notice. A power of arrest may still be attached to an occupation order if the criteria in FLA 1996, Part IV, s 47 are fulfilled.

As the consequences of breach of a non-molestation order are potentially very severe, it is important that these orders are drafted so that it is clear to the respondent, and to any court having to deal with an alleged breach, exactly what forms of behaviour are prohibited. For this reason it will usually be preferable for non-molestation orders to be expressed in specific rather than in general terms. Whether in the context of a criminal prosecution or committal proceedings, if the order is not clear as to what can and cannot be done before a breach occurs enforcement of the order will be ineffective.

The form of words used in general non-molestation orders, not to intimidate, harass or pester, is not sufficiently clear. It is good practice for non-molestation orders to be specifically directed to those aspects of the respondent's behaviour that it is sought to curb, for example telephone calls or other direct forms of communication, sending text messages or making contact via social media, or coming within 25m of a particular address.

4.12   Service of orders

Unless the court has made any other order as to service, orders must be served personally on the respondent.

No enforcement by committal proceedings may be taken in respect of any breach of the order before service has been effected. However s 42A(1), when read in conjunction with s 42A(2), suggests that even if the respondent has not been served with the order, if he is aware of its terms a breach may leave him open to prosecution.

When the court makes a non-molestation order a copy of the order must be sent to the applicant's local police station. This is the duty of the applicant, or the court if the applicant is acting in person and so requests.[20] The order must be accompanied by a statement showing that the respondent has been served with the order or informed of its terms.[21]

The Domestic Abuse Committee of the Family Justice Council has issued a Protocol for Process servers that should be followed in every case.[22]

---

[20]   FPR 2010, r 10.10(3).
[21]   FPR 2010, r 10.10(2).
[22]   *Protocol of November 2011 for Process servers: non-molestation orders* (Family Court Practice, Part V).

4.13   Duration of orders

A non-molestation order may be made for a specified period or until further order. An order made by the court of its own motion in other family proceedings ceases to have effect if those proceedings are withdrawn or dismissed.

Non-molestation orders made after a hearing on notice are generally made for a fixed period, rather than expressed as lasting until further order. Orders should be made to last for as long as is necessary in each particular case.

Non-molestation orders are now generally made for an initial period of up to 6 months or for a longer period if it is likely that ancillary issues such as finances or Children Act 1989 applications are likely to continue to bring the parties into conflict. Orders will not usually last for longer than 12 months, but they may if the particular circumstances warrant it.

Non-molestation orders should be open-ended ('until further order') in only exceptional or unusual circumstances.[23]

In view of the potential for criminal liability if a non-molestation order is breached, it will be good practice for the time as well as the date of expiry to be stated on the face of the order.

4.14   Application without notice for a non-molestation order

There is power to make a non-molestation order without notice to the respondent in any case in which the court considers it is just and convenient to do so.[24] Alternatively, the court may abridge time for service of the application so that it may be heard without giving two clear working days' notice to the respondent.

Where an application is made without notice, the witness statement in support must state the grounds for making the application without giving the respondent an opportunity to be heard. The judge will check the statement for this information and if it is not included the statement will have to be amended before the application may proceed. When drafting the witness statement, consider the criteria to be applied by the court under Part IV,[25] namely all the circumstances, including:

(a) any risk of significant harm to the applicant or a relevant child attributable to the conduct of the respondent if an order is not made immediately;

(b) the likelihood of the applicant being deterred from pursuing the application if an order is not made immediately; and

---

23   *M v W (Non-Molestation Order: Duration)* [2000] 1 FLR 107.
24   FLA 1996, s 45.
25   See s 45 and FPR 2010 r 10.2(4).

(c)   whether there is reason to believe that the respondent is evading service, and the delay in effecting service, in the case of an application in the family proceedings court, or in effecting service by an alternative method, will cause serious prejudice to the applicant or a relevant child.

Although the court staff will produce the order, it will be helpful for the judge to have a draft of the specific terms sought in a non-molestation order.

In October 2014 the President of the Family Division issued important Practice Guidance.[26] This set out the principles with which compliance is essential whenever an application is made without notice for an injunctive order. This includes the following:

(1)   an ex parte injunctive order must always have a fixed end date that the date and time of its expiry must be clearly stated on the face of the order.

(2)   The duration of the order should not normally exceed 14 days.

(3)   A hearing on notice must be fixed and the date, time and place of the hearing set out in the order.

(4)   The order must contain a clear statement of the respondent's right to apply to set aside or vary the order under r 18.11 before the hearing on notice. It is not sufficient that the order gives 'liberty to apply'.

(5)   Any such application must be listed for hearing as a matter of urgency.

At the same time as the Practice Guidance was issued there were released omnibuses of draft non-molestation and occupation orders prepared by the Family Orders Project Team. Both the Practice Guidance and the draft orders are available on the Family Law website.[27]

4.15 Power of arrest

Since 1 July 2007 it has no longer been possible to attach a power of arrest to a non-molestation order. This is because breach of a non-molestation order without reasonable excuse is a criminal offence.

Section 47 does still apply to occupation orders.

4.16 Undertakings

Although DVCVA 2004 amended the provisions of Part IV of the FLA 1996 in relation to undertakings, there is little, if any, practical difference. The position remains unchanged when the court is considering accepting an undertaking instead of making an occupation order. Where an undertaking is offered in place of a non-molestation order, the court will also have to specifically consider whether there has been the use or threat of violence to the applicant or

---

[26]   *Practice Guidance: Family Court – Duration of Ex Parte (Without Notice) Orders* 13 October 2014.

[27]   See www.familylaw.co.uk.

a relevant child, and whether for the protection of the applicant or the child it is necessary to make an order so that any breach may be punishable as a criminal offence under s 42A.

If an undertaking is accepted, a power of arrest may not be attached to it. However, although breach of an undertaking is not a criminal offence under s 42A, it is possible to apply for a warrant of arrest in the event of any alleged breach of an undertaking and for this to be dealt with in committal proceedings.

An undertaking will be in Form N117 and should set out in clear terms what the party giving the undertaking is promising to the court. Before the court accepts the undertaking, the judge must be satisfied that its terms and the consequences of breach are fully understood. The undertaking should be signed by the person giving it to confirm that understanding. A copy of the undertaking must be given to the person who has given the undertaking, ideally by hand immediately after the hearing.

Occupation orders

4.17   Who may apply for an occupation order?

The parties to an application for an occupation order, as for a non-molestation order, must be associated persons. In addition they must share, have shared, or have intended to share, a dwelling-house as their home. 'Dwelling-house' is construed widely to include any structure which is or has been a shared home, or which was intended to be a shared home.[28] It is important to know the respective rights and interests, if any, in the shared home of the associated persons, as this will determine the section of Part IV of the FLA 1996 under which the application may be made, and thus the court's powers.

If an application is made under the incorrect section, the court may remedy the defect using its powers under s 39(3).

It will be common in practice for one application to be made for both non-molestation and occupation orders.

An order that excludes one party from the shared home is regarded as a serious remedy.[29]

4.18   Which level of judiciary?

An application may be made to the same level of judiciary as for a non-molestation order, but it should be borne in mind that the Lay Justices have no power to deal with any application or make any order where there is a

---

[28]   FLA 1996, s 63.
[29]   *Chalmers v Johns* [1999] 1 FLR 392, CA.

dispute as to a party's entitlement to occupy the subject property, unless it is unnecessary to determine the dispute in order to deal with the application.

4.19   Which section will apply?

Occupation orders in relation to associated persons who are not and who never have been married can be made under ss 33, 36 and 38 of the FLA 1996. The decision as to which section to use is determined by whether or not the applicant and/or respondent is entitled to occupy the home. A party is entitled to occupy the home if he or she has a beneficial interest in it, or some contractual or statutory right to occupy, for example a tenancy or licence.

If the applicant is entitled to occupy, then regardless of whether the respondent is so entitled, s 33 applies.

Section 33 is open to all within the definition of associated persons. However, ss 36 and 38 apply only to cohabitants or former cohabitants. Section 36 applies where the applicant is not entitled to occupy but the respondent is. Section 38 applies where neither the applicant nor the respondent is entitled to occupy.

Put simply, an occupation order is available only to those who share or have shared a home as cohabitants (or spouses and former spouses) unless the applicant from the wider class of associated persons is entitled to occupy the home.

The court's powers and the exercise of its discretion are slightly different for each section.

Occupation orders under section 33

4.20   Who may apply?

An application may be made under s 33 by an entitled applicant against any person with whom he or she is associated. This will include many domestic arrangements in which parties live together, for example, students sharing accommodation, relatives living in the same household, friends living together, as well as those living together as husband and wife or if of the same sex, in an equivalent relationship (cohabitants).

It is important to note that in order for the court to have jurisdiction to hear an application from one of the wider class of associated person, the applicant must be entitled to occupy the home. If the applicant is not entitled, Part IV of the FLA 1996 will only offer a remedy to those who are not and never have been married to one another if the applicant and respondent are associated by virtue of being cohabitants or former cohabitants.

4.21 The court's powers under section 33

In relation to parties to proceedings who are not and have never been married to one another the court may make an occupation order in respect of a dwelling-house that they share or shared, or intended to share, and include any of the following provisions:

- declare the applicant's entitlement to occupy;[30]
- enforce the applicant's entitlement to remain in occupation as against the respondent;
- require the respondent to allow the applicant to enter and remain in the home or part of it;
- regulate the occupation of the home by either the applicant and/or the respondent;
- prohibit, suspend or restrict the respondent's exercise of any right to occupy;
- require the respondent to leave the home or part of it;
- exclude the respondent from a defined area around the home.

An occupation order cannot be made in respect of a property occupied by the applicant, at which the respondent is an unwelcome visitor, if the parties never lived there together, or never intended to do so. This situation is encountered quite frequently in practice where, for example the applicant moves out of the shared house at the end of the period of cohabitation, but continues to be pestered by the respondent. The court can make an order restraining the molestation, but cannot exclude the respondent from the applicant's new home or the immediate area. One solution in this type of situation is to ask the court to make a specific non-molestation order which expressly prohibits the respondent from attending at the applicant's new address.[31]

4.22 The balance of harm test under section 33

Before making an occupation order under s 33 of the FLA 1996 and deciding what (if any) provision to make, the court must first decide whether the applicant has established that there is a likelihood of significant harm to him or her or to a relevant child attributable to the conduct of the respondent. This is a duty imposed on the court. Harm in relation to an adult means ill-treatment or impairment of health. In relation to a child it also includes impairment of development. Ill-treatment includes non-physical ill-treatment, and in relation to a child includes sexual abuse. Health includes mental as well as physical well-being. Significant harm is construed in the same way as it is for the purposes of the CA 1989.[32]

---

[30] See s 33(4).

[31] For example: 'The respondent is forbidden to intimidate, harass or pester the applicant by entering or attempting to enter or going within 25 metres of (*applicant's new address*)'.

[32] CA 1989, ss 31 and 105, interpreted in *Humberside County Council v B* [1993] 1 FLR 257 by Booth J as, 'considerable, noteworthy or important'.

If it appears to the court that the applicant or a relevant child is likely to suffer significant harm attributable to the respondent if an occupation order is not made, then an order must be made, unless it appears that the respondent or a relevant child is likely to suffer significant harm if an order is made, and such harm is as great or greater than the harm attributable to the respondent that the applicant or a relevant child would suffer if an order were not made. If the respondent makes out significant harm, the court has to weigh up the relative positions of the applicant and respondent and make an order only if on balance there will be greater harm to the applicant if an order is not made.

In relation to the respondent, the harm alleged may emanate from any source, ie the source does not have to be the applicant. In the case of the applicant, the harm in question must be attributable to the respondent.

4.23 The exercise of the court's discretion under section 33

If the 'balance of harm' test results in the court finding that the harm to the respondent or a relevant child if an order were made would be as great or greater than that to the applicant or a relevant child if an order were not made, or where there is no finding of significant harm to either applicant or respondent, the court must look at all the circumstances to decide whether or not an order should be made.[33]

All the circumstances, for the purposes of s 33 of the FLA 1996, will include:
–   the housing needs and resources of each of the parties and any relevant child;
–   the financial resources of each of the parties;
–   the likely effect of any order, or the refusal of an order, on the health, safety or well-being of the parties and of any relevant child; and
–   the conduct of the parties to one another and otherwise.

In *G v G*[34] the Court of Appeal refused a respondent husband permission to appeal against the making of an occupation order. Whilst recognising that it was a serious order to make, it was relevant to the exercise of the court's discretion under s 33(6) that the respondent had alternative accommodation that was available to him, and although there had not been any findings of violence, his bullying behaviour made it imperative that the parties should live separately.

In *Dolan v Corby*[35] the Court of Appeal again emphasised the breadth of the court's discretion when conducting the balance of harm test under s 33(6). The use or threat of violence was not of itself determinative. It was for the judge *to*

---

[33]   See *Chalmers v Johns* [1999] 1 FLR 392, CA, as to the relationship between s 33(6) and (7); see also *Banks v Banks* [1999] 1 FLR 726, *B v B (Occupation Order)* [1999] 1 FLR 715 and *Re Y (Children) (Occupation Order)* [2000] 2 FCR 470, for the exercise of the balance of harm test.
[34]   [2011] 1 FLR 687.
[35]   [2012] 2 FLR 1031.

identify and weigh up all the relevant features of the case whatever their nature.[36] In that case the poor state of the applicant's psychiatric health carried great weight with the judge at first instance. The judge found the respondent to be of a dominating disposition and to have verbally abused the applicant and frequently belittled her. His decision to exclude the respondent from the property was held to be well within the ambit of his discretion even though the respondent was himself disabled. His conclusion was that of the two of them the respondent was better equipped to find alternative accommodation.

4.24 Additional provision under section 40

The court may at any time on or after making an occupation order under s 33 (and s 36) of the FLA 1996:

- impose on either party obligations to repair and maintain the home, or pay the rent, mortgage subscription or other outgoings of the home;
- require a party in occupation to pay an occupation rent to the party out of occupation if that party was, but for the terms of the occupation order, entitled to occupy;
- allow either party use of furniture or other contents;
- require either party to take reasonable care of any furniture or other contents; and
- require either party to keep the home and contents secure.

Note, however, that there are currently no statutory provisions for enforcement of these additional provisions.[37]

4.25 Exercise of additional powers when an occupation order is made under section 33

In deciding whether and if so how to exercise its additional powers the court must have regard to all the circumstances, including:

- the financial needs and financial resources of the parties; and
- the financial obligations which they have or are likely to have in the foreseeable future, including financial obligations to each other and to any relevant child.

4.26 Duration of orders under section 33

Occupation orders made under s 33 of the FLA 1996 will be expressed to last for a specified period, until a specified event (eg until the determination of any application for transfer of tenancy) or until further order. There will not be a final order, but orders need not be limited in duration. Any additional provision

---

[36] Per Black LJ at para 27 p 1039.
[37] See *Nwogbe v Nwogbe* [2000] 2 FLR 744.

made under s 40 of the FLA 1996 will come to an end when the occupation order to which it relates comes to an end.

Occupation orders under section 36

4.27 Who may apply?

This section applies only to cohabitants or former cohabitants who share, shared or intended to share a home, where the applicant is not entitled to occupy the home but the respondent is.

4.28 The court's powers under section 36

If the court decides to make an occupation order under s 36 of the FLA 1996, it must contain similar provisions to the home rights:

–   giving the applicant the right not to be evicted or excluded from the home or part of it by the respondent or if he or she is out of occupation the right to return and remain; and

–   prohibiting the respondent from evicting or excluding the applicant or if he or she is given the right to return and remain, from interfering with that right.

If an occupation order is made, it may also contain any of the following provisions:

–   to regulate the occupation of the home by either or both of the parties;

–   to require the respondent to leave all or part of the home;

–   to exclude the respondent from a defined area around the home; and

–   to prohibit, suspend or restrict the respondent's rights of occupation.

4.29 The exercise of the court's discretion under section 36

The court's discretion is exercised in two stages. In the first stage, the court decides whether or not to make an occupation order, and if an order is made, the court must give the applicant what amount to rights of occupation. In the second stage, the court considers whether to make any further provision. The criteria for each stage are different.

4.30 First stage in the exercise of the court's discretion under section 36

Before the court can make an occupation order under s 36 of the FLA 1996 in favour of the cohabitant or former cohabitant who is not entitled to occupy the home, it must have regard to all the circumstances, including:

–   the housing needs and resources of each of the parties and of any relevant child;

- the financial resources of each of the parties;
- the likely effect of any order, or the refusal of an order, on the health, safety or well-being of either of parties and any relevant child;
- the conduct of the parties towards one another and otherwise;
- the nature of the parties' relationship and in particular the level of commitment involved in it;
- the length of time they have cohabited;
- whether they have any children in common;
- the length of time that has elapsed since they last lived together; and
- the existence of any pending proceedings relating to financial relief or the legal or beneficial ownership of the home.

If, after considering all the circumstances, the court makes an occupation order, it must give the applicant rights of occupation.

4.31 Second stage in the exercise of the court's discretion under section 36

In deciding whether to make any further provisions, for example in relation to the regulation of the occupation of the home or restricting the respondent's right to occupy, the court must take into account all the circumstances, including:

- the housing needs and resources of each of the parties and of any relevant child;
- the financial resources of each of the parties;
- the likely effect of any order or the refusal of an order on the health, safety or well-being of either of the parties or any relevant child; and
- the conduct of the parties towards one another and otherwise.

4.32 The balance of harm test under section 36

In addition to the considerations outlined above, the court must carry out a balance of harm test by asking two questions.

The first question is whether the applicant or any relevant child is likely to suffer significant harm attributable to the conduct of the respondent if the additional provision (eg to exclude the respondent) is not included in the order.

The second question is whether the harm likely to be suffered by the respondent or a child if such provision is included is likely to be as great or greater than the harm attributable to the conduct of the respondent which is likely to be suffered by the applicant or a child if the provision is not included.

Unlike the balance of harm test under s 33 of the FLA 1996, this test is not overriding. The court retains its discretion regardless of the outcome of the balance of harm test.

4.33   Additional provision under section 40

The court may make additional provision pursuant to s 40 and the provision the court may make, and the criteria to be considered are identical to those under s 33 of the FLA 1996.[38]

4.34   Duration of orders under section 36

An occupation order made under s 36 of the FLA 1996 cannot last longer than six months in the first instance, and can be renewed on one occasion only, again for a period not exceeding six months. Therefore the maximum duration possible is 12 months.

Occupation orders under section 38

4.35   Who may apply?

Cohabitants and former cohabitants, neither of which is entitled to occupy the home, may apply under s 38 of the FLA 1996 for an occupation order. For the court to have jurisdiction at least one of the parties must be in occupation of the home. So if the applicant leaves the home because of the respondent's violence, and the respondent then leaves the home and the applicant remains out, there is apparently no power to make an occupation order under Part IV of the FLA 1996.

4.36   The court's powers under section 38

Where the court makes an occupation order under s 38 of the FLA 1996 in favour of an applicant with no entitlement to occupy, and the respondent is also not entitled to occupy, the court may make the following provisions:

–   to regulate the occupation of the home;

–   to require the respondent to allow the applicant to occupy the home and afford him or her peaceful occupation;

–   to exclude the respondent from the home (or part of it) and a defined area around it; and

–   to prohibit respondent from returning to the home and a defined area around it.

---

[38]   See **4.25** above.

4.37 The exercise of the court's discretion under section 38

Before the court can make an occupation order under s 38, it must have regard to all the circumstances, including:

–   the housing needs and housing resources of each of the parties and of any relevant child;

–   the financial resources of each of the parties;

–   the likely effect of any order, or the refusal of an order, on the health, safety, or well-being of either of the parties and of any relevant child;

–   the conduct of the parties towards one another and otherwise; and

–   the balance of harm.

4.38 The balance of harm test under section 38

The court must ask the two questions it would ask for the purposes of s 36 of the FLA 1996.

The first question is whether the applicant or any relevant child is likely to suffer significant harm attributable to the conduct of the respondent if the additional provision (eg to exclude the respondent) is not included in the order.

The second question is whether the harm likely to be suffered by the respondent or a child if provision is included is likely to be as great, or greater than the harm attributable to conduct of the respondent which is likely to be suffered by the applicant or a child if the provision is not included.

As is the case with s 36 of the FLA 1996, the balance of harm test is not overriding.

4.39 Duration of orders under section 38

An order under s 38 of the FLA 1996 may be made for a period not exceeding six months in the first instance and may be renewed on one occasion only for a further period not exceeding six months. Therefore, like orders under s 36, orders under s 38 may not last for longer than 12 months in total.

Procedure on application for an occupation order

4.40 Issuing the application

The procedure for occupation orders is the same as that for applications for non-molestation orders save that the application in Form FL401 must:

–   specify that an occupation order is sought;

–   give the section of Part IV of the FLA 1996 that is relied upon; and

– give details of the property in question and of the interest that the applicant and respondent have in it.

The application in Form FL401 must be supported by a witness statement.

In practice, it will be common for one application to be made for both an occupation order and a non-molestation order. If an application is made for both, only one Form FL 401 and witness statement in support is required.

On being presented with the Form FL401, the witness statement (with sufficient copies for the court and service on all parties) the court will issue the Notice of Proceedings endorsed with a return date. A fee is no longer payable.[39]

4.41   Service

Copies of Form FL401, the witness statement in support and Notice of Proceedings must be served on the respondent personally no less than two clear days before the return date, unless the application is made without notice to the respondent or the court has ordered that time for service be abridged.

In addition, copies must be served by the applicant on the mortgagee or landlord of the home, except in the case of applications under s 38 of the FLA 1996. Service is effected by ordinary first-class post.

A Certificate of Service in Form FL415, recording service on all relevant persons, must be filed after service.

4.42   Application for an occupation order without notice to the respondent

Application may be made for an occupation order without giving notice to the respondent, but because occupation orders are potentially more significant and more likely to interfere with the respondent's personal or property rights than a non-molestation order, these orders will generally be made without notice only in the most extreme cases. If it is felt that an application without notice is justified, the procedure to be followed and the criteria to be considered by the court are the same as for applications for non-molestation orders without notice.

4.43   The hearing

The hearing will be in private unless the court directs otherwise and the court will keep a record of the hearing in Form FL405.

---

[39]   Family Proceedings Fees (Amendment) Order 2014 (SI 2014/877).

At a hearing on notice, if the respondent does not appear, the judge will need to have proof of personal service of the application and supporting documents in order for the matter to proceed. In the absence of this, the hearing will usually be adjourned to another date.

If the respondent attends a hearing on notice but is not represented and the court considers that the interests of justice require that he has an opportunity to seek advice and representation, the hearing may be adjourned to another date. To avoid having to serve the respondent personally with the new hearing date, the court has the power to fix the date and time there and then and communicate it to the respondent or to ask the respondent if he is prepared to accept service of the notice of hearing by ordinary first-class post.

If the respondent appears at the hearing and is represented but denies the allegations against him, the hearing will have to be adjourned for a hearing on another date with an adequate time estimate to enable evidence to be heard from both sides. Directions will usually be given as to filing of witness statements.

4.44   Undertakings

If the respondent denies the matters alleged but does not wish to have a fully contested hearing, he may offer to give an undertaking to the court, for example not to return to the home or within 25 metres of it. Although Part IV of the FLA 1996 provides that the court has power to accept an undertaking in order to dispose of an application,[40] the circumstances in which it may do so have led to a difference of judicial opinion as to whether it is an appropriate way of proceeding. FLA 1996, s 46 provides that the court may only accept an undertaking when, if it were a case in which an occupation order would to be made, the mandatory power of arrest would not attach. In other words, the use of undertakings in place of occupation orders is restricted to those cases in which there has not been the use of or threat of violence, unless the court is satisfied that if in that particular case it were making an occupation order following admissions or findings of violence, used or threatened, it would not attach a power of arrest because it could be satisfied that the applicant would be adequately protected without it.[41]

If an undertaking is accepted, a power of arrest may not be attached to it.

If the court will not accept an undertaking, it may make an order on the basis that the respondent has offered no evidence.

If the court is not prepared to accept an undertaking, and the applicant does not wish to pursue his or her application to a contested hearing he or she will have to withdraw her application or have it dismissed.

---

[40]   See s 46(1).
[41]   See also 4.45 below.

4.45   Power of arrest

Part IV of the FLA 1996 evidenced a change in attitude to the power of arrest.

This was in response to research findings that the majority of applicants wanted the court to make an order with a power of arrest attached to it, rather than to accept an undertaking. Under the previous legislation, powers of arrest were used sparingly. Part IV imposed a duty to attach a power of arrest to one or more provisions of a non-molestation or occupation order made on notice if it appeared to the court that the respondent had used or threatened violence against the applicant or a relevant child, unless the court was satisfied that the applicant or child will be adequately protected without it.

Following the amendments made to Part IV FLA 1996 by DVCVA 2004, it is no longer possible to attach a power of arrest to a non-molestation order. However, the position in relation to occupation orders has not changed. Where an occupation order is made without notice, a power of arrest may be attached if the court finds actual or threatened violence on the part of the respondent and there is a risk that significant harm will result to the respondent or a relevant child.

Whether the application is made with notice to the respondent or without, the violence or threats of violence complained of generally will have to be within the timescale of the events immediately leading up to the application for it to be considered in the context of attaching a power of arrest.

4.46   Duration of power of arrest

Section 47(4) of the FLA 1996 provides that where a power of arrest is attached to any provisions of an occupation order made without notice to the respondent under Part IV, it may have effect for a shorter period of time than the order itself. The court has a similar discretion when a power of arrest is attached to an order made on notice.[42]

4.47   Procedure for power of arrest

Where the court makes an order with a power of arrest attached, and the respondent was either not given notice of the hearing or was not present at the hearing this must be announced by a judge in open court at the earliest opportunity.[43]

Where the court makes an occupation order containing one or more provisions to which a power of arrest is attached, each provision to which a power of arrest attaches must be set out in a separate paragraph. A provision to which a

---

[42]   *Re B-J (Power of Arrest)* [2000] 2 FLR 443.
[43]   FPR 2010, PD 10A, para 3.1.

power of arrest is attached must not be contained in the same paragraph as a provision to which a power of arrest has not been attached.[44]

The power of arrest is issued in Form FL406. When the occupation order has been served on the respondent, a copy of Form FL406 and the order must be sent to the applicant's local police so that they are aware of it. This is the duty of the applicant unless the applicant is acting in person and has requested that the court do so. A statement must accompany those documents, which confirms that the respondent has been served with the order or informed of its terms, whether by being present when the order was made, by telephone or otherwise. If the local police operate a domestic violence unit, generally it will be better to send the Form FL406 and order there as it is more likely to be acted upon should the need arise. Check the practice in your area.

Enforcement of orders under Part IV

4.48 Enforcement as a criminal offence under s 42A

Since 1 July 2007, breach of a non-molestation order without reasonable excuse has been a criminal offence. The penalty on conviction is a term of imprisonment of up to five years. However, the sentencing options are much wider than those available to a court punishing for contempt of court. They include community penalties that can, for example, require attendance at an anger management course. This may be more appropriate than imprisonment for less serious cases, and is more likely to promote a change in behaviour for the better.

Subject to the views of the police and the CPS, an applicant has the choice of pursuing a remedy either in the criminal courts or as before, in the civil courts, in committal proceedings for contempt of court. It is not every applicant that wishes to see the respondent criminalised.

A respondent cannot be punished twice for the same breach, and the civil court has no jurisdiction to entertain committal proceedings when a respondent has been convicted in the criminal courts of an offence arising out of the same breach, and vice versa.

4.49 Enforcement by power of arrest

If a power of arrest has been attached to any provision in an occupation order that the respondent is believed to have breached, the applicant will call the police at the office holding the copy of the order. If on investigation the police officer has reasonable cause to suspect that the respondent has breached the part of the order to which a power of arrest has been attached, the respondent may be arrested. Note that this is only a power, not a duty.

---

[44] FPR 2010, r 10.9.

Where there has been an arrest pursuant to a power of arrest, the respondent must be brought to the court that made the order within 24 hours of the arrest. Only Sundays, Christmas Day and Good Friday are excluded from the reckoning. The effect of this is that where the arrest was made on a Friday evening, a court will have to be convened on a Saturday. As it is unlikely that the respondent will be legally represented at the first hearing, the proceedings will usually be adjourned, and the respondent released or remanded on bail or in custody depending upon the gravity of the alleged breach and any other relevant circumstances. The resumed hearing must take place within 14 days of the day of the arrest, and the respondent must have at least two clear days' notice of the hearing.

If the respondent is not brought to court within the required timescale, or there has not been personal service of the order before the alleged breaches, the court will have no power to deal with a committal pursuant to the power of arrest. The applicant will not be able to apply for a warrant of arrest,[45] and it seems that the only procedure open to the applicant will be to apply to show cause why the respondent should not be committed under CPR 1998, Sch 2, CCR Ord 29.

The procedure at the committal hearing is dealt with at **4.57** below.

4.50   Application for a warrant of arrest

An application for a warrant of arrest may be made at any time after the respondent has been served with either a non-molestation or occupation order if the applicant considers that the respondent has breached the order or part of it, provided that a power of arrest was not attached to the order or to that part of the order that the applicant considers that the respondent has breached. In the case of a non-molestation order no power of arrest can be attached, but it will be important to know whether or not the respondent has already pleaded or been found guilty of an offence under s 42A before proceeding as the respondent cannot be punished both in the criminal courts and in the civil courts for contempt of court for the same breach.

An application may also be made for a warrant of arrest where it is alleged that the terms of an undertaking given under s 46 have been breached.

4.51   Which court?

Application must be made to the same level of judiciary that made the order. Any judge apart from a deputy district judge has jurisdiction to deal with the application.

---

[45]   See **4.50** below.

4.52 Procedure

Application is made on Form FL407 detailing the terms of the order alleged to have been breached and how it is alleged that the respondent is in breach.

A sworn statement must be filed in support.[46]

4.53 The exercise of the court's discretion

The court considers the application and sworn statement and if there are reasonable grounds for believing that the respondent has failed to comply with the order, a warrant for arrest in Form FL408 is issued and will be executed by the court bailiff or in the case of lay justices the police.

Where a respondent is arrested pursuant to a warrant of arrest, he must be brought before the court immediately, and in any event within 24 hours of his arrest. Sundays, Christmas Day and Good Friday are excluded from the reckoning.

The procedure for the committal hearing is set out at **4.57** below.

4.54 Committal for contempt of court

Breach of a non-molestation[47] and/or an occupation order or an undertaking is a contempt of court and can be dealt with by committal proceedings. FPR 2010 Part 37 applies. This procedure will only be followed:

(a) where an undertaking has been broken;

(b) where a power of arrest was attached to the term of the order breached, but the police declined to exercise the power of arrest;

(c) where a power of arrest was attached to the term of the order breached but the respondent was either not brought before the court within 24 hours of his arrest or not brought back to court following an adjournment within 14 days; and

(d) where there was no power of arrest attached to the term of the order breached and the court declined to issue a warrant of arrest.

4.55 Which court?

Application is made to the court which made the order that is alleged to have been breached. Judges at every level have the power to commit for breach of orders made under Part IV of the FLA 1996, but deputy district judges do not have any jurisdiction in enforcement of Part IV orders.

---

[46] FPR 2010, PD 4.1.

[47] Since DVCVA 2004 it is expected that most alleged breaches of a non-molestation order will follow the criminal route.

4.56   Procedure on application to commit

The applicant issues Form N78 (Notice to Show Cause why the respondent should not be committed), listing the breaches alleged, and files a witness statement in support, setting out all the circumstances. Form N78 endorsed with a return date and copy affidavit is served personally on the respondent.

The procedure at the committal hearing is set out at **4.57** below.

4.57   The committal hearing

Whether the respondent is arrested and brought to court under a power of arrest, pursuant to a warrant of arrest or comes to court following issue of a Form N78 Notice to show cause or the similar procedure in the family proceedings court, the procedure thereafter is the same.

Any judge apart from a deputy district judge may deal with the alleged breach. A district judge may deal with the alleged breach of an order made by a circuit judge. The hearing is in public.[48]

The applicant and his or her solicitor should be present at the hearing, and the respondent should have the opportunity of having legal representation. If the respondent is not legally represented, the proceedings will almost certainly be adjourned to enable him or her to be represented. The court will be mindful that if the breaches are proved, the respondent may be deprived of his or her liberty, and so the proceedings must comply with Art 6(3) of the European Convention for the Protection of Human Rights and Fundamental Freedoms 1950.[49] This gives the respondent the right to be legally represented, if necessary at the public expense.

At the first hearing, the following courses are open to the court.

(1)   To determine after hearing evidence/admissions whether the order has been breached and to decide upon the appropriate penalty for the breach. This course is only likely if the respondent is represented.

(2)   To adjourn the hearing to another date and remand the respondent in custody for a maximum of 8 days. If the remand is for more than 3 days, the court will have to arrange for the respondent to be escorted to prison, otherwise the respondent may be detained in custody by the local police. The court will issue a remand order in Form FL409.

(3)   To adjourn the hearing to another date and remand the respondent on bail with or without sureties/recognisances. The court will issue a remand order in Form FL409 and bail notice in Form FL412, together with Recognisance/Surety Forms FL410/FL411 as appropriate.

---

[48]   See *Practice Guidance 3 May 2013 and 4 June 2013 (Committal for Contempt of Court) Family Court Practice* Part V.
[49]   *Hammerton v Hammerton* [2007] EWCA Civ 248, [2007] 2 FLR 1133.

(4) To release the respondent and adjourn the hearing to a date no more than 14 days from the date of the arrest. The respondent must be given at least two clear days' notice of the adjourned hearing date.

When the court deals with the alleged breach of the order, either immediately following arrest or at an adjourned hearing, the procedure is as follows.

(1) The judge will need to be satisfied that the court had jurisdiction to make the order in the first place, that it was served on the respondent before the alleged breach and that the arrest was lawful. For example, the arrest will be unlawful if made pursuant to a power of arrest that did not attach to the part of the order in respect of which a breach is alleged.

(2) The judge will want to be satisfied that the applicant can establish each of the breaches alleged, and unless admissions are made by the respondent, oral evidence will be heard.

(3) The judge will record his finding in respect of each alleged breach and give reasons. The standard of proof is the criminal standard ie he must be sure.[50] The breach will be proved only if the respondent is in breach of the terms of the order literally construed and the respondent's conduct was deliberate.

(4) The judge will give a punishment for each breach proved, having given the respondent an opportunity to address him on any mitigating factors, and having heard the applicant's views on the appropriate punishment. A separate penalty should be imposed for each breach proved, and these can be expressed to be concurrent or consecutive. The court's powers are limited. Lay justices may not impose a term of imprisonment exceeding two months whereas District or Circuit judges may imprison for up to two years. In either case any fine must not exceed level 5 on the standard scale.[51]

4.58 Sentencing

The options are as follows:

(1) an immediate prison sentence of up to two years;

(2) a new order coupled with a custodial sentence suspended on strict compliance with the new order until it expires;

(3) a new order coupled with an adjournment of sentence until the expiry of the new order with liberty to the applicant to restore for sentence to be imposed before then. In the absence of an application to restore before the expiry of the new order the respondent to be relieved of his liability to be punished for the breach;

(4) a fine, on its own or in combination with any of the above. As a matter of practice, a fine is an unlikely punishment as most respondents to applications of this nature will be without the means to pay; or

---

[50] *Dean v Dean* [1987] 1 FLR 517.
[51] Family Court (Contempt of Court) (Powers) Regulations 2014 (SI 2014/833).

(5) a stern warning but no penalty.

The sentence should reflect the frequency and severity of the breach, whether the respondent is an habitual offender against court orders, and his personal circumstances.

A first offender need not consider that he may not be imprisoned. There has been a move away from the tacit acceptance of 'one free strike'.[52]

In *Wilson v Webster*,[53] on the applicant's appeal, the Court of Appeal substituted a sentence of three months' imprisonment for that of 14 days imposed by the court below. The respondent had broken an undertaking within one month of giving it by attacking the applicant in the street, knocking her to the ground and punching her in the face.

Similarly, in *Neil v Ryan*[54] the Court of Appeal allowed an appeal by an applicant against a suspended sentence for the first breach of a non-molestation order:

'... When all is said and done, here was a woman in her own home, the victim of a serious attack when she, not unreasonably, would have believed that the court's order had given her a measure of protection from violence. If this sort of attack is not met by an immediate committal to prison, the likely message will be that the first attack in breach of an order of the court in effect will attract no immediate consequences ... If that were the message then the protection which the court order is meant to provide would be illusory. The whole point of the order is that it should bite immediately, and that the person in serious breach of it should understand that there will be immediate punishment.'

In *Atrill v O'Donnell*,[55] a two-month sentence of imprisonment for the first breach of an undertaking was upheld on appeal. In *Hale v Tanner*[56] Hale LJ (as she then was) took the opportunity to give some guidance as to the length of sentence that should be contemplated for breaches of orders in family cases. In that case, she emphasised that the approach to punishing a breach of an order in a family case would be quite different from any other type of case, because of 'the heightened emotional tensions that arise between family members and often the need for those family members to continue to be in contact with one another because they have children together'. The judgment of Hale LJ also sets out the various factors that the courts should take into account when sentencing for contempt for breach of a non-molestation order. Among these are the following:

---

52 *Brewer v Brewer* [1989] Fam Law 352; *Ansah v Ansah* [1977] 2 All ER 638; *McIntosh v McIntosh* [1990] FCR 351; and *Thorpe v Thorpe* [1998] 2 FLR 127.
53 [1998] 1 FLR 1097.
54 [1998] 2 FLR 1068.
55 Unreported, 27 November 1998.
56 [2000] 2 FLR 879.

- If imprisonment was appropriate, the length of the committal should be considered without reference to whether or not the committal was to be suspended.

- The length of the committal depended on the two objectives in contempt proceedings:
  (a) marking the court's disapproval of disobedience to its orders, and
  (b) securing future compliance.

- The length had to bear some relationship to the maximum of two years available.

- Suspension was available in a much wider range of circumstances than in the criminal justice system.

- The length of any suspension required a separate consideration, although it would often be linked to continued compliance with the underlying order.

- The context in which the breach had occurred had to be borne in mind, for example, the emotions involved in family break-ups.

- In many cases, the court would have to bear in mind that there were concurrent proceedings in another court based on the same or substantially the same facts. The court could not ignore those proceedings and might have to take their outcome into account. A court would not want to cause a contemnor to suffer punishment twice.

- It would usually be desirable for the court to explain why it was making the order it was making.

In *Lomas v Parle*[57] this guidance was supplemented. That case concerned the appeal by an applicant against the sentence imposed for the admitted breach of two non-molestation orders. The two concurrent sentences of four months' imprisonment were substituted with sentences of nine months' imprisonment concurrent by the Court of Appeal. There was a background of persistent intimidation and threats of violence. The respondent was also the subject of criminal proceedings and proceedings under the Protection from Harassment Act 1997 arising out of the incident that gave rise to the breach of the injunction and the Court of Appeal also dealt with the sentencing considerations in these circumstances.

In *Murray v Robinson*,[58] a sentence of eight months for each of three breaches of a non-molestation order, to run concurrently, was upheld by the Court of Appeal. There had been no actual violence to the victim, but the court took a serious view of the great distress and anxiety caused by the respondent's behaviour.

Notwithstanding the courts' increasingly tough approach, it is as well to remember that the court is punishing the respondent's contempt of court in breaching the order, not for the behaviour resulting in the breach.

---

[57] [2004] 1 FLR 812.
[58] [2006] 1 FLR 365.

Whenever a punishment is imposed for being in contempt of court, it is open to the contemnor to apply to the court to purge his contempt.

Since 1 July 2007 breach of a non-molestation order without reasonable excuse has been a criminal offence and so many alleged breaches of a non-molestation order without reasonable excuse will be dealt with in the criminal jurisdiction. This will be the better course for the more serious breaches where the full sentencing powers of the criminal courts will provide a more effective sanction.

SECTION 2   OTHER REMEDIES

4.59   The Protection from Harassment Act 1997

The PHA 1997 creates civil (and criminal) remedies to protect individuals from 'stalking', which can cover a wide range of anti-social behaviour, including that between cohabitants.

There is no requirement for parties to be associated, unlike Part IV of the FLA 1996, nor even for there to be or to have been a relationship between them.[59]

The PHA 1997 creates a statutory tort of harassment, and for the purposes of the Act the three-year primary period of limitation of actions that applies to torts resulting in personal injury is disapplied.[60] The usual tortious limitation period under s 2 of the Limitation Act 1980 will apply, that is 6 years.

4.60   *Which court?*

As with any action in tort, the proceedings may be commenced in any county court or in the High Court and the same procedural requirements apply as to actions in tort generally.

4.61   *Prohibition of harassment*

Section 1 of the PHA 1997 prohibits harassment and provides that a person must not pursue a course of conduct:
(a)   which amounts to harassment of another; and
(b)   which he knows or ought to know amounts to the harassment of the other.

It amounts to harassment of another if a reasonable person in possession of the same information would think the course of conduct amounted to harassment of the other, ie it is an objective test.

Section 3 provides for a cause of action in damages for an actual or apprehended breach of s 1.

---

[59]   *R v Hills* [2000] TLR 893.
[60]   PHA 1997, s 6 and Limitation Act 1980, s 11(1A).

Damages may be awarded for anxiety caused by the harassment and financial loss resulting from the harassment.

The right to apply for an injunction to restrain harassment is not mentioned in the PHA 1997, but the court's inherent jurisdiction to grant an injunction is not affected.

There is no definition of harassment but references to harassing a person include alarming the person or causing distress.

A course of conduct must involve conduct on at least two occasions.

Conduct includes speech.[61] However, the fewer the incidents relied upon, and the farther apart in time they are, the less likely it is that it will be reasonable to describe them as a course of conduct.[62]

The prohibition of harassment does not apply to a course of conduct if the person who pursued it shows that:
(a) it was pursued for the purpose of preventing or detecting crime;
(b) it was pursued under any enactment or rule of law or to comply with any condition or requirement imposed by any person under any enactment; or
(c) in the particular circumstances, the pursuit of the course of conduct was reasonable.

4.62 Procedure

Proceedings under PHA 1997 are civil proceedings and are governed by CPR 1998 Part 65.

The claim will usually be issued in the county court[63] although the High Court does have jurisdiction. The claimant issues a claim form under Part 7. The nature of the claim must be set out concisely and the remedy sought must be specified. If personal injury damages are claimed, the claim form must contain a statement as to whether the claimant expects to recover more than £1,000 under that heading.

Separate particulars of claim may be served and, if this course is followed, the claim form must indicate that they are to follow.

If, as is likely, an injunction is required, a separate application must be made which is supported by a witness statement. Application may be made without notice to the defendant in an appropriate case, but the witness statement must set out why the claimant is asking the court to make an order without giving notice to the defendant.

---

[61] See s 7(4).
[62] *Lau v DPP* [2000] 1 FLR 799.
[63] Any county court as these are not family proceedings.

The claim must be served on each of the defendants in accordance with CPR 1998, Part 6. Personal service of an application for an injunction will be necessary.

As well as the claim form and any particulars of claim, the defendant will receive a response pack from the court in Form N1C. This includes an acknowledgement form which should be returned within 14 days of service indicating whether or not the claim is contested. Any defence should be filed and served 28 days after service of the particulars of claim if the defendant has filed an acknowledgement form, otherwise the defence must be filed and served within 14 days of service of the claim.

In practice, most claims will merely be the vehicle for obtaining an injunction to restrain the harassment and if the matter is disposed of at the injunction hearing (as is usually the case), the balance of the claim will be adjourned generally, requiring the defendant to do nothing further.

However, if the damages claim is pursued, the claim will be allocated to a track and case managed to a trial or disposal hearing.

Enforcement

4.63   Criminal liability

Breach of an injunction granted by the High Court or county court to restrain conduct which amounts to harassment without reasonable excuse is an offence with a remedy under the criminal law.

4.64   Contempt of court

Alternatively, if the defendant has done anything which the claimant believes is prohibited by the injunction and is thereby in contempt of court, the claimant may apply for the issue of an arrest warrant. There is no provision for a power of arrest to be attached to an order made under PHA 1997.

CPR 1998, Part 81 applies. The application for a warrant must be substantiated on oath and a warrant must not be issued unless the judge/district judge has reasonable grounds for believing that the defendant has breached the terms of the injunction.

Following arrest the defendant must be brought to court immediately.[64] Only a circuit judge or recorder has the power to commit, and there is no provision for remanding the defendant in custody or on bail. This means that the committal must either be dealt with immediately or adjourned to a later date.

---

[64]   Contrast this with the position under Part IV FLA 1996, ie within 24 hours.

4.65   Other remedies in tort

Despite the powers given to the courts by Part IV of the FLA 1996 and the PHA 1997 to deal with personal protection, there are still occasions when it may be necessary to make an application for relief under the common law tort jurisdiction to deal with assault, battery, trespass to the person or to land, or nuisance. Before the PHA 1997 was enacted, the case-law had evolved to the extent that it was possible to bring an action in nuisance for behaviour that amounted to harassment, thereby avoiding the need for there to be physical violence before a cause of action arose.

In *Burnett v George*[65] it was held to be sufficient to warrant the granting of an injunction restraining the defendant from 'molesting or otherwise interfering with the claimant by doing acts calculated to do her harm' that the defendant had been making persistent telephone calls to her in the middle of the night that had a harmful effect on the claimant's mental health.

In *Khorasandjian v Bush*[66] the court took the view that harassment by telephone could amount to private nuisance where it interfered with the use and enjoyment of property. However, since *Hunter v London Docklands Development Corporation and Hunter v Canary Wharf Limited*[67] and *Burris v Azadani*[68] it has been clear that a licensee may not sue in private nuisance, and to this extent *Khorasandjian v Bush* has been overruled.

4.66   *Procedure*

The procedure for bringing an action in the common law tort jurisdiction is the same as for bringing an action in the statutory tort of harassment. The action may be commenced in any county court, save for actions relating to trespass to land or nuisance relating to land which must be commenced in the court for the district in which the land or property is situated.

A Part 7 Claim Form must be issued and, if injunctive relief is sought, an application for an injunction must be issued supported by an affidavit.

4.67   Housing Act 1985

The Housing Act 1985 (HA 1985), as amended by the HA 1996, provides a discretionary ground for possession of a dwelling-house let under a secure tenancy where one partner in a marriage, civil partnership or cohabitation relationship has left the property as a result of the violence of the other and the court is satisfied that he or she is unlikely to return.

---

[65]   [1992] 1 FLR 525.
[66]   [1993] 3 All ER 669.
[67]   [1997] 2 All ER 426.
[68]   [1996] 1 FLR 266.

PART B PROCEDURAL GUIDES

Non-molestation and/or occupation order under Family Law Act 1996, Pt IV

4.68 Legal background

An application under FLA 1996, Pt IV can be made to the Family Court either as a freestanding application or within existing proceedings. By FC(CDB)R 2014, r 17, an application within existing proceedings will be allocated to the level of judge dealing with the existing proceedings.

An application by a person under the age of 18, or for leave under s 43 (applications by children under 16) will be allocated to the first available judge other than a lay justice (FC(CDB)R 2014, r 16).

Personal protection in the form of a 'non-molestation order' is available to 'associated persons', a term widely defined in s 62(3). 'Molestation' is not defined in the Act. It includes violence and threats of violence but is not confined to such acts (see s 42). It includes controlling, coercive or threatening behaviour and all forms of abuse.

'Occupation orders' are available under ss 33, 35, 36, 37 and 38. Each section is self-contained, setting out who may apply and the court's powers. In practice, most applications will be under s 33. If an application is made under the wrong section, the court can make an order under another section (s 39). The court can include ancillary provisions (s 40).

Power of arrest may be attached to an occupation order. However, it is not possible to attach a power of arrest to a non-molestation order (s 42A). A breach of a non-molestation order is a criminal offence.

Where injunctive relief from harassment within the meaning of PHA 1997 is sought, see **4.72** below. Thus a person who is not an 'associated person' within FLA 1996, Pt IV may need to sue under PHA 1997. Compensatory damages can be awarded under PHA 1997 and thus that Act (and/or proceedings in tort for, eg, assault) should be used where such a claim is pursued. Concurrent proceedings under the FLA 1996 and PHA 1997 can be brought and should be consolidated (see *Lomas v Parle*[69]).

---

[69] [2004] 1 FLR 812.

4.69 Procedure

What is a 'non-molestation' order?	An order prohibiting the respondent from molesting another person who is associated with the respondent and/or a relevant child	FLA 1996, s 42(1)
Who may apply for a 'non-molestation' order?	An associated person; a person is associated with another person if: they are or have been married to each other	FLA 1996, s 62(3)
	they are or have been civil partners of each other	
	they are cohabitants or former cohabitants	
	they live or have lived in the same household, otherwise than merely by reason of one of them being the other's employee, tenant, lodger or boarder	
	they are relatives (as defined)	FLA 1996, s 63(1)
	they have agreed to marry one another (whether or not that agreement has been terminated)	
	they have entered into a civil partnership agreement (whether or not that agreement has been terminated)	CPA 2004, s 73
	they have or have had an intimate personal relationship with each other which is or was of significant duration	FLA 1996, s 62(3)
	in relation to a child both persons are parents or have or have had parental responsibility for the child	FLA 1996, s 62(4)
	they are parties to the same family proceedings	FLA 1996, s 63(1), (2)

Who may apply for an 'occupation order' under s 33?	An applicant who is entitled to occupy a dwelling-house by virtue of a beneficial estate or interest or contract or by virtue of any enactment giving him the right to remain in occupation or who has home rights	FLA 1996, s 30
	The respondent is an 'associated person'	FLA 1996, s 62(3)
	The dwelling-house must be, have been, or have been intended to be, the home of the applicant and respondent	FLA 1996, s 33
Who may apply for an 'occupation order' under s 35?	An applicant former spouse or former civil partner who is not entitled to occupy; the respondent is entitled to occupy; the dwelling-house was or was intended to be their home	FLA 1996, s 35
Who may apply for an 'occupation order' under s 36?	An applicant cohabitant or former cohabitant who is not entitled to occupy; the respondent is entitled to occupy; the dwelling-house is, was, or was intended to be the home where they live(d) together	FLA 1996, s 36
Who may apply for an 'occupation order' under s 37?	An applicant spouse former spouse, civil partner or former civil partner where neither applicant nor respondent is entitled to occupy; the dwelling-house must be or have been their home	FLA 1996, s 37
Who may apply for an 'occupation order' under s 38?	An applicant cohabitant or former cohabitant where neither applicant nor respondent is entitled to occupy. The dwelling-house must be or have been the home in which they live(d) together	FLA 1996, s 38

How is the application made?	In all cases, on Form FL401 supported by a witness statement (which must state the grounds)	FPR 2010, r 10.2
Fee	No fee is payable on an application for a non-molestation or occupation order	
Ex parte applications	In any case where it considers it is 'just and convenient' to do so the court can make a non-molestation order or an occupation order on an ex parte basis. The court must have regard to 'all the circumstances', including the criteria in s 45(2)	FLA 1996, s 45(1), (2)
	The witness statement must state the reasons why notice was not given	FPR 2010, r 10.2(4)
	If an ex parte order is made there must be a 'full hearing' as soon as just and convenient	FLA 1996, s 45(3)
Form of order	An occupation order is in Form FL404. A non-molestation order is in Form FL404a	
Service of ex parte order	Respondent must be personally served with: a copy of the order made a copy of the application in Form FL401 a copy of the witness statement in support of the application notice of the date of the full hearing in Form FL402.	FPR 2010, r 10.6; FJC Protocol of November 2011: *Process Servers: Non-Molestation Orders*

Application on notice	Notice in Form FL402, together with a copy of the application in Form FL401 and the witness statement in support must be served on the respondent personally not less than 2 days before the application is to be heard	FPR 2010, r 10.3
	Before the application is served, the court can abridge time for service	FPR 2010, r 10.3(1)(*b*)(ii)
	If the application is for an occupation order under ss 33, 35 or 36 a copy of the application and notice in Form FL416 must be served by first class post on the mortgagee or landlord	FPR 2010, r 10.3(3)
Proof of service	After service, the applicant must file a statement in Form FL415	FPR 2010, r 6.37
Response	Respondent may, but is not required to, serve a statement in reply and/or make a cross-application	
Hearing	An application for a non-molestation order or an occupation order is dealt with in private unless the court otherwise directs	FPR 2010, r 10.5
	The application in the County Court is heard by a district judge or circuit judge	FP(AJ)D 2009
	The court keeps a record of the hearing in Form FL405	
Orders available	*Non-molestation order* An order may forbid molestation in general or particular acts of molestation or both	FLA 1996, s 42(6)

The better modern practice is
to make the order as specific as
is appropriate whether or not it
also contains a
clause forbidding molestation
in general. In particular, an
order can require the
respondent to 'keep-away'
from a specified address (but
not to 'get out', which needs to
be part of an occupation
order).

Boness v R [2005]
EWCA Crim 2395

Occupation order under s 33
An order may:
enforce the applicant's
entitlement to remain in
occupation as against the
respondent

require the respondent to
permit the applicant to enter
and remain in the
dwelling-house or part of the
dwelling-house

regulate the occupation of the
dwelling-house by either or
both of the parties

if the respondent is entitled to
occupy, prohibit, suspend or
restrict the exercise by him of
his right to occupy the
dwelling-house

if the respondent has home
rights in relation to the
dwelling-house, restrict or
terminate those rights

require the respondent to leave
the dwelling-house or part of
the dwelling-house

exclude the respondent from a
defined area in which the
dwelling-house is included

For additional provisions, see
s 40

	Occupation orders under ss 35, 36 Mandatory provisions are set out in ss 35(3), (4), 36(3), (4), and discretionary provisions in ss 35(5), 36(6)	
	For additional provisions, see s 40	
	Occupation orders under ss 37, 38 See ss 37(3), 38(3)	
Duration of non-molestation orders	For a specified period or until further order	FLA 1996, s 42(7)
	Application for extension of the order is made in Form FL403	FPR 2010, r 10.8
Duration of occupation orders	*Applicant with estate or interest etc or with home rights* for a specified period	
	until the occurrence of a specified event	
	or until further order	FLA 1996, s 33(10)
	Application for extension of the order is made in Form FL403	FPR 2010, r 10.8
	Spouse, former spouse, civil partner or former civil partner not entitled to an interest for a maximum of 6 months, but can be renewed any number of times	FLA 1996, ss 35(10), 37(5)
	Application for extension of the order is made in Form FL403	FPR 2010, r 10.8
	Cohabitant or former cohabitant not entitled to an interest for a maximum of 6 months, but can be renewed only once	FLA 1996, ss 36(10), 38(6)

	Application for extension of the order is made in Form FL403	FPR 2010, r 10.8
Penal notice	A penal notice must be endorsed on an order before it can be enforced by committal	FPR 2010, rr 10.12, 37.9, PD 37A
	The prescribed forms of order (FL404 and FL404a) include an appropriately worded penal notice. Because the sanction for breach is different, the wording of the penal notice for breach of a non-molestation order is unique to that form of order. Thus two separate orders are required if the court makes both types of order	FPR 2010, rr 10.12, PD 37A
Power of arrest	The court '*shall* attach a power of arrest to one or more provisions of an occupation order unless satisfied that ... the applicant ... will be adequately protected without [it]' if the respondent has used or threatened violence	FLA 1996, s 47(2)
	If the order is made ex parte, the court *may* attach a power of arrest to an occupation order if 'the respondent has used or threatened violence ...' and 'there is a risk of significant harm ... if the power of arrest is not attached ...'	FLA 1996, s 47(3)
	It is not possible to attach a power of arrest to a non-molestation order. Breach of such an order is a criminal offence	FLA 1996, s 42A

Undertakings	The court may accept an undertaking. The court 'shall not accept an undertaking ... instead of making an occupation order in any case where ... a power of arrest would be attached' nor instead of making a non-molestation order where 'it is necessary ... that any breach may be punishable under s 42A'	FLA 1996, s 46(1), (3), (3A)
	The court must deliver a copy of the undertaking to the party giving the undertaking	FPR 2010, r 37.7
	A warrant of arrest can be issued to enforce an undertaking	FLA 1996, s 46(4)
Damages	It is not possible to claim damages under the FLA 1996. However, damages can be claimed under PHA 1997, s 3. If concurrent proceedings are brought they should be consolidated	*Lomas v Parle* [2004] 1 FLR 812
Service of injunction	Personal service of an order is required	FPR 2010, r 10.6; FJC Protocol of November 2011: *Process Servers: Non-Molestation Orders*
	The applicant's solicitor should endeavour to effect service as soon as possible	
	An injunction directing an act to be done cannot be enforced unless it is served before the time within which the act is to be done has expired; an injunction cannot be enforced unless the respondent knows about it. Service should be effected in accordance with the terms of the Protocol	FPR 2010, r 37.5; FJC Protocol of November 2011: *Process Servers: Non-Molestation Orders*

Form 404a (non-molestation order) and/or Form FL406 (containing only those provisions of the occupation order to which a power of arrest has been attached) must be delivered to the officer in charge of any police station for the applicant's address or such other police station as the court may specify. The form must be served together with a statement showing that the respondent has been served with the order(s) or otherwise informed of its terms	FPR 2010, r 10.10
A copy of an occupation order made under s 33, 35 or 36 must be served by the applicant by first class post on the mortgagee or landlord	FPR 2010, r 10.6(3)

Transfer of a Tenancy under Family Law Act 1996, Pt IV, s 53 and Sch 7

4.70 Legal background

Since the coming into force of FLA 1996, Pt IV on 1 October 1997, the court is empowered to transfer tenancies, both contractual and statutory, between cohabitants who no longer live together as husband and wife, as well as between spouses and former spouses. As set out in FLA 1996, Sch 7, para 10, the person to whom the tenancy is transferred can be ordered to pay compensation to the other party. The power to transfer the tenancy to a former spouse arises on decree nisi; the order becomes effective on decree absolute; and there is a prohibition on applying if that former spouse has remarried. If there is a decree of judicial separation, the power to transfer arises after the decree is pronounced. A tenancy in the other spouse's name, or in joint names, can be destroyed by the unilateral surrender or giving of notice to quit by one tenant without consultation with the other (*Hammersmith and Fulham London Borough Council v Monk*[70]). A party should ask for an undertaking that the tenancy will not be surrendered and then serve that undertaking on the landlord. If the undertaking is not given the applicant should apply for an injunction and serve the order on the landlord (*Bater v Greenwich London Borough Council*[71]).

---

[70] [1992] 1 AC 478, [1992] 1 FLR 465.
[71] [1999] 2 FLR 993.

An application under FLA 1996, s 53 and Sch 7 is governed by the procedure in FPR 2010, rr 8.29–8.34.

4.71   Procedure

Who may apply	Either spouse, but a matrimonial/civil partnership order must be granted before the order is made	FLA 1996, Sch 7, para 2(2)
	Either former spouse, but a decree nisi must be granted before the order is made and the applicant must not have remarried; if application is for the transfer of a statutory tenancy or contractual tenancy containing a prohibition on assignment, it must be made before decree absolute	FLA 1996, Sch 7, para 13
	A cohabitant who is no longer living with the other cohabitant as husband and wife	FLA 1996, Sch 7, para 3
Application	To the Family Court or the same court as existing matrimonial/civil partnership proceedings	FLA 1996, Sch 7, para 2(2); FPR 2010, r 8.30, PD8A, para 1.1(a)
Fee	£75	FPFO 2008, fee 1.4
Service	The court will serve the respondent and the landlord unless the applicant is directed to serve	FPR 2010, r 8.31
	A landlord may be made a party to proceedings	FPR 2010, r 8.32
Respondent	The other spouse or cohabitant	
Interlocutory injunction	The court may grant an injunction if ancillary or incidental to the assistance sought; an application for an injunction must be in accordance with procedure under FPR 2010, r 20.4	FPR 2010, r 8.34

Orders for disclosure	Any party may apply to the court under r 21.2 for any person to attend a production appointment to produce documents specified or described in the order	FPR 2010, r 8.33
Order	Transfer of tenancy or statutory tenancy	FLA 1996, Sch 7, paras 7–9
	Payment by the spouse or cohabitant to whom the tenancy is transferred, to the other; deferment of payment or payment by instalments if transferee's financial hardship greater than transferor's	FLA 1996, Sch 7, para 10
	Order that both liable to discharge obligations prior to date of transfer and indemnity	FLA 1996, Sch 7, para 11

Claims under the Protection from Harassment Act 1997

4.72 Legal background

The High Court and the County Court have jurisdiction to grant an injunction for personal protection by forbidding harassment under PHA 1997 or any conduct which amounts to a recognised form of tort (*Khorasandjian v Bush*[72]). Such proceedings are not 'family proceedings'; however, a warrant of arrest can be granted in respect of a breach (PHA 1997, s 3(3), (5)). Unlike FLA 1996, the court can award damages under the PHA 1997 (see *Singh v Bhakar*,[73] where damages of £35,000 were awarded). In *Burris v Azadani*,[74] the Court of Appeal held that, where it is necessary to make the injunction effective for the protection of the applicant, an 'exclusion zone' can be ordered forbidding the defendant to go within a specified area around the applicant's home. In *Silverton v Gravett*,[75] the 'exclusion zone' included also the claimant's place of work.

Where the victim and the perpetrator of harassment or molestation are 'associated persons' within FLA 1996, s 62(3), the remedies under that Act are more comprehensive, particularly if occupation of the family home is an issue.

For precedents, see *Emergency Remedies in the Family Courts* (Family Law).

---

[72] [1993] 2 FLR 66.
[73] [2007] 1 FLR 880.
[74] [1996] 1 FLR 266.
[75] [2001] All ER (D) 282.

4.73   Injunctions under the Protection from Harassment Act 1997

An injunction can be granted in the County Court (as in the High Court) without a claim for damages or other relief, by virtue of CCA 1984, s 38. Whereas an injunction under FLA 1996 is applied for by way of an application in Form FL401 under FPR 2010, Pt 10, an application for an injunction under PHA 1997 is governed by CPR 1998, Pt 65 which requires the claim to be brought under CPR, Pt 8.

Under the CPR, proceedings are commenced by 'claim form'. Claims under the PHA 1997 must be brought under the Pt 8 procedure (see r 65.28 and CPR 1998, Pt 8). Generally, a Pt 8 claim form (N208) should not contain the same amount of detail as in a Pt 7 claim. A Pt 8 claim form should set out in summary form the issue which the claimant wants the court to decide and the remedy sought. If an interim remedy is also sought (eg a without notice injunction) see also Pt 25 CPR and in particular CPR PD25A (see Part III) which supplements Pt 25. Best practice for making a free-standing application is to file N208 incorporating short particulars of claim, which can, but need not, include a claim for damages, together with an application in Form N16A (County Court) or Application Notice in Form N244 (High Court), provided that the evidence setting out the relevant facts is given in Form N16A or N244, or in witness statement(s), verified by a statement of truth (see para 3 of PD25A).

4.74   Assault and battery

If protection is required but is not available under the FLA 1996 (eg because the parties are not 'associated persons') nor under the PHA 1997 (eg because there is no 'course of conduct': in *Andreson v Lovell* [2009] EWHC 3397 (QB) a 'one-off unwanted grope' was an isolated incident and not harassment, but it would be an assault) it may be possible to sue in tort and seek an injunction in those proceedings.

4.75   Procedure

Who may apply	A person who is or may be the victim of a course of conduct prohibited by PHA 1997, s 1	PHA 1997, s 3(1)
	Application for an interim injunction may be made by the defendant to the claim	*Huntingdon Life Sciences v Stop Huntingdon Animal Cruelty* [2003] EWHC 810; CPR 1998, rr 25.1(1)(*a*), 25.2(1)

Which court?	High Court or the County Court at the hearing centre for the area where the claimant or defendant resides	
	A district judge has jurisdiction to deal with all claims under PHA 1997	PHA 1997, s 3(3); CPR 1998, r 65.28
Application	Claim Form N208 must be issued, unless the court allows the application to be made before proceedings are started because the matter is urgent or there are good reasons for not giving notice	
	A claimant must file any written evidence on which he intends to rely when he files his claim form. A claimant may rely on the matters set out in the claim form if it is verified by a statement of truth.	CPR 1998, rr 65.28, 25.2(1)(2), 25.3(1); PD25A, para 4.4 CPR 1998, rr 8.5 and 8.6
	An urgent application for an injunction should be made as an interim application in pending proceedings by application notice in Form N16A (County Court) or Form N244 (High Court)	CPR 1998, Pt 23; PD23A; CPR 1998, r 25.1(1)(*a*); PD25A, para 2.1
	A form of acknowledgement of service (N210) must be served with the claim form. The defendant must file an acknowledgement of service. If he does not do so, he may attend the hearing but may not take part unless the court gives permission	PD8, para 3; CPR 1998, rr 8.3 and 8.4
	Damages can be claimed, but need not be	PHA 1997, s 3; CCA 1984, s 38; CPR 1998; PD2, para 8.1(*d*)(ii)

	An application for an interim injunction must be supported by evidence, ie a witness statement, unless the court orders otherwise	CPR 1998, r 25.3(2)
Fee	High Court: £480 County Court: £280 (non-money claim) payable on issue of application in Form N16A or N244 together with Claim Form N208	CPFO 2008 (as amended), fee 1.5
Oral application without documents	The court can dispense with the requirement for an application notice and in cases of extreme urgency can grant an interim injunction by telephone. However, the court should be expected to require an undertaking to file evidence, verified by a statement of truth, notice of application and, if not yet done, to issue a claim form Such an undertaking must be strictly complied with	CPR 1998, r 23.3(2)(*b*); PD25A, paras 4.2, 4.5, 5.1(2) *Re S (A Child) (Family Division: Without Notice Orders)* [2001] 1 All ER 362
Application begun without notice	An interim injunction can be granted without notice of the application having been given, where the matter is urgent and the court considers that there are good reasons for not giving notice Any applicant without notice is under a duty to give full and frank disclosure of all relevant facts	CPR 1998, rr 25.2(1), (2), 25.3(1) *W v H* [2001] 1 All ER 300; *B v A (Wasted Costs Order)* [2013] 2 FLR 958

	In an urgent case informal notice, ie short notice, of application for a personal protection injunction is better practice than no notice, unless the circumstances require secrecy	CPR PD23A, para 4.2
	If a claim form has already been served, the applicant should take steps to tell the respondent that the application is being made without full notice unless secrecy is essential	CPR PD25A, para 4.3
	The reasons for not giving notice must be stated in the evidence in support	CPR 1998, r 25.3(3); PD25A, para 3.4
	If the application is made before the application notice has been issued, the notice and evidence in support and fee must be filed on the same or next working day (or as ordered by the court), as should the claim form and fee, if not already issued	CPR PD25A, paras 4.4(3), 5.1(4), (5)
	The respondent against whom an interim injunction is granted may apply to have it set aside or varied, but must apply within 7 days after it is served or at the return date provided in the order	CPR 1998, r 23.10(1), (2); PD25A, para 5.1(3)
Evidence	Applications for interim injunctions must be supported by evidence, ie set out in a document verified by a statement of truth, which may be in a witness statement or the statement of case or the application itself	CPR 1998, r 25.3(2); PD25, para 3.2
	The evidence must set out the facts on which the applicant relies for the claim including all material facts of which the court should be made aware	CPR PD25A, para 3.3

	The witness statement must be verified by a statement of truth	CPR 1998, rr 8.2 and 22.1(1)
Service of notice	The application and evidence in support must be served as soon as practicable after it is filed and at least 3 working days before the hearing to give valid notice, unless the court shortens the time	CPR 1998, rr 2.8, 3.1(2)(*a*), 23.7(1)(*a*); PD25A, para 2.2
	Informal notice (ie less than 3 days) is better than no notice	*G v G* [1990] 1 FLR 395
	Where proceedings have commenced, informal notice should be given unless secrecy is essential	CPR PD25A, para 4.3(3)
Response	The defendant must file an acknowledgment of service. A defendant who intends to rely on written evidence must file it when he files his acknowledgment of service. (A claimant may file further written evidence in reply.) If the defendant fails to acknowledge service, he may attend the hearing but may not take part unless the court gives permission	CPR 1998, rr 8.3–8.5; PD8A, para 3,
	Respondent to application for injunction may: (i) elect not to oppose (ii) oppose in whole or in part by filing and serving evidence (iii) make his own application in like form	CPR 1998, r 23.11(1)
Hearing	CPR 1998 do not require the hearing of an interim application to be conducted in open court in public	CPR 1998, rr 23.8, 25.1, 25.2, 39.2(1)

	The applicant should submit a draft of the injunction in typescript (in Form N16 in the County Court) and on disk (in a format compatible with the word processing format used by the court) if he has not filed one already	CPR 1998, r 23.7(3)(*b*); PD25A, paras 2.4, 4.3
	Breach of an order under PHA 1997, s 3 is both a crime and a contempt of court. The facts on which the order is obtained need to be proven to the civil standard	*Hipgrave and Hipgrave v Jones* [2005] 2 FLR 174
Orders available	The court may grant an injunction restraining the defendant from pursuing any conduct which amounts to harassment. The order may prohibit specific conduct and/or harassment in general.	
	Where necessary for the protection of the applicant, an exclusion zone can be provided around her home or her place of work	*Burris v Azadani* [1996] 1 FLR 266; *Silverton v Gravett* [2001] All ER (D) 282
	Power of arrest is not available (though a warrant of arrest can be granted after the event)	PHA 1997, s 3(3), (4)
Order made without notice: duration and review	If an injunction is granted at a hearing of which the respondent has not been given notice:	
	a return date must (unless the court orders otherwise) be given for a hearing at which the respondent can be present	CPR PD25A, para 5.1(3)
	the respondent is in any event entitled within 7 days of service on him to apply to have the order set aside	CPR 1998, r 23.10; Form N16

	Where an injunction is granted without notice having been given, it is good practice for the court to order that it runs to a date later than the return date, so that there is no hiatus until an injunction granted on notice can be served.	
Damages	The court can award damages under the PHA 1997	PHA 1997, s 3, eg, *Singh v Bhakar* [2007] 1 FLR 880
	Concurrent proceedings under the FLA 1996 and the PHA 1997 should be consolidated and tried together	*Lomas v Parle* [2004] 1 FLR 812
Undertakings	An enforceable undertaking can be accepted by the court	*Hussain v Hussain* [1986] 2 FLR 271; CPR 1998, rr 81.4-81.11
Form of injunction order or undertaking: penal notice and clear instructions	To be enforceable, when served an injunction order must have prominently displayed on the front a warning notice of the consequences of disobedience	CPR PD81, paras 1, 2; Form N16A
	Any order for an injunction must set out clearly what the respondent must do or not do (in the County Court the injunction should be issued in Form N138)	CPR PD25A, para 5.2
	An undertaking given to a county court must be recorded in Form N117	

Service of injunction or delivery of form of undertaking	Before an injunction can be enforced it must have been personally served on the respondent, before any alleged breach, unless the court has dispensed with service or he was present when the order was made or he has been notified of the terms of the order. Service should be effected in accordance with the Protocol (see "Introduction" in the Protocol, which extends it to "harassment")	CPR 1998, r 81.5; Family Justice Council *Protocol for Process Servers*, November 2011
	An undertaking becomes enforceable when and because it is given to the court; however, unless a record of it is given to the person who gave it, difficulties can arise on enforcement proceedings, and in the County Court a copy is required to be delivered to the giver by the court or, failing that, served by the applicant	CPR 1998, r 81.7; *Hussain v Hussain* [1986] 2 FLR 271
Duration of interim injunction made on notice	An interim injunction granted on notice can be ordered to last until a fixed date or trial or further order	CPR PD25A, para 5.2
	If the claim is stayed other than by agreement between the parties, an interim injunction shall be set aside unless the court orders that it should continue to have effect	CPR 1998, r 25.10
Warrant for arrest	Application for a warrant of arrest in respect of disobedience of an injunction prohibiting harassment should be made in the High Court if the order was made there or, if the order was made in the County Court, the application may be made in any County Court office	PHA 1997, s 3(4), (5)

The formal requirements upon making application for a warrant are provided by rules	CPR 1998, r 65.29

Committal and arrest for disobedience of an injunctive order or breach of an undertaking in the Family Court, the High Court and the County Court

4.76   Legal background

An injunctive order (including a non-molestation order or occupation order under FLA 1996, Pt IV; a CA 1989, s 8 order to which a penal notice has been attached; and an order under PHA 1997) directing a person to do an act at or within a specified time, or to abstain from doing an act, or an undertaking to like effect which incorporates a penal warning notice, may be enforced by committal proceedings initiated by the person entitled to the benefit of the direction or undertaking. Any undertaking for the payment of money that has effect as if it was an order under Matrimonial Causes Act 1973, Pt II may be enforced as if it was an order and FPR 2010, Pt 33 applies (FPR PD 33A). Some money orders may be enforceable by judgment summons under the Debtors Acts 1869 and 1878. Personal service of an injunctive order is required by CPR 1998, r 81.5 and FPR 2010, r 37.5. The court can dispense with service or provide for some other form of service, but an injunction cannot be enforced unless it can be proved that the person to whom it was directed knew about the order and, where an act is directed to be done, the order must have been served before the time set for the act to be done. 'Any procedural defect in the commencement or conduct by the applicant of a committal application may be waived by the court if satisfied that no injustice has been caused to the respondent by the defect' (*Nicholls v Nicholls* [1997] 1 FLR 649; CPR PD81, para 16.2). However, grave procedural errors will result in the findings and sentences being quashed (*Hammerton v Hammerton*[76]).

The President issued Practice Guidance on 3 May 2013 on 'Committal for Contempt of Court'. Although it is described as 'guidance' rather than a 'direction', it should be followed because 'liberty of the subject' is so important. No one is to be committed by the Family Court (whether sentence is immediate or suspended) without (a) the name of the contemnor, (b) proper details of the contempt and (c) reasons for the committal being made publicly available in a judgment published on the BAILII website.

4.77   Which rules of court

Applications for committal in respect of injunctive orders are interlocutory in nature (*Savings and Investment Bank v Gasco Investments (Netherlands) BV*

---

[76]   [2007] 2 FLR 1133.

(No 2)[77]. Consequently, if the injunctive order was made in family proceedings an application for committal is made in family proceedings and is now governed by FPR 2010, Pt 37. In civil proceedings, committal proceedings are governed by CPR 1998, Pt 81. However, Pt 81 does not apply to family proceedings. If the injunctive order was made in non-family civil proceedings, eg under the PHA 1997, then the CPR 1998 apply. In family cases, see generally FPR PD37A.

4.78 Committal proceedings begun by notice to show good reason

The standard procedure for beginning proceedings for committal for enforcement of an injunction or an undertaking is by way of notice to show good reason why an order for committal should not be made, begun by application notice or Pt 8 claim form (High Court), Form N78 (County Court) or FL418 (magistrates' court).

4.79 Committal proceedings begun by arrest under a power of arrest

The power to arrest, for breach of an occupation order granted under FLA 1996, s 47(3) or for breach of a forced marriage protection order granted under FLA 1996, s 63I(2), provides the police with authority to intervene and stop a breach while it is happening or where they have reason to believe that such a breach has occurred. A power of arrest can also be exercised after the disobedience has ended and after an arrest for a criminal offence (*Wheeldon v Wheeldon*[78]). Where the police use the civil power of arrest the arrested person must be brought before the civil court within 24 hours (FLA 1996, s 47(7)). Breach of a non-molestation order in Form 404a made after 30 June 2007 is a criminal offence in respect of which the police may use their criminal powers of arrest.

There is no power to attach a power of arrest to an injunction under the PHA 1997 or at common law. Further, as from 1 July 2007, the power of arrest is abolished for non-molestation orders (see now FLA 1996, s 42A).

4.80 Committal proceedings begun by arrest under a warrant of arrest

FLA 1996, s 47(8), (9) extended to the High Court and County Court a power to issue a warrant of arrest. This power is available where no power of arrest was attached to the breached direction (s 47(8)). The court can issue a warrant for the arrest of a person where the court has reasonable grounds, substantiated on oath (s 47(9)), to believe that he has failed to comply with a non-molestation or occupation order made under FLA 1996, Pt IV.

---

[77] [1988] Ch 422.
[78] [1998] 1 FLR 463.

PHA 1997, s 3(3)–(5) provides the High Court and County Court with the power to issue a warrant of arrest where the court has reasonable grounds, substantiated on oath (s 3(5)), to believe that the respondent has failed to comply with an injunction which forbids harassment.

4.81   Remand following arrest

Once an arrested respondent is before the court, the court can immediately deal with the breach for which he has been arrested or adjourn (whether or not upon enlarged injunctive provisions). If adjourning, the court may remand. In FLA 1996 cases the power to remand is given to the High Court and County Court by s 47(11) and Sch 5, and exists in a magistrates' court by virtue of MCA 1980, ss 128 and 129. The remand can be in custody or on bail. Under FLA 1996, s 48, the power to remand can be exercised to enable a medical report to be made on the respondent.

There is no power to remand under PHA 1997.

4.82   Conduct of committal proceedings where the respondent is before the court following an arrest – preliminaries

Where a respondent is before the court for an alleged breach of an injunction, in order to ensure a fair trial there are essential preliminaries which the judge will consider. Is the respondent before the court within 24 hours of the arrest and is a lawful arrest admitted or proved? Is there proof of service of the injunction? Have the alleged breaches been reduced to writing and is Form N78 required? Is the respondent represented and, if not, does he seek an adjournment to obtain it or require time to prepare? Does he appreciate that he may be entitled to legal aid? Is the applicant present or represented and, if not, is an adjournment required? If adjourning, what directions are required and should the respondent be remanded? If remanded, should it be on bail or in custody?

An arrest is effected on the basis of a particular alleged breach. Earlier breaches cannot be dealt with unless Form N78 is also served (see FPR 2010, r 10.11 and, in the case of the PHA 1997, CPR 1998, r 65.29).

4.83   Conduct of committal proceedings when the respondent is before the court, whether on notice or following an arrest

Whether the respondent appears on notice in answer to a notice to show good reason, or following an arrest, the procedure to be followed for the determination of whether the respondent has disobeyed an order or breached an undertaking, and the disposal powers of the court, are the same. The breach must be proved to the criminal standard of proof. Thus, if not admitted, the applicant's evidence is heard first.

4.84   Absence of respondent

Provided that the court is satisfied that the respondent has been duly served, and has had the opportunity to obtain legal advice, the court can proceed in his absence. In *Begum v Anam*[79] a committal order was set aside as the respondent had not had the opportunity to obtain legal representation nor to arrange a production warrant to secure his attendance from prison.

4.85   Penalties

The court can order imprisonment (immediate or suspended) and/or a fine, or adjourn consideration of penalty for a fixed period and/or extend or enlarge the injunction. The common disposal orders are set out in County Court Form N79 and family proceedings court Form FL419. For the differing powers of judges of the Family Court, see the Family Court (Contempt of Court) (Powers) Regulations 2014.

4.86   Procedure

Preliminary matters	An injunctive order must be served personally on the person to whom it is directed, unless there has been an order for substituted service or dispensing with service	CPR 1998, r 81.5 (civil); FPR 2010, r 37.5 (family)
	However, pending service, if the respondent disobeys an injunctive order which requires him to abstain from doing an act, the court can impose a penalty if it is satisfied that he knew about the terms of the order	CPR 1998, r 81.8 (civil); FPR 2010, r 37.8 (family)
	Proof of service of the order is required. In all courts this is usually by Form FL415. Service should be effected in accordance with the Protocol	Family Justice Council *Protocol for Process Servers*, November 2011
	A mandatory injunctive order directing a person to do an act cannot be enforced unless it was served before the time at or by which the act was directed to be done	CPR 1998, r 81.5 (civil); FPR 2010, r 37.5 (family)

---

[79]   [2004] EWCA Civ 578.

	An undertaking becomes enforceable on being given to and accepted by the court; however the court can require the giver to sign a statement to the effect that he understands the terms of his undertaking and the consequences of failure to comply with it	*Hussain v Hussain* [1986] 2 FLR 271; CPR PD81, para 2.2
	A copy of the undertaking in Form N117 in the County Court, D787 in the Principal Registry or FL422 in a family proceedings court, is required to be delivered to the giver of the undertaking, but the giver is bound even if he does not receive a copy	CPR 1998, r 81.7 (civil); FPR 2010, r 37.7 (family)
Who may apply for committal or enforcement?	Person in whose favour the injunctive order was granted or the undertaking was given	CPR 1998, r 81.3 (civil); FPR 2010, r 37.3 (family)
Which court?	The court which granted the injunctive order or undertaking	CPR 1998, PD81, para 10 (civil); FPR 2010, r 37.10 (family)
	The powers of the County Court to deal with disobedience or breach are the same as the High Court	Contempt of Court Act 1981; CCA 1984, s 38
	Lay justices' statutory powers to deal with disobedience or breach are limited to imposing immediate or suspended committal, fine or adjourning consideration of penalty	Family Court (Contempt of Court) (Powers) Regulations 2014
Committal applications (general)	The affidavit or statement in support should narrate the facts relied on, but the list of alleged breaches must be given in the application notice	CPR 1998, r 81.10 (civil); FPR 2010, r 37.10 (family); *Harmsworth v Harmsworth* [1988] 1 FLR 349 at 354D–355B

	Fee on application in the Family Court: £155	FPFO 2008, fee 5.3
Application for warrant of arrest under FLA 1996, s 47(8) or s 63J	Application is made, without notice to the respondent, in Form FL408, to 'the relevant judicial authority', ie the convenient hearing centre in whichever tier of court the injunctive order was granted	FLA 1996, ss 47(8), 63(1) and 63J
	The application must be substantiated on oath and the court must have reasonable grounds for believing that the respondent has failed to comply with an order, or part of an order to which no power of arrest had been attached	FLA 1996, s 47(9), s 63J
	Breach of a non-molestation order is a criminal offence. However, the respondent cannot be both punished for a criminal offence and a contempt of court for the same breach. An application for a warrant of arrest to a civil court should confirm that there is no conviction	FLA 1996, s 42A(3), (4)
	The warrant is executed in the High Court by the Tipstaff, in the County Court by the bailiffs (or, in each case, by the police on request), and in the magistrates' court by the police	Form FL408
	In the magistrates' court the justices' clerk is responsible for delivering the warrant to the police	
Application for warrant of arrest under PHA 1997, s 3(3)	Application must be made in accordance with CPR Pt 23 and may be made without notice	PHA 1997, s 3(4); CPR 1998, r 65.29

	The application must be supported by affidavit evidence setting out the grounds for the application and state whether the claimant has informed the police and whether criminal proceedings are being pursued	PHA 1997, s 3(5); CPR 1998, r 65.29
Production in court following arrest under FLA 1996, s 47 or s 63I	A person arrested under a power of arrest must be brought before the relevant judicial authority within 24 hours not including Sunday, Christmas Day or Good Friday	FLA 1996, s 47(7), s 63I
	Neither FLA 1996 nor the rules prescribe how soon a person arrested under a warrant of arrest must be brought before the court. Nevertheless it must be as soon as practicable	FLA 1996, s 47(8)–(10), s 63J
Procedures open to court under FLA 1996, ss 47, 48 when arrested person produced in court and under ss 63I–63M	The court may hear the facts upon which the arrest was based, and decide penalty or adjourn, in which case the respondent must be given not less than 2 days' notice of the adjourned hearing, or	FLA 1996, s 47(7)(*b*), (10); FPR 2010, r 10.11(3)
	remand in custody for a period not exceeding 8 days, or	FLA 1996, ss 47(11), 63K, Sch 5 para 2(5)
	remand on bail on conditions and/or recognisances	FLA 1996, s 47(11), (12), Sch 5 para 2(5)
	where the court has reason to suspect mental illness or severe mental impairment, the court may remand, to enable a medical examination and report, for not more than 3 weeks if in custody, or 4 weeks if on bail	FLA 1996, s 48, s 63L

Powers of court under PHA 1997, s 3(5) when arrested person produced in court	The court may hear the facts upon which the arrest was based, and decide penalty, or adjourn for not more than 28 days, in which case the defendant must be given not less than 2 days' notice of the adjourned hearing	CPR 1998, r 65.30
Hearing without notice to the respondent	In exceptional circumstances, the court may, without notice having been given to the respondent, deal with an application begun by notice to show good reason, by dispensing with service of the summons or notice	CPR 1998, rr 39.3, 81.28 (civil); FPR 2010, r 37.27 (family)
	It is not appropriate for a court to proceed without notice where arrest under a power or warrant can be achieved under FLA 1996, s 47, or under PHA 1997, s 3(5). However, where a power or warrant of arrest is not available, proceeding without notice may exceptionally be appropriate. When the court takes this exceptional step and imposes imprisonment, the court should fix a date and time for the contemnor to be brought before the court	CPR 1998, r 81.28 (civil); FPR 2010, r 37.27 (family)
Service of application to commit	Personal service of the application is required	FPR 2010, r 37.27
	In both family and civil proceedings a period of 14 clear days after service is required unless the court directs otherwise by using its powers to abridge time for service	CPR 1998, PD81, para 15.2 (civil); FPR 2010, PD37A, para 12.1 (family)

	In exceptional cases, the court can dispense with service	see Hearing without notice to the respondent (above)
Service of notice of adjourned hearing	Where a hearing is adjourned, personal service of notice of the adjourned hearing is required, unless the respondent was present in court and was told when and where the adjourned hearing would resume and/or was remanded under FLA 1996, s 47(7),(10), Sch 5 or MCA 1980, ss 128, 129	*Chiltern DC v Keane* [1985] 1 WLR 619 at 622H–623C
Case management	The court can make directions at any time as to service of evidence and conduct of the proceedings, or strike out an inappropriate application	CPR 1998, PD81, paras 15 and 16 (civil); FPR 2010, PD37A, para 12.3 (family)
The hearing	District judges as well as High Court and circuit judges have power to hear committal proceedings under FLA 1996, Parts 4 and 4A	FLA 1996, ss 58, 63(1), 63O, 63S
	However district judges do not have power to hear committal proceedings under PHA 1997	PHA 1997, s 3(3),(4) only gives power to issue a warrant; CPR PDCommittal, para 11
	Normally held in open court	CPR 1998, rr 39.2, 81.28 (civil); President's Guidance of 3 May 2013 (family)
	If it is just to do so, the court can proceed if the respondent, having been duly served, fails to attend	*Begum v Anam* [2004] EWCA Civ 578; CPR 1998, r 39.3

	Committal proceedings, although technically civil proceedings, are treated as criminal proceedings for the purposes of ECHR, Art 6. Consequently, persons in danger of losing their liberty are, subject to means, eligible for legal aid. (Contempt in the face of the court is separately dealt with in LASPOA 2012, s 14(g))	LASPOA 2012, Schs 1 and 3; *Chelmsford County Court v Ramet* [2014] EWHC 56
	Procedure is akin to criminal trial. The criminal standard of proof ('beyond reasonable doubt') applies	*Dean v Dean* [1987] 1 FLR 517
	An application notice can be amended with the permission of the court but not otherwise	CPR 1998, PD81, paras 12(2), 13.2(2) (civil); FPR 2010, r 37.27 (family)
	An alleged contemnor cannot be directed or compelled to give information	CPR 1998, r 81.28 (civil); FPR 2010, r 37.27(3) (family)
	A deliberate act or failure to act (actus reus) with knowledge of the terms of the order (mens rea) must be proved	*DG of Fair Trading v Smiths Concrete* [1992] QB 213
Powers of court	The disposal must be proportionate to the seriousness of the contempt, reflect the court's disapproval and be designed to secure compliance in future. The principles of sentencing in the CJA 2003 apply. The judge cannot sentence again for matters already dealt with by the criminal court. The court should briefly explain its reasons for the choice of disposal	*Murray v Robinson* [2006] 1 FLR 365 *Hale v Tanner* [2000] 2 FLR 879; *Lomas v Parle* [2003] EWCA Civ 1804; *Slade v Slade* [2009] EWCA Civ 748

Committal to prison is appropriate only where no reasonable alternative exists	*Hale v Tanner* (above)
Imprisonment is restricted to total of 2 years in the High Court or a county court, 2 months in a magistrates' court, and must be for a fixed term	CCA 1981, s 14; MCA 1980, s 63(3)
Sentence can be suspended or adjourned on terms	CPR 1998, r 81.29 (civil); FPR 2010, r 37.28 (family)
Any time spent on remand in custody must be taken into account in the sentence	*Kerai v Patel* [2008] EWCA (Civ) 600
Person under the age of 21 can be detained under Powers of Criminal Courts (Sentencing) Act 2000, s 96	*R v Selby Justices ex parte Frame* [1991] 2 WLR 965
Person under the age of 18 cannot be committed to any form of detention for contempt of court (but could be prosecuted for breach of a non-molestation order)	*R v Selby Justices* (above); FLA 1996, s 42A
MHA powers are available	CCA 1981, s 14; MHA 1983, ss 35, 37, 38
Fine can be imposed	*Hale v Tanner* [2000] 2 FLR 879
A fresh injunction can be granted	*Coats v Chadwick* [1894] 1 Ch 347
A power of arrest can be attached, if available, to the injunctive order	*Ansah v Ansah* (1976) FLR Rep 9; FLA 1996, s 47
Sequestration is available only in the High Court	CPR 1998, rr 81.19-81.27 (civil); FPR 2010, r 37.25 (family)

Form of order	The order must specify 'exact details' of each contempt found proved and specify the disposal ordered	*Nguyen v Phung* [1984] FLR 773 at 778C; *Re C (A Minor) (Contempt)* [1986] 1 FLR 578 at 585A
	Where sentence is suspended or adjourned, the period of suspension or adjournment and the precise terms for activation must be specified	*Pidduck v Molloy* [1992] 2 FLR 202; CPR 1998, r 81.29 (civil); FPR 2010, r 37.28 (family)
	In the High Court, the order is issued in Form A85 and warrant in Form PF303. In the County Court, Form N79 and warrant in Form N80. In a magistrates' court, Form FL419 and warrant in Form FL420	
Service of order	Where immediate imprisonment or detention is imposed, the court serves the order	CPR 1998, r 81.30 (civil); FPR 2010, r 37.29 (family); *Clarke v Clarke* [1990] 2 FLR 115
	Where sentence is suspended, the applicant must serve the order, unless the court directs otherwise	CPR 1998, r 81.29(2) (civil); FPR 2010, r 37.28 (family)
Review by Official Solicitor	The court sends a copy of every committal order and relevant details to the Official Solicitor, who reviews the case and may apply or appeal of his own motion or at the contemnor's request	*Lord Chancellor's Direction of 29 May 1963; Secretary's Circular of 28 September 1981*
Discharge of contemnor	A contemnor is entitled to apply to purge his contempt and be discharged from prison	CPR 1998, r 81.31 (civil); FPR 2010, r 37.30 (family)

The application should be made in accordance with CPR 1998, Pt 23 or FPR 2010, Pt 18 but in practice a letter from the contemnor usually suffices	*CJ v Flintshire Borough Council* [2010] 2 FLR 1224
If the committal was made in civil proceedings, the application notice must be served as soon as practicable after it is filed and at least 3 days before the hearing. If made in family proceedings, the application must be served at least 7 days before the hearing	CPR 1998, r 23.7(1) (civil); FPR 2010, r 18.8 (family)
The contemnor should be in court	*PD of 25 July 1983*
On an application to purge, the court can say 'yes', 'no' or 'not yet'	*Harris v Harris* [2001] EWCA Civ 1645, [2002] 1 FLR 248

PART C   CHECKLISTS

4.87   Checklist for first instructions for applications under Part IV of the Family Law Act 1996

A   General:

(1)   full name and date of birth of client;

(2)   full name and date of birth/age of respondent;

(3)   names and dates of birth of any relevant children and relationship to each party;

(4)   client's permanent address;

(5)   client's temporary address;

(6)   should an application be made not to disclose present address?

(7)   client's contact telephone numbers;

(8)   are the parties associated persons?
   –   have they cohabited? and/or
   –   do they have a child? and/or
   –   do they or have they had an intimate personal relationship with each other of significant duration?
   –   do they fall within any of the other categories within s 62 of the FLA 1996? (See **4.1** above);

(9)   are there any 'relevant' children within s 62(2) of the FLA 1996?

(10) period of cohabitation;

(11) duration of relationship;

(12) parties' financial position.

B   Non-molestation order:

(1)   history of behaviour complained of;

(2)   recent incidents;

(3)   final incident;

(4)   effect of behaviour on applicant;

(5)   effect of behaviour on any relevant children;

(6)   behaviour directed at any relevant children;

(7)   any witnesses?

(8)   client's own behaviour;

(9)   police intervention?

(10) has either party any criminal convictions?

(11) hospital or medical treatment required?

(12) obtain consent for release of medical records/to obtain medical report;

(13) are social services involved? And if so details of office and officer concerned;

(14) any previous injunctions?

(15) with whom are the children currently living?

(16) are any urgent steps necessary under the CA 1989?

(17) description/photograph of respondent, and where most likely to be found, for process server;

(18) advise that breach of non-molestation order without reasonable excuse can be an offence and lead to criminal liability.

C   *Occupation order:*

(1)   address of property;

(2)   property is/was intended to be shared home?

(3)   if client has left does he/she wish to return?

(4)   if so, as a temporary measure/long term?

(5)   is property rented/owner-occupied?

(6)   name and address of landlord/mortgagee;

(7)   in whose name is tenancy/title?

(8)   if rented, should an application be made to restrain service of notice to quit?

(9)   make application for transfer of tenancy?

(10) if property is owner-occupied or other property in issue, see checklists at **1.115** and **1.116**.

4.88   Checklist of steps for application under Part IV of the Family Law Act 1996

(1)   public funding;

(2)   warning letter, if appropriate;

(3)   application for non-molestation and/or occupation order; prepare schedule of specific behaviour to be prohibited by non-molestation order;

(4)   with/without a power of arrest in the case of an occupation order?

(5)   Form FL401 and sworn statement in support;

(6)   application without notice to respondent, if appropriate;

(7)   contact court if urgent hearing without notice required;

(8)   arrange to meet client at court;

(9)   application for transfer of tenancy?

(10) application for injunction to restrain service of notice to quit?

(11) contact process server;

(12) service on landlord/mortgagee of application for occupation order (including transfer of tenancy) by first-class post;

(13) arrange personal service on respondent of application/order;

(14) file statement of service in Form FL415;

(15) police provided with any power of arrest attached to an occupation order (after respondent served);

(16) client notified about return date.

PART D   PRECEDENTS

4.89   Application in Form FL401 for non-molestation or occupation order under Family Law Act 1996, s 36

Application for:	To be completed by the court
a non-molestation order	Date issued
an occupation order	
Family Law Act 1996 (Part IV)	Case number
The court	

Please read the accompanying notes as you complete this form.

1   About you (the applicant)

State your title (Mr, Mrs etc), full name, address, telephone number and date of birth (if under 18):

Ms MARY HAWTHORN
19 POPLAR COURT
OAKWOOD
ELMSHIRE   01213 641633

State your solicitor's name, address, reference, telephone, FAX and DX numbers:

PLANE & PARTNERS
LAW CHAMBERS
HIGH STREET
OAKWOOD
DX 12345 OAKWOOD
Tel: 01213 613000   Ref: J Shaw

2   About the respondent

State the respondent's name, address and date of birth (if known):

PETER ROWAN
c/o MAPLE ENTERPRISES
OAKWOOD INDUSTRIAL ESTATE
OAKWOOD
ELMSHIRE

3   The Order(s) for which you are applying

This application is for:

☑   a non-molestation order

☑   an occupation order

☐   Tick this box if you wish the court to hear your application without notice being given to the respondent. The reasons relied on for an application being heard without notice must be stated in the statement in support.

1

**4   Your relationship to the respondent
(the person to be served with this
application)**

Your relationship to the respondent is:

(Please tick only one of the following)

1   ☐ Married

2   ☐ Civil Partners

3   ☐ Were married

4   ☐ Former civil partners

5   ☐ Cohabiting

6   ☑ Were cohabiting

7   ☐ Both of you live or have lived in the same
       household

8   ☐ Relative
       State how related:

9   ☐ Agreed to marry.
       Give the date the agreement was made.
       If the agreement has ended, state when.

10 ☐ Agreed to form a civil partnership.
       Give the date the agreement was made.
       If the agreement has ended, state when.

11 ☐ Both of you are parents of, or have parental
       responsibility for, a child

12 ☐ One of you is a parent of a child and the other
       has parental responsibility for that child

13 ☐ One of you is the natural parent or
grandparent of a child adopted, placed or freed
for adoption, and the other is:

    (i)   the adoptive parent

or (ii) a person who has applied for an
        adoption order for the child

or (iii) a person with whom the child has
        been placed for adoption

or (iv) the child who has been adopted,
        placed or freed for adoption.

State whether (i), (ii), (iii) or (iv):

14 ☐ Both of you are the parties to the same family
proceedings (see also Section 11 below).

5   Application for a non-molestation order

If you wish to apply for a non-molestation order,
state briefly in this section the order you want.

Give full details in support of your application in
your supporting evidence.

*I want the respondent to stop making threats and
being violent. I want him to stop ringing my mobile
and sending me text messages.*

6   Application for an occupation order

*If you do not wish to apply for an occupation order,
please go to section 9 of this form.*

(A) State the address of the dwelling-house to which
your application relates:

*19 Poplar Court
Oakwood
Elmshire*

(B) State whether it is occupied by you or the respondent
now or in the past, or whether it was intended to be
occupied by you or the respondent:

*I am living in the flat now.
I asked the respondent to leave.
We lived there together before that.
I have a licence to occupy but the respondent now
wants me out.*

(C) State whether you are entitled to occupy the
dwelling-house: ☐ Yes   ☑ No

If yes, explain why:

(D) State whether the respondent is entitled to occupy
    the dwelling-house: ☑ Yes   ☐ No

    If yes, explain why:

He owns it.

**On the basis of your answers to (C) and (D) above,
tick one of the boxes 1 to 6 below to show the category
into which you fit**

1 ☐ a spouse or civil partner who has home rights
     in the dwelling-house, or a person who is
     entitled to occupy it by virtue of a beneficial
     estate or interest or contract or by virtue of
     any enactment giving him or her the right to
     remain in occupation.

     If you tick box 1, state whether there is a
     dispute or pending proceedings between you
     and the respondent about your right to occupy
     the dwelling-house.

2 ☐ a former spouse or former civil partner with no
     existing right to occupy, where the respondent
     spouse or civil partner is so entitled.

3 ☑ a cohabitant or former cohabitant with no
     existing right to occupy, where the respondent
     cohabitant or former cohabitant is so entitled.

4 ☐ a spouse or former spouse who is not entitled
     to occupy, where the respondent spouse or
     former spouse is also not entitled.

5 ☐ a civil partner or former civil partner who is not
     entitled to occupy, where the respondent civil
     partner or former civil partner is also not entitled.

6 ☐ a cohabitant or former cohabitant who is
     not entitled to occupy, where the respondent
     cohabitant or former cohabitant is also not
     entitled.

Home Rights

If you do have home rights please:

State whether the title to the land is registered or unregistered (if known):

If registered, state the Land Registry title number (if known):

If you wish to apply for an occupation order, state briefly here the order you want. Give full details in support of your application in your supporting evidence:

I want to be able to stay in the flat and for the respondent to be excluded

7   Application for additional order(s) about the dwelling-house

If you want to apply for any of the orders listed in the notes to this section, state what order you would like the court to make:

I want an order making the respondent pay all the outgoings on the flat. I also want the use of the furniture in the flat.

8   Mortgage and rent

Is the dwelling-house subject to a mortgage?

☑ Yes   ☐ No

If yes, please provide the name and address of the mortgagee:

Elmsfield Building Society
Construction House
Oakwood
Elmshire

Is the dwelling-house rented?

☐ Yes   ☑ No

If yes, please provide the name and address of the landlord:

9   At the court

Will you need an interpreter at court?

☐ Yes   ☑ No

If yes, specify the language:

If you require an interpreter, you must notify the court immediately so that one can be arranged.

If you have a disability for which you require special assistance or special facilities, please state what your needs are. The court staff will get in touch with you about your requirements.

10   Other information

State the name and date of birth of any child living with or staying with, or likely to live with or stay with, you or the respondent: *N / A*

State the name of any other person living in the same household as you and the respondent, and say why they live there: *N / A*

11   Other Proceedings and Orders

If there are any other current family proceedings or orders in force involving you and the respondent, state the type of proceedings or orders, the court and the case number. This includes any application for an occupation order or non-molestation order against   *N / A*
you by the respondent.

This application is to be served upon the respondent

Signed: Date:

Application for non-molestation order or occupation order
Notes for guidance

Section 1

If you do not wish your address to be made known to the respondent, leave the space on the form blank and complete Confidential Address Form C8. The court can give you this form.

If you are under 18, someone over 18 must help you make this application. That person, who might be one of your parents, is called a 'next friend'.

If you are under 16, you need permission to make this application. You must apply to the High Court for permission, using this form. If the High Court gives you permission to make this application, it will then either hear the application itself or transfer it to a county court.

Section 3

An urgent order made by the court before the notice of the application is served on the respondent is called an ex-parte order. In deciding whether to make an ex-parte order the court will consider all the circumstances of the case, including:

- any risk of significant harm to the applicant or a relevant child, attributable to conduct of the respondent, if the order is not made immediately

- whether it is likely that the applicant will be deterred or prevented from pursuing the application if an order is not made immediately

- whether there is reason to believe that the respondent is aware of the proceedings but is deliberately evading service and that the applicant or a relevant child will be seriously prejudiced by the delay involved.

If the court makes an ex-parte order, it must give the respondent an opportunity to make representations about the order as soon as just and convenient at a full hearing.

'Harm' in relation to a person who has reached the age of 18 means ill-treatment or the impairment of health, and in relation to a child means ill-treatment or the impairment of health and development.

'Ill-treatment' includes forms of ill-treatment which are not physical and, in relation to a child, includes sexual abuse. The court will require evidence of any harm which you allege in support of your application.

Section 4

For you to be able to apply for an order you must be related to the respondent in one of the ways listed in this section of the form. If you are not related in one of these ways you should seek legal advice.

Cohabitants are two persons who, although not married to each other, nor civil partners of each other, are living together as husband and wife or civil partners. People who have cohabited, but have then married or formed a civil partnership will not fall within this category but will fall within the category of married people or people who are civil partners of each other.

Those who live or have lived in the same household do not include people who share the same household because one of them is the other's employee, tenant, lodger or boarder.

You will only be able to apply as a relative of the respondent if you are:

(A) the father, mother, stepfather, stepmother, son, daughter, stepson, stepdaughter, grandmother, grandfather, grandson, granddaughter of the respondent or of the respondent's spouse, former spouse, civil partner or former civil partner.

(B) the brother, sister, uncle, aunt, niece, nephew or first cousin (whether of the full blood or of the half blood or by marriage or by civil partnership) of the respondent or of the respondent's spouse, former spouse, civil partner or former civil partner.

This includes, in relation to a person who is living or has lived with another person as husband and wife or as civil partners, any person who would fall within (A) or (B) if the parties were married to, or civil partners of, each other (for example, your cohabitee's father or brother).

Agreements to marry: You will fall within this category only if you make this application within three years of the termination of the agreement. The court will require the following evidence of the agreement:

     evidence in writing

or   the gift of an engagement ring in contemplation of marriage

or   evidence that a ceremony has been entered into in the presence of one or more other persons assembled for the purpose of witnessing it.

Agreements to form a civil partnership: You will fall within this category only if you make this application within three years of the termination of the agreement. The court will require the following evidence of the agreement:

     evidence in writing

or   a gift from one party to the agreement to the other as a token of the agreement

or   evidence that a ceremony has been entered into in the presence of one or more other persons assembled for the purpose of witnessing it.

Section 4 continued

Parents and parental responsibility:
You will fall within this category if

both you and the respondent are either the parents of the child or have parental responsibility for that child

or if one of you is the parent and the other has parental responsibility.

Under the Children Act 1989, parental responsibility is held automatically by a child's mother, and by the child's father if he and the mother were married to each other at the time of the child's birth or have married subsequently. Where, a child's father and mother are not married to each other at the time of the child's birth, the father may also acquire parental responsibility for that child, if he registers the birth after 1st December 2003, in accordance with section 4(1)(a) of the Children Act 1989. Where neither of these circumstances apply, the father, in accordance with the provisions of the Children Act 1989, can acquire parental responsibility.

From 30 December 2005, where a person who is not the child's parent ("the step-parent") is married to, or a civil partner of, a parent who has parental responsibility for that child, he or she may also acquire parental responsibility for the child in accordance with the provisions of the Children Act 1989.

Section 5

A non-molestation order can forbid the respondent from molesting you or a relevant child. Molestation can include, for example, violence, threats, pestering and other forms of harassment. The court can forbid particular acts of the respondent, molestation in general, or both.

Section 6

If you wish to apply for an occupation order but you are uncertain about your answer to any question in this part of the application form, you should seek legal advice.

(A) A dwelling-house includes any building or part of a building which is occupied as a dwelling; any caravan, houseboat or structure which is occupied as a dwelling; and any yard, garden, garage or outhouse belonging to it and occupied with it.

(C) & (D) The following questions give examples to help you to decide if you or the respondent, or both of you, are entitled to occupy the dwelling-house:

(a) Are you the sole legal owner of the dwelling-house?

(b) Are you and the respondent joint legal owners of the dwelling-house?

(c) Is the respondent the sole legal owner of the dwelling-house?

(d) Do you rent the dwelling-house as a sole tenant?

(e) Do you and the respondent rent the dwelling-house as joint tenants?

(f) Does the respondent rent the dwelling-house as a sole tenant?

If you answer

- **Yes** to (a), (b), (d) or (e) you are likely to be entitled to occupy the dwelling-house

- **Yes** to (c) or (f) you may not be entitled (unless, for example, you are a spouse or civil partner and have home rights – see notes under 'Home Rights' below)

- **Yes** to (b), (c), (e) or (f), the respondent is likely to be entitled to occupy the dwelling-house

- **Yes** to (a) or (d) the respondent may not be entitled (unless, for example, he or she is a spouse or civil partner and has home rights).

Box 1 For example, if you are sole owner, joint owner or if you rent the property. If you are not a spouse, former spouse, civil partner, former civil partner, cohabitant or former cohabitant of the respondent, you will only be able to apply for an occupation order if you fall within this category.

If you answer yes to this question, it will not be possible for a magistrates' court to deal with the application, unless the court decides that it is unnecessary for it to decide this question in order to deal with the application or make the order. If the court decides that it cannot deal with the application, it will transfer the application to a county court.

Box 2 For example, if the respondent is or was married to you, or if you and the respondent are or were civil partners, and he or she is sole owner or rents the property.

Box 3 For example, if the respondent is or was cohabiting with you and is sole owner or rents the property.

Home Rights
Where one spouse or civil partner **"(A)"** is entitled to occupy the dwelling-house by virtue of a beneficial estate or interest or contract or by virtue of any enactment giving him or her the right to remain in occupation, and the other spouse or civil partner **"(B)"** is not so entitled, then **B** (who is not entitled) has home rights.

The rights are

(a) if **B** is in occupation, not to be evicted or excluded from the dwelling-house except with the leave of the court; and

(b) if **B** is not in occupation, the right, with the leave of the court, to enter into and occupy the dwelling-house.

Note: Home Rights do not exist if the dwelling-house has never been, and was never intended to be, the matrimonial or civil partnership home of the two spouses or civil partners. If the marriage or civil partnership has come to an end, home rights will also have ceased, unless a court order has been made during the marriage or civil partnership for the rights to continue after the end of that relationship.

Section 6 (continued)

Occupation Orders
The possible orders are:

If you have ticked box 1 above, an order under section 33 of the Act may:

- enforce the applicant's entitlement to remain in occupation as against the respondent
- require the respondent to permit the applicant to enter and remain in the dwelling-house or part of it
- regulate the occupation of the dwelling-house by either or both parties
- if the respondent is also entitled to occupy, the order may prohibit, suspend or restrict the exercise by him, of that right
- restrict or terminate any home rights of the respondent
- require the respondent to leave the dwelling-house or part of it
- exclude the respondent from a defined area around the dwelling-house
- declare that the applicant is entitled to occupy the dwelling-house or has home rights in it
- provide that the home rights of the applicant are not brought to an end by the death of the other spouse or civil partner or termination of the marriage or civil partnership.

If you have ticked box 2 or box 3 above, an order under section 35 or 36 of the Act may:

- give the applicant the right not to be evicted or excluded from the dwelling-house or any part of it by the respondent for a specified period
- prohibit the respondent from evicting or excluding the applicant during that period
- give the applicant the right to enter and occupy the dwelling-house for a specified period
- require the respondent to permit the exercise of that right
- regulate the occupation of the dwelling-house by either or both of the parties
- prohibit, suspend or restrict the exercise by the respondent of his right to occupy
- require the respondent to leave the dwelling-house or part of it
- exclude the respondent from a defined area around the dwelling-house.

If you have ticked box 4 or box 5 above, an order under section 37 or 38 of the Act may:

- require the respondent to permit the applicant to enter and remain in the dwelling-house or part of it
- regulate the occupation of the dwelling-house by either or both of the parties
- require the respondent to leave the dwelling-house or part of it
- exclude the respondent from a defined area around the dwelling-house.

You should provide any evidence which you have on the following matters in your evidence in support of this application. If necessary, further statements may be submitted after the application has been issued.

If you have ticked box 1, box 4 or box 5 above, the court will need any available evidence of the following:

- the housing needs and resources of you, the respondent and any relevant child
- the financial needs of you and the respondent
- the likely effect of any order, or any decision not to make an order, on the health, safety and well-being of you, the respondent and any relevant child
- the conduct of you and the respondent in relation to each other and otherwise.

If you have ticked box 2 above, the court will need any available evidence of:

- the housing needs and resources of you, the respondent and any relevant child
- the financial resources of you and the respondent
- the likely effect of any order, or of any decision not to make an order on the health, safety and well-being of you, the respondent and any relevant child
- the conduct of you and the respondent in relation to each other and otherwise
- the length of time that has elapsed since you and the respondent ceased to live together
- where you and the respondent were married, the length of time that has elapsed since the marriage was dissolved or annulled
- where you and the respondent were civil partners, the length of time that has elapsed since the dissolution or annulment of the civil partnership

Section 6 (continued)

- the existence of any pending proceedings between you and the respondent:

    under section 23A of the Matrimonial Causes Act 1973 (property adjustment orders in connection with divorce proceedings etc.)

    or under Part 2 of Schedule 5 to the Civil Partnership Act 2004 (property adjustment on or after dissolution, nullity or separation)

    or under Schedule 1 para 1(2)(d) or (e) of the Children Act 1989 (orders for financial relief against parents)

    or relating to the legal or beneficial ownership of the dwelling-house.

If you have ticked box 3 above, the court will need any available evidence of:

- the housing needs and resources of you, the respondent and any relevant child

- the financial resources of you and the respondent

- the likely effect of any order, or of any decision not to make an order, on the health, safety and well-being of you, the respondent and any relevant child

- the conduct of you and the respondent in relation to each other and otherwise

- the nature of your and the respondent's relationship

- the length of time during which you have lived together as husband and wife or civil partners

- whether you and the respondent have had any children, or have both had parental responsibility for any children

- the length of time that has elapsed since you and the respondent ceased to live together

- the existence of any pending proceedings between you and the respondent under Schedule 1 para 1(2)(d) or (e) of the Children Act 1989 or relating to the legal or beneficial ownership of the dwelling-house.

Section 7

Under section 40 of the Act the court may make the following additional orders when making an occupation order:

- impose on either party obligations as to the repair and maintenance of the dwelling-house

- impose on either party obligations as to the payment of rent, mortgage or other outgoings affecting it

- order a party occupying the dwelling-house to make periodical payments to the other party in respect of the accommodation, if the other party would (but for the order) be entitled to occupy it

- grant either party possession or use of furniture or other contents

- order either party to take reasonable care of any furniture or other contents

- order either party to take reasonable steps to keep the dwelling-house and any furniture or other contents secure.

Section 8

If the dwelling-house is rented or subject to a mortgage, the landlord or mortgagee must be served with notice of the proceedings in Form FL416. He or she will then be able to make representations to the court regarding the rent or mortgage.

Section 10

A person living in the same household may, for example, be a member of the family or a tenant or employee of you or the respondent.

4.90 **Witness statement in support of application without notice for non-molestation and occupation orders under s 33 of the Family Law Act 1996**

1st statement
made by applicant
on [date]

IN THE [ ] COUNTY COURT   CASE NUMBER

BETWEEN:

A   Applicant

And

B   Respondent

STATEMENT OF APPLICANT IN SUPPORT OF APPLICATION FOR
NON-MOLESTATION AND OCCUPATION ORDERS

(1)   I, [name], of [address] make this affidavit in support of my applications for a non-molestation order against the respondent and an order that he be restrained from coming within 50 metres of [address]. This is a property that I rent from the local council, and which used to be the home that I shared with the respondent until he left in [date].

(2)   My relationship with the respondent began in [date] and he moved in with me in [date]. We have a child, [name], who was born on [date] and who is now [age] years old. [name] remained living with me after the respondent moved out.

(3)   Throughout our relationship the respondent was violent towards me and it was his violence that brought our relationship to an end. He would think nothing of pushing and shoving me around the bedroom, or pulling me across the room by my hair when he came home from the pub the worse for drink. He would also go into very bad moods and his temper then was uncontrollable. On one occasion [date] he came home from work having had a disagreement with his foreman. The first thing he did when he came in was to take it out on me, shouting abuse at me, calling me fat and lazy, and asking me why I was serving up a meal that he said was only fit for a dog to eat. When I protested at this he responded by throwing his plate of food across the room at me. Fortunately I ducked out of the way and the plate and its contents landed in a great mess on the kitchen worktop. However the respondent then came charging across the kitchen towards me and grabbed me by the throat. I thought he was going to strangle me and I am sure he would have done had a neighbour not called round to see what was going on, having heard all the shouting and commotion. Incidents like this would take place at least once every couple of months, and eventually I became so tired of it that in [date] I asked the respondent to leave, and to my surprise he did.

(4)   After the respondent moved out I would see him every week when he came to the house to see [name] and we remained on reasonable terms. However, earlier this year I started a relationship with another man and although we do not have any plans to live together the respondent turned very nasty about it. He started off by making snide comments and then he started threatening that he would take [child] away from me because he said I was an unfit mother. On another occasion he came round to see [child] and wanted to take him out for the afternoon. It was clear to me that the respondent had been drinking and so I refused, whereupon the respondent slapped me round the face, called me a slag, and would only leave when I enlisted the help of a friend to physically remove him from the house.

(5)   On [date] things came to a head. He came to the house and walked in without knocking. He walked straight upstairs and into my bedroom and without saying a word grabbed the first thing that was to hand, a table lamp. He smashed this against the wall. I had followed him upstairs and ordered him out of the house. He refused to leave and so I went downstairs to telephone the police. He followed me, grabbed the telephone from me and then grabbed me by the throat with great force. He then pushed me onto the sofa and held me down, shouting abuse at me. Eventually he calmed down and he left but not before saying that he would kill me if he saw my boyfriend anywhere near [child]. I am very concerned that he will carry out this threat. Certainly he has shown himself capable of inflicting extreme violence on me in the past and I am very much in fear of him and what he may do next time he comes to the house. He has sent me a large number of threatening text messages and has called me on my mobile 'phone telling me that he is going to get me.

(6)   In view of the history of violence towards me and the respondent's unpredictability I would like the protection of an order made without giving notice to the respondent. I am sure that if the respondent were to have notice of my application he would fly into a rage and come round straight away and harm me.[80]

(7)   In the circumstances I seek an order that the respondent be restrained from using or threatening violence against me, and from contacting me by telephone or by sending text messages. I also seek an order that the respondent having left the home we used to share at [address], he be forbidden to return to it or go within 50 metres of it.

I believe that the facts stated in this witness statement are true.

---

[80]   See **4.14**.

4.91   Witness statement in support of application for service by an alternative method

1ST statement
Made by [name]
On behalf of the
applicant
On [date]

IN THE [ ] COUNTY COURT   CASE NUMBER

BETWEEN:

A

Applicant

And

B

Respondent

STATEMENT IN SUPPORT OF APPLICATION
FOR SERVICE BY AN ALTERNATIVE METHOD

(1)   I, [name], of [address], a solicitor of the Supreme Court and a partner in [firm] say as follows:

(2)   I have the conduct of this matter on behalf of the applicant and I am authorised by her to make this statement in support of an application for an order for service of the application herein on the respondent by an alternative method.

(3)   In these proceedings the applicant seeks relief under Part IV of the Family Law Act 1996, in particular a non-molestation order against the respondent. The grounds of her application are set out in her statement dated [...] to which I shall refer.

(4)   It will be apparent from the applicant's statement that although the respondent has left the property in which they were living together, he retains a key to the property and has on a number of occasions returned there unannounced. If the applicant has been out he has ransacked the place, and if she has been in he has subjected her to verbal and sometimes physical abuse.

(5)   The problem in relation to service of the application and supporting documents is that the applicant has no idea where the respondent is living. She believes that he is staying with friends, but is not certain which friends. She is aware however that the respondent is still working at [address], and I duly made arrangements for a process server to attend at those premises in order to serve the respondent. However, the respondent had obviously been tipped off that a process server was looking for him, and several attempts to effect personal service of the respondent at his work address have been blocked by the receptionist who refuses to co-operate with the process server. The process server did confirm to me that on each of his visits to the [address] he saw that the respondent's

motor vehicle as described to him by the applicant was in the car park leading him to believe that the respondent was there and was evading service.

(6) In the circumstances, I believe that the respondent would receive the documents to be served on him if they were posted to him by ordinary first-class mail at his work address, and I ask for an order that this method of service be substituted for personal service.

I believe that the facts stated in this witness statement are true.

4.92 Letter to mortgagee/landlord of dwelling-house the subject of an application for an occupation order under s 33 or s 36 of the Family Law Act 1996

FIRST-CLASS POST

Dear Sir/Madam,

Address of Property

Roll Number (in the case of mortgaged property)

Names of Mortgagors/Tenants

We act for who is (one of) the mortgagor(s)/tenant(s) of the above-mentioned property.

Pursuant to Rule 10.3(3) of the Family Procedure Rules 2010, we enclose a copy of our client's application for an occupation order in respect of the property.

We also enclose notice in the prescribed Form FL416 informing you of your right to make representations in writing, or at any hearing.

Please acknowledge receipt of this letter within 7 days.

Yours faithfully,

CHAPTER 5

CHILDREN

PART A   LAW AND PRACTICE
SECTION 1   REGISTRATION OF BIRTHS; PARENTAL RESPONSIBILITY

5.1   Introduction

It has been some time since marriage was universally accepted as the only appropriate relationship within which to bring up children. Over forty seven per cent of all children in the UK are now born outside marriage,[1] and some 1.9 million children now live with cohabiting couples, including an increasing number of children living with same sex cohabitants.[2]

Over the years, legislation has slowly removed the distinction between children born within marriage and those born outside it. First, references to legitimate and illegitimate children were largely removed from family law legislation and replaced with a description of their parents as either married to one another or not. In 2003 changes were made to the CA 1989 so that fathers named on the birth certificate would automatically acquire parental responsibility even if not married to the mother.

Most recently, the HFEA 2008 updated the definitions of parenthood for parents undergoing assisted reproduction treatment and provided a mechanism under which a female partner could, in certain circumstances, acquire parental responsibility on registration in the same way as her male counterpart. For this reason, references in this section are generally to the 'mother' and the 'other parent' except in situations where the law could only possibly apply to a male second parent.

5.2   Registration of births

Every birth within England and Wales must be registered with the registrar of births and deaths for the sub-district in which the child was born.[3]

---

[1]   2014 Office for National Statistics.
[2]   2013 Office for National Statistics.
[3]   BDRA 1953, s 1.

A 'qualified informant' must provide the required information within 42 days of the date of birth. In the case of parents who are not married to one another at the time of the birth, the mother has a duty to register the birth, although the other parent[4] will be a 'qualified informant' and may register it.

If both parents sign the birth register together they will both be recorded as parents on the child's birth certificate. If the other parent does not attend then only the mother will be recorded as a parent unless she provides one of the following:

- a statutory declaration from the other parent confirming parentage;
- a parental responsibility order or agreement in relation to the child and makes a statutory declaration that any agreement complies with s 4 or s 4ZA of the CA 1989, and that there is no order bringing the order or agreement to an end; or
- an order made under Sch 1 to the CA 1989 for financial provision to be made by the other parent, and makes a statutory declaration that the order has not been discharged.

If the parent of a child who is not married to the mother of the child wishes to be named as the parent on the child's birth certificate, in the absence of a joint request for his or her name to be registered, that parent may apply for registration of their details in any one of the following circumstances:

- they produce statutory declarations from themselves and from the mother that they are the parent of the child;
- they produce a parental responsibility order or agreement in relation to the child and make a statutory declaration that the agreement complies with the requirements of s 4 or s 4ZA of the CA 1989 and that there is no order bringing the order or agreement to an end;
- they produce an order requiring them to make financial provision for the child under Sch 1 to the CA 1989 and make a statutory declaration that the order has not been discharged.

In practice, since the introduction of the Child Support Agency,[5] there will be relatively few cases in which either parent will be able to produce a financial provision order within the first 42 days of a child's life. It is also unlikely that a court would be in a position to make a parental responsibility order on a contested application within six weeks of the birth of the child, and so the opportunity for one or other parent to register the parent's details where there is no agreement between them will be limited.

If the parents of a child born outside marriage subsequently marry one another the child becomes legitimated and the birth should be re-registered.[6]

---

4   Usually the father, but the same rules apply to a second female parent pursuant to an agreement under HFEA 2008, s 43.

5   And its successors, the Child Maintenance and Enforcement Commission (CMEC) and most recently the Child Maintenance Service (CMS).

6   BDRA 1953, s 14(1).

5.3 Determination of parentage

Where a child is born to a woman who is married, there is a presumption that her husband is the father of the child, provided that the parties were married at the estimated date of conception.[7] There is no such presumption of paternity even where the unmarried parents of a child were living together in a stable relationship at the time of the birth.

However, if a man's name is recorded in the Register of Births as the father of a child this is *prima facie* evidence of paternity and therefore the burden of proof will be on the father if he subsequently disputes it.

Under CSA 1991, s 26(2), the circumstances in which the Child Maintenance Service may assume that a man is the father of a child in the face of his denial of paternity were enlarged, and the burden of proof falls on him to prove he is not the father. These circumstances include a case in which the man is named as the father on the child's birth certificate, and where he refuses to submit to scientific testing to establish paternity.

As well as being an issue for parents who may wish to avoid or confirm paternity (whether for reasons connected with parental responsibility, contact and residence, or financial support), parentage may also be a matter that a child may wish to bring before the court.

5.4 Declaration of parentage

In any case in which parentage is disputed a declaration of parentage can be sought from the court under FLA 1986, s 55A.

A parent (or alleged parent), the child or anyone else with sufficient personal interest may apply for a declaration of parentage (including the Secretary of State in circumstances where an alleged parent objects to a child maintenance calculation on the basis that they are not a parent of the child). The alleged parents and the person whose parentage is in issue must be respondents to the application. There is provision for the Attorney General to intervene to minimise the incidence of fraudulent applications proceeding unopposed.

5.5 Evidence on an application for declaration of parentage

CSPSSA 2000 effected an important change to the court's powers under FLRA 1969 to order testing in order to establish paternity. Before CSPSSA 2000 the position was that if the parent of a child aged under 16 years refused to allow the child to be subjected to tests the court could not compel the taking of a

---

[7]   Although the relevance of such a presumption in the age of DNA testing has been questioned, see for example the comments of Thorpe LJ in *Re H and A (Paternity: Blood Tests)* [2002] 1 FLR 1145.

sample.[8] The position now is that where the parent refuses to allow testing when directed by the court, the court may consent to a test if it is in the best interests of the child to do so.[9]

The approach of the court was considered in *Re T (Paternity: Ordering Blood Tests)*.[10] In that case the child's mother and her husband agreed that as they were unable to conceive together the mother would have a sexual relationship with a family friend with a view to conceiving a child that would be brought up by the mother and her husband. She did not conceive. However, some years later she resumed her sexual relationship with the family friend and three other men. She became pregnant and she brought up the child with her husband. The family friend saw the child in the normal course of events, but before long the mother took the view that he was overstepping the mark and brought an end to his visits. He applied for parental responsibility and contact but was unsuccessful. Subsequently, he made it known publicly that he believed himself to be the father of the child and the judge found that there was a significant risk that the child would learn of the situation sooner rather than later. He made a further application to the court six years later for a direction for DNA testing to establish paternity.[11]

Confirming that the earlier authorities of *S v S; W v Official Solicitor*[12] and *Re H (Paternity: Blood Test)*[13] remained good law, Bodey J held that:

> 'Under domestic law the child's best interests were to be weighed against the competing interests of the adults affected. In most cases it was likely to be in the child's best interests that the truth about paternity was known and under Art 8 ECPHRFF 1950 all parties had the right to respect for private and family life. The child had a right to know his true identity and to have the possibility of contact with each of his natural parents; also a competing right to have the current stability of his family life protected. Similarly the mother and her husband, and the applicant ... had conflicting rights. When the various Convention rights pulled in different directions, the rights and best interests of the child concerned fell particularly to be considered, and in this case the child's right to know, perhaps with certainty, his true identity, emerged as the weightiest consideration. The interference with other rights which would result from going ahead with the tests was proportionate to the legitimate aim of providing the child with the possibility of certainty as to his real paternity.'[14]

---

8   See *Re O (A Minor) (Blood Tests: Constraint)* [2000] 1 FLR 418 in which Wall J, as he then was, disagreed with the approach of Hale J, as she then was, in *Re R (Blood Test; Constraint)* [1998] 1 FLR 745 where she had given temporary care and control of the child to the Official Solicitor to enable him to consent to the taking of samples.

9   FLRA 1969, s 21(3).

10   [2001] 2 FLR 1190.

11   See *Re F (Children) DNA Evidence* [2008] 1 FLR 348 for guidelines for orders for DNA testing.

12   [1972] AC 24.

13   [1996] 2 FLR 65.

14   For the circumstances in which the court may decline to make an order requiring the mother to disclose to a child the identity of his father see *Re K (Specific Issue Order)* [1999] 2 FLR 280; *Re J (Paternity: Welfare of Child)* [2007] 1 FLR 1064; *Re F (Paternity: Jurisdiction)* [2008] 1 FLR 225.

5.6 Refusal to submit to testing

The refusal of a parent to consent to the scientific testing of a child need no longer create evidential difficulties in view of the court's powers under FLRA 1969, s 21 to give consent in appropriate cases. Where a man against whom a declaration of parentage is sought fails to submit to testing directed by the court he cannot be compelled to take part in testing, but the court is entitled to draw an adverse inference from his reluctance to do so.

In *Secretary of State for Work and Pensions v Jones*[15] an application was made by the Secretary of State for Work and Pensions for a declaration of parentage under FLA 1986, s 55A. An application for a maintenance calculation had been made to the Child Support Agency naming Mr Jones as the child's father. He denied paternity. A direction was made by the family proceedings court that Mr Jones should submit to a DNA test to establish paternity. He refused to do so.

The President of the Family Division at that time held that on the subsequent hearing on the issue of paternity the magistrates had been wrong not to follow the authority of the Court of Appeal in *Re A (A Minor) (Paternity: Refusal of Blood Test)*[16] and *Re G (Parentage: Blood Sample)*[17] and draw the inference from Mr Jones' refusal to be tested that he was the father of the child.[18]

5.7 Assisted reproduction

A woman who has carried a child as a result of the placing in her of an embryo or of sperm and eggs is treated as the child's mother regardless of whether her eggs or donor eggs were used.[19]

At common law, the genetic father is considered to be the legal father. Where an unmarried couple have undergone in vitro fertilisation using the man's sperm they will both be the child's parents (regardless of whether a donor egg was used).

The situation becomes more complicated where donor sperm is used. Since the coming into force of HFEA 2008 on 1 April 2009, the mother's unmarried partner (whether male or female) will be treated with the mother as the child's parent where, at the time the treatment takes place:[20]

---

[15] [2004] 1 FLR 282.
[16] [1994] 2 FLR 463.
[17] [1997] 1 FLR 360.
[18] The interesting question of what inference to draw when a refusal accompanies an assertion of paternity, rather than a denial, was raised but not answered by the current President in *Re Z (Children)* [2014] EWHC 1999 (Fam).
[19] HFEA 2008, s 33(1), also HFEA 1990, s 27.
[20] Specifically, at the time the embryo or the sperm and eggs are placed in the mother, or at which she is artificially inseminated.

–   the mother was not married or in a civil partnership (or, if she was, her husband/wife/civil partner did not consent to the treatment);

–   both the mother and her partner provided the appropriate notices under s 37 (male) or s 44 (female) of the HFEA 2008;

–   the treatment is provide by an appropriately licensed clinic; and

–   the partner is still alive.

HFEA 2008 did not apply retrospectively, and earlier treatments (between 1 August 1991 and 31 March 2009) are still determined by HFEA 1990. Under this Act the requirements for unmarried fathers were similar to the 2008 regime, except that there was no equivalent to s 37 requiring formal notice to be given.[21] There was no equivalent provision for a female partner.

The case of *AB v CD and the Z Fertility Clinic*[22] concerned a situation where the course of fertility treatment straddled the cross-over between the 1990 and 2008 regimes. When the new regime came into force the clinic did not ensure that the appropriate consent forms were completed and, in particular, did not ensure that both partners received the necessary counselling required by the terms of its licence. As a result, the mother's female partner was deemed not to be the children's parent. In light of this case and other similar situations, the Human Fertility and Embryology Authority has instructed all clinics to conduct a complete audit of patient records since April 2009 for unmarried couples[23] and it may well be the case that further instances arise where partners do not have the legal parental status they expected.

A child born by donor insemination before 1 August 1991 will not be regarded as the child of the male partner, whether he was married to the mother or not.[24]

5.8   Parental responsibility

CA 1989, s 3(1) defines parental responsibility as 'all the rights, powers, responsibilities and authority which by law a parent of a child has in relation to the child and his property'.

Until CA 1989 was amended by the ACA 2002,[25] if the parents of a child were not married to one another at the time of the birth the mother would automatically have parental responsibility but the father would not.

The effect of this was that an unmarried father without parental responsibility was potentially disadvantaged. He may not have been consulted in adoption

---

21   HFEA 1990, s 28(3).
22   [2013] 2 FLR 1357.
23   HFEA (CE(14)01, 2014).
24   *Re M (Child Support Act: Parentage)* [1997] 2 FLR 90.
25   Adoption and Children Act 2002, s 111.

proceedings[26] or if the mother wished to change the child's name, nor would he be entitled to receive information from the child's doctor or school, or give consent for medical treatment.

CA 1989, s 4(1)(a)[27] provides that a parent[28] who registers the child's birth jointly with the child's mother will automatically have parental responsibility. Where circumstances at the time of the birth do not make this possible, the procedure for entering into a parental responsibility agreement is retained, and a parent without parental responsibility may still apply for a parental responsibility order.

It is also possible for a parent's name to be placed on the birth certificate by making an application to re-register the birth.[29]

These measures go some way to removing the discrimination between unmarried mothers and the other parent but it should be noted that whereas a mother may lose parental responsibility only if an adoption order is made in respect of the child, the other parent may also lose the automatically conferred parental responsibility if the court orders it under CA 1989, s 4(2A).[30]

5.9 Acquiring parental responsibility

An unmarried father or second female parent may acquire parental responsibility for their child by any one of the following means:

- jointly registering the child's birth with the child's mother;[31]

- marrying (or entering into a civil partnership with) the child's mother;[32]

- entering into a parental responsibility agreement with the child's mother;[33]

- obtaining a parental responsibility order;[34]

- being appointed as the child's guardian;[35]

- being named in a child arrangements order as a person with whom the child shall live;[36] or

- having an adoption order made in their favour.

More than one person may have parental responsibility for the same child.

---

[26] *Re R (Adoption: Father's Involvement)* [2001] 1 FLR 302; *Re H; Re G (Adoption: Consultation of Unmarried Fathers)* [2001] 1 FLR 646.

[27] And, since 1 April 2009, s 4ZA(1)(a) for second female parents.

[28] Either a biological father or, since the enactment of HFEA 2008, either a man or woman who is a legal parent by virtue of being the partner of a woman who has undergone licensed assisted reproduction treatment, see *Assisted Reproduction* at 5.7.

[29] Births and Deaths Registration Act 1953, s 10A.

[30] Section 4ZA(5) in respect of second female parents.

[31] CA 1989, ss 4(1)(a) and 4ZA(1)(a).

[32] CA 1989, s 2(3) indirectly recognises the effect of the LA 1976, s 2.

[33] CA 1989, ss 4(1)(b) and 4ZA(1)(b).

[34] CA 1989, ss 4(1)(a) and 4ZA(1)(a).

[35] CA 1989, s 5.

[36] CA 1989, ss 8 and 12.

5.10 Jointly registering the birth

CA 1989, ss 4(1)(a) and 4ZA(1)(a) provide that a parent who jointly registers the child's birth with the child's mother or re-registers it will automatically have parental responsibility. The birth certificate will be evidence of this. However, such a parent may lose parental responsibility acquired under s 4(1)(a) or s 4ZA(1)(a) if the court orders it under CA 1989, s 4(2A) or s 4ZA(5). Re-registration of a child born to unmarried parents can be effected at any time subject to the requirements that if the child has reached the age of 16 the child's written consent must be given. Furthermore, an amendment to the birth certificate made automatically following a declaration of parentage will not impart parental responsibility on the other parent.

It follows from this that a birth certificate is not necessarily conclusive evidence of a father or second female parent's parental responsibility since the birth may have been re-registered subsequently, or indeed superseded by an order removing parental responsibility, or an adoption order.

5.11 Parental responsibility agreement

If the parents of a child who are not married to one another at the time of the birth agree, they can enter into a parental responsibility agreement which, if all the formalities are complied with, will mean that they will then both have parental responsibility for the child. There is nothing to prevent unmarried parents from entering into a parental responsibility agreement even where a care order in respect of the child has been granted in favour of a local authority.[37]

A parental responsibility agreement is not necessary if both parents jointly register the child's birth.[38]

5.12 Procedure

The form for a parental responsibility agreement is prescribed by the PRAR 1991,[39] as amended, and available as court forms C(PRA1) and C(PRA3). The parents' signatures must be witnessed by a Justice of the Peace or an officer of the court[40] and filed (with sufficient copies for each parent) at the Principal Registry of the Family Division. On receipt, the copy agreements will be sealed and one sent to each parent. There must be a separate agreement for each child. The original agreement remains at the Principal Registry and is a public document. Unless all the formalities are observed, the agreement will not take effect.

---

[37] *Re X (Parental Responsibility Agreement: Children in Care)* [2000] 1 FLR 517.
[38] CA 1989, ss 4(1)(a) and 4ZA(1)(a).
[39] SI 1991/1478.
[40] This does not include solicitors.

In view of the cumbersome procedure, and a tendency not to have recourse to the law before it is absolutely necessary, it is hardly surprising that the number of parental responsibility agreements registered each year accounts for little more than 1 per cent of all live births outside marriage.

5.13 *Duration of agreements*

A parental responsibility agreement will automatically come to an end on the child's 18th birthday.[41]

An agreement cannot be revoked unilaterally, and can only be brought to an end before the child's 18th birthday by an order of the court.[42]

An application to terminate a parental responsibility agreement may be made by either party to the agreement or any other person with parental responsibility for the child. With the court's leave, the child may apply to terminate the agreement.

5.14 Parental responsibility order

If parents of a child who are not married to one another (or in a civil partnership) at the time of the birth, and who have not jointly registered the birth, cannot agree that the father (or second female parent) should have parental responsibility that parent can apply to the court under s 4(1)(c) or s 4ZA(1)(c) of CA 1989 for an order giving them parental responsibility.[43] A parental responsibility order is intended to confer status on an unmarried parent so that they are in no worse position than a married parent would be. The effect of a parental responsibility order is not to give the parent a right to interfere in what the person with day-to-day care of the child is doing.[44]

The issue of parental responsibility is quite separate from those of where the child should live and who they should spend time with, and different considerations apply.[45]

The effect of a parental responsibility order was summarised by the Court of Appeal in *Re S (Parental Responsibility)*:[46]

---

[41] CA 1989, s 91(8).

[42] CA 1989, s 4(3).

[43] If the father or second female parent is not named on the birth certificate then, in the absence of agreement from the mother, they cannot simply circumvent the need for a parental responsibility order by obtaining a declaration of parentage and subsequent amendment of the birth certificate as re-registration under BDRA 1953, s 14A is not one of the specified enactments under CA 1989, s 4(1A) – see *M v F and H (Legal Paternity)* [2014] 1 FLR 352 at para 31.

[44] *Re P (A Minor) (Parental Responsibility Order)* [1994] 1 FLR 578 and *Re A (A Minor) (Parental Responsibility)* [1996] 1 FCR 562.

[45] *Re C and V (Contact and Parental Responsibility)* [1998] 1 FLR 392.

[46] [1995] 2 FLR 648 at 648F.

'… The granting of a parental responsibility order was the granting of a status … It was wrong to place undue and false emphasis on the rights and duties and powers comprised in "parental responsibility" and not to concentrate on the fact that what was at issue was the conferring on a committed father of the status of parenthood for which nature had already ordained that he must bear responsibility, and there was all too frequently a failure to appreciate that any abuse of the exercise of parental responsibility which was adverse to the welfare of the child could be controlled by the wide exercise of s 8 orders …'

5.15 Procedure

The application is made in Form C1 (accompanied by a Form FM1) to the Family Court.

The respondent(s) to the application will be the mother and any other person having parental responsibility for the child, or having the day-to-day care of the child. They will need to be served with notice of the application.

5.16 The exercise of the court's discretion

When deciding whether or not to make an order for parental responsibility in favour of a parent, the court will apply the principle that the child's welfare is the paramount consideration.[47] Under the CFA 2014, new sections[48] have been written into the CA 1989 introducing a presumption that involvement of a parent in its life will further the child's welfare.[49] The presumption will apply to all cases commenced on or after 22 October 2014, but not those already commenced but not disposed of prior to that date.[50] In addition, the court will have regard to the general principle that unless it considers that it would be better for the child that an order be made, no order should be made on any application under the CA 1989.[51]

These considerations apart, the CA 1989 does not prescribe any matters to which the court must have specific regard. However, reported cases suggest that the factors that will guide the court include:

– the reasons for the parent's application;

– the degree of commitment shown by the parent to the child;

– the degree of attachment between the parent and the child;[52]

– the nature of the relationship between the mother and the other parent of the child.

---

[47] CA 1989, s 1(1).

[48] Which will be ss 1(2A) and (2B)

[49] CFA 2014, s 11

[50] Although FPR PD12J was amended as early as April 2014 to include the words: 'the Family Court presumes that the involvement of a parent in a child's life will further a child's welfare, so long as the parent can be involved in a way that does not put the child or other parent at risk of suffering harm' (at para 4).

[51] CA 1989, s 1(5).

[52] *Re H (Illegitimate Children: Father: Parental Rights) (No 2)* [1991] 1 FLR 214.

The fact that a parent may not be able to exercise one or more of the parental rights that a parental responsibility order would confer upon him should not necessarily deter the court from making an order in his favour.[53]

Whether the presumption imported by the CFA 2014 will significantly alter the approach of the court remains to be seen.

A parental responsibility order can be made in favour of the other parent even where the child is in the care of the local authority, thereby giving him the right to be heard in the care proceedings.[54]

In *Re S (Parental Responsibility)*[55] it followed from the fact that a parental responsibility order did no more than confer status that the judge at first instance had been wrong to refuse a parental responsibility order to the father of a six-year-old girl who although he had been convicted of being in possession of paedophilic material was nonetheless a genuine, attached and committed father.

In reaching his decision, Ward LJ's review of the authorities up to that point remains the leading exposition on how to apply the welfare test in CA 1989, s 1 to the question of parental responsibility. In *Re M (Parental Responsibility Order)*[56] Ryder LJ condensed this into a list of non-exhaustive factors which he described as the '*Re S (Parental Responsibility)* factors':

(1) The court should take into account the degree of commitment which the father has shown towards the child, the degree of attachment which exists between the father and the child and the reasons of the father for applying for the court order.

(2) It is a relevant but not an overriding consideration that the court considers the prospective enforceability of parental rights.

(3) It is important to observe the interrelation between the rights and the status and the exercise of those rights and the restrictions upon the exercise of those rights that exists or can be imposed. One of the examples given of this was the 'cruel and callous' behaviour of a father who abducted a child from her mother for a few days who was not granted parental responsibility and other circumstances where a misuse of 'rights' could be controlled by a specific issue or prohibited steps order or in the last resort the discharge of a parental responsibility order.

(4) While not wholly irrelevant to each other, the s 8 welfare decision and a decision whether to grant a father parental responsibility are separate and distinct questions to be examined from different perspectives.

(5) Where a concerned though absent father has established a degree of commitment to a child, there is a degree of attachment between them and his reasons for applying for parental responsibility are neither

---

[53] *Re C (Minors) (Parental Rights)* [1992] 1 FLR 1.
[54] *Re G (A Minor) (Parental Responsibility Order)* [1994] 1 FLR 504.
[55] [1995] 2 FLR 648.
[56] [2014] 1 FLR 339.

demonstrably improper or wrong, then prima facie, it would be in the interests of the child for a parental responsibility order to be made and the court will need cogent evidence that the child's welfare would be adversely affected before considering otherwise.

In *Re H (Parental Responsibility)*[57] a father appealed against the refusal of a parental responsibility order on the basis that he had demonstrated commitment to the child, the child was attached to him, and the motivation behind his application was genuine. The Court of Appeal held that those factors:[58]

> '... though a starting-point, were not intended to be exhaustive. Notwithstanding that parental responsibility was a question of status and different in concept from orders made under s 8 ... the court had a duty to take into account all the relevant circumstances bearing in mind that s 1 applied, under which the welfare of the child was paramount. If the judge considered that there were factors adverse to the father sufficient to tip the balance ... it would not be right to make the order even though the three requirements could be shown by the father.'

What concerned the court in that case was that the father was unable to accept responsibility for his actions, having inflicted injuries on the four-year-old child that the court considered could only have been caused deliberately and sadistically.

In *Re J-S (Contact: Parental Responsibility)*[59] it was held by the Court of Appeal that the case for granting parental responsibility to a father who had, until the parents separated, played an important part in the child's life and whose devotion to him was overwhelming, despite findings by the trial judge of violence and harassment of the mother by the father. The father easily established the recognised criteria of commitment, attachment and appropriate motivation as set out in *Re H (Parental Responsibility)*.

In *Re C and V (Contact and Parental Responsibility)*[60] the court confirmed that a parental responsibility order did no more than confer on a natural father the state of fatherhood enjoyed by a father who was married to the child's mother.

In *Re P (Parental Responsibility)*[61] the court exercised its discretion to refuse a parental responsibility order having found that the father would use the status if conferred to try to interfere with and possibly undermine the mother's care of the child. The Court of Appeal upheld the judge's decision, holding that it was not sufficient to say that the father's potential for interference could be controlled by orders that could be made under s 8 of the CA 1989.

---

[57]   [1998] 1 FLR 855; followed in *Re P (Parental Responsibility)* [1998] 2 FLR 96.
[58]   At p 855F.
[59]   [2002] EWCA Civ 1028.
[60]   [1998] 1 FLR 392.
[61]   [1998] 2 FLR 96.

It will be inappropriate for the court to withhold a parental responsibility order until the applicant has demonstrated his commitment by assisting in the financial upkeep of the child.[62]

The fact that the mother displays a negative reaction to a parental responsibility order which would adversely affect her child was held in *Re K*[63] to be sufficient reason to refuse the order.

Where the purpose of the father's application was to obtain the precise information that a child (of sufficient age and understanding) wished to conceal then the application should be refused. Also, parental responsibility is not to be 'automatically conferred' if the father poses a risk to the child or if his reasons for applying were 'demonstrably wrong'. Case-law is clear that the likely misuse of parental responsibility could lead to it being refused.[64]

The court may entertain an application for a parental responsibility order even if the child is born out of the jurisdiction, and/or is permanently outside the jurisdiction. There would be no jurisdiction to grant s 8 orders however.[65]

Note that a parent will acquire parental responsibility where an order is made that the child is to live with them.[66] This is true even if the application is made without notice to the mother, for example in a situation in which the other parent contends that the court should intervene in an emergency situation. It may be that the order regarding who the child is to live with is discharged when the mother has had an opportunity to be heard, and yet the other parent has still acquired parental responsibility by default.

5.17 Duration of order

An order giving a parent parental responsibility will automatically end on the child's 18th birthday or the marriage of the parties,[67] but otherwise it cannot be discharged except by a further order of the court.

5.18 Discharge of order

Any person with parental responsibility may apply to discharge the order, and with leave the child may also apply. The welfare principle will apply to applications to terminate parental responsibility. It has been noted that courts should be slow to terminate a parental responsibility order '… not least because they can only do so in the case of unmarried fathers'.[68]

---

62 *Re H (Parental Responsibility: Maintenance)* [1996] 1 FLR 867.
63 [1998] Fam Law 567.
64 *Re M (Parental Responsibility Order)* [2014] 1 FLR 339.
65 *Re S (Parental Responsibility: Jurisdiction)* [1998] 2 FLR 921.
66 CA 1989, s 12(1).
67 CA 1989, s 21(1).
68 *Re C (A Child)* [2002] EWCA Civ 446, para 13.

In *Re P (Terminating Parental Responsibility)*[69] a father was said to have forfeited his parental responsibility by causing serious injuries to his child for which he was convicted and imprisoned. The court noted that the welfare of the child is paramount and that an order terminating parental responsibility should only be used as an appropriate step in the regulation of the child's life where the circumstances really do warrant it and not otherwise. *Re D (A Child)*[70] confirmed that the introduction of ACA 2002 and HRA 1998 had not changed the test as expounded in *Re P*. Although in this case the court did terminate the father's parental responsibility, Ryder LJ was clear that the case should not be construed as making it easier to remove an unmarried parent's parental responsibility.

No order can be made to discharge a parental responsibility order where the father also has a residence order (or child arrangements order that the child live with him) in his favour.[71]

The discharge of a residence or child arrangements order does not automatically revoke the parental responsibility order, which has to be considered separately.

Parental responsibility, once acquired, cannot be given up or transferred to any other person. The mother of a child can only lose parental responsibility through adoption or a freeing order, likewise the other parent if they were married to (or in a civil partnership with) the mother at the time of the child's conception.

A parent who automatically acquires parental responsibility by jointly registering the child's birth with the mother can lose that status by court order under CA 1989, s 4(2A).

5.19 Applications for orders under s 8 of the Children Act 1989

Whether the parent of a child has parental responsibility or not, he or she may apply to the court without leave for a child arrangements order (regulating who the child is to live, spend time or otherwise have contact with), for the determination of a specific issue or to prohibit certain steps being taken.

Quite often in practice an application for a child arrangements order for contact will be combined with an application for a parental responsibility order where the parent has not already acquired it.

The same principles will guide the court when deciding whether to make an order under s 8, regardless of whether a parent was married to (or in a civil partnership with) the child's mother at the time of the birth or not, namely that

---

[69]   [1995] 1 FLR 1048.
[70]   [2014] EWCA Civ 315.
[71]   CA 1989, s 12(4).

the welfare of the child is the paramount consideration. The court will have regard in particular to the matters set out in s 1(3) of the CA 1989 (the 'welfare checklist'):

(a) the ascertainable wishes and feelings of the child concerned (considered in the light of the child's age and understanding);

(b) his physical, emotional and educational needs;

(c) the likely effect on the child of any change in his or her circumstances;

(d) the child's age, sex, background and any characteristics the court considers relevant;

(e) any harm which the child has suffered or is at risk of suffering;

(f) how capable each of the child's parents, and any other person in relation to whom the court considers the question to be relevant, is of meeting the child's needs; and

(g) the range of powers available to the court under the CA 1989 in the proceedings in question.

The court will also have regard to the general principle that any delay is likely to prejudice the child, and that it will not make an order unless it would be better for the child than making no order at all.

In addition, for cases commencing on or after 22 October 2014, CFA 2014, s 11 introduces a presumption[72] that involvement of a parent in its life will further the child's welfare.

If an order is made that a child should live with a parent without parental responsibility, even if that order is made on an interim basis, the court must also make a parental responsibility order in that parent's favour.[73]

If an order is made that the child should live with one parent where both parents have parental responsibility, and if those parents subsequently cohabit for a continuous period exceeding six months, the child arrangements order will cease to have effect.[74] This will not operate to deprive a parent of the benefit of parental responsibility when that parental responsibility was acquired as a result of a child arrangements order specifying them as a person with whom the child was to live.

Notice of an application under CA 1989, s 8 must be given to any person with parental responsibility, any person caring for the child at the time the application is made, any person who is believed by the applicant to be named in a current relevant court order affecting the child, and any person with whom the child has lived for at least three years prior to the application. There will be circumstances, therefore, where a s 8 application could be sought without an unmarried parent having to be notified. In relation to care proceedings,

---

[72] At CA 1989, ss 1(2A) and (2B).

[73] See **5.16** above.

[74] CA 1989, s 11(5).

however, notice must be given to any person whom the applicant believes to be a parent of the child, whether or not that person has parental responsibility.

In the context of a relationship breakdown, grandparents and other relatives apart from a child's parents may wish to apply for s 8 orders. Unless they (unusually) fall within the categories of persons specified in s 10 of the CA 1989, they will need the permission of the court to bring an application.

Section 10(9) sets out the matters to which the court will have particular regard when deciding whether or not to give permission:

(a)   the nature of the proposed application for the s 8 order;

(b)   the applicant's connection with the child; and

(c)   any risk there might be of the proposed application disrupting the child's life to such an extent that he or she would be harmed by it.

Whilst the welfare checklist does not specifically apply, the matters set out in it clearly will be relevant to the court's consideration of the application for leave and the court will take into account the likely prospects of success of the proposed substantive application when deciding whether or not to grant leave.[75]

5.20   Procedure

The procedure for applying for and dealing with s 8 applications after 22 April 2014 is set out in the Child Arrangments Programme, which was incorporated into FPR PD 12B on the same date.

Applications for a child arrangements order are made on Form C100. Where there are allegations of harm or domestic violence a Form C1A should accompany the application.

Parents are expected to consider whether dispute resolution services, including mediation, would be appropriate and can be safely attempted before issuing an application for a s 8 order. Other than in exceptional circumstances[76] the applicant will be expected to have attended a Mediation Information and Assessment Meeting (MIAM) to obtain information about mediation and consider the suitability of mediation as a way of resolving the dispute. The mediator will sign the C100 to confirm their attendance. Where a judge considers that the parties have not taken sufficient steps to explore alternative forms of dispute resolution the court may direct that proceedings, or a hearing in the proceedings, be adjourned to enable the parties to obtain further

---

[75]   *Re C (Residence: Child's Application for Leave)* [1995] 1 FLR 927; *Re SC (A Minor) (Leave to Seek Residence Order)* [1994] 1 FLR 96; *Re M (Care: Contact: Grandmother's Application for Leave)* [1995] 2 FLR 86.

[76]   Set out in full at FPR r 3.8 but essentially in cases where the application is urgent, where there is a history of domestic violence or there are child protection concerns.

information about non-court dispute resolution and, if the parties agree, to enable such dispute resolution to be attempted.[77]

Where an application is made for a child arrangements order, Cafcass[78] or CAFCASS Cymru will be notified and carry out initial safeguarding enquiries, including seeking information from local authorities and carrying out police checks on the parties. Where possible, they will also undertake telephone risk identification interviews with the parties. Any safety issues identified will be reported to the court in a safeguarding letter.

A First Hearing Dispute Resolution Appointment (FHDRA) should ordinarily be listed five to six weeks after the application is filed at court. All parties should attend. Local practices vary as to whether children should attend this first meeting but should be made clear on the notice of hearing provided by the court.[79]

The FHDRA provides an opportunity for the parties to be helped to an understanding of the issues between them and to reach an agreement. If an agreement can be reached the court will be able to make an order reflecting that agreement. If not, the court will make directions for the future conduct of the case – this may include the preparation of a welfare report under CA 1989, s 7, fact-finding and/or dispute resolution hearings and detailed statements from the parties.

Orders made at the FHDRA should be made on an order CAP02.

5.21 Change of name

The issue of the surname by which a child is to be known is one that can frequently arise where the parents of a child are not married and so do not share the same surname, unless one of them has chosen formally to adopt the surname of the other.[80] Similarly, the name of the mother may change on

---

[77] FPR PD 12B, para 6.3.

[78] The Children and Family Court Advisory and Support Service.

[79] The District Judge's Direction: Children: Conciliation [2004] 1 FLR 974 stated that the practice in the Principal Registry of the Family Division from 22 April 2004 was for 'any child aged 9 or over to whom the conciliation appointment relates *must* attend (unless otherwise directed) and that when a child of 9 or over attends, any younger child to whom the application relates *may* also attend. This direction related to the PRFD conciliation program, and continued in practice even though no subsequent guidance was issued after that program was superseded first by the Private Law Programme (November 2004), then the Revised Private Law Programme (April 2010) and most recently the Child Arrangements Programme (April 2014).

[80] See, generally, Nasreen Pearce *Name-changing: A Practical Guide* (Fourmat Publishing, 1990). Broadly speaking, a person can be called by whatever name he or she chooses. This is provided he does not do so for any fraudulent purpose or in order to deceive and inflict economic loss on another (*Du Boulay v Du Boulay* (1869) LR 2 PC 430; *Cowley v Cowley* [1901] AC 450) or for purely frivolous reasons such as 'Pudsey Bear' in the infamous case of Eileen De Bont. No formalities are necessary, and a name can be acquired simply by habit and repute. See *Dancer v Dancer* [1949] P 147. It was stated by Justice Harry Vaisey in *re Parrott, Cox and Parrott* [1946] Ch 183 that a Christian name given to a person on baptism cannot be changed by deed

marriage or remarriage, or she may choose to revert to a former surname on divorce, raising the question of whether the name of the child should be changed as well. Understandably, both parents may hold strong opinions about why their own surname should be used, and the courts have viewed any application to change a child's name as a matter of utmost importance and have shown a reluctance to accede to such a request lightly.

5.22   Who may change the surname of a child?

Except where there has been a clerical error or a mistake, the entry of a child's name in the Register of Births cannot be changed. However, the name by which a child is known can be changed, and if a child's parents are in agreement they may execute a change of name deed to record this.[81]

However, the birth may be re-registered to include the father's surname on the birth certificate if the mother consents, if there is an order or agreement giving the father parental responsibility or if there is a court order for the father to maintain the child. This procedure cannot be used to change the child's name.[82]

In cases in which a child arrangements order regulating where a child is to live or a care order is in force in respect of any child, the permission of the court is required before a child may be known by a new surname unless the written consent of every person with parental responsibility has been obtained.[83]

A Practice Direction governs the formal procedure for changing a child's surname by deed poll.[84]

Re PC (Change of Surname)[85] concerned three legitimate children whose mother effected a change of their surname by deed poll following her remarriage. The children lived with the mother and her new husband and, initially, there was contact with the father. The father discovered the change of

---

poll and can therefore only be changed on confirmation, by Act of Parliament or by adding a name when a child is adopted. In a few cases authority to take a new forename has been given by royal licence.

[81]   At some stage somebody is likely to require evidence of the change of name, and so it is usual practice to document a change of name by means of one of the more formal procedures, such as executing a deed or making a statutory declaration. Other methods include Notarial Instrument, Royal Licence, and even a private Act of Parliament. Where a change of name deed is to be enrolled in the Central Office of the Supreme Court, the enrolment regulations distinguish between children who have attained the age of 16, and those who have not (Enrolment of Deeds (Change of Name) Regulations 1983 (SI 1983/680), reg 8). A child of 16 or over can either execute the deed poll himself or endorse his consent on the deed executed by his parent or guardian on his behalf. (See Enrolment of Deeds (Change of Name) Regulations 1983, reg 8(3).) Where a child is under 16 the deed poll must be executed by his parent or guardian, and the application for enrolment must be supported by an affidavit showing that the change of name is for the child's benefit (1983 Regulations, reg 8(5); see also *Practice Direction of 24 May 1976* [1977] 1 WLR 1065).

[82]   BDRA 1953.

[83]   CA 1989, ss 13(1)(a) and 33(7)(a).

[84]   *Practice Direction of 20 December 1994 (Child: Change of Surname)* [1995] 1 FLR 458.

[85]   [1997] 2 FLR 730.

name from the headmaster of the children's school who had rightly refused to register the change of name without evidence of the consent of every person with parental responsibility. The mother applied for a specific issue order to compel the school to register the change of name. The mother's argument that she could exercise her parental responsibility unilaterally and so change the children's names without reference to any other person with parental responsibility, ie their father, was rejected. For the avoidance of doubt in the future, the court set out as follows who might apply to change a child's surname.

(1) Where only one person has parental responsibility for a child (eg a surviving parent after the death of the other, or the mother of a child born outside marriage where there has been no order or agreement for parental responsibility), that person has the right and power lawfully to cause a change of surname without any other permission or consent.

(2) Where two or more people have parental responsibility for a child, one of those people can lawfully cause a change of surname only if all other people having parental responsibility consent or agree. Subject to (3) below, there is no necessary requirement that that consent be in writing.

(3) Where two or more people have parental responsibility for a child and either a residence or a care order is in force, then one of those people can lawfully cause a change of surname only if all other people having parental responsibility consent in writing.

(4) In any other situation an appropriate order of the court is required.

The court also pointed out that in the case of children over 16 none of the above may apply as generally their wishes and feelings would prevail.

5.23 Procedure

It is clear from the authorities that one parent wishing to change a child's name against the wishes of the other will be well advised to bring the matter to court for determination.

If there is a residence order in force, a free-standing application should be made for leave to cause the child to be known by a new surname under the jurisdiction given by CA 1989, s 13. In any other case, an application should be made for a specific issue order under CA 1989, s 8.

Where the change of name has already been effected unilaterally, application by a concerned parent or party with parental responsibility should be made under s 8 for an order requiring the name to be changed back, and a prohibition against any future change. The court might also be invited to make a residence order, thereby invoking the general prohibition in s 13(1)(a) against a unilateral change.

As a matter of practice, any application to change a child's name back following a unilateral change should be made as swiftly as possible because any delay may lend support to the 'status quo' argument.

5.24   Exercise of the court's discretion

If an application is made under s 8 of the CA 1989 for a specific issue order relating to a child's surname, the court will have to apply the criteria in s 1 of the CA 1989, including the 'welfare checklist'. Although technically CA 1989, s 1(4) does not make it mandatory for the court to have regard to the 'welfare checklist' set out at s 1(3) when considering an application under s 13 it is clear that the court will consider all the factors in the welfare checklist in the exercise of its discretion. Indeed, in reviewing the authorities of *Dawson v Wearmouth* and *Re W, Re A, Re B (Change of Name)* (both set out below) Ryder LJ went so far as to say *'The test is welfare, pure and simple'*.[86]

In *Dawson v Wearmouth*[87] the House of Lords dealt with the criteria to be applied in determining an application to change a child's surname. In that case, a child born to unmarried parents was registered by the mother with the surname used by her and the child's half siblings. The father objected and applied for an order that the child should be known by his surname instead. At first instance, the judge had made an order that the child should be known by the father's surname. The mother appealed. The Court of Appeal said that the judge at first instance had failed to give sufficient weight to the fact the child was registered with the mother's surname, albeit also that of her former husband, but one shared by her other children. The father's appeal to the House of Lords was dismissed. The salient points of the decision of the House of Lords were that:

(1)   changing a child's name was a serious matter, and not one for unilateral action;

(2)   the welfare checklist applied to the exercise of discretion;

(3)   the name in which the child was registered was a factor to be taken into account but was not necessarily decisive in each case; and

(4)   any change of name should lead to an improvement from the point of view of the welfare of the child.

Further guidance was given in *Re W, Re A, Re B (Change of Name)*[88] as follows:

(1)   If the parents were married, they both had the power and duty to register their child's name.

(2)   If they were not married, the mother had the sole duty and power to do so.

---

[86]   *Re W (Change of Name)* [2014] 2 FLR 221.
[87]   [1999] 1 FLR 1167.
[88]   [1999] 2 FLR 930.

(3) After the registration of the child's name, the grant of a residence order obliged any person wishing to change the surname to obtain the leave of the court or the written consent of all those who had parental responsibility.

(4) In the absence of a residence order,[89] the person wishing to change the surname from the registered name had to obtain the relevant written consent or the leave of the court by making an application for a specific issue order.

(5) On any application, the welfare of the child was paramount.

(6) Among the factors to which the court should have regard was the registered surname of the child and the reasons for the registration, for instance recognition of the biological link with the child's father. Registration was always a relevant and important consideration, but it was not in itself decisive.

(7) Relevant considerations should include factors which could arise in the future as well as the present.

(8) Reasons given for changing or seeking to change a child's name based on the fact that the child's name was not the same as the parent making the application did not generally carry much weight.

(9) The reasons for an earlier unilateral decision to change a child's name might be relevant.

(10) Any change of circumstances of the child since the original registration might be relevant.

(11) In the case of a child whose parents were married to each other, the fact of the marriage was important and there would have to be strong reasons to change the name from the father's surname if the child was so registered.

(12) Where the child's parents were not married to each other, the mother had control over registration. Consequently, on an application to change the surname of the child, the degree of commitment of the father to the child, the quality of contact, if it occurred, between father and child, and the existence or absence of parental responsibility were all relevant factors to take into account.

In *Re P (Parental Responsibility)*[90] two children born outside marriage had been registered with the father's surname. After the breakdown of the parents' relationship, largely as a result of the father persistently committing criminal offences and serving long terms of imprisonment, the mother moved to a new area for a fresh start, and she and the children assumed her maiden surname. The father's appeal against the decision of the circuit judge that they should continue to be known by their new surname was dismissed. The Court of Appeal said that the judge at first instance had applied the correct criteria. In addition to the requirement that the court must consider the welfare of the child

---

[89] Or since 22 April 2014 a child arrangements order stating that the child is to live with the applicant.

[90] [1997] 2 FLR 722.

to be paramount, these were identified as those set out in the judgment of Dunn LJ in *W v A (Minors: Surname)*:[91]

> 'When considering the question of a change of name, that is to be regarded as an important matter ... It is a matter for the discretion of the individual judge hearing the case, seeing the witnesses, seeing the parents, possibly seeing the children, to decide whether or not it is in the interests of the child in the particular circumstances of the case that his surname should or should not be changed; and the judge will take into account all the circumstances of the case, including no doubt where appropriate any embarrassment which may be caused to the child by not changing his name and, on the other hand, the long-term interests of the child, the importance of maintaining the child's links with his paternal family, and the stability or otherwise of the mother's remarriage. I only mention those as typical examples of the kind of considerations which arise in these cases, but the judge will take into account all the relevant circumstances in the particular case before him.'

In *Re C (Change of Surname)*[92] the question of preserving family ties by the use of a parent's surname was considered. In that case, two children born outside marriage lived with their father. There was a residence order in force. The children had been registered at birth with their mother's maiden name, and ignorant of the prohibition against it the father had caused the children to be known by his own surname. He had by then started to live with another woman and she and her three children also adopted his surname. The mother had remarried and so no longer used the surname with which the children had been registered. The court granted the father's application for leave for the children to be known formally by his surname, and the Court of Appeal refused the mother's application for leave to appeal. The basis of the decision was that, although it was important to recognise the link with their mother that their official surname gave them, in this case, as the mother acknowledged that they would be known by their father's name on a day-to-day basis in any event, and she no longer used the original surname herself, it was hard to see how keeping her name would assist in preserving the link.

In *Re C (Change of Surname)*[93] the Court of Appeal considered that it was not in the child's best interests for her surname to be changed back to the father's name three years after the mother had changed her surname to her own by deed poll. Nonetheless the mother's actions were wrong and it was emphasised that there was:

> '... a heavy responsibility on those who seek to effect a change of name, as a matter of prudence if not of direct law, to take the issue of dispute to the court and to appreciate that good reasons have to be shown before the judge will allow such a change in the future.'

---

[91]   [1981] Fam 14 at p 21.
[92]   [1998] 1 FLR 549.
[93]   [1998] 2 FLR 656.

In *Re T (Change of Surname)*,[94] however, the Court of Appeal held that the children's surname should be changed back to that of their father. The convenience to the mother of having the same surname for all her children was of slight weight against the strength of the father's application to check the mother's ill-considered act.

In *A v Y (Child's Surname)*[95] an application by a father to change the surname of a four-year-old child was dismissed. The child had been known by the mother's surname since birth and a change to the father's surname would cause confusion. The delay in making the application was relevant. Further, there would be no benefit in giving the child a double surname as suggested by the father.

However, in *Re R (Surname: Using Both Parents')*[96] the use of both surnames was adopted by the Court of Appeal as a pragmatic solution to disputes between parents over the use of surnames. In that case the children of unmarried parents were to be removed by the mother to live in Spain. Although initially opposed by the father, he subsequently agreed to this, leaving only the issue as to the surname by which the children were to be known. The mother had changed the names unilaterally by deed poll to her own surname. Thorpe LJ proposed that as the children were to live in Spain, the Spanish custom of combining maternal and paternal surnames should be adopted. Hale LJ, as she then was, agreed but went further and proposed that in appropriate cases the use of both parental surnames was to be encouraged so as to make the child's parentage transparent.

In *Re F (Contact)*[97] Sumner J allowed a change of name on the basis that it would provide some extra protection against the threat of abduction by the children's father.

In some cases cultural issues will be relevant to the court's decision. In *Re A (Change of Name)*,[98] it was held that with the child's welfare being the paramount consideration it was appropriate to the cultural mores of the society into which he was born that his names should protect his mother from the loss of dignity and prestige in the community of acknowledging her adultery, even if this meant that his names did not reflect his true parentage.

5.25 Appointment of a guardian

There is provision in the CA 1989 for any parent having parental responsibility for a child, or the court, to appoint a guardian of that child to take over parental responsibility for the child on the parent's death.

---

[94] [1998] 2 FLR 620.
[95] [1999] 2 FLR 5.
[96] [2001] 2 FLR 1358.
[97] [2007] 1 FLR 1663.
[98] [2003] 2 FLR 1.

The appointment usually takes effect when there is no parent with parental responsibility for the child by reason of death. So, for example, if the mother of the child dies having appointed her mother as guardian of the child, if the other parent of the child had parental responsibility the mother's appointment of a guardian would not be operative until after that parent's death or such other time as he or she might cease to have parental responsibility for the child.

A parent of a child who was not married to the mother of the child at the time of birth will not have power to appoint a guardian unless he or she has parental responsibility, although the child's mother could appoint them to be the child's guardian in the event of her death. In this event, the other parent would then have parental responsibility for the child on the mother's death, and would have the power to appoint a guardian to act after his or her own death.

Should the mother of a child appoint as guardian any person other than the other parent (without parental responsibility), any dispute over who should bring up the child will be resolved by way of proceedings under s 8 of the CA 1989. The other parent may wish to apply for an order that the child live with them, for example, or may simply wish to have some specific issue determined.

Where, immediately before her death, there is an order in place that the child should live with the mother, even if the other parent has parental responsibility, the appointment of any other person as the child's guardian will take effect from her death. However, where the mother does not have a residence order and the other parent has parental responsibility, any appointment of a guardian by the mother will not take effect upon her death, but on the death of both parents.[99] If the person appointed as guardian wishes to act as such an application must be made to court for a special guardianship order.[100]

To be effective the appointment of a guardian must be in writing and, except in certain specified circumstances,[101] must be dated and signed by the person making the appointment. The most convenient way to appoint a guardian is by will, but this is not essential if the formalities are complied with.

SECTION 2   ADOPTION

5.26   Introduction

Adoption is a specialist topic and it is intended merely to highlight those areas of particular concern to the unmarried family.[102]

---

[99]   CA 1989, s 5(8).
[100]   CA 1989, ss 14A–14G.
[101]   CA 1989, s 5(5)(a) and (b).
[102]   Practitioners are referred to a specialist work such as *Child Care and Adoption Law: A Practical Guide*, McFarlane and Reardon, Family Law (2010).

5.27 The Adoption and Children Act 2002

The ACA 2002 replaced the AA 1976. ACA 2002 made significant changes to adoption generally, and, in particular, how adoption affects unmarried adopters.[103]

One of the main aims of the legislation was to increase the pool of those eligible to apply for adoption orders and so reduce the numbers of children caught up in the care system.

In addition to adoption orders, the court may make special guardianship orders. This stops short of severing the child's legal ties with his birth family, but provides a degree of stability and permanence. Parental responsibility can also be granted to step-parents.

5.28 The Adoption and Children Act 2002 and applications by cohabitants

Section 14 of the AA 1976 precluded a joint application to adopt a child except where the applicants were married to one another. This did not prevent one of the parties from applying for an adoption order, and if successful asking the court to make a residence order in favour of the other. It was also possible for couples of the same sex to use this procedure.[104] This less than satisfactory and discriminatory situation was remedied by ss 49 and 50 of the ACA 2002. These provide that an application for an adoption order may be made by either a couple, or one person, while s 144 defined 'a couple' as either a married couple or 'two people (whether of different sexes or the same sex) living as partners in an enduring family relationship'.[105]

5.29 Adoption by one person

Whilst AA 1976 allowed a single unmarried person to apply for an adoption order, ACA 2002 extended this to include a person who the court is satisfied is the partner of a parent of the child who is the subject of the application (s 51(2)). A partner is one of a couple as defined by ACA 2002, s 144(4) who is not the child's parent.

This provision enables a step-parent to adopt the child of his or her spouse or civil partner without the need for there to be a joint application with the child's parent, as had been the case under AA 1976, and allows one member of a cohabiting couple to adopt his or her partner's child.

---

[103] For an outline to the key changes brought about by ACA 2002 see *President's Guidance (Adoption: The New Law And Procedure)* March 2006 [2006] 1 FLR 1234.

[104] *Re W (Adoption: Homosexual Adopter)* [1997] 2 FLR 406.

[105] Those with close blood ties are excluded from the definition of 'couple' – ACA 2002, s 144(5) and (6).

5.30   Preliminaries to adoption

A child may be placed for adoption either voluntarily by a parent (s 19) or by order of the court on the application of a local authority in circumstances in which the local authority is satisfied that the child should be adopted but either the parents do not consent or have withdrawn their consent (s 21). There will of course be circumstances in which adoption is an agreed course between private individuals, for example where one of a couple applies to adopt the child of the other.

Before an application for an adoption order is made conditions as to residence must be met.

Where the child is placed for adoption by an adoption agency the child must have had his home with the applicant(s) for at least 10 weeks before an order can be made (s 42(2)). Where the application is by a step-parent or partner of the child's parent the child must have had his home with the applicant for a continuous period of at least six months preceding the application. In the case of local authority foster parents the period is 12 months, and in all other non-agency cases for three years out of the five years preceding the application, unless the court gives leave to make an application before the condition is met.

The relevant adoption agency or local authority will provide a report for the court that deals with the suitability of the applicant(s), issues of the child's welfare, and in the case of unmarried couples whether or not they have an 'enduring family relationship'.

5.31   Consent to adoption

The court cannot make an adoption order without the consent of the child's parent or guardian unless the court is satisfied that in the interests of the child such consent should be dispensed with.

5.32   Dispensing with consent

The giving of parental consent is always subject to the court's powers to dispense with consent in cases in which either the parent cannot be found or is incapable of giving consent, or the welfare of the child requires it. This is determined by reference to the welfare checklist contained in s 1(4).

5.33   The status of the unmarried father

The father of a child who was not married to the child's mother at the time of the birth is not a 'parent' for the purposes of the ACA 2002 unless he has parental responsibility for the child (s 52(6)).

The practical effect of this is that unless he has parental responsibility his consent will not be required before a placement or an adoption order can be made (s 19(1)).

ACA 2002 provides for a child's father who was not married to the child's mother at the time of the birth to register the birth jointly with the mother and so acquire parental responsibility. This is in addition to the routes to parental responsibility that existed before ACA 2002 (see 5.8 above).

Although a father with parental responsibility will have the right to give, or withhold, his consent to adoption, a father who acquires parental responsibility after the mother has given her consent to the child being placed for adoption will be deemed to have given his consent. This is subject to the provisions for withdrawing consent to the placement only. However, once an application has been made for an adoption order the making of an order can be opposed only with the permission of the court if the court is satisfied that there has been a change of circumstances since the consent was given or the placement order made (s 47).

5.34   Unmarried fathers and party status

Although for the purposes of AA 1976 a father without parental responsibility had no right to consent to freeing for adoption or the making of an adoption order, nor any right under the Adoption Rules 1984 (AR 1984) to be given notice of the proceedings, r 15(3), AR 1984 allowed the court to direct that any person be made a respondent. Largely as a result of the impact of the ECHR and the acknowledgement that such fathers had a right to respect for family life under Art 8 where there had been a significant relationship with the child, it became established that fathers without parental responsibility would be informed of the proceedings unless there was good reason not to do so. In *Re R (Adoption: Father's Involvement)* [2001] 1 FLR 302 the President of the Family Division at that time said that each case will

> '... have to be decided on its merits as to whether or not it is appropriate that [the father] should be joined as a respondent ... there will be extreme cases such as rape where it would be wholly inappropriate for such a father to be joined. There is a spectrum and the question is: at what point does each father without parental responsibility stand on that spectrum?'

The considerations that would weigh in favour of the involvement in adoption proceedings of a father without parental responsibility were developed further by the President in *Re H; Re G (Adoption: Consultation of Unmarried Fathers)* [2001] 1 FLR 646 in which she held that as a matter of general principle judges giving directions in adoption applications would be expected to inform such fathers of the proceedings unless, for good reason, it was inappropriate to do so.

5.35   The exercise of the court's discretion

ACA 2002 brought adoption proceedings in line with CA 1989 in making the child's welfare the paramount consideration for the courts when deciding whether to make an adoption order. Furthermore, it is the child's welfare throughout his or her life that must be considered, and the principles of delay, and non-intervention apply as they do in CA 1989. A comprehensive welfare checklist is set out in ACA 2002, s 1(4).

Increasingly, the making of adoption orders has not been considered incompatible with the child maintaining links with his or her birth family and it was possible for concurrent contact orders to be made under s 8, CA 1989. ACA 2002 imposes a duty on the court before making an adoption order to consider whether there should be any arrangements for allowing any person to have contact with the child.

SECTION 3   CHILD ABDUCTION

5.36   Removal of children from the jurisdiction

The detailed provisions of the law relating to child abduction are outside the scope of this book, and specialist publications should be consulted. This section is designed to serve as a brief introduction to this complex area and to highlight the importance to an unmarried parent of having parental responsibility.

5.37   The unmarried parent without parental responsibility

Where more than one person has parental responsibility for a child who is habitually resident in the UK, the removal of that child from the jurisdiction by one parent without the consent of the other may be unlawful. In particular, if there is a child arrangements order in force concerning who a child is to live with, then under s 13(1) of the CA 1989 the child may not be removed from the UK unless everyone with parental responsibility for the child consents, or the court gives permission.

Where the mother is the only parent with parental responsibility, however, there will generally be nothing in English civil law to prevent her from removing the child from the UK. In cases where there is no residence order, the Child Abduction and Custody Act 1985 provides a remedy only to those with parental responsibility.

Detailed guidance on the form and requirements of court applications relating to wrongful removal (both to prevent unlawful removal and to secure the return of a child taken away unlawfully) is provided in FPR PD 12F.

5.38   Rights of custody

Where a parent does not have parental responsibility, it may be possible to argue that there has been 'wrongful removal' or 'wrongful retention' under the terms of the Hague Convention on the Civil Aspects of International Child Abduction (the Hague Convention) if the removal or retention was in breach of that parent's 'rights of custody'.

'Rights of custody' is a concept to be determined within the context of the Hague Convention and not with reference to any particular domestic definition. However, it will include rights relating to the care of the child, and the decision as to where the child should live.

On 17 October 1997 the Lord Chancellor's Child Abduction Unit issued a practice note[106] setting out the policies at that time in respect of the acceptance of applications by fathers for the return of children for whom they do not have parental responsibility.

The importance of the practice note was the recognition that in certain circumstances a parent of a child who does not have parental responsibility may nonetheless have 'rights of custody' for the purposes of the Hague Convention.

The 1996 Hague Convention on Parental Responsibility came into force on 1 November 2012. Under Art 16, if a parent has acquired parental responsibility abroad (including under mechanisms that do not require judicial or administrative involvement, eg by agreement or unilateral act), that parent will retain parental responsibility when the child's habitual residence changes to the UK.[107]

In *Re B (A Minor) (Abduction)*[108] and *Re O (Child Abduction: Custody Rights)*[109] it was held that a father who was exercising parental functions over a substantial period of time may have 'inchoate' rights of custody sufficient to amount to 'rights of custody' for the purposes of the Hague Convention.

In *Re W; Re B (Child Abduction: Unmarried Father)*[110] Hale J, as she then was, considered applications by two unmarried fathers for declarations under Art 15 of the Hague Convention that the removal of their respective children from

---

[106] [1998] 1 FLR 491.
[107] Whether parental responsibility has been so acquired is a question to be referred to the foreign court under Art 15, see *Re K (Rights of Custody: Spain)* [2010] 1 FLR 57 and *Kennedy v Kennedy* [2010] 1 FLR 782.
[108] [1994] 2 FLR 249.
[109] [1997] 2 FLR 702.
[110] [1998] 2 FLR 146.

England and Wales was wrongful within the meaning of Art 3 on the ground that the removal was in breach of the rights of custody held by the father in one case, and the court in the other.[111]

In *Re W*, there were pending proceedings before the family proceedings court for parental responsibility and contact orders. Indeed, the children were removed from the jurisdiction only a matter of days before the final hearing at which orders were granted in favour of the father. Hale J held that the removal of the child from the jurisdiction was a breach of the rights of custody attributable to the court, and made the declaration sought.

No such declaration was given in *Re B (Abduction: Rights of Custody)*.[112] The father had never applied for parental responsibility, and his application for a prohibited steps order preventing the removal of the children from the jurisdiction was ultimately compromised and a residence order made in favour of the mother.[113]

It was stated by Hale J, *per curiam*, that unmarried parents should be advised that removal by the mother of a child who is habitually resident here will be wrongful under the Hague Convention if:

(a)   the father has parental responsibility either by agreement or court order or by jointly registering the birth;

(b)   there is a court order in force prohibiting it;

(c)   there are relevant proceedings pending in a court in England and Wales; or

(d)   where the father is currently the primary carer for the child, at least if the mother has delegated such care to him.

In *Re H (Child Abduction) (Unmarried Father: Rights of Custody)*[114] Holman J held that removal from the jurisdiction was a breach of rights of custody of a father without parental responsibility on the basis that correspondence between the parents' solicitors concerning the child's proposed removal from the jurisdiction established the father's inchoate right to determine the child's place of residence. The mother's solicitors had written to those acting for the father stating that it was not the mother's intention, as was believed by the father, to remove the child to Spain. Holman J regarded this as amounting to an undertaking that this was the case, and observed:

> 'The practice was that when responsible and reputable solicitors wrote to each other in these sorts of terms, their letters could be relied upon. The mother's solicitors could have responded that the father had no parental responsibility and that the question of the child's residence was therefore none of his business, but they did not do so. The positive terms in which the mother's solicitors in fact wrote involved a determination of the child's place of residence into the foreseeable

---

[111] See also *Re E (Abduction Rights of Custody)* [2005] 2 FLR 759 regarding the court's right of custody while seised of the right to determine the child's place of residence.

[112] [1997] 2 FLR 594.

[113] See also *B v UK* [2000] 1 FLR 1, ECHR.

[114] [2003] 2 FLR 153.

future at the request of the father. For so long as the terms of the letter of the mother's solicitors remained operative and not withdrawn, the father clearly had a right of custody in relation to the child.'

In *Re F (Abduction: Unmarried Father: Sole Carer)*[115] the mother of four children had moved to Australia taking all but the youngest child with her. The youngest child remained with the man who believed himself to be the father and he applied for a residence order. He was the father of and had parental responsibility for the other children. All the children had been substantially in his care, the mother having lived with them only intermittently. The mother did not initially dispute the man's paternity as far as the youngest child was concerned but subsequently denied it and it was agreed that there would be paternity tests. Before the outcome of the tests was known and the application for a residence order processed, the mother was party to the abduction of the youngest child to join her and her siblings in Australia. Following the abduction, the father made an application for the child's return under the Hague Convention on the Civil Aspects of International Child Abduction 1980 and an order was made on an ex parte basis. The mother applied to set aside the order but was unsuccessful. The court held that:

'(1) There were circumstances in which a person who was not related by blood to a child, but who fell into a quasi-parental role and had exclusive care of the child, might be found to have inchoate rights of custody in relation to the child for the purposes of making an application under the Hague Convention.

(2) Inchoate rights of custody were those which were capable of being affected by court applications in which there was a reasonable prospect of success. The father here, even if he were not the natural father, had good prospects of obtaining a residence order under s 8 of the Children Act 1989 and consequently had inchoate rights of custody which were capable of being perfected.'

A parent without parental responsibility whether or not they are the primary carer of the child may be well advised not to delay in making an application to the court to prevent the removal of the child from the jurisdiction if they believe they have sufficient evidence of the mother's intention to remove the child.[116]

It is increasingly the case that the court will consider that if it is seised of proceedings to determine rights of custody, removal of the child from the jurisdiction without the court's permission while the proceedings are pending is a breach of the rights of custody attributable to the court. This was the case in *Re J (Abduction: Declaration of Wrongful Removal)*,[117] *Re C (Abduction: Wrongful Removal)*[118] and *Re H (Abduction: Rights of Custody)*.[119] In the latter case, the House of Lords held that the court acquired rights of custody if its jurisdiction had been invoked in respect of matters of custody within the

---

[115] [2003] 1 FLR 839.
[116] See Helen L Conway 'Feared Abduction – Jumping the Gun?' [2000] Fam Law 272.
[117] [1999] 2 FLR 653.
[118] [1999] 2 FLR 859.
[119] [2000] 1 FLR 374.

meaning of the Hague Convention. Proceedings which called upon the court to determine a child's place of residence gave the court a right of custody. The date on which the court's jurisdiction was invoked was, at the latest, the date on which proceedings raising matters of custody were served; in special cases, the court's jurisdiction might be invoked before service of such an application.

This raises the question of whether a hearing without notice to the mother deprives her of her right to a fair trial under Art 6(1) of the Convention. This was considered in *Re J (Abduction: Wrongful Removal)*.[120] The Court of Appeal considered whether in making an order without notice to the mother, as Hale J, as she then was, had done in this case, she had deprived the mother of a fair trial. It was held that the mother had not been deprived of a fair trial. Cases concerning children often had to be dealt with as a matter of great urgency, and in the circumstances of that case the father had been entitled to make both applications without notice to the mother. It was certainly possible that there might be a breach of the right to a fair trial if no opportunity were provided by the law to challenge an order made without notice, but it was always open to a party against whom an order had been made without notice to apply to the court to have it set aside.

A recital in a court order that a child is not to be removed from the jurisdiction without prior written agreement of the parties or a court order confers rights of custody on the other parent.[121]

SECTION 4   FINANCIAL PROVISION FOR CHILDREN

5.39   Introduction

A parent's obligation to maintain his or her child will not depend upon whether he or she has parental responsibility. It is an absolute obligation and the only circumstances in which this obligation will be removed is on the making of an adoption order in respect of the child.

5.40   Agreement or court application

Financial provision can be made for children from capital and from income:
(1)   by agreement of the parties;
(2)   by application under the CA 1989, s 15 and Sch 1;
(3)   income only: under the CSA 1991 in respect of qualifying children (see below).

This section looks first at the general law in relation to provision for children where agreement cannot be reached between the parties; and then provides an

---

[120] [2000] 1 FLR 78.
[121] *Re P (Abduction: Consent)* [2004] 2 FLR 1057.

overview of the particular provisions which govern child maintenance and the administrative scheme set up by the Child Support Act 1991.

Child maintenance

5.41 Terminology

The terms which will be used to denote child maintenance in this section are as follows:

(1) Child periodical payments: eg CA 1989, Sch 1.

(2) Child support maintenance: CSA 1991.

(3) Child maintenance: used for all periodic payments of maintenance for children, including for provision in private agreements.

The first two are statutorily defined (see respectively CSA 1991, s 3(6); CA 1989, Sch 1, para 1(2)(a): the third is not specifically defined, but consists of words which can be given their ordinary meaning (the same terminology is used in the Matrimonial Causes Act 1973, s 23(1)(a))). Child maintenance is commonly used, and is used here, as a generic term which comprises all forms of periodic payments for children and which also includes the two forms of statutory financial provision.

In the provision of each form of maintenance there is no distinction between whether parents are married or unmarried or of the same gender or heterosexual. In most cases parentage is the pre-requisite for financial provision, not the fact that parents are cohabiting.

Cohabitation prevents one of a couple seeking maintenance under any statutory scheme. Where there has been a separation and child support maintenance or periodical payments are being paid, if cohabitation is resumed, it will terminate continuing payments as follows:

(1) *Child support maintenance* under CSA 1991: on resumption of cohabitation there is no longer a non-resident parent and therefore no longer any qualifying children (CSA 1991, s 3). The calculation terminates after cohabitation for more than six months (and see CSA 1991, Sch 1, para 16(1)(d); *Brough v Law and CMEC*[122]).

(2) *Periodical payments* under CA 1989, upon the parents living together for more than six months (Sch 1, para 3(4)).

In *Brough v Law and CMEC* at para [58] Lewison LJ suggest that during the period of resumed cohabitation and until the six months has expired the surviving duty to pay child maintenance would be 'suspended ... and cease at the expiry of six months'.

---

[122] [2011] EWCA Civ 1183.

5.42   Forms of child maintenance

There are five main ways for child maintenance to be provided:

(1)   By unwritten voluntary arrangement between the parties.

(2)   By written agreement.

(3)   By court consent order (though note difficulties with this in cases under CA 1989, Sch 1).

(4)   Under the child support scheme (CSA 1991).

(5)   By top-up order normally ancillary to proceedings under CA 1989, Sch 1, para 1 (or eg the MCA 1973, s 23); though the application may be free-standing.

In what follows the means of obtaining child maintenance under (4) and (5) will be considered, starting with the scheme under CSA 1991.

5.43   Child support scheme

The child support scheme was set up in 1993 (under the CSA 1991) to provide an administrative means whereby maintenance could be quantified and then be payable by a separated parent ('non-resident parent': 'NRP') to the main carer (normally the other parent: the 'parent with care': 'PWC') for their qualifying children; and to set up a scheme for enforcement of unpaid maintenance.

In respect of a qualifying child (one who is eligible to be paid child support maintenance) his parents are statutorily prevented from seeking a court order for child periodical payments (CSA 1991, s 8) save:

(1)   By consent order.

(2)   Top-up orders under s 8(6)—(8).

Application can be made to court where, for example, there is a step-child; one or more of the parents or qualifying children are habitually outside the UK (CSA 1991, s 44); or to vary an existing court order (see eg *V v V (Child Maintenance)*[123]).

Nothing in CSA 1991 is intended to prevent parents reaching agreement if they are able to do so; and indeed the £20 application fee that was introduced in June 2014 was designed primarily to give applicants cause to consider whether it would be better to reach agreement directly with the other parent.[124]

5.44   Qualifying child: meaning of 'child'

Child support is payable in respect of one or more 'qualifying children', who are defined as children, both of whose natural parents are living apart, or are

---

[123] [2001] 2 FLR 799.

[124] Application fees are not payable by applicants who are under 19 or who are victims of domestic violence or abuse.

living apart from the qualifying child (CSA 1991, s 3(1)). It cannot therefore apply to step-children whose periodical payments are covered by MCA 1973 or CA 1989 (who may also be entitled to child support maintenance from their natural parent).

Child support maintenance is payable whist the qualifying child is a 'child' within the terms of CSA 1991, s 55, that is:

(a)   Under 16 (CSA 1991, s 55(1)(a));

(b)   Under 20[125] and in full-time education (but not advanced education) (CSA 1991, s 55(1)(b); nor if he or she is married or formerly married (CSA 1991, s 55(2)).

5.45   *Child support scheme*

The scheme set up under the CSA 1991 has been extensively amended four times (1995, 1998, 2000 and most recently by the CMOPA 2008). The original 1991 Act remains in force; but its original provisions are overlaid by an extensive variety of amendment.

A wholly different understanding of finance on family breakdown is demanded by the child support scheme. For example:

(1)   The scheme works from, and is dependent upon, a decision made by what is now branded as the Child Maintenance Service (CMS), the decision maker whose scope for exercise of any discretion is restricted as far as possible by thickets of regulations (the antithesis of the wide judicial discretion vested in courts under eg CA 1989, Sch 1, para 4).

(2)   The decision gives both parents an automatic right of appeal to an appeal tribunal (First-tier Tribunal (Social Entitlement Chamber)[126]) which considers the issues afresh. The tribunal judge makes a fresh decision on behalf of the CMS.

(3)   Once parents are in the scheme there is no scope for negotiation with the CMS. Negotiation is permitted – where possible – with the other parent and an agreement can result outside the statutory scheme (and see CSA 1991, s 9 below).

Once an assessment has been made, parties are encouraged to make private 'direct pay' arrangements for the calculated maintenance to be paid. If either party insists on using the CMS's 'Collect and Pay' service administration fees will be added to every amount collected. This results in a 20% increase in the amount paid by the payer and a 4% deduction from the amount received by the recipient, so that for every £100 assessed the NRP will pay £120 and the PWC will receive £96.[127]

---

[125]   The maximum age was increased from 'has not attained the age of 19' to 'has not attained the age of 20' by CMOPA 2008, s 42 on 10 December 2012.

[126]   Considered further in Chapter 9.

[127]   On the face of it there is a clear opportunity here for a PWC to inflict financial pain on the NRP at limited cost to herself. It remains to be seen whether this will be used tactically by

Other than referring the matter to the Collect and Pay service, the PWC is not permitted to control enforcement of collection of arrears for the children: this is left to the administrators.[128] There is almost no remedy for the PWC if CMS fails to enforce payments.

5.46   The child support calculation

Since the repeal of CSA 1991, s 6 the tie of the scheme to welfare benefits claimants has been broken: there is now no compulsion for a claimant for income support to apply as there was until July 2009.

An application for child support maintenance is made under CSA 1991, s 4 by either parent or a person with care (a non-parent looking after the qualifying child). This triggers a calculation which produces a figure for child support maintenance.

Since the CSA was established in 1991 there have been three mechanisms for calculating the required level of child support. The initial scheme (colloquially known now as 'CM1' or the 'old' scheme) was heavily criticised for being overcomplicated but continued to operate from enactment until March 2003. Plans to move existing cases from the old scheme to 'CM2' (the 'net income' scheme) never materialised and consequently there will remain, even now, children whose child support is regulated through this scheme.

Calculations under CM2 were based on a percentage of the payer's net income, and most existing child maintenance calculations will have been made under this scheme. This scheme was gradually phased out for new applicants in December 2012. All existing cases started under CM1 and CM2 will continue to be operated through the CSA as a department within the Department for Work and Pensions for the time being. It is intended, however, that all existing cases will be closed by the end of 2017.[129] No automatic transition onto 'CS3' is planned, meaning that parents who wish to continue to use the CSA/CMS will have to reapply in due course under the new scheme, incurring an application fee and becoming liable for collection charges in the process. The exception to this closure policy is where the youngest qualifying child will be 20 years old before 31 December 2017, in which case the case will be allowed to run to its conclusion under its existing scheme.

All applications since 25 November 2013 have been operated under CS3 (the 'gross income' scheme).

Stage 1: The new, gross income, calculation is as follows:

---

vindictive PWCs. Early indications are that the £20 charge is putting a significant number of parents off applying to the CMS at all, with applications down 38% between May and August 2014.

[128] *R (Kehoe) v Secretary of State for Work and Pensions* [2005] UKHL 48, [2005] 3 WLR 252.

[129] The first tranche of CM1 and CM2 file closures will take place in early 2015.

(1) A 'nil rate' for payers who fall into certain categories, such as students and those with an income of less than £5 per week;

(2) A 'flat rate' of £7 per week for paying parents with a gross income of less than £100 per week or in receipt of certain prescribed benefits;

(3) A 'reduced rate' for paying parents with a gross income of between £100 and £200 per week;[130]

(4) The 'basic rate':
  (a) for income up to £800 per week:
    (i) 12% for one qualifying child;
    (ii) 16% for two qualifying children;
    (iii) 19% for three or more qualifying children;
  (b) and for further income between £800 and £3,000 per week:
    (i) 9% for one qualifying child;
    (ii) 12% for two qualifying children;
    (iii) 15% for three or more qualifying children.

Stage 2: Where the NRP is living in a household where there are other dependent children his income will be reduced in the following proportion before the calculation is carried out:

(1) 11% for one other relevant child;

(2) 14% for two other relevant children;

(3) 16% for three other relevant children.

Stage 3: Where the NRP shares the care of the children, his payments will be (further) reduced by the following proportions based on the number of nights the children spend with him:

(1) 1/7 for 52 to 103 nights per year;

(2) 2/7 for 104 to 155 nights per year;

(3) 3/7 for 156 to 174 nights per year; and

(4) 1/2 plus a further £7 for 175+ nights per year.

Once an initial calculation has been carried out, either parent may make a variation application to the CMS, at which point the CMS will also be able to incorporate into their calculation the following:

(1) 'Special expenses' (including the costs of contact, costs relating to the illness or disability of another child and the maintenance (but not educational) element of boarding school fees);

(2) Unearned income of more than £2,500 pa;

---

[130] Set out in the Child Support and Claims and Payments (Miscellaneous Amendments and Change to the Minimum Amount of Liability) Regulations 2013 (SI 2013/1654) but designed to achieve a straight line increase from £7 for those earning £100 per week to the basic rate for those earning £200 per week. The precise calculation can perhaps be carried out most easily using the government's child maintenance calculator at https://www.gov.uk/calculate-your-child-maintenance.

(3) Income that, in the opinion of the Secretary of State, has been unreasonably diverted to other destinations in order to reduce his liability to pay maintenance.

It should be noted that the there are fewer categories available for variation under CS3 than under CS2. For some parents forced to reapply under CS3 when their existing CS2 case is closed the difference could be significant.[131]

5.47   Top-up orders: discretionary principles

The Child Support Act 1991, ss 8(6)–(8) provides for orders to be made in financial remedy proceedings in terms that CSA 1991, s 8 'shall not prevent a court from exercising any power ... to make a [child] maintenance order' where:

(1) a maintenance calculation has been carried out and the NRP's gross weekly income exceeds £3,000 per week (s 8(6));[132]

(2) for educational expenses 'for the instruction or training of the child' (s 8(7)); and

(3) where disability living allowance or a personal independence payment is paid for a child or is otherwise disabled, to cover 'expenses attributable' to that disability.

Such an application is made in existing or free-standing CA 1989, Sch 1 proceedings and is subject to the court exercising discretion in accordance with Sch 1, para 4 principles.

5.48   Agreements and child maintenance

Nothing in the 1991 Act is intended to prevent the parents from agreeing their own figure for child periodical payments (s 9(2)) with each other – whether with or without advice or through dispute resolution; though their agreement may not in any way exclude operation of the child support scheme (s 9(4)) in the event that either parent later wishes to apply (s 9(3)). Such an application will override any terms previously agreed between the parents.

---

[131] For example, under CS2 the CSA is entitled to look at an NRP's capital (excluding his home, business and a few other exceptions). Any such capital over £65,000 under CS2 was treated as being capable of achieving a notional return of 8% pa which was then added to his income for the purpose of the calculation. Similarly, under CS2 the CSA was able to look at the NRP's lifestyle and increase its award if that lifestyle was not consistent with that parent's declared income. A switch from CS2 to CS3 could have a significant impact where the NRP is asset-rich but income-poor.

[132] It had generally been thought that a court application could not be made until a maximum assessment had been obtained from the CSA (or one of its successors). In *CF v KM (Financial Provision for Child: Costs of Legal Proceedings)* [2011] 1 FLR 208, however, Charles J considered it arguable that the court was entitled to decide for itself whether the non-resident parent's income exceeded that required for a maximum assessment.

At the same time as introducing the latest scheme for child support, the government has also been keen to encourage parents to reach their own agreements if possible. To this end its Child Maintenance Options website[133] includes a 'Family Based Arrangements Form' that parents are encouraged to complete together (albeit that the document specifically states that it is not a legal document). As noted at **5.43** above, the introduction of the application fee for applications to the CMS was primarily to give applicants cause to consider whether it would be better to reach agreement directly with the other parent.

Tribunal rules[134] require the respective tribunals to 'bring to the attention of parties [before them] the availability of any appropriate' dispute resolution scheme and 'to facilitate the use of the (*sic*) procedure'.

5.49 Schedule 1 to the Children Act 1989

Although the CMS will be the starting point for those asked to advise anyone with children in their care following the breakdown of a relationship with the other parent, generally it will be necessary to consider the financial provision in addition to periodical payments that can be made for children under Sch 1 to the CA 1989.

5.50 *What relief is available?*

Schedule 1, para 1(2) to the CA 1989 enables the court to make the following orders in respect of children:
- periodical payments;
- secured periodical payments;[135]
- lump sum;
- settlement of property; and
- transfer of property.

Although only one substantive order can be made for settlement or transfer of property,[136] there is no bar to multiple applications for lump sum payments.[137]

In addition, the court may make orders for interim periodical payments, subject to the CSA 1991,[138] and has power to alter the provision contained in a maintenance agreement.[139]

---

[133] See www.cmoptions.org.

[134] Tribunal Procedure (First-tier Tribunal) (Social Entitlement Chamber) Rules 2008, r 3 and the Tribunal Procedure (Upper Tribunal) Rules 2008, r 3.

[135] The court's jurisdiction to make a periodical payments order, secured or otherwise, will be subject to the operation of the CSA 1991, as amended by CSPSSA 2000, see **5.46**.

[136] CA 1989, Sch 1, para 1(5)(b).

[137] CA 1989, Sch 1, para 1(5)(a).

[138] CA 1989, Sch 1, para 9.

[139] CA 1989, Sch 1, para 10.

5.51   Which court?

An application should be made to the Family Court, who will then allocate it to the appropriate level of judge.[140]

5.52   Who may apply?

Schedule 1, para 1(1) to the CA 1989 provides that applications may be made by:

–   the parent of a child ('parent' includes a step-parent);
–   the guardian of a child;
–   the special guardian of a child;
–   any person named in a child arrangements order as a person with whom a child is to live; or
–   in certain limited circumstances a child over 18.[141]

With the exception of those in the latter category, the court has jurisdiction to make orders for children under the age of 18, although an order for periodical payments will usually be expressed to last until a child's 17th birthday unless he or she is in full-time education or training, or has a disability.

There is no definition of 'parent' in CA 1989 and in *T v B (Parental Responsibility: Financial Provision)*[142] Moylan J held that for the purposes of Sch 1 it should be strictly interpreted to include only a legal parent. In that case a child was born to a lesbian couple as a result of their joint application for treatment by way of artificial insemination by donor. They had not entered into a civil partnership. On the breakdown of their relationship a shared residence order was made which had the effect of conferring parental responsibility also upon the woman who had not borne the child. The other applied for financial provision for the child under Sch 1. The court rejected the submissions of the applicant that the definition of 'parent' could extend to a social and psychological parent as the respondent clearly was in that case.

5.53   Pre-application protocol

The pre-application protocol introduced by the FPR 2010 is intended to apply to all applications for a financial remedy, including applications under Sch 1 CA 1989, however straightforward or complex.

---

[140] Applications for a top-up order where the maximum calculation following a maximum assessment (CSA, s 8(6)) should generally be listed at High Court level: *Re P (Child: Financial Provision)* [2003] 2 FLR 865.

[141] Schedule 1, para 2(1). Where the child is or will be undergoing education or training or where there are special circumstances, and a periodical payments order was not in force immediately before the child's 16th birthday, and the child's parents are not living together.

[142] [2010] 2 FLR 1966.

The aim is to exchange financial and other relevant information at an early stage to assist the parties to identify and resolve their differences speedily and fairly, or at least narrow the issues. This is with a view to saving costs and is in line with the overriding objective.

Even if the parties are unable to reach agreement, adherence to the protocol will assist the court in dealing justly with the case and as speedily and cost-effectively as possible. The court will therefore expect the parties to comply with the terms of the protocol.

5.54 Procedure in the Family Court

Since 22 April 2014 applications under CA 1989, Sch 1 have been dealt with under the 'short cut' procedure set out at Chapter 5 of FPR 9 and not the full procedure used for other financial remedies (such as financial division on divorce). This can provide faster access to a final contested hearing but does not include the opportunity to attempt a Financial Dispute Resolution hearing (which is generally considered to be a useful opportunity to bring about a settlement using 'early neutral evaluation' from a judge). Parties who would like their application to be dealt with under the full procedure must make a specific application for this.[143]

The application for an order under Sch 1 to the CA 1989 is in Form A1 together with any documents stated to be required or referred to in the application. A copy of the Form A1 with sufficient copies for service on the respondent, together with the court fee, must be sent to court for issue. On receipt, the court will endorse the date of the first hearing that will be not less than four weeks and not more than eight weeks after the date of filing of the application. The court will then either effect service of the application upon the respondent within four days, or send the papers to the applicant's solicitors for service by them within four days of receipt. If service is not effected by the court a certificate of service must be filed at court before the date fixed for the first appointment.

Where there is also to be an application under TLATA 1996 generally speaking it will be preferable for the application to be conjoined and case managed together.[144]

5.55 Procedure after issue

Not more than 14 days after the issue of the application the parties must simultaneously exchange a financial statement in Form E1, accompanied by the prescribed documents only.[145]

---

[143] FPR 2010, r 9.18.
[144] *W v W (Joinder of Trusts of Land Act and Children Act Applications)* [2004] 2 FLR 321.
[145] FPR 2010, r 9.19(1).

No additional disclosure or inspection of documents may be given until the court has given its approval.[146]

5.56   Procedure at first hearing

The first appointment must be conducted with the aim of defining the issues and saving costs in pursuance of the overriding objective.

Both parties must personally attend the first hearing unless the court directs otherwise.

If the court is able to determine the application at the first hearing it may do so, otherwise it will direct that further evidence be filed and a date set for a directions hearing or appointment or final hearing.[147]

5.57   The exercise of the court's discretion

The matters to which the court must have regard when deciding whether or not to make one or more orders for financial relief are similar to those considered when the court is exercising its discretion under s 25(3) of the MCA 1973. However, there is no explicit requirement that the child's welfare is to be either the court's 'first consideration',[148] or the 'paramount consideration'.[149] Nonetheless it is apparent from *J v C*[150] and *Re P*[151] that the child's welfare will assume a greater importance in the exercise of the court's discretion than simply being one of the relevant circumstances. It will be 'in the generality of cases, a constant influence on the discretionary outcome', as Thorpe LJ put it in *Re P*.

The court must have regard to all the circumstances, including:
–   the financial needs of the child;
–   the income, earning capacity (if any), property and other financial resources of the child;
–   any physical or mental disability of the child; and
–   the manner in which the child was being, or was expected to be, educated or trained.

In addition, the court will look at income, earning capacity, property and other financial resources, and financial needs, obligations and responsibilities, at the time of the hearing and in the foreseeable future, in the following cases:
–   where the court is considering an application made by a parent, special guardian, or guardian of the child, or someone named in a child arrangements order as someone with whom the child is to live, it will look

---

146   FPR 2010, r 9.19(4).
147   FPR 2010, r 9.20.
148   MCA 1973, s 25(1).
149   CA 1989, s 1(1).
150   [1999] 1 FLR 152.
151   [2003] 2 FLR 865.

at the financial position of the child's parents, which definition will include a step-parent or former step-parent, and that of the applicant and any other person in whose favour the court proposes to make the order, for example a person with such a child arrangements order;

– when the court is considering an application made by a child over 18, it will look at the financial position of the parents of the child as well the applicant for the order; and

– when the court is asked to make an order against a person who is not the parent of the child, for example a step-parent or former step-parent, it will in addition have regard to matters set out in Sch 1, para 4(2). These concern the degree of the assumption of responsibility, whether this was in the knowledge that the child was not his, and the liability of any other person to maintain the child.

Note that the definition of 'parent' for these purposes, will include any party to a marriage, whether or not that marriage is still subsisting, in relation to whom the child is or was a child of the family. It will not include parties who cohabit, and so under Sch 1 one cohabitant will have no liability for the children of the other cohabitant alone.

The court's approach

5.58 *Periodical payments*

An order for periodical payments will only be made if the CMS does not have jurisdiction, or where the court retains a residual jurisdiction under CSA 1991, ss 8(6)-(8) and so in practice such applications tend to be limited either to cases where the paying party is particularly affluent, or special circumstances apply.

An order in favour of a child can reflect the contribution of the parent with care to the child's upbringing by including an allowance for that parent.[152]

In *W v J (Child: variation of financial provision)*[153] Bennett J held that there was no jurisdiction to make an allowance for the legal fees of one parent in an order for periodical payments, even though the application had been brought for the benefit of the child. However, since then the courts have begun to recognise the need for there to be equality of arms between parties to these applications.

In *MT v T*[154] Charles J made an allowance for legal costs in an application for interim periodical payments. This was on the basis that since the application

---

[152] *Haroutunian v Jennings* (1980) 1 FLR 62, followed in *A v A* [1994] 1 FLR 657; *FG v MBW (Financial Remedy for Child)* [2012] 1 FLR 152.
[153] [2004] 2 FLR 300.
[154] [2007] 2 FLR 925.

was brought by the mother effectively on behalf of and for the benefit of the child, she was acting in a quasi-fiduciary or representative capacity and should not have to bear the costs personally.

In *G v G*[155] Moylan J made an award of interim periodical payments of £40,000 as a contribution to the costs of the applicant mother. The court held that there was jurisdiction to make such an order under Sch 1 if it was considered appropriate to do so for the benefit of the children. In that case Moylan J took the view that it would be of benefit to the children if the mother were properly represented. It was relevant to his decision that there was a significant financial imbalance between the parents, the applicant was conducting the litigation in an entirely responsible way, and the respondent could well afford to pay.

In *CF v KM*[156] the question arose as to whether the court had the jurisdiction to make interim provision for legal costs where there had as yet been no determination by CMEC as to the non-resident parent's liability to pay the maximum assessment. In practice, applications for periodical payments, interim or otherwise, and for costs allowances within such provision, will be confined to those cases in which the court retains jurisdiction, generally where there is power to make a top-up order. In this case Charles J determined the issue by making a lump sum order sufficient to cover the applicant's legal costs. The basis for the decision was that there was nothing in para 9 of Sch 1 to prevent the court from making a lump sum order other than on a final basis in cases in which the court did not retain the jurisdiction to make a periodical payments order. It was of course necessary for the court to find, which it did in that case, that on a balance of probabilities it would benefit the child if the mother had legal representation in both the Sch 1 and s 8 proceedings.

In *PG v TW (No 1)*[157] Theis J ordered interim provision for costs of £80,000, together with a further £27,000 which would only fall to be paid if the father did not withdraw his strike out application. It is interesting to note that in the substantive hearing that followed (*PG v TW (No 2)*[158]) HHJ Horowicz ordered that the mother's costs be met by the father in full on an indemnity basis because to leave the mother with unpaid legal fees would have had an impact on the child's welfare.[159]

Although a principle has therefore been established that the court has power under Sch 1 to make an allowance for costs by way of an interim periodical payments or lump sum order, in exercising its discretion the court will always be mindful that the pursuit of the substantive claim must be for the benefit of the child and not to satisfy the applicant's desire to litigate.

---

[155] [2009] EWHC 2080 (Fam).
[156] [2011] 1 FLR 208.
[157] [2014] 1 FLR 508.
[158] [2014] 1 FLR 923.
[159] So following the approach of Peter Hughes QC in *H v M* (unreported) which went unchallenged when the case reached the Court of Appeal as *Morgan v Hill* [2007] 1 FLR 1480.

5.59 Lump sum

There is no limit to the size, or indeed number, of lump sum orders that may be made in the Family Court.[160]

A lump sum order may be payable by instalments, and although the size of the lump sum cannot be varied, the size and frequency of the instalments may be.

It is not possible to order a lump sum payable by instalments as a back door route to a periodical payments order.[161]

In *Phillips v Peace*[162] although the court could not make an order for income provision for the child against the very rich father who had arranged his financial affairs so that the assessment of the Child Support Agency (as it was then) was nil, the court made a lump sum order that took into account the medical costs associated with the birth, the equipping of the nursery and the cost of furnishing a new flat for the mother and child to live in. The total lump sum awarded was just short of £25,000. In addition, a settlement of £90,000 was ordered to enable a suitable flat to be purchased on trust, the terms of the trust being to provide a home for the child until she finished university, and thereafter the mother to have the right to buy the property from the trustees at the market value. Although the lump sum included a small sum to reimburse the mother for the cost of registering the child at a private school, the mother's claim for the cost of private education was rejected on the basis that it was too early at that stage to make any decision about what would best suit the child's needs. This would not preclude a further application for lump sum provision to cover school fees at a later stage.

In reaching his decision as to the level of provision, Johnson J took into account that whilst the child was the daughter of a rich and successful businessman and would have had a certain standard of living commensurate with that had her parents lived together, her mother with whom she would live was of modest means, claiming income support.

In *J v C (Child: Financial Provision)*[163] the father of a child born after the breakdown of his relationship with the mother to whom he was never married, won £1.4m on the national lottery. The mother applied for lump sum, transfer and settlement of property orders to benefit the child.

The court made it clear that it attached little weight to the length or the quality of the parents' relationship (short and turbulent), nor to the fact that the windfall was received over a year after the relationship ended:[164]

---

[160] *CF v KM* [2011] 1 FLR 208.
[161] *Phillips v Peace* [1996] 2 FLR 230.
[162] [1996] 2 FLR 230.
[163] [1999] 1 FLR 152.
[164] Per Hale J at 160B–D.

'Parents are responsible for their children throughout their dependency. The fact that such riches as they have came after the breakup of the relationship cannot affect that. This case is not the same as *Phillips v Peace* where the parents came from two very different backgrounds, or what in the olden days used to be called "stations in life". These two parents are reasonably equivalent ... There is a further point of public policy that, where resources allow, the family obligation should be respected in such a way as to reduce, or even eliminate, the need for children to be supported by public funds.'

Accordingly an order was made requiring the father to buy a four-bedroomed house for the child to live in with her mother and half sisters. The property would be held on trust for the child's benefit during her dependency and would revert to her father thereafter. The mother's cohabitation or remarriage would not affect the situation. There was also lump sum provision to enable the mother to buy a car and furnish the new property.

The court was at pains to ensure that no element of the child's income needs was reflected in the lump sum, as this would offend against the principle of the CSA 1991.

In *B v V (Children: Financial Provision: Unmarried Parents)*[165] the parties had cohabited for three years and had a child, aged four at the date of the hearing. The father's income was about £38,000 and he had capital assets of about £174,000. The mother had the care of the child. She did not work, but the judge found that she had a part-time earning capacity. The mother had no assets. The judge ordered payment of a lump sum of £55,000 to enable the mother to purchase a small flat, leaving it up to her to improve on that by fulfilling her earning capacity. The property was to be held on trust until the child reached 21 years or finished full-time education, whichever was later, at which point the proportion contributed by the father would revert to him.

In *Re P (Child: Financial Provision)*[166] the parents of a two year-old child were not married and had not lived together. The father had unlimited resources and a lifestyle that reflected this. He had told the trial judge that he could afford to pay £10m if required to do so. The mother came from an affluent background but had little or no earning capacity.

The court at first instance made an order for an allowance of £450,000 for a house, a lump sum of £30,000 for furnishings, £20,000 for a car and periodical payments of £35,360 per annum, to be reduced by £9,333 on the child's 7th birthday.

The mother's appeal against the housing allowance and periodical payments was allowed and an order was made for a housing fund of £1m, £100,000 for interior decoration and periodical payments of £70,000 per annum.

---

[165] *Current Law* September 1999, para 248.
[166] [2003] 2 FLR 865.

Thorpe LJ set out his view as to the approach the court should take where both of the parents were affluent, although similar principles would apply in other cases. The starting point would be the provision and equipping of a home, then any lump sum and finally a 'broad common-sense assessment' of the budget that the applicant would need to maintain the home and lifestyle. He acknowledged that in cases in which there was sufficient money available to take into account the parent's needs as the carer of the child, this set up a tension between the parents, the paying party tending to resist any payment that may confer an incidental benefit on the carer. In determining all these matters Thorpe LJ expressed the view that it was necessary to:[167]

> 'recognise the responsibility, and often the sacrifice, of the unmarried parent (generally the mother) who is to be the primary carer for the child ... In order to discharge this responsibility the carer must have control of a budget that reflects her position and the position of the father, both social and financial. On the one hand she should not be burdened with unnecessary financial anxiety or have to resort to parsimony when the other parent chooses to live lavishly. On the other hand whatever is provided is to be spent at the expiration of the year ... There can be no slack to ... fund a pension ... or otherwise to put money away for a rainy day.'

5.60   Transfer or settlement of property

In many cases the main purpose of an application under Sch 1 will be to secure a home for the benefit of the child and the applicant. Where provision for a child under Sch 1 includes an allowance for housing, the court tends to take the view that the provision is to be for the child during his minority, and only exceptionally will provision be carried beyond a child's 18th birthday or the completion of full-time tertiary education.

In practice, this means that any property that is transferred for the benefit of a child will usually revert to the transferor when the child reaches 18, or ceases full-time education, whichever occurs first.[168]

The question of how long property could be settled for the benefit of a child was considered by Munby J, as he then was, in *Re N (Payments for benefit of child)*.[169] In that case the respondent father successfully appealed the decision of the district judge to settle property until the child was 21. The court held that in the absence of the circumstances set out in Sch 1,[170] orders for financial provision for children cannot extend beyond their minority. This means the child's 18th birthday, in the absence of special circumstances or completion of the child's tertiary education. The latter could include a gap year either before or after university.

---

[167] At para 49.
[168] *H v P (Illegitimate Child: Capital Provision)* [1993] Fam Law 515; *A v A (A Minor: Financial Provision)* [1994] 1 FLR 657; *T v S (Financial Provision for Children)* [1994] 2 FLR 883; *Phillips v Peace* [1996] 2 FLR 230; *J v C (Child: Financial Provision)* [1999] 1 FLR 152.
[169] [2009] 1 FLR 1442.
[170] Schedule 1, paras 2, 3 and 6.

The definition of 'property' will include a tenancy. Before Part IV of the FLA 1996 came into force, applications for the transfer of a tenancy for the benefit of a child were frequently used as an incidental means of securing accommodation for the parent with care.[171]

However, whilst there may remain cases to which Sch 1 to the CA 1989 will be appropriate, it is likely that most cohabitants will now seek an outright transfer of tenancy under the provisions of s 53 of and Sch 7 to the FLA 1996.[172]

Alternatively, in appropriate circumstances, an occupation order may be made under Part IV of the FLA 1996.[173]

5.61 Interim orders

The court has power to make an interim order for periodical payments that will expire no later than the final determination of the substantive application.

5.62 Variation of orders

Orders for periodical payments, secured or otherwise, may be varied on the application of the payer or payee.

The amount of a lump sum order may not be varied, but where the lump sum is payable by instalments the frequency and amount of the instalments may be varied.

However, there is no prohibition on subsequent applications for further lump sum orders.

5.63 Termination of payments

Dependency of a child is the likely arbiter of termination of payments in private agreements or where an order has been made under CA 1989, Sch 1. Each agreement should have its own terms incorporated into it.

Dependency is expressed in statutory terms as not extending past the child's seventeenth birthday 'unless the court thinks it right in the circumstances';[174] and in any event not beyond the child's eighteenth birthday (para 3(1)(b)).[175] It can be extended beyond 18, however, in the case of a child's continuing in education or training[176] or in 'special circumstances'.[177]

---

[171] *K v K (Minors: Property Transfer)* [1992] 2 FLR 220.
[172] See **1.175**.
[173] See **4.18**.
[174] CA 1989, Sch 1 para 3(1)(a).
[175] CA 1989, Sch 1 para 3(1)(b).
[176] CA 1989, Sch 1 para 3(2)(a).
[177] CA 1989, Sch 1 para 3(2)(b).

Child support maintenance terminates when the qualifying child ceases to be a 'child' under s 55 (see above) or in a variety of more or less technical circumstances set out in CSA Sch 1, para 16. Some para 16 conditions beg the question in issue: for example, para 16(1)(b) provides for termination where there are no longer any qualifying children; but this demands the reader's ability to detect, say, that where jurisdiction of the CMS ceases under s 44 (habitual residence of one or more of qualifying children, PWC or NRP outside UK) then the child is no longer a qualifying child.

5.64 Termination by resumption of cohabitation

As mentioned above maintenance terminates on resumption of cohabitation by operation of law; and by operation of any agreement in the case of a private agreement. As far as is known, the common law does not imply a term for duration of cohabitation to cause termination by resumption of cohabitation.

5.65 Enforcement of financial provision orders

This book can deal only briefly with the subject of enforcement of orders and agreements (mostly, though not exclusively, for child maintenance). More detail and appropriate references can be found in *The Family Court Practice*.

5.66 Enforcement of payment of child maintenance arrears and other financial provision

Enforcement of arrears and other payments as between cohabitants may be under three schemes according to the nature of the underlying statutory basis for payment:

(1) by civil claim in restitution or contract where there is a private agreement;

(2) by statutory enforcement of statutory provision and orders under Family Procedure Rules 2010 Part 33 (with Civil Procedure Rules 1998 Parts 70 to 73); and

(3) by the CSA or CMS only under CSA 1991, ss 28–40 (this part of the 1991 Act was extensively amended and extended by CMOPA 2008).

The schemes for enforcement are divided irreconcilably (in procedural terms) between the private law remedies available at (1) and (2) and the public or administrative law scheme under (3).

The introduction of the single Family Court in April 2014 went some way towards simplifying the process for applicants wishing to enforce child maintenance orders, with a new single point of entry for all family law applications. Nevertheless, the options and complexity can remain overwhelming, to the extent that the Law Commission is currently commissioned to report on the enforcement of family financial orders.

5.67   *Enforcement of arrears of child support maintenance following an assessment by CMS*

Arrears of child support maintenance can be pursued only by the CSA/CMS and the recipient parent has no involvement in the process. As a very last resort any serious failure on the part of the CSA or CMS may be addressed by an application for judicial review and/or a claim for maladministration.

A parent with care who wishes to sidestep the CSA enforcement machinery must dispense altogether with the child support scheme. However, the arrears that have accrued under the CSA maintenance liability can never be the subject of the enforcement proceedings brought by the parent with care. Only those arrears that have accrued from the date of any request 'to cease acting' (CSA 1991, s 4(5)) and payments thereafter can be enforced outside the statutory regime. In *Kehoe*[178] the House of Lords made it clear that there can be no cross-over between the private and the administrative schemes.

5.68   *Enforcement of child periodical payments*

By contrast with payments due under a CMS assessment, there are no restrictions upon the payee of an order made under Sch 1 of the CA 1989 to take any necessary enforcement steps.

These orders may be for substantive provision or a top-up order.[179] In the latter case the Family Court has jurisdiction to back-date the payment of that order according to the earlier of the first effective date of the calculation (which can be many months, even years before) or six months prior to the CA 1989, Sch 1 application.[180] This in itself creates potential for arrears which may remain unpaid:[181]

(1)   Civil Procedure Rules 1998 – where there is an agreement (oral or written) a parent must first obtain an order by the CPR 1998, Part 8 procedure before that order can be enforced. The usual civil means of enforcement are then available upon application (see Tables below).

(2)   Family Procedure Rules 2010 – for orders made under Sch 1 of the CA 1989 the applicant has the range of enforcement methods available under FPR 2010, Part 33 (see tables and enforcement in the Family Court below).

---

[178]   *R (on the application of Kehoe) v Secretary of State for Work and Pensions* [2005] UKHL 48, [2006] 1 AC 42, [2005] 4 All ER 905, [2005] 3 WLR 252.
[179]   CSA 1991, s 8(6)–(8).
[180]   CA 1989, Sch 1, para 3(5) and (6); and see *Re P (Child; Financial Provision)* [2003] 2 FLR 865, CA.
[181]   See eg *H v C* [2009] 2 FLR 1540.

5.69 Enforcement procedures for financial provision and child maintenance

Tables 1 and 2 list the main forms of application for enforcement (including reference to the MEA 1991) arising in proceedings between cohabitants. Parallel child support maintenance enforcement under CSA 1991 is referred to; and reference to lump sum and capital orders (charging orders and orders for sale) is included briefly. Enforcement of arrears of child periodical payments may become necessary by charging order and sale of property (CPR 1998, r 73.10).

5.70 Using the tables

Table 1 lists the main forms of financial provision likely to be covered by agreements and orders in this book. It then lists in reference figures codes for the forms of enforcement available in respect of each. Parallel forms of child support maintenance enforcement (CSA 1991) are also given.

Table 2 lists each of the codes referred to in Table 1 and sets out the source reference for the form of enforcement, the procedural rules reference and the court in which enforcement is available.

5.71 *Table 1 – Enforceable forms of agreement and order: child maintenance and lump sums: procedure under which enforcement proceeds*

Enforceable order	Family proceedings (covered by FPR 2010)	Family proceedings (covered by CPR 1998)	Child support maintenance (CSA 1991)
Agreed child maintenance		(2)(3)	
Periodical payments order (no default)	(1)(1A)(1B)		
Periodical payments orders (default)	(1)(1A)(1B)(3)		(3A)(3B)
(1) Lump sum; and (2) Arrears of periodical payments (accumulated)[182]	(4)(5)(6)(7)(8)	(4)(5)(6)(7)(8)	(4A)(4B)(5A) (6A)(7)(8A)
Enforcement of charging order by foreclosure and order for sale	(9)	(9)	(9)

[182] In the case of periodical payments orders under MCA 1973 and CA 1989, Sch 1 permission is needed to enforce arrears more than a year old (MCA 1973, s 32: there appears to be no equivalent provision in CA 1989, Sch 1).

5.72 *Table 2 – Main forms of enforcement of orders for payments of child maintenance and for payment of lump sums or accumulated arrears of child maintenance*

	Form of enforcement	Statutory or other source	Procedure	Court for issue of enforcement proceedings
1	Payment by standing order or direct debit on nominated bank account	Maintenance Enforcement Act 1991	(1) By consent (as part of order); or (2) as FPR 2010, Part 18 application	High court or family court
1A	Payment into court	Maintenance Enforcement Act 1991	FPR 2010, Part 18 application	Family court
1B	Collection through CMS/CSA	Maintenance Enforcement Act 1991	FPR 2010, Part 18 application	Family court
2	Breach of contract	Common law	CPR 1998, Part 8	County court
3	Attachment of earnings	Attachment of Earnings Act 1971	County Court Rules 1981, Order 27 (found in CPR 1998, Sch 2); in family proceedings as applied by FPR 2010, r 33.19A	High court (for high court orders) or family court (for high court or family court orders)
3A	Deduction from earnings order(+)[183]	CSA 1991, s 31	Appeal: Child Support (Collection and Enforcement) Regulations 1992, reg 22	Appeal: family court

---

[183] These 'orders' (indicated by (+)) are imposed by administrative direction, and are not orders in the conventional 'court order' sense of the word in the rest of this table: they are appealed against to the court: DEO – to a magistrates' court (or by judicial review); RDO and LSDO – to the county court.

	Form of enforcement	Statutory or other source	Procedure	Court for issue of enforcement proceedings
3B	Regular deduction order (+)	CSA 1991, s32A	Appeal: Child Support (Collection and Enforcement) Regulations 1992, reg 25AB	Appeal: family court
4	Charging Order	Charging Orders Act 1979	CPR 1998, Part 73 (in FPR 2010 proceedings per and as amended by FPR 2010, r 33.25)	High court, family court or county court[184]
4A	Charging order: child support maintenance only	CSA 1991, s 36	CPR 1998, Part 73	County court
4B	Lump sum deduction order (+);	CSA 1991, ss 32E–32H	Appeal: Child Support (Collection and Enforcement) Regulations 1992, reg 25AB	Appeal: family court
5	Third party debt order	Common law (and see Senior Courts Act, s 40)	CPR 1998, Part 72 (in FPR 2010 proceedings: per and as amended by FPR 2010, r 33.24)	As for 4 Charging order above
5A	Third party debt order: child support maintenance only	CSA 1991, s 36	CPR 1998, Part 72	County court

---

[184] Which one is prescribed at COA 1979, s 1(2).

	Form of enforcement	Statutory or other source	Procedure	Court for issue of enforcement proceedings
6	*Parasitic enforcement orders* Avoidance of disposition Restraint of disposal Freezing (*Mareva*) orders	(a) MCA 1973, s 37(2)(a) and (c);[185] (b) MCA 1973, s 37(2)(b) (c) Common law; and see Civil Procedure Act 1997, s 7	CPR 1998, Parts 23 and 25; FPR 2010, Parts 18 and 20	Court where order made
6A	Orders preventing avoidance	CSA 1991, s 32L	FPR 2010, rr 8.35–40	High court or family court
7	Distress	Powers in civil courts and under CSA 1991, s 28		
8	Judgment summons	Debtors Act 1869, s 5	FPR 2010, r 33.9–33.18	High court or family court
8A	Committal	CSA 1991, ss 39A and 40	Child Support (Collection and Enforcement) Regulations 1992	Magistrates court (civil proceedings)
9	Foreclosure and sale	Common law	CPR 1998, r 73.10 (as applied by FPR 2010, r 33.25)	Originating application (CPR 1998, Part 8 or FPR 2010, Part 19[186]) in court where order made. If charge over £30,000 in High court only

---

[185] There is no equivalent power to MCA, s 37(2) in CA 1989, Sch 1; and in the light of such cases as *Wicks v Wicks* [1998] 1 FLR 470, CA it is unlikely the court would assume an inherent jurisdiction. In certain circumstances a freezing order may be available; but it may be necessary to transfer to the High Court if this remedy is sought.

[186] There is no specific reference to part 19 in the r 33.25 amendments; but it must follow from the references to the Part 8 procedure in CPR 1998, r 73.10(3).

5.73 Procedures available in the High Court and Family Court for enforcement

FPR 2010, r 33.3 has provided a procedure, new to family proceedings, which enables an applicant in the High Court or Family Court[187] to opt in his or her application to leave it to the court to decide on 'such method of enforcement as the court may consider appropriate'. The rules use the term 'judgment creditor' for the person 'entitled to enforce a judgment or order'; and 'judgement debtor' is the person against whom the order was made.[188] FPR 2010, r 33.2 applies CPR 1998, Part 70 to family proceedings. This rule applies throughout Part 33 where application is made for enforcement of an order for payment of money.

The CPR Practice Direction 70 – Enforcements of judgments and orders at para 1.1 summarises the forms of enforcement as follows:

'A judgment creditor may enforce a judgment or order for the payment of money by any of the following methods:
(1)   a writ of *fieri facias* or warrant of execution (see RSC Orders 46 and 47 and CCR Order 26);
(2)   a third party debt order (see Part 72);
(3)   a charging order, stop order or stop notice (see Part 73);
(4)   in a county court, an attachment of earnings order (see CCR Order 27);
(5)   the appointment of a receiver (see Part 69).'

Of these, (2), (3) and (4) will be considered here. Application for enforcement of an order for payment of money is made as follows:

(1)   By any means of enforcement available to him/her[189] from the list set out above (either as specified in the application or by such means as 'the court may consider appropriate').[190]

(2)   By appropriate notice of application.

(3)   Accompanied by a statement (verified by a statement of truth) which shows the amount due under the order and how that amount is calculated.[191]

A judgment creditor who applies for enforcement by one of these means can apply by more than one means of enforcement and do so 'either at the same time or [by one means] after another'.[192] Plainly a judgment creditor can only be paid once; but cumulatively that can be by more than one method of enforcement.

Rule 33.3(2)(b) leaves it open to a judgment creditor to apply for enforcement, but leaves it to the court to decide by what means enforcement should proceed.

---

[187] FPR 2010, r 33.1(1).
[188] CPR 1998, r 70.1(2).
[189] CPR 1998, r 70.2(2)(a).
[190] FPR 2010, r 33.3(2)(b): see below.
[191] FPR 2010, r 33.3(1)(a).
[192] CPR 1998, r 70.2(2)(b).

Thus, if a judgment creditor asks the court to decide what method of enforcement the court considers appropriate:

(1)   'An order to attend court will be issued' and CPR 1998, r 71.2(6) and (7)[193] apply.

(2)   The order to attend will be endorsed with a penal notice,[194] and, though the rules do not say so, it will presumably have to be served personally (the rules do not give any indication as to by whom or at whose expense).

(3)   The judgment debtor will be required to attend court and to produce there such 'documents in his control [as] are described in the order [to attend court]'.[195]

(4)   The judgment debtor will be required at court to answer such questions on oath as are put to him by the court.[196]

There appears to be no requirement that the judgment creditor attend nor that s/he can ask questions or make submissions as to the means of enforcement once evidence has been heard. Presumably questions could be put through the judge in any event; and the court would not refuse to hear how enforcement could be achieved in the view of the creditor. The final decision is for the court:[197] a novel departure leaving the court, in effect, to advise on disposal and then to dispose of the case (no adjudication is involved, since no issue is before the court) on the basis of its own advice.

5.74   Registration for enforcement in the Family Court

The Maintenance Orders Act 1958 (MOA 1958) aims to enable certain orders[198] to be registered in the Family Court for enforcement purposes. Application is made in the originating court which, if it so decides, may order registration in the payer's court.[199]

Application for enforcement proceeds in the Family Court; and any variation of maintenance application can be dealt with there.[200] Collection of arrears and current payments can be arranged through the Family Court.

---

[193] CPR 1998, r 71.2 as a whole applies where a judgment creditor applies for a judgment debtor to attend court to give information as to his means or about his ability to pay a judgment (r 71.2(1)). This paragraph of r 71.2 has not been applied to family proceedings.
[194] CPR 1998, r 71.2(7).
[195] CPR 1998, r 71.2(6)(a) and (b).
[196] CPR 1998 r 71.2(6)(c).
[197] FPR 2010, r 33.3(2)(b).
[198] Primarily orders made in the High Court, but the list does include orders made in the Magistrates' Court under DPMCA 1978, Pt I, see AJA 1970, Sch 8.
[199] MOA 1958, s 2(1).
[200] MOA 1958, ss 1(1), 4 and 4A.

PART B   PROCEDURAL GUIDES

Scientific test direction

5.75   *Legal background*

In any civil proceedings in which an issue as to parentage arises, a party may apply to the court for a direction for the use of scientific tests or bodily samples to determine the issue, or the court may, on its own initiative, issue such a direction (FLRA 1969, s 20(1)). An application cannot be made on a freestanding basis but only in existing proceedings (eg FLA 1986, s 55A, CA 1989, s 9 or CSA 1991, s 27, TLATA 1996, s 14 or under I(PFD)A 1975). The court issues a direction (see also *Re H (Paternity: Blood Test)*[201]). No sample can be taken without consent (FLRA 1969, s 21(1)) or by direction of the court where a person having care and control of a child refuses consent (FLRA 1969, s 21(3)): failure to comply with a direction enables the court to draw such inferences as appear proper in the circumstances of the particular case (FLRA 1969, s 23(1)). Procedure is governed by CPR PD23B imported into family proceedings by the FPR PD that describes those practice directions relating to family proceedings in force before 6 April 2011 that support the FPR 2010, para 2.1: although no procedure is prescribed by CPR PD23B the fact that it accompanies CPR 1998, Pt 23 implies that in family proceedings its equivalent, Pt 18, would apply.

A child under 16 or who lacks capacity acts by a 'responsible adult' as defined in CPR PD23B, para 1.1(3).

5.76   *Procedure*

Who may apply	Any party to the proceedings; or the court on own initiative	FLRA 1969, s 20(1)
The proceedings	Any civil proceedings in which parentage is in issue	FLRA 1969, s 20(1)
The application	By FPR 2010, Pt 18 procedure application notice (Form D11)	FPR 2010, r 18.1(2)(*a*)
	The application must specify who is to carry out the tests	FLRA 1969, s 20(1A)
	If application is regarding (1) a person under 16 or (2) who is a protected party (per FPR 2010, Pt 15), the name and address of the responsible adult must be given	CPR PD23B, para 1.2

---

[201] [1996] 2 FLR 65, CA.

Respondent/ Other parties	(1) All other parties to the existing proceedings (2) Anyone else from whom samples may be required	See, for example, FPR 2010, r 8.20 for declarations under r 8.18
Notice	(1) FPR 2010 proceedings: 7 days before hearing	FPR 2010, r 18.8(1)(*b*)(ii)
	(2) CPR 1998 proceedings: 3 days before hearing	CPR 1998, r 23.7(1)(*b*)
Joinder	Application for joinder in proceedings: (1) FPR 2010 proceedings	No procedure: quaere on analogy with CPR 1998 procedure (per *Goldstone v Goldstone & ors* [2011] EWCA Civ 39)
	(2) CPR 1998 proceedings	CPR 1998, r 19.2
Direction	Court gives a direction in form proposed in *Re H*	*Re H* [1996] 2 FLR 65 at 83
	The name of the tester must be included in the direction	
Service of direction	By the court (1) on parties to proceedings	CPR PD23B, para 1.4(1)
	(2) anyone from whom sample is to be taken	CPR PD23B, para 1.4(2)
Report	Made to the court by the tester	FLRA 1969, s 20(2)
	Report in form prescribed by Blood Tests (Evidence of Paternity) Regs 1971	FLRA 1969, ss 20(3), 22
	Served by the court on (1) parties to proceedings, (2) responsible adult (as applicable) and (3) anyone from whom sample to be taken	CPR PD23B, para 1.5
Fees and costs	Fee for report payable by applicant for direction; but treated as costs in the main proceedings	FLRA 1969, s 20(6)

Parental responsibility order

5.77   *Legal background*

Parental responsibility comprises all the rights, duties, powers, responsibilities and authority which, by law, a parent has in relation to a child and his property, or which a guardian of a child's estate has in relation to his property (CA 1989, s 3).

A child's mother always has parental responsibility for the child; however, if she was not married to the child's father at the time of the birth, the father will only acquire parental responsibility by marrying the mother, by making a formal parental responsibility agreement with her (using Form C(PRA1)) or by obtaining an order from the court (CA 1989, s 4, to be read in conjunction with FLRA 1987, s 1(2)) or if his name is placed on the birth certificate at registration or re-registration of the birth under the Births and Deaths Registration Act 1953 (see CA 1989, s 4(1)(a)). A step-parent may acquire parental responsibility for a child of his spouse or civil partner by agreement (using Form C(PRA2)), or by order of the court (CA 1989, s 4A). A second female parent may acquire responsibility for a child by agreement (using Form C(PRA3)) or by order of the court (CA 1989, s 4ZA). The court must make such an order where it makes a residence order in favour of the father (CA 1989, s 12(1)) and care should therefore be taken to consider this requirement when making or opposing an interim residence application; otherwise, it is in the court's discretion whether to grant a specific application under CA 1989, s 4.

On making an application to the court, the applicant should also file a completed Form FM1 confirming attendance at a mediation information and assessment meeting or giving reasons for not attending (FPR PD3A, Annex A).

The court may subsequently revoke such an order and also a parental responsibility agreement (which may not be revoked merely by agreement).

5.78 *Procedure*

Who may apply	Father without parental responsibility	CA 1989, s 4(1)(*a*)
	The spouse or civil partner of a parent with parental responsibility	CA 1989, s 4A
	The second female parent of a child	CA 1989, s 4ZA; HFEA 2008, s 43
Which court	Family court (lay justices) if none of the criteria in the schedule to the *Guidance* apply	CA 1989, ss 10(1); FC(CDB)R 2014; President's Guidance *Allocation and Gatekeeping*
	Proceedings can be transferred sideways, upwards or downwards, using order in Form C49	FC(CDB)R 2014
Which proceedings	Freestanding application	CA 1989, s 4(1), s 4ZA(1)

	Court must make order on making a child arrangements order that the child shall live with the second parent without parental responsibility even if no specific application is made; it has a discretion whether or not to make a parental responsibility order where the child is to have contact with the second parent	CA 1989, s 12(1)
Application	On Form C1 (or Forms C(PRA1), C(PRA2) or C(PRA3) as appropriate), together with Form FM1, with sufficient copies for each respondent. Where it is alleged that the child who is the subject of the application has suffered, or is at risk of suffering, any harm from (*a*) any form of domestic abuse; (*b*) violence within the household; (*c*) child abduction; or (*d*) other conduct or behaviour, supplemental Form C1A must also be completed	FPR PD3A, PD5A, PD12B
	Fee: £215	FPFO 2008, Sch 1, fee 2.1(*a*), (*b*);
Respondents	Notice to be served in Form C6 on every person with parental responsibility and on every person with parental responsibility before care order	FPR 2010, r 12.3
Additional persons to be served with notice of the proceedings	Notice to be served in Form C6A on local authority, if providing accommodation, and on person caring for child or providing refuge	FPR PD12C, para 3.1
Service	Applicant must serve a copy of the application, together with Form C6 (endorsed with date fixed for hearing), on each respondent at least 14 days before the hearing; notice of the proceedings must be served in Form C6A (endorsed with date fixed for hearing) on other persons to be served at least 14 days before the hearing	FPR PD12B, para 8.8; FPR PD12C, Annex B
	At or before first directions appointment or hearing, applicant must file statement in Form C9 to prove that requirements for service have been complied with	FPR PD5A

Answer to application	Respondent to an application must file a written answer and serve it on the other parties to the proceedings within 14 days of the date on which the application is served	FPR 2010, r 12.32
Joinder or removal of parties	By court order, of its own initiative or on written request on Form C2 together with Form C1A if necessary (see under 'Application' above)	FPR 2010, rr 4.3, 12.3(3)
Directions	As to applications for directions, see —	FPR 2010, r 12.12
	NB A written request for directions must be made on Form C2 and C1A if necessary (see under 'Application' above)	
	Directions which may be given (eg timetable for the proceedings, submission of evidence or transfer of proceedings to another court)	FPR 2010, r 12.12
	Timing of proceedings	FPR 2010, r 12.13
	Attendance at the directions hearing	FPR 2010, r 12.14
Order	Conferring parental responsibility on the father, spouse, civil partner or second female parent, in Form C45	CA 1989, ss 4(1)(*a*), 12(1); FPR PD12B
Transitional arrangements	Implementation of CFA 2014	Children and Families Act 2014 (Transitional Proceedings) Order 2014

Discharge of a parental responsibility order or a parental responsibility agreement

Legal background

For parental responsibility orders, see above.

5.79 Procedure

Who may apply	Any person with parental responsibility; the child (with permission)	CA 1989, s 4(3) and s 4A
Which court	Family Court (lay justices) if none of the criteria in the schedule to the *Guidance* apply	CA 1989, ss 10(1); FC(CDB)R 2014; President's Guidance *Allocation and Gatekeeping*

	Proceedings can be transferred sideways, upwards or downwards, using order in Form C49	FC(CDB)R 2014
Which proceedings	Freestanding application	CA 1989, s 4(3)
Application	On Form C1, together with Form FM1, with sufficient copies for each respondent. Where it is alleged that the child who is the subject of the application has suffered, or is at risk of suffering, any harm from (a) any form of domestic abuse; (b) violence within the household; (c) child abduction; or (d) other conduct or behaviour supplemental Form C1A must also be completed.	FPR PD3A
	Fee: £215	FPFO 2008, Sch 1, para 2.1(a),(b);
	Child should obtain the necessary permission, using Form C2	FPR 2010, rr 18.1–18.13; PD12B
Respondents	Notice to be served in Form C6 on every person with parental responsibility; every person with parental responsibility before care order and on other parties to original proceedings (where the appointment had been by the court)	FPR 2010, r 12.3
Additional persons to be served with notice of the proceedings	Notice to be served in Form C6A on local authority, if providing accommodation, and on person caring for child or providing refuge	FPR PD12C, para 3.1
Service	Applicant must serve a copy of the application, together with Form C6 (endorsed with date fixed for hearing), on each respondent at least 14 days before the hearing; notice of the proceedings must be served in Form C6A (endorsed with date fixed for hearing) on other persons to be served at least 14 days before the hearing	FPR PD12B, para 8.8; FPR PD12C, Annex B
	At or before first directions appointment or hearing, applicant must file statement in Form C9 to prove that requirements for service have been complied with	FPR PD5A
Answer to application	Respondent must file a written answer and serve it on the other parties to the proceedings within 14 days of the date on which the application is served	FPR 2010, r 12.32

Joinder or removal of parties	By court order, of its own initiative or on written request on Form C2 and Form C1A if necessary (see under 'Application' above)	FPR 2010, rr 4.3, 12.3(3)
Directions	As to applications for directions, see —	FPR 2010, r 5.1; PD5A, PD12B
	NB A written request for directions must be made on Form C2 and Form C1A if necessary (see under 'Application' above)	
	Directions which may be given (eg as to timetable for the proceedings, submission of evidence or transfer of proceedings to another court)	FPR 2010, r 12.12
	Timing of proceedings	FPR 2010, r 12.13
	Attendance at the directions hearing	FPR 2010, r 12.14
Order	Form C45, for termination of parental responsibility order or parental responsibility agreement	FPR PD12B
Transitional arrangements	Implementation of CFA 2014	Children and Families Act 2014 (Transitional Proceedings) Order 2014

Appointment or removal of a guardian

5.80 Legal background

A guardian usually stands in the shoes of a parent when a child no longer has a parent with parental responsibility living (although one may also be appointed where a parent who had the benefit of a residence order dies regardless of whether the non-resident parent survives).

Under CA 1989, s 5, a guardian may be appointed in writing by a parent with parental responsibility, the appointment to take effect when he dies (if he has a residence order) or when the last surviving parent with parental responsibility dies. In default (or in addition), the court has a concurrent right of appointment. The court may also terminate (under CA 1989, s 6(7)) the appointment of a guardian, whether he had been appointed by the court or a parent.

On making an application to the court, the applicant should also file a completed Form FM1 confirming attendance at a mediation information and assessment meeting or giving reasons for not attending (FPR PD3A, Annex A).

5.81   *Procedure*

Who may apply	*Appointment* Any person (the proposed guardian)	CA 1989, s 5(1)
	Removal Any person with parental responsibility or, with permission, the child	CA 1989, s 6(7)
Which court	Family court (lay justices) if none of the criteria in the schedule to the *Guidance* apply	CA 1989, ss 10(1); FC(CDB)R 2014; President's Guidance *Allocation and* *Gatekeeping*
	Proceedings can be transferred sideways, upwards or downwards, using order in Form C49	FC(CDB)R 2014
Which proceedings	Freestanding application; own initiative order in any family proceedings	CA 1989, ss 5(1), (2), 6(7)
Application	*Appointment* On Form C1, together with Form FM1	FPR PD3A, PD5A
	Fee: £215	FPFO 2008, Sch 1, para 2.1(*c*);
	Removal On Form C1, together with Form FM1, with sufficient copies for each respondent	FPR 2010, r 5.1; PD3A, PD5A, PD12B
	Fee: £215	FPFO 2008, Sch 1, para 2.1(*c*);
Respondents	Notice to be served in Form C6 on every person with parental responsibility, every person with parental responsibility before a care order, and (on application to discharge court-appointed guardian) parties to the original proceedings	FPR 2010, r 12.3
Additional persons to whom notice in Form C6A is to be given	Local authority, if providing accommodation Person caring for child or providing refuge If application is for appointment, father without parental responsibility	FPR PD12C, para 3.1

Service	Applicant must serve a copy of the application, together with Form C6 (endorsed with date fixed for hearing), on each respondent at least 14 days before the hearing; notice of the proceedings must be served in Form C6A (endorsed with date fixed for hearing) on other persons to be served at least 14 days before the hearing	FPR PD12C
	At or before first directions appointment or hearing, applicant must file statement in Form C9 to prove that requirements for service have been complied with	FPR PD5A, PD12B
Joinder of parties	By court order, of its own initiative or on written request on Form C2	FPR 2010, rr 4.3, 12.3(3)
Answer to application	Respondent must file a written answer and serve it on the other parties to the proceedings within 14 days of the date on which the application is served	FPR 2010, r 12.32
Directions	Applications for directions	FPR 2010, r 5.1; PD5A, PD12B
	NB A written request for directions must be made on Form C2	
	Directions which may be given (eg as to timetable for the proceedings, submission of evidence or transfer of proceedings to another court)	FPR 2010, r 12.12
	Timing of proceedings	FPR 2010, r 12.13
	Attendance at the directions hearing	FPR 2010, r 12.14
Order	On Form C46, appointing a guardian, in which case the appointee assumes parental responsibility until the appointment is brought to an end by the court	CA 1989, ss 5(1), (6), 6(7); FPR PD12B
	On Form C46, bringing to an end the appointment of a guardian under CA 1989, s 5 (whether made by the court or not)	CA 1989, s 6(7); FPR PD12B
Transitional arrangements	Implementation of CFA 2014	Children and Families Act 2014 (Transitional Proceedings) Order 2014

Financial relief for a child under the Children Act 1989, Sch 1

5.82 Legal background

Subject to the provisions of CSA 1991, which leave the court with a limited role in ordering maintenance or variation of maintenance agreements in respect of children, CA 1989, Sch 1 provides three forms of financial relief for a child: first, para 1 enables a maintenance order, settlement and transfer of property order to be made in favour of a child against either or both of its parents; secondly, para 2 enables a periodical payments order and lump sum order to be made in favour of a child who has reached 18 where: (i) the child's parents are not living with each other, (ii) there was not in force a periodical payments order for the child immediately before he reached 16, and (iii) he is undergoing education or training or there are special circumstances (orders under both paras 1 and 2 may be varied or extended under para 6); and, thirdly, by paras 10 and 11, the court may vary a maintenance agreement containing financial arrangements for the child either during the lifetime of the parent or after the death of one of them. For the reasons set out under s 15, if a child's parents are married, the greater procedural powers that are available make it more advantageous for an application for financial relief against a parent by a child to be brought under MCA 1973, ss 23, 24 and 27 and for an alteration of a maintenance agreement to be brought under MCA 1973, ss 35 and 36; however, where the parents are not married, there is no jurisdiction apart from CA 1989, Sch 1.

An application under CA 1989, Sch 1 is defined as a financial remedy under FPR 2010, r 2.3. The procedure under Pt 9 applies. The application may be made to the Family Court.

5.83 Procedure

Who may apply	*Application for child under 18* Parent or guardian or special guardian of child or holder of residence order	CA 1989, Sch 1, para 1(1); FPR 2010, r 9.10
	The order will be made either on the application of the above or without an application on the making, varying or discharging of a residence order	CA 1989, Sch 1, para 1(6)
	Application by child over 18 The child who is over 18 and:	
	who is or will be undergoing education or training or where there are special circumstances	CA 1989, Sch 1, para 2(1)(*a*), (*b*)
	who has not had in force a periodical payments order immediately before he was 16	CA 1989, Sch 1, para 2(3), (6)

	whose parents are not living together	CA 1989, Sch 1, para 2(4)
	Variation application Any of the persons set out above, with, additionally on an application under CA 1989, Sch 1, para 1, the child himself if he has reached 16	CA 1989, Sch 1, para 6(4)
	Application to alter maintenance agreement Either party to the agreement or a personal representative	CA 1989, Sch 1, paras 10(2), 11(1)
Application	Preliminary requirement for proposed parties to attend a MIAM before application, subject to exemptions.	CFA 2014, s10(1); FPR 2010, Ch 3; PD3A, para 13(1)(b); FPR 2010
	To the Family Court	FPR 2010, r 9.5(2)
	The application is on Form A1 together with any documents stated to be required or referred to in the application. Proceedings start when a court officer issues an application, and are issued on that date	FPR 2010, rr 5.1–5.3, PD5A
	The application is dealt with by the 'short cut' procedure in FPR, Pt 9, Ch 5	FPR 2010, rr 9.18-9.20, PD9A
	On application, the court may direct that the full procedure in FPR 2010, Pt 9, Ch 4 is followed, for example where there are contested issues about the settlement of property. This is determined on paper without notice to the parties before the first hearing	FPR 2010, r 9.18A
Fee	£215	FPFO 2008, fee 2.1(v)
Service	Within 4 days of the date on which the application was filed, a court officer will serve a copy of the application on the respondent and give notice of the date of the first hearing to both parties.	
	Alternatively, the applicant must serve the respondent within 4 days, beginning with the date on which the copy of the application was received from the court, and file a certificate of service on or before the first appointment	FPR 2010, r 9.12(1), (2)

Respondents	Any parent who is not an applicant, or both parents, where the holder of a residence order or special guardianship order applies	CA 1989, Sch 1, para 1(2)
Directions/Interim orders	The court may make an interim order for periodical payments. FPR 2010, Pt 18 procedure applies to applications for interim orders	CA 1989, Sch 1, para 9; FPR 2010, r 9.7(2)
Procedure	The shorter procedure under FPR 2010, Pt 9, Ch 5 applies	FPR 2010, r 9.18A
	The court will fix a first appointment not less than 4 weeks and not more than 8 weeks after the filing of the application	FPR 2010, r 9.12
	Not more than 14 days after the issue of the application, the parties must simultaneously exchange a financial statement on Form E1, accompanied by a limited category of documents. No disclosure or inspection of the parties' documents may be given between the filing of the application and the first appointment, save as laid down in FPR 2010, r 9.19(4)	FPR PD5A; FPR 2010, r 9.19(4)
	Unless the court is able to determine the application at the first hearing, the court may direct further evidence and set a date for a directions hearing or final hearing	FPR 2010, r 9.20
Order	*Application for child under 18* Periodical payments	
	Secured periodical payments	
	Lump sum	
	Settlement of property or transfer of property	
	Application by child over 18 Periodical payments	
	Lump sum	
	Application to alter maintenance agreement Varying or revoking any financial arrangements contained in the maintenance agreement, including inserting provision for periodical payments or for security for increasing or decreasing the level of periodical payments	

PART C PRECEDENTS

5.84 Parental Responsibility Agreement

Parental Responsibility Agreement
Section 4(1)(b) Children Act 1989

Keep this form in a safe place
*Date recorded at the Principal Registry
of the Family Division:*

**Read the notes on the other side
before you make this agreement.**

This is a Parental Responsibility Agreement regarding

the Child   *Full Name* _____

| *Boy or Girl* | *Date of birth* | *Date of 18th birthday* |

Between
the Mother   *Name* _____

     Address

and   the Father   *Name* _____

     Address

We declare that   we are the mother and father of the above child and we agree that the child's father shall have parental responsibility for the child (in addition to the mother having parental responsibility).

Signed (Mother)	Signed (Father)
Date	Date

Certificate of witness

The following evidence of identity was produced by the person signing above:	The following evidence of identity was produced by the person signing above:
Signed in the presence of: *Name of Witness*	Signed in the presence of: *Name of Witness*
Address	*Address*
Signature of Witness	*Signature of Witness*
[A Justice of the Peace] [Justices' Clerk] [An assistant to a justices' clerk] [An officer of the court authorised by the judge to administer oaths]	[A Justice of the Peace] [Justices' Clerk] [An assistant to a justices' clerk] [An Officer of the Court authorised by the judge to administer oaths]

C(PRA1) (12.05)   HMCS

Notes about the Parental Responsibility Agreement

Read these notes before you make the agreement.

About the Parental Responsibility Agreement

The making of this agreement will affect the legal position of the mother and the father. You should both seek legal advice before you make the Agreement. You can obtain the name and address of a solicitor from the Children Panel (020 7242 1222)

or from
- your local family proceedings court, or county court
- a Citizens Advice Bureau
- a Law Centre
- a local library.

You may be eligible for public funding.

When you fill in the Agreement

Please use black ink (the Agreement will be copied). Put the name of one child only. If the father is to have parental responsibility for more than one child, fill in a separate form for each child. **Do not sign the Agreement.**

When you have filled in the Agreement

Take it to a local family proceedings court, or county court, or the Principal Registry of the Family Division (the address is below).

A justice of the peace, a justices' clerk, an assistant to a justices' clerk, or a court official who is authorised by the judge to administer oaths, will witness your signature and he or she will sign the certificate of the witness. **A solicitor cannot witness your signature.**

To the mother: When you make the declaration you will have to prove that you are the child's mother so take to the court the child's full birth certificate.

                You will also need evidence of your identity showing a photograph and signature (for example, a photocard, official pass or passport). **Please note that the child's birth certificate cannot be accepted as sufficient proof of your identity.**

To the father: You will need evidence of your identity showing a photograph and signature (for example, a photocard, official pass or passport).

When the Certificate has been signed and witnessed

Make 2 copies of the Agreement form. You do not need to copy these notes.

Take, or send, this form and the copies to **The Principal Registry of the Family Division, First Avenue House, 42-49 High Holborn, London, WC1V 6NP.**

The Registry will record the Agreement and keep this form. The copies will be stamped and sent back to each parent at the address on the Agreement. The Agreement will not take effect until it has been received and recorded at the Principal Registry of the Family Division.

Ending the Agreement

Once a parental responsibility agreement has been made it can only end
- by an order of the court made on the application of any person who has parental responsibility for the child
- by an order of the court made on the application of the child with permission of the court
- when the child reaches the age of 18.

C(PRA1) (Notes) (12.05)

Step-Parent Parental Responsibility Agreement
Section 4A(1)(a) Children Act 1989

Keep this form in a safe place
Date recorded at the Principal Registry of the Family Division:

Read the notes on the other side before you make this agreement.

This is a Step-Parent Parental Responsibility Agreement regarding

the Child — *Full Name* _____

_____

Gender _____ *Date of birth* _____ *Date of 18th birthday* _____

Between
Parent A — *Name*

Address

and
the other parent (with parental responsibility) — *Name*

Address

and
the step-parent — *Name*

Address

We declare that — we are the parents and step-parent of the above child and we agree that the above mentioned step-parent shall have parental responsibility for the child (in addition to those already having parental responsibility).

Signed **(Parent A)**	*Signed **(Other Parent)**	Signed **(Step-Parent)**
Date	Date	Date

Certificate of witness

The following evidence of identity was produced by the person signing above:	The following evidence of identity was produced by the person signing above:	The following evidence of identity was produced by the person signing above:
Signed in the presence of: *Name of Witness*	Signed in the presence of: *Name of Witness*	Signed in the presence of: *Name of Witness*
Address	Address	Address

*If there is only one parent with parental responsibility, please delete this section.

Signature of Witness	*Signature of Witness*	*Signature of Witness*
[A Justice of the Peace] [Justices' Clerk] [An assistant to a justices' clerk] [An Officer of the Court authorised by the judge to administer oaths]	[A Justice of the Peace] [Justices' Clerk] [An assistant to a justices' clerk] [An Officer of the Court authorised by the judge to administer oaths]	[A Justice of the Peace] [Justices' Clerk] [An assistant to a justices' clerk] [An Officer of the Court authorised by the judge to administer oaths]

C(PRA2) (09.09)   ht 2009

Notes about the Step-Parent Parental Responsibility Form
Read these notes before you make the Agreement

About the Step-Parent Parental Responsibility Agreement

The making of this agreement will affect the legal position of the parent(s) and the step-parent. You should seek legal advice before you make the Agreement. You can obtain the name and address of a solicitor from the Children Panel (020 7242 1222) or from:

- your local family proceedings court, or county court,
- a Citizens Advice Bureau,
- a Law Centre,
- a local library.

You may be eligible for public funding.

When you fill in the Agreement

Please use black ink (the Agreement will be copied). Put the name of one child only. If the step-parent is to have parental responsibility for more than one child, fill in a separate form for each child. **Do not sign the Agreement.**

When you have filled in the Agreement

Take it to a local family proceedings court, or county court, or the Principal Registry of the Family Division (the address is below).

A justice of the peace, a justices' clerk, an assistant to a justices' clerk, or a court official who is authorised by the judge to administer oaths, will witness your signature and he or she will sign the certificate of the witness. **A solicitor cannot witness your signature.**

To Parent A and the Other Parent with parental responsibility:

When you make the declaration you will have to prove that you have parental responsibility for the child. You should therefore take with you to the court one of the following documents:

- the child's full birth certificate and a marriage certificate or civil partnership certificate to show that the parents were married to each other or were in a civil partnership with each other at the time of birth or subsequently,
- a court order granting parental responsibility,
- a registered Parental Responsibility Agreement Form between the child's mother and father or other parent

- if the birth was registered after the 1 December 2003, the child's full birth certificate showing that the parents jointly registered the child's birth.

You will also require evidence of your (both parents') identity showing a photograph and signature (for example, a photocard, official pass or passport) **(Please note that the child's birth certificate cannot be accepted as sufficient proof of your identity.)**

To the step-parent: When you make the declaration you will have to prove that you are married to, or the civil partner of, a parent of the child so take to the court your marriage certificate or certificate of civil partnership.

You will also need evidence of your identity showing a photograph and signature (for example, a photocard, official pass or passport).

When the Certificate has been signed and witnessed

Make sufficient copies of the Agreement Form for each person who has signed the form. You do not need to copy these notes.

Take, or send, the original form and the copies to: **The Principal Registry of the Family Division, First Avenue House, 42-49 High Holborn, London, WC1V 6NP.**

The Registry will record the Agreement and retain the original form. The copies will be stamped with the seal of the court and sent back to every person with parental responsibility who has signed the Agreement Form and to the step-parent. The Agreement will not take effect until it has been received and recorded at the Principal Registry of the Family Division.

Ending the Agreement

Once a step-parent parental responsibility agreement has been made it can only end:

- by an order of the court made on the application of any person who has parental responsibility for the child,
- by an order of the court made on the application of the child with permission of the court,
- when the child reaches the age of 18.

5.85 Application by an unmarried father for a parental responsibility order

Application for an order	Form C1

Children Act 1989

The court	To be completed by the court
	Date issued
	Case number
The full name(s) of the child(ren)	Child(ren)'s number(s)

Important Note
You should only answer question 7 if you are asking the court to make one of the following orders:
a Contact Order, a Residence Order, a Prohibited Steps Order, a Specific Issue Order or a
Parental Responsibility Order.

1 **About you (the person completing this form known as 'the applicant')**

State:
* *your title, full name, address, telephone number, date of birth and relationship to each child above*
* *your solicitor's name, address, reference, telephone, FAX and DX numbers.*

2 **The child(ren) and the order(s) you are applying for**

For each child state:
* *the full name, date of birth and sex*
* *the type of order(s) you are applying for (for example, residence order, contact order, supervision order).*

3 Other cases which concern the child(ren)

If there have ever been, or there are pending, any court cases which concern:
- *a child whose name you have put in paragraph 2*
- *a full, half or step brother or sister of a child whose name you have put in paragraph 2*
- *a person in this case who is or has been, involved in caring for a child whose name you have put in paragraph 2*

attach a copy of the relevant order and give:
- *the name of the court*
- *the name and contact address (if known) of the children's guardian, if appointed*
- *the name and contact address (if known) of the children and family reporter, if appointed*
- *the name and contact address (if known) of the welfare officer, if appointed*
- *the name and contact address (if known) of the solicitor appointed for the child(ren).*

4 The respondent(s)

Appendix 3 Family Proceedings Rules 1991; Schedule 2 Family Proceedings Courts (Children Act 1989) Rules 1991

For each respondent state:
- *the title, full name and address*
- *the date of birth (if known) or the age*
- *the relationship to each child.*

5 Others to whom notice is to be given

Appendix 3 Family Proceedings Rules 1991; Schedule 2 Family Proceedings Courts (Children Act 1989) Rules 1991

For each person state:
*   *the title, full name and address*
*   *the date of birth (if known) or the age*
*   *the relationship to each child.*

6 The care of the child(ren)

For each child in paragraph 2 state:
*   *the child's current address and how long the child has lived there*
*   *whether it is the child's usual address and who cares for the child there*
*   *the child's relationship to the other children (if any).*

7 Domestic abuse, violence or harm

Do you believe that the child(ren) named above have suffered or are at risk of suffering any harm from any of the following:
*   *any form of domestic abuse*
*   *violence within the household*
*   *child abduction*
*   *other conduct or behaviour*
by any person who is or has been involved in caring for the child(ren) or lives with, or has contact with, the child(ren)?

Yes □   No □

Please tick the box which applies

If you tick the Yes box, you must also fill in Supplemental Information Form (form C1A). *You can obtain a copy of this from a court office if one has not been enclosed with the papers served on you.*

8 Social Services

For each child in paragraph 2 state:
- *whether the child is known to the Social Services. If so, give the name of the social worker and the address of the Social Services department.*
- *whether the child is, or has been, on the Child Protection Register. If so, give details of registration.*

9 The education and health of the child(ren)

For each child state:
- *the name of the school, college or place of training which the child attends*
- *whether the child is in good health. Give details of any serious disabilities or ill health.*
- *whether the child has any special needs.*

10 The parents of the child(ren)

For each child state:
- *the full name of the child's parents*
- *whether the parents are, or have been, married to each other or civil partners of each other*
- *whether the parents live together. If so, where.*
- *whether, to your knowledge, either of the parents have been involved in a court case concerning a child. If so, give the date and the name of the court.*

11 The family of the child(ren) (other children)

For any other child not already mentioned in the family (for example, a brother or half sister)
state:
* *the full name and address*
* *the date of birth (if known) or age*
* *the relationship of the child to you.*

12 Other adults

State:
* *the full name of any other adults (for example, lodgers) who live at the same address as any child named in paragraph 2*
* *whether they live there all the time*
* *whether, to your knowledge, the adult has been involved in a court case concerning a child. If so, give the date and the name of the court.*

13 Your reason(s) for applying and any plans for the child(ren)

State briefly your reasons for applying and what you want the court to order.
* ***Do not** give a full statement if you are applying for an order under Section 8 of Children Act 1989. You may be asked to provide a full statement later.*
* ***Do not** complete this section if this form is accompanied by a supplementary form.*

14 Attending the court

State:

* *whether you will need an interpreter at court. If so, please indicate what language interpreter you will use. If you require an interpreter you must notify the court immediately so that one can be arranged.*
* *whether you have a disability for which you require special assistance or special facilities. If so, please say what your needs are. The court staff will get in touch with you about your requirements.*

15 Parenting Information – Arrangements after Separation

	Yes	No
Have you received a Parenting Plan booklet? *(If No, you may obtain a copy from a court office,* *a citizen's advice bureau or other family advice service.)*	☐	☐
Have you agreed to a Parenting Plan? *(If Yes, please include a copy of the Plan when you send* *your application to the court)*	☐	☐
If you did agree a Parenting Plan, has the Plan *broken down?*	☐	☐

If Yes, please explain briefly why the Plan broke down –

Signed   Date
(Applicant)

5.86 Change of name deed made by a mother on behalf of her child: not intended for enrolment[202]

THIS CHANGE OF NAME DEED made on (*date*)
BY me (*mother's name*) of (*address*).
WITNESSES that:

1   I am
    (1.1)   the mother of (*child's forename(s) and old surname*) ('*child*')[203] who was born on (*date*); and
    (1.2)   the only person who has parental responsibility for (*child*).[204]

2   On (*child's*) behalf:
    (2.1)   I completely renounce and abandon the use of (his)/(her) surname (*old surname*); and
    (2.2)   I now adopt and assume for (him)/(her) the surname (*new surname*); and
    (2.3)   I ask and authorise all persons at all times when addressing, describing and identifying (*child*) to use (his)/(her) new surname (*new surname*).

3   From now onwards (*child*) will be known as (*child's forename(s) and new surname*):

(3.1) in all deeds, documents, forms, records and other written instruments; and
    (3.2)   in all actions and proceedings; and
    (3.3)   in all dealings and transactions; and
    (3.4)   on all occasions.

SIGNED as a Deed by me (*mother's name*) on behalf of my (son)/(daughter) (*child's forename(s) and new surname*) in the presence of:

---

[202] For changing a child's name generally, see Nasreen Pearce *Name-changing: A Practical Guide* (Fourmat Publishing, 1990) at Chapter 3. See also **5.21** et seq.

[203] Insert the child's usual forename for future reference in the deed.

[204] See CA 1989, s 2(2). If the mother is not the only person with parental responsibility, see CA 1989, ss 13 and 33(7).

5.87   Informal appointment of a guardian by one parent[205]

Children Act 1989, s 5

I (*name*) of (*address*) APPOINT (*name*) of (*address*) to be the Guardian of my (son)/(daughter) (*child's name*) in the event of my death.

Dated

Signed

5.88   Informal appointment of a guardian by both parents

Children Act 1989, s 5

WE (*father's name*) and (*mother's name*) of (*address*) JOINTLY APPOINT[206] (*name*) of (*address*) to be the Guardian of our (son)/(daughter) (*child's name*) in the event that both of us die before (he)/(she) reaches the age of eighteen.[207]

Dated

Signed

Signed

5.89   Child maintenance agreement[208]

THIS MAINTENANCE AGREEMENT made on (*date*)

BETWEEN (1) (*father's name*) of (*address*) ('*name 1*') and (2) (*mother's name*) of (*address*) ('*name 2*')

WITNESSES as follows:

(1)   Recitals

(1.1)   On (*date*) (*name 2*) gave birth to a (son)/(daughter) whose name is (*child's name*) ('*name 3*').

(1.2)   (*Name 1*) acknowledges that he is (*name 3's*) father.

---

[205] Informal insofar as it is not contained in a will or deed. CA 1989, s 5(5) allows a parent or guardian to appoint a guardian provided that the appointment 'is made in writing, is dated and is signed by the person making the appointment'. This form of appointment would be particularly suitable for a parent under the age of 18, who, by virtue of the Wills Act 1837, s 7 (as amended), would not be able to execute a valid will.

[206] CA 1989, s 5(10): 'Nothing in this section shall be taken to prevent an appointment under subsection (3) or (4) being made by two or more persons acting jointly.'

[207] Unless it is brought to an end earlier in accordance with the provisions of s 6, the appointment of the guardian will continue until the child reaches 18 (CA 1989, s 91(8)).

[208] See, generally, 5.39 above.

(2)   Maintenance agreement

(*Name 1*) agrees that:

(2.1)   he will pay to (*name 2*) maintenance for (*name 3's*) benefit;

(2.2)   the maintenance payable will start at £   a year;

(2.3)   the maintenance payable each year will be paid in 12 equal monthly instalments;

(2.4)   each instalment will be paid in advance by standing order on the (first) day of each month;

(2.5)   the first instalment will be paid on (*date*);

(2.6)   the maintenance payable will be reviewed in (April) each year when:

   (a)   the amount of maintenance payable until then will be multiplied by the extent to which the Retail Prices Index has changed during the year which ended on (31 March) immediately before the review; and

   (b)   the revised amount of maintenance payable will take effect with the payment of the instalment due on (1 May) immediately after the review and will continue to be payable at the same rate until it is reviewed again immediately after the payment of the instalment due on the following (1 April)

(2.7)   he will continue to pay maintenance in accordance with the terms of this Agreement until the date on which a maintenance assessment made under the Child Support Act 1991 with respect to (*name 3*):

   (a)   takes effect;[209] or

   (b)   would, if a maintenance assessment had been made, cease to have effect.[210]

(3)   Right to apply for maintenance assessment

The existence of this Agreement does not prevent either party, or any other person, from applying to the Secretary of State for a maintenance assessment to be made with respect to (*name 3*).[211]

SIGNED as a Deed by (*name 1*) in the presence of:

SIGNED as a Deed by (*name 2*) in the presence of:

---

[209] For the effective date of the maintenance assessment, see CSA 1991, Sch 1, para 11. A maintenance assessment will take effect on such date as may be determined in accordance with regulations made by the Secretary of State (which date may be earlier than the date on which the assessment is made).

[210] For the termination of maintenance assessments, see CSA 1991, Sch 1, para 16.

[211] CSA 1991, s 9(3).

5.90   Notice of [intention to proceed with] an application for a financial remedy (other than a financial order) in the county or High Court

Notice of [intention to proceed with] an application for a financial remedy (other than a financial order) in the county or High Court

To be completed by the Applicant	
Name of court	Case No.
Name of Applicant	
Name of Respondent	

Please note that this form should only be completed if you are applying for a financial remedy other than a financial order in the county court.

If you are applying for

- a financial order in the county court please complete Form A
- a financial remedy in the magistrates court please complete Form A2
- financial relief after overseas divorce etc under Part 3 of the Matrimonial and Family Proceedings Act 1984 please complete D50F
- financial provision under section 27 of the Matrimonial Causes Act 1973/Part 9 of Schedule 5 to the Civil Partnership Act 2004 please complete D50C
- alteration of a maintenance agreement under section 35 of the Matrimonial Causes Act 1973/ paragraph 69 of Schedule 5 to the Civil Partnership Act 2004 please complete D50H

1. The Applicant intends: **(please tick the appropriate boxes)**

   ☐ **to apply** to the Court for:

   ☐ **to apply to vary**:

   ☐ a periodical payment order
   ☐ a lump sum order
   ☐ a secured periodical payments order
   ☐ Other (please specify)

   ☐ a settlement of property for the benefit of the child(ren) (please provide address below)
   ☐ a transfer of property for the benefit of the child(ren) (please provide address below)

2. **If an application is made for** any periodical payments or secured periodical payments for children please complete this section:

   ☐ there is a written agreement made before 5 April 1993 about maintenance for the benefit of children;

   ☐ there is a written agreement made on or after 5 April 1993 about maintenance for the benefit of children; or

   ☐ there is no agreement, tick any of the boxes below to show if you are applying for payment:

      ☐ for a stepchild or stepchildren
      ☐ in addition to child support maintenance already paid under a Child Support Agency assessment
      ☐ to meet expenses arising from a child's disability
      ☐ to meet expenses incurred by a child in being educated or training for work
      ☐ when either the child **or** the person with care of the child **or** the absent parent of the child is not
      ☐ habitually resident in the United Kingdom

   If none of the above applies, the court may not have jurisdiction to hear the application for periodical payments.

3. Has the Child Support Agency made any calculation of maintenance in respect of the child(ren)

☐ Yes　　☐ No

If Yes, state briefly your reasons for making this application to the court including any reasons why the Child Support Agency is no longer dealing with your claim or any reasons why you need additional maintenance to top up payments made through the Child Support Agency:

4. Have you attended a mediation information/assessment meeting as provided in the pre-action protocol and/or attached Form FM1?

☐ Yes　　☐ No

5. **Applicant's details**	6. **Respondent's details**
Name of Applicant	Name of Respondent
Applicant's address (including postcode)	Respondent's address (including postcode)
Postcode ☐☐☐ ☐☐☐	Postcode ☐☐☐ ☐☐☐
Telephone no.	Telephone no.
Ref.	Ref.
Email address	Email address

7. Have there been any previous court orders or written agreements regarding financial arrangements?

☐ Yes　　☐ No

If Yes, please attach a copy of the order, or if the order is not available please state the date, the terms, the parties and the court below:

8. Are you applying for a financial remedy in relation to a child?

☐ Yes   ☐ No   (If No, please complete the statement of truth)

(If Yes, please complete the tables below for each child continuing on additional sheets if necessary, and then complete the statement of truth)

Name of child 1	
Date of birth	D D / M M / Y Y Y Y
Gender	☐ Male ☐ Female
Relationship to Applicant	
Relationship to Respondent	
Country of residence (if not England or Wales)	

Name of child 2	
Date of birth	D D / M M / Y Y Y Y
Gender	☐ Male ☐ Female
Relationship to Applicant	
Relationship to Respondent	
Country of residence (if not England or Wales)	

Statement of Truth   *delete as appropriate

*[I believe] [the Applicant believes] that the facts stated in this application are true

*I am duly authorised by the Applicant to sign this statement

Print full name	
Name of Applicant's solicitor's firm	

Signed _____   Dated D D / M M / Y Y Y Y

(Applicant) (Litigation friend) (Applicant's solicitor)

Position or office held
(if signing on behalf of firm
or company)   _____

Proceedings for contempt of court may be brought against a person who makes or causes to be made, a false statement in a document verified by a statement of truth.

3

5.91 Financial statement for a financial remedy (other than a financial order or financial relief after an overseas divorce or dissolution etc) in the county or High Court

Financial Statement for a financial remedy (other than a financial order or financial relief after an overseas divorce or dissolution etc) in the county or High Court

Name of court	Case No.
Name of Applicant	
Name of Respondent	

(please tick the appropriate boxes)

This is the Financial Statement of the

☐ Applicant
☐ Respondent

in this application

This form should only be completed if you are applying for a financial remedy other than a financial order or financial relief after an overseas divorce or dissolution etc. in the county or high court.

If you are applying for a financial order or financial relief after an overseas divorce or dissolution etc. in the county court you should complete Form E

If you are applying for a financial remedy in the magistrate's court you should complete Form E2.

Please fill in this form fully and accurately. Where any box is not applicable, write 'N/A'.

You have a duty to the court to give a full, frank and clear disclosure of all your financial and other relevant circumstances.

A failure to give full and accurate disclosure may result in any order the court makes being set aside.

If you are found to have been deliberately untruthful, criminal proceedings may be brought against you for fraud under the Fraud Act 2006.

The information given in this form must be confirmed by an affidavit. Proceedings for perjury may be brought against a person who makes or causes to be made, a false statement in a document confirmed by an affidavit.

You must attach documents to the form where they are specifically sought and you may attach other documents where it is necessary to explain or clarify any of the information that you give.

If there is not enough room on the form for any particular piece of information, you may continue on an attached sheet of paper.

If you are in doubt about how to complete any part of this form you should seek legal advice.

This statement is filed by

Name and address of solicitor

1. General information

1.1   Full name

1.2   Date of birth   `D D / M M / Y Y Y Y`

1.3   Are you married/in a civil partnership?   ☐ Yes   ☐ No

1.4   If you are not married or in a civil partnership   ☐ Yes   ☐ No
are you living with a partner?

1.5   Your present residence and the occupants of it and on what terms you occupy it
(e.g. tenant, owner-occupier).

Address	Occupants	Terms of occupation

1.6   Children living with you

Names	Date of birth
	`D D / M M / Y Y Y Y`
	`D D / M M / Y Y Y Y`
	`D D / M M / Y Y Y Y`
	`D D / M M / Y Y Y Y`
	`D D / M M / Y Y Y Y`
	`D D / M M / Y Y Y Y`

1.7   Children not living with you

Names	Date of birth
	`D D / M M / Y Y Y Y`
	`D D / M M / Y Y Y Y`
	`D D / M M / Y Y Y Y`
	`D D / M M / Y Y Y Y`
	`D D / M M / Y Y Y Y`
	`D D / M M / Y Y Y Y`
Amount of any maintenance being paid	£

1.8 Other dependents
(Give details – including whether you have these responsibilities on a permanent basis).

Names	Details

1.9 Details of the state of health of yourself and the children if you think this should be taken into account.

Yourself	Children

1.10 Details of the present and proposed future educational arrangements for the children.

Present arrangements	Future arrangements

1.11 Details of any child support maintenance calculation or any maintenance order or agreement made in respect of any children of the family. If no calculation, order or agreement has been made, give an estimate of the liability of the non-resident parent in respect of the children of the family under the Child Support Act 1991.

3

1.12 Details of any other court cases between you and your spouse/civil partner, whether in relation to money, property, children or anything else.

Case No.	Court	Type of proceedings

2. Employment

2.1   I am   ☐ employed (complete 2.2)

☐ self employed (complete 2.3)

☐ unemployed (go to 3.)

☐ a pensioner (go to 3.)

2.2 Details of earned income from employment. Complete one page for each employment.

> Documentation required for attachment to this section:
> a) P60 for the last financial year (you should have received this from your employer shortly after the last 5th April)
> b) Your last three payslips
> c) Your last Form P11D if you have been issued with one

Name and address of your employer	
Job title and brief details of the type of work you do	
Hours worked per week in this employment	
How long have you been with this employer?	
Explain the basis of your income i.e. state whether it is based on an annual salary or an hourly rate of pay and whether it includes commissions or bonuses	
Gross income for the last financial year as shown on your P60Net income for the last financial year i.e. gross income less income tax and national insurance	
Average net income for the last three months i.e. total income less income tax and national insurance divided by three	
Briefly explain any other entries on the attached payslips other than basic income, income tax and national insurance	
If the payslips attached for the last three months are not an accurate reflection of your normal income briefly explain why	
Details and value of any bonuses or other occasional payments that you receive from this employment not otherwise already shown, including the basis upon which they are paid	
Details and value of any benefits in kind, perks or other remuneration received from this employer in the last year (e.g. provision of a car, payment of travel, accommodation, meal expenses, etc.)	
Your estimate of your net income from this employment for the next 12 months.	

Estimated TOTAL of ALL net earned income from employment for the next 12 months: Total A £

5

2.3 *Income from self-employment or partnership*

Complete this section giving details of your income from your business. Complete one page for each business.

Documentation required for attachment to this section:

a) Copies of your business accounts for the last 2 years

b) A copy of your last tax assessment or, if that is not available, a letter from your accountant confirming your tax liability

c) If net income from the last financial year and estimated net income for the next 12 months is significantly different, a copy of management accounts for the period since your last account

Name of the business	
Date to which your last accounts were completed	
Your share of gross business profit from the last completed accounts	
Income tax and national insurance payable on your share of gross business profit above	
Net income for that year (using the two figures directly above, gross business profit less income tax and national insurance payable)	
Details and value of any benefits in kind, perks or other remuneration received from this business in the last year e.g. provision of a car, payment of travel, accommodation, meal expenses, etc.	
Amount of any regular monthly or other drawings that you take from this business	
If the estimated figure directly below is different from the net income as at the end date of the last completed accounts, briefly explain the reason(s)	
Your estimate of your net annual income for the next 12 months	
Estimated TOTAL of ALL net income from self-employment or partnership for the next 12 months: Total B	£

3. Other income

3.1 Details of income from investments (e.g. dividends, interest or rental income) received in the last financial year (the year ended last 5th April), and your estimate of your income for the current financial year. Indicate whether the income was paid gross or net of income tax. You are not required to calculate any tax payable that may arise.

Nature of income and the asset from which it derived	Paid gross or net	Income received in the last financial year	Estimated income for the next 12 months

Estimated TOTAL investment income for the next 12 months: Total C £

3.2 Details of all state benefits (including state pension and child benefit) that you are currently receiving.

Name of benefit	Amount paid	Frequency of payment	Estimated income for the next 12 months

Estimated TOTAL investment income for the next 12 months: Total D £

3.3 Details of any other income not disclosed above.
INCLUDE:
Any source including a Pension (excluding State Pension), and Pension Protection Fund (PPF) compensation
- from which income has been received during the last 12 months (even if it has now ceased)
- from which income is likely to be received during the next 12 months
You are reminded of your obligation to give full disclosure of your financial circumstances.

Nature of income	Paid gross or net	Income received in the last financial year	Estimated income for the next 12 months

Estimated TOTAL other income for the next 12 months: Total E £

7

4. Capital

4.1   Details of your interest in property, land or buildings. Complete one page for each property you
      have an interest in.

> Documentation required for attachment to this section:
> a) A copy of any valuation of the property obtained within the last six months. If you cannot
>   provide this document, please give your own realistic estimate of the current market value
> b) A recent mortgage statement confirming the sum outstanding on each mortgage

Property name and address	
Land Registry title number	
Mortgage company name(s) and address(es) and account number(s)	
Type of mortgage	
Details of who owns the property and the extent of your legal and beneficial interest in it (i.e. state if it is owned by you solely or jointly owned with your spouse/civil partner or with others)	
If you consider that the legal ownership as recorded at the Land Registry does not reflect the true position, state why	
Current market value of the property	
Balance outstanding on any mortgage(s)	
If a sale at this stage would result in penalties payable under the mortgage, state amount	
Estimate the costs of sale of the property	
Total equity in the property (i.e. market value less outstanding mortgage(s), penalties if any and the costs of sale)	

TOTAL value of your interest in ALL other property: Total F | £

4.2 Details of all personal bank, building society and National Savings Accounts that you hold or have held at any time in the last twelve months and which are or were either in your own name or in which you have or have had any interest. This applies whether any such account is in credit or in debit. For joint accounts give your interest and the name of the other account holder. If the account is overdrawn, show a minus figure.

Documentation required for attachment to this section:
For each account listed, all statements covering the last 12 months.

Name of bank or building society, including branch name	Type of account (e.g. current)	Account number	Name of other account holder (if applicable)	Balance at the date of this statement	Total current value of your interest

TOTAL value of your interest in ALL accounts: (G1) | £

4.3 Details of all investments, including shares, PEPs, ISAs, TESSAs, National Savings Investments (other than already shown above), bonds, stocks, unit trusts, investment trusts, gilts and other quoted securities that you hold or have an interest in. (Do not include dividend income as this will be dealt with separately later on.)

Documentation required for attachment to this section:
Latest statement or dividend counterfoil relating to each investment.

Name	Type of Investment	Size of holding	Current value	Name of any other account holder (if applicable)	Total current value of your interest

TOTAL value of your interest in ALL holdings: (G2) | £

9

4.4   Details of all life insurance policies including endowment policies that you hold or have an interest in. Include those that do not have a surrender value. Complete one page for each policy.

> Documentation required for attachment to this section:
> A surrender valuation of each policy that has a surrender value.

Name of company

Policy type

Policy number

If policy is assigned, state in whose favour and amount of charge

Name of any other owner and the extent of your interest in the policy

Maturity date (if applicable)   D D / M M / Y Y Y Y

Current surrender value (if applicable)

If policy includes life insurance, the amount of the insurance and the name of the person whose life is insured

Total current surrender value of your interest in this policy

TOTAL value of your interest in ALL policies: (G3)   £

Add together the totals of G1 to G3 to give TOTAL G   £

10

4.5 Give details of any other assets not listed above.
INCLUDE (the following list is not exhaustive):
- Any personal or business assets not yet disclosed
- Any monies owed to you
- Any cash sums held in excess of £500
- Any other personal belonging individually worth more than £500
- Trust interests (including interests under a discretionary trust), stating your estimate of the value of the interest and when it is likely to become realisable. If you say it will never be realisable, or has no value, give your reasons
- Any asset that is likely to be received in the foreseeable future
- Any asset held on your behalf by a third party
- Any asset not disclosed elsewhere on this form even if held outside England and Wales
- You are reminded of your obligation to disclose all your financial assets and interests of ANY nature.

Type of asset	Value	Total NET value of your interest

TOTAL value of ALL your other assets: Total H £

4.6 Details of any liabilities you have.
EXCLUDE liabilities already shown such as:
Mortgages
Any overdrawn bank, building society or National Savings accounts
INCLUDE:
Money owed on credit cards and store cards
Bank loans
Hire purchase agreements
List all credit and store cards held including those with a nil or positive balance. Where the liability is not solely your own, give the name(s) of the other account holder(s) and the amount of your share of the liability.

Liability	Name(s) of other account holder(s) (if applicable)	Total liability	Total current value of your interest in the liability

TOTAL value of your interest in ALL liabilities: Total I £

11

5. Income needs
(Do not include any payments made by other members of the household out of their own income)

5.1 I have regular expenses as follows:
(do not include payments on any arrears)

	Amounts are per ☐ week ☐ month
Mortgage	
Rent	
Council Tax	
Gas	
Electricity	
Water charges	
TV rental/licence	
HP repayments	
Mail order	
Housekeeping, food, school meals	
Travelling expenses	
Children's clothing and pocket money	
Maintenance Payments	
Car Expenses	
Insurance – House	
Insurance – Other (please give details)	
Others	
Total payments:	£

5.2 Income needs for children living with you or provided for by you.
INCLUDE:
• Only those income needs that are different to those of your household shown above

Item	Current cost	Estimated future cost
SUB-TOTAL children's income needs:		£
TOTAL of ALL income needs:		£

6. Financial resources of child(ren)

Income	Property	Other
TOTAL:	TOTAL:	TOTAL:

7. Financial Details *Summaries*

7.1 Summary of your estimated income for the next 12 months (Parts 2 to 3).

Description	Reference of the section on this statement	Value
Estimated net total of income from employment	A	
Estimated net total of income from self-employment or partnership	B	
Estimated net total of investment income	C	
Estimated state benefit receipts	D	
Estimated net total of all other income	E	

Estimated TOTAL income for the next 12 months (Totals A to E): £

7.2 Summary of your capital (Part 4).

Description	Reference of the section on this statement	Value
Current value of your interest in property	F	
Current value of personal assets	G	
Current value of all your other assets	H	
Current value of your liabilities	I	

TOTAL value of your assets (Totals F to H minus I): £

Sworn confirmation of the information

I,		Enter your full name
of		Enter your full residential address

The above named ☐ Applicant
☐ Respondent

☐ make oath
☐ affirm

and confirm that the information given above is a full, frank, clear and accurate disclosure of my financial and other relevant circumstances.

SWORN / AFFIRMED at

in the County of

on ☐D ☐D / ☐M ☐M / ☐Y ☐Y ☐Y ☐Y

Before me,

☐ A Commissioner for Oaths
☐ Officer of the Court appointed by the Judge to take Affidavits

---

Address all communications to the Court Manager of the Court and quote the case number.
If you do not quote this number, your correspondence may be returned.

Schedule of Documents to accompany Form E1

The following list shows the documents you must attach to your Form E1 if applicable. You may attach other documents where it is necessary to explain or clarify any of the information that you give in the Form E1.

Form E1 paragraph	Document	Attached	Not applicable	To follow
		Please tick		
2.2	**Employment income:** your P60 for the last financial year in respect of each employment that you have.	☐	☐	☐
2.2	**Employment income:** your last three payslips in respect of each employment that you have.	☐	☐	☐
2.2	**Employment income:** your last form P11D if you have been issued with one.	☐	☐	☐
2.3	**Self-employment or partnership income:** a copy of your last tax assessment or if that is not available, a letter from your accountant confirming your tax liability and business accounts for the last 2 years.	☐	☐	☐
2.3	**Self-employment or partnership income:** if net income from the last financial year and the estimated income for the next twelve months is significantly different, a copy of the management accounts for the period since your last accounts.	☐	☐	☐
4.1	a copy of any valuation relating to each other property disclosed that has been obtained in the last six months.	☐	☐	☐
4.1	a recent mortgage statement in respect of each mortgage on each other property disclosed confirming the amount outstanding.	☐	☐	☐
4.2	**Personal bank, building society and National Savings accounts:** copies of statements for the last 12 months for each account that has been held in the last twelve months, either in your own name or in which you have or have had any interest.	☐	☐	☐
4.3	**Other investments:** the latest statement or dividend counterfoil relating to each investment as disclosed in paragraph 4.3.	☐	☐	☐
4.4	**Life insurance (including endowment) policies:** a surrender valuation for each policy that has a surrender value as disclosed under paragraph 4.4.	☐	☐	☐
State relevant Form E1 paragraph	Description of other documents attached:			

15

CHAPTER 6

DEATH AND SUCCESSION

PART A   LAW AND PRACTICE

SECTION 1   MAKING PROVISION FOR DEATH

6.1   Introduction

Cohabitants are not able to benefit under the rules that govern intestacy, and so if it is intended that provision should be made for one cohabitant on the death of another, positive steps must be taken during the lifetime of both parties.

If cohabitants wish to make provision for one another after death, they may do one or more of the following:

– make a will in favour of the other;
– hold property in joint names so that on death the survivor will automatically succeed to ownership;
– nominate the surviving cohabitant to receive benefits payable on death under the terms of a life assurance policy or pension scheme;
– make a lifetime gift of property.

However, all of the above are subject to the powers of the court under the Inheritance (Provision for Family and Dependants) Act 1975 (I(PFD)A 1975) to set aside transactions, deem jointly owned property part of the deceased's net estate, and make orders for financial provision out of the estate.[1]

The Law Commission published a Consultation Paper on 28 October 2009 asking (inter alia) whether certain cohabitants should have a place in the intestacy rules, the conditions which have to be met, and how much of the estate they should receive. That project is now complete and certain of the recommendations have been enacted in the Inheritance and Trustees' Powers Act 2014 (ITPA 2014) that received Royal Assent on 14 May 2014. This includes reforms that amend the legal rules which had disadvantaged unmarried fathers when a child died intestate, and remove arbitrary obstacles to family provision claims by dependants of the deceased and anyone treated by the deceased as a child of his or her family outside the context of a marriage or civil partnership.

---

[1]   I(PFD)A 1975, ss 10, 9 and 2.

However, the recommendations set out in Part 8 of the Report to extend rights to cohabitants under the intestacy rules are not to be implemented in the foreseeable future.

6.2 Wills

In principle there should be no difference between the contents of the wills of those who are married or in a civil partnership and those who are not, and, with the notable exception of inheritance tax planning, there is little difference in practice. However, the law itself distinguishes between those who are married or in a civil partnership and those who are not in a number of ways. Among them are the following.

(1) *Wills Act 1837, s 15*[2] states that a gift to a beneficiary is void if the will is witnessed by the beneficiary or his or her spouse or civil partner.[3] However, if a cohabitant were to witness a will conferring a benefit on his or her partner, the gift would be valid.

(2) *Wills Act 1837, s 18* provides that, except in certain circumstances, a will is revoked if the testator subsequently marries or enters in to a civil partnership[4] Subsequent cohabitation outside the marriage or civil partnership will not revoke an existing will.

(3) *Wills Act 1837, s 18A*[5] provides that on the dissolution or annulment of a marriage or civil partnership, a will takes effect as if the appointment of the former spouse or former civil partner as an executor or trustee were omitted, and any devise or bequest to the former spouse or former civil partner lapses.[6] These provisions apply automatically, unless a contrary intention appears by the will. The section does not apply on the termination of the relationship of a couple who are not married or in a civil partnership.[7]

(4) *Administration of Justice Act 1982, s 22* states a presumption. Unless a contrary intention is shown, it is presumed that where a testator gives property to his spouse in terms which in themselves would give an absolute interest to the spouse, but also purports to give his issue an interest in the same property, the gift to the spouse is absolute notwithstanding the purported gift to the issue. The presumption does not apply in the case of an unmarried couple. So, if the testator were to say, 'I give all my property to (*cohabitant*) and after her death to my children', the surviving partner would receive only a life interest, not an absolute interest.

---

[2]   As amended by CPA 2004.

[3]   This was the problem in the well-known negligence case of *Ross v Caunters* [1980] Ch 297.

[4]   The main exception is where the will is expressly made in expectation of marriage.

[5]   Added by the Administration of Justice Act 1982, ss 18(2) and 73(6), with effect from 1 January 1983.

[6]   It is unfortunate that s 18A did not provide that for all the purposes of the testator's will the former spouse should be treated as having predeceased him (*Re Sinclair* [1985] Ch 446). The Law Commission has published an informal consultation paper: 'The Effect of Divorce on Wills' (November 1992).

[7]   A new will or codicil should be executed (see Precedent **6.150** below).

(5) *Inheritance Tax Act 1984, s 18.* Generally speaking, transfers of value
between spouses and civil partners are wholly exempt.[8] This exemption
does not apply to unmarried couples.

6.3   Describing the cohabitant

A testator should describe his partner clearly, accurately and unambiguously.
The best course of action is simply to state the cohabitant's full and correct
forenames and surname (and any alias) and his or her address. To abbreviate
any later references in the will, the partner's forename, or some other concise
and accurate description, can be placed in brackets immediately after the first
occurrence of the full name. For example: Mary Jane Smith ('Mary').

A description on its own – 'my partner', 'my cohabitant', 'my boyfriend' – must
never be used. However, where it is stated in addition to the full and correct
name it will probably be innocuous. Several reported decisions reveal a
tendency among some unmarried couples to refer to each other as 'my husband'
or 'my wife'.[9] When it comes to making their wills, these terms should be
avoided for the obvious reason that they have led, and could continue to lead,
to litigation. However, in most cases where the inaccurate or euphemistic
expression 'my wife' has been used in addition to the partner's full and correct
name, the courts have applied the *falsa demonstratio* rule,[10] and the gift has not
been invalidated.

6.4   'Cohabitation' and wills

The words used in a will are given their ordinary, grammatical meaning.[11]
However, it is the testator's privilege to be able to use 'his own dictionary' and
make words mean whatever he wishes:[12] 'He can make "black" mean "white"
if he makes the dictionary sufficiently clear in his will.'[13] References in a will to
'cohabitation' are likely to occur in two sets of circumstances. First, in the
context of the testator's own relationship, where a gift to the surviving
cohabitant is made subject to the condition precedent that the couple are still
living together when the testator dies.[14] The second, and more usual,
occurrence is where a life interest is given to the surviving cohabitant and it is
expressed to be determinable on cohabitation.[15] The underlying purpose is
usually economic. If the survivor enters into a new relationship, the testator –
or his estate – will no longer be responsible for maintaining her or him.

---

[8]   If the transferor/deceased is domiciled in the UK and the spouse is domiciled outside the UK,
the exemption applies only to the first £55,000. This figure has not been increased since 1982.
[9]   For example: *Re Smalley* [1929] 2 Ch 112; and *Re Lynch* [1943] 1 All ER 168.
[10] In this context, the full maxim is *falsa demonstratio non nocet dummodo constet de persona* (a
false description does no harm provided that it is clear who the person is). The ambiguity can
be cured by extrinsic evidence.
[11] *Gorringe v Mahlstedt* [1907] AC 225 at 227.
[12] *Re Lynch* [1943] 1 All ER 168.
[13] Parry and Kerridge *The Law of Succession* (Sweet & Maxwell, 12th edn).
[14] For an example and further comment, see **6.122** below.
[15] For examples, see **6.115** and **6.133** below.

Where a life interest is determinable on cohabitation, the very act of cohabiting, whatever that may be, will operate as a disqualification. The burden of proof is on those who are seeking to disqualify. It is notoriously difficult to establish whether or not a couple are cohabiting.[16] Sometimes the couple are uncertain themselves. By referring to 'cohabitation' in his will the testator is asking someone – primarily the executors and trustees, but perhaps also the remaindermen, the surviving cohabitant, and the court – to make a value judgment as to which incidents of such a relationship are to be treated as essential, and which incidents can be discarded as superfluous. In order to shield the trustees it has become common practice to impose a discretionary trust, which probably makes their evidential burden lighter, extends their immunities, and circumscribes the scope for any appeal against their decision.[17] Although a discretionary trust has its uses, the testator must still make his intentions clear to the trustees, perhaps by way of an off-the-record memorandum. But neither the trust nor the memorandum will resolve the underlying difficulties in answering the question of whether a couple is cohabiting. In addition, consideration must be given to the tax treatment of the ongoing trust.

6.5 Joint property

If property, whether real or personal, is held in the joint names of cohabitants as beneficial joint tenants, on the death of one of them the survivor will automatically succeed to the ownership of the property. Jointly owned property will not ordinarily[18] form part of the deceased's estate.

In the case of land, care must be taken when the property is acquired to ensure that the beneficial interests are expressly declared, and not left open to interpretation.[19]

The contents of bank accounts in joint names will belong to the survivor and will be immediately accessible without the need to produce a grant of representation in respect of the estate.

6.6 Nominations

There is no provision in the state pension scheme for benefits to be paid to a surviving cohabitant, but many occupational and private schemes will enable the trustees or fund managers to make payments to a person with whom the deceased was living as spouse or civil partner at the date of death, as well as to dependants, within which category a cohabitant may be included. The rules of each scheme will be different, and it is prudent to establish what benefits will be

---

[16] See the DWP Guidance for Decision-Makers, Vol 3, Ch 11: Living together as husband and wife or as civil partners.

[17] For an 80-year discretionary trust, see **6.135** below); for a two-year discretionary trust, see **6.136** below; for a life interest subject to the trustees' power of revocation, see **6.134** below.

[18] Subject to I(PFD)A 1975, s 9, where application is made for an order under s 2 of the Act.

[19] See **1.3**.

payable in the event of death in service or death after retirement (usually very limited) and who will be eligible to receive them.

Most schemes, whilst giving the trustees or fund managers unfettered discretion to distribute certain benefits payable on death as they see fit between those eligible, will also allow them to take into account any expression by the scheme member of a preference as to how the discretion should be exercised. Such schemes will generally have a standard form 'Expression of wishes', which can be completed by the scheme member and kept on file by the pension provider.

Trustees are not obliged to take into account any expression of wishes by the scheme member, but they do have to exercise their discretion in accordance with the rules of the scheme. In *Wild v Pensions Ombudsman*[20] a complaint about the decision of the trustees to exercise their discretion in favour of a woman with whom the deceased had been living before his death was upheld on the basis that she was not in fact dependent upon the deceased and so could not be brought within the category of persons eligible to be considered for provision, namely, 'dependants, relatives or legal representatives of the member'.

6.7 Lifetime gifts

Subject to taxation considerations (for example the annual gift exemption limit of £3,000 and inheritance tax on gifts made within seven years of death) cohabitants are free to make one another gifts of property during their joint lives. It is important to bear in mind the court's powers to set aside transactions that were intended to defeat a claim for provision under the I(PFD)A 1975.[21] For this reason, as well as from the point of view of inheritance tax, the more time that has elapsed between the gift and death the better.

6.8 Donationes mortis causa

In some cases a person who is approaching death, and who has not made formal provision for another, may seek to remedy this by making a gift in contemplation of his or her death, and conditional upon it. Certain formalities have to be complied with for the gift to be effective to transfer ownership, but in one case it was held that a cohabitant was entitled to land that was given to her by her dying cohabitant merely by his handing to her the keys to the box in which the title deeds to the land were kept, and his clear statement to her that she was to have the land as a gift.[22]

In *Woodard v Woodard*[23] it was held by the Court of Appeal that the act of the deceased, who was then within days of dying from leukaemia, of handing to his

---

20 [1996] 2 FLR 680.
21 I(PFD)A 1975, s 10.
22 *Sen v Headley* [1991] 2 FLR 449.
23 [1996] 1 FLR 399.

son the keys to his car, together with his words that he could, 'keep the keys, I won't be driving it any more', was sufficient to satisfy the requirements for a valid *donatio mortis causa*.

SECTION 2   DEATH OF A COHABITANT

6.9   Introduction

On the death of a cohabitant, a number of situations may arise, depending upon whether there are children of the parties or a previous marriage or relationship, or even a surviving spouse or civil partner, and whether the cohabitant dies intestate, or leaves a valid will.

6.10   Cohabitant leaves a valid will

If a deceased cohabitant has left a valid will, the estate should be administered in accordance with the will subject to any question of interpretation[24] and to any order that may be made by the court where application is made for provision under the I(PFD)A 1975.

6.11   Cohabitant dies intestate

If there is an intestacy, the distribution of the estate is dealt with in accordance with the provisions of s 46 of the Administration of Estates Act 1925, as amended by the Intestates' Estates Act 1952, the Family Provision Act 1966, successive Family Provision (Intestate Succession) Orders and the Inheritance and Trustees' Powers Act 2014.

The effect of the latest rules governing intestacy is that if there is a surviving spouse or civil partner but no children, the estate will pass in its entirety to the surviving spouse or civil partner.

If there is a surviving spouse or civil partner and children, the children will receive nothing unless the value of the estate exceeds £250,000. In this case the surviving spouse or civil partner will take £250,000, the personal chattels and half of the remainder outright. The other half of the remainder will be divided between the children in equal shares, at the age of 18. If any of the children predecease their deceased parent, but leave children who survive, those children will take the share their deceased parent would otherwise have taken.

There is no provision for a surviving cohabitant if there is an intestacy and it is therefore important that cohabitants are encouraged to make a will. However, it should be borne in mind that certain property will not form part of the deceased's estate for the purposes of any will or intestacy in any event. Jointly owned property, such as a house or bank account in joint names, will pass to

---

[24]   See **6.4**.

the surviving joint owner automatically on death. Similarly, certain benefits from insurance and pension policies can be the subject of a nomination in favour of a particular beneficiary or beneficiaries that will exclude those assets from the deceased's estate.[25] It should be borne in mind however, that where an application is made for provision under the I(PFD)A 1975, the court has power to deem certain property which otherwise would be excluded from the estate to be part of the net estate for the purposes of that Act[26] or set aside lifetime transactions.[27] This may mean for example that an attempt by the deceased to provide for the surviving cohabitant by a lifetime gift may prove ineffective.

If no provision has been made outside the estate for a surviving cohabitant, then the only course where there has been an intestacy is to make application under the I(PFD)A 1975.

In very rare cases where there are no eligible beneficiaries under an intestacy, a surviving cohabitant may apply to the Crown to whom the estate will have passed *bona vacantia* for provision as someone 'for whom the intestate may reasonably have been expected to make provision'.[28]

6.12 Surviving spouses and civil partners and the effect of a decree of judicial separation or separation order

Many cohabitants may find themselves in the position of living with a person who is married to, or in a civil partnership with, someone else. If a cohabitant dies intestate and there is a surviving spouse or civil partner, the spouse or civil partner will benefit unless, in the case of married parties, there has been a decree of judicial separation or in the case of civil partners, a separation order.

If there is a decree of judicial separation or separation order and the separation was continuing at the date of death, the deceased's estate will devolve as if the other party to the proceedings were dead. Therefore, there will be no provision for the spouse or civil partner on intestacy and any testamentary provision in his or her favour will lapse.

Note, however, the power of the court under I(PFD)A 1975, s 14 and s 14A[29] on an application for provision under s 2, to disregard a decree of divorce or judicial separation, or in the case of a civil partnership a dissolution order, nullity order, separation order or presumption of death order, in circumstances in which the death of one of the parties occurred within 12 months of the decree or order and a financial provision order had not been made.

If there is a failure to change the terms of any will following dissolution or annulment of a marriage or civil partnership, in the case of individuals who

---

[25] See **6.6**.
[26] I(PFD)A 1975, s 9.
[27] I(PFD)A 1975, s 10.
[28] Administration of Estates Act 1925, s 46(1); *Cameron v Treasury Solicitor* [1996] 2 FLR 716.
[29] Inserted by CPA 2004.

have died on or after 1 January 1996, Law Reform (Succession) Act 1995, s 3 provides that where an appointment of a former spouse or civil partner as an executor or trustee exists, that former spouse or civil partner shall be treated as having died on the date the marriage or civil partnership was dissolved or annulled and the same applies to any provision made in a will for a former spouse or civil partner.

A former spouse or civil partner who has not remarried or entered into another civil partnership may be a potential applicant under the I(PFD)A 1975. Enquiry should be made as to whether any order was made in the dissolution proceedings which precludes such an application.[30]

6.13   Children of a deceased cohabitant

There is no difference between the treatment of the illegitimate children of a deceased cohabitant and the legitimate children for succession purposes.

If there is an intestacy, they are included in the category of children, without discrimination.[31]

If their deceased parent leaves a valid will, they are similarly included in the general category of children unless children are referred to specifically by name and unless the will specifies that only legitimate children may benefit.

Whether or not they benefit from the will or any intestacy, children of parents who are not married or in a civil partnership may apply to the court under the I(PFD)A 1975 for reasonable financial provision out of the estate. Even a child who is not a natural child of the deceased cohabitant could make a claim against the estate if he or she was being maintained, wholly or in part by the deceased immediately before the death.

Applicants may be minor or adult children although there is a reluctance on the part of the courts to make significant awards to adult children who are independent and self-supporting.[32]

The definition of 'child' will also include a child *en ventre sa mère* at the date of the death of the deceased parent.

Children who have been adopted by the deceased are eligible to apply, but not the natural children of parents where there is an adoption order in favour of another party as this operates to sever all legal obligations.

---

[30]   I(PFD)A 1975, s 15.
[31]   FLRA 1969, s 15; FLRA 1987, s 19.
[32]   See, for example, Ilott v Mitson & *Others* [2014] EWHC 542 (Fam).

6.14 Proprietary estoppel

A surviving cohabitant may find that, on the death of the other cohabitant, provision that was promised has not been made. The omission may have been deliberate or merely neglectful. In certain situations, equity will step in to assist the disappointed party. See the discussion at **1.29**.

The essentials for an application for relief in reliance upon the equitable doctrine of estoppel are that the applicant must have acted to his or her detriment in reliance upon a promise that he or she would be given an interest in property, subject to there being sufficient connection between the promise and the detrimental conduct. There should also be knowledge on the part of the promissor that the other party was relying upon the promise and acting detrimentally as a result, yet taking no steps to disabuse him or her, thereby making it unconscionable for the promissor to go back on his word.[33]

In *Wayling v Jones*[34] the parties lived together in a homosexual relationship. The deceased was the owner of an hotel and the applicant had worked in the hotel for pocket money and expenses alone. The applicant, a much younger man, went along with this on the basis that the deceased had promised that he would leave him the hotel in his will. In the event he did not, and the applicant claimed against the estate. He was unsuccessful at first instance, but on appeal the Court of Appeal held that:[35]

> '... On the facts it was clear that the promises had been made, that the plaintiff's conduct was such that inducement might be inferred, and that since the plaintiff had stated in examination-in-chief that he would have left the deceased if the promises had been withdrawn, the defendants had not discharged the burden of establishing that the plaintiff had not relied on the promises ...'

An order was made for the applicant to receive the net proceeds of sale of the hotel which by that time had been sold, and so the estate was held to the promise made by the deceased.[36]

Applications under the Inheritance (Provision for Family and Dependants) Act 1975

6.15 Introduction

Although a testator's freedom to dispose of his property by will remains a fundamental right, since the introduction of the Inheritance (Family Provision)

---

[33] *Gillett v Holt and Another* [2000] 2 All ER 289, CA.
[34] [1995] 2 FLR 1029.
[35] At 1029G.
[36] See also *Re Basham (Deceased)* [1987] 2 FLR 264, not followed in *Taylor v Dickens* [1998] 1 FLR 806: '... there was a difference between saying you will make a will and saying you will not revoke a will ...' (at 806G). This stricter approach was also evident in *Coombes v Smith* [1987] 1 FLR 352. See also *Thorner v Major* [2008] EWCA Civ 732.

Act 1938 this has been subject to the power of the court in statutorily prescribed circumstances to alter the provision that has been made. The categories of applicant were extended in the I(PFD)A 1975 to include children of the family, and further extended to cohabitants of at least two years' standing by an amendment to the I(PFD)A 1975 following the Law Reform (Succession) Act 1995. The Civil Partnership Act 2004 contained provision for the categories of applicant to be extended to include civil partners. Further amendments have been made by the Inheritance and Trustees' Powers Act 2014 (ITPA 2014) that include extending the category of potential applicants in s 1(1)(d) from children of the family in the context of marriage and civil partnership to any child in respect of whom the deceased stood in the role of parent.

The emphasis in the successive legislation and its interpretation has remained the same. The legislation is not intended to give the court *carte blanche* to rewrite the terms of the will or interfere with the operation of the intestacy rules.

6.16   What relief is available?

Certain categories of applicant may apply to the court for financial provision if the deceased's estate failed to make 'reasonable financial provision', either directly by will or indirectly by the operation of the law relating to intestacy. If so satisfied, the court may exercise its discretion to make one or more of the following orders in favour of the applicant:

- periodical payments;[37]
- variation, discharge, suspension, revival of periodical payments order;[38]
- lump sum;[39]
- transfer of property;[40]
- settlement of property;[41]
- variation of settlement;[42]
- variation of trusts;[43]
- variation or discharge of secured periodical payments;[44]
- variation or revocation of maintenance agreements;[45]
- setting aside a disposition intended to defeat a claim;[46]

---

[37]   I(PFD)A 1975, s 2(1)(a).
[38]   Ibid, s 6.
[39]   Ibid, s 2(1)(b).
[40]   Ibid, s 2(1)(c).
[41]   Ibid, s 2(1)(d).
[42]   Ibid, s 2(1)(e).
[43]   Ibid, s 2(1)(h).
[44]   Ibid, s 16.
[45]   Ibid, s 17.
[46]   Ibid, ss 10 and 11.

– interim relief.[47]

6.17   Who may apply?

According to s 1(1) of the I(PFD)A 1975, the potential applicants are:

(a)   a surviving spouse or civil partner;

(b)   a former spouse who has not remarried, or a former civil partner who has not entered into another civil partnership;

(ba) a surviving cohabitant whether someone living with the deceased as spouse or civil partner who had lived with the deceased throughout the whole of the period of at least two years immediately before the death;[48]

(c)   a child of the deceased;

(d)   any person other than a child of the deceased who was treated by the deceased as a child of the family within the context of a marriage or civil partnership,[49] or in relation to any family in which the deceased stood in the role of parent, any person who was treated by the deceased as a child of the family; and

(e)   any person not included in categories (a)–(d) above who was being maintained in whole or in part by the deceased immediately before the death.

6.18   The parties to the application

If there is more than one applicant and there is no conflict of interest between them, they may make an application jointly. Otherwise there will have to be separate applications which may then be consolidated.

The personal representatives should always be named as respondents to the application together with any significant beneficiary under a will or intestacy, ie a person who is likely to be affected financially by any order made, or any other person affected by the claim.

The court may direct that other persons who are not already parties be joined in the proceedings.

6.19   Which court?

The High Court and any county court have unlimited jurisdiction to hear claims under the I(PFD)A 1975. In practice, most claims will be dealt with in the county court.

---

[47] Ibid, s 10.

[48] CPA 2004 inserted s1(1A) and s1(1B) to further define a surviving cohabitant as a person who has lived in the same household as the deceased for the whole of the period of two years ending immediately before the deceased died, either as husband and wife (s 1(1A)) or as civil partner s1(1B) of the deceased.

[49] Ie a step-child.

In the High Court, application may be made to either the Chancery Division or the Family Division. The choice of Division in the High Court will depend largely on the issues involved. For example, if there will be detailed accounts to be taken the Chancery Division may be preferred, but the broader issues generally raised by these cases may, as a rule, be better suited to the Family Division.

In any event, the court has power to transfer between Divisions, and between the county court and High Court and vice versa.

In the county court the application may be made to the county court local to the deceased's residence at the date of death. If the deceased was resident abroad, the application may be filed at the county court local to a respondent to the application, or where the estate or part of it is situated.

In the High Court, application may be made in London or any district registry.

Note that although the place of death is irrelevant, the deceased must have been habitually resident in England and Wales at the date of death for the court to have jurisdiction under the I(PFD)A 1975.

6.20 Procedure

Proceedings under the I(PFD)A 1975 are not family proceedings and are governed by the CPR 1998. The claim is made under CPR 8. CPR, rr 57.14-16 and the accompanying Practice Direction contain additional provisions for claims under the I(PFD)A 1975 in both the county court and High Court.

The application is made by Part 8 Claim Form N208 which gives details of the claim and contains a statement of truth. Where a grant has been taken out, the claim form must be accompanied by a witness statement that exhibits an office copy of the grant of representation and any relevant will. Although not specifically required by CPR 1998, it will be good practice to include:

(a) the name of the deceased, the date of death and country of domicile at that time;

(b) the category or categories of potential applicant to which the applicant claims to belong;

(c) the date of the grant of representation and the names and addresses of the personal representatives;

(d) whether any provision is made for the applicant by will or the law of intestacy, and if so, the nature of that provision;

(e) any other persons interested in the estate, and the nature of that interest;

(f) particulars of the applicant's financial resources at the time of the application and in the foreseeable future; and

(g) the nature of the provision sought.

In addition, the death certificate should be exhibited together with any other relevant documentation. Where a child is applying, the child's birth certificate should be exhibited.

Following amendments made to I(PFD)A by ITPA 2014 it is possible to make a claim before a grant is taken out. In those circumstances CPR, r 57.16(3A) provides that the evidence in support must explain the reasons why it has not been possible for a grant to be obtained, exhibit a copy of the will if available and set out brief details of the estate and those interested in it.

In either case the witness statement must also comply with the requirements of the CPR, Pt 22 and contain a statement of truth.

When the court issues the claim, it will provide a response pack for service on the defendants along with sealed copies of the claim form and witness statement. The claimant will receive Notice of Issue.

CPR 1998, Part 57 provides that within 21 days of service of the claim form, inclusive of the day of service, a defendant must acknowledge service and a defendant who is a personal representative must, and any other category of defendant may, file and serve a statement in answer to the claim.

If a defendant is a personal representative, the statement must contain the following information to the best of that person's ability:[50]

(a)   the full particulars of the estate;

(b)   the names and addresses of all the beneficiaries of the estate, and the extent of their interest in the estate;

(c)   the name of any beneficiary who is a child or who lacks mental capacity; and

(d)   any facts that may affect the exercise of the court's discretion.

On receipt of the acknowledgement, or after the time for doing so has expired, the papers are put before the district judge. The district judge will usually direct a hearing when case management directions will be given. These will include provision for allocation, usually to the multi-track, disclosure of documents, filing of further evidence, and there will be consideration given to transfer of proceedings, joinder of parties, and whether certain parties should have separate representation because of a potential conflict of interest. The directions given will be subject to a strict timetable which will have to be adhered to. This will usually include provision for a further case management conference so that the district judge can ensure that the case will be ready for trial.

If there is an application for permission to bring a claim out of time, or for interim provision, a further interlocutory hearing will be fixed.

---

[50]   CPR 1998, Part 57, PD 16.

In the event that one or more defendants do not appear at the case management conference it will be necessary for the claimant to prove service of the claim.[51]

6.21 Time for making the application

The application must be made within six months of the date of the grant of representation. In calculating the six-month period, the day on which the grant of representation was issued is included. However, nothing now prevents the making of an application before the grant of representation is first taken out.[52]

6.22 Application for permission to apply out of time

There is provision for the court to allow applications made outside the time-limit imposed by I(PFD)A 1975, s 4, but permission must be expressly requested in the claim form. The claimant's witness statement/affidavit must set out the grounds for the application and give a full explanation as to why the application was not made within the time-limit. A defendant wishing to oppose the application will signify as much in the acknowledgement form.

The application for permission will be dealt with as a preliminary issue and the district judge will give directions at the first hearing if it is not possible to dispose of it on that occasion.

6.23 The exercise of the court's discretion on an application for permission

The court's power to allow the application to proceed notwithstanding that it was issued out of time is discretionary. The matters to which the court will have regard in the exercise of its discretion, as well as all the circumstances of the case and the interests of justice will include:

- the length of the delay;
- the reason for the delay, and in particular whether any fault rests with the claimant or the claimant's solicitors;
- whether the defendant was aware of the potential claim before proceedings commenced;
- whether negotiations were on foot when the time-limit expired;
- whether the estate has already been distributed;
- whether the claim stands any realistic prospect of success; and
- whether the claimant could pursue a claim against his or her solicitors in the event that permission were not given.

These general guidelines can be found in the judgments in *Re Salmon, Coard v National Westminster Bank Limited*.[53] That case also made it clear that it is for

---

[51] CPR 1998, Part 6.
[52] Inserted by ITPA 2014, s 6, Sch 2.
[53] [1980] 3 All ER 532.

the claimant to establish sufficient grounds for disapplying the time-limit, as to do so necessarily deprives the defendant of the benefit of it.

The exercise of the judge's discretion is unfettered, but it must be exercised with regard to the interests of justice.

There are cases in which the court has exercised its discretion in favour of the applicant. For example, in *Re Ruttie; Ruttie v Saul*[54] an application made six weeks out of time was allowed where negotiations were well advanced and there would have been serious hardship to the impecunious applicant and no prejudice to the defendant save for the loss of advantage of the expiry of the time-limit. In *Re C (Deceased) (Leave to Apply for Provision)*[55] a claim was made on behalf of the deceased's illegitimate daughter, by her mother. The claim was made four years after the death and two years after the grant of probate was taken out. At the hearing before the district judge no explanation was given for the delay and leave to proceed with the claim was refused. Allowing the mother's appeal, Wilson J, as he then was, said that 'the task is to determine whether the net weight of the relevant factors is such as to justify permission to claim outside the normal period'.[56]

Whilst pointing out that there was no general principle that applications on behalf of minors to bring claims out of time should be treated more sympathetically, he said that a significant factor in the balance was the fact that if leave was not allowed the child in this case would be left without any remedy. He was guided by the judgments given in *Re Salmon* and suggested that other relevant factors in the exercise of the court's discretion were the extent of and reasons for the delay, any prejudice there may be to beneficiaries, for example where the estate has already been distributed, and the merits of the application. In this case, the merits were very good and the estate had not been distributed.

Stock v Brown[57] was described as an exceptional case in which leave was given to a very elderly widow to make a claim in respect of her late husband's estate nearly six years out of time. The provision in the will gave her a life interest in his estate. For some years this provided her with an adequate income and she was content. However, interest rates then fell dramatically and her income was insufficient. On appeal, leave was given to bring a claim out of time. The court took the view that the exceptional delay was more than offset by the 'combination of extenuating circumstances and meritorious need'.[58] See also *Re B (Deceased)*.[59]

---

[54] [1969] 3 All ER 1633.
[55] [1995] 2 FLR 24; also reported as *Re W (A Minor) (Claim from Deceased's Estate)* [1995] 2 FCR 689.
[56] At 29E.
[57] [1994] 1 FLR 840.
[58] At 842.
[59] [2000] 1 All ER 665 at 668.

The court refused an application to proceed out of time in *Re Dennis (Deceased)*.[60] Following the guidelines set down in *Re Salmon*, the court said that in addition to the 19-month delay in bringing the claim that was partly unexplained, the case was not an arguable one. A son of the deceased, described by the judge as something of a 'rolling stone', claimed a lump sum by way of provision from the large estate to meet the capital transfer tax he had to pay on substantial lifetime gifts from his father. The court held that as this need was not in the nature of maintenance, and this was the only provision that could be made to a child of the deceased, his claim had little or no prospect of success and he should not have leave to proceed.

In *Re Longley (Deceased), Longley and Longley v Longley*[61] the court took the view that as the estate had been distributed by the time an application was made, long after the time-limit had expired, the disappointed claimant could sue her solicitors against whom she had a good claim. It was not the duty of the court to protect negligent solicitors.

After taking legal advice, the claimant in *Escritt v Escritt*[62] decided against making application for provision within the time-limit, but did make an application three years later after a slight change in her circumstances. Leave was not granted and the application was struck out.

In *Berger v Berger*[63] permission to make a claim six and a half years after the deceased's death was refused. The Court of Appeal disagreed with the trial judge that the claim had no prospects of success because the will did make reasonable financial provision for the claimant, the widow of the deceased. However, it agreed that the main factor in the exercise of his discretion to refuse permission was the very significant delay in commencing proceedings. Even though the claimant was elderly and had not been in particularly good health, the factors that ultimately led her to seek advice had been evident from an early stage and she had enlisted professional help at that time. Nothing changed, but it took another four or five years before she contemplated a claim under I(PFD)A 1975. It was the absence of the 'extraneous circumstances' in *Stock v Brown*, namely the dramatic fall in interest rates that distinguished this case and failed to provide a sufficient excuse for the delay.

6.24   Standing search

Although it is now possible to make a claim before the issue of a grant, to avoid falling foul of the time-limit imposed by I(PFD)A 1975, s 2, there is a facility to set up a standing search at the Central Probate Registry or any District Registry or sub-registry which ensures that notice is given of any application for a grant. Application is made on Form PA1S, accompanied by the fee payable.[64]

---

[60]   [1981] 2 All ER 140.
[61]   [1981] CLY 2885.
[62]   (1982) 3 FLR 280.
[63]   [2013] EWCA Civ 1305.
[64]   See **6.156**.

On receipt, the court will supply a copy of any grant fitting the details given on Form PA1S that was issued not more than 12 months before the receipt of the application for the search or within 6 months thereafter. If necessary, the search can be extended by submitting the appropriate request and fee to the court within the last month of the 6-month period.[65]

6.25   The ground for the application

I(PFD)A 1975, s 1(1) provides that for every category of applicant the ground for making an application for an order under s 2 is 'that the disposition of the deceased's estate effected by his will or the law relating to intestacy, or the combination of his will and that law, is not such as to make reasonable financial provision for the applicant'.

In the case of applicants other than a spouse or civil partner, this is qualified by s 1(2)(b) which provides that 'reasonable financial provision' shall mean 'such financial provision as it would be reasonable in all the circumstances of the case for the applicant to receive for his maintenance'.

The ITPA 2014 has slightly altered the position regarding those falling into the residuary category 1(1)(e), namely any person not included in the other categories who was being maintained in whole or in part by the deceased immediately before the death. Previously s 1(3) stated that a person shall be treated as being maintained by the deceased if the deceased was, otherwise than for full valuable consideration, making a substantial contribution towards that person's reasonable needs. The courts therefore balanced the contribution made by the deceased towards the needs of the applicant against any benefits flowing from the applicant to the deceased. This was the case even if the applicant and the deceased were living in an interdependent domestic relationship without any commercial aspect. The new wording of s 1(3) still requires the deceased to have been making a substantial contribution towards the reasonable needs of the applicant but the words 'otherwise than for full valuable consideration' are omitted. Instead, there is a narrower exception for any contribution that was made for full valuable consideration pursuant to an arrangement of a commercial nature. This means that contributions made between people in a domestic context should not now be weighed against one another.

6.26   Reasonable financial provision for applicant to receive for maintenance

Reasonable financial provision for the applicant to receive for maintenance has been variously defined:

> 'What is proper maintenance depends on all the facts and circumstances of the case being considered; but although it does not mean just enough to enable an applicant

---

[65]   Non-Contentious Probate Rules 1987, r 43(1), *Practice Direction (Probate: Standing Search for Grant of Representation)* [1975] 3 All ER 403 and *Practice Direction (Probate: Minors' Grants)* [1991] 1 WLR 1069.

to get by on, neither does it mean anything which it may be regarded as reasonably desirable for the applicant's general benefit or welfare.'[66]

'[reasonable financial provision] is the provision sufficient to enable the dependent to live neither luxuriously nor miserably, but decently and comfortably according to his or her station in life.'[67]

'... only payments which would, directly or indirectly, enable the applicant to discharge the recurring costs of his living expenses ...'[68]

'... only those payments which will directly or indirectly enable the applicant in the future to discharge the cost of his daily living at whatever standard is appropriate to him ...'[69]

In *Negus v Bahouse*[70] Goff LJ whilst acknowledging that *maintenance is the touchstone*[71] took into account the lifestyle that the claimant had enjoyed with the deceased over the eight years they were together in assessing what it was appropriate for her to receive for her maintenance.

6.27   The court's approach to whether reasonable financial provision has been made

Before the court can decide what, if any, order to make in favour of the applicant, it has to make a finding that the provision that has been made following the death does not make such financial provision as it would be reasonable in all the circumstances of the case for the applicant to receive for his or her maintenance.

This is an objective test. In other words, the question is not whether the deceased acted unreasonably in the provision that was made, but whether the effect of the devolution of the deceased's estate is to produce an unreasonable result in terms of provision for the maintenance of the applicant. It does not necessarily follow that if no provision is made, the provision, or lack of it, is unreasonable. If the deceased had not in his or her lifetime assumed any financial responsibility for the applicant, it is unlikely that a failure to make provision after death would be found to be unreasonable.

It is implicit in this that the applicant must satisfy the court that there is some kind of obligation on the estate to provide for his or her maintenance.

The applicant's dire financial circumstances or need for maintenance are not in themselves sufficient to establish a claim.

---

[66]   Per curiam in *Re Coventry (Deceased)* [1979] 3 All ER 815 at 816D.
[67]   *Re Duranceau* [1952] 3 DLR 714 at 720.
[68]   *Re Dennis (Deceased)* [1981] 2 All ER 140 at 140H.
[69]   *Re Jennings (Deceased)* [1994] 3 All ER 27 at 35J.
[70]   [2008] 1 FLR 381.
[71]   At para 88.

In determining this question, which is essentially a question of fact, the court must have regard to the matters set out in s 3 of the I(PFD)A 1975. As well as the matters set out in s 3(1)(a)–(g) to which regard must be had in every case, the court must look at the additional matters set out in s 3. The subsection that will apply depends upon the particular category of applicant. Section 3(2A) applies to applications by cohabitants under s 1(1)(ba); s 3(3) applies to applications by children under s 1(1)(c) and (d); and s 3(4) to applications under s 1(1)(e) by dependants. Section 3(2) applies to claims by a spouse or former spouse who has not remarried or civil partner or former civil partner who has not entered into another civil partnership. These additional requirements are considered at **6.35–6.63** below.

6.28 Matters to which the court must have regard in every case in determining whether reasonable financial provision has been made for the applicant

Section 3(1) of the I(PFD)A 1975 states that the court must have regard to:

(a) the financial needs and resources of the applicant at the date of the hearing and in the foreseeable future;

(b) the financial needs and resources of any other applicant at the date of the hearing and in the foreseeable future;

(c) the financial needs and resources of any beneficiary of the estate at the date of the hearing and in the foreseeable future;

(d) any obligations and responsibilities of the deceased towards any applicant or beneficiary of the estate;

(e) the size and nature of the estate;

(f) any physical or mental deficiency of the applicant or any beneficiary of the estate; and

(g) any other matter, including the conduct of the applicant or any other person, which in the circumstances of the case the court may consider relevant.

6.29 Financial resources and financial needs

These require consideration of earning capacity and financial obligations and responsibilities.[72]

The court will be able to ascribe earnings in cases in which a party's true earning capacity is being suppressed.

The court may take into account contingent resources such as the possibility of an inheritance, unless it is very remote.

---

[72] I(PFD)A 1975, s 3(6).

Although financial needs means reasonable requirements, the assessment of a party's financial needs can take into account the standard of living enjoyed during the deceased's lifetime.

6.30   Obligations and responsibilities

What constitutes reasonable financial provision for the applicant must be viewed in the light of the deceased's obligations and responsibilities to any other applicant or beneficiary and his or her financial position.[73]

However generally only those obligations that the deceased had immediately before death will be relevant. As a rule, mere blood ties without obligations will not suffice.[74]

Obligations will include moral as well as legal obligations.[75]

6.31   Size and nature of the net estate[76]

The courts discourage claims against estates where the assets are small on the basis that the costs of the proceedings will make significant inroads into what is available to satisfy the competing interests in the estate.

Although, generally, the costs will be met out of the estate, the court will have no hesitation in making an order for costs against an unsuccessful applicant who has pursued an unmeritorious claim. In *Re Vrint*[77] the estate was valued at a little over £138[78] and the claim by the deceased's estranged widow was dismissed with costs. The court said that given the size of the estate, the claim ought never to have been brought.[79]

It was held in *Re Fullard*[80] that before making an order that the estate pay the costs of an unsuccessful applicant, the court should look closely at the merits of the application.

However, the fact that an estate is large enough to make adequate provision for all interested parties, whilst making the balancing exercise easier, does not remove the need for the applicant to satisfy the court that reasonable financial provision has not been made and that it should have been.

---

[73]   I(PFD)A 1975, s 3(1)(b), (c) and (d).
[74]   *Re Jennings (Deceased)* [1994] 3 All ER 27.
[75]   *Re Goodchild (Deceased) and Another* [1997] 2 FLR 644; and *Re Debenham (Deceased)* [1986] 1 FLR 404.
[76]   I(PFD)A 1975, s 3(1)(e).
[77]   [1940] 3 All ER 470.
[78]   Present day value approximately £3,600.
[79]   See also *Re Joslin* [1941] 1 All ER 302.
[80]   [1981] 2 All ER 796.

6.32   Any physical or mental disability of an applicant or a beneficiary[81]

In *Re Debenham*[82] the court awarded provision for an adult daughter of the deceased even though there was no legal obligation towards her. The deceased had abandoned her at birth and thereafter heartlessly rejected all her attempts to establish a relationship. The court said that although the deceased had made no effort during her lifetime to help the applicant, because of her health problems there was nonetheless a moral obligation on the estate to make provision for her.

6.33   Any other relevant matter, including conduct

The court will admit evidence of facts from which can be inferred the deceased's reasons for disposing of his estate as he did.[83]

In *Re Snoek (Deceased)*[84] it was held that the vicious and atrocious behaviour of the applicant in the later years of her marriage to the deceased did not entirely cancel out her earlier contribution to the home and family, and provision was made for her.

In *Baynes v Hedger*[85] the court considered that the conduct of one of the claimants in pressurising, if not bullying, the deceased into baling her out of a succession of financial crises was an important factor in the case.

6.34   The Forfeiture Act 1982

The Forfeiture Act 1982 gives the court discretion to modify the application of the forfeiture rule if it takes the view that, bearing in mind the extent of the applicant's moral culpability, it would be unjust to deny him or her any benefit as a result of unlawfully killing the deceased. In *Royse v Royse*[86] Mrs Royse was convicted of killing her husband. The forfeiture rule prevented her from benefiting under his will of which she was the sole beneficiary. The Forfeiture Act 1982 was not in force when Mrs Royse made her application for provision from the estate which the court said should fail for the same reasons, namely that she should not be able to profit from her unlawful act in killing her husband.

In *Jones v Roberts*[87] the decision in *Royse* was followed, and there are very few decisions in which the court has exercised its discretion to modify the operation of the forfeiture rule.[88]

---

[81]   I(PFD)A 1975, s 3(1)(f).
[82]   [1986] 1 FLR 404.
[83]   *Re Smallwood, Smallwood v Martins Bank* [1951] 1 All ER 372.
[84]   (1983) 13 Fam Law 18.
[85]   [2008] 3 FCR 151.
[86]   [1984] 3 All ER 339.
[87]   [1995] 2 FLR 422.
[88]   *Re H (Deceased)* [1990] 1 FLR 441.

In *Re S*[89] a husband murdered his wife. On her death, the proceeds of a joint policy became payable. The insurance company did not oppose the modification of the forfeiture rule to enable the deceased's estate, which was effectively the proceeds of the policy, to be held in trust for the parties' young son.

6.35   Application by a surviving cohabitant under Inheritance (Provision for Family and Dependants) Act 1975, s 1(1)(ba)

The requirements for an application under the section are set out in s 1(1A)[90] and s 1(1B).[91] Whilst recognising the existence of cohabitation, the threshold criteria are less generous than for a surviving spouse or civil partner. Although cohabitants of at least two years' standing no longer have to establish dependency on the deceased, I(PFD)A 1975, s 1(2)(b) makes a clear distinction between applications made by a surviving spouse or civil partner and all other categories of applicant. The question of whether or not reasonable financial provision has been made for a surviving spouse or civil partner is determined without regard to whether that provision is required for his or her maintenance. The other categories of applicant are restricted by the requirement to show that reasonable provision for their maintenance has not been made.

6.36   Who is eligible to apply?

To qualify to make an application under the category of a cohabitant of at least two years' standing the following criteria must be satisfied:

(a)   the deceased must have died on or after 1 January 1996; and
(b)   for the whole of the two years immediately preceding the death of the deceased, the applicant and the deceased must have:
   –   lived in the same household;
   –   as spouse or civil partner.

These requirements raise questions of interpretation.

6.37   For the whole of the two years immediately preceding the death of the deceased

Until *Re Watson (Deceased)*[92] there had been no reported decisions for guidance on how strictly the courts may construe this requirement. Although in that case it was not argued that the application should fail because the deceased had spent the last three weeks of his life in hospital, Neuberger J, as he then was, commented that it was:[93]

---

[89]   [1996] 1 FLR 910.
[90]   Inserted by the Law Reform (Succession) Act 1995 in respect of those living together as spouses.
[91]   Inserted by CPA 2004 in relation to those living together as civil partners.
[92]   [1999] 1 FLR 878.
[93]   At 882H–883A.

'... not an argument which could respectably have been advanced. In the first place, as a matter of ordinary language, the fact that someone is in hospital for a period, possibly for a long period, at the end of which he dies, does not mean that, before his death, he ceased to be part of the household of which he was part, until he was forced by illness to go to hospital, and to which he would have returned had he not died.'

This approach reflects the case-law in related areas. For example, when considering whether for the purposes of applications under I(PFD)A 1975, s 1(1)(e) the applicant was being maintained by the deceased 'immediately before the death', the courts have tended to look at the general arrangement between the parties up to the date of death rather than construe the section so as to exclude applications where the dependency had as a matter of fact ceased before the date of death.[94]

It was held in *Re Beaumont (Deceased)* that the court should look, 'not at the *de facto* state of maintenance existing at the moment of death, but at the settled and enduring basis or arrangement then generally existing between the parties, using the date of death as the day on which that arrangement was to be considered'.[95]

That case was referred to in *Jelley v Iliffe and Others*[96] in which it was said that 'a relationship of dependence which has persisted for years will not be defeated by its termination during a few weeks of mortal sickness'.[97]

In *Re Dix*,[98] the Court of Appeal held that notwithstanding that the claimant had lived apart from the deceased for the last three months of his life, she was entitled to claim against his estate under s 1(1)(ba) and s 1(1)(e). In that case the parties had lived together in a settled relationship for 27 years in spite of the problems that resulted from the deceased's alcoholism. Eventually, the situation became intolerable for the claimant and she left with a suitcase of clothes to stay with her daughter. The question for the court was whether the relationship was at an end or merely suspended. The Court of Appeal said that the judge at first instance was right to conclude on the evidence that the parties did not regard their relationship at an end. The judge had accepted the claimant's case that she was forced by a combination of the deceased's behaviour and her own ill health to leave, but that she always intended to return. It was likely that she would have returned, as she had following previous separations, had the claimant's daughter not deliberately failed to tell her of the deceased's attempts to contact her to plead for her return.

In *Kourkgy v Lusher*[99] the court found that the applicant was not being maintained by the deceased immediately before his death. The deceased had

---

[94] *Re Beaumont (Deceased)* [1980] 1 All ER 266.
[95] At 267E.
[96] [1981] 2 All ER 29.
[97] Per Stephenson LJ at 35A.
[98] [2004] 1 FLR 918, [2004] 1 WLR 1339.
[99] (1983) 4 FLR 65.

only a matter of days before his death returned to live with his wife, although there had been cohabitation with the applicant for some six years immediately preceding that. The court took the view on the evidence that the deceased had been moving towards a position of divesting himself of responsibility for the applicant for some months before his death, and this was finally achieved when he returned to live with his wife, albeit days before his death.

In *Layton v Martin*[100] it was held that a former cohabitant had no claim under the I(PFD)A 1975 as she had ceased to live with the deceased about two years before his death.

In *Witkowska v Kaminski*[101] the claimant was a Polish national. She had originally entered the United Kingdom on a tourist visa and, when that expired, she became an illegal overstayer. Shortly after they met, the claimant moved in to live with the deceased. Over the five years they were together, the pattern was that she would return to Poland on frequent visits, and during this time the deceased would send money for her support. The claimant was in Poland on a 14-week visit when the deceased had an accident as a result of which he shortly thereafter died. When she heard of the accident she returned to the United Kingdom but arrived just too late. It was not in issue that the claimant and the deceased had lived together in the same household as spouses, but it was in dispute that the cohabitation had subsisted up to the deceased's death. The case of the defendant, the deceased's son, was that there was evidence that the claimant had decided not to return to live with the deceased. However, the court considered that evidence of payments sent by the deceased to the claimant in Poland up to seven weeks before his death, correspondence and telephone calls between them during her absence and the fact that she had left some of her possessions at the deceased's home all pointed to the relationship continuing up to the time of his death.

In *Kaur v Dhaliwal*[102] the Court of Appeal dismissed the appeal by the sons of the deceased from a decision that the deceased and the applicant had lived together for the requisite period. Although the applicant and the deceased had cohabited for just short of 2 years immediately preceding the deceased's death, they had a settled relationship that continued until the deceased's death, and the interruption in their living arrangements was for reasons unconnected with the state of their relationship.

6.38   Living in the same household

Even if there is an intimate relationship and the parties spent periods of time together on holidays and the like, without a shared household there can be no basis for an application under this section.[103]

---

[100] [1986] 2 FLR 227.
[101] [2007] 1 FLR 1547.
[102] [2014] EWHC 1991 (Ch).
[103] *Malone v Harrison* [1979] 1 WLR 1353.

In the Law Commission's report, *Cohabitation: The Financial Consequences of Relationship Breakdown*[104] it is recommended that for the purposes of the legislation then proposed that cohabitants should be defined as those who *are living as a couple in a joint household.*

Reference is made in the Report to the 'six signposts' currently used in the social security context[105] as a starting point for the central factors that a court may have in mind when deciding the issue. These factors are:

(1) existence of a joint household;
(2) financial arrangements;
(3) stability of the relationship;
(4) responsibility for children;
(5) sexual relationship;
(6) public recognition of the relationship.

In *Churchill v Roach*[106] the court found that the claimant and the deceased were not living in the same household at the material time but were maintaining two separate households. The judge did not consider that it was necessarily fatal to the application that there were two houses, and he accepted that there was a degree of sharing when the parties met at weekends and for more extended periods of time, but on the facts of that case the claimant failed to satisfy the criteria as he understood it to be:

> '... living in the same household ... seems to me to have elements of permanence, to involve a consideration of the frequency and intimacy of contact, to contain an element of mutual support, to require some consideration of the degree of voluntary restraint upon personal freedom which each party undertakes, and to involve an element of community of resources. None of these factors is of itself sufficient, but each may provide an indicator.'

This question was considered by Lewison J, as he then was, in *Baynes v Hedger*[107] in relation to one of the two claimants whose application was not the subject of the later appeal to the Court of Appeal. In that case it was held[108] that:

> 'Whether two people lived together in the same household was a question of fact. It was not simply a matter of living under the same roof but of the public and private acknowledgement of their society and the mutual protection and support that bound them together. Nor did two people living in the same household cease to do so because they became physically separated.'

It was determinative of the court's finding in *Baynes v Hedger* that one of the applicants and the deceased had not shared a household for the requisite

---

[104] Law Com No 307.
[105] See also chapter 9.
[106] [2004] 2 FLR 989.
[107] [2008] 3 FCR 151.
[108] At p 152.

period, that although historically they had lived together in a same-sex relationship, there had for at least the 30 years before the death of the deceased, been a settled pattern whereby they each maintained their own households and only 'stayed' with or 'visited' the other periodically.

There may be a dispute as to whether the applicant and the deceased lived in the same household, even if they lived under the same roof. However, if the court finds that the applicant satisfied the requirements for living together as spouse or civil partner,[109] it will generally be the case that this requirement will be satisfied.

Brief periods of separation will not necessarily prevent a finding that the parties were living in the same household,[110] nor will the fact that one party had another household as well as the shared household.[111]

HHJ Behrens provided a helpful review of the authorities in *Lindop v Agus, Bass and Hedley*.[112] In that case he concluded that although it ran counter to the applicant's case that she retained her father's address for correspondence and for the purposes of the electoral roll, on the totality of the evidence she and the deceased had lived together as husband and wife openly and her claim under s 1(1A) was made out.

Cases decided in other jurisdictions may also be of relevance here.

For the purposes of establishing separation in the context of divorce proceedings, the parties in *Mouncer v Mouncer*[113] were held not to be living in a separate household because although they slept in separate rooms and the wife no longer did the husband's washing, they shared the cleaning and continued to take meals together.

In *Kimber v Kimber*[114] HHJ Tyrer concluded that whilst it was impossible to draw up an exhaustive list of the criteria for determining the existence of cohabitation, certain factors were relevant derived from the authorities, and the Social Security Contributions and Benefits Act 1992. The judge's approach was approved by the Court of Appeal in *Grey v Grey*.[115]

In proceedings under the DVMPA 1976 the parties were held to be living together even where they had completely severed their living arrangements but were still under the same roof.[116]

---

[109] I(PFD)A 1975, s 1(1A)(b), see **6.39** below.
[110] *Pounder v London Underground Limited and Others* [1995] PIQR 217.
[111] *Jessop v Jessop* [1992] 1 FLR 591.
[112] [2010] 1 FLR 631.
[113] [1972] 1 All ER 289.
[114] [2000] 1 FLR 383.
[115] [2010] 1 FLR 1764.
[116] *Adeoso (otherwise Ametepe) v Adeoso* [1981] 1 All ER 107.

Kotke v Saffarini[117] concerned a claim under the Fatal Accidents Act 1976 for loss of dependency. An issue arose as to whether the claimant and the deceased had been living in the same household as spouses for at least two years before the death. The Court of Appeal upheld the decision of the trial judge that, although the claimant and the deceased were living together as spouses at the date of his death, the claimant had not made out her case that they had done so for at least two years before the date of death. The court held that whilst the retention of a separate property by the deceased would not in itself prevent a finding that the parties were living in one household, on the facts of this case, '... the extent to which ... the deceased maintained and made use of it and treated himself as still resident there, indicated that he and the claimant had not [two years before the date of death] reached the position of treating [the claimant's house] as their mutual home.'

6.39 Living together as spouse or civil partner

This was an issue in *Re Watson (Deceased)*,[118] a case decided before the amendment to I(PFD)A 1975 made by CPA 2004. The parties had shared the home of the deceased for the last 11 years of his life. Although they had known one another for over 30 years, and in their younger days had enjoyed an intimate relationship, they had never married. During the time that they shared a home the deceased had worked long hours outside the home, and the applicant had worked long hours in the home, cooking, washing, cleaning and the like. They had separate bedrooms, but shared the other accommodation, took meals together and were otherwise companionable. Although the applicant owned her own home elsewhere and had a small income, the deceased provided the accommodation without charge, and the outgoings were shared on an informal basis. In finding that the applicant satisfied the requirements of s 1(1)(ba) of the I(PFD)A 1975 as a person living in the same household as the deceased, and as his wife, Neuberger J, as he then was, said that:

> '... when considering that question, one must beware of indulging in too much over-analysis. Anyone who reads newspapers or law reports does not need to be told that marriages, like, perhaps even more than, other human relationships, can vary from each other in multifarious ways. However, in my judgment, when considering whether two people are living together as husband and wife, it would be wrong to conclude that they do so simply because their relationship is one which a husband and wife could have. If the test were as wide as that, then, bearing in mind the enormous variety of relationships that can exist between husband and wife, virtually every relationship between a man and a woman living in the same household would fall within s 1(1A). It seems to me that, when considering the question, the court should ask itself whether, in the opinion of a reasonable person with normal perceptions, it could be said that the two people in question were living together as husband and wife; but, when considering that question, one should not ignore the multifarious nature of marital relationships.'[119]

---

[117] [2005] 2 FLR 517.
[118] [1999] 1 FLR 878.
[119] At 883E–G.

In what is thought to be the first reported decision of a claim under s 1(1B), it was the view of Lewison J, as he then was, in *Baynes v Hedger* in relation to one of two claimants whose application was not subject to a later appeal to the Court of Appeal that 'it is not possible to establish that two persons have lived together as civil partners unless their relationship as a couple is an acknowledged one'.[120] In that case the deceased and one of the claimants had formed an intimate relationship and had lived together as a family with the claimant's children. This continued for some years until they established their own households after which they would visit one another from time to time. As the judge observed they, 'were of a generation for whom a same-sex relationship was not an acceptable lifestyle, and their relationship was not openly acknowledged' and although he found that initially they shared a bedroom and probably had a sexual relationship, he concluded that later when they had each their own house this may not have been the case. Although he was satisfied that they were emotionally committed to one another right up until the deceased's death, he concluded that their relationship was a private one, and they did not themselves acknowledge that they were a couple.'

6.40 Making out the ground for the application

If the court is satisfied that the applicant fulfils the criteria for eligibility under s 1(1)(ba), it will go on to consider whether or not the ground for applying for provision is made out, namely that the disposition of the deceased's estate does not make reasonable financial provision for the maintenance of the surviving cohabitant.

This is essentially a question of fact for the court, but one that it was held in *Re Coventry (Deceased)*[121] involved '… the judge making a value judgment (or qualitative decision) whether in the circumstances, looked at objectively, it was unreasonable that the provisions governing the estate did not provide for the applicant['s maintenance], and not merely by deciding whether the deceased had acted unreasonably or unfairly in leaving his estate as he had.'[122]

6.41 Matters to which the court must have regard

The matters to which the court must have regard when making a finding about the provision that has been made are those set out in I(PFD)A 1975, s 3. As well as the matters set out in s 3(1)(a)–(g), which are common to all applicants and which are considered at **6.28** above, in the case of applications by a cohabitant under s 1(1)(ba), s 3(2A) requires the court to have regard to:

> '(a) the age of the applicant and the length of the period during which the applicant lived as the spouse or civil partner of the deceased and in the same household as the deceased;

---

[120] At para 150.
[121] [1979] 3 All ER 815.
[122] At p 815J.

(b)   the contribution made by the applicant to the welfare of the family of the deceased, including any contribution made by looking after the home or caring for the family.'

These matters mirror those which the court must consider under s 3(2) of the I(PFD)A 1975 when exercising its powers in favour of a spouse or former spouse who has not remarried or civil partner or former civil partner who has not entered into another civil partnership. They were considered in *Re Watson (Deceased)*.[123]

6.42   Age of the applicant and length of cohabitation

Clearly the older the applicant, and the longer he or she has put the family's interests first, the less likely it is that he or she will be able to achieve financial independence.

In the case of elderly applicants, the court will bear in mind that the purpose of the I(PFD)A 1975 is to make provision for the applicant, and so any order made will be geared to the applicant's life expectancy so as not to provide a windfall for the applicant's survivors.

6.43   Applicant's contribution to the welfare of the family

There would appear to be no reason why, when considering this matter in a claim by a surviving cohabitant, the court should not look at it in the same way as when considering an application by a surviving spouse or former spouse who has not remarried, or surviving civil partner or former civil partner who has not entered into another civil partnership. This is subject to the proviso that the question of whether reasonable financial provision has been made must be decided on the basis of what is reasonable for the applicant to receive for his or her maintenance.

In *Re Watson (Deceased)*[124] the applicant's contribution by taking on and discharging the responsibility for all aspects of the day-to-day running and management of the household for the 11 years the parties lived together was regarded as substantial.

6.44   The exercise of the court's discretion

If, after considering all the matters in s 3(1) and (2A) of the I(PFD)A 1975, the court has found as a fact that reasonable provision has not been made for the applicant's maintenance, it must then go on to decide what, if any, provision to make. It does not necessarily follow from a finding that reasonable provision has not been made that the court will make a substantive order. The court must exercise its discretion at this second stage and, in so doing, is required by s 3 to take into account once again all the matters set out in s 3(1)(a)–(g) and (2A).

---

[123]   [1999] 1 FLR 878.
[124]   [1999] 1 FLR 878.

In *Musa v Holliday*[125] the Court of Appeal upheld the first instance decision to award the transfer to the deceased's cohabitant of the bulk of the deceased's UK property. The Court of Appeal found that on the unusual facts of that case HHJ Kushner had correctly made a determination that the applicant needed a home outright and sufficient income to maintain the mortgage repayments and other outgoings, and to provide for the income needs of herself and her son. The income could only be provided by the transfer to the applicant of the deceased's business in the UK. Although by this award the applicant received most of the UK assets of the estate, the judge was satisfied that the six competing beneficiaries had sufficient to meet their needs from the deceased's assets in Northern Cyprus. It is unlikely that a surviving spouse could have done better but there is little doubt that the result owes a good deal to the bad blood evident between the parties, and the need for all financial ties to be severed.

In *Cattle v Evans*[126] the parties had been together for around 18 years but had lived together for only the last five years. They bought a property in Spain in joint names as their shared home using funds from the sale of the property owned by the deceased. The applicant used the sale proceeds of her own property to buy a property to rent out, and she contributed to renovation work at the Spanish property. They subsequently decided to sell the Spanish property and live in Wales but before the purchase of the property in Wales could be completed, the deceased received a diagnosis of terminal cancer. He proceeded with the purchase in his sole name using his half share of the proceeds of sale of the Spanish property and the parties lived there until his death shortly afterwards. He died intestate.

In awarding the applicant a life interest in a modest property to be purchased by the estate the court took into account that apart from the Spanish property the parties had kept their property and finances separate and the property in Wales had been funded almost entirely by the deceased.

6.45 Application by a 'dependant' under section 1(1)(e) of the Inheritance (Provision for Family and Dependants) Act 1975

If a surviving cohabitant is not eligible to apply under s 1(1)(ba) because there has not been the required cohabitation for two years immediately preceding the death, or the other conditions of eligibility cannot be satisfied, the only alternative is to make an application under s 1(1)(e).

6.46 Who is eligible to apply?

Applications under this section are not limited to those living together as spouse or civil partner who do not qualify to apply under s 1(1)(ba). Any person who

---

[125] [2013] 1 FLR 806.
[126] [2011] 2 FLR 843.

can claim dependency upon the deceased may apply. This category will include, for example, friends and family members.[127]

From 1 October 2014 ITPA 2014 has made important changes to claims made under this section. First, the definition of a dependant for the purposes of s 1(1)(e) is now qualified as follows:[128]

'... a person is to be treated as being maintained by the deceased (either wholly or partly, as the case may be) only if the deceased was making a substantial contribution in money or money's worth towards the reasonable needs of that person, other than a contribution made for full valuable consideration pursuant to an agreement of a commercial nature.'

Before this amendment, the court was required to balance the respective contributions of the applicant and the deceased up to the date of death and only if there was a net contribution by the deceased to the applicant would the applicant be eligible to make a claim. The balancing exercise is no longer required, and the only vitiating factor will be the payment of money by the deceased to the applicant for full valuable consideration pursuant to an arrangement of a commercial nature.

This will exclude, for example, claims where there has been a landlord/lodger relationship where the rental paid is the full commercial value. However, it allows for a situation in which the consideration falls short of that either from the outset, or over time.

The amendments also deal with the difficulty that had arisen whereby the courts had tended to interpret the eligibility criteria as requiring the applicant to prove that the deceased had assumed responsibility for his or her maintenance.[129] This was specifically addressed by the Law Commission in the report that gave rise to ITPA 2014.[130] The consequent amendment to s 3(4), specifically subsection (b), admits the possibility of the deceased having maintained the applicant as required by s 1(1)(e) without there being any assumption of responsibility, thereby making it clear that no such evaluation is required for the purposes of determining eligibility.

6.47 Immediately before the death

The requirement for the maintenance of the applicant by the deceased to be current at the time of death is not changed by ITPA 2014. However, courts have

---

[127] See *Re B (Deceased)* [2000] 1 All ER 665, in which a mother with the full-time care of a severely disabled child was held to fall into this category by virtue of the incidental benefits received by the mother from payments made from the child's personal injury damages for the child's maintenance.

[128] IPFDA, s 1(3).

[129] *Jelley v Iliffe* [1981] Fam 128; *Bouette v Rose* [1999] All ER (D) 1458; *Martin v Midland Bank Trust Co Ltd* [1980] 1 Ch 444; [1980] 1 All ER 266; *Baynes v Hedger* [2009] EWCA Civ 374, [2009] 2 FLR 767.

[130] *Intestacy and Family Provisions Claims on Death* Law Com 331 (TSO), 2011.

tended to look at the general arrangement between the parties up to the date of death rather than construe the section so as to exclude applications where the dependency had as a matter of fact ceased before the date of death. In *Re Beaumont (Deceased)*[131] it was held that the court should look 'not at the *de facto* state of maintenance existing at the moment of death, but at the settled and enduring basis or arrangement then generally existing between the parties, using the date of death as the day on which that arrangement was to be considered'.[132]

That case was referred to in *Jelley v Iliffe and Others*,[133] in which it was said that 'a relationship of dependence which has persisted for years will not be defeated by its termination during a few weeks of mortal sickness'.[134]

In *Re Dix*,[135] the Court of Appeal held that notwithstanding that the claimant had lived apart from the deceased for the last three months of his life, she came within s 1(1)(e) and was also entitled to claim against his estate under s 1(1)(ba). In that case the parties had lived together in a settled relationship for 27 years in spite of the problems that resulted from the deceased's alcoholism. Eventually, the situation became intolerable for the claimant and she left with a suitcase of clothes to stay with her daughter. The question for the court was whether the relationship was at an end or merely suspended. The Court of Appeal said that the judge at first instance was right to conclude on the evidence that the parties did not regard their relationship at an end. The judge had accepted the claimant's case that she was forced by a combination of the deceased's behaviour and her own ill health to leave, but that she always intended to return. It was likely that she would have returned, as she had following previous separations, had the claimant's daughter not deliberately failed to tell her of the deceased's attempts to contact her to plead for her return.

In *Kourkgy v Lusher*,[136] however, the court found that the applicant was not being maintained by the deceased immediately before his death. The deceased had returned to live with his wife only a matter of days before his death, although there had been cohabitation with the applicant for some six years immediately preceding that. The court took the view on the evidence that the deceased had been moving towards a position of divesting himself of responsibility for the applicant for some months before his death, and this was finally achieved when he returned to live with his wife, albeit days before his death.

---

[131] [1980] 1 All ER 266.
[132] At 267E.
[133] [1981] 2 All ER 29.
[134] Per Stephenson LJ at 35A; see also *Re Watson* [1999] 1 FLR 878.
[135] [2004] 1 FLR 918.
[136] (1983) 4 FLR 65.

In *Layton v Martin*[137] it was held that the former cohabitant had no claim under the I(PFD)A 1975, as she had ceased to live with the deceased about two years before his death.

In *Witkowska v Kaminski*[138] the claimant was a Polish national. She had originally entered the United Kingdom on a tourist visa and when that expired she became an illegal overstayer. Shortly after they met, the claimant moved in to live with the deceased. Over the five years they were together, the pattern was that she would return to Poland on frequent visits, and during this time the deceased would send money for her support. The claimant was in Poland on a 14-week visit when the deceased had an accident as a result of which he shortly thereafter died. When she heard of the accident she returned to the United Kingdom but arrived just too late. It was not in issue that the claimant and the deceased had lived together in the same household as spouses, but it was in dispute that the cohabitation had subsisted up to the deceased's death. The case of the defendant, the deceased's son, was that there was evidence that the claimant had decided not to return to live with the deceased. However, the court considered that evidence of payments sent by the deceased to the claimant in Poland up to seven weeks before his death, correspondence and telephone calls between them during her absence and the fact that she had left some of her possessions at the deceased's home all pointed to the relationship continuing up to the time of his death.

In *Kaur v Dhaliwal*,[139] a claim made under s 1(1)(ba), the Court of Appeal dismissed the appeal by the sons of the deceased from a decision that the deceased and the applicant had lived together for the requisite period. Although the applicant and the deceased had cohabited for just short of 2 years immediately preceding the deceased's death, they had a settled relationship that continued until the deceased's death, and the interruption in their living arrangements was for reasons unconnected with the state of their own relationship.

6.48   Being maintained

Following the amendment to s 1(1)-(3) I(PFD)A 1975 the court will no longer have to balance the respective contributions in order to ascertain whether there is a net gain to the applicant. The only matter for the court will be whether there is a substantial contribution, in cash or in kind, other than by way of a commercial arrangement.

It is possible that an arrangement that began on a business footing may in time evolve to become one in which there is a degree of dependency.

There is no statutory definition to assist the court in deciding whether any sums paid to the applicant by the deceased can be regarded as maintenance sufficient

---

[137] [1986] 2 FLR 227.
[138] [2007] 1 FLR 1547.
[139] [2014] EWHC 1991 (Ch).

to satisfy the eligibility criteria. The case-law suggests that such sums should enable the applicant directly or indirectly to *discharge the cost of his daily living at whatever standard of living is appropriate to him.*[140]

6.49   Making out the ground for the application

If the applicant has satisfied the court that he or she is within the category eligible to apply for provision under s 1(1)(e) of the I(PFD)A 1975, the court will then look at the provision that has been made and whether in the light of the evidence and the matters referred to in s 3 that provision is such as it would be reasonable in all the circumstances of the case for the applicant to receive for his or her maintenance. This is essentially a question of fact for the court, but one that it was held in *Re Coventry (Deceased)*[141] involved 'the judge making a value judgment (or qualitative decision) whether in the circumstances, looked at objectively, it was unreasonable that the provisions governing the estate did not provide for the applicant, and not merely by deciding whether the deceased had acted unreasonably or unfairly in leaving his estate as he had'.[142]

6.50   Matters to which the court must have regard

The matters to which the court must have regard when making a finding about the provision that has been made are those set out in s 3(1) of the I(PFD)A 1975. As well as the matters set out in s 3(1)(a)–(g) which are common to all applicants and which are considered at **6.28** above, in the case of applications under s 1(1)(e), s 3(4), as amended by IPTA, requires the court to have regard to 'the length of time for which and basis on which the deceased maintained the applicant, and to the extent of the contribution made by way of maintenance, and to whether and, if so, to what extent the deceased assumed responsibility for the maintenance of the applicant'.

6.51   Assumption of responsibility for maintenance by the deceased

Although much of the existing case-law looks at the assumption of responsibility in the context of eligibility, the decided cases may offer some assistance when the court is considering the assumption of responsibility for the purposes of s 3.

In *Jelley v Iliffe and Others*[143] the court determined that:

> 'The bare fact that the applicant was being maintained by the deceased under an agreement subsisting at the deceased's death was sufficient to, and generally did, raise a presumption that the deceased had assumed responsibility for [the applicant's] maintenance ... and it was unnecessary to prove any other overt act demonstrating the assumption of responsibility because ... the words "assumed

---

[140]   *Re Dennis (deceased)* [1981] 2 All ER 140.
[141]   [1979] 3 All ER 815.
[142]   At 815J.
[143]   [1981] 2 All ER 29.

responsibility for" in s 3(4) meant "had undertaken" to provide maintenance. Moreover it was not necessary for an applicant to prove that the deceased had intended to maintain [the applicant] after his or her death, and it was sufficient if the deceased's conduct was such that the applicant had been made wholly or partially dependent on the deceased for his maintenance during the deceased's lifetime …'

This approach was confirmed in *Rees v Newbery and the Institute of Cancer Research*.[144] The assumption of maintenance could be inferred from the fact that the deceased in his lifetime undertook such maintenance.[145] In *Malone v Harrison and Another*,[146] although the applicant and the deceased had never lived together, for 12 years they took holidays together that were paid for by the deceased, and for the rest of the time the applicant made herself available to the deceased. He discouraged her from working so that she could be at his beck and call. He bought a flat in joint names for her occupation, and a flat in Malta for their holidays, also in joint names. He gave her a car and some shares. The deceased made no provision in his will for the applicant, but before his death had brought to her attention that she may be able to make a claim against his estate. It was held that the deceased had assumed full responsibility for the applicant for the last 12 years of his life.

However, in *Rhodes v Dean*,[147] despite satisfying the court that she had been maintained by the deceased, the Court of Appeal considered that the trial judge had correctly applied the provisions of s 3(1)(a)–(g) and in particular s 3(4) in finding that the deceased had not assumed responsibility for the applicant's maintenance. The deceased had provided the applicant with accommodation for two years and two months, but had not assumed financial responsibility for all her maintenance needs. Bearing in mind the sum of £36,000 that the applicant had received from a joint bank account on the death of the deceased, the judge had been right to conclude that it was not unreasonable that no provision had been made for the applicant in the deceased's will.

In *Baynes v Hedger*[148] the deceased had become closely involved with the first claimant and her family, including a daughter, the second claimant, who was also her goddaughter. Over the course of many years the deceased generously provided financial help. In relation to the first claimant, the deceased had some thirty years before provided her with a large sum of money with which to buy

---

[144] [1998] 1 FLR 1041.

[145] The applicant, a 50-year-old actor with modest earnings, applied for financial provision out of the deceased's £700,000 estate. The two had become friends through their work. The basis for the application was that for nearly 10 years the applicant had been living in a flat owned by the deceased at substantially less than the market rent. The deceased's motives appeared to have been entirely philanthropic. The deceased had intended to make a new will to make continued provision after his death, but died before the will was executed. The court held, granting the application, that the provision of accommodation at less than the market rent amounted to maintenance of the applicant, and by inference that the deceased had assumed responsibility for the applicant.

[146] [1979] 1 WLR 1353.

[147] [1996] CLY 555.

[148] [2008] 3 FCR 151, [2009] 2 FLR 767.

a house, and made her a beneficiary of a trust fund that gave her an income. Since then she had made occasional one-off payments and some much smaller payments on a more regular basis.

At first instance Lewison J, as he then was, decided that this claimant could not satisfy the requirements of s 1(1)(e) as there was no evidence that she had been maintained by the deceased immediately before the death. He rejected the argument that the fact that the source of the first claimant's home and major part of her income was the deceased pointed to dependency. She did not fall within the category and her claim must fail. However, the judge went on expressly to consider in the context of s 3(4) the extent to which the deceased had assumed responsibility for her maintenance. He concluded that a one off gift of money for a house in the distant past did not show any assumption of responsibility for future maintenance. The creation of the settlement indicated the clear extent of the responsibility assumed and that it was this, rather than the deceased's free assets, that was to be the source of the maintenance.

The second claimant had been the recipient of very generous financial support from the deceased throughout her adult life that continued up to a few months before her death. Latterly the financial assistance had been at the second claimant's request, if not insistence, as a result of the precarious state of her finances. Some of the payments were gifts, others were expressed to be 'soft' loans that it was doubtful would be repaid in full. On this basis the judge held that she qualified to make a claim under s 1(1)(e).

In the exercise of his discretion under s 3(1) and 3(4) the judge went on to determine that the financial arrangements between the second claimant and the deceased did not amount to an assumption of responsibility for her continued support. Her primary concern was to help the second claimant to pay off her debts so that she could then support herself on her own earnings. For this and other reasons he concluded that the second claimant had failed to establish that the deceased's will had failed to make reasonable provision for her and so her claim failed.

6.52   The exercise of the court's discretion

If after considering all the matters in s 3(1)(a)–(g) and s 3(4) of the I(PFD)A 1975 the court is satisfied that reasonable provision has not been made for the applicant's maintenance, it must go on to decide what if, any provision, to make. It does not follow from a finding that reasonable provision has not been made that the court will make a substantive order.[149] This stage also involves the court in the exercise of its discretion, and in so doing it must take into account once again all the matters set out in s 3(1)(a)–(g) and s 3(4).

---

[149] *Rhodes v Dean* [1996] CLY 555.

6.53 Applications under the Inheritance (Provision for Family and Dependants) Act 1975 by children

The amendments to IPFDA by ITPA 2014 introduce a new category of applicant, namely any person towards whom the deceased has stood in the role of parent. There is no requirement for any blood or family tie.

Children may therefore qualify to apply for an order under the I(PFD)A 1975 by virtue of being either the natural child of the deceased,[150] a person treated by the deceased as a child of the family in relation to any marriage or civil partnership,[151] or a child who in relation to any family in which the deceased at any time stood in the role of a parent, was treated by the deceased as a child of the family.[152] A child claiming under s 1(1)(d) could be the child of a spouse or former spouse, civil partner or former civil partner, who had been treated by the deceased as a child of the family in relation to that marriage or civil partnership. A claimant could also be someone with no connection to any marriage or cohabitation to which the deceased may have been a party[153] as long as the deceased had stood in the role of parent to that child.

The definition of 'child' for the purposes of the I(PFD)A 1975 will not preclude applications by adult children.

A child in respect of whom an adoption order has been made cannot claim against the estate of a biological parent, unless the child has a contingent interest in the deceased parent's estate immediately before the adoption.[154]

A child will include a child *en ventre sa mère* at the date of the deceased parent's death.

There is no distinction made between a legitimate child and an illegitimate child.

6.54 Who is eligible to apply under section 1(1)(c)?

This section applies only to the natural children of the deceased, be they minor children or adults. Unlike other categories of applicant, the question of the eligibility of a natural child to apply under this section should be easily determined.

6.55 Who is eligible to apply under section 1(1)(d)?

The enactment of ITPA 2014 extends the category of applicant under this subsection to include not only children of the family in the context of marriage

---

[150] Section 1(1)(c).
[151] Ie a step-child.
[152] Section 1(1)(d) as amended by ITPA 2014.
[153] And since the implementation of ITPA 2014, the child of a surviving cohabitant.
[154] Section 69(4) ACA 2002 as amended by ITPA 2014.

and civil partnership, but also a child with no connection to any marriage or cohabitation to which the deceased may have been a party[155] as long as the deceased had stood in the role of parent to that child.

In its report, *Intestacy and Family Provisions Claims on Death*,[156] The Law Commission rejected views gathered during the consultation process that extending the potential applicants under s 1(1)(d) would create problems:[157]

> '... A court would not find that a child who was simply sponsored by the deceased or with whom the deceased undertook voluntary work was treated as a child of the family, unless the quality and intensity of that help could be characterized as parental. Nor would simply helping an elderly neighbour, without much more, merit such a description...There may be a risk of speculative, ill-judged litigation to test the boundaries of this new category but this is no reason not to cure what appears to us ... as an undesirable anomaly in the law[158] ... Nothing has emerged from consultation which alters our preliminary view that section 1(1)(d) is outdated and may operate in an arbitrary and unfair manner. Applicants with the same quality of relationship with the deceased may be treated quite differently from one another depending on whether the deceased was married or in a civil partnership, cohabiting, or single. It is ... no answer to say that some children of the family excluded because of the wording of section 1(1)(d) may have standing to apply ...as dependants under section 1(1)(e). That subsection imposes a quite different set of threshold requirements and sets a much higher hurdle.'

The definition of a child treated as a child of the family in the context of marriage or civil partnership has been given a wide interpretation by the courts, and the case-law will be relevant to the assessment of the relationship in other contexts.

In *Re Leach, Leach v Lindeman*[159] the 55-year-old stepdaughter of the deceased was eligible to apply under s 1(1)(d). The basis for this decision was that, even though the deceased had married the applicant's father late in life, and at a time when the applicant was living independently, the relationship between them was in the nature of a close mother/daughter relationship, and this continued even after the death of the applicant's father. It was held that the applicant had been treated by the deceased as a child of the family that was formed when she married the applicant's father.

Re Callaghan (Deceased)[160] concerned an application by the adult stepson of the deceased. In that case, the deceased had come into the applicant's life when he was about 13, although he had not married the applicant's mother until long after the applicant had himself married and left home. Nonetheless, Booth J found on the particular facts of the case that:

---

[155] And since the implementation of ITPA 2014, the child of a surviving cohabitant.
[156] Law Com 331 (TSO, 2011).
[157] At para 6.40.
[158] At para 6.38.
[159] [1985] 2 All ER 754.
[160] [1984] 3 All ER 790.

'… the acknowledgement by the deceased of his own role of grandfather to the plaintiff's children, the confidences as to his property and financial affairs which he placed in the plaintiff and his dependence on the plaintiff to care for him in his last illness are examples of the deceased's treatment of the plaintiff as a child, albeit an adult child, of the family. All these things are part of the privileges and duties of two persons who, in regard to each other, stand in the relationship of parent and child; it is the existence of that relationship that enables the plaintiff to apply under s 1(1)(d) of [the I(PFD)A 1975].'

6.56 Who is eligible to apply under section 1(1)(e)?

Children who are not eligible to apply under s 1(1)(c) or (d) may be able to make a claim against the deceased's estate on the basis of dependency.

6.57 The ground for the application

As with the other categories of applicant, apart from a surviving spouse, the ground for making the application as a child under s 1(1)(c), or (d)[161] is that the disposition of the deceased's estate does not make such financial provision as it would be reasonable in all the circumstances of the case for the applicant to receive for his or her maintenance.

The effect of this in relation to claims by infant children is that provision is considered on the basis that it is designed to last until the child's majority, or at the latest until he or she has finished higher education.

Provision for a child's maintenance can include the cost of private education, although in view of the wording of s 3(1) and (3) it is unlikely that a court will view provision to cover the cost of school fees as reasonable if private education would not have been considered in the lifetime of the deceased parent or it would otherwise be inappropriate for the child in question.[162]

In relation to claims by adult children, the applicant's financial circumstances will be of great significance. The definition of 'maintenance' will not extend to payment of capital debts incurred by an adult child[163] nor topping up the pension fund of an adult child who in every other respect, including income, was well provided for.[164]

It will be one of the prerequisites for a successful claim that the applicant is in need of maintenance from the estate, although the existence of that need will not of itself lead to provision being made.[165]

---

[161] Or possibly (e) if very unusual circumstances exist.
[162] *Re W (A Minor) (Claim from Deceased's Estate)* [1995] 2 FLR 24.
[163] *Re Dennis (Deceased)* [1981] 2 All ER 140.
[164] *Re Jennings (Deceased)* [1994] 3 All ER 27.
[165] *Re Coventry* [1979] 3 All ER 815; *Re Dennis (Deceased)* (above).

6.58   Matters to which the court must have regard

The matters to which the court must have regard when making a finding about the provision that has been made are those set out in s 3 of the I(PFD)A 1975. As well as the matters set out in s 3(1)(a)–(g) which are common to all applicants and which are considered at **6.28** above, in the case of applications by children there are additional matters to which the court must have regard.

6.59   Additional matters to which the court must have regard in applications under section 1(1)(c) and section 1(1)(d): Education and training

In the case of a claim by a natural child of the deceased under s 1(1)(c) or a child eligible to apply under s 1(1)(d), the court must also, without prejudice to the generality of s 3(1)(g), have regard to the manner in which the applicant was being or in which he might expect to be educated or trained.

This will only be a matter of relevance to claims by infant children or at least those still undergoing full-time education or training. The fact that there are sufficient funds in the estate to provide for private education will not of itself mean that any order will take such an expense into account. As the wording of the subsection suggests, it will depend upon whether the applicant was in fact receiving private education or could expect to by reason of his family circumstances.[166]

6.60   Additional matters to which the court must have regard in an application under section 1(1)(d): Assumption of responsibility by deceased/liability of another to maintain

In the case of applications by a child under this section, in addition to the matters to be considered under s 3(1) of the I(PFD)A 1975, the court must also have regard to s 3(3),[167] namely:

(a)   to whether the deceased maintained the applicant and, if so, to the length of time for which and basis on which the deceased did so, and to the extent of the contribution made by way of maintenance;

(aa)   to whether and, if so, to what extent the deceased assumed responsibility for the maintenance of the applicant;

(b)   to whether in maintaining or assuming responsibility for maintaining the applicant the deceased did so knowing that the applicant was not his own child;

(c)   to the liability of any other person to maintain the applicant.

These subsections do not qualify or limit the scope of s 1(1)(d).[168] In other words, the matters referred to in s 3(3)(a)–(c) are not preconditions to eligibility under s 1(1)(d).

---

[166] *Re C (Deceased) (Leave to Apply for Provision)* [1995] 2 FLR 24.
[167] As amended by IPTA 2014.
[168] *Re Callaghan* [1985] FLR 116.

6.61 The exercise of the court's discretion

If after considering all the relevant matters in s 3 of the I(PFD)A 1975 the court has found as a fact that the disposition of the deceased's estate failed to make reasonable financial provision for the applicant's maintenance, it will go on to the second stage and decide whether an order should be made.

Even if the court has found the ground for the application made out, it does not follow that a substantive order will be made. It is subject to discretion, which is exercised by looking once again at the matters set out in s 3.

Generally speaking, the court will take a broad view and try to balance the applicant's claim with the interests of the beneficiaries and any other applicants.

6.62 Approach of the court to claims by minor children

Minor children, in particular a natural or adopted child of the deceased, will generally be in a very strong position when making a claim for provision out of the deceased's estate. After all, unless they are fortunate enough to be of independent means, they will look to their parents or the adults with whom they are living for financial support, and morally and in the case of parents as a matter of law,[169] they are under an obligation to provide such support. They clearly fall into the category of individual that the I(PFD)A 1975 is designed to assist, namely those who are placed in a position of dependence by the deceased but are not adequately provided for on his or her death.

The matters to which the court must have regard under s 3(1) and s 3(3) are unlikely to present any difficulty to an applicant who is the natural infant child of the deceased, save that there may be competing claims. For example, the natural child of the deceased's spouse or former spouse may be in competition with the cohabitant and illegitimate child of the deceased. In such a situation, it is likely that the court will also look at the financial situation of each surviving parent, and their relative ability to make provision for the child in their care.[170]

6.63 Approach of the court to claims by adult children

Since the decision of the Court of Appeal in *Re Jennings (Deceased)*,[171] the circumstances in which a claim by an adult child will succeed are likely to be relatively limited. That case endorsed the rationale of Oliver J at first instance in *Re Coventry (Deceased)*.[172] His decision to dismiss the applicant's claim for provision from the estate of his late father was upheld by the Court of Appeal, quoting approvingly from the judgment in the court below:[173]

---

[169] CSA 1991 and CSA 1995.
[170] *Re H (A Minor)* (1976) Fam Law 172.
[171] [1994] 3 All ER 27.
[172] [1979] 3 All ER 815.
[173] At 822A.

'It cannot be enough to say, "Here is a son of the deceased, he is in necessitous circumstances, there is property of the deceased which could be made available to assist him but which is not available if the deceased's dispositions stand; therefore those dispositions do not make reasonable provision for the applicant." There must ... be established some sort of moral claim by the applicant to be maintained by the deceased or at the expense of his estate beyond the mere fact of a blood relationship, some reason why it can be said that, in the circumstances, it is unreasonable that no or no greater provision was made.'

In *Re Jennings (Deceased)* the Court of Appeal overturned Wall J's finding that the deceased father's failure to support his son, the applicant, during his minority, produced a moral obligation that would make a failure to make provision for the applicant on his death unreasonable: 'An Act intended to facilitate the making of reasonable financial provision cannot have been intended to revive defunct obligations and responsibilities as a basis for making it.'[174] 'It is not the purpose of [the I(PFD)A 1975] to punish or redress past bad or unfeeling parental behaviour where that behaviour does not still impinge on the applicant's present financial situation.'[175]

It was affirmed in *Re Jennings (Deceased)* that for an able-bodied adult child of the deceased to succeed in an application for provision from the estate, 'there must be some special circumstance, typically a moral obligation of the deceased towards [the child]'.[176] This is not to import into the statute a moral obligation as a pre-condition to a successful application by an adult child, rather to underline that an adult child who does not demonstrate a financial need for provision is likely to have to show some special circumstance, such as a moral obligation, in order to succeed.

In *Re Abram (Deceased)*[177] the court found a special circumstance leading to the conclusion that the deceased mother's failure to make provision in her will for her adult son who was clearly in need of maintenance was unreasonable. The facts were that the son had for most of his working life worked for his mother in the family business. He had worked for a very low wage on the basis that in due course the business would be his. In the event, he could no longer support his family on the wages he received and he had no alternative but to leave the business. This led to a rift between mother and son and although this was repaired before her death, she never revoked the will that she had made when they were estranged that left her estate elsewhere. Looking at all the circumstances of the case, the court found that the applicant had established a moral claim to provision from the estate.

In *Re Goodchild (Deceased) and Another*,[178] decided at first instance before *Re Abrams*, the Court of Appeal upheld a finding that the applicant's father owed him a moral obligation to ensure that as much of the estate of his late mother

---

[174] Per Nourse LJ at 34G.
[175] Per Henry LJ at 39F.
[176] Per Nourse LJ at 33J.
[177] [1996] 2 FLR 379.
[178] [1997] 2 FLR 644.

would devolve to him on his father's death as it would have done if he had not changed his will in favour of his new wife on his remarriage. This decision was based on the mutual intention of the applicant's parents in the wills they prepared that the survivor of them would succeed to the estate of the first to die and on the death of the survivor the estate would devolve on the applicant.

In *Re Hancock (Deceased)*[179] Butler-Sloss LJ indicated that it may not be necessary in every case for an adult child to show moral obligation or some other special circumstance. In that case, no provision had been made for the deceased's eldest daughter from a relatively modest estate. However, a parcel of land comprised in the estate had realised over six times its probate value and, therefore, there was scope to make provision for her. The court found on the evidence that the deceased was well-disposed towards his daughter and would have made provision for her if his means had allowed, and this was considered to be a matter that could be taken into account under s 3(1)(g). It was held by the House of Lords that, in view of the windfall, the Court of Appeal had been right to uphold the decision of the court at first instance to make provision for the applicant daughter, even though the court had found that it was not unreasonable for no provision to have been made for her.

In *Garland v Morris*,[180] the judge weighed in the balance the factors set out in s 3(1) and concluded that the claimant, one of two daughters of the deceased, had failed to establish that it was unreasonable in all the circumstances for her father to fail to make any provision for her in his will. In that case, following her parents' divorce, the claimant had severed all links with her father and aligned herself with her mother. Her mother committed suicide and left her small estate entirely to the claimant. Her sister remained on good terms with their father and he gave financial assistance to her and her family during his lifetime and left the bulk of his estate to her on his death. The judge found that, although the claimant was in very difficult financial circumstances, her sister was also in genuine need of the benefit that she had received under the will and the claimant had already had the benefit of receiving the mother's estate. It was also relevant that there had been no effort by the claimant to speak to or contact the deceased for the last 15 years of his life, whereas he had enjoyed a close relationship with his other daughter and had helped her out financially. Against this background it was not unreasonable for the father to consider that he had no further obligations towards the claimant.

In *Illot v Mitson*[181] the Court of Appeal overturned the decision of Eleanor King J as she then was by way of cross appeal by the defendant that the claimant had not established that the estate of her deceased mother had failed to make reasonable provision for her. The analysis conducted by Eleanor King J

---

[179] [1998] 2 FLR 346.
[180] [2007] 2 FLR 528.
[181] [2011] EWCA Civ 346.

of Court of Appeal authorities in the course of which she produced a list of the key matters to be borne in mind when deciding an application by an adult child nonetheless remains relevant:[182]

(1)　it is for the claimant to prove his or her case;

(2)　nothing in the 1975 Act undermines the basic proposition that a citizen of England and Wales is at liberty at his death to dispose of his own property in whatever way he pleases;

(3)　section 3 of the Act does not 'rank' the matters to be taken into consideration. The weight of each of the matters specified in the section will depend upon the facts of the particular case. That is not to say that in an individual case one or two factors may not have a magnetic or even decisive influence on the outcome;

(4)　the question is not whether the deceased acted unreasonably but whether, looked at objectively, the lack of disposition produces an unreasonable result; in that it does not make any or any greater provision for the claimant;

(5)　there is no threshold requirement that an adult child claimant has to establish some form of moral obligation or special circumstance;

(6)　necessitous circumstances cannot, in themselves, be a reason to alter the testator's dispositions;

(7)　the ability of the claimant to earn a living is a significant factor;

(8)　an express reason for rejecting an applicant is a relevant consideration.

The claimant's own appeal against quantum was directed to be heard by a different judge of the High Court, and Parker J[183] upheld the award of £50,000 made by the district judge. The total estate was a little under £500,000 and the majority of the balance went to the charities named in the deceased's will.

Both at first instance and on appeal, the decision in *Ilot v Mitson* gives useful guidance on claims by adult children.

In relation to the 'value judgment' by the court as to whether the deceased's will made reasonable financial provision for the claimant, the district judge referred to the following factors that led to a conclusion that it did not:

• the claimant was in financial need;

• the resources and needs of the defendant charities were not relevant;

• the estate whilst not large was nonetheless significant;

• the deceased owed the ordinary family obligations to the claimant, her only child;

• the deceased had acted harshly towards the claimant in rejecting her when she left home at the age of 17 to live with a man whom she then married;

---

[182]　At para [49].
[183]　[2014] EWHC 542 (Fam).

- a child is entitled to make her own life choices and for these to be respected and accepted by a parent.

Having concluded that the deceased's will did not make reasonable financial provision for the claimant, the district judge awarded £50,000 by way of capitalised maintenance. This was not overturned on appeal. Although the claimant lived in straitened circumstances with her husband and five children, relied upon state benefits and had little or no earning capacity, it was relevant to the trial judge's exercise of his discretion under s 3 that the claimant had lived like this for many years and had never had any expectation of receiving a legacy from her mother.

Taken together, the decisions in *Ilott v Mitson* can be said to uphold the principles already enshrined in case-law that a testator is at liberty to dispose of his estate as he sees fit, and an impecunious adult child will not necessarily succeed in his claim.

6.64 Circumstances at the date of the hearing

When the court is considering the matters to which it is required to have regard under s 3 of the I(PFD)A 1975, it will be the circumstances at the date of the hearing that will be relevant, not those at the date of death or at any other time.[184]

In *Re Hancock (Deceased)*[185] a parcel of land comprised in the estate was sold for £663,000 net as against its earlier valuation for probate at £100,000. The appropriate figure for the court to take into account was the later figure.

6.65 Orders that may be made

If the court, after consideration of the matters referred to in s 3 of the I(PFD)A 1975, concludes that reasonable financial provision has not been made for the applicant from the deceased's estate, it will then decide what if any provision should be made, again by reference to the factors in s 3.

The applicant will already have made out a need for maintenance from the estate in order to reach this second stage, and the question will therefore be whether any provision is appropriate in the light of the s 3 factors, and if so what form it should take.

The court has power to make any one or more of the following orders in order to make reasonable financial provision for the maintenance of an applicant.

---

[184] I(PFD)A 1975, s 3(5).
[185] [1998] 2 FLR 346.

6.66   Periodical payments

A periodical payments order will usually be expressed to have commenced at the date of the deceased's death as the provision made by the order is intended to have effect as a substitution for the actual disposition of the deceased's estate. However, if the applicant has delayed excessively in making or pursuing the application, the court may exercise its discretion to order the payments to begin on the date of the application, or even from the date of the order.

If there has been an interim order, this may affect the timing of the final order.

Unless an earlier date is specified, a periodical payments order will terminate on the death of the applicant, or in the case of a spouse or former spouse, on remarriage.

The duration of the order will be intended to reflect the extent of the deceased's obligations towards the applicant. So, for example, periodical payments to a minor child will generally cease when the child attains his or her majority or ceases full-time education or training.

6.67   Lump sum

An order for a lump sum payment out of the net estate will be the order that is most commonly encountered, even where the applicant is limited to receiving provision for his or her maintenance only. The lump sum may represent capitalised periodical payments calculated on the basis of the approach used in *Duxbury v Duxbury*.[186] Alternatively, a lump sum may be provided to enable the applicant to be rehoused during his or her lifetime, or to pay for such other expenditure that the court deems appropriate for the applicant's maintenance. In *Re Besterman (Deceased)*[187] a capital sum was awarded to provide a 'financial cushion'.

There is no power to vary a lump sum order except as to the terms of a lump sum payable by instalments, and it has been held that the court therefore must take into account the effects of inflation and other variables when considering the appropriate amount of a lump sum order.

Transfer of property

6.68   Settlement of property

The provision of a home for the lifetime of the applicant will be regarded as a legitimate maintenance requirement. This may be achieved either by the outright transfer of property or as part of a settlement. If there is no property or

---

[186] [1987] 1 FLR 7.
[187] [1984] 2 All ER 656.

no property that is suitable already comprised in the net estate, s 2(1)(f) of the I(PFD)A 1975 allows property to be acquired for the purpose out of the net estate.

6.69 *Variation of settlement*

Children of a marriage or children treated as a child of the family in relation to any marriage or civil partnership (or a surviving spouse or civil partner) may benefit from an order varying a settlement made by the deceased.

6.70 The order

A copy of every order made on an application under s 2 of the I(PFD)A 1975 must be sent to the Principal Registry of the Family Division for filing, and a memorandum of the order should be endorsed on the grant of representation of the estate.

6.71 Variation of orders

An order for periodical payments under s 2(1)(a) of the I(PFD)A 1975 can be varied on application by the applicant who has the benefit of the order, or by the personal representatives of the deceased, any beneficiary of the estate, or any other person who did or could have applied for an order under s 2.

The court has power to vary the order upwards or downwards, temporarily suspend any part of it, discharge the order, or make a lump sum or transfer of property order instead.

In exercising its powers of variation, the court must have regard to all the circumstances of the case, including any change in the factors to which the court had regard under s 3 when making the original order.[188]

A lump sum order can be varied only if it was ordered to be paid by instalments, and the variation can only be as to the terms of the instalment payments, whether the amount, or the time for payment.[189]

6.72 Transactions and dispositions intended to defeat claims under Inheritance (Provision for Family and Dependants) Act 1975, s 2

When an application is made for provision under I(PFD)A 1975, s 2, the court has power to set aside transactions or dispositions made less than six years before the deceased's death if they were made other than for full valuable consideration and with the intention of defeating an applicant's claim for provision, if to do so would facilitate the making of financial provision for the applicant.

---

[188] I(PFD)A 1975, s 6(7).
[189] I(PFD)A 1975, s 7.

Section 12 provides that when deciding whether or not the deceased intended to defeat the operation of the I(PFD)A 1975, either by making it impossible to make an order or by reducing the amount of any order, the court has to be satisfied on a balance of probabilities that this was the intention, although it need not have been the sole intention.

Section 10(6) provides that when deciding whether and if so how to exercise its powers to set aside transactions and dispositions, the court must have regard to the circumstances in which the disposition was made, any consideration that was given for it, the relationship between the deceased and the donee, the financial resources of the donee and all the circumstances of the case.

A disposition for the purposes of s 10 will not include any *donatio mortis causa*.

6.73   Procedure

An application to set aside a transaction or disposition will be made in the application for an order under s 2, the applicant setting out as much information about the matter as possible.

Interlocutory applications

6.74   Striking out a claim as disclosing no reasonable cause of action

Many of the reported cases concern applications made at the interlocutory stage to strike out a claim as disclosing no reasonable cause of action.

The making of such applications as a purely tactical measure should be avoided because of the cost, but there will be occasions when it is entirely appropriate to make an application, which if successful will almost certainly result in a saving of costs to the estate.

Where an application is made under either s 1(1)(ba) or (e) there may be scope for arguing that the applicant does not satisfy the eligibility criteria.

An application by an adult child under s 1(1)(c) or (d) may be struck out if it is clear that the applicant has no need for provision out of the estate for his or her maintenance.

6.75   Procedure

As soon as possible after the claim has been issued, any respondent wishing to make application to strike out the claim should issue an application notice and file and serve a witness statement or affidavit in support. On issue, the application should be listed for a short appointment before the district judge when directions can be given as to the filing of further evidence and listing for the hearing of the application.

6.76   Interim orders

The court has power to make an order for interim provision from the deceased's net estate for an applicant for an order under s 2 of the I(PFD)A 1975. The criteria to be satisfied are that the applicant is in immediate need of financial assistance and there are funds available from the net estate to meet that need.

Although interim orders have of necessity to be made before the court has decided the merits of the application, the court is required to have regard to the factors set out in s 3, 'so far as the urgency of the case admits' before making an order.

There is scope for a payment or payments of capital and/or income to be made on an interim basis, and these can be expressed to be on account of any sums received when the application under s 2 is finally determined. Any sum or sums awarded on an interim basis must be 'reasonable'.

There is no explicit provision for the court to order repayment of sums paid on account if no substantive order is made at the end of the day, but this could be imposed as one of the conditions or restrictions that the court may include in any interim order.

6.77   *Procedure*

An applicant who is in immediate need of financial assistance by way of an interim order should make an application as soon as possible after the issue of the application for an order under s 2. The application should be supported by a witness statement or affidavit setting out details of the applicant's financial position so as to illustrate the urgency of the need for financial assistance. Details of the deceased's estate should be provided so far as they are known to the applicant. Insofar as it is not apparent from the claim form, the applicant should deal with the merits of the substantive claim as an interim order is unlikely if there is any prospect that the claim under s 2 may fail.

The application will be listed for a short appointment before the district judge so that directions can be given as to filing of evidence by the respondents, and the matter listed for hearing with an appropriate time estimate.

Respondents wishing to defend an application for an interim order will need to address the merits of the substantive claim and, if appropriate, challenge the financial grounds for the application. The court will expect the respondents to give as much detail as possible of the size and nature of the net estate, and how much of it, if any, would be available to meet any interim order that was made.

6.78   Preservation of property

As the court has power under the I(PFD)A 1975 to make orders relating to specific property comprised in the estate,[190] it is possible for orders to be made under the court's inherent jurisdiction to safeguard such property pending the final determination of an application under s 2.

6.79   *Procedure*

An application for an injunction will be made in the usual way, accompanied by a witness statement or affidavit setting out the background, the grounds for the application and the relief sought. Except in very exceptional cases, the application should be on notice in the first instance. If the matter cannot be resolved on the return date, directions will be given for evidence to be filed by the respondent to the application and a date fixed for the resumed hearing.

6.80   Costs

As is generally the case, the costs of an application will be at the discretion of the court.

Whilst there is no reason why costs should not follow the event, it is not unusual in cases in which the applicant has been unsuccessful for an order to be made for each side to bear its own costs. Indeed, it was the practice for an order for costs against an unsuccessful applicant to be made in only exceptional cases.[191]

In *Re Fullard (Deceased)*[192] a former wife unsuccessfully applied for provision from the estate of her deceased former husband. Ormrod LJ enjoined judges to 'reconsider the practice of ordering the costs of both sides to be paid out of the estate',[193] but upheld the decision of the court below to dismiss her claim with her costs to be paid out of the estate.

In *Graham v Murphy and Another*[194] a *Calderbank* offer was made on behalf of the estate that came very close to the order that was made. In order to do justice between the parties, the judge made an order for the estate to pay one-third of the successful applicant's costs on the standard basis, as well as the costs of the estate's administrators, on an indemnity basis.

---

[190] See s 2(1)(c) and (d).
[191] See **6.31** above.
[192] [1981] 2 All ER 796.
[193] At 799C.
[194] [1997] 1 FLR 860.

6.81 Tax implications of orders under the Inheritance (Provision for Family and Dependants) Act 1975

Orders for provision made by the court have the same effect as if the provision had been made direct to the applicant by will or on intestacy, that is, they are treated as operating from death.[195]

As between cohabitants, and parents and children there are no inheritance tax exemptions that will apply to gifts on death.

Claims by dependants following fatal accidents

6.82 Fatal Accidents Act 1976

If death has been caused by the tortious act of a third party, such that if the deceased had lived there would have been a right of action against the tortfeasor, the tortfeasor can be liable at the suit of a dependant of the deceased.

The category of dependants includes spouses, civil partners and former spouses or civil partners of the deceased, parents and other ascendants, children (whether natural or merely treated as the deceased's children) and children of the family of any marriage, siblings, aunts, uncles and cousins of the deceased.

In addition, any person who was living with the deceased as husband and wife in the same household immediately before, and for at least two years before the death,[196] may apply. It has been held that brief interruptions in the period of two years will not be fatal to a claim.[197]

In relation to the question of eligibility there is no requirement to prove dependency as such, but unless the applicant can show a loss as a result of the deceased's death there can be no claim.

When the court is assessing the dependency claim of a cohabitant, it is required by the FAA 1976 to take into account '… (together with any other matter that appears to the court to be relevant to the action) the fact that the dependant [cohabitant] had no enforceable right to financial support by the deceased as a result of their living together'.[198] In other words, the court must be aware that the relationship of dependency could have been brought to an end by either party without obligation, unlike a married relationship.

It will be appropriate for the court to hear evidence about the nature and duration of the relationship in order that it may assess its stability, and apply the appropriate multiplier.

---

[195] I(PFD)A) 1975, s 19(1).
[196] *Kotke v Saffarrini* [2005] 2 FLR 517.
[197] *Pounder v London Underground* [1995] PIQR 217.
[198] FAA 1976, s 3(4).

This situation could be affected by the provisions of any cohabitation agreement.[199]

The fact that a cohabitant may not be eligible to make a claim for damages under the FAA 1976 may not necessarily mean that his or her dependency is not taken into account. In *K v JMP Co Ltd*[200] a claim was made by the children of the deceased. They had been living with him immediately before his death, together with their mother, the deceased's cohabitant. The court took into account expenses of the cohabitant that had been paid by the deceased when assessing the multiplicand. This increased the value of the claim and indirectly benefitted the cohabitant.

6.83   Law Reform (Miscellaneous Provisions) Act 1934

Damages can be claimed for the benefit of the estate of the deceased in respect of pain and suffering between the date of the tortious act and the death. However, there can be no claim for loss of earnings beyond the date of death.[201]

A cohabitant who is entitled to share in the estate on death or following a claim under the I(PFD)A 1975 clearly will benefit if the estate is enlarged by an award of damages.

6.84   Criminal Injuries Compensation Scheme

In fatal cases, dependants or relatives of someone who died as a result of a criminal injury, or someone who was criminally injured but died from some other cause, are eligible to apply for compensation.

6.85   Who may apply?

The categories of applicant include a person who at the time of the deceased's death had been living together as husband or wife or as same-sex partner in the same household as the deceased and for the two years immediately leading up to the death. An exception is made if for reasons of infirmity or ill health physical proximity in the same house is not possible.

6.86   Time-limit for application

A claim must be submitted to the Criminal Injuries Compensation Authority within two years of the date of death.

---

[199] See generally Chapter 2.
[200] [1975] 1 All ER 1030.
[201] LR(MP)A 1934, s 1(2)(a)(ii).

6.87   Procedure

Application should be made in Form TS14, which can be obtained by request from the Criminal Injuries Compensation Authority or online.[202] Details of the Criminal Injuries Compensation Scheme (Form TS1) and a Guide to the Criminal Injuries Compensation Scheme set out the procedure for application and assessment.

Where death has occurred as a result of a criminal injury, the Criminal Injuries Compensation Authority will assess eligibility for compensation in the form of a fatal injury award and/or a dependants award and/or an award for loss of parental services.

An application may be made notwithstanding that an award was made to the victim before death.

If death follows but is not the result of a criminal injury, an award of supplementary compensation may be made to an applicant who was financially dependent upon the deceased. This is intended to cover loss of earnings, expenses and liabilities incurred by the victim as a result of the crime of violence.

SECTION 3   ILLNESS OR INCAPACITY OF A COHABITANT

6.88   Introduction

When one cohabitant falls ill, or is diagnosed as having a terminal illness, there may be uncertainty as to the status of the other cohabitant when it comes to consent to medical treatment, especially if there are family members who have differing views as to how the patient should be treated and cared for. On admission to hospital, a patient will be asked to give the name of his or her 'next of kin', or contact in the event of an emergency.

A little thought and forward planning can help to minimise any tension between relatives and cohabitants when these situations arise.

The questions of consent to medical treatment and who should be allowed to have information and be consulted about the patient are matters for the patient himself. However, necessity may justify medical intervention without consent. If a patient is unable to give consent, then in the absence of an advance decision, it will be a matter for the clinical judgment of the medical team, subject to the jurisdiction of the High Court to make a declaration that the proposed treatment is in the best interests of the patient.[203]

---

[202]   Tay House, 300 Bath Street, Glasgow G2 4JZ, tel: 0141 331 2726, fax: 0141 331 2287.
[203]   *Re F (Sterilisation: Mental Patient)* [1989] 2 FLR 376.

As a matter of law, therefore, a cohabitant is in no different position than a civil partner, spouse or relative, when it comes to consultation and decision-making about a patient. However, from a practical point of view, the hospital staff will generally limit the people involved to close family, unless they are aware of any request from the patient to consult, for example, a cohabitant.

6.89   Advance decisions or 'living wills'

Advance decisions to refuse medical treatment were given legal effect for the first time by the MCA 2005.[204] An advance decision, more commonly referred to as a living will, is a means by which a person of full capacity may specify that if in the future he should lack the capacity to make a decision about medical treatment, the advance decision is to be acted upon by the relevant health care professionals. Such documents often include wishes regarding the refusal of life-sustaining treatment in situations where the person is in a coma or has very little quality of life. Advance decisions are likely to be considered if a person is diagnosed as suffering from a terminal illness, or is to undergo a course of medical treatment.

Those in cohabitation relationships, in particular, may wish to make provision in this way, especially if there is scope for differences of opinion between the relatives of the patient and the other cohabitant.

6.90   *The content of an advance decision*

An advance decision may only relate to the refusal of specified treatment. It cannot require particular treatment or care to be given.

Except where the advance decision relates to life-sustaining treatment, there is no prescribed form of words, and it may even be an oral statement.

In the case of an advance decision that relates to life-sustaining treatment the following formalities must be observed. It must
–   be in writing;
–   be signed by the person making it, or by another person in his presence and at his direction;
–   be witnessed;
–   set out that it is to apply to the specified treatment even if life is at risk.

Euthanasia is outside the scope of advance decisions.

6.91   *The legal status of an advance decision*

To be effective, an advance decision must be both valid, and applicable.

---

[204]   MCA 2005, ss 24–26.

If both valid and applicable, an advance decision has the same effect as if the maker of it had capacity to make that decision at the time the question of refusing medical treatment arises.

If there is any doubt about the existence, validity or applicability of an advance decision application may be made to the Court of Protection for a declaration.

6.92   *Validity of an advance decision*

An advance decision will not be valid in the following circumstances:
- the person who made the advance decision has withdrawn it at a time when he had the capacity to do so;
- the advance decision has been overtaken by a lasting power of attorney that gives the donee the power to give or refuse consent to the specified treatment;
- the person who made the advance decision has acted in way that is clearly inconsistent with the advance decision remaining his fixed position.

6.93   *Applicability of an advance decision*

For an advance decision to be applicable the following must apply:
- the person who made the advance decision must lack capacity at the time it is sought to act upon it;
- the treatment specified in the advance decision must be that which it is proposed to carry out;
- any circumstances specified in the advance decision must be present.

In addition, if there are reasonable grounds for believing that circumstances exist that were not anticipated at the time the advance decision was made and that would have affected the decision had they been anticipated, the advance decision will not be applicable.

6.94   Lasting Powers of Attorney (LPAs)

There are two types of Lasting Power of Attorney. One is for Health and Welfare and the other is for Property and Financial Affairs.

Cohabitees can grant each other Lasting Powers of Attorney for Health and Welfare as an alternative to an advance decision as the document enables the attorney to make decisions relating to the health and welfare of the donor. This type of LPA can specifically give power to the attorney to give or refuse consent to life-sustaining treatment. The documents can cover any decision about healthcare and medical treatment as well as day to day decisions about personal welfare.

The second type is a Lasting Power of Attorney for Property and Financial Affairs. Such Lasting Powers of Attorney replaced Enduring Powers of Attorney from 1 October 2007.

Both types of LPA have to be registered with the Office of the Public Guardian before they can be used. For more information on LPAs and procedures see *Elderly Clients – A Precedent Manual* (Jordan Publishing 2013).

PART B   PROCEDURAL GUIDE

Claim for Financial Provision under the Inheritance (Provision for Family and Dependants) Act 1975

6.95   *Legal background*

A claim may be made against the estate of a deceased person by certain members of the deceased's family and dependants categorised in the I(PFD)A 1975, s 1 (as amended by the Law Reform (Succession) Act 1995) and CPA 2004 (CPA 2005) for financial provision out of the net estate of the deceased, on the ground that the disposition of the deceased's estate effected by his will and/or under the laws of intestacy is not such as to make reasonable financial provision for the applicant. Unless the court gives permission extending the time limit, the application must be made within six months of the date on which representation is first granted (s 4) although nothing prevents the application being made before the grant is taken out.

The procedure for both the High Court and County Court is governed by CPR 1998, Pt 57. See also CPR PD57 and CPR PD8A. Before issuing proceedings practitioners must comply with the CPR Protocol. Non-compliance could result in the court making an order for costs against the non-complying party (CPR 1998, r 44.3).

6.96   *Procedure*

Who may apply	The spouse of the deceased	I(PFD)A 1975, s 1(*a*)
	The registered civil partner of the deceased	I(PFD)A 1975, s 1(*a*); CPA 2004, s 71, Sch 4
	The former spouse of the deceased who has not remarried	I(PFD)A 1975, s 1(*b*)
	The former civil partner of the deceased who has not formed a subsequent civil partnership	I(PFD)A 1975, s 1(*b*); CPA 2004, s 71, Sch 4
	A cohabitant of the deceased	I(PFD)A 1975, s 1(*ba*), s 1A as amended by the Law Reform (Succession) Act 1995

	A person who lived in the same household as the deceased as his/her civil partner	I(PFD)A 1975, s 1(*ba*), s 1B; CPA 2004, s 71, Sch 4
	A child of the deceased	I(PFD)A 1975, s 1(*c*)
	Any person who was treated as a child of the family by the deceased	I(PFD)A 1975, s 1(*d*)
	Any other person who immediately before the death of the deceased was being maintained by him	I(PFD)A 1975, s 1(e); CPA 2004
Which court	High Court (Chancery or Family Division) or county court	CPR 1998, r 57.15; CCA 1984, s 25
	District judges (including district judges of the Principal Registry of the Family Division) have jurisdiction to hear such applications	CPR 1998, r 57.15; I(PFD)A 1975, s 22
Application	*High Court/county court* By Pt 8 claim form which should be entitled 'In the estate of … deceased' and 'In the matter of I(PFD)A 1975'	CPR 1998, rr 57.16, 8.2
Time limit	The claim must be issued either before or within 6 months of the date on which representation is taken out (unless extended by the court). Application to extend the time limit must be included in the claim form	I(PFD)A 1975, s 4
Documents	The applicant must file with the claim form a witness statement/affidavit in support exhibiting an official copy of the grant of representation and of every testamentary document admitted to proof	CPR 1998, rr 57.16(3), 8.5(1), (2)

Defendants	Personal representatives Beneficiaries Other persons affected by the claim Any other person directed by the court to be added	CPR 1998, r 19.7
Service	The claim form must be served within 4 months after date of issue	
	Extension of time must be sought under CPR 1998, r 7.6	
	Acknowledgement of service must be filed within 21 days after service of the claim form and served on the claimant and other parties if served within the jurisdiction If served outside the jurisdiction extended period is permitted by CPR 1998, r 57.16(4A)	CPR 1998, rr 57.16(4), 6.19, 6.22, 8.3(1), 10.3(1)
	For service on children and patients see CPR 1998, r 6.6	
	otherwise, in accordance with CPR 1998, r 10.3(2)	CPR 1998, r 10.3(2)
Statement/ Affidavit in answer	Must be filed by the personal representatives within 21 days after service of the claim form (it should include the matters set out in CPR PD57, para 16)	CPR 1998, r 57.16(4),(5); PD57, para 16
	May be filed by other defendants within 21 days after service of the claim form	CPR 1998, r 57.16(4)
Service of answer	Every defendant who files any written evidence within 21 days in answer must serve a copy on the claimant and every other defendant who is not represented by the same solicitor	CPR 1998, r 57.16(4)

Reply	A claimant may serve a statement in reply on all other parties within 14 days of service of the defendant's evidence on him	CPR 1998, r 8.5(5), (6)
Directions/case management conference pre-trial hearing	At the same time as issuing the claim form a directions hearing may be requested	CPR PD8A, para 4.1
	The court will in any event give directions after the defendant has filed the acknowledgement of service or after the time for filing it has expired. Parties must complete the listing questionnaire in Form N170 and provide an estimate of costs, following which the court will consider whether to hold a pre-trial review, set a timetable and fix the date for the trial	CPR PD8A, para 4.2 CPR 1998, rr 29.6–29.8
Fee	High Court: £480	CPFO 2008, fee 1.5
	County court: £280	CPFO 2008, fee 1.5
Order	Periodical payments	I(PFD)A 1975, s 2(1)(*a*)
	Lump sum	I(PFD)A 1975, s 2(1)(*b*)
	Transfer of property	I(PFD)A 1975, s 2(1)(*c*)
	Settlement of property	I(PFD)A 1975, s 2(1)(*d*)
	Acquisition, transfer and settlement of property	I(PFD)A 1975, s 2(1)(*e*)
	Variation of ante-nuptial and post-nuptial settlement	I(PFD)A 1975, s 2(1)(*f*)
	Variation of trusts of the estate	
	Variation or discharge of secured periodical payments	I(PFD)A 1975, s 16

Variation or revocation of maintenance agreements	I(PFD)A 1975, s 17
Order setting aside disposition intended to defeat a claim under the Act	I(PFD)A 1975, ss 10, 11
Treatment of deceased's former beneficial interest in joint property as part of his estate and not passing by survivorship	I(PFD)A 1975, s 9
Interim order	I(PFD)A 1975, s 5
Consequential orders	I(PFD)A 1975, s 2(4)

PART C CHECKLISTS

6.97 Checklist for first instructions on making a claim under the Inheritance (Provision for Family and Dependants) Act 1975

- Deceased habitually resident in England and Wales?
- Full name of deceased.
- Address at date of death.
- Date and place of death.
- In the event of an application by a cohabitant under s 1(1)(ba), was the date of death after January 1996?
- Is there a valid will?
- If so, who are the executors and beneficiaries?
- What provision, if any, has been made for the surviving cohabitant?
- If no provision has been made, did the deceased make any promises to make provision after his death?
- If there is no valid will, who will benefit under the statutory trusts?
- Has a Grant of Representation been taken out, and if so, by whom?
- Date of the issue of the Grant.
- If more than six months has elapsed since the date of the Grant, why were steps not taken to issue an application before the expiry of the six months?
- Date cohabitation with deceased commenced.
- Was the period of cohabitation unbroken – if not, dates and reasons for break in cohabitation.
- Was cohabitation continuing right up to the date of death (subject to deceased ending life in hospital/hospice)?
- Does the cohabitation exceed two years?
- Does surviving cohabitant remain living in the shared home?
- Details of acquisition and ownership of the shared home.
- Details of assets and liabilities of deceased, ie the likely value of the estate.
- Details of any joint assets/liabilities.
- Details of any nominations in respect of insurance policies/pensions.
- Details of deceased's pension arrangements.
- Details of financial circumstances of surviving cohabitant.
- If cohabitation less than two years immediately preceding the date of death, can dependency be established? In particular, did the deceased provide a home and/or financial support, and what did the surviving cohabitant give in return? Full details required.
- What other financial obligations and responsibilities did the deceased have?
- Are there likely to be conflicting claims?

PART D   PRECEDENTS

Section 1   Non-contentious precedents

Clauses

6.98   Combined commencement and revocation clause[205]

I (*name*)[206] of (*address*) DECLARE that this is my Will[207] and that it revokes[208] my earlier Wills.

6.99   Commencement including date: separate revocation clause[209]

THIS WILL is made on (*date*)[210] by me (*name*)[211] of (*address*).

I REVOKE my earlier Wills.[212]

6.100   Will in expectation of marriage[213]

THIS WILL will not be revoked by my expected marriage to (*cohabitant*).

6.101   Will in expectation of marriage: some provisions applying before marriage and others on marriage[214]

(1)   THIS WILL will not be revoked by my expected marriage to (*cohabitant*).

(2)   PART I[215] of this Will applies at all times.

(3)   PART II will apply until my expected marriage is solemnised.

(4)   PART III will apply when my expected marriage has been solemnised.

---

[205] For separate commencement and revocation clauses, see **6.99** below.

[206] The testator's full and correct forenames and surname should be stated. If any assets are registered in another name, it may be sensible to add after the full and correct name '(also known as   )'. This would facilitate the inclusion of the other name in the grant of representation. See, generally, Non-Contentious Probate Rules 1987 (SI 1987/2024), r 9.

[207] The words 'last will', which are often used, are probably of no significance.

[208] It is usual practice to revoke all earlier wills, even when it is clear that there are none to revoke.

[209] For a combined commencement and revocation clause, see **6.98** above.

[210] If the date is not included in the commencement it is usually stated in the testimonium at the end of the will.

[211] See footnote 2 at **6.98** above.

[212] See footnote 4 at **6.98** above.

[213] Except in certain cases, a will is revoked by the testator's marriage or civil partnership (Wills Act 1837, s 18(1), as amended). Section 18(3) states that 'where it appears from a will that at the time it was made the testator was expecting to be married to a particular person and that he intended that the will should not be revoked by the marriage, the will shall not be revoked by his marriage to that person'. Until s 18 was substituted by the Administration of Justice Act 1982, such wills were known as 'wills in contemplation of marriage', by virtue of the wording of LPA 1925, s 177.

[214] For wills made in expectation of marriage, see footnote 1 to **6.100** above.

[215] Division into 'parts' may be considered preferable to division into 'schedules' as it enables each clause of the will to continue in numerical order (*cf* MCA 1973, etc).

PART I

(Insert the provisions which will apply regardless of whether or not the marriage has been solemnised, for example funeral wishes, specific bequests, trustee powers, etc.)

PART II

(Insert provisions which apply immediately.)

PART III

(Insert the provisions which will apply on the solemnisation of the expected marriage.)

6.102 Declaration of mutuality[216]

I HAVE AGREED with (*cohabitant*) that if I survive (him)/(her) I will not revoke or change this Will.

6.103 Declaration of non-mutuality[217]

ALTHOUGH (*cohabitant*) and I are making Wills in similar terms they are not 'Mutual Wills' and each of us can alter or revoke his or her Will at any time.

---

[216] **Warning.** A 'mutual will' is made when testators contractually agree that neither of them will revoke or alter his will. If, after the first death, the survivor revokes the mutual will, equity will enforce the original agreement by imposing a constructive trust on the survivor's death. The disadvantages of a mutual will are: (a) the will is revoked on marriage; (b) it is very difficult to identify the assets which are subject to the constructive trust; and (c) the agreement can be frustrated by lifetime alienation or dissipation of the assets. The advantages of a mutual will are that the survivor's ability to renege on the agreement is curtailed, and the survivor is free to enjoy the assets without being subject to a trust. Mutual wills can cause many practical difficulties and should be used with caution. A mutual will, made by an unmarried person, may be contrary to public policy because it acts in restraint of marriage (*Robinson v Ommanney* (1883) 23 Ch D 285, CA).

See, generally, *Williams on Wills* (Lexis Nexis Butterworths, 8th edn, 2008); A J Oakley *Constructive Trusts* (Sweet & Maxwell, 3rd edn, 1996); Law Reform Committee's 22nd Report (1980), 'The making and revocation of wills', at paras 3.50–3.52; and the articles by Professor C E F Rickett 'Mutual Wills and the Law of Restitution' (1989) 105 LQR 534, and 'Extending Equity's Reach through the Mutual Wills Doctrine' (1991) MLR 581. See also *Cleaver (Deceased)* [1981] 1 WLR 939; *Re Goodchild* [1997] 1 WLR 1216.

[217] See footnotes to **6.102** above. It is important to distinguish between 'mutual wills' in the lay sense and 'mutual wills' in the legal sense.

Survivorship clause[218]

6.104   General applicability

ANYONE who does not survive me by (14) days[219] will be treated as having died before me for all the purposes of this Will.

6.105   Specific to cohabitant[220]

IF (*cohabitant*) does not survive me by (14) days (he)/(she) will be treated as having died before me for all the purposes of this Will.

6.106   *Funeral wishes*[221]

If possible and practicable I would like:

– any part of my body which may be of use to others to be made available for treatment or transplantation;[222]

– my (kidneys)/(corneas)/(heart)/(lungs)/(liver)/(pancreas) to be used for transplantation;[223]

– (*name of firm*) to be my funeral directors;

– an obituary notice to be inserted in (*name of newspaper, journal, etc*);

– my funeral service to be conducted in accordance with the (rites)/(usages) of (*name of faith or denomination*);

---

[218] The Law Reform (Succession) Act 1995 inserted a 28-day survivorship clause between husband and wife on intestacy.

The object of a survivorship clause is to stop the assets of both partners passing to the parents or relatives of the second to die in cases of not quite simultaneous death, usually in accidents. See also the statutory presumption that where uncertainty exists as to the order in which two or more persons have died, 'the younger shall be deemed to have survived the elder' (LPA 1925, s 184). There may also be inheritance tax advantages in including a survivorship clause in a will (Inheritance Tax Act 1984, s 92).

[219] Law Com No 187, para 57 states: 'We consider that an appropriate length for such a survivorship clause is 14 days. Any longer might lead to unacceptable delays in the administration of estates'.

[220] See footnotes at **6.104** above.

[221] A binding disposition of the body of the deceased cannot be made by will so as to oust the executors' rights and duties as to its disposal. Many precedent books suggest that it is unnecessary or even undesirable to incorporate funeral wishes in a will. The main arguments for *excluding* such wishes include:

(a) the will might not be found until it is too late;

(b) the wishes are generally not binding; and

(c) it adds to the cost of preparing the will, or having to prepare another will or codicil if the testator changes his mind about any of these wishes.

Reasons for *including* funeral wishes in a will include:

(a) they require the testator to make his wishes known;

(b) others are relieved of the duty of making such decisions;

(c) there is less likelihood of conflict between executors, relatives, beneficiaries, etc;

(d) such wishes are usually honoured and rarely changed; and

(e) expenditure can be formally authorised.

[222] This sub-clause is based on the wording of the standard 'Donor Card'.

[223] This sub-clause is based on the wording of the standard 'Donor Card'.

– my funeral service to be held at (*location*);

– there to be no religious formalities at my funeral;

– (*hymns, songs, tunes, music, etc*) to be played or sung at my funeral;

– (scriptural, poetry or other readings) to be read at my funeral;

– family flowers only;

– donations, if desired, to be made to (*Charity*);

– to be cremated;

– my ashes to be scattered (in the grounds of the Crematorium [*OR*] (*wherever*);

– my ashes to be interred in (*location*);

– to be buried;

– to be buried in (*location*) [*OR*] (wherever is most convenient)/(at sea);[224]

– a headstone to be placed on my grave;

– (*cohabitant*) to decide what wording should be inscribed on the headstone;

– refreshments to be provided for those attending my funeral;

– my funeral arrangements to be as simple (and inexpensive) as possible;

– (*cohabitant*) to decide on any other funeral arrangements;

– the expenses incurred in carrying out these wishes (and *cohabitant's* wishes) to be paid out of my estate.

6.107   *Appointment of cohabitant as executor*[225]

I APPOINT (*cohabitant*) of (*address*) to be the Executor of this Will but if (he)/(she) dies before me or is unwilling or unable to act as Executor I APPOINT (*name*) of (*address*) (and (*name*) of (*address*)) to be the Executor(s) (and Trustees)[226] of this Will instead.

6.108   *Appointment of cohabitant as sole executor and universal beneficiary*[227]

IF (he)/(she) survives me by (14) days[228] I GIVE all of my estate[229] to (*cohabitant*) of (*address*) AND APPOINT (him)/(her) to be my Executor[230] but if (he)/(she) fails to survive me by (14) days the following clauses will apply.[231]

---

[224] Those with an appetite for black comedy might enjoy the Scottish case *Herron v Diack and Newlands* 1973 SLT (Sh Ct) 27 which involved an unsuccessful burial at sea.

[225] If the cohabitant is also the universal beneficiary use **6.108** instead.

[226] It is only necessary to appoint trustees where there is or could be an ongoing trust.

[227] The sole executor and universal beneficiary must be an adult.

[228] A survivorship clause is not essential but advisable.

[229] For the meaning of 'estate' see, generally, *Williams on Wills* (Lexis Nexis Butterworths, 8th edn 2008).

[230] As the sole executor and universal beneficiary has all the powers needed to administer the estate, no further powers or provisions are necessary. There is no continuing trust, so there is no need to appoint the executor as a trustee.

[231] It is virtually essential to include substitutionary gifts, appointments and provisions.

6.109 *Appointment of executors and trustees including a professional charging clause*[232]

1   I APPOINT (*name*) of (*address*) and (*name*) of (*address*)[233] to be the Executors and Trustees of this Will.

2   In this Will 'my trustees' means my personal representatives and the persons who at any time are the trustees of any trusts created by this Will.

3   A professionally qualified trustee can charge and be paid in priority to the gifts in this Will for all the work done by him or his firm in obtaining probate, administering my estate, and acting as a trustee, even though some of the work could have been done by a person who is not professionally qualified.[234]

6.110 *Appointment of guardians*[235]

I APPOINT (*name*) of (*address*) (and (*name*) of (*address*))[236] to be the Guardian(s) of my children under eighteen.[237]

6.111 *Appointment of guardian and substitute guardian*[238]

I APPOINT (*name*) of (*address*) to be the Guardian of my children under eighteen but if this appointment fails for any reason[239] I APPOINT (*name*) of (*address*) to be the Guardian instead.

---

[232] It seems logical to include a professional charging clause (where appropriate) in the appointment itself. This generally happens where trust corporations are appointed. Despite the Trustee Act 2000, it is still desirable to include such a clause.

[233] The maximum number that can be appointed is four (Trustee Act 1925, s 34; Supreme Court Act 1981, s 114(1)).

[234] Trustee Act 2000, s 28 now allows a trustee who is a trust corporation or is acting in a professional capacity to receive payment in respect of services, even if they are services which are capable of being provided by a lay trustee. This applies except where excluded by the trust instrument. Section 28(4) provides that any payment is to be treated as remuneration for services for the purposes of s 15 of the Wills Act 1837, so a professional trustee who witnesses the will no longer forfeits the right to payment for services, which was previously treated as a general legacy.

[235] A guardian can only be appointed in accordance with the provisions of s 5 of the CA 1989 (s 5(13)). See, generally, 'Appointment of a Guardian' at **5.25** above.

[236] More than one person may have parental responsibility for the same child at the same time (CA 1989, s 2(5)).

[237] Unless it is brought to an end earlier, the appointment of a guardian continues until the child reaches the age of 18 (CA 1989, s 91(8)).

[238] A guardian can only be appointed in accordance with the provisions of CA 1989, s 5(13). See, generally, 'Appointment of a Guardian' at **5.25** above.

[239] For example, the guardian could predecease the testator; the guardian could die before the child reaches 18; the guardian could disclaim; or the appointment could be brought to an end by order of the court. See, generally, CA 1989, s 6(5), (6) and (7).

Guardianship

6.112   Statement of wishes concerning children under 18[240]

IT IS MY WISH that, as far as circumstances and finances permit, my children will be:

–   kept together;

–   allowed to retain their present surname(s);[241]

–   encouraged to keep in contact with their (grandparents, uncles, aunts, cousins, godparents, etc as the case may be);[242]

–   brought up in the (Christian) faith;[243]

–   educated at (a single sex)/(an independent) school;

–   (other wishes, as appropriate).

6.113   Trustees' power to lend capital to guardians[244]

MY TRUSTEES can at any time raise capital from my residuary estate and lend it to the Guardian(s) of any child of mine:

–   on such terms and conditions (including repayment, interest, and security) as they consider appropriate in the circumstances;

–   even if they exhaust my residuary estate in the process;

–   even if one of the Guardians is also a trustee of this Will;

–   without being liable for any loss incurred;

–   but only if they consider that doing so would be better for the child than not doing so.

6.114   Absolute gift of (a share of) a house

(1)   I GIVE to (*cohabitant*) my (*share of the*) property known as (*address*) or failing which the property that is my principal residence at the time of my death ('the property').[245]

---

[240]   The wishes of the parent are only permitted to prevail if they are not inconsistent with other considerations relating to the child's welfare (*Ward v Laverty* [1925] AC 101). See also CA 1989, s 1.

[241]   See, generally, Nasreen Pearce *Change of Name – The Law & Practice*, Caliph Publishing.

[242]   For 'contact orders', see CA 1989, s 8(1).

[243]   'In accordance with the *Gillick* principle, the parent's wishes over religious upbringing yield to the child's right to make his own decision once he has reached sufficient intellect and understanding to be capable of doing so' (H K Bevan *Child Law* (Butterworths, 1989), at para 11.06).

[244]   If the children are the beneficiaries under the will, the cost of looking after them will generally be met (so far as funds are available) by the trustees under their statutory powers of maintenance and advancement. There may be circumstances in which it would be helpful for the trustees to have power to lend capital to the guardians, for example the guardians may need to acquire a larger house in order to accommodate the children. For potential inheritance tax difficulties with such a power, see *Butterworth's Wills, Probate and Administration Service* (Butterworths) at paras A[1027]–[1030].

[245]   A specific devise or specific legacy will fail by ademption if its subject-matter has ceased to form

(2)   IF when I die:
  (a)   there is any doubt as to which of two or more properties is my principal residence the decision of my Trustees will be final;[246]
  (b)   the property is subject to a binding but uncompleted contract of sale then this gift will take effect as a gift of (my share of) its net proceeds of sale;[247]
  (c)   the property has been sold then I GIVE to (*cohabitant*) the sum of pounds (£   ) (free of tax) instead.

(3)   THIS GIFT is subject to any legal or equitable charge affecting the property immediately before my death AND I GIVE to (*cohabitant*) (free of tax) the full benefit of and all sums payable under any policies of insurance on my life which have been given as security for the repayment of such charges.[248]

[OR]

(3)   ANY legal or equitable charge affecting the property immediately before my death will (if not automatically discharged by any policies of insurance on my life given as security for this purpose) be paid and discharged from my residuary estate in exoneration of the property.[249]

(4)   THIS GIFT will bear its own share of any tax which is payable on or by reason of my death.[250]

[OR]

(4)   ANY tax attributable to the property which is payable on or by reason of my death will be paid and discharged from my residuary estate in exoneration of the property.[251]

---

part of the testator's estate at the time of his death. If the testator sells the property, the disappointed devisee is not entitled to the traceable net proceeds of sale (*Re Bagot's Settlement* (1862) 31 LJ Ch 772 at 774).

[246]   If there is any doubt about which of two or more residences is 'the principal residence', it may be considered preferable that the surviving partner should choose, rather than the trustees. For example: 'If (*address*) has been sold in my lifetime and if there is any doubt as to which of two or more properties is my principal residence at the time of my death this gift will apply only to the one property that (*cohabitee*) selects within (6 weeks) of my death'. Compare the prior rights of a surviving spouse on an intestacy in the dwelling house in Scottish Law (Succession (Scotland) Act 1964, s 8(1)).

[247]   A binding contract for sale will effect an ademption (*Farrar v Earl of Winterton* (1842) 5 Beav 1).

[248]   In the absence of any provision to the contrary the specific devisee would be primarily liable for any money charged on the property (AEA 1925, s 35).

[249]   In the absence of any provision to the contrary the specific devisee would be primarily liable for any money charged on the property (AEA 1925, s 35).

[250]   See, generally, *Butterworth's Wills, Probate and Administration Service* (Butterworths), Vol 1, at paras 1031–1035, 'Tax Free or Not Tax Free'.

[251]   See, generally, *Butterworth's Wills, Probate and Administration Service* (Butterworths), Vol 1, at paras 1031–1035, 'Tax Free or Not Tax Free'.

(5)   ALL expenses incurred in transferring the property to (*cohabitant*) and registering (his)/(her) title at the Land Registry will be paid by (*cohabitant*).[252]

[OR]

(5)   ALL expenses incurred in transferring the property to (*cohabitant*) and registering (his)/(her) title at the Land Registry will be paid from my residuary estate.[253]

6.115   Life or lesser interest in (a share of) a dwelling and its net proceeds of sale[254]

(1)   I GIVE my (share of the) property known as (*address*) or failing which the property that is my principal residence at the time of my death[255] to my Trustees on a trust of land.[256]

(2)   MY TRUSTEES can invest the net proceeds of sale of that property as freely as if it were their own money and can purchase and improve any replacement property or a share in any replacement property for (*cohabitant*) to live in.[257]

(3)   ANY property which is subject to these trusts is referred to as 'the property', and the property and any cash or investments representing it are referred to as 'the property fund'.

(4)   MY TRUSTEES will allow (*cohabitant*) live in the property on the terms mentioned below and will pay any income from the property fund to (him)/(her) during (his)/(her) lifetime until (he)/(she) cohabits[258] ('the termination of these trusts').

(5)   UNTIL the termination of these trusts (*cohabitant*) can live in the property rent free on the terms that (he)/(she):
      (a)   pays the outgoings;
      (b)   keeps it in reasonable repair and condition;
      (c)   keeps it insured to its full reinstatement value;
      (d)   complies with the covenants and conditions to which it is subject.

(6)   MY TRUSTEES will not:

---

[252] In the absence of a direction to the contrary, the expense incurred in vesting a specific devise in the devisee is borne by the devisee personally (*Re Grosvenor* [1916] 2 Ch 375).

[253] In the absence of a direction to the contrary, the expense incurred in vesting a specific devise in the devisee is borne by the devisee personally (*Re Grosvenor* [1916] 2 Ch 375).

[254] Contrast this clause with a clause giving the surviving partner a life or lesser interest in the whole of the estate (**6.132** below) and a clause conferring mere occupation rights that do not extend to an interest in the proceeds of sale (**6.116** below).

[255] This wording is designed to avoid the problem of abatement.

[256] Trustees of land have power under the Trusts of Land and Appointment of Trustees Act 1996 to delegate any of their functions as trustees to any beneficiary entitled to an interest in possession. Such delegation can be used to give a life tenant powers equivalent to those of a life tenant under the Settled Land Act 1925. Since that Act, it has no longer been possible to create a strict settlement.

[257] For the powers of trustees to purchase and improve land for occupation by a beneficiary, see the footnotes to **6.137** below.

[258] For difficulties which arise when a life interest is terminable on cohabitation, see **6.4**.

(a) exercise their trust for sale without reasonable cause before the termination of these trusts;

(b) be personally liable for the failure of (*cohabitant*) to comply with any of the obligations imposed on (him)/(her);

(c) be personally liable for paying any income from the property fund to (*cohabitant*) after the termination of these trusts unless they have knowledge of the event causing the termination.

(7) SUBJECT to these provisions my Trustees will hold the property fund (as part of my residuary estate)/(on trust for   )/(for   ).

6.116 Occupation rights restricted to a particular property: variation lifting that restriction

(1) I GIVE my (share of the) property known as (*address*) or failing which the property that is my principal residence at the time of my death ('the property') to my Trustees on a trust of land.

(2) MY TRUSTEES will allow (*cohabitant*) live in the property for as long as (he)/(she) wishes on the terms that (he)/(she):
(a) pays the outgoings;
(b) keeps it in reasonable repair and condition;
(c) keeps it insured to its full reinstatement value;
(d) complies with the covenants and conditions to which it is subject.

(IF (*cohabitant*) wishes to live elsewhere my Trustees can sell the property and apply the proceeds in or towards the purchase of another property or a share in another property which will be held on exactly the same trusts as the property itself (but if the purchase price of the other property or a share in it is less than the net proceeds of sale of the property itself the surplus cash will immediately (form part of my residuary estate)/(be paid by my Trustees to   ))).

(3) MY TRUSTEES will not:
(a) require (*cohabitant*) to pay an occupation rent;
(b) require (*cohabitant*) to share the property with anyone else;
(c) be personally liable for the failure of (*cohabitant*) to comply with any of the obligations imposed on (him)/(her);
(d) exercise their power of sale without reasonable cause unless or until (*cohabitant*) ceases to occupy the property on a permanent basis[259] or fails to comply with any of the obligations imposed on (him)/(her).

(4) SUBJECT to these provisions my Trustees will hold (my share of) the property and its net proceeds of sale (as part of my residuary estate)/(on trust for   )/(for   ).

6.117 Option to purchase (a share of) a dwelling[260]

(1) I GIVE to:

---

[259] For consideration of the meaning of expressions such as 'permanently ceases to reside', see *Re Coxen* [1948] 2 All ER 492 at 500.

[260] An option to purchase can be very useful. It allows the surviving partner to buy the whole property and, where the testator permits his partner to purchase at an undervalue, there is an

    (a)   my Trustees my (share of the) property known as (*address*) or failing which the property that is my principal residence at the time of my death ('the property') on a trust of land.

    (b)   (*cohabitant*) the option to purchase the property from my Trustees at the price and on the terms and conditions stated below.

(2) THE PROPERTY will be valued on the basis that:

    (a)   it is being sold at arm's length on the open market with vacant possession;

    (b)   all the fixtures and fittings and carpets and curtains are included in the sale;

    (c)   there is no discount for joint ownership.[261]

(3) THE PRICE will be (75% of) the value of (my share of) the property.

(4) FROM the date of my death, within a period of:

    (a)   (4) weeks the property will be valued by a professionally qualified valuer appointed by my Trustees;

    (b)   (6) weeks my Trustees will give written notice of this option to (*cohabitant*);

    (c)   (8) weeks (*cohabitant*) will give written notice to my Trustees exercising this option;

    (d)   (12) weeks (*cohabitant*) will complete the purchase of the property.

(5) MY TRUSTEES can:

    (a)   compromise on the price if (*cohabitant*) obtains a valuation of the property which differs from that obtained by them;

    (b)   let (*cohabitant*) live in the property rent free until it is sold provided that (he)/(she) pays all the outgoings and keeps it insured to its full reinstatement value;

    (c)   enforce their trust for sale after the end of the period of (12) weeks from the date of my death;

    (d)   extend any of the time-limits set out in this clause if they consider that such an extension is reasonable in the circumstances.

(6) MY ESTATE will pay:

    (a)   the cost of obtaining the valuation;

    (b)   the costs of transferring the property to (*cohabitant*); including Stamp Duty Land Tax, Land Registry fees and legal fees;

    (c)   any inheritance tax payable because the price is less than the open market value.

(7) THIS OPTION:

    (a)   is personal to (*cohabitant*) and cannot be exercised by anyone else;

---

    added incentive to buy. It frees the property from an ongoing trust of land, and it releases cash for distribution to other beneficiaries. Note the Law of Property (Miscellaneous Provisions) Act 1989, s 2.

[261] See *Wight and Another v IRC* (1982) 264 EG 935, Lands Tribunal, which related to the valuation of a property held as tenants in common. It was held that for capital transfer tax purposes the discount for joint ownership should be 15%, rather than the 10% which had become customary following the earlier decision in *Cust v CIR* (1917) 91 EG 11. See also *Arkwright v IRC* [2004] STC 1323.

(b) can be exercised by (*cohabitant*) even though (he)/(she) is one of my Trustees;

(c) will lapse if it has not been exercised by (*cohabitant*) within (8) weeks from the date of my death or within such later period as my Trustees consider to be reasonable in the circumstances.

(8) SUBJECT to these provisions my Trustees will hold (my share of) the net proceeds of sale of the property (as part of my residuary estate)/(on trust for   )/(for   ).

6.118 Bequest of personal chattels

I GIVE free of tax to (*cohabitant*) all my personal chattels (as defined in the Administration of Estates Act 1925)[262] that have not been specifically bequeathed to others.

6.119 Bequest of personal chattels: cohabitant to choose

(1) I GIVE free of tax to (*cohabitant*) such of my personal chattels (as defined in the Administration of Estates Act 1925)[263] that have not been specifically bequeathed to others as (he)/(she) may choose within the period of (6) weeks beginning with the date of my death.

(2) Any personal chattels that (he)/(she) has not chosen within that period will form part of my residuary estate.

Specific bequest

6.120 Jewellery[264]

I GIVE all my jewellery including watches[265] to my daughter (*name*) free of tax (and my Trustees can let her wear my jewellery when she reaches the age of (14)).

---

[262] Until 1 October 2014 'Personal chattels' were defined under s 55(1)(x) Administration of Estates Act 1925 as carriages, horses, stable furniture and effects (not used for business purposes), motor cars and accessories (not used for business purposes), garden effects, domestic animals, plate, plated articles, linen, china, glass, books, pictures, prints, furniture, jewellery, articles of household or personal use or ornament, musical and scientific instruments and apparatus, wines, liquors and consumable stores, but do not include any chattels used at the death of the intestate for business purposes nor money or securities for money'). For wills executed after 1 October 2014 or on an intestacy after that date, 'Personal chattels' are defined under s 3 ITPA 2014 as tangible movable property, other than any such property which consists of money or securities for money, or was used at the death of the intestate solely or mainly for business purposes, or was held at the death of the intestate solely as an investment.

[263] For definition of personal chattels, see footnote to **6.118** (above).

[264] Unless they are particularly valuable, it is usually preferable that specific chattels vest in a minor immediately, rather than be made contingent on the child reaching 18. Strictly speaking, the chattels should be kept until the child is 18 and can give a valid receipt for them.

[265] D T Davies *Will Precedents and Inheritance Tax* (Butterworths, 4th edn) at p 176, contains a more comprehensive definition: 'all my jewellery and all other articles of a like nature including tiaras, rings, necklaces, earrings, brooches, pendants, bracelets and watches.'

6.121   Car on hire purchase, etc[266]

I GIVE to (*cohabitant*) (free of tax) any car I own or lawfully have in my possession at the time of my death.

IF the car is subject to a hire purchase or conditional sale agreement ...[267] I GIVE to (*cohabitant*) all my rights under that agreement on condition that (he)/(she) pays all sums, performs all obligations and indemnifies my estate against all liabilities arising under it.

[OR]

... my Trustees will do what they can to complete the purchase of the car and to transfer it to (*cohabitant*) at the expense of my residuary estate.

6.122   Cohabitation as a condition precedent:[268] pecuniary legacy[269]

IF (*cohabitant*) and I are still living together at the time of my death, I GIVE (him)/(her) the sum of   pounds (£   ) free of tax.

6.123   Pecuniary legacy: index-linked[270]

(1)   I GIVE to (*cohabitant*) the sum of £   free of tax ('this legacy').

(2)   This legacy will be index-linked by reference to the extent by which the Retail Prices Index has changed between the month in which I sign this Will and the month in which I die.

---

[266] Although this clause relates to a car, the same principles would apply in respect of other goods being acquired on HP. Clauses of this nature are fraught with difficulties and, wherever possible, the practitioner should inspect the HP, etc, agreement. For comments and precedents on goods subject to a credit sale agreement and leasing agreement, see *Butterworth's Wills, Probate and Administration Service* (Butterworths) Vol 1, para A[736].

[267] The ownership of goods under an HP agreement is not vested in the testator (compare credit sale agreements).

[268] Wills Act 1837, s 18A contains provisions relating to the effect on wills of a decree of dissolution or annulment of marriage. Nothing comparable exists in respect of the end of an unmarried couple's relationship. If the couple split up, it is imperative that they review their wills as soon as possible. For example, see **6.151** below. If a testator specifically wishes to make a gift to the cohabitee conditional on their still living together, he should appoint independent executors who could apply to the court for directions if there were any problems over compliance with the condition precedent.

[269] The pecuniary legacy is merely an illustration of the condition precedent. The same rules would apply in respect of other gifts. If the cohabitee does not satisfy the condition specified, the pecuniary legacy will fail.

[270] The Retail Prices Index (RPI) is designed to measure the changes in the prices of good and services purchased by householders from their net income, and is, therefore, indicative of the purchasing power of money. The figures are published by the Office of National Statistics monthly.

(3) If the Retail Prices Index no longer exists at the time of my death my trustees may apply whatever formula they consider appropriate to ensure that the value of this legacy is the same at my death as it was when I signed this Will.[271]

6.124   Release of debt[272]

I RELEASE (*cohabitant*) free of tax from any debt and the interest on any debt which (he)/(she) may owe me at the time of my death.

6.125   Lump sum to buy an annuity[273]

I GIVE free of tax to (*cohabitant*) the sum that my Trustees consider sufficient to enable (him)/(her) to purchase from a reputable insurance company a gross annuity of £   payable quarterly from the date of my death AND I HOPE that (*cohabitant*) will use the sum to purchase such an annuity.

6.126   Administration trusts and definition of residuary estate[274]

I GIVE all (the rest)[275] of my estate to my Trustees on trust to:

(1) sell or retain;

(2) pay my debts, funeral expenses, testamentary expenses, and any inheritance tax (that is not charged on or primarily payable out of other property),[276] and

---

[271] This sub-clause is probably unnecessarily cautious. The original 'Cost-of-Living Index' was introduced in 1914, and was superseded by the RPI in June 1947. A new base for the RPI was set in January 1987.

[272] The release of a debt constitutes a pecuniary legacy to the debtor (*Attorney-General v Holbrook* (1823) 3 Y & J 114). If the debtor dies before the testator, the release will lapse like any other legacy, unless the will contains express provisions against lapse, for example: '... but if (he)/(she) dies before me (his)/(her) personal representatives will have the benefit of this release'. Cohabitants often make loans to each other, with varying degrees of formality, and it is sensible to ascertain exactly what the testator's wishes are in order to avoid any misunderstanding. A declaration in the will that moneys advanced by the testator were gifts, not loans, to the cohabitee would, in theory, produce the same result, but there are constructional difficulties in such a declaration. The clause would 'speak' from the date of the will, rather than from the date of death.

[273] This is probably the easiest way of providing the surviving cohabitant with an annuity. More complicated provisions, including index-linking, can be found in the standard will precedent books. If the surviving cohabitee is or is likely to be receiving income-related benefits from the DSS, the notional capital rule under reg 51 of the Income Support (General) Regulations 1987 (SI 1987/1967) must be considered.

[274] It may be considered preferable to separate the administration trusts from the trusts of residue. Compare, Statutory Will Forms 1925, Form 8 'Administration Trusts'.

[275] The words 'the rest' should be included if this clause is preceded by a legacy or legacies.

[276] In the absence of a direction to the contrary, the residue will bear the inheritance tax. The testator may prefer to state 'pay ... any inheritance tax attributable to property which I hold as a joint tenant'. Care should be taken where part of the residue is exempt from inheritance tax (eg a gift to charity) and part is not to make it clear whether the division into shares is before or after deduction of inheritance tax. See *Re Benham's Will Trusts* [1995] STC 210; *Re Ratcliffe* [1999] STC 262.

(3) hold what remains ('my residuary estate') on the following trusts.

Residuary estate

6.127   *Cohabitant entitled absolutely*[277]

MY TRUSTEES will pay or transfer any residuary estate to (*cohabitant*) absolutely.

IF (*cohabitant*) dies before me, my Trustees will pay or transfer my residuary estate to (or hold it on trust for) ...[278]

6.128   *Cohabitant and other adults equally entitled: no gifts over*[279]

MY TRUSTEES will pay or transfer my residuary estate to (*cohabitant*) and (*name*) and (*name*) in equal shares or to the survivor of them absolutely.

6.129   *Cohabitant and testator's children given specified shares: provisions for their 'separate families'*[280]

MY TRUSTEES will divide my residuary estate into (*number*) equal shares which they will hold as follows:

(1) (number) shares ('the (cohabitant's family name) Fund' for (cohabitant);

(2) (*number*) shares ('the (*testator's family name*) Fund' for my children (*name*) and (*name*) in equal shares or for the survivor absolutely;

(3) if (*cohabitant*) dies before me my Trustees will hold the (*cohabitant's family name*) Fund for (his)/(her) children (*name*) in equal shares or for the survivor absolutely;

(4) if any of my children or (*cohabitant's*) children dies before me leaving a child or children living at my death, that child or those children on reaching the age of (18) will take, and if more than one in equal shares, the share of my residuary estate which his, her or their parent would have taken if he or she had survived me;

(5) if the trusts affecting either Fund completely fail that Fund will be added to the other Fund.

6.130   *The 'slice system'*

MY TRUSTEES will pay or transfer to (*cohabitant*):

(1) (75) % of the first (£100,000) of my residuary estate; and

---

[277] This clause assumes that 'my residuary estate' has already been defined (see **6.126** above).

[278] It is advisable to include a gift over.

[279] This clause assumes that 'my residuary estate' has already been defined. The words 'pay or transfer' are probably preferable to, and less misleading than, 'hold on trust for' where there is no on-going trust.

[280] This clause assumes that 'my residuary estate' has already been defined. It is designed to cover 'funds' of equal or unequal size.

(2)   (50) % of my residuary estate in so far as it exceeds (£100,000).[281]

IN DEFAULT of and subject to this gift my Trustees will hold my residuary estate (on trust) for (*names*).

6.131   Cohabitant's entitlement based on the duration of the relationship[282]

MY TRUSTEES will pay or transfer to (*cohabitant*) (10) % of my residuary estate[283] for each complete year which has elapsed between (*date*) [OR] (the date of this Will)[284] and the date of my death[285] and no apportionment will be made in respect of any period of less than a year.

IN DEFAULT of and subject to this gift my Trustees will hold my residuary estate (on trust) for (*names*).

6.132   Life interest

(1)   MY TRUSTEES will hold my residuary estate on trust to pay its income[286] to (*cohabitant*) during (his)/(her) lifetime.

(2)   AFTER the death of (*cohabitant*) my Trustees will hold the capital and income of my residuary estate on trust for those of my children who survive me[287] and reach the age of (18) and if more than one in equal shares.

(3)   IF any of my children dies before me[288] or before reaching the age of (18) leaving a child or children who do reach that age that child or those children equally will take the share of my residuary estate that his, her or their parent would otherwise have taken.

6.133   Life interest determinable on cohabitation[289]

(1)   MY TRUSTEES will hold my residuary estate on trust to pay its income to (*cohabitant*) during (his)/(her) lifetime until (he)/(she) cohabits.[290]

---

[281] The percentages and figures can be adapted to suit the testator's requirements; those quoted are merely illustrative. The clause can be adapted to provide alternatives where the testator is survived by the cohabitee and issue, and where the testator dies without issue and is survived by the cohabitee. For example: 'If I die without issue and (*cohabitant*) survives me …'; and 'If I die leaving issue and (*cohabitant*) survives me …'.

[282] The same concept could be applied to a pecuniary legacy.

[283] The percentage can be adapted to suit the testator's requirements.

[284] If any date other than the date of the will is stated it must be precise: e g day, month, year.

[285] If it is considered necessary, the following words could be added: '… so that if I die on or after (*date*), (*cohabitant*) will be entitled to all of my residuary estate …'.

[286] The income may be insufficient for the surviving partner's needs. Consider whether the trustees should have power to advance capital or make loans.

[287] Note that the interests of the remaindermen are contingent on their surviving the testator, not the life tenant. If the alternative is preferred, delete the word 'me' and replace it with the life tenant's name or description.

[288] Note that the interests of the remaindermen are contingent on their surviving the testator, not the life tenant. If the alternative is preferred, delete the word 'me' and replace it with the life tenant's name or description.

[289] For a brief discussion of the definition of 'cohabits' and the evidential problems experienced in

(2)   SUBJECT to the above trust my Trustees will hold my residuary estate (on trust) for.

6.134   *Revocable life interest*[291]

(1)   MY TRUSTEES will hold my residuary estate on trust to pay the income from it to (*cohabitant*) during (his)/(her) lifetime subject to the powers and provisions that follow.

(2)   MY TRUSTEES can revoke the life interest of (*cohabitant*) and hold my residuary estate as if (he)/(she) had died on the date of revocation.

(3)   THE REVOCATION can only be made:
    (a)   by my Trustees, provided that they are at least two in number or a trust corporation;
    (b)   by deed.

(4)   THE REVOCATION can be made:
    (a)   in respect of (*cohabitant's*) interest in all of my residuary estate or any asset comprised in it;
    (b)   before Probate of this Will has been granted;
    (c)   before the administration of my estate has been completed;
    (d)   at any time during the lifetime of (*cohabitant*).

(5)   IN EXERCISING their power of revocation:
    (a)   my Trustees will have absolute discretion;
    (b)   my Trustees can have regard to, or disregard, any wishes I may have communicated to them;
    (c)   the decision of my Trustees will be final and binding.

(6)   MY TRUSTEES can:
    (a)   appoint any person, professional trustee or trust corporation to be a new trustee of all or any part of my residuary estate and, where appropriate, provide for their remuneration;
    (b)   provided that they are at least two in number or a trust corporation, execute any deed or deeds extinguishing or restricting the future exercise of their power of revocation.

(7)   SUBJECT to the above trusts, powers and provisions my Trustees will hold the capital and income of my residuary estate (on trust) for.

6.135   *Full discretionary trust*[292]

(1)   MY TRUSTEES will hold the capital and income of my residuary estate on trust for any one or more of the Beneficiaries whom they appoint.

---

trying to establish whether a couple are cohabiting, see **6.146** below.
For alternative provisions in respect of the residuary estate, consider a revocable life interest (**6.134** below), and a discretionary trust (**6.135** below).

[290] It is considered that the word 'marries' in the expression 'until (he)/(she) marries or cohabits (whichever happens first)' is probably otiose.

[291] A revocable life interest is one of the devices used by some practitioners to overcome some of the difficulties that arise when a testator wishes to give his partner a life interest, but also wishes it to terminate as soon as she enters into a new relationship. It is not entirely clear how successful such a clause is in practical and human terms.

[292] Discretionary trusts allow the trustees great flexibility, enabling them to react to changing

(2) THE BENEFICIARIES are:

    (a) (cohabitant);

    (b) anyone with whom I am living at the time of my death;

    (c) my (husband)/(wife), if any;

    (d) my former (husband)/(wife), if any;

    (e) my children and remoter issue;

    (f) my parents;

    (g) my brothers and sisters and their children and remoter issue;

    (h) the children and remoter issue of (*cohabitant*), anyone with whom I am living at the time of my death, my (husband)/(wife) and my former (husband)/(wife).

(3) THE APPOINTMENT(S) can only be made:

    (a) by my Trustees, provided that they are at least two in number or a trust corporation;

    (b) by deed;

    (c) within the period of 125[293] years (less three days) beginning with the date of my death ('the 125-year period').

(4) THE APPOINTMENT(S) can be made:

    (a) as one appointment or as several appointments;

    (b) at any time during the 125-year period;

    (c) before Probate of this Will has been granted;

    (d) before the administration of my estate has been completed;

    (e) revocably or irrevocably;

    (f) even though one or more of my Trustees stands to benefit personally from the appointment(s).

(5) IN MAKING any appointment my Trustees:

    (a) have total discretion;

    (b) have the same powers that they would have if my residuary estate belonged to them personally;

    (c) may have regard to, or disregard, any wishes I may have communicated to them;

    (d) are under no obligation to ensure equality among the Beneficiaries or any class of Beneficiaries;

    (e) can create interests that are free from any trust;

---

family and tax circumstances. In the context of cohabitation they are occasionally used for the purpose of varying the financial provision made for the surviving partner according to any changes in his or her personal circumstances. The trustees have extremely wide-ranging powers. It is essential to establish whether the testator really wishes to leave his family's welfare and finances in the hands of trustees on a long-term basis.

A discretionary trust gives no qualifying interest in possession for the purposes of the Inheritance Tax Act 1984, s 58. No inheritance tax arises on the death of any of the potential beneficiaries, but the trust is subject to a 10-yearly charge and exit charges (ibid, ss 64 and 65). For a full discussion of the tax implications and the advantages and disadvantages of these trusts, see D T Davies *Wills Precedents and Inheritance Tax* (Butterworths, 4th edn) and *Butterworth's Wills, Probate and Administration Service* (Butterworths).

[293] The Perpetuities and Accumulations Act 2009 increased the perpetuity period from 80 to 125 years for all purposes and no other period can now be specified. It also abolished the rule against excessive accumulations of income which was previously restricted to 21 years but can now last for the whole of the trust period specified.

(f)   can create any kind of trust;

(g)   can stipulate any age or date at which a Beneficiary may be entitled;

(h)   can confer any powers and discretions they think fit;

(i)   can impose any restrictions, limitations, terms and conditions they think fit;

(j)   can make any provisions they think fit;

(k)   will not invalidate any earlier payment or application of any part(s) of the capital or income of my residuary estate.

(6)   MY TRUSTEES can:

(a)   appoint any person, professional trustee or trust corporation to be a new trustee of the whole or any part of my residuary estate and, where appropriate, provide for their remuneration;

(b)   provided that they are at least two in number or a trust corporation, execute at any time(s) a deed or deeds extinguishing or restricting the future exercise of their powers.

(7)   IN DEFAULT of any appointment and subject to any appointment the following provisions apply.

(8)   DURING the 125-year period my Trustees:

(a)   will pay all or any part of the income of my residuary estate to any one or more of the Beneficiaries or apply it for his, her or their benefit, education, maintenance and support in whatever manner they think fit;

(b)   can pay or apply any accumulations of income from past years as if they were the income of the present year.

(9)   AT THE END of the 125-year period my Trustees will hold the capital and income of my residuary estate for my children and remoter issue who are alive at that time and if more than one in equal shares according to their stocks, so that no issue whose parent is still alive will be entitled.

6.136   *Two-year discretionary trust*[294]

(1)   MY TRUSTEES will hold the capital and income of my residuary estate on trust for any one or more of the Beneficiaries whom they appoint.

(2)   THE BENEFICIARIES are:

(a)   (cohabitant);

(b)   anyone with whom I am living at the time of my death;

(c)   my (husband)/(wife), if any;

(d)   my former (husband)/(wife), if any;

---

[294]   A two-year discretionary trust is widely used as an inheritance tax planning device, and takes advantage of the provisions of the Inheritance Tax Act 1984, s 144. For a fuller discussion see *Butterworth's Wills, Probate and Administration Service* (Butterworths) at paras A[967–970]. In the context of cohabitation a 'mini discretionary trust' might be regarded as a useful 'wait and see' vehicle, where the testator wishes to make provision for the surviving partner, but also wishes to withdraw such provision as soon as the survivor has entered into a new, stable relationship.

The testator should make his wishes clear to his trustees, preferably in a written 'off-the-record' memorandum.

The interaction of 'mini discretionary trusts' and the I(PFD)A 1975 has not yet been fully explored by the courts.

(e) my children and remoter issue;

(f) my parents;

(g) my brothers and sisters and their children and remoter issue;

(h) the children and remoter issue of (*cohabitant*), anyone with whom I am living at the time of my death, my (husband)/(wife) and my former (husband)/(wife).

(3) THE APPOINTMENT(S) can only be made:

(a) by my Trustees, provided that they are at least two in number or a trust corporation;

(b) by deed;

(c) within the period of two years (less three days) beginning with the date of my death ('the two-year period').

(4) THE APPOINTMENT(S) can be made:

(a) as one appointment or as several appointments;

(b) at any time during the two-year period;

(c) before Probate of this Will has been granted;

(d) before the administration of my estate has been completed;

(e) revocably or irrevocably;

(f) even though one or more of my Trustees stands to benefit personally from the appointment(s).

(5) IN MAKING any appointment my Trustees:

(a) have total discretion;

(b) have the same powers that they would have if my residuary estate belonged to them personally;

(c) may have regard to, or disregard, any wishes I may have communicated to them;

(d) are under no obligation to ensure equality among the Beneficiaries or any class of Beneficiaries;

(e) can create interests that are free from any trust;

(f) can create any kind of trust;

(g) can stipulate any age or date at which a Beneficiary may be entitled;

(h) can confer any powers and discretions they think fit;

(i) can impose any restrictions, limitations, terms and conditions they think fit;

(j) can make any provisions they think fit;

(k) will not invalidate any earlier payment or application of any part(s) of the capital or income of my residuary estate.

(6) MY TRUSTEES can:

(a) appoint any person, professional trustee or trust corporation to be a new trustee of the whole or any part of my residuary estate and, where appropriate, provide for their remuneration;

(b) provided that they are at least two in number or a trust corporation, execute at any time(s) a deed or deeds extinguishing or restricting the future exercise of their powers.

(7) IN DEFAULT of any appointment and subject to any appointment the following provisions apply.

(8) DURING the two-year period my Trustees:

(a)   will pay all or any part of the income of my residuary estate to any one or more of the Beneficiaries or apply it for his, her or their benefit, education, maintenance and support in whatever manner they think fit;

(b)   can accumulate the income;

(c)   can add accumulations of income to the capital of my residuary estate.

(9)   AT THE END of the two-year period my Trustees will hold the capital and income of my residuary estate (on trust) for ...

Trustee's power[295]

6.137   Investment[296]

(MY TRUSTEES can) invest as freely as if the assets of my residuary estate were their own and can acquire assets which produce no income[297] and can purchase[298] and improve[299] any property for the purpose of providing a home for a beneficiary.[300]

6.138   Delegation of investment management[301]

(MY TRUSTEES can) delegate their powers of investing, managing and administering trust assets to any person or company (whether UK resident or not) and allow trust assets to be held in the name of that person or company as their nominee on whatever terms (including remuneration) they think appropriate.

---

[295] Trustee Act 2000, s 1 now lays down a statutory duty of care for trustees.

[296] Trustee Act 2000, s 3 now contains wide investment powers. It is, however, recommended that a specific power be included for the benefit of the testator. Even where the investment power is express, the trustees must have regard to the standard investment criteria laid down in s 4 of the Trustee Act 2000.

[297] Assets which produce no income are not 'investments', and are, therefore, unauthorised (*Re Wragg* [1919] 2 Ch 58).

[298] Although trustees of land can now purchase land for occupation by a beneficiary (Trusts of Land and Appointment of Trustees Act 1996, s 6(4)(b)), it is still advisable to include these powers.

[299] A very limited power to raise money for improvements is conferred by LTA 1927, s 13.

[300] A power to invest in the purchase of land did not automatically authorise the trustees to acquire a vacant freehold house for occupation by the testator's family; because it produced no income it was not an investment (*Re Power's Will Trusts* [1947] Ch 572). Trustee Act 2000, s 8 now allows the acquisition of freehold or leasehold land in the United Kingdom for occupation by a beneficiary.

[301] Trustee Act 2000, Part IV allows the appointment of agents, nominees and custodians and lays down the criteria and conditions applicable.

6.139   Maintenance[302]

(MY TRUSTEES can) apply all or any part of the income of that share of my residuary estate to which a beneficiary is or may in future be entitled for that beneficiary's maintenance, education or benefit in whatever manner they in their absolute discretion think fit, regardless of whether other funds are available for these purposes, and regardless of whether anyone has a legal duty to provide for that beneficiary's maintenance or education.[303]

6.140   Advancement[304]

(MY TRUSTEES can) apply all or any part of the capital of that share of my residuary estate to which a beneficiary is or may in future be entitled for that beneficiary's advancement or benefit[305] in whatever manner they in their absolute discretion think fit.[306]

6.141   Insurance[307]

(MY TRUSTEES can):

(1)   insure any asset in my estate against any insurable risk[308] and for any amount even though a beneficiary is absolutely entitled to it;[309]

(2)   pay insurance premiums out of income or capital[310] in whatever manner they think fit;

(3)   use any insurance money they receive to restore the asset or alternatively treat that money as if it were the net proceeds of sale of the asset insured.

---

[302]   The statutory power to apply income for maintenance and to accumulate surplus income during a minority is contained in Trustee Act 1925, s 31. It is submitted that the standard will clauses which refer to this section and amend it are unintelligible to the ordinary testator.

[303]   If necessary, the clause could prohibit any payment being made while the father has anything to do with the child's education or upbringing (*Re Borwicks Settlement* [1916] 2 Ch 304).

[304]   The statutory power of advancement is contained in Trustee Act 1925, s 32. It is submitted that the widely used type of clause which refers to the section and amends it is unintelligible to the ordinary testator.

[305]   'Advancement' suggests establishing the beneficiary in life. The wider-term 'benefit' includes (*inter alia*) payments for the beneficiary's maintenance or education. The trustees must have good reason for making the advance, and must see that its purpose is carried out (*Re Pauling (No 1)* [1965] Ch 303).

[306]   Trustee Act 1925, s 32(1), proviso (b), which requires that the advances be brought into account, will apply unless specifically excluded.

[307]   For the existing statutory powers, see the Trustee Act 1925, s 19 as amended by the Trustee Act 2000.

[308]   The statutory power now applies to 'loss or damage due to any event' (Trustee Act 1925, s 19(1)).

[309]   Ibid, s 19(2) includes the trustees' statutory power of insurance where they hold on a bare trust subject to directions by the beneficiaries.

[310]   The statutory power is exercised at the expense of income (ibid, s 19(1)).

6.142 Appropriation[311]

(MY TRUSTEES can) appropriate any part of my estate in its then actual condition or state of investment in or towards the satisfaction of any legacy, interest or share in my estate without having to obtain any consent and regardless of whether they are acting as personal representatives or trustees.[312]

6.143 Remuneration

(MY TRUSTEES can) if they are professionally qualified trustees or a trust corporation[313] charge and be paid for all the work they do in obtaining probate, administering my estate and acting as trustees, even though some of that work could have been done by a person who is not professionally qualified.

6.144 Statement for the purposes of the Inheritance (Provision for Family and Dependants) Act 1975[314]

I HAVE NOT MADE (greater)/(any) provision[315] in this Will for (*cohabitant*) (not through any lack of love or affection for (him)/(her) but) because:

(a) I consider that (he)/(she) already has adequate financial resources;[316]

(b) (he)/(she) is not maintained by me or financially dependent on me;[317]

(c) our relationship has been of a comparatively short duration;[318]

(d) I believe that my (children) have a greater claim on my estate;

(e) (other reasons, if any).[319]

---

[311] See, generally, AEA 1925, s 41.

[312] The statutory power applies only to personal representatives. It does not apply to trustees. For comment and proposed reform see the Law Commission Report LC 260, published 21 July 1999. No amendments were made to this power in the Trustee Act 2000.

[313] Express authorisation to charge is not required where the Public Trustee takes on the appointment (Public Trustee Act 1906, s 5).

[314] For the admissibility as evidence of statements made by the deceased, see I(PFD)A 1975, s 21. If the statement is defamatory, objectionable, or distressing to 'the family' it will be excluded from the probate (*In the Estate of Hall* [1943] 1 All ER 159).

[315] For anyone other than a spouse 'reasonable financial provision' means 'such financial provision as it would be reasonable in all the circumstances of the case for the applicant to receive for his maintenance' (I(PFD)A 1975, s 1(2)(b)).

[316] See I(PFD)A 1975, s 3.

[317] See I(PFD)A 1975, s 2(3). However, the situation could change between the date of the will and the testator's death.

[318] See I(PFD)A 1975, s 3(4). Likewise, the situation could change between the date of the will and the testator's death.

[319] For example: there could be a nomination in the cohabitant's favour; various assets could pass to the cohabitant by the *ius accrescendi*; the testator may have made lifetime gifts to the cohabitant; the cohabitant may have expectations under the will of someone else; the origin of the deceased's assets may be relevant; the couple might even have signed a cohabitation contract waiving the right to apply to the court for an order under the Act. See **2.108** above. See also clause 10 at **6.155** below.

The word 'cohabits' in wills

6.145   Definitions

For the purposes of this Will 'cohabitation' exists where two people who are not married to each other or in a civil partnership together live together in the same household as spouses or civil partners, and 'cohabits' will be interpreted accordingly.[320] [OR]

For the purposes of this Will 'cohabitation' exists where two people who are not married to each other or in civil partnership together live together in the same household as spouses or civil partners for a period of (*number*) months in any (*number*) month period, and 'cohabits' will be interpreted accordingly.[321] [OR]

For the purposes of this Will (*cohabitant*) will be treated as cohabiting if (he)/(she) lives in the same household with a person of either sex who is not a blood relative of (his)/(hers) or mine.[322] [OR]

For the purposes of this Will 'cohabits' means 'has sexual relations'.[323]

6.146   Miscellaneous

–   For the purposes of deciding whether or not (*cohabitant*) is cohabiting, my Trustees may have regard to the criteria applied by the Department of Work and Pensions for the purposes of deciding whether or not a claimant is cohabiting.[324]

–   The fact that (*cohabitant*) is living in the same household with someone who is not (his)/(her) or my blood relative will give rise to a presumption that they are cohabiting and the burden of proving that (he)/(she) is not cohabiting will lie with (*cohabitant*).

–   My Trustees will not be liable for paying the income from (my residuary estate) to (*cohabitant*) after (his)/(her) interest in it has terminated unless they have knowledge of the event causing the termination.[325]

---

[320]   This definition is based partly on the wording of the DVMPA 1976, s 1(2) and the Social Security Act 1986, s 20(11).

[321]   This definition is based partly on the Solicitors' Family Law Association *Precedents for Consent Orders* (5th edn), Precedent 32. Cf Barton, above, at p 3: 'sharing a bedroom during at least four nights per week during at least three consecutive months with someone of the opposite sex.'

[322]   This definition could include those living with friends.

[323]   Cf the euphemistic expression '*dum casta vixerit*'. It is submitted that some testators would construe 'cohabits' in exactly this way.

[324]   See Guidance for Decision-Makers Vol 3 Ch 11: Living together as husband and wife or as civil partners.

[325]   Trustee Act 1925, s 61 provides that 'if it appears to the court that a trustee ... is or may be personally liable for any breach of trust ... but has acted honestly and reasonably, and ought fairly to be excused ... the court may relieve him either wholly or partly from personal liability'. This relief may also be extended to executors.

–   The decision of my Trustees as to whether or not (*cohabitant*) is cohabiting will be final and binding.[326]

6.147   Testimonium[327]

AS WITNESS my hand on (*date*)

[OR]

SIGNED by me on (*date*).

6.148   Attestation clause[328]

SIGNED by (*testator*) in our joint presence and then by us in (his)/(hers).

---

[326] Any clause in a will which purports to make the trustees' decision final and binding is invalid (*Re Wynn* [1952] 1 All ER 341). The reason for this is that the court exercises a general controlling influence over all trustees, and a clause which attempts to oust its jurisdiction is thereby repugnant and contrary to public policy.

[327] The testimonium will be needed if the date does not appear in the commencement of the will.

[328] The formal requirements for the execution of a valid will are set out in the Wills Act 1837, s 9 (as substituted by the Administration of Justice Act 1982, s 17). This section ends with the statement that 'no form of attestation shall be necessary'.

This clause is for use in normal cases. For attestation clauses where the testator is unable to read or write, or is visually handicapped, or when another person signs on the testator's behalf, see the standard will precedent books.

Forms

6.149 *Pension scheme: request to trustees*[329]

(Full Name and Address of Member)

(date)

To: The Trustees
The *(name)* Pension Scheme
(address)

Dear Sirs,

Statement of wishes concerning death benefits

Although I am aware that you have an absolute discretion in respect of the payment of any lump sum and other benefits on my death, I would be grateful if you could have regard to my wishes, as stated below, until you receive a further statement from me.

I would like the following people to receive the following shares:

Name	Relationship	Address	Percentage

Yours faithfully,

(member's signature)[330]

6.150 *Codicil 'disinheriting' former cohabitant*[331]

THIS (SECOND) CODICIL is made by me *(testator)* of *(address)* on *(date)* and is supplemental to my Will dated *(date)* (and the Codicil(s) to it dated   ).

---

[329] It would be sensible to check the terms of the scheme to see whether or not such a nomination is possible.
As this is a 'non-statutory' nomination, the benefits do not form part of the deceased's estate for the purposes of an order under the I(PFD)A 1975 (s 8(1)). See also *Re Cairnes* (1983) 4 FLR 225, 12 Fam Law 177.

[330] A nomination of this kind is not a 'testamentary disposition' (*Re Danish Bacon Co Staff Pension Fund* [1971] 1 All ER 486).
The member should send the letter to the trustees in a sealed envelope stating his full name, the date, and the words 'Statement of Wishes relating to the *(name)* Pension Scheme'.

[331] For unmarried couples there is no equivalent to Wills Act 1837, s 18A, which describes the effect on a will of a decree of dissolution or annulment of marriage. Therefore, if cohabitants

(1) I REVOKE the appointment of (*cohabitant*) as an Executor and Trustee of my Will.

(2) I REVOKE every devise, bequest, legacy, benefit and privilege given to or conferred on (*cohabitant*) in my Will.

(3) I INTEND that my Will will be interpreted and take effect as if (*cohabitant*) had died before me.[332]

(4) I CONFIRM my Will (and Codicil(s)) in all other respects.

SIGNED by (*testator*) in our joint presence and then by us in (his)/(hers).

6.151 Will: unmarried mother leaving her entire estate to her child under 18

THIS WILL is made on (*date*) by me (*testatrix*) of (*address*).

(1) I REVOKE my earlier Wills.

(2) I WOULD LIKE to be (cremated).

(3) I APPOINT my parents (*name*) and (*name*) of (*address*) ('my Trustees') to be my Executors and Trustees and the Guardians of my (son)/(daughter) (*child's name*).[333]

(4) I GIVE all my estate to my Trustees on trust to:
    (a) sell or retain;
    (b) pay my debts, funeral expenses and testamentary expenses; and
    (c) hold what remains ('my residuary estate') as follows.

(5) MY TRUSTEES will hold my residuary estate on trust for my (son)/(daughter) (*child's name*) if and when (he)/(she) reaches the age of (18).

(6) IF my (son)/(daughter) dies before me or before (he)/(she) reaches (18) leaving issue, my Trustees will hold my residuary estate on trust for such issue who reach (18) and if more than one in equal shares.[334]

(7) IF all of the above trusts fail, my Trustees will pay or transfer my residuary estate to my parents in equal shares or to the survivor of them absolutely.

(8) MY TRUSTEES can:

---

split up, it is vitally important that they should review their respective wills immediately. A codicil of this nature should only be executed if the will contains suitable alternative appointments and gifts unless, of course, the testator consciously wishes to bring about a potential intestacy or partial intestacy. A codicil of this nature could also be executed by a married person in the throes of a divorce but where no decree of the court has yet been made.

[332] Cf *Re Sinclair* [1985] Ch 446.

[333] It is assumed that the child's father has not acquired parental responsibility. See, generally, CA 1989, s 4.

[334] Although the reference to the testatrix's grandchildren may seem completely inappropriate, it would not be possible in these circumstances to rely on the provisions of Wills Act 1837, s 33. In order for that section to apply, the son or daughter would have to die before the testatrix, leaving issue living at her death. Furthermore, the gift over to the parents, which is probably sensible, could be construed as 'a contrary intention' for the purposes of s 33.

(a) invest as freely as if the assets of my residuary estate were their own and can acquire assets which produce no income and can purchase and improve any property for the purpose of providing a home for a beneficiary;

(b) apply all or any part of the income of that share of my residuary estate to which a beneficiary is or may in future be entitled for that beneficiary's maintenance, education or benefit in whatever manner they in their absolute discretion think fit, regardless of whether other funds are available for these purposes, and regardless of whether anyone has a legal duty to provide for the beneficiary's maintenance or education;[335]

(c) apply all or any part of the capital of that share of my residuary estate to which a beneficiary is or may in future be entitled for that beneficiary's advancement or benefit in whatever manner they in their absolute discretion think fit.

SIGNED by (*testatrix*) in our joint presence and then by us in hers.

6.152 Will: childless unmarried couple: all to the surviving partner: gift over to their respective parents

THIS WILL is made on (*date*) by me (*testator*) of (*address*).

(1) I REVOKE my earlier Wills.

(2) I WOULD LIKE:
   (a) any part of my body which may be of use to others to be made available for treatment or transplantation;
   (b) to be cremated;
   (c) donations to be made to (*Charity*).

(3) IF (he)/(she) survives me by (7) days I GIVE my estate to (*cohabitant*) of (*address*) AND I APPOINT (him)/(her) to be my Executor, but if (he)/(she) fails to survive me by (7) days the following clauses will apply.

(4) I APPOINT (*name*) of (*address*) and (*name*) of (*address*) ('my Trustees') to be the Executors and Trustees of this Will.

(5) I GIVE my estate to my Trustees on trust to:
   (a) sell or retain;
   (b) pay my debts, funeral expenses, testamentary expenses and Inheritance Tax; and
   (c) hold what remains ('my residuary estate') as follows.

(6) MY TRUSTEES will divide my residuary estate into two equal shares and if the trusts of one of these shares fail, that share will be added to the other share.

(7) MY TRUSTEES will pay or transfer one share to my parents (*name*) and (*name*) of (*address*) equally or to the survivor of them.

---

[335] For example, a maintenance assessment may have been made under the CSA 1991, requiring the absent parent to make periodical payments.

(8)   MY TRUSTEES will pay or transfer the other share to (*cohabitant's*) parents (*name*) and (*name*) of (*address*) equally or to the survivor of them.

SIGNED by (*testator*) in our joint presence and then by us in (his)/(hers).

6.153   Will: unmarried couple with minor children: both parents have parental responsibility: all to the surviving partner: gift over to children: further gift over in case of a family catastrophe

THIS WILL is made on (*date*) by me (*testator*) of (*address*).

(1)   I REVOKE my earlier Wills.

(2)   I WOULD LIKE to be (cremated).[336]

(3)   IF (he)/(she) survives me by (7) days I GIVE my estate to (*cohabitant*) of (address) AND I APPOINT (him)/(her) to be my Executor, but if (he)/(she) fails to survive me by (7) days the following clauses will apply.

(4)   I APPOINT (*name*) of (*address*) and (*name*) of (*address*) ('my Trustees') to be the Executors and Trustees of this Will.

(5)   I APPOINT (*name*) of (*address*) to be the Guardian of my children.

(6)   I GIVE all my estate to my Trustees on trust to:
   (a)   sell or retain;
   (b)   pay my debts, funeral expenses, testamentary expenses and Inheritance Tax; and
   (c)   hold what remains ('my residuary estate') as follows.

(7)   MY TRUSTEES will hold my residuary estate on trust for my children who survive me and reach the age of (18) and if more than one in equal shares.

(8)   IF a child of mine dies before me or before reaching (18) leaving a child or children who do reach that age that child or those children equally will take the share of my residuary estate that his, her or their parent would otherwise have taken.

(9)   IF all the above trusts fail my Trustees will divide my residuary estate into two equal shares and if the trusts of one of these shares fail that share will be added to the other share.

(10) MY TRUSTEES will pay or transfer one share:
   (a)   to my parents (*name*) and (*name*) equally or to the survivor of them; or
   (b)   if both of my parents die before me, to my brothers and sisters (*names*) equally or to the survivor of them.

(11) MY TRUSTEES will pay or transfer the other share:
   (a)   to (*cohabitant's*) parents (*name*) and (*name*) equally or to the survivor of them; or

---

[336] If this is the woman's will, and the man does not have parental responsibility for the child(ren), insert a guardianship appointment at this stage. For example, 'I APPOINT (*cohabitant*) to be the Guardian of our children'.

(b)   if both of (*cohabitant's*) parents die before me, to (his)/(her) brothers and sisters (*names*) equally or to the survivor of them.

(12) (Trustees' powers.)

SIGNED by (*testator*) in our joint presence and then by us in (his)/(hers).

6.154   *Will: older unmarried couple: life interest to the survivor*

THIS WILL is made on (*date*) by me (*testator*) of (*address*).

(1)   I REVOKE my earlier Wills.

(2)   I WOULD LIKE to be cremated.

(3)   I APPOINT (*name*) of (*address*) and (*name*) of (*address*) ('my Trustees') to be my Executors and Trustees.

(4)   I GIVE all my personal chattels (as defined in the Administration of Estates Act 1925) to (*cohabitant*) free of tax.

(5)   I GIVE the rest of my estate to my Trustees on trust to:
(a)   sell or retain;
(b)   pay my debts, funeral expenses, testamentary expenses and inheritance tax; and
(c)   hold what remains ('my residuary estate') as follows.

(6)   MY TRUSTEES will hold my residuary estate on trust to pay its income to (*cohabitant*) during (his)/(her) lifetime.

(7)   AFTER the death of (*cohabitant*) my Trustees will pay or transfer the capital and income of my residuary estate to those of my children (*name*), (*name*) and (*name*) who survive me and if more than one in equal shares.

(8)   IF any of my children dies before me leaving a child or children living at my death that child or those children equally on reaching the age of (18) will take the share of my residuary estate that his, her or their parent would otherwise have taken.

(9)   (Trustees' powers, including a clause excluding the operation of the apportionment rules.)

SIGNED by (*testator*) in our joint presence and then by us in (his)/(hers).

6.155   *Will: older unmarried couple: limited provision for the surviving partner: residue to the testator's children*

THIS WILL is made on (*date*) by me (*testator*) of (*address*).

(1)   I REVOKE my earlier Wills.

(2)   I WOULD LIKE:
(a)   to be cremated;
(b)   my ashes to be scattered;
(c)   (*cohabitant*) to decide what other funeral arrangements should be made;

(d) the expenses incurred in carrying out these wishes to be paid out of my estate.

(3) I APPOINT my children (*name*) of (*address*) and (*name*) of (*address*) ('my Trustees') to be the Executors and Trustees of this Will.

(4) I GIVE to (*cohabitant*) free of tax all my personal chattels (as defined in the Administration of Estates Act 1925) and without imposing an obligation or creating a trust I would like (him)/(her), either by Will or lifetime gifts, to pass on to my children and grandchildren any articles which have particular associations with my family.

(5) I GIVE to (*cohabitant*)   pounds (£   ) free of tax.

(6) I RELEASE (*cohabitant*), free of tax, from any sum of money that (he)/(she) may owe me at the time of my death.

(7) I GIVE the rest of my estate to my Trustees on trust to:
    (a) sell or retain;
    (b) pay my debts, funeral expenses, testamentary expenses and inheritance tax including the tax attributable to property that I hold as a joint tenant; and
    (c) hold what remains ('my residuary estate') as follows.

(8) MY TRUSTEES will pay or transfer my residuary estate to my children (*name*) and (*name*) equally or to the survivor of them but if either of them dies before me leaving a child or children who reach the age of (18) that child or those children equally will take the share of my residuary estate that (his)/(her)/(their) parent would otherwise have taken.

(9) (Trustees' powers, including a clause excluding the operation of the apportionment rules.[337])

(10) I HAVE NOT MADE greater provision for (*cohabitant*) in this Will because:
    (a) the house and bank accounts that we hold as joint tenants will automatically pass to (him)/(her) by right of survivorship;
    (b) I am satisfied that (he)/(she) has adequate resources to enable (him)/(her) to live comfortably for the rest of (his)/(her) life;
    (c) of the possibility that if I had left the whole of my estate to (him)/(her) my family could be disinherited and (his)/(her) family commensurately enriched.

SIGNED by (*testator*) in our joint presence and then by us in (his)/(hers).

---

[337] Bearing in mind that the Trusts (Capital and Income) Act 2013 excluded the majority of the rules of apportionment.

6.156   *Application for a standing search*

(NCPR 43(1))

In the High Court of Justice

Family Division

The Principal [*or*   District Probate] Registry

I/We apply for the entry of a standing search so that there shall be sent to me/us an office copy of every grant of representation in England and Wales in the estate of—

Full name of deceased:

Full address:

Alternative or alias names:
Exact date of death:

which either has issued not more than 12 months before the entry of this application or issues within six months thereafter.

Signed:
Name in block letters:
Full address:
Reference No. (if any):

(NCPR 1988, Form 2.)

Section 2   Contentious precedents

6.157   *Claim form for application by surviving cohabitant for provision from the estate of a deceased cohabitant*

	Claim Form (CPR Part 8)	In the
		OAKWOOD COUNTY COURT
		Claim No.

Claimant

    JENNY PINE

SEAL

Defendant(s)   ROBERT FOREST and JOHN BEECH, the personal representatives of PAUL BEECH, deceased   (1)
RICHARD BEECH   (2)
MARY OAK   (3)
JAMES BEECH   (4)

Details of claim (see also overleaf)

    Pursuant to the Inheritance (Provision for Family and Dependants) Act 1975 the claimant claims:
        1.   Financial provision from the net estate of Paul Beech, deceased
        2.   The costs of the claim to be paid out of the estate

Defendant's name and address   £

ROBERT FOREST & JOHN BEECH of RICHARD BEECH of MARY OAK of JAMES BEECH of	Court fee	
	Solicitor's costs	
	Issue date	

The court office at

is open between 10 am and 4 pm Monday to Friday. When corresponding with the court, please address forms or letters to the Court Manager and quote the case number.

N208 Claim form (CPR Part 8) (4.99)   *Printed on behalf of The Court Service*

Claim No.	

Details of claim (continued)

See witness statement attached.

Statement of Truth
*~~I believe~~ (The Claimant believes) that the facts stated in these particulars of claim are true.
*~~I am duly authorised by the claimant to sign this statement~~

Full name ___JANE PLANE_____

Name of claimant's solicitor's firm_____

signed _____ position or office held _____
*(Claimant)(~~Litigation friend~~)   (if signing on behalf of firm or company)
(~~Claimant's solicitor~~)

delete as appropriate

Claimant's or claimant's solicitor's address to which documents should be sent if different from overleaf. If you are prepared to accept service by DX, fax or e-mail, please add details.

6.158   Claim form for application by dependant for provision from estate and permission to proceed out of time

Claim Form (CPR Part 8)	In the
	OAKWOOD COUNTY COURT
	Claim No.

Claimant

JONATHAN CHERRY

(SEAL)

Defendant(s)   JOHN HAZEL, Administrator of the Estate
of Mary Hazel, deceased   (1)
DORIS HAZEL   (2)
JOHN HAZEL   (3)

Details of claim (see also overleaf)

Pursuant to the Inheritance (Provision for Family and Dependants) Act 1975 the claimant claims:
1.   Financial provision from the net estate of Mary Hazel deceased
2.   The costs of the claim to be paid out of the estate
3.   Permission to proceed with the claim notwithstanding that the time for doing so has expired, on the grounds set out in the witness statement served herewith.

Defendant's name and address   £

JOHN HAZEL of . . .

DORIS HAZEL of . . .

	£
Court fee	
Solicitor's costs	
Issue date	

The court office at

is open between 10 am and 4 pm Monday to Friday. When corresponding with the court, please address forms or letters to the Court Manager and quote the case number.
N208 Claim form (CPR Part 8) (4.99)   *Printed on behalf of The Court Service*

Claim No.	

Details of claim (continued)

Statement of Truth

*I believe(~~The Claimant believes~~) that the facts stated in these particulars of claim are true.

*I am duly authorised by the claimant to sign this statement

Full name ___JONATHAN CHERRY_____

Name of claimant's solicitor's firm___PLANE & PARTNERS_____

signed ___*Jonathan Cherry*___ position or office held _____

*(Claimant)(~~Litigation friend~~)   (if signing on behalf of firm or company)

(~~Claimant's solicitor~~)

delete as appropriate

PLANE & PARTNERS

Claimant's or claimant's solicitor's address to which documents should be sent if different from overleaf. If you are prepared to accept service by DX, fax or e-mail, please add details.

Notes for claimant on completing a Part 8 claim form

- Please read all of these guidance notes before you begin completing the claim form. The notes follow the order in which information is required on the form.
- Court staff can help you fill in the claim form and give information about procedure once it has been issued. But they cannot give legal advice. If you need legal advice, for example, about the likely success of your claim or the evidence you need to prove it, you should contact a solicitor or a Citizens Advice Bureau.
- If you are filling in the claim form by hand, please use black ink and write in block capitals.
- You must file any written evidence to support your claim either in or with the claim form. Your written evidence must be verified by a statement of truth.
- Copy the completed claim form, the defendant's notes for guidance and your written evidence so that you have one copy for yourself, one copy for the court and one copy for each defendant. Send or take the forms and evidence to the court office with the appropriate fee. The court will tell you how much this is.

Notes on completing the claim form

Heading

You must fill in the heading of the form to indicate whether you want the claim to be issued in a county court or in the High Court (The High Court means either a District Registry (attached to a county court) or the Royal Courts of Justice in London).

Use whichever of the following is appropriate:

'In the .... County Court'
(inserting the name of the court)

or

'In the High Court of Justice .... Division'
(inserting eg. 'Queen's Bench' or 'Chancery' as appropriate)
'...................... District Registry'
(inserting the name of the District Registry)

or

'In the High Court of Justice .... Division,
(inserting eg. 'Queen's Bench' or 'Chancery' as appropriate)
Royal Courts of Justice'

Claimant and defendant details

As the person issuing the claim, you are called the 'claimant'; the person you are suing is called the 'defendant'. Claimants who are under 18 years old (unless otherwise permitted by the court) and patients within the meaning of the Mental Health Act 1983 must have a litigation friend to issue and conduct court proceedings on their behalf. Court staff will tell you more about what you need to do if this applies to you.

You must provide the following information about yourself **and** the defendant according to the capacity in which you are suing and in which the defendant is being sued. When suing or being sued as:-

an individual:

All known forenames and surname, whether Mr, Mrs, Miss, Ms or other (e.g. Dr) and residential address (**including** postcode and telephone and any fax or e-mail number) in England and Wales. Where the defendant is a proprietor of a business, a partner in a firm or an individual sued in the name of a club or other unincorporated association, the address for service should be the usual or last known place of residence **or** principal place of business of the company, firm or club or other unincorporated association.

Where the individual is:

under 18 write '(a child by Mr Joe Bloggs his litigation friend)' after the child's name.

a patient within the meaning of the Mental Health Act 1983 write '(by Mr Joe Bloggs his litigation friend)' after the patient's name.

trading under another name

you must add the words 'trading as' and the trading name e.g. 'Mr John Smith trading as Smith's Groceries'.

suing or being sued in a representative capacity

you must say what that capacity is e.g. 'Mr Joe Bloggs as the representative of Mrs Sharon Bloggs (deceased)'.

suing or being sued in the name of a club or other unincorporated association

add the words 'suing/sued on behalf of' followed by the name of the club or other unincorporated association.

a firm

enter the name of the firm followed by the words 'a firm' e.g. 'Bankbox – a firm' and an address for service which is either a partner's residential address or the principal or last known place of business.

a corporation (other than a company)

enter the full name of the corporation and the address which is either its principal office **or** any other place where the corporation carries on activities and which has a real connection with the claim.

a company registered in England and Wales

enter the name of the company and an address which is either the company's registered office **or** any place of business that has a real, or the most, connection with the claim e.g. the shop where the goods were bought.

an overseas company (defined by s744 of the Companies Act 1985)

Enter the name of the company and either the address registered under s691 of the Act **or** the address of the place of business having a real, or the most, connection with the claim.

Details of claim

Under this heading you must set out either
- the question(s) you wish the court ot decide; **or**
- the remedy you are seeking and the legal basis for your claim; **and**
- if your claim is being made under a specific CPR Part or practice direction, you must state which.

Defendant's name and address

Enter in this box the full name and address of the defendant to be served with the claim form (i.e. one claim form for each defendant). If the defendant is to be served outside England and Wales, you may need to obtain the court's permission.

Address for documents

Insert in this box the address at which you wish to receive documents, if different from the address you have already given under the heading 'Claimant'. The address you give must be either that of your solicitors or your residential or business address and must be in England or Wales. If you live or carry on business outside England and Wales, you can give some other address within England and Wales.

Statement of truth

This must be signed by you, by your solicitor or your litigation friend, as appropriate.

Where the claimant is a registered company or a corporation the claim must be signed by either the director, treasurer, secretary, chief executive, manager or other officer of the company or (in the case of a corporation) the mayor, chairman, president or town clerk.

Notes for defendant (Part 8 claim form)

Please read these notes carefully – they will help you to decide what to do about this claim.

- You have 14 days from the date on which you were served with the claim form (see below) in which to respond to the claim by completing and returning the acknowledgment of service enclosed with this claim form.

- If you **do not return** the acknowledgment of service, you will be allowed to attend any hearing of this claim but you will **not** be allowed to take part in the hearing unless the court gives you permission to do so.

Court staff can tell you about procedures but they cannot give legal advice. If you need legal advice, you should contact a solicitor or Citizens Advice Bureau immediately

Responding to this claim

Time for responding

The completed acknowledgment of service must be returned to the court office within 14 days of the date on which the claim form was served on you. If the claim form was

- sent by post, the 14 days begins 2 days from the date of the postmark on the envelope.
- delivered or left at your address, the 14 days begins the day after it was delivered.
- handed to you personally, the 14 days begins on the day it was given to you.

Completing the acknowledgment of service

You should complete section A, B, **or** C as appropriate **and all** of section D.

Section A – contesting the claim

If you wish to contest the remedy sought by the claimant in the claim form, you should complete section A. If you seek a remedy different from that sought by the claimant, you should give full details in the space provided.

Section B – disputing the court's jurisdiction

You should indicate your intention by completing section B and filing an application disputing the courts jurisdiction within 14 days of filing of your acknowledgment of service at the court. The court will arrange a hearing date for the application and tell you and the claimant when and where to attend.

Section C – objecting to use of procedure

If you believe that the claimant should not have issued the claim under Part 8 because:

- there **is** a substantial dispute of fact involved and
- you do not agree that the rule or practice direction stated does provide for the claimant to use this procedure

you should complete section C setting out your reasons in the space provided.

Written evidence

If you wish to file written evidence in reply to the claimant's written evidence, you must send it to the court with your acknowledgment of service. Your written evidence must be verified by a statement of truth or the court may disallow it.

Serving other parties

At the same time as you file your completed acknowledgment of service (and any written evidence) with the court, you must also send copies of both the form and any written evidence to any other party named on the claim form.

What happens next

The claimant may, within 14 days of receiving any written evidence from you, file further evidence in reply. On receipt of your acknowledgment of service and any evidence from the claimant in reply, the court file will be referred to the judge for directions for the disposal of the claim. The court will contact you and tell you what to do next.

Note: The court may already have given directions or arranged a hearing. If so, you will have received a copy with the claim form. You should comply with any directions and attend any hearing in addition to completing, filing and serving your acknowledgment of service.

Statement of truth

This must be signed by you, by your solicitor or your litigation friend, as appropriate.

Where the claimant is a registered company or a corporation the claim must be signed by either the director, treasurer, secretary, chief executive, manager or other officer of the company or (in the case of a corporation) the mayor, chairman, president or town clerk.

6.159 Witness statement in support of a claim by a surviving cohabitant for provision from estate of deceased cohabitant and application for an interim order

IN THE [ ] COUNTY COURT   CLAIM NUMBER

IN THE MATTER OF

An application under section 1 of the Inheritance (Provision for Family and Dependants) Act 1975

AND IN THE
MATTER OF

The estate of [name] deceased

BETWEEN:

	[name]	Claimant
and		
	[name(s)] Personal Representatives of [name], deceased	1st Defendants
and		
	[name]	2nd Defendant
and		
	[name]	3rd Defendant
and		
	[name]	4th Defendant

WITNESS STATEMENT OF [name]

I, [name], of [address] say as follows:

(1) I make this statement in support of my claim for provision from the estate of [name] ('the deceased') and in support of my application for an interim payment from the estate.

(2) The deceased and I began to cohabit six years ago when I moved into his home. We continued to cohabit right up until his death [*date*]. We had known one another for about two years before we began to live together. The deceased was 59 at the date of his death. I am 42.

(3) A Grant of Probate of the deceased's will was taken out on [*date*] and the personal representatives are the deceased's brother and his solicitor.

(4) The will of the deceased made no provision for me apart from a small legacy of £5,000. The will provides for the deceased's residuary estate to be shared between his three adult children, who are defendants to this claim.

(5) The deceased made his will on [*date*], about a year after we met, and before we started to live together. I believe that the provision that he made in his will recognised the depth of our friendship. Although he talked about changing his will after we began to live together this is something he did not get round to doing.

(6) When I first met the deceased I was working as a personal assistant earning enough to live in a comfortable way. Like the deceased, I had recently been divorced and had a lump sum of £125,000 as my share of the matrimonial assets. I intended to buy my own house, but as the relationship developed with the deceased it looked as though it may be a lasting relationship and so I continued to live in rented accommodation. Eventually we decided to live together and as the deceased owned his own home it was agreed that I would move in with him. Over the years that we lived together I was very happy to use my savings to pay for holidays and other treats, and to improve the deceased's home. For example, four years ago I paid £30,000 to have the kitchen and bathroom refitted. Although the deceased earned far more than I did, we shared the household outgoings. The deceased would pay all the bills, and I would buy the food and pay for dry cleaning, newspapers and the like. I was not able to save anything from my earnings and I now have only £48,000 remaining of my lump sum. I have no other assets apart from the car that the deceased bought for me two years ago that is now worth about £4,500. My net monthly income is £1,300 and I exhibit to this statement a schedule setting out my income needs.

(7) I believe the deceased's house to be worth in the region of £350,000. I am unsure as to the extent of the other assets in the estate, but I know that there is a share portfolio, and a car worth about £9,000. The deceased was a member of his employer's pension scheme.

(8) Given the settled and committed nature of my relationship with the deceased, my contribution in looking after the deceased and the home for six years, I ask the court to find that in all the circumstances it is unreasonable for there to be no provision for me from the deceased's estate apart from the legacy of £5,000. The beneficiaries of the residuary estate are all over 25 years and have good jobs and own their own homes. I am left after six years with very little capital. Had I invested my lump sum in a property as I had initially intended I would have been in a much better financial position than I am now. Although my earnings are sufficient to live on in a modest way, since living with the deceased I have become accustomed to living to a much higher standard.

(9) I therefore ask for sufficient financial provision to be made for me from the estate by way of a lump sum payment to enable me to rehouse myself and provide a financial cushion.

DATED this   day of

Statement of Truth

The claimant believes that the facts stated in this witness statement are true.

Signed . . . .

6.160 *Witness statement of dependant in support of claim for provision from estate and application for permission to proceed outside the time-limits*

IN THE [ ] COUNTY COURT   CLAIM NUMBER

IN THE MATTER OF

An application under section 1 of the Inheritance (Provision for Family and Dependants) Act 1975

AND IN THE
MATTER OF

The estate of [name] deceased

BETWEEN:

	[name]	Claimant
And		
	[name]	1st Defendant
	Administrator of	
	[name], deceased	
And		
	[name]	2nd Defendant
And		
	[name]	3rd Defendant

WITNESS STATEMENT OF [name]

I, [name], of [name] say as follows:

(1)   I make this statement in support of my claim for provision from the estate of [name] ('the deceased') and in support of my application for permission to proceed with my claim notwithstanding that the time-limit for bringing a claim has expired.

(2)   The deceased died on [*date*] and a Grant of Letters of Administration was taken out by the deceased's brother, [name] on [*date*]. The deceased's mother, [name] and her brother are the only beneficiaries of the estate. To my knowledge they are both very comfortable financially and have no particular need of the windfall that the deceased's death will bring them.

(3)   I believe that the deceased's estate to be valued at a figure in the region of £850,000.

(4)   The deceased and I had known each other from our schooldays, and after leaving school had always kept in touch. About five years ago we began to see one another on a more serious basis, and although we never lived together, we had a very close relationship. I am now 38 and the deceased was 36 when she died from cancer.

(5)   The deceased had a very successful career as an actuary and had never married. She had very high earnings and had also amassed savings. I was at that time, and I still am trying to make a living as an artist. Initially I was fortunate to be able to use rooms rent free in a friend's office as a studio, but about four years ago my friend sold the offices and I had nowhere to go. I could not afford to pay a market rent. The deceased offered to pay the rent on a studio for me and so I signed a seven-year lease and every month since then until her death she gave me £650 for this purpose. This was paid by standing order direct to the landlord's bank account. She was very generous in other ways as well because she was aware that I was always struggling financially. She would frequently write out cheques to pay my bills when she knew that I did not have enough to pay them and she bought most of my clothes. The deceased invariably paid when we went out for meals and she always paid for a holiday for the two of us twice a year.

(6)   As will be apparent from my trading accounts for the last two financial years, copies of which are exhibited to this statement as [ ], my income from my business is not sufficient to discharge all my outgoings that are set out on the schedule exhibited as [ ]. The plain fact is that I was unable to make ends meet without the considerable cash injections I received from the deceased, which I would estimate at about £900 per month taking into account everything that the deceased paid for on my behalf. I am now very heavily overdrawn at the bank having had to meet the cost of my studio myself for several months as well as having to pay for many things that the deceased would have helped me with had she been alive.

(7)   In these circumstances I ask the court to find that the deceased was maintaining me at the date of her death and that it is unreasonable that I receive no provision from her estate.

(8)   I am aware that my claim is brought outside the time-limit but for the reasons set out below I ask the court to give me permission to proceed with my claim.

(9)   The deceased was diagnosed with cancer and died within a very short space of time. When she knew she was ill, her mother moved into her home to be with her. I visited her every day, and did what I could to make her final days comfortable.

(10) I was not sure whether or not her mother knew the extent to which the deceased supported me and I did not mention it until after her death when I felt I had to say something about the standing order for the rent for my studio. The deceased's mother discussed it with her brother and they agreed that they would continue to pay it for a few months until I could make other arrangements. This they did for three months.

(11) The deceased's brother then wrote to me to say that the payments would end with immediate effect. I was grateful to them for continuing the payments for as long as they had so I did not say anything. However, a few months later when I realised that I was getting into a mess financially, I went to see my bank manager.

(12) He advised me to see a solicitor which I did. He said I should get Counsel's opinion on whether I could make a claim against the estate. I was rather put off by the cost of this, and also I felt it was rather distasteful. However, after another interview with my bank manager I decided that I had no alternative and I instructed my solicitor to proceed.

(13) By this time the Grant had been taken out and eight months had elapsed. I realise that I should have taken action sooner, but I was reluctant to do so largely because it seemed rather grasping. However, the reality is that for over three years the deceased subsidised my living expenses to a very large degree, and I find it impossible to make ends meet without that financial help.

(14) Furthermore, I would not have taken on the commitment of rented studio accommodation if the deceased had not offered to pay for it.

(15) In the circumstances I ask the court to accept that I have a good claim for provision from the deceased's estate and that it would be unjust to prevent me from proceeding with that claim because for good reasons I did not start my claim until two months after the expiry of the time-limit.

DATED this   day of

Statement of Truth

The claimant believes that the facts stated in this witness statement are true.

Signed . . . .

6.161 Witness statement of cohabitant in support of claim for provision for herself and child of the family, for an interim payment and for the deceased's beneficial interest in jointly owned property to be treated as part of his net estate

IN THE [ ] COUNTY COURT   CLAIM NUMBER

IN THE MATTER
OF

An application under section 1 of the Inheritance (Provision for Family and Dependants) Act 1975

AND IN THE
MATTER OF

The estate of [name], deceased

BETWEEN:

A	Claimant

And

Personal Representative(s) of [name], deceased	1st Defendants

And

B	2nd Defendant

WITNESS STATEMENT OF [name]

I, [name], of [address] say as follows:

(1) I make this statement in support of my claim for provision from the estate of [name] ('the deceased').

(2) The deceased and I began to cohabit eight years ago, when he moved into my house. We continued to live together until the deceased was killed in a road traffic accident on [*date*]. There are two children of our relationship, C born on [*date*] who is five and D born on [*date*] who is three. I am 36 years old and the deceased was 48 when he died.

(3) A Grant of Probate of the deceased's will was taken out by his wife, B, and his solicitor on [*date*].

(4) As far as I am aware, the estate comprises savings and investments of about £280,000. The deceased's beneficial interest in his former matrimonial home passed to B as the surviving joint owner on his death. I estimate the value of that interest at £230,000 and I ask the court to direct that this be treated as part of the deceased's net estate. If this is not treated as part of the deceased's net estate I would say that the net estate will not be of sufficient size to make reasonable provision for myself and the children.

(5) The deceased remained married to B up until his death. They did not have any children. He had left her in order to live with me and she has never agreed to a divorce. Even though he could have divorced her after five years' separation he said that he could not be bothered getting involved with solicitors and he did not want to have an argument with her over the financial side of things. We never discussed the question of a will. I simply took it that he had made provision for me and the children. As it was, he had made a will soon after he was married to B in which he left everything to her, and he had clearly forgotten to revise it in the light of his changed circumstances.

(6) The house in which I live is in my sole name. It is worth about £275,000 and is subject to a mortgage. The equity in the property is about £140,000. I had bought the property with my divorce settlement before I met the deceased. At the time I met the deceased I was working and earning enough to pay the mortgage and live in a modest way. I continued to work after the deceased came to live with me, but because we then pooled our resources we lived to a much better standard.

(7)   When C was born, I gave up work and the deceased then had to support us entirely from his earnings. D was born a couple of years later and I have not returned to work. I would find it difficult to earn enough to keep the family afloat because of my limited earning capacity and the cost of child care. As at the date of his death, the deceased was earning £5,300 net per month and he paid £2,250 per month into my bank account for the mortgage and housekeeping. I doubt that I could earn much more than £800 per month in a full-time job. As will be seen from the schedule of outgoings exhibited at [ ] the mortgage repayments alone are £525 and the shortfall of my present income from State benefits over routine expenditure is considerable. I exhibit to this statement marked SB2, a letter from my bank manager dated [*date*] warning me that I have exceeded my overdraft limit, together with my bank statements since the death of the deceased. It will be apparent that I am getting very heavily into debt simply by discharging the routine household accounts without the standing order payment of £2,250 that was paid into my account every month by the deceased.

(8)   I am in a desperate financial situation. I have no capital other than the equity in my house, and no prospect of being able to earn enough to support myself and the two children. B has a good job and was not in need of maintenance from the deceased. I am aware that the former matrimonial home has a small mortgage and that it is larger than is necessary for one person. B could rehouse herself in a suitable property mortgage free with her own share of the former matrimonial home.

(9)   In the circumstances, I ask for provision to be made for me and the children from the deceased's estate, for the deceased's share of his former matrimonial home to be treated as part of his net estate, and for interim provision to be made for me from the estate so that the children and I can pay the bills as they fall due and repay my overdraft.

DATED this   day of

Statement of Truth

The claimant believes that the facts stated in this witness statement are true.

Signed . . . .

6.162   *Witness statement of adult in support of claim for provision from estate of deceased step-parent*

IN THE [ ] COUNTY COURT   CLAIM NUMBER

IN THE MATTER
OF

An application under section 1 of the Inheritance (Provision for Family and Dependants) Act 1975

AND IN THE
MATTER OF

The estate of [name], deceased

BETWEEN:

A	Claimant

and

AB and CD the personal representatives of the estate of [name], deceased	1st Defendants

and

B	2nd Defendant

STATEMENT OF [name]

I, [name], of [address] make this statement in support of my claim for provision from the estate of my late step-father, [name] ('the deceased').

(1) The deceased died on [*date*] aged 83. A Grant of Probate was taken out by the executors of his will, the first defendants. The sole beneficiary of the will, as my mother pre-deceased him, is his daughter, my step-sister, B.

(2) I am 53 years of age. My mother and the deceased were married when I was three years of age. B was born eight years after their marriage. She is 45 and for the past 20 years has lived in New Zealand.

(3) My mother was never married to my father and I have never had any knowledge of his identity or whereabouts. The deceased treated me as his own child, but once B was born I did not feel that our relationship was quite the same as it had been before. He clearly preferred B to me, and this obviously had implications for my own relationship with my half-sister.

(4) I have never moved out of Oakwood. I have a job working at the local library. I have never married. About 15 years ago my mother's health began to fail. I took on the shopping and household chores which the deceased was not inclined to do himself and effectively ran the house for them. In addition, I took my mother to medical appointments, and generally ran them both about as the deceased could not drive.

(5) My mother died three years ago. She left her estate to the deceased. After her death I continued to look after the deceased and his house, and to do the garden and such other chores as I could manage. About a year before his death the deceased agreed that I could stay in the house with him so that I would be there if he needed any help in the night. The deceased was never one for spending money on outside help if someone would do it for him for nothing. I kept my own home although I did not live there, and I paid my own way in terms of food. Even though I know that the deceased was grateful for what I did, my impression was that he saw me as doing my duty, effectively repaying his kindness in bringing me up as his daughter.

(6) I have not been as fortunate in life as my half-sister. She has married well and has no particular need of the deceased's estate. I have always put my mother and the deceased first, and have attended to their needs selflessly. I own a modest home, and have earnings of £1,250 per month net. Otherwise I have no assets or income. Had the deceased pre-deceased my mother, I would have inherited half the combined estates on her death, and it seems grossly unfair that I should now inherit nothing, particularly bearing in mind the contribution I made in caring for them both.

(7) I therefore ask the court to find that it is unreasonable for no provision to have been made for me from the deceased's estate and to make provision for me by way of a lump sum.

DATED this   day of

Statement of Truth

The claimant believes that the facts stated in this witness statement are true.

Signed . . . .

6.163 *Witness statement of personal representatives in answer to claim*

IN THE [ ] COUNTY COURT   CLAIM NUMBER

IN THE MATTER
OF

An application under section 1 of the Inheritance (Provision for Family and Dependants) Act 1975

AND IN THE
MATTER OF

The estate of [name], deceased

BETWEEN:

A		Claimant

and

Personal Representatives of [name], deceased	1st Defendant(s)

and

B		2nd Defendant

WITNESS STATEMENT OF 1st DEFENDANTS

I/WE, [name(s)] of [*address*]

Make this statement in answer to the application by A for provision from the estate of [name], deceased ('the deceased').

(1)   We are the personal representatives of the deceased.

(2)   The grant of probate was granted to us out of the [ ] District Registry on [*date*]. Exhibited to this statement as PR1 is a true copy of the grant of probate.

(3)   The gross value of the deceased's estate for probate purposes was £280,245 consisting of the following:

Cash at	£6,500
Cash at	£3,400
Shares per schedule PR2	£270,345

(4)   The deceased was in addition entitled to receive a death benefit from his employers under the terms of the company pension scheme. No nomination was made in respect of this and the payment will be made at the discretion of the trustees of the scheme. The death benefit amounts to £144,000.

(5)   The liabilities of the deceased at the date of his death, including funeral expenses, are set out in the schedule marked PR3 annexed hereto.

(6)   The estate has not yet been fully administered.

(7)   The sole beneficiary of the estate in accordance with the deceased's will is his widow, B. A copy of the deceased's will dated [*date*] is exhibited and marked PR4.

(8)   The following matters are relevant to the exercise of the court's discretion:

[*give details*]

DATED this   day of

Statement of Truth

The first defendants believe that the facts stated in this witness statement are true.

Signed . . . .

6.164   Specimen directions on application for provision from estate

IN THE [ ] COUNTY COURT   CLAIM NUMBER

IN THE MATTER
OF

An application under section 1 of the Inheritance (Provision for Family and Dependants) Act 1975

AND IN THE
MATTER OF

The estate of [name], deceased

BETWEEN:

	A	Claimant
and		
	Personal Representative(s) of [name], deceased	1st Defendant(s)
and		
	B	2nd Defendant

UPON HEARING the solicitors for all parties

IT IS ORDERED THAT:

(1) The application for an interim payment will be heard on the first available date after 28 days with a time estimate of one hour.

(2) The 2nd Defendant shall by 4pm on [*date*] file and serve a witness statement in answer to the application for provision from the estate.

(3) The Claimant shall by 4pm on [*date*] file and serve a witness statement in reply, if so advised.

(4) The claim for provision from the estate will be heard on the first available date after 56 days with a time estimate of one day.

(5) Costs in the case.

6.165   Order on application for interim payment

IN THE [ ] COUNTY COURT   CLAIM NUMBER

IN THE MATTER
OF

An application under section 1 of the Inheritance (Provision for Family and Dependants) Act 1975

AND IN THE
MATTER OF

The estate of [name], deceased

BETWEEN:

	A	Claimant
and		
	Personal Representative(s) of [name], deceased	1st Defendant(s)

and

B   2nd Defendant

UPON HEARING the solicitors for both parties

IT IS ORDERED THAT

(1) [name] and [name] as the executors of the will of [name] deceased shall pay to the Claimant from the net estate of the deceased
   (a) a lump sum payment of £2,500 by 4 pm on [*date*]
   (b) periodical payments at the rate of £750 per month payable monthly in advance from the date of this order until the final hearing of the claim or further order.

(2) The payments ordered to be made by paragraph (1) of this order shall be made on condition that they are accounted for by the claimant following the making of a final order herein.

(3) The costs of this application shall be reserved to the final hearing.

DATED this   day of

6.166   *Order on application for provision from estate*

IN THE [ ] COUNTY COURT   CLAIM NUMBER

IN THE MATTER
OF

An application under section 1 of the Inheritance (Provision for Family and Dependants) Act 1975

AND IN THE
MATTER OF

The estate of [name], deceased

BETWEEN:

A   Claimant

and

Personal Representative(s) of   1st Defendant(s)
[name], deceased

and

B   2nd Defendant

UPON HEARING COUNSEL FOR ALL PARTIES

AND UPON the court being satisfied that the disposition of the deceased's estate by his will dated [*date*] is not such as to make reasonable provision for the claimant and the children of the deceased [name] d.o.b. [*date*] and [name] d.o.b. [*date*].

IT IS ORDERED THAT:

(1) The beneficial half share of the deceased in the property [address] shall be treated as part of the net estate of the deceased.

(2) [name] and [name], the executors of the will of the deceased dated [*date*] shall pay the claimant a lump sum of £120,000, payable as to £50,000 by 4pm on [*date*] And as to the balance, less the sums to be accounted for by the claimant pursuant to the order dated [*date*], by 4pm on [*date*].

(3) The will of the deceased shall have effect and shall be deemed to have had such effect as from the death of the deceased.

(4) The costs of the claimant shall be subject to a detailed assessment in default of agreement and paid out of the net estate of the deceased.

DATED this   day of

CHAPTER 7

PENSION RIGHTS OF COHABITANTS

LAW AND PRACTICE

7.1 Introduction

Individuals may acquire rights to pensions benefits during their lifetimes. If the individual lives to pension age, a pension becomes payable until death. However, there are benefits which are paid to other persons on the basis of the individual's contributions and entitlement. In many cases, these benefits are restricted to pensions for widows and widowers and dependent children. However, there are circumstances under which dependants or other persons who are not married to the person entitled to the pension can benefit. The purpose of this chapter is to look at the circumstances in which a cohabitant may benefit from the pension arrangements of his or her partner. For ease of reference, the person having the primary pension rights is referred to as 'the pension holder'.

The position of a married couple who are divorced has been altered radically over the past two decades in relation to pension benefits. 'Earmarking' (or 'pension attachment' as it is now termed), under which a divorced spouse may be awarded a lump sum or pension benefits out of the pension entitlement of the other spouse when that benefit becomes payable, was introduced by the Pension Act 1995.

The Welfare Reform and Pensions Act 1999 introduced pension sharing on divorce (or nullity, but not judicial separation), under which courts have the power on the breakdown of a marriage to split existing pension benefits between the spouses. The non-pension holder may be awarded a pension credit which creates an indefeasible pension for that person and can (depending on the circumstances) either be left in the existing scheme as specific benefits for that former spouse ('internal transfer') or transferred out to other permitted pension arrangements ('external transfer').

None of these provisions apply to unmarried partners.

The Civil Partnership Act 2004[1] enabled amendments to be made to pensions legislation by statutory instrument to implement the changes necessary for

---

[1]   Civil Partnership Act 2004, c 33, s 255.

same-sex civil partners to be treated in the same way as married couples. State pension rights have been extended to civil partners so that female civil partners are able to claim a basic state pension using their civil partner's NI contribution record, where the contributing civil partner was born on or after 5 April 1950 and has attained state pension age. However, because of the difference in state pension ages, male civil partners will only qualify from 2015. Surviving civil partners of members of contracted-out schemes are eligible for survivors' benefits based on contracted-out rights earned by service from 6 April 1988. Additionally, they are eligible for survivors' benefits based upon pensionable service from 5 December 2005. Civil partners do not, therefore, enjoy full equality with married couples in relation to survivors' benefits. Survivors' benefits in respect of pre-5 December 2005 non-contracted-out service depend upon an amendment to the relevant scheme rules.[2]

7.2 State retirement pension

The state retirement pension (SRP) is a state benefit payable on reaching pensionable age to those with a sufficient National Insurance record. Pensionable age is currently 65 for men born before 6 December 1953. The age at which women can claim their SRP was 60 until April 2010. This is to be equalised at 65 for both men and women by November 2018. The change is being gradually phased in. Women born before 6 April 1950 will not be affected by the change; women born after 6 December 1953 will have a new pensionable age of 65. Further changes mean that the age at which a person will be able to claim their SRP will reach (a) age 66 for both men and women by between 2018 and October 2020; (b) age 67 by between 2026 and 2028; (c) age 68 by between 2044 and 2046.[3]

A state pension age calculator can be found at www.direct.gov.uk.

Category A SRP is currently payable on a person's own NIC record, a full record being 30 years' worth. Those who are divorced or former civil partners, however, may combine their own NICs, if insufficient alone, with those of their former spouse or former civil partner to produce a category A SRP. Subsequent re-partnering as cohabitants does not interfere with such an entitlement; marriage or civil partnership post-divorce/dissolution and prior to the SRP claim, however, does prevent the entitlement based on joint NICs. Such clients should be advised carefully about the pitfalls of too early a re-marriage or new civil partnership.

Married people and civil partners also currently can become entitled to a Category B SRP pension by virtue of their spouse's or civil partner's contributions. Widows, widowers and surviving civil partners can also claim a category B pension based on their late spouse's or late civil partner's NICs.

---

2   Equality Act 2010, Sch 9, para 18(1).
3   Pensions Act 1995, Sch 4, Part 1 as amended by the Pensions Act 2007, the Pensions Act 2011 and the Pensions Act 2014, ss 26 and 27.

These rules are complex. However, for cohabitants, no such claim can be made: there is no provision to base an SRP entitlement on the NICs of a cohabitant.

Bereavement benefits can be claimed by widow(er)s and surviving civil partners who are bereaved under pension age. Again, no such benefits can be claimed by the other partner if one partner in an unmarried couple dies.

It is currently possible to defer a SRP claim so as to enhance its value (or receive a lump sum). Whilst spouses and civil partners can inherit the benefits of such deferral should their spouse or civil partner die whilst deferring, this inheritance is not available to cohabitants: for them the value of the late partner's deferral is lost.

7.3   State Second Pension

Additional State Pension (ASP) consists of the State Second Pension (S2P) and the State Earnings Related Pension Scheme (SERPS), which S2P replaced as from April 2002. However, existing SERPS entitlements are preserved. ASP is payable as an addition to the SRP. Consequently, its application to cohabitants is the same. Employees generally pay additional contributions to qualify for ASP, unless they are a member of an occupational pension scheme and their employment is contracted out of ASP. Contracting out for defined contribution pension schemes (both occupational and personal pension schemes) was abolished from 6 April 2012.[4] Members of such schemes are contracted back into ASP for the future. However, contracting out is still currently possible in relation to defined benefit pension schemes. Contracting out of such schemes will be abolished when the new single tier state pension is brought into effect on 6 April 2016.[5] Provisions which allow widow(er)s and surviving civil partners to inherit a proportion of their late spouse's or late civil partner's ASP do not benefit cohabitants who are not married or civil partners. For those reaching pensionable age on or after 6 April 2016, there will be a single tier pension (see 7.4) and no ASP.

7.4   State single tier pension

The new state single tier pension (STP) was introduced by the Pensions Act 2014 and will come into force on 6 April 2016. It will apply to those who reach pensionable age on or after 6 April 2016, ie men who were born on or after 6 April 1951 and women who were born on or after 6 April 1953. There will be a qualifying period of 35 years of NI contributions in order to qualify for the full rate as compared with the 30 year qualifying period under the current scheme. STP will be a single, flat rate payment with no ASP. A person who has fewer than 35 qualifying years (but not less than 10 qualifying years) will be entitled to a reduced rate of STP. Contributions made after a person has already accrued 35 qualifying years will not provide any increased pension. A

---

4   Pensions Act 2007, s 15(1) and Sch 4.
5   Pensions Act 2014, s 24.

transitional rate of STP will be payable to a person falling within the new scheme, who has at least the minimum number of qualifying years and at least one qualifying year attributable to tax years prior to the introduction of STP. Such a person will be entitled to a 'foundation amount' representing the higher of their entitlement under the new scheme or under the current scheme. There is no equivalent (with very limited exceptions) to the category B pension under the current scheme, whereby a person may obtain a pension in reliance on their spouse's/civil partner's contributions record.

7.5   Taxation of pension schemes

The taxation of pension schemes is a complex area, a detailed discussion of which is outside the scope of this work. The Finance Act 2004 introduced provisions intended to simplify the taxation of pension schemes as from April 2006. There are two limits on pension contributions: the lifetime allowance and the annual allowance. For 2014/15, the lifetime allowance (the total amount of pension savings that can benefit from tax relief) is £1.25m. The annual allowance (the annual limit of tax relief on contributions) is £40,000 for 2014/15. Significant changes to the access to money purchase pension funds were introduced by the Taxation of Pensions Act 2014 with effect from 6 April 2015. They permit an individual with defined contribution arrangements, who is above the minimum pension age, to take an unlimited amount of income from their pension fund by what is known as 'flexi access drawdown' and which will be available alongside 'capped pension drawdown' arrangements in place prior to 6 April 2015.[6] It was also possible prior to 6 April 2015 for an individual, who has a secure pension income from specified sources of £12,000 per annum to take an unlimited income under 'flexible pension draw down'. Such arrangements automatically become flexi access drawdown from 6 April 2015. Under flexi access drawdown, 25% will be available tax-free with the balance being taxed at the individual's marginal rate of income tax. Those who take an income from their pension by way of flexi access drawdown will have their further pension contributions restricted to a newly-introduced money purchase annual allowance of £10,000 per annum aimed at restricting the ability to recycle income into a new pension arrangement to take further tax-free lump sum payments. For funds not in drawdown, it will be possible to offer an uncrystallised funds pension lump sum, which may be in the form of a single payment representing all benefits within the scheme or by way of stage payments. Each payment will be considered as part tax-free cash (25%) and the remainder (75%) will be taxed at the individual's marginal rate.

Changes were also made in relation to the tax charge on defined contribution pension funds on death. Prior to 6 April 2015, where death occurred before age 75, the pension fund, when crystallised (that is, already in a drawdown

---

6   A method by which an individual could draw an income directly from their pension fund rather than secure an annuity. The maximum income that can be drawn (providing the capped drawdown arrangement was in place prior to 6 April 2015) is 150% of the income available from the factors provided by the Government Actuary's Department, which are broadly equivalent to a single life, non-increasing annuity.

account), was subject to a 55% tax charge if paid as a lump sum or at the dependant's marginal rate, if drawn down. If the fund was uncrystallised, it could be taken tax-free as a lump sum or at the dependant's marginal rate, if drawn down. Where death occurred at age 75 or over, the position was – in the case of both crystallised and uncrystallised benefits – that there was a tax charge of 55% if the funds were paid as a lump sum or at the dependant's marginal rate, if drawn down. Under the system in relation to payments made on or after 6 April 2015 (rather than in respect of deaths occurring on or after that date), where death occurs before age 75, the fund (whether crystallised or uncrystallised) may be taken tax-free either as a lump sum or as a drawn down pension by any beneficiary. Where death occurs at age 75 or over, there will be a tax charge of 45% (or the recipient's marginal rate from 2016/17) if paid as a lump sum or at the recipient's marginal rate, if drawn down. These proposals may increase the flexibility available to cohabitants in their financial planning.

Currently, individuals cannot commence taking their pensions before age 55, unless they have a 'protected retirement age'.[7] There are also some other exceptions, most notably, the uniformed services schemes and those suffering from a terminal illness. The minimum pension age will increase from age 55 to age 57 in2028. It will then remain 10 years below the state pension age.

The payment of a pension may be guaranteed for a fixed period. Where the pension holder dies before the end of that period and payments continue to be paid to the estate, they will be subject to inheritance tax. However, pension payments made to the deceased's widow, widower or surviving civil partner are not subject to inheritance tax. If a lump sum death benefit is payable to the deceased pension holder's personal representatives either by right or because there is no-one else who qualifies for the payment, or if the deceased could, up until death, have signed a nomination, which bound the trustees of a pension scheme to make payment to a person named by the deceased, the lump sum will be an asset of the deceased's estate liable to inheritance tax. A binding nomination is different from a letter of wishes. A letter of wishes records what the deceased would like to happen with the death benefit and does not bind the trustees of a pension scheme. Many pension schemes and policies provide a form referred to as a nomination, but which usually contains a statement that the trustees are not bound to follow the deceased's wishes. If this is the case, the form is a letter of wishes and not a binding nomination. Most pension schemes and personal pension policies allow a member to dispose of the death benefits and to make changes to the benefits that they are entitled to. Usually, the member can nominate or appoint the death benefits to someone else, assign the death benefits into a trust, or make changes to the pension benefits they intend to take and when they intend to take them. If the deceased made a nomination, appointment or assignment or made any changes to the pension benefits in the two years prior to death, a liability to inheritance tax may have arisen. Where the death benefits are assigned into a trust, the pension scheme trustees will not exercise any discretion and are obliged to make payment to the trustees

---

7   Ie those who had unqualified rights, as at 5 April 2006, to take a pension before the normal minimum pension age.

appointed by the pension holder, who also nominates the potential beneficiaries who may be considered by those trustees. In order to keep the lump sum death benefits outside the pension holder's estate for inheritance tax purposes, the trust needs to provide for the distribution of the lump sum death benefits to someone other than the policy holder's estate. This mechanism does give the policy holder greater certainty over the distribution of the lump sum death benefits. The policy holder may normally alter the trustees and preferred beneficiaries at a later stage.

7.6   Occupational pension schemes

Occupational pension schemes are schemes that are provided by employers and in the private sector are set up under a trust deed so that the assets are independent of the employer. There are also various schemes for public sector workers (eg the police, the civil service and the armed forces), which are statutorily based and have their own regulations.[8]

The vast majority of private sector occupational pension schemes qualify for income tax relief on contributions and the scheme itself is exempt from income tax and capital gains tax so that the fund accumulates tax free.[9]

As the benefits from registered schemes are limited both as to contributions and benefits, it is possible for employers to top up or replace these schemes with unapproved schemes which do not qualify for tax relief and so are not restricted as to the benefits that they can provide. Such schemes are usually set up for individuals or small groups of employees and there is no reason why their rules should not include benefits for unmarried couples.

Registered pension schemes

7.7   Pensions for surviving dependants

The statutory framework for these schemes[10] formerly restricted all benefits that could be paid to persons other than the pension holder. In the case of the death in service of the pension holder, pensions can only be paid to the pension holder's (former) widow or widower, (former) civil partner or for children and dependants. The widow or widower's or civil partner's pension is restricted to two-thirds of the maximum pension that the pension holder would have been entitled to at pension age.

Cohabitants or their children may qualify for a death in service pension as *dependants* of the pension holder. A dependant is a person who was financially

---

[8]   Such schemes were the subject of major reforms contained in the Public Service Pensions Act 2013, which take effect (other than in relation to the Local Government Pension Scheme where the reforms took effect in April 2014) from April 2015.

[9]   Pensions Act 2004, c 35.

[10]   Finance Act 2004, s 167 (pension death benefit rules).

dependent on the employee, was mutually financially dependent[11] or dependent by virtue of physical or mental impairment.[12] Although the regulations allow pensions to be paid to adult dependants in these circumstances, some company schemes restrict pensions to widows and widowers or civil partners and this would need to be checked in the scheme's booklet issued to members. Some schemes restrict dependant's pension for a surviving cohabitant to those who have, for example, lived together as a couple (whether married or in a civil partnership) for, say, two years or more.

Pensions for children have to cease when the child ceases to be dependent. This is defined as under the age of 23. If a child is dependent because of physical or mental impairment, dependence can be indefinite. Natural and adopted children qualify automatically, but other children, such as those of a partner from a previous relationship, only qualify if they were dependent financially or by reason of physical or mental impairment at the date of death of the pension holder.

Under the provisions of the Taxation of Pensions Act 2015, Sch 2, Pt 1 (see 7.5), it is possible from 6 April 2015 for death benefits from a drawdown fund to be paid to any beneficiary, eg adult children, a former cohabitant or other non-dependants.

7.8 Lump sum death in service benefits

In addition to pensions for surviving dependants, registered schemes can also provide lump sum benefits in the event of the death in service of the pension holder. From April 2006, the limits are calculated by reference to the individual's lifetime allowance. If the maximum is payable under the scheme, it can amount to a substantial amount. As discussed at 7.5, the taxation position changed significantly under the provisions contained in the Taxation of Pensions Act 2014.

To avoid the sum being liable to inheritance tax on the death of the employee, the lump sum death benefit is invariably subject to discretionary trusts exercisable by the trustees of the pension scheme. Under the HMRC guidelines,[13] tax rules do not set any conditions on who is able to receive lump sum death in service benefits. However, the pension scheme rules may do so. Beneficiaries of the lump sum can include the employee's personal representatives, potential beneficiaries in the employee's will or a nominated beneficiary as well as dependants. See, further, 7.5.

Therefore, it is essential that where a pension holder wishes to benefit his cohabitant in the event of death in service, he should complete a letter of wishes form provided by the pension scheme or, if none is provided, a letter of wishes

---

[11] This can include an unmarried partner of the same or opposite sex who relies on the other's income to maintain a standard of living that depended on the joint income.

[12] Finance Act 2004, Sch 28 para 15(3).

[13] Registered Pension Schemes Manual.

(see **6.149**). This should be sent to the trustees of the pension scheme. It will not bind the trustees; however, they are unlikely to exercise their discretion in favour of an unmarried partner if no letter of wishes has been signed and there are other competing beneficiaries. The jurisdiction of the Pensions Ombudsman may be invoked to overturn the exercise of the trustees' discretion.[14] The trustees have two years in which to distribute the lump sum.[15] Where there are competing beneficiaries, trustees often pay the lump sum over to the personal representatives of the employee's estate where it will be dealt with under his will or intestacy. This again underlines the importance of cohabitants making wills if they wish to benefit each other.

Most pension schemes allow lump sums to be paid to a trust for eligible beneficiaries. This is primarily to allow minor children to be provided for, but also gives scope for tax planning through the use of a discretionary trust with the cohabitant as one of the beneficiaries. See, further, **7.5**.

7.9   Personal pension schemes

Personal pension schemes were introduced in 1988 (replacing retirement annuity contracts for the self-employed) to encourage mobility of pensions for employees and also to provide a vehicle for the self-employed and those with no company pension scheme. A group personal pension is a collection of personal pensions provided by an employer for employees. Contributions are made to an insurance company or other pension provider with similar tax reliefs to those available to company schemes. On retirement, the fund accumulated may be accessed by the purchase of an annuity (which is currently unusual because of the poor rates now on offer) or by various means of income drawdown, which were liberalised under the Taxation of Pensions Act 2014 (see **7.5**). There is no longer any requirement to purchase an annuity at age 75.

A self-invested personal pension (SIPP) is a type of personal pension, in which the member has some control over the underlying investments.

7.10   Pensions for surviving dependants

If the pension holder dies before drawing benefits, the personal pension scheme can provide for a survivor's pension. In this context, a survivor means a widow or widower or dependant and the criteria are the same as for company pension schemes as discussed above.

---

[14]   See, for example, *Wild v Pensions Ombudsman* [1996] 2 FLR 680 (see **6.6**) and *McGurk v Royal Mail Pension Trustees Limited* (2009) 6 July, ref 74946/2, where the exercise of discretion by the trustee to pay part of a lump sum benefit to a cohabitant was upheld, notwithstanding the existence of a separated spouse and children, as the trustee had all the relevant information that the cohabitant satisfied the criteria for financial dependency.

[15]   If the lump sum is distributed after this period, it is an unauthorised payment and a tax charge will be payable.

As the terms of personal pension policies differ, any cohabitant wanting to benefit a partner should check when the pension policy is bought that it is capable of providing a survivor's pension for the surviving cohabitant. If the policy does provide a survivor's pension, the survivor should be nominated.

7.11 Lump sum death-in-service benefits

In the event of death in service, the personal pension policy itself will specify what lump sum benefit can be paid. Usually, this will be a return of the member's fund that has been built up over the years, less an amount required to purchase any survivor's annuity. Personal pension policies differ in the treatment of these payments. This will depend, for example, on whether death occurs before or after age 75, whether or not benefits have crystallised and whether an annuity has been purchased (in which event an annuity may continue for a dependant at the same or a reduced rate). A lump sum death benefit may be paid in accordance with the contract itself, or to a valid trust (so as not to be subject to inheritance tax as part of the pension holder's estate). See, further, 7.5.

In the context of cohabitation, it is essential that the pension holder either sets up a trust to receive the return of fund or other benefit with the cohabitant as a beneficiary or sends a letter of wishes for the benefit of their cohabitant to the scheme administrator. If the fund becomes payable to the pension holder's personal representatives, it will form part of his or her estate and be liable to inheritance tax because, of course, there is no spouse exemption applicable in the case of cohabitants.

7.12 Stakeholder pensions

Stakeholder pensions were introduced by the Welfare Reform and Pensions Act 1999. The intention was to provide a system of low-cost money purchase pension provision starting on 6 April 2001. Charges on stakeholder pensions are limited. Stakeholder pensions are available to both employees and the self-employed. Employers had to facilitate access to such schemes by their employees from 8 October 2001. This applied to all employers with more than five employees. Thus, employers have to have at least one designated scheme to which their employees can contribute. Take up since the introduction has been particularly poor and many companies have set up schemes that have not attracted any members. Because of the introduction of auto-enrolment with effect from 1 October 2012, the requirement to designate access to a stakeholder pension was removed, although employers may still choose to offer a stakeholder pension, if they so wish, to meet their automatic enrolment obligations, or as an additional savings option.

Contributions are limited to £3,600 gross per annum. Non-earners are able to make contributions up to this limit. Stakeholder pensions have, therefore, been used as a vehicle for tax planning by enabling a non-working cohabitant to build up a pension. Furthermore, on relationship breakdown, a non-working cohabitant may be able to set up a stakeholder pension with contributions funded by voluntary maintenance.

Stakeholder schemes can be set up either under trust in the same way as an occupational scheme or under contract like a personal pension scheme.

The regulations introducing stakeholder pensions[16] did not introduce any new provisions relating to HMRC approval and so schemes have to achieve approval either as a registered scheme if written under trust or as personal pension schemes if under contract.

Therefore, the rules on who can benefit are the same as described above for those two types of scheme. Any cohabitant who contributes to a stakeholder pension will have to establish which type of scheme he or she is joining and how he or she can best ensure that any benefits accrue to his or her partner in the event of his or her death.

7.13   Auto-enrolment/National Employment Savings Trust (NEST)

A new compulsory pension scheme for employees came into force on 1 October 2012 under the Pensions Act 2008. All eligible employees (but not the self-employed) must be enrolled by their employer in an automatic enrolment (auto-enrolment) scheme, which may be either their employer's pension scheme or a new national pension scheme called NEST. The requirement to enrol employees applies to workers who are aged 22 or over, but under state pension age, who have earnings of more than £10,000 per annum and who work or ordinarily work in the UK. Employees' contributions are supplemented by contributions from employers (a minimum of 3%) and tax relief from the Government. Employees must make a specific choice to opt out, if they do not wish to be enrolled in the scheme. NEST is intended to offer low-cost, simple pension provision for those on low to moderate earnings.

7.14   Other pensions

Pensions come in all shapes and sizes. The main types of pensions available have been discussed above. However, an awareness when advising cohabitants is required of other types of pensions which may be encountered. For example, small self-administered schemes (SSAS) are a form of occupational pension scheme limited to 12 or fewer members frequently encountered in family businesses.

The Pension Protection Fund (PPF) was established in 2005 by the Pensions Act 2004, Part 2 to act as a form of insurance to ensure the payment of certain defined benefit occupational pension scheme benefits up to a certain level, if a scheme is underfunded and of insufficient funds to pay liabilities, where the

---

16   Stakeholder Pension Schemes Regulations 2000 (SI 2000/1403).

employer is insolvent. Increasingly, given the modern trend towards mobility of employment, foreign pensions are encountered, such as international pension plans established by multi-national companies, Qualifying Recognised Overseas Pensions Schemes (QROPS), Qualifying Non-UK Pension Schemes (QNUPS) and Off-Shore Employer Finance Retirement Benefits Schemes (EFRBS). Specialist advice from an independent financial adviser will be required, when such pensions are encountered.

7.15   Children

Pensions may not be an obvious consideration for cohabitants planning for the future of their children. However, it is possible to put £2,880 per annum into a pension (for example, a stakeholder pension or other personal pension), which with automatic tax relief will equate to a gross contribution of £3,600 per annum. The child will not be able to access the pension until minimum pension age and will not, therefore, be able to use the funds to purchase a house or to fund education. It is, nonetheless, a savings option for cohabitants alongside, for example, a Junior ISA or premium bonds.

7.16   Conclusions

Pensions are a complex area both for cohabitants and the lawyers advising them. Whether on the formation of a relationship or on the breakdown of cohabitation, the advice of an independent financial adviser will be useful and, in many instances, essential, particularly in the light of the flexibilities now available under the Taxation of Pensions Act 2014. It is always important with such advice to check the particular terms of the pension scheme or policy involved and, where possible, to sign a letter of wishes in favour of the cohabitant intended to benefit. Without such action, it may be necessary to resort to an application under the Inheritance (Provision for Family and Dependants) Act 1975. Any such letter of wishes needs to be kept under review (eg on the birth of a child). Cohabitants need to view pensions in the wider context of financial planning for retirement and on death alongside other savings and wills.

CHAPTER 8

PRE-NUPTIAL AGREEMENTS

PART A   LAW AND PRACTICE

Introduction

8.1   The law of coverture

> 'The law supposes that your wife acts under your direction'. Mr. Bumble: 'If the law supposes that, the law is a ass — a idiot. If that's the eye of the law, the law is a bachelor; and the worst I wish the law is that his eye may be opened by experience — by experience.' (Charles Dickens, *Oliver Twist*)

This statement to the parish beadle in the 1838 novel following the confession by his wife that she had, for personal gain, disposed of another's jewellery, whilst provoking the memorable response, reflected an accurate summary of the law of coverture up to that time, whereby the married woman or 'feme covert' was not recognised, in most situations, as having legal rights and obligations separate from those of her husband.

From the Norman invasion of 1066 until the Married Women's Property Act 1882 came into force, the wife's existence became one with that of her husband and such property as she might be possessed of upon her marriage or became possessed of during the marriage belonged, by the *ius mariti*, to him.[1] Prior to 1066, the Vikings had first started their forays into Britain in 789AD and, thereafter, over time their influence ensured a growing diminution in the role of women in society from that which it had been under the Anglo-Saxons, who had, in certain respects, followed the example of their Roman pre-decessors and permitted women to hold certain positions of authority,[2] to own property, as single women to decide whether or not to enter into marriage and on entering marriage to receive a dowry from their husbands, which they were permitted to keep.[3] The Norman invasion, however, somewhat uniquely when compared with the rest of Europe where, mostly, a 'law of community of

---

[1] 'The very being or legal existence of the woman is suspended during the marriage, or at least is incorporated and consolidated into that of the husband, under whose wing protection and cover she performs everything' (Blackstone: *Commentaries on the Law of England* (23rd edn 1854), Vol 1, p 554).

[2] Hilda of Whitby (c 614–680) a Christian saint and the original abbess of Whitby monastery, whose counsel was sought by kings, according to The Venerable Bede in his 'The Ecclesiastical History of the English'.

[3] The 'law of dower' see Cnut's law post 1016. Divorce too was permitted, although only

property' applied, introduced the Law of Normandy, under which the woman's role in marriage was little more than one of servitude to her husband with the woman regarded as a 'subservient chattel' with no independent legal personality, no rights to own property and on breakdown of the marital relationship only limited rights to maintenance.[4]

This role for women under the law in England was to continue for many centuries, so that by the start of Victoria's reign in 1837, married women's rights were few.[5] Accordingly, pre-nuptial or ante-nuptial[6] settlements, whereby the bride-to-be transferred her property to trustees to hold on her behalf, were, therefore, commonly used by wealthier families as a means of, at the very least, protecting the woman's pre-owned assets.

8.2 Reform

The 1882 Married Womens' Property Act was a milestone in the gathering, albeit tortuous, campaign for women's rights.

Of course, that piece of legislation was very much towards the end of a half century of Victorian zeal by a small army of women protesters whose fervor for the cause of their rights was to revolutionise both the rights of women within the family and in property ownership and within a couple of decades thereafter to wrestle into their possession also the right to vote.

In 1839, the Infants and Child Custody Act had allowed wives to take custody of their children under the age of seven (later extended to 16 in the 1883 Custody Acts), if divorced or separated, albeit they could not take custody if they had been found to be adulterous. This legislation was very much the result of the campaigning zeal of one woman, Lady Caroline Norton, who with the use of pamphlets and in conjunction with the MP, Sir Thomas Taulford, obtained Parliamentary support for this reforming measure.[7]

---

officially recorded if occasioned by adultery and if the wife left with the children of the union then she was entitled to half of the couple's assets.

4   'What is Marriage? What should it be?' Mostyn J's speech to the All Party Parliamentary Group on Family Law (2010).

5   Even sexual relations were at the demand of husbands and a charge of marital rape was not permissible until exceptions to the established rule were allowed from 1949 (R v Clarke [1949] 2 All ER 448) onwards and the rule itself only finally overturned as late as *R v R* (1991) by the House of Lords.

6   'Ante-nuptial' – '131. The issue in this case is simple: what weight should the court hearing a claim for ancillary relief under the Matrimonial Causes Act 1973 give to an agreement entered into between the parties before they got married which purported to determine the result? I propose to call these "ante-nuptial agreements" because our legislation already uses the term "ante-nuptial" to refer to things done before a marriage' – Lady Hale: *Radmacher (formerly Granatino) v Granatino* [2010] UKSC 42.

7   'As it stands at present, the law is entirely in favour of the husband and oppressive to the wife. A man who may be drunken, immoral, vicious, and utterly brutalized, may place his wife, who seeks to live separately from him, in this cruel dilemma – "You shall either continue to live with me, or you shall be deprived of your children." The wife, in such a case, has no redress.' Sir Thomas Taulford; House of Commons debate 1839.

Caroline Norton, the granddaughter of the famous playwright, Richard Sheridan, was no feminist or suffragette by nature, but as a gifted poet and a society beauty, who had caught the eye of the rising political star of the day, Lord Melbourne, the future Whig prime minister, she was well placed to assert her independent and liberal views about the role of women before the law. Poignantly, this was particularly so because she was herself the victim of domestic violence from her own husband, George Norton, the MP for Guildford, from whom she separated on two occasions because of his regular beatings, only to return for the sake of her three children. Following, the spurious accusation by the jealous husband of Caroline's infidelity with Lord Melbourne, which caused a political scandal of the day, but which a jury in the subsequent court action was to reject as false, Caroline was to be ejected by her husband from the family home without any basis at that time for pursuing her own divorce and no right to claim the custody of the children, as the law then stood.[8]

In 1857, again after a period of further pamphleteering by Caroline Norton and others, secular divorce was established in England and Wales through the Matrimonial Causes Act of that year. That Act established, free, for the first time, of the control of the Ecclesiastical Court, a new civil court system, which was a forerunner of today's Family Court; and again for the first time, both men and women were permitted to obtain divorce with the right to remarry on the ground of adultery, albeit, the woman had to also establish her husband had, in addition, committed incest, rape, sodomy, bestiality, bigamy or two years' desertion. Women also gained their first autonomy in financial matters, being permitted, as divorcees, to retain any monies received by inheritance or investments and to secure separate 'needs' based maintenance for themselves – again, the inception of the divorce 'needs' based test today.

For Caroline Norton, ironically, none of these legislative campaigns were to assist her personal plight. Her husband removed their three children out of the jurisdiction to the care of his appointed guardian in Scotland and only in 1842, upon the death of the youngest boy (8) in a riding accident at the time, did he eventually relent and permit the remaining children to return to their mother's care. His unrequited jealousy for his wife meant that when Melbourne died in 1848 leaving Caroline a small legacy, Norton then claimed that gift for himself as her husband and he further refused her maintenance support for the children when they returned to her and being envious of her literary success, he further claimed her publishing earnings as his own, as in law he was entitled to do. His

---

8   Married parties under the rule of the Ecclesiastical Courts, could gain 'a separation' upon proof of adultery, sodomy or physical violence, but thereafter they could not remarry, albeit their separation was permanent. The reasoning being that their marriage had been a promise made before God which no man could put asunder.

Divorce with the right to remarry was only possible (as on offshoot from King Henry's Protest) before 1857 by a private Act of Parliament on the grounds of adultery, if prosecuted by the husband or if sought by the wife but then the adultery by the husband had also to be accompanied with proof of life threatening cruelty. Unsurprisingly, only the very wealthy could pursue this course of action and for 150 years after 1700 only 314 such Acts were successfully obtained, almost all by men.

last denial of her was to refuse to instigate divorce proceedings himself and Caroline was only able to remarry upon Norton's own death, albeit, sadly, just three months before her own demise.

Women such as Millicent Fawcett and Emilene Pankhurst and many others were, clearly encouraged by the example of Caroline Norton, to continue similar campaigns for greater women's rights at this time. In 1870, the Married Women's Property Act of that year entitled women to keep their own earnings and even inherit personal property and money, but again, everything else (subject to the outmoded 'law of dower' and 'paraphernalia') still belonged to the husband, whether the wife had acquired it before or after marriage.

By the Married Women's Property Act 1882, following the efforts of Ursula Bright and others and a manifesto promise of the incoming Gladstone Government (1880), a woman was, finally, permitted to keep all personal and real property, which she had obtained before or gained during her marriage. This meant that marriage no longer affected the woman's property rights[9] and as soon as married women became entitled to hold property in their own right, the need for pre-nuptial settlements, at that stage, diminished. Of course, it was only to be after a World War (1914—18) that women would also be able to wrestle into their possession also their entitlement to equal suffrage with men.[10]

8.3 Current position

Now in the twenty-first century, there should be cause for reflection that it has only been in the last 130 years that Parliament has been prepared to recognise the entitlement of a married woman to retain her own property. Many would recognise that the struggle for full recognition of the wife's rights in this area of the law continues unabated in what still remains a male dominated legislature and judiciary. However, some progress has been made and following the House of Lords decision in *White v White*,[11] reference back to the pre-*White* case-law in regard to distribution of the resources of spouses on divorce makes uncomfortable reading against the now familiar post-*White* signposts of 'fairness without discrimination' and the rationales of 'needs, compensation and sharing'. Despite this, neither *White* nor the conjoined appeal decisions of *Miller v Miller: McFarlane v McFarlane*[12] have yet completed the task of full recognition of the wife's equal entitlement to that of the husband. Indeed, some would say that such an endeavour is not the responsibility of the judiciary in any event, but rather the role of democratic debate within Parliament.[13]

---

9   Most of the rest of Europe as well as some US states operated the 'community of property' regime, where marriage did affect the parties' property ownership rights creating thereby a pool of jointly owned assets which provided the non-earning spouse with some financial security.
10   Qualification of Women Act 1918.
11   [2000] UKHL 54.
12   [2006] UKHL 24.
13   See Lady Hale in *Radmacher (formerly Granatino) v Granatino* [2010] UKSC 42 and '*What is Marriage? What should it be?*' and see Mostyn J's address to the All Party Parliamentary Group on Family Law (2010).

However, pending legislative reform, lip-service to a non-discriminatory approach upon divorce has continued in certain respects and some may still detect in the High Court decision of *VB v JP*[14] and the Court of Appeal decision in *B v B*,[15] a lingering intellectual reluctance against full acknowledgment of the wife's equal contribution and, thereby, her entitlement to an equal share. After early signs in *Charman v Charman*[16], with the promotion of the 'principle of equality', that the then[17] newly appointed President may have been willing to champion real equality of approach for women in divorce, his later judgment in *VB v JP*[18] and his, curiously, concurring judgment in *B v B*[19] gave every sign of the gears in this area being put into reverse or, at the very least, into neutral. Certainly, the judgment of Wall LJ, as he then was, in *B v B*,[20] denying the existence of a 'principle' of equality, was an ominous indication of the re-emergence of the more historic judicial approach to such issues.

Inherited land,[21] family business contributions[22] and an exceptional wealth creative ability of a spouse (almost invariably husbands)[23] are still paraded as three of the more obvious bases for departure from equality. Others, such as 'non matrimonial'[24] and, more recently, needs 'generously interpreted'[25] and the parties' 'autonomy and personal choices in a relationship'[26] have, almost predictably, developed as areas for further veiled discrimination against wives.

Given that the historical development of our society in regard to women's rights has within it an in-built discrimination against women attaining positions of landed wealth or commercial influence even to this day, then the present approach of our law still inherently continues to perpetuate a discrimination against the woman's role within marriage generally. For it remains the woman, who is the less likely spouse to have developed a career by the start of the marriage and the more likely by its end to have given up her chance for the same level of earnings potential in order to care for the children of a marriage. Sir Mark Potter's promised development of the 'yardstick of equality' into 'the

---

[14] [2008] EWHC 112 (Fam).
[15] [2008] EWCA Civ 543.
[16] [2007] EWCA Civ 50.
[17] Sir Mark Potter.
[18] See note 9 above.
[19] [2008] EWCA Civ 543.
[20] See note 14 above.
[21] *P v P (Inherited Property)* [2005] 1 FLR 576, Munby J and *Robson v Robson* [2010] EWCA 1171, Ward LJ.
[22] *Miller v Miller: McFarlane v McFarlane* see note 4 above.
[23] *Charman* [2007] EWCA Civ 50.
[24] [2006] UKHL 24; *Jones v Jones* [2011] EWCA 41 Civ, *K v L* [2011] 550 Civ and *N v F* [2011] EWHC 586 Fam.
[25] *VB v JP* above, but see Ward LJ in *Robson v Robson* [2010] EWCA 1171 disapproving of the phraseology.
[26] *Charman's* case (see note 11 above) and *J v J* [2009] EWHC 2654 (Fam), Charles J in relation to ancillary relief applications and *Radmacher's* case (see note 27 below) in relation to ante-nuptial agreements.

sharing principle' in *Charman*[27] has proved, as yet, to be a false dawn for the belief that, finally, the law had, within nearly a century and a half of reforms and development, reached the position where each spouse could stand 'shoulder to shoulder' at the beginning of the statutory exercise under s 25 of the 1973 Matrimonial Causes Act. At the same time, wives have also suffered the double blow of a diminishment by the courts of their chances of compensation after, again, earlier signs of advancement (cf *Miller v Miller: McFarlane v McFarlane, H v H*[28] and *VB v JP*[29] and most recently, Mostyn J in *SA v PA (Pre-marital agreement: Compensation)*[30]).

Against such a background, the content of the Majority decision of the extraordinary assembly of some nine[31] Justices of the Supreme Court in the *Radmacher (formerly Granatino) v Granatino* appeal[32] and the delivery of the Minority dissenting judgment by the only woman Justice sitting, who was also the only family law specialist of the Court, did little to dispel the impression that the determined direction of the law of England and Wales in relation to marital breakdown was again moving away from a position of securing complete equality for women in this area.

Most recently, the publication of the long awaited Law Commission's report entitled 'Matrimonial Property Needs and Agreements'[33] was expected to suggest not only reforms to the law following the Supreme Court's decision in *Radmacher's*[34] case upon pre-nuptial agreements, but also to better define the use of the concepts of spousal 'needs' and 'non matrimonial' property within divorce financial remedy law and, possibly, to advance percentage formulae to assist spouses to better predict the likely outcome of such matrimonial applications. The anticipation has, in parts, been fulfilled, but in other respects left unsatisfied.[35] However, the principal recommendation of the Law Commission is that, for the first time within this jurisdiction, by statutory reform, there should be introduced into the law of England and Wales the concept of 'Qualifying Nuptial Agreements' to enable couples, including those contemplating marriage, to contract out of the Court's discretionary powers within financial remedy applications upon divorce.

---

[27] [2007] EWCA Civ 50.

[28] [2007] EWHC 459 (Fam), Charles J.

[29] [2008] EWHC 112 (Fam).

[30] [2014] EWHC 392.

[31] Historically, the former Appellate Committee of the House of Lords rarely sat with more than five Law Lords and the few exceptions have related mainly to appeals involving terrorism/constitutional cases.

[32] [2010] UKSC 42.

[33] Published February 2014 – Commission Terms of Reference set out in its Tenth Program of Law Reform (2007) Law Comm No 317. The project was commenced in 2009, the consultation opened in January 2011 and extended in 2012 in agreement with the Ministry of Justice to include 'needs' and 'non matrimonial' property with a supplementary consultation which itself opened in September 2012.

[34] Ibid.

[35] The Commission has referred the question of what is meant by 'needs' to the Family Justice Council for guidance and suggested that to develop any formulae will require considerable further research to be undertaken.

8.4   Modern relevance of the pre-nuptial agreement

Prior to the Supreme Court's decision,[36] pre-nuptial agreements had remained contractually unenforceable in the courts of England and Wales. This position had been based on the grounds of public policy that such agreements undermined 'the concept of marriage as a lifelong union'[37] or, where it applied, that the terms of the same purported to oust the court's jurisdiction on an application for ancillary relief (now financial remedy). However, as set out later, the courts have, progressively, over the last two decades, shown themselves to be more willing to take such agreements into account under 'all the circumstances of the case' or as 'conduct' within the s 25 exercise under the Matrimonial Causes Act 1973 when redistributing resources between parties upon a divorce.

The increasing incidence of cohabitation, as opposed to marriage, between couples and the effects of the court's more liberal and non-discriminatory approach to the exercise of its redistributive powers on divorce, have led to the increasing re-emergence of pre-nuptial agreements in a more modern form designed to protect the separate property of either or both of the spouses on the dissolution of their marriage.

Ironically, against such a historical backdrop, the pre-nuptial agreement, which was, initially, intended to shield the wife-to-be's property from the full rigour of the husband's coverture rights in marriage, is now, almost invariably, being used to attempt to shield the husband's property rights against the wife's entitlement upon a divorce. As the use and greater recognition of such a device has increased in this modern context, so the ground gained by women in financial remedy relief upon divorce prior to 2006[38] has continued to be at risk of being progressively and systematically eroded.[39]

This is because the modern use of the pre-nuptial agreement is almost invariably an attempt by the male and/or his family to ensure that the wife-to-be's full rights against him upon a divorce are more restricted than the law would otherwise permit under the 'statutory exercise' of s 25 of the Matrimonial Causes Act 1973, as it stands presently, before any reform consequent upon the Law Commission's Report, is introduced.. The wife-to-be may be persuaded in such pre-marriage discussions that there is something in it for her, whereas the reality is, usually, that there will be far more in it for her future husband. Indeed, Lady Hale in *Radmacher*'s case expressed concern that the provisions of some pre-nuptial agreements in use are such that they seek to limit the wife's claim to a pre-determined sum based upon buying her wifely services by the year.[40]

---

[36]   [2010] UKSC 42.

[37]   Per Wall J in *N v N (Jurisdiction: Pre-Nuptial Agreement)* [1999] 2 FLR 745 at 752.

[38]   See *Miller v Miller: McFarlane v McFarlane* [2006] 1 FLR 1186.

[39]   See Baroness Hale in *Macleod v Macleod* [2008] UKPC 64 and Baron J in *NG v KR* [2008] below.

[40]   See [2010] UKSC 42, at para 137. 'Would any self-respecting young woman sign up to an

As 'fairness' is the approach to the present law concerning financial re-distribution upon divorce, then the only justification for a pre-nuptial agreement between a couple preparing to marry is that it is an attempt by the parties to introduce in advance certainty of distribution and provision between them to reduce the risk of litigation and the costs attendant upon a subsequent divorce[41] and further that the same reflects the autonomy of the parties to regulate their own financial affairs in the event that their marital relationship fails. These are, of course, laudable objectives, but, again, in reality, such considerations are likely to be less influential in the creation of a pre-nuptial agreement at the beginning of a married life together than the concern of the husband, with present wealth or an expectation of the same, of securing, in advance, a damage limitation outcome should 'wedded bliss' descend into disharmony.

In addition, of course, within the context of saving future litigation costs, the existence of a pre-nuptial agreement may, in a given case, be a 'magnetic factor' indicative of an obvious outcome,[42] but cannot, as yet (and without eg the legislative introduction of 'a Qualifying Nuptial Agreement'), prevent the court process, within which the imprimatur of the court is required to authorise any financial arrangement between the parties following a divorce.[43] In this context, the notion that the law would adopt a 'presumptively dispositive' approach to the existence of a pre-nuptial agreement upon divorce following the Supreme Court's decision in *Radmacher*'s case, has, subsequently, received progressive encouragement by a number of judgments, including by Mostyn J in a trilogy of cases *Kremen v Agrest (No 11)*,[44] *B v S*[45] and *SA v PA (Pre-marital agreement: Compensation)*.[46]

When advising a female client, who is being pressed by her husband-to-be or his family to enter into a pre-nuptial agreement, the advice must almost, invariably, be first to suggest that she resists and says 'no' and, when advising a male client wishing to press for such an agreement, he should be cautioned, under the present law, that, if he wishes to give himself the best chance of securing the

---

agreement which assumed that she would be the only one who might otherwise have a claim, thus placing no limit on the claims that might be made against her, and then limit her claim to a pre-determined sum for each year of marriage regardless of the circumstances, as if her wifely services were being bought by the year? Yet that is what these precedents do. In short, there is a gender dimension to the issue which some may think ill-suited to decision by a court consisting of eight men and one woman.' See also 'The effect of *Radmacher* on the average person' Penny Booth, 20 October, 2010, Fam Law Week.

[41] Eg in the case of *Moore v Moore* [2007] EWCA Civ 361, approximately £1.6m had been expended on the wife's endeavours to achieve a London award, rather than a 'Marbella' award, despite the application of the Regulations of Brussels II and see *J v J* [2014] EWHC 3654 (Fam) Mostyn J, where parties had spent c £920k on legal and expert witness costs representing some 325 of the value of the assets under consideration.

[42] See *Crossley v Crossley* [2007] EWCA Civ 1491.

[43] *Xydhias v Xydhias* [1999] 1 FLR 683 CA, but cf Ward LJ in *Soulsbury v Soulsbury* [2007] EWCA Civ 969. See also *NG v KR (pre-nuptial contract)* [2008] EWHC 1532 (Fam) below.

[44] [2012] EWHC 45 (Fam), [2012] 2 FLR 414.

[45] [2012] EWHC 265 (Fam), [2012] 2 FLR 502.

[46] [2014] EWHC 392 (Fam).

approval of the other lawyer involved, he should first seek to ensure that the proposed agreement is as general and generous as possible, without losing its underlying purpose of restricting the other's eventual recovery.[47]

Is the effort worth it? Following the Supreme Court's decision, undoubtedly, it is for any spouse-to-be with significant prospects or substantial property/asset worth. Indeed, even before the *Radmacher* appeal, the courts had, clearly, shown themselves more prepared to have regard to the contents of such an agreement in determining what is 'fair' in any given case. The Supreme Court has now strongly signalled that the entry into a pre-nuptial agreement, following their decision, will in future be a compelling factor in the s 25 exercise; it being natural to infer that parties who enter into a pre-nuptial agreement to which English law is likely to be applied intend that effect should be given to it.[48] The subsequent case-law[49] has further emphasised the 'magnetic factor' of such an agreement, unless the court considers its provisions attempt to leave the other spouse with less than a 'reasonable needs' level of resources. Furthermore and in any event, the court's approach under the present developed case-law to what is fair under the s 25 exercise is likely to be significantly affected by the terms of any pre-nuptial agreement in existence and which reflects the parties' prevailing circumstances upon divorce whether or not, ultimately, its provisions are precisely adhered to by the court within the s 25 'statutory exercise'.[50]

For the financially weaker spouse-to-be, unless the terms struck are sufficiently generous and she (as it usually is) fears that a short marriage may be the reality, then the answer as to whether the effort is worth it, is, in terms of legal and financial benefit to her, that she would, having regard to the usual contents of such an agreement, be better off upon a divorce without such an agreement in place.

Of course, these observations also assume that both male and female regard the priority of securing the certainty of such financial benefits as foremost in the decision to marry in the first place – an assumption, which, certainly, many women would, undoubtedly, challenge as false; advocating instead the importance of the wider family and emotional benefits of marriage as opposed to financial self-interest as one of their primary motivations.[51]

---

[47] See Emma Hitchings *From Pre-Nups to Post-Nups: Dealing with Marital Property Agreements*, School of Law, Bristol University, [2009] Fam Law 1056.

[48] See Lord Phillips at para 70 of decision.

[49] See footnotes 45 to 47 above.

[50] '*Radmacher* – Fettering but not ousting' Sandra Davis, 20 October 2010, Fam Law; see now below *Z v Z* [2011] 2878 Moor J and more recently *AH V PH ((Scandinavian Marriage Settlement)* [2013] EWHC 3873 (Fam) and *Luckwell v Limata* [2014] EWHC 502 (Fam).

[51] A viewpoint which it is submitted was (inevitably) rejected by an all male Court of Appeal and the eight male Justices of the nine Justices of the Supreme Court sitting on the appeals in *Radmacher's* case.

8.5 A decade of development

Despite the recommendation of the Government's 1998 Consultation Document, '*Supporting Families*',[52] to make pre-nuptial agreements relating to property binding, legislative reform was deferred following the initial lukewarm *Response of the Judges of the Family Division* ((1999) Family Law 159 – expressed as a 'unanimous lack of enthusiasm for the pre-nuptial agreement') and the profession to the proposal.

However, there followed gathering support for such a change, 'unless significant injustice would be caused', in the report of the SFLA Law Reform Committee ((22 November 2004) *A More Certain Future – Recognition of Prenuptial Contracts in England and Wales*) and, again, in 2005 Resolution published a well-argued report urging the Government to give statutory force to nuptial contracts.[53] The latter report was, subsequently, fully supported by the Money and Property Sub-Committee of the Family Justice Council.

Sir Mark Potter, as the then President of the Family Division, added his weight to this recommendation in the Court of Appeal decision in *Charman*[54] and Thorpe LJ, as a late convert to the cause, repeated such a call in *Crossley v Crossley*.[55]

With mounting media coverage and discussion of the topic, the Law Commission in 2008 announced[56] its intention to examine the status and enforceability of marital property and finance agreements made either before or during the course of a marriage with the aim of presenting draft legislation by 2012.

---

[52] *Supporting Families* (Stationery Office, October 1998) at p 31. This view did not receive any immediate support from the judiciary or the profession. There were 157 responses to the Consultation Document, 80 were in favour of allowing the agreements and 77 against: see *The Response of the Judges of the Family Division to Government Proposals* (made by way of submission to Chancellor's Ancillary Relief Advisory Group) [1999] Fam Law 159 and the Law Society's Report (May 2003) *Financial Provision on Divorce – Clarity and fairness – Proposals for Reform;* the latter recommending that there could be 'significant unfairness' if the law was changed to make pre-nuptial contracts binding and that in financial provision on divorce the same should remain as one of the factors only: para 312–315. However, the SFLA's Law Reform Committee's report (22 November 2004) *A More Certain Future – Recognition of Pre-marital Contracts in England and Wales* recommended that pre-nuptial contracts should be made binding unless significant injustice would be caused. See also S Bruce 'Pre-marital Agreements Following *White v White*' and 'Introduction to Precedents for Pre-marital Contracts' and Professor Barton 'The SFLA and Pre-marital Agreements: A More Lucrative Future?' Fam Law [2005] 47.

[53] In 2009, the Centre for Social Justice 'Every Family Matters' suggested a similar reform with the courts being able to intervene where the terms of the agreement would cause 'significant injustice' with safeguards imposed of disclosure, advice and a minimum 28 day pre-marriage period. Resoultion echoed these suggestions in a further report 'Family Agreements – Seeking Certainty to Reduce Disputes' of the same year suggesting a 42 day pre-marriage period.

[54] [2007] EWCA Civ 50.

[55] [2008] EWCH Civ 1491.

[56] [2008] June Law Comm 311; Tenth Programme of Law Reform.

With little attempt at concealing the politics of their decision, the three man[57] Court of Appeal in the *Radmacher* case by their judgments on the appeal, somewhat blatantly, sought to force the hand of the newly formed Supreme Court to judicially legislate in advance of the Law Commission's recommendations upon the status of pre-nuptial agreements and the weight to be given to them upon divorce. Diplomatically, however, the Supreme Court's decision avoided an outcome which wholly undermined the Law Commission's brief upon the subject, but, in the process, gave further impetus to the primacy of the parties' right to autonomy in determining in advance the outcome of the division of their resources upon divorce and, in the experienced view of Lady Hale, the decision of the Majority, further diminished the prospect, in that exercise, of achieving 'fairness' for the financially weaker spouse.

8.6 The case-law – *Hyman* to *Radmacher*

The Supreme Court, clearly, stated that in future cases involving English pre-nuptial agreements entered into after the *Radmacher* case, it will now be natural for a court to infer that the parties to such an agreement intended that effect should be given to terms of the same.

However, in regard to pre-nuptial agreements, which pre-date the decision, there remains the real possibility that one or both parties may have been advised that such agreements were void or would carry little weight with the court. In such cases, therefore, the parties' intentions will not be subject to the same inference and it will remain important for the court to determine if the parties intended the pre-nuptial agreement in question to be given effect. Accordingly, it will remain necessary, in such a case, to have an understanding of the development of the law concerning pre-nuptial agreements pre-*Radmacher*.

The modern development of the law concerning pre-nuptial agreements since the start of the last century is to be traced in the following cases:

In *Hyman v Hyman*,[58] a wife by a deed of separation (as opposed to a pre-nuptial agreement) had covenanted not to take proceedings against her husband to provide her with maintenance beyond the provision made for her by the deed. When, subsequently, she obtained a decree of divorce on the grounds of her husband's adultery, it was held that she was not prevented by her covenant from applying for maintenance. The House of Lords decided that, on public policy grounds, parties could not by agreement preclude the divorce court from exercising its jurisdiction in financial matters. In the speech of Lord Hailsham LC, the fact that there had been such an agreement remained relevant to the 'conduct of the parties' within the statutory exercise (then under s 190 of the Supreme Court of Judicature (Consolidation) Act 1925) that the court had to undertake in determining what provision was reasonable.

---

[57] Thorpe, Rix, Wilson LJJ.
[58] [1929] AC 601.

Thereafter, it was not until 1981 and *Edgar v Edgar*[59] that the status and effect of agreements between parties to a marriage was, effectively, developed within the modern context. In that case, the Court of Appeal, in upholding the effect of an agreement (made upon separation and which did not seek to oust the court's jurisdiction) between two married parties, who had each received the benefit of independent legal advice, made it plain that, whilst the court retained its overriding discretion under the s 25 exercise of the 1973 Act, the terms reached would not be avoided in such a case, unless justice demanded. In a well-known extract from the judgment, Ormrod LJ stated:[60]

> '... formal agreements, properly and fairly arrived at with competent legal advice, should not be displaced unless there are good and substantial grounds for concluding that an injustice will be done by holding the parties to the terms of their agreement.' (see fuller extract in notes below).

Of course, these words were directed towards a settlement reached at court between spouses already separated and pursuing an outcome to a financial relief application already brought; but they served, by analogy, to highlight the potential advantages of seeking to reach terms of agreement, more generally, either before or after marriage, as well as after an eventual separation.

In 1995, in *F v F (Ancillary Relief: Substantial Assets)*,[61] which involved pre-nuptial agreements governed under the laws of Germany and Austria, the husband had made his application for financial relief within this jurisdiction, following his petition for divorce in England. Thorpe J, as he was then, expressed himself, in the particular circumstances of the case, as unwilling to attach much significance to the agreements reached, stating:[62]

> 'In this jurisdiction [pre-nuptial agreements] must be of very limited significance. The rights and responsibilities of those whose financial affairs are regulated by statute cannot be much influenced by contractual terms which were devised for the control and limitation of standards that are intended to be of universal application throughout our society.'

---

[59] (1981) 2 FLR 19. 'To decide what weight should be given, in order to reach a just result, to a prior agreement not to claim a lump sum, regard must be had to the conduct of both parties leading up to the prior agreement, and to their subsequent conduct in consequence of it. It is not necessary in this connection to think in formal legal terms, such as misrepresentation or estoppel; all the circumstances as they affect each of two human beings must be considered in the complex relationship of marriage. So the circumstances surrounding the making of the agreement are relevant. Undue pressure by one side, exploitation of a dominant position to secure an unreasonable advantage, inadequate knowledge, possibly bad legal advice, an important change of circumstances, unforeseen or overlooked at the time of making the agreement, are all relevant to the question of justice between the parties. Important, too, is the general proposition that, formal agreements, properly and fairly arrived at with competent legal advice, should not be displaced unless there are good and substantial grounds for concluding that an injustice will be done by holding the parties to the terms of their agreement. There may well be other considerations which affect the justice of this case; the above list is not intended to be an exclusive catalogue' – per Ormrod LJ at 893.

[60] (1981) 2 FLR 19.

[61] [1995] 2 FLR 45.

[62] [1995] 2 FLR 45 at 66.

However, these comments (repeated as they were, obiter, the following year by the same judge in *Dart v Dart*),[63] have to be set against the facts of the case, where the provision made in the agreements for the wife was (although, apparently, as was stated in the judgment, then comparable to the salary of a German judge) almost negligible, when contrasted to the fact that it was to be made out of some £200m of assets held by the husband.

The next year, Cazalet J in *N v N (Foreign Divorce: Financial Relief)*[64] considered that a pre-nuptial agreement, which would have been binding in Sweden, was to be treated 'as being no more than a material consideration for the court under the statutory exercise'.

In the same year, in *S v S (Divorce: Staying Proceedings)*,[65] Wilson J, as he then was, effectively opened the stable door to such agreements, when, after reviewing the earlier dicta of Thorpe J, he said:[66]

> 'I am aware of the growing belief that, in the dispatch of a claim for ancillary relief in this jurisdiction, no significant weight will be afforded to a pre-nuptial agreement, whatever the circumstances. I would like to sound a cautionary note, in that respect ... but there will come a case ... where the circumstances surrounding the pre-nuptial agreement and the provision therein contained might, when viewed in the context of the other circumstances of the case, prove influential or even crucial. Where other jurisdictions, both in the US and in the European Community, have been persuaded that there are cases where justice can only be served by confining the parties to their rights under pre-nuptial agreements, we should be cautious about too categorically asserting the contrary. I can find nothing in [the Matrimonial Causes Act 1973] s 25 to compel a conclusion, so much at odds with personal freedoms to make arrangements for ourselves, that escape from solemn bargains, carefully struck by informed adults, is readily available here ... The matter must be left open.'

By 1999, Wall J, as he then was, in *N v N (divorce: pre-nuptial agreement)*,[67] accepted that, whilst pre-nuptial agreements were, at that time, unenforceable, they could be taken into account, where justice required it, in the s 25 exercise. He stated:

> 'However, the fact that a pre nuptial agreement, or an agreement between spouses, that neither will make a claim for ancillary relief in future divorce proceedings is unenforceable does not mean that the court will not, in appropriate circumstances, hold the parties to that agreement, provided it is just to do so: see, for example, *Edgar v Edgar* ... The existence of the agreement, and the weight to be given to it, are both factors to be taken into account in the overall balance when the court is deciding (on the facts of the individual case) whether or not to exercise its discretion under s 25 of the Matrimonial Causes Act 1973 to make orders for financial provision under ss 23 and 24.'

---

63 [1996] 2 FLR 286.
64 [1997] 1 FLR 900.
65 [1997] 2 FLR 100.
66 [1997] 2 FLR 100 at 103.
67 [1999] 2 FLR 745 at 751–755.

Of course, in 1999, in *Xydhias v Xydhias*[68] Thorpe LJ, concluded that as within the matrimonial jurisdiction post separation agreements were not specifically enforceable without the approval of the court, ordinary contractual principles did not apply to such agreements (a view not fully shared by Ward LJ in the case of *Soulsbury v Soulsbury*[69] and now further explained and developed by Lord Phillips in the *Radmacher* case[70]). Instead, he held that the court would carry out a discretionary review of the negotiations and surrounding circumstances in order to determine whether the parties had reached an agreement or 'an accord' to which they should be held, requiring the court to determine only those matters that remain outstanding.

Following this decision, applications were made, increasingly in practice, within ancillary relief applications, whenever there existed evidence of a concluded separation agreement (Edgar) or a final hearing compromise agreement (akin to the *Xydhias* case facts), for the other party to show cause why a final order should not be made in the terms of the agreement alleged to have been reached. This position also served to strengthen the status and effect of other post marital agreements reached between the parties and also that of pre-nuptial agreements within the statutory exercise upon divorce. The paradigm example of this process, where even a pre-nuptial agreement could be accepted by a court as wholly determinative of the parties' divorce distribution, arose, eventually, in *Crossley v Crossley*[71] (see below and see also *S v S*[72] and Baroness Hale in *Macleod v Macleod*[73]).

In 2000 in *Smith v Smith*,[74] the parties' pre-nuptial agreement provided for a lump sum payment to the wife of £16k in full settlement. The judge, at first instance, in reliance, dismissed the wife's claim. The Court of Appeal stated that the judge had been wrong to dismiss her claim on this basis. The existence of a prior agreement between the parties for a lump sum payment in full and final settlement was said to be only one of the considerations to which a judge had to give weight on an application for ancillary relief.

The following year, Johnson J, in *C v C (Divorce: Stay of English Proceedings)*[75] held that the existence of a French pre-nuptial agreement was a 'significant factor' in deciding to stay the English proceedings.

In 2002 in *M v M (Pre-nuptial Agreement)*[76] Connell J stated:

---

[68]   [1999] 1 FLR 683 CA.
[69]   [2007] EWCA Civ 969. See also Baron J in *NG v KR (pre-nuptial contract)* [2008] EWHC 1532 (Fam) below.
[70]   *Radmacher (formerly Granatino) v Granatino* [2010] UKSC 42.
[71]   [2007] EWCA 1491.
[72]   [2008] EWHC 2038 (Fam), [2008] All ER (D) 16 (Sep).
[73]   [2008] UKPC 64.
[74]   [2000] 3 FCR 374.
[75]   [2001] 1 FLR 624.
[76]   [2002] 1 FLR 654.

'I do bear the (pre-nuptial) agreement in mind as one of the more relevant circumstances of this case, but the court's over-riding duty remains to attempt to arrive at a solution that is fair in all the circumstances, applying s 25 of the Act.'

In the event, his award then provided the wife with a lump sum payment of £875,000, compared with the provision in the agreement of just £275,000. It had been a short five-year marriage and there was a five-year-old child. Overall, the husband's worth was a net £6.5m; the wife had an asset worth of £300,000. It was acknowledged that the court's award was more than the pre-nuptial agreement provision, but was much less than if there had been no agreement at all.

K v K (Ancillary Relief: Pre-nuptial Agreement)[77] in 2002 was the first of the more modern court decisions in which the party seeking to avoid the pre-nuptial agreement entered into was held to its terms. The parties had entered into a pre-nuptial agreement, which the wife wanted to avoid. Rodger Hayward-Smith QC, sitting as a deputy High Court judge, accepted that the husband had been pressurised to marry on the understanding that the wife's capital claims, in the event of an early breakdown, would be as provided for in the pre-nuptial agreement. In the event, the marriage lasted 14 months. The wife already had trust assets of £1m and she was held to the agreement's capital provision of £120,000, although she had claimed £1.6m. The husband had, at least, £25m. The court's approach was that entry into the agreement should be considered as 'conduct which it would be inequitable to disregard' under MCA 1973, s 25(2)(g). By the pre-nuptial agreement, provision was made that, in the event of the separation of the parties for a period of six months or more or the dissolution of the marriage within five calendar years of the date of the agreement, the husband would pay to the wife £100,000, to be increased by 10 per cent compound interest per annum. This provision and the nature of the negotiations preceding the agreement made it apparent that the parties intended the agreement to have effect only in the event of a short marriage. However, as the agreement provided for reasonable financial provision for any children, but made no income provision for the wife, the court concluded that the agreement did not prevent an order for periodical payments for the wife, and, in any event, such a prohibition, in the circumstances, would be unjust to the wife.

Whilst the wife had signed the pre-nuptial agreement just three days before the marriage, she was, nevertheless, to be held to its terms having fully understood the agreement and having been properly advised as to its terms, at the time. Specifically, it was found that she had not been put under pressure to sign the agreement nor had she felt under any other pressure at the time. The court found she exercised her own free will and the husband had not exploited a dominant position. Again, whilst there had not been full disclosure, it had been the wife, as advised, who had decided not to pursue any valuation of the assets disclosed. She was, however, fully aware that the husband was very wealthy. Furthermore, the agreement had been entered into in the knowledge that there

---

[77] [2003] 1 FLR 120. See also *NG v KR (pre-nuptial contract)* [2008] EWHC 1532 (Fam).

would be a child and there had, therefore, been no unforeseen circumstances, which had arisen since the agreement to make it unjust to hold the wife to it.

Upon a review of the law, the judge distilled therefrom a number of questions that he considered were important in determining whether the pre-nuptial agreement was binding or influential. These may remain helpful pointers for the legal advisor as to the approach of a court whenever a pre-nuptial agreement dated pre *Radmacher*'s case is involved and are summarised below:

	Question	Answer
1.	Did she understand the agreement?	Yes.
2.	Was she properly advised as to its terms?	Yes.
3.	Did the husband put her under any pressure to sign?	No.
4.	Was there full disclosure?	No. There was disclosure of assets, but the wife decided not to press for values and she was aware that the husband was very wealthy.
5.	Was the wife under any other pressure?	Yes from the circumstances she found herself in and from her family; but whilst she had signed the day before the marriage, she had discussed the terms before and had had plenty of time and had felt no pressure when she actually signed.
6.	Did she willingly sign the agreement?	Yes.
7.	Did the husband exploit a dominant position, either financially or otherwise?	No.
8.	Was the agreement entered into in the knowledge that there would be a child?	Yes.
9.	Has any unforeseen circumstance arisen since the agreement was made that would make it unjust to hold the parties to it?	No.
10.	What does the agreement mean?	The agreement is clear as to the capital provision to be made for the wife if the marriage broke down within five years and the provision for the child was to be either agreed or adjudicated upon by the court.
11.	Does the agreement preclude an order for periodical payments for the wife?	No. It does not say so.
12.	Are there any grounds for concluding that an injustice would be done by holding the parties to the terms of the agreement?	No. Indeed, an injustice would be done to the husband if the agreement was ignored.

	Question	Answer
13.	Is the agreement one of the circumstances of the case to be considered under s 25?	Yes.
14.	Does the entry into this agreement constitute conduct which it would be inequitable to disregard under s 25(2)(g)?	Yes.
15.	Am I breaking new ground by holding the wife to the capital terms of the agreement?	No. See previous cases.
16.	If the agreement does preclude a maintenance claim, would it be unjust to hold the parties to that aspect of the agreement?	Yes to the wife because of her continuing contribution for the child and the effect thereof upon her earning capacity.

In 2003 in *J v V (Disclosure: Offshore Corporations)*,[78] where the agreement was made on the wedding night and where there was no disclosure, no legal advice and no provision for the arrival of children, despite what had happened in *K v K*, Coleridge J stated that 'Nowadays [pre-nuptial agreements] can be of some significance, but not in this case.' By contrast and it should be said somewhat exceptionally, the lack of independent legal advice and disclosure in the subsequent *Radmacher* case[79] were not found by the Supreme Court to have been *material* in the husband's decision in that case to sign up to such an agreement.

In 2004, Baron J in *A v T (ancillary relief: cultural factors)*,[80] under 'all the circumstances' of the case, decided that the English court should also take into consideration cultural factors, where the parties are from an ethnic background and, within this process, the court may have regard to the manner in which the case would be dealt with by courts of a foreign country where such a reference is relevant. In consequence, it was relevant to consider a pre-nuptial agreement that had been made under Sharia law. Again, in *Radmacher's* case, the fact that each of the parties' own national legal systems (German and French) would, in the circumstances, have upheld the pre-nuptial agreement entered into was an important factor in the decision of both appeal courts concluding that it was not unfair to keep the husband to the agreement he had signed.

In the same year in *G v G (financial provision: separation agreement)*,[81] the Court of Appeal held that the judge was right to give weight to both the pre-nuptial and separation agreements, since both parties had intentionally chosen to regulate their marital affairs by agreement in the light of their individual experiences of previous marital breakdowns.

---

[78]   [2003] EWHC 3110 (Fam).
[79]   [2010] UKSC 42.
[80]   [2004] 1 FLR 977.
[81]   [2004] 1 FLR 1011, CA.

In 2007 in *Ella v Ella*,[82] where the two spouses had dual nationality in this jurisdiction and in Israel, the Court of Appeal stayed the English proceedings commenced by the wife, who was then living in London, in favour of the Israeli court jurisdiction on the basis of the then existing parallel Israeli proceedings brought by the husband and the existence of a pre-nuptial agreement between the parties, which, clearly, provided for the law of Israel to apply.

Again, that same year, Baron J in *A v A*,[83] considered a post-nuptial agreement where the parties, having separated, entered into the agreement, at the insistence of the husband, as a pre-condition of their reconciliation, following the wife's earlier adultery. The case is helpful in the analysis of the court's approach to the effect of duress or undue pressure, which has resulted in an agreement between the parties to resume their marital cohabitation. The husband had during their marriage come into an inheritance and the agreement sought to limit the wife's claims. The wife signed when the husband gave her the ultimatum that she was to leave the family home if she had not signed by a given date. The husband then discovered she had renewed the adulterous relationship and divorce proceedings followed. The wife claimed in the ancillary relief proceedings that she had been put under pressure to sign and the agreement should not be relied upon.

The court acknowledged the greater use of pre-nuptial agreements than before and that the same were much more likely to be accepted by the courts in governing the parties' financial affairs on breakdown. Their effectiveness, however, it was stated, depended upon fairness and how the parties had come to enter into the agreement. To render the agreement ineffective, it would be necessary to show the husband had exercised undue pressure or influence, by which the wife's free will had been overborne. It was held that, in the circumstances, her will had, indeed, been overborne and the post-nuptial agreement, therefore, would not be determinative and the s 25 exercise would be undertaken in the ordinary way.

Thereafter, in 2008, the Court of Appeal in *Crossley v Crossley*[84] held that the 'overriding objective' enables the court in exceptional circumstances to follow the proportionate approach of rejecting a hearing upon full disclosure where spouses of significant personal wealth (H £45m and W £18m) had entered into a pre-marital agreement some seven weeks before a childless marriage that lasted just 14 months. The pre-nuptial agreement had provided that only jointly acquired assets would be divided (there were none) and each party would retain assets they had introduced. The judge, hearing the ancillary relief application, had set aside the requirement for full disclosure and adjourned the First Appointment and listed the matter for a hearing of the issue of the effect of the pre-nuptial agreement directing bare Form E's and a solicitors letter, in place of questionnaires, setting out the wife's case as to whether there had been relevant non-disclosure upon entering the pre-nuptial agreement. On the facts of the

---

[82] [2007] 2 FLR 35.
[83] [2007] 1 FLR 1760.
[84] [2007] EWCA 1491.

case, the existence of the pre-nuptial agreement was considered to be a 'magnetic factor' in all the circumstances under the statutory exercise and the agreement's terms represented the fair outcome. The example of robust case management given by this case was later followed in relation to where an *Edgar* agreement had been entered into in the case of *S v S*.[85]

It has transpired that the most significant judgment in this area of the law was, in hindsight to have been that given by Baron J in 2008 in the *NG v KR (pre-nuptial contract)*,[86] now known to all upon appeal as *Radmacher v Granatino*.[87] In this case, it was the wife, who held vast wealth (c £100m), derived from her family in Germany. She sought to have the nil provision pre-nuptial agreement enforced within the husband's applications for financial relief upon divorce after an eight-year marriage in which two children, then aged nine and six, had been born and who were the subject of a shared residence order. In contrast, at first instance, the husband claimed relief of over £6.9m. The High Court, finally, awarded him over £5.56m, within which were provisions for a home in the United Kingdom, use of a home in Germany and certain capital awards, including capitalised maintenance.

In what was then seen as a welcomed development, the court's more structured approach to the content and effect of the pre-nuptial agreement was to ask whether the agreement satisfied the six safeguards set out in the Government's 1998 Consultation Document, Supporting Families[88] (see below). In what many saw as an astute judgment, Baron J, whilst clear that the agreement failed the safeguard test in several regards, was equally clear that the husband, nevertheless, was fully aware that he was signing an agreement which was intended to deny him any provision upon a divorce and, accordingly, concluded that the existence of the agreement, which would have been, she found, enforceable in the birthplaces of both of the parties, namely Germany and France, was an important factor that should limit the husband's claim overall when carrying out the s 25 statutory exercise. Had the agreement satisfied the six safeguard test, the learned judge considered that the existence of the agreement would have become 'a magnetic factor' within the discretionary exercise under 'all the circumstances of the case' and the result and the court order, in that event, would more likely have mirrored its provisions.

Before, the Court of Appeal heard the first appeal from Baron J's decision. The Privy Council in *Macleod v Macleod*,[89] dealt with an appeal by a husband from an award in ancillary relief made by the Manx Courts under mirror legislation to s 25 in a case where the parties had entered into a post-nuptial agreement, which, in part, contained provisions from an earlier pre-nuptial agreement. The Board expressly resisted the temptation to attempt a judicial reform of the then

---

[85] [1997] 2 FLR 100.
[86] [2008] EWHC 1532 (Fam).
[87] [2010] UKSC 42 (Supreme Court) and [2009] EWCA Civ 649 (Court of Appeal).
[88] *Supporting Families* (Stationery Office, October 1998).
[89] [2008] UKPC 64.

current developed approach of the courts, as latterly reflected in NG's case, to pre-nuptial agreements. Lady Hale, in delivering the decision of the Board, specifically, stated that such a task was for Parliament in the light of the Law Commission's announced review[90] of this area. However, when laying down guidance as to a more uniform approach to be adopted in ancillary relief to the existence and, in appropriate cases, paramountcy of marital agreements between parties, whether in the form of a post nuptial, an *Edgar* separation or a *Xydhias* compromise agreement, her Ladyship sought to emphasise the importance of the existing statutory review powers under ss 34 and 35 of the 1973 Act in relation to such marital (post as opposed to pre-nuptial) agreements as the 'starting point' for the court's s 25 exercise and further suggested that in any future legislative reform, which may validate pre-nuptial agreements, it was essential that the court should retain a similar review power.

Her Ladyship's suggestion that all post-nuptial agreements were merely 'maintenance agreements' under another name and that even the Court of Appeal in *Edgar v Edgar*[91] (and, of significance, presided over by Ormrod LJ) had missed the significance of ss 34 and 35 of the 1973 Act in dealing with the weight to be given to post-nuptial agreements within the s 25 exercise,[92] was a surprise to many practitioners in the field of ancillary relief. This gauntlet of interpretation was not to be left unchallenged long and, subsequently, the Court of Appeal and, in particular, Wilson LJ., as he then was, upon the hearing of the first appeal in *Radmacher's* case, took issue with her Ladyship's approach, suggesting, obiter, that ss 34 and 35 had been 'dead letters' in ancillary relief law for many years and their resurrection in such a context was now inappropriate.[93]

Again, in 2009, before the Supreme Court's decision, Eleanor King J dealt, in *F v F*,[94] with a husband's appeal from a district judge's decision, which itself had relied upon the Court of Appeal's decision in *Radmacher*. On the facts, the parties had, before their wedding, travelled to France where they had signed a separation of property agreement. The district judge had decided that the

---

90   Law Commission: [2008] June; Tenth Programme of Law Reform.
91   [1980] 3 All ER 887, [1980] 1 WLR 1410, 2 FLR 19.
92   See Baroness Hale's speech in *Macleod*'s case [2008] UKPC 64.
93   Such a debate, which was continued, obiter, in the Supreme Court in *Radmacher's* case as to the applicability of ss 34 and 35 to post nuptial agreements is of interest in the present context in the limited sense that strictly, the same remains persuasive as to the current approach to be adopted to post nuptial agreements. However, the Privy Council decision in *Macleod* was in relation to a post nuptial agreement whereas *Radmacher's* case was, clearly, a decision, on its facts, dealing with a pre-nuptial agreement. Whilst a Privy Council decision is also of persuasive authority, the Board's decision was delivered by Lady Hale, who in delivering the Minority speech in *Radmacher's* case in the Supreme Court, clearly considered that the Majority's expressed view in relation to post-nuptial agreements was indeed strictly obiter. This suggests that *Macleod* should, until clarification is provided by a subsequent case or by the Law Commission's review, continue to be the principal authority dealing with the approach to post-nuptial agreements under the s 25 exercise. Indeed, the Majority in *Radmacher's* case expressly approved the approach in *Macleod* whenever the post nuptial agreement being considered was either an *Edgar* or *Xydhias* type agreement dealing with an imminent or actual separation between the parties.
94   [2009] EWHC 2485 (Fam).

parties had only entered into the agreement because on their understanding it was required by French law. In fact, the signed document was entirely in French as drafted by a French lawyer. The parties had never previously met with the lawyer in question. In addition, the agreement referred to parts of the French Code Civil with which the parties had no previous knowledge. In the circumstances, after signature, neither party gave any further thought to the agreement whilst they remained married. King J, therefore, found that the circumstances leading to the signing of the agreement were fundamentally different to those in *Radmacher v Granatino*. She found that, accordingly, the parties' understanding had been that their signatures were required as some form of administrative obligation imposed upon them in France. The agreement was, in consequence, neither decisive nor magnetic as a factor in the case.

Radmacher v Granatino – the appeals

8.7 Decision of the Court of Appeal

The first appeal by the wife[95] came before Thorpe, Rix and Wilson LJJ as he then was. The appeal was successful.

Thorpe LJ in delivering the leading judgment, considered that the primary problem was the difficulty in reconciling the civil law and common law jurisdictions of Europe and the UK. The former applying formulaic property outcomes to marriage and divorce and the latter applying, in contrast, a broad judicial discretion to property distribution upon divorce. By example, he contrasted the outcomes of these two regimes on the facts of the case, where in the parties' birthplaces (Germany and France) the pre-nuptial agreement entered into would have resulted in no award to the husband, whereas under the English system of law, the husband had received £5.6m.

His Lordship acknowledged the change in judicial attitude from his own decision in *F v F* in 1995 in which he had suggested that the statutory exercise under s 25 'cannot be much influenced by contractual terms ...' to the decision in *Crossley* in 2008, where, again, in giving judgment, he had accepted that especially in short childless marriages of independently wealthy individuals, a pre-nuptial agreement would be regarded as a factor of magnetic importance.

Thorpe LJ considered that this movement had been necessary to modernise the law from that reflecting the laws and morals of earlier generations to the current position of recognising the autonomy of adults to govern their future financial relationship by agreement in an age when divorce had become commonplace. By such a process, also, the distinctions between the law in this jurisdiction would be reduced from those applying in the majority of the member states of Europe and the wider common law world.

---

[95] [2009] EWCA Civ 649.

His Lordship recognised that in regard to pre-nuptial agreements there still needed to be appropriate safeguards, which should be that:

(1) any term which purported to oust the court's jurisdiction would be void, albeit severable;

(2) where the appropriate safeguards had not been followed or, under contractual principles, there were grounds which vitiated an agreement, then the agreement would be voidable;

(3) a pre-nuptial agreement would remain, under the s 25 exercise, subject to the judge's discretionary review where it was contended that its terms were unfair.

Against such considerations, whilst the judge at first instance had directed herself appropriately in relation to her reference to the 'safeguards' set out in the 1998 Government Green Paper and the previous case-law, Thorpe LJ, along with the other judges sitting, did not accept her findings that, as measured against such criteria, the pre-nuptial agreement signed was 'flawed', as she had found it to be. Nor, in the light of her findings that she would yet take into account, in limiting his recovery, the fact that the husband had entered into the 'flawed' agreement, was the Court of Appeal satisfied that the judge had properly reflected such an approach in the award she made.

In consequence, Thorpe LJ considered that the appropriate approach on the facts of the case was to adopt the methodology of the award made by Baron J, but to limit its duration only to the period whilst the children were dependent and they enjoyed the shared care arrangement reached between the parties. Hence, the provision made over to the husband for a home for himself and the children and the other capital provision made for him as a father and part time carer of the children would continue, but only in regard to the latter until the youngest child attained 22 years of age. As a result, in the light of the agreement reached, the husband received no capital provision for himself as a husband.

The Court of Appeal directly addressed the approach to be adopted to those matters previously considered as safeguards or pre-conditions to a pre-nuptial agreement being taken into consideration by the court (ie independent legal advice, prior full and frank disclosure, needs or the absence of provision for children).

Thorpe LJ emphasised the husband's experience in international banking and Wilson LJ considered that s 25 enabled the court to apply common sense to the facts of any given situation and, therefore, as the husband had, clearly, understood the effect of the pre-nuptial agreement and had had the chance to seek independent legal advice, but had chosen not to do so, then the absence of such advice would not enable him to escape the impact of the agreement.

As to disclosure, neither party had made specific disclosure to the other before the pre-nuptial agreement was signed, albeit the wife had deliberately ensured that her finances were kept secret. However, the husband was well aware the wife was from a very wealthy family and the Court of Appeal stated that would be sufficient in the circumstances. Wilson LJ considered that lack of disclosure alone would not be a sufficient 'flaw' and any party so relying on such an alleged failure would need to show that the effect of any non-disclosure would have been material eg as to reaching the agreement or entering into the marriage.

In regard to needs, Wilson LJ was, plainly, of the view that a pre-nuptial agreement, which purported to exclude recovery by a claimant spouse on divorce with basic needs unmet, could not, without more, be said to be unfair, if the same had been agreed to with full knowledge of such consequential effect. At the very least, His Lordship considered that a court should, in such circumstances, only allow such a party to claim to the extent necessary for the service of that 'real need' and, in this respect, the husband in *Radmacher's* case was seen as having received an award at first instance as 'home maker' for the children, which more than provided for his own basic needs and fairness, in the light of the agreement entered into should, instead, have limited his award to that period only and not have permitted an extension covering his statistical lifetime following the independence of the children, when it was unlikely that he would have been in 'real need'.

As to the absence of any provision for children within a pre-nuptial agreement, the Court of Appeal remained untroubled and because any children's provision could not be limited by agreement, Wilson LJ did not regard the absence or express limitation of such provision as a 'flaw' which would significantly affect the weight to be ascribed to the pre nuptial agreement, subsequently, upon a divorce etc. Indeed, in *Radmacher's* case, such an absence of written provision, permitted the court, in the event, to make very substantial provision for the husband as the children's shared carer.

8.8   Decision of the Supreme Court

The Supreme Court had before them in the hearing before them in 2010 an appeal by the husband in which the questions for them to decide were whether the Court of Appeal:

(1)   had erred in finding that a freely entered into pre-nuptial agreement ought to be given decisive weight under the s 25 assessment; and

(2)   in coming to its decision, had, in error, judicially legislated in contravention of the decision of *Macleod*.[96]

8.9   The majority

The Supreme Court's decision by a majority of 8 to 1 was that the Court of Appeal had correctly found that on the facts of the case contained it was not unfair under s 25 to hold the husband to the pre-nuptial agreement. The

---

[96]   [2008] UKPC 64.

President of the Court, Lord Phillips gave the majority judgment with Lord Mance adding further commentary in support and Lady Hale, as the sole experienced family judge sitting, delivering the only dissenting judgment.

In a review of the current law of division of assets upon divorce, Lord Phillips, specifically, highlighted the fact that in *Miller*[97] it had been recognised that assets may be treated differently where the parties during the marriage had themselves treated the same as separate property and that this had been seen as a cautious '… movement in the law towards a more frequent distribution of property upon divorce in accordance with what, by words or conduct, the parties appear previously to have agreed' (see para 30 of Speech).

His Lordship noted that it had been contrary to public policy for a married couple, who were living together or a couple about to get married, to make an agreement that provided for the contingency that they might separate. Such agreements had, therefore, been treated as void and the court would pay no regard to them. But this rule had not applied to an actual agreement to separate or an agreement that governed a separation that had already taken place (see *Hyman*[98]). Subsequently, the Maintenance Agreements Act 1957, which, as a prelude to ss 34 and 35 of the later Matrimonial Causes Act 1973 had advanced this situation, so that the Court could determine the validity of an agreement to separate ('maintenance agreement') and whether there was a need to alter the terms of the same and the existence of such an agreement to separate could have a considerable effect upon the Court's exercise of the discretionary powers under s 25 upon a divorce.

However, the approach to other post nuptial and pre nuptial agreements had remained that they were void and the courts had only been prepared to give their terms limited weight within the statutory exercise under s 25 (see paras 35–42). Progressively, this position had changed, so that the situation had now been reached whereby in *Crossley*[99] the court had been prepared to regard the existence of a pre nuptial agreement as a factor of 'magnetic importance' when determining the fair division of resources upon divorce (see paras 45–46).

Lord Phillips agreed with the Board in *Macleod*'s case that the old public policy rule against agreements providing for future separations was now obsolete and should be swept away; but, unlike the Board's view that this did not apply to pre-nuptial agreements, the Majority of the Supreme Court considered that such an approach applied to all nuptial agreements whether pre or post nuptial, all of which should and could, in His Lordship's opinion, be equally enforced (see para 52). This was for two reasons, namely that it was doubtful that ss 34 and 35 applied to all nuptial agreements as opposed to only *Edgar* type separation agreements and *Xydhias* type compromise agreements and there was no material distinction between the nature of pre and post nuptial agreements as contracts (see paras 53–63).

---

97   [2006] UKHL 24.
98   [1929] AC 601.
99   [2007] EWCA Civ 1491.

There may be good reason why a court should start with the agreement and consider initially whether any changes had occurred. In relation to both *Edgar* and *Xydhias* type agreements, by their nature and timing, they were likely to be more contemporary with the circumstances prevailing at the time of ancillary relief proceedings and therefore more relevant. Whereas, by contrast, the terms of a pre-nuptial or other early post nuptial agreement may not be as relevant. Hence, whilst the Board's approach in *Macleod* may be appropriate in relation to *Edgar* or *Xydhias* type agreements, it would not be so in relation to pre-nuptial and such other post nuptial agreements (paras 64–66).

Lord Phillips identified three issues for the court's decision (para 67). They were:

(1)   Did circumstances attending the making of the agreement exist that detracted from the weight to be accorded to it?

(2)   Did circumstances attending the making of the agreement exist that enhanced the weight to be accorded to it; ie the foreign element?

(3)   Did the circumstances prevailing when the court's order was made make it fair or just to depart from the agreement?

As to (1) (weight): The Court considered, under the s 25 exercise, that a pre or post nuptial agreement would only carry full weight if both parties entered it with free will, without undue influence or pressure and informed of its implications (see 3rd, 5th and 6th safeguards in Government's Green Paper (1998)). Whilst the Court accepted that the six safeguards of the Green Paper would, in most cases, be highly relevant considerations, the real question for a court in this context was whether there was any material lack of disclosure, information or advice. If it is clear that a party is fully aware of the implications of a pre-nuptial agreement and yet indifferent to detailed particulars of the other party's assets, there will be no need to accord the agreement reduced weight because he or she is unaware of those particulars. What is essential is that each party should have all the information that is material to his or her decision and should intend that the agreement should govern the financial consequences of the marriage coming to an end (paras 68 to 69).

Lord Phillips considered that it must follow that, whilst before this appeal decision it may not have been right to infer from an agreement's existence alone that the parties had intended it to take effect; in future, it will be natural to infer that parties who enter into a pre-nuptial agreement to which English law is likely to be applied intend that effect should be given to it (para 70).

Guidance as to the future approach included:

(i)   asking first the question, whether there are any of the standard vitiating factors, being duress, fraud or misrepresentation, present. Such factors will negate any effect the agreement might otherwise have, whether contractually enforceable or not. Akin to *Edgar*, unconscionable conduct such as undue pressure (falling short of duress) will also be likely to eliminate the weight to be attached to the agreement and other unworthy conduct eg exploitation of a dominant position to secure an unfair advantage, would reduce or eliminate it (para 71).

(ii) taking account of a party's emotional state, and what pressures he or she was under to agree. However, this should not be in isolation from what would have happened had he or she not been under those pressures. All the circumstances of the parties at the time of the agreement will be relevant, including eg their age and maturity, and whether previously married or in long-term relationships. Such previous relationships may explain the terms of the agreement, and reveal what they foresaw when they entered into the agreement. Matters not foreseeable for less mature couples may well be fully in contemplation of more mature couples. It may be an important factor, either way, that the marriage would still have gone ahead without an agreement, or without certain of the terms agreed (para 72).

(iii) an unfair agreement at inception will reduce its weight, albeit, in practice, this question will be subsumed within the wider question under s 25 whether the agreement operates unfairly, having regard to the circumstances prevailing at the time of the breakdown of the marriage (para 73).

As to (2) (foreign element): Lord Phillips, whilst noting the foreign element of the case, with the husband being French and the wife German and the agreement having a German law jurisdiction clause, commented that in future it was unlikely, with agreements made contemporaneously and, a fortiori, any made after the judgment, that there would be any live issue between the parties that they intended to be bound by the agreement and, therefore, foreign law would not need to be considered in such cases. However, when dealing with agreements concluded in the past (here 1998), such foreign elements may continue to bear on the important question of whether or not the parties intended their agreement to be effective (para 74).

As to (3) (fairness): Following *White* and *Miller*, under the s 25 exercise, where the pre-nuptial agreement's provisions conflict with what the court would otherwise consider to be the requirements of fairness, then the fact of the agreement is an important factor to be weighed in the balance and is capable of altering what is fair. The proposition, in substitution for the previous approach of Macleod, should be in both pre and post nuptial agreement cases that:

> 'The court should give effect to a nuptial agreement that is freely entered into by each party with a full appreciation of its implications *unless in the circumstances prevailing it would not be fair to hold the parties to their agreement*' (para 75).

What is fair is fact sensitive to the particular facts of the case under consideration, but any nuptial agreement cannot be allowed to prejudice the reasonable requirements of any children of the family.

Respect for individual autonomy and the right to determine the division of their resources on divorce is a good reason why it would be fair to give weight to a nuptial agreement reached between parties, especially if the agreement addresses existing circumstances and not merely the contingencies of an uncertain future. Another good reason may be where parties wish to make provision for existing property owned by one or other, or property that one or other anticipates receiving from a third party. Another may be where the nuptial agreement makes provision for what is termed non matrimonial and matrimonial property, as distinguished in White and Miller (paras 76–80).

Lord Phillips considered, however, that where the pre-nuptial agreement attempts to address contingencies, unknown and unforeseen, of the couple's future relationship, there is more scope for events over the years to make it unfair to hold them to their agreement. The longer the marriage, the more likely it is that this will be the case, eg where a pre-nuptial agreement made no provision on divorce and the parties started their marriage with no particular wealth and, over time, by mutual contribution, one of them has accumulated significant wealth.

In His Lordship's view, 'need' and/or 'compensation' are the most likely of the three strands of fairness to make it unfair to hold the parties to a pre-nuptial agreement and the parties to such an agreement are unlikely to have intended that their agreement should result, upon marital breakdown, in one partner being left in a predicament of 'real need', while the other enjoys a sufficiency or more, and such an outcome is likely to render it unfair to hold the parties to their agreement. Similarly where the devotion of one partner to looking after the family and the home has left the other free to accumulate wealth, then again, it is likely to be unfair to hold them to an agreement that entitles the latter to retain all that he or she has earned.

In contrast, where each can meet his or her needs, fairness may well not require a departure from their agreement in the circumstances that have come to pass. Hence, it is in regard to the third strand of 'sharing', that the court will be most likely to make an order in the terms of the nuptial agreement in place of the order that it would otherwise have made. However, a court will now be more willing to ascribe the appropriate weight to the agreement under 'all the circumstances of the case' under s 25 and, in the right case, the existence of the agreement will be the most compelling factor (see paras 81–83).

Lord Phillips highlighted certain facts of the appeal case, which resulted in the majority upholding the decision of the Court of Appeal. These were:

(1) that whilst the husband had not taken independent legal advice, he had well understood the effect of the agreement, had had the opportunity to take independent advice, but had failed to do so and, in such circumstances, he could not rely on the fact that he had not taken independent legal advice;

(2) that whilst the wife had failed to disclose the approximate value of her assets, the husband knew she had substantial wealth and had shown no

interest in ascertaining its approximate extent and he had never suggested that this would have had any effect on his readiness to enter into the agreement;

(3)   that whilst there had been no negotiation, it was unclear why this should be a vitiating factor as Baron J had maintained and it merely reflected the fact that the background of the parties rendered the entry into such an agreement commonplace;

(4)   that it was not apparent that Baron J had made any significant reduction in her award to reflect the fact of the agreement.

However, Lord Phillips was not prepared to endorse the stance of Wilson LJ that there was nothing unfair about an absence of provision within the agreement for the possibility that the husband might be reduced to circumstances of 'real need'. If the husband had been incapacitated in the course of the marriage, affecting his ability to meet his needs, then, in the interests of fairness, it may have been unfair to hold him to the full rigours of the pre-nuptial agreement. On the facts, this was, in the prevailing circumstances, far from the case. The husband was a very able and well qualified individual and had received generous relief given to meet the needs of the two children, which would indirectly provide in large measure for his own need until his children reached independence and further the court orders had provided separately for the discharge of his personal debts.

There was no compensation factor in the case as the husband's decision to abandon his lucrative career in the city for the fields of academia was not motivated by the demands of his family, but reflected his own choice. In the light of the husband's initial agreement that he should have no part in the wife's family wealth and the fact that the same had been acquired mainly before the marriage and/or independently of any contribution by the husband, it was fair that he should be held to the pre-nuptial agreement and unfair to depart from it (paras 120–122).

A succinct summary of the consequences of the Supreme Court's decision upon the court's approach to pre-nuptial agreements is to be found in the recent case of *Luckwell v Limata*,[100] where Holman J endorsed the following joint statement by leading counsel before him of the law in this area post *Radmacher* as follows:

'129. There is no doubt that the decision of the Supreme Court in *Granatino v Radmacher* [2010] UKSC 42, [2011] 1 AC 534 represented, and now requires, a significant shift in the approach to, and weight to be given to, negotiated, drafted and freely signed nuptial agreements of the kinds in the present case when there is no vitiating factor.

130. I said at the outset of this judgment that the law is not difficult to state. Such agreements must always be given weight, and often decisive weight as part of the circumstances of the case. They may affect not only whether to make any award at

---

[100] [2014] EWHC 502 (Fam).

all, but also the size and the structure of any award. I could at this point cite passages from the majority judgment in *Granatino v Radmacher* but, helpfully, all three counsel have agreed the following propositions of law which are drawn from *Granatino v Radmacher* and which I gratefully adopt. (They were first drafted by Mr Marks and Miss Faggionato, but I quote them with the additions made by Mr Howard.)

1.   It is the court, and not the parties, that decides the ultimate question of what provision is to be made;

2.   The over-arching criterion remains the search for 'fairness', in accordance with section 25 as explained by the House of Lords in Miller/McFarlane (i.e. needs, sharing and compensation). But an agreement is capable of altering what is fair, including in relation to 'need';

3.   An agreement (assuming it is not 'impugned' for procedural unfairness, such as duress) should be given weight in that process, although that weight may be anything from slight to decisive in an appropriate case;

4.   The weight to be given to an agreement may be enhanced or reduced by a variety of factors;

5.   Effect should be given to an agreement that is entered into freely with full appreciation of the implications unless in the circumstances prevailing it would not be fair to hold the parties to that agreement. i.e. There is, at least, a burden on the [the other spouse] to show that the agreement should not prevail;

6.   Whether it will 'not be fair to hold the parties to the agreement' will necessarily depend on the facts, but some guidance can be given:

    i)   A nuptial agreement cannot be allowed to prejudice the reasonable requirements of any children;

    ii)   Respect for autonomy, including a decision as to the manner in which their financial affairs should be regulated, may be particularly relevant where the agreement addresses the existing circumstances and not merely the contingencies of an uncertain future;

    iii) There is nothing inherently unfair in an agreement making provision dealing with existing non-marital property, including anticipated future receipts, and there may be good objective justifications for it, such as obligations towards family members;

    iv)   The longer the marriage has lasted the more likely it is that events have rendered what might have seemed fair at the time of the making of the agreement unfair now, particularly if the position is not as envisaged;

    v)   It is unlikely to be fair that one party is left in a predicament of 'real need' while the other has 'a sufficiency or more';

    vi)   Where each party is able to meet his or her needs, fairness may well not require a departure from the agreement.

131. In elaboration of proposition 6(i) above, I should stress that part of the express statutory duty of the court under section 25(1) is to give first consideration to the welfare while a minor of any child of the family, who has not attained the age of eighteen. As in *Granatino v Radmacher*, the children in the present case spend time with each of their parents, and the financial circumstances of each of their parents are likely to impact upon their welfare. The facts of the two cases differ markedly – Mrs Radmacher was far, far richer than is [the wife in this case] – but in *Granatino v Radmacher* quite significant financial provision was made for the husband, in his role as father, until the younger child attained 22. In that case, however, the children were broadly evenly residing with each of the parents.

132. To counsel's propositions of law, I add one other, which needs no citation of authority. The court must be scrupulous to avoid gender discrimination or gender bias. Of course, gender may, and often does, impact heavily on outcome. If in fact a wife, in her role as mother, is the primary carer for the children, then her need for secure and suitable accommodation may outweigh that of the husband. If a wife, due to her commitments to caring for the children, is less able to work than is the husband, then that is likely to impact upon maintenance needs. So, too, if it is a fact of a case that a wife has lower earning capacity because of gender discrimination in the relevant employment markets. But there must be no discrimination or bias based on gender alone, nor on any stereo–typical view that a wife may be dependent upon her husband but not vice versa.'

8.10   The minority

Lady Hale in her minority judgment, repeated her view, as in *Macleod*, that modern marriage still holds an 'irreducible minimum', including a couple's mutual duty to support each other and their children. In her view, the issue was how far individuals should be free to rewrite that essential feature of the marital relationship. She considered that it remained for Parliament to achieve comprehensive and principled reform following the Law Commission's report (see paras 132 to 135). She accepted that the Board's decision in *Macleod* had gone too far in referring to 'manifestly unjust' as opposed to 'unjust', which was the wording of ss 34 and 35 of the 1973 Act and in applying the test under ss 34 and 35 to all post nuptial agreements without adjustment. However, she confirmed that in relation to *Edgar* and *Xydhias* type agreements, *Macleod* remained good law.

Her Ladyship differed (para 138 and following) from the majority decision in a number of respects, being that:

(1)   she rejected the view that pre-nuptial agreements are legally enforceable contracts;

(2)   she rejected the view that it is open to the Supreme Court to hold that they are;

(3)   she also rejected the upholding of the Court of Appeal's decision on the facts of the case; since the Court of Appeal had appeared to treat the parties as cohabitees as opposed to married partners and had failed to recognise the expectation of many parents of continuing to be a resource for their grown-up children. Hence, whilst the first instance decision should have given more weight to the fact of the pre-nuptial agreement, the majority's lack of additional provision to the husband was not, in Her Ladyship's view, generous enough and should have included the retention by him of the home for his lifetime and not just the dependency of the children;

(4)   in her view, policy considerations justified a different approach for agreements made before and after a marriage;

(5) she considered that the test to be applied by the court when approaching a pre-nuptial agreement should not be to introduce the 'impermissible gloss' on the statute of a presumption or starting point in favour of holding the parties to the agreement;

(6) she considered also that the approach of the Court of Appeal and the majority decision did not give sufficient importance to the status of marriage in English law;

(7) she believed that reform of this area should be in regard to both pre and post nuptial agreements and not limited to pre-nuptial agreements alone;

(8) in her view, fairness should be the sole touchstone in the light of the actual and foreseeable circumstances at the time when the court comes to make its order. No pre-nuptial agreement should prevent the court reaching a fair outcome on divorce (see para 168).

8.11 Case-law – post Radmacher

There have now been a number of cases decided since the Supreme Court's decision in the *Radmacher* case.

The first to be reported was *Z v Z*,[101] a judgment in 2011 of Moor J. This decision served to emphasise two aspects of the current law pending any reform. The first is that whatever the terms of a pre-nuptial agreement between the parties, the court will not countenance a distribution under the s 25 exercise, which fails to meet either parties' 'needs' level for accommodation and income (or for that matter any entitlement to 'compensation'). Secondly, the existence of a valid pre-nuptial agreement which remains 'material to the prevailing circumstances' and which seeks to limit or extinguish a party's entitlement under the 'sharing principle' is likely to be considered as fair and followed by the court upon divorce.

In the *Z v Z* case, the parties aged 53 (H) and 50 (W) had three dependent children. They had cohabited for 4 years and thereafter been married for 14 years before their final separation. As French nationals they had in 1994 signed a separation of property pre-nuptial agreement in Paris before two Notaries in which they opted out of the community of property default system. During the marriage, the parties had moved around with H's employment and latterly, as the marriage was failing, they had moved to London, having already consulted lawyers over their possible separation. Following a trial separation, H finally left W in their family home in London and W issued divorce proceedings in the UK.

Ryder J granted permission to proceed in the UK, determining that the parties' habitual residence had, latterly, been in the jurisdiction. Accordingly, upon the pursuit of W's claims for financial orders, the fact of the pre-nuptial agreement became a focal issue. W claimed H had promised orally not to enforce the same and maintained it was fair under s 25 to divide a marital pot then of £15m

---

[101] [2011] EWHC 2878 (Fam).

equally between the parties. H contended that it was fair to apply the terms of the pre-nuptial agreement, but accepted that as the same did not include 'maintenance' he was vulnerable to W claiming, at least, a recovery to meet her 'reasonable requirements' (a la pre *White* [2000]).

Moor J considered that the Supreme Court in *Radmacher* had brought about a *'seismic change'* in the Law pending any further review by the Law Commission or Parliament in cases where a pre-nuptial agreement had been signed. Such agreements would be followed '… unless in the prevailing circumstances, it would not be fair to hold the parties to the agreement' (see Lord Phillips in *Radmacher*). Accordingly, whilst in other circumstances this was a case of equal contributions and, therefore, equal sharing between the parties, the presence of the agreement allowed the Court to depart from the 'sharing principle' to the extent that only W's needs for accommodation and her *Duxbury* capitalised income needs would be met together with child maintenance, resulting in a clean break upon W recovering around £6m or 40 per cent plus child maintenance (assuming H met the risk of certain unlikely but possible contingent tax liabilities).

In the same year (2011), Charles J considered the case of *V v V*.[102] This was an appeal by H against a district judge's order in the ancillary relief proceedings in which, before the marriage, a 'marriage settlement' (ie pre-nuptial agreement) had been signed. The settlement provided for H to keep all of his pre-marital property (c £1 million).

The district judge had ordered a charge back in favour of H on the home to be bought by W with the lump sum that she was awarded as part of the settlement. The appeal centered upon whether the court had been right to make such an order. Charles J, decided that the district judge had wrongly approached the settlement as if the case had been dectermined before the *Radmacher* decision in holding that because the settlement did not specify what was to happen upon divorce, then the weight to be attached to it was limited. On the contrary, Charles J emphasised the decision of the Supreme Court required a significant change to the approach to be taken now in relation to such agreements. The priority, on the same level of importance as the established principles of 'need, compensation and sharing', was the need to recognise the weight to be given to autonomy and the choices and agreements made by the parties to a marriage. Hence, autonomous agreements and choices made by the parties could alter an award that would otherwise have been made.

---

[102] [2011] EWHC 3230 (Fam). See also *GS v L* [2011] EWHC 1759 (Fam), King J. Financial remedies application where H sought ring fencing of £1.49m of assets as pre-acquired or subject to a community of property agreement signed in Spain in 2002. Parties married 10 years with two children and now all living in Spain. Their foremost intention had been to give W financial security in the event of H's death. In addition, the impact of the existence of the agreement in Spanish law was itself controversial and uncertain and, accordingly, Her Ladyship considered the same provided the court with scant assistance in the s 25 exercise. Save for H's pension, this was a needs case which required all the assets to be considered and which would be equally divided with W's maintenance capitalized on top £4m. King J found that neither party had a full appreciation of the implications of the community of property agreement.

Charles J decided that, in view of the lower court's findings that the parties had intended the settlement to be effective, were fully aware of its obvious purpose despite W not having legal advice prior to signing and that W had been unconcerned as to the precise value of the H's property, there had, therefore, been no material non-disclosure and the terms of the settlement, taken together with the district judge's findings, did not justify a conclusion that the agreement was to be given limited weight.

Charles J further considered that whilst the district judge found that the wife had been in the weaker bargaining position, this factor was not sufficient to give only limited weight to the marriage settlement. Without more, the agreement had been willingly and honestly entered into by both sides. Accordingly, the district judge had been wrong in law in her approach to the assessment of the weight to be given to the marriage settlement and in concluding that it should only be given little weight in the s 25 exercise. Incorrectly, she had adopted a pre-*Radmacher* approach to the pre-nuptial agreement under consideration.

By contrast, Charles J concluded that the agreement was a factor that should be given weight to reflect the autonomy of both parties, who had freely and knowingly entered into it and in the circumstances it provided a good reason for departing from an equal division of the available assets which in His Lordship's judgment should by fresh assessment under the statutory exercise result in a chargeback of 33.3% of the value of the wife's property in favour of the husband and this percentage was increased to 35.8% when accounting for the wife's liability to pay the husbands costs on appeal.

In a trilogy of cases determined by Mostyn J between 2012 and 2013, the impact of a pre-nuptial agreement post *Radmacher* was further considered

The first of these was *Kremen v Agrest* (No 11) *(Financial Remedy: Non-Disclosure: Post-Nuptial Agreement)*[103] In this case, there had been a number of proceedings in this jurisdiction and abroad, including Israel. W was seeking financial orders under Part III of the Matrimonial and Family Proceedings Act 1984. Both parties were Russian and their marriage had been in Moscow in 1991. In 2001, they had signed a post-nuptial agreement in Israel in which W's entitlement was limited to $1.5m. This agreement was to be approved by the court in Israel and such approval was reaffirmed upon the parties' divorce in Israel in 2003. In fact, belatedly, H claimed the marriage and the agreement were invalid as he had been married to another at the time and in 2010 on this basis the court in Russia granted him a marriage annulment. In the proceedings brought by W in this jurisdiction, Mostyn J found H to have failed to disclose assets and he also found that W had been subjected to undue pressure and that she had had no independent legal advice and, therefore, His Lordship concluded that no reliance could be placed upon a post nuptial agreement signed by the parties in 2001. Assessing H's wealth at circa £20m to £30m, he awarded W £12.5m, being the court's assessment of her housing and

---

[103] [2012] EWHC 45 (Fam).

maintenance needs and reflecting her contribution and her overall fair share. In reaching his judgment, he summarised the impact of the *Radmacher* case in relation to the approach to be adopted to nuptial agreements, as follows (see para 72 of judgment):

(1) A nuptial agreement freely entered into by each party with a full appreciation of its implications should be followed by the court unless in the circumstances prevailing it would not be fair to hold the parties to their agreement.

(2) There is no absolute rule for what amounts to full disclosure or independent legal advice – instead, the question is there has been a *material lack* of disclosure, information or advice. Each party must have all the information that is *material* to his or her decision that the agreement should govern the financial consequences of the marriage coming to an end.

(3) The presence of any of the standard vitiating factors of duress, fraud or misrepresentation will negate any effect the agreement might otherwise have. Further, unconscionable conduct such as undue pressure (falling short of duress) will likely eliminate the weight to be attached to the agreement (ibid). Other unworthy conduct, such as exploitation of a dominant position to secure an unfair advantage, will reduce or eliminate the weight to be attached to the agreement (ibid). The court may take into account a party's emotional state, and what pressures he or she was under to agree, as well as their age and maturity, and whether either or both had been married or been in long-term relationships before. The court may take into account foreign elements to determine whether or not the parties intended their agreement to be effective.

(4) In determining whether 'in the circumstances prevailing it would not be fair to hold the parties to their agreement':

    (a) The agreement cannot be allowed to prejudice the reasonable requirements of any children of the family.

    (b) Respect should be accorded to the decision of a married couple as to the manner in which their financial affairs should be regulated particularly where the agreement addresses existing circumstances and not merely the contingencies of an uncertain future. This is likely to be so where the agreement seeks to protect pre-marital property. By contrast it is less likely to be so where the agreement leaves in the hands of one spouse rather than the other the most part of a fortune which each spouse has played an equal role in their different ways in creating. If the devotion of one partner to looking after the family and the home has left the other free to accumulate wealth, it is likely to be unfair to hold the parties to an agreement that entitles the latter to retain all that he or she has earned.

    (c) Is likely to be unfair to hold the parties to an agreement which leaves one spouse in a predicament of *real need*, while the other enjoys a sufficiency or more. However, need may be interpreted as being that minimum amount required to keep a spouse from destitution. For example, if the claimant spouse had been incapacitated in the course of the marriage, so that he or she was incapable of earning a living, this might well justify, in the interests of fairness, not holding him or her to the full rigours of the pre-nuptial agreement.

His Lordship added at para 73 of the judgment:

'73. It seems to me that it will only be in an unusual case where it can be said that, absent independent legal advice and full disclosure, a party can be taken to have freely entered into a marital agreement with a full appreciation of its implications. After all, almost every common law country that has legislated in this field has as a key pre-condition these requirements as well as a safety-net where the agreement is judged to be "unfair" (e.g. British Columbia) or "unjust" (e.g. New Zealand) or "unconscionable" (e.g. Australia). It would surely have to be shown that the spouse, like Mr Granatino, had a high degree of financial and legal sophistication in order to have a full appreciation of what legal rights he or she is signing away. Equally, it seems to me that there would have to be clear evidence of significant economic capacity on the part of the claimant spouse before the assessment of needs was suppressed to that minimal level imposed on Mr Granatino. There would surely have to be an equivalent finding to that in para 119 viz "on the evidence he is extremely able, and has added to his qualifications by pursuing a D Phil in biotechnology". I have noted that in the recent decision of *Z v Z (No. 2)* [2011] EWHC 2878 (Fam), which concerned a French pre-nuptial agreement, Moor J generously assessed the wife's needs to include the outright ownership of valuable property and a Duxbury fund to provide a high level of income for the remainder of her life. There was no question of imposing on her an arrangement akin to an award under Schedule 1 Children Act 1989.'

In the second of these cases, in *B v S (Financial Remedy: Marital Property Regime)*[104] the parties had been married for 14 years and there were two children aged 10 and 12. W, who was Spanish had made an application for financial remedy orders against H, a national of another country. The family had been in the UK since 2004 and divorce proceedings had commenced in 2009. Mostyn J had to consider what weight was to be attached, first to an alleged tacit agreement between the parties whereby they had adopted a default matrimonial property regime of 'separate property' upon their marriage in Catalonia as endorsed also by a second 'separation of property' agreement made in 2000 in another country, the identity of which could not be reported because of the requirement of anonymity. The second agreement having come into existence to deal specifically with certain property of W's, which would otherwise have fallen under the default 'community of property' regime of the other country.

H had established a widget company in 2000, which was now under a discretionary trust of which the parties and their children were beneficiaries and, therefore, the agreement was a 'nuptial settlement' and, plainly, a resource of H – however, the company was sited in a 'failed state' where the parties security could not be guaranteed and the company profits had been very volatile. It was contended that the company had $9.5m in accessible assets and

---

[104] [2012] EWHC 425 (Fam).

that H had had access to over £8m in company loans in recent years. Mostyn J determined, having rejected the applicability of either agreement ventured, that W should have £3m (being half of the value of the company assets value found), payable by instalments with a capitalised maintenance sum of £344k paid on the last instalment when the decreasing interim spousal maintenance for W would then terminate.

Mostyn J considered that as the law of England and Wales applied to all issues engaged, the only relevance of the foreign law involved was as to the evidence it provided as to the parties' intentions when they entered into the agreements. In a review of the *Radmacher* decision and the cases determined since in respect of pre and post nuptial agreements, His Lordship's view was that the established requirement of 'a full appreciation of [the agreement's] implications' did not carry with it a requirement to have received specific advice as to the operation of English law on the agreement in question. If it were otherwise then many nuptial agreements would fall at that hurdle. Rather, for the agreement entered into to have a relevance to the court's decision as to what was fair under the s 25 exercise on divorce, the reference to a 'full appreciation ... etc' must mean more than having a mere understanding that the agreement would just govern in the country in which it was made – indeed the parties must have intended the agreement to have effect, wherever they might be divorced and, most particularly, were they to be divorced in a jurisdiction that operated a system of discretionary equitable distribution.

His Lordship rejected H's case that the parties had tacitly adopted the Catalan default system of 'separation of property', without more; but rather, he found, they had intended the Catalan system to apply but subject to its 'lax judicial discretionary adjustment (powers) to effect compensatory redress for resultant economic inequality' – akin to that operated within this jurisdiction. He also found that the parties when entering into the second 'separation of property' agreement had simply intended only that the general Catalan law, as described above, would be applied thereby and in relation to neither agreement had the parties been advised whether the same may apply should they be divorced elsewhere or whether either agreement may restrict their rights to seek the statutory exercise of discretion under an equitable distribution jurisdiction such as that of England and Wales. Accordingly, neither party had entered either agreement with a full appreciation of the implications.

In the last of these cases, in *BN v MA*,[105] the parties with international backgrounds had had a relationship since 2002 and a child in 2005 and they had become committed to one another by 2007. They eventually married in 2012 and by 2013 a second child was expected by W, but then there was a separation after a violent incident occurred. W issued full applications for financial remedies upon filing her petition for divorce. In 2010, however, whilst both were abroad albeit living in different countries, they signed a comprehensive pre-nuptial agreement which was headed with an enlarged caution not to sign unless they wished to be bound by its terms and in which

---

[105] [2013] EWHC 4250 (Fam).

the terms provided a set amount for W and any children dependent upon the length of the marriage capped at 30% of H's wealth.

Mostyn J found that the law adopts 'a strict policy of requiring the demonstration of something unfair before it will open the Pandora's Box of litigation' after an agreement of this nature. He queried on what legal basis W had supposed it appropriate to file application for financial relief, including interim remedial relief, after signing such an agreement just 15 months before. His Lordship considered post *Radmacher* that there was only one approach to apply (to all nuptial agreements no matter if signed before or after a marriage), namely to give effect to such agreements, unless, in circumstances prevailing, it would be unfair to do so. In His Lordship's view, the autonomy of the parties, especially where, as here, they were of some sophistication and independently advised, was of particular importance and that particular weight should be given to agreements, which addressed present circumstances and sought to protect pre-owned property; although, he acknowledged that no provision could overreach basic need. (Of course, it is to be commented that the Law Commission's proposals for reform relating to the effect of a duly signed Qualifying Nuptial Agreement would make all, but the issue of the parties 'needs', irrelevant as to the implementation of the terms of the agreement.)

In Mostyn J's judgment, under the current law, all that was needed was that there should have been such 'material' disclosure and legal advice that was enough to enable the parties to have understood what was being given up and to have given their free consent. Accordingly, His Lordship found, in this case, there was nothing to suggest it would be unfair to uphold the terms of the pre-nuptial, which would be applied as closely as possible.

In 2013, Moor J in *AH v PH (Scandanavian Marriage Settlement)*,[106] dealt with two spouses of Scandanavian origin. Their marriage was relatively short, just over 4 years, although they had two young children. H's wealth of c £76m was mainly inherited. There had been a marriage settlement with the benefit of legal advice signed in the parties' home country and providing W with c £850,000 to buy a home upon a separation, but with no spousal or child maintenance provision. W wanted over £12m on a clean break and H submitted £4.6m to her was appropriate.

Moor J approached the case on the basis that as all the assets were essentially 'non matrimonial' in origin then he should address W's claims on the basis of her 'reasonable needs' only. His Lordship acknowledged that the *Radmacher* decision had altered the court's previous approach to the existence of a nuptial settlement, which had been entered into by parties with a full appreciation of the implications and, even if the court considered after analysis of the circumstances that the agreement should not be binding, the fact of its existence would still be relevant within 'all the circumstances of the case'. In His Lordship's judgment, the agreement had a number of failings. It would not, on the basis of expert evidence received by the court, be binding in Scandinavia, it

---

[106] [2013] EWHC 3878 (Fam).

did not provide for English housing or maintenance, the parties had not obtained legal advice as to its effect in this jurisdiction before signing and it did not relinquish all of W's claims in any event. Overall, W, therefore, entered into the same without a full appreciation of its implications and, therefore, the agreement would carry little weight, save only to have regard to the intention to protect H's inherited wealth, subject to W's reasonable needs – however, as Moor J observed, because of the shortness of the marriage, this would have been the approach in any event. Moor J, therefore, awarded W £5m of housing needs and her annual maintenance was to be capitalised on the basis of 17 years of child care to tertiary education and not on the basis of her lifetime.

In 2014, Mostyn J gave judgment in *SA v PA (Pre-Marital Agreement: Compensation)*[107]. In this case the parties (H, a Dutch solicitor aged 50 and earning £600k p a net who intended to retire at 55 and W, English aged 48 and not employed, although a qualified lawyer) had been married 18 years and had four children aged 13 to 19. They had signed a pre-nuptial agreement before a notary the day before their marriage in Amsterdam, the purpose of which had been to provide that there would on separation be an equal division of jointly created capital and a separate entitlement to any capital acquired by each party post-marriage from outside sources to be kept separate. There was no provision in the agreement for spousal maintenance. In the event, H had received family gifts of over £363k out of non-pension asset values of £3.8m and pension asset value held by H of £1.14m.

His Lordship determined that he should transfer the family home (value £2.2m subject to (£600k) mortgage to W plus a lump sum of £120k, with H to be responsible for the joint debts and there to be an equal split by pension share of the pension funds with over £10k pm periodical payments for W and with child support and education costs paid by H. In the Court's view W had had sufficient advice as to the implications of the agreement and had known exactly what she was agreeing to and the parties had intended that the agreement should cover a divorce in whatever jurisdiction that might take place. Because the agreement did not cover maintenance, the Court adjudicated upon that aspect, but otherwise W was to be held to the bargain she had struck, it being determined that her claim that this was a compensation case of a lost career had not been made out. However, because under both the law of this jurisdiction and that of Holland a pre-nuptial agreement was subject to adjustment for the parties' needs, there would be provision to W, which permitted her to build up a Duxbury fund from enhanced maintenance payments for a period and it was reasonable for her to live in the former martial home, without a sale, for a further 5 years.

Mostyn J again set out the applicable current law, as he had done in the *BN v MA* case and his previous decisions in this area, as above. He laid particular emphasis, however, in the circumstances of this case, upon the meaning of the requirement that parties to a pre-nuptial agreement should have been given within the independent legal advice they received upon the agreement 'a full

---

[107] [2014] EWHC 392 (Fam).

appreciation of its implications'. In His Lordship's view, to have effect within the jurisdiction of England and Wales, parties who entered into a pre-nuptial agreement abroad must have had advice not specifically about the law as it applied to divorce and inheritance distribution within this jurisdiction, but, at least, to the effect that the agreement would apply wherever they might be divorced including, in particular, in a regime that operated a system of 'discretionary equitable distribution' and it would be wise to insert a clause dealing with this in the agreement (see also Moor J in the *AH v PH (Scandinavian Marriage Settlement)* case above.

By way of comment, in this respect, it is to be noted that the Law Commission's proposals for reform have avoided a requirement which stipulates the content of the advice upon the effect of the agreement which is to be given. Accordingly, the Commission is of the view that this would remain the judgment of the individual lawyer who advises. However, clearly it would include advising what may be the outcome on divorce without a Qualifying Nuptial Agreement in place, emphasis upon the fact that by the time of a divorce etc the nature of the parties' resources may be wholly different to when the agreement was signed and, of course, the potential, as in the present case, of either party commencing divorce proceedings in another jurisdiction.

Again Mostyn J further emphasised the fact that a marital agreement does not have to deal with all aspects of the parties' resources in order to be presumptively binding over the assets or resources which it addresses (see *L v C*, Hong Kong CA[108]). Hence, for example, an agreement under current law may deal with the capital, whilst leaving maintenance at large or it may deal with certain assets, which each party wished to retain and ringfence from the eventual pot. In this event, the court would ordinarily give effect to such an intention, albeit that would not prevent a court, upon the s 25 exercise, taking the values of those excluded assets into account overall in the assessment of the fairness of the division of the remaining resources. Of course, under the Law Commission's proposals for reform, where a duly signed Qualifying Nuptial Agreement is in existence, there would no longer be a need in the court to consider the fairness of the same, subject to the condition that the terms of that agreement are not inconsistent with the financial needs of a party to it or the interests of any child of the family.

In the same year, Holman J in *Luckwell v Limata*[109] had to consider a case where there were not just one but several pre and post nuptial agreements signed by the parties with independent legal advice and all with the express purpose of limiting/excluding the recovery to be made upon any future divorce by H. The parties had been married 8 years (H 45 and W 37) and there were 3 children (aged 2 to 8). The pre-nuptial signed excluded H from claiming against W's separate property of gifts to her. Two further post-nuptial agreements between the parties on the same basis followed at times when W's family were to make specific advances to her. It was accepted that had these agreements not

---

[108] [2007] 3 HKLRD 819, Hong Kong CA.
[109] [2014] EWHC 502 (Fam).

been in place then neither the marriage nor the advances would have occurred. At the time of the divorce the only asset, the former marital home, which had been a parental gift to W in her sole name was valued at £6.7m and the family were supported by £100k pa from W's parents. H was in debt to the tune of £226k and had been unemployed since his redundancy two years before and was studying for an Open University degree.

Holman J considered that whilst very great weight had to be given to the agreements freely entered into by H as a mature man after expert legal advice and where there had been a realisation of the implications of doing so, the factor of H's present and future needs would have the effect that the agreements should not be applied rigorously. Whilst 'need' is not a trump card it can outweigh the fact of an agreement in a particular case, especially as here where the agreements made no provision at all for H in any circumstances and where it was clear he was in a predicament of real need having no home, no current income, no capital, considerable debts and no borrowing capacity. Furthermore, His Lordship, considered that it was in the children's welfare interests that each parent should have appropriate homes in which the children could visit and stay with each parent (see *Radmacher's* case).

Holman J, therefore, directed a sale of the former marital home, even though her father had said in evidence that if this was done he would withdraw all further support for his daughter. In His Lordship's judgment, W's mother would still provide her with some support. In any event, the sale was required so that W could specifically buy a house for £900k for H's use and in which H could be provided with a home under lease at a peppercorn rent to be sold only when the youngest child reached 22 at which time 45% of the net sale proceeds of the property would return to W and H would retain the balance to acquire a more modest home based on his reasonably predicted needs then. W was ordered also to pay H a lump sum of £292k to buy furniture, a car and to pay his debts. Again by way of comment, the Law Commission's proposals for reform (see more below) would not have altered this position in view of the Commission's recognition that 'needs' must take precedence and on this the Commission was not in favour of any distinction being made between 'needs' and 'real needs', which has been otherwise canvassed in some of the above post *Radmacher* cases.

Again in 2014, Roberts J gave judgment in *Y v Y (Financial Remedy – Marriage Contract)*,[110] which involved W's application for financial remedy orders upon divorce, where H and W, as French nationals, had 2 days before the marriage entered into a marriage contract under French law in which the parties elected to apply to their marriage the *separation de biens* regime, in which they retained their own separate property. In France, such an agreement would be binding upon divorce. Instead, W now sought her equal share of their marital acquest. H contended that the choice made by the parties of the applicable

---

[110] [2014] EWHC 2920 (Fam).

marital property regime was equivalent in effect to a pre-nuptial agreement and, therefore, this agreement should be determinative in excluding assets the parties accrued in marriage.

Roberts J found that W had appreciated that the agreement she was signing would determine how the parties would conduct their marital financial dealings together. Whilst the judge did not accept the W had been confronted with the contract just 2 weeks before the marriage ceremony, as she claimed, she did accept the guidance of Mostyn J in *Kremen v Agrest* (as further explained by His Lordship in *B v S) (above)*, namely:

> 'Each party must have all the information that is material to his or her decision that the agreement should govern the financial consequences of the marriage coming to an end.'

Accordingly, Her Ladyship accepted, in the circumstances, that, in the absence of independent legal advice, W, on the facts of the case, would not have had all the information she needed to fully understand all of the legal consequences which her entering the contract would have upon divorce or the entitlements which she would be surrendering as a result. In particular, she would not have appreciated that whatever their financial circumstances upon divorce, she was agreeing to a financial recovery substantially less than equality. However, that did not mean that the contract was irrelevant to the outcome; but rather the weight to be attributed to its terms was to the effect that fairness required that, subject to the wife's needs, the non-matrimonial property owned by each of the parties should be excluded from the sharing exercise to be conducted.

8.12   Other jurisdictions and human rights

Irrespective of the nationality or domicile of the parties, their habitual residence at the time of, or during the marriage, their making of a pre or post nuptial agreement or any choice of law clause within it, it remains the position after *Radmacher's* case that an English court seised of the matter on divorce and making an order for financial relief under the Matrimonial Causes Act 1973 will apply English law.[111]

The relevance of any foreign element in any pre-nuptial agreement in the case will, therefore, be, primarily, in respect of the intention of the parties that the terms of the agreement would apply.

The United Kingdom has made a policy decision not to participate in the results of the work done by the European Community and the Hague Conference on Private International Law to apply uniform rules of private international law in relation to 'maintenance' obligations. Although, the United Kingdom Government has opted in to Council Regulation (EC) No 4/2009 of 18

---

[111]   See Dicey, Morris and Collins, *Conflict of Laws*, vol 2, (14th edn, 2006), Rule 9 1(7), and eg C *v C (Ancillary Relief: Nuptial Settlement)* [2004] EWCA Civ 1030, [2005] Fam 250, at para 31.

December, 2008 on jurisdiction, applicable law and enforcement of decisions and co-operation in matters relating to 'maintenance' obligations, the rules relating to applicable law will not apply in the United Kingdom. This is the result of the effect of Art 15 of the Council Regulation in that the law applicable to 'maintenance' obligations is to be determined in accordance with the 2007 Hague Protocol, but only in those Member States bound by the Hague Protocol. The United Kingdom will not be bound by the Hague Protocol, because it agreed to participate in the Council Regulation only on the basis that it would not be obliged to join in accession to the Hague Protocol by the EU. The United Kingdom Government's position was that there was very little application of foreign law in family matters within the United Kingdom and in 'maintenance' cases, in particular, the expense of proving the content of that law would be disproportionate to the low value of the vast majority of maintenance claims.

In *Radmacher's* case, the Majority noted that had the Hague Protocol applied, its terms not only allowed the parties to designate the law applicable to a 'maintenance' obligation, but also provided that, unless at the time of the designation, the parties were fully informed and aware of the consequences of their designation, the law designated by the parties will not apply where the application of that law would lead to manifestly unfair or unreasonable consequences for any of the parties (Art 8(1) and (5)).

In summary, most other countries in Europe, the North American states and Canada, as well as South Africa, Australia, New Zealand and many other nations in the civilised world, including China, have statutory as opposed to common law provision for the recognition of some form of pre-nuptial agreements upon divorce.[112] Many of these countries operate under a community of property regime and, by the pre-nuptial agreement, parties will exercise an opt out of the consequences of the same in relation to certain identified assets, which they each hold.

The approach of this jurisdiction, even after the Supreme Court's decision in the *Radmacher* case, of leaving the relevance and weight upon divorce of such an agreement to the discretion of the individual judge in the circumstances of the particular case is almost exceptional. Of course, short of legislation, the Supreme Court's decision has, at least, ensured, for now, that the presence of a pre-nuptial agreement will be taken into account under 'all the circumstances of the case' and, where its terms remain relevant to the parties' prevailing circumstances and do not attempt to impede the rights of any dependent children, the same will have significant, if not compelling weight in the s 25 exercise and it will be for the party seeking to avoid the terms of the signed agreement to establish that it would be unfair to be bound to that agreement.[113]

---

[112] For a comprehensive survey of the approach of different jurisdictions; see Resolutions 2010 Report '*Family Agreements: Seeking Certainty to Reduce Disputes*' Annex 1 – Jurisdictions other than England and Wales.

[113] See, by contrast, the pre-*Radmacher* position as criticised by Hoffmann LJ in *Pounds v Pounds* [1994] 1 WLR 1535, 1550–1551.

This element of uncertainty of outcome was one of the aspects of the challenge under the Human Rights Act and the Article of the First Protocol (protection of property rights etc) mounted on behalf of the wife in the first instance decision of the *Radmacher* case, *NG v KR (pre-nuptial contract)*[114] against the husband's claims for financial relief brought in the face of the nil provision pre-nuptial agreement signed by the parties. It was argued that the wife, under the pre-nuptial agreement signed by the parties, had a valid contractual right that should be protected as 'property' under the Protocol by the courts and, thereby, the agreement should be the central and inescapable focus of the s 25 statutory exercise.

In a comprehensive review of the law in this area up to that point, Baron J concluded that it remained the position in English matrimonial law that neither party could sue upon a pre-nuptial agreement since the enforceability of any such agreement, in the absence of statutory exceptions, depended not upon the agreement but upon the subsequent court order incorporating its terms (*de Lasala v de Lasala*,[115] *Xydhias v Xydhias*[116] and *Soulsbury v Soulsbury*[117]) and, accordingly, the pre-nuptial agreement was not a binding legal contract and the Protocol, therefore, had no application. Further, there was, stated Baron J, no 'arbitrary' uncertainty of outcome within the s 25 exercise that might infringe the Protocol, but rather 'a fair balance between existing property rights and the entitlement of the claiming party to share, to receive compensation or have his needs met. This fair balance was well within "the margin of appreciation" afforded to this country.'

Of course, the Supreme Court has since, in the same case on appeal, held that pre-nuptial agreements are, indeed, legally enforceable and accordingly, Baron J's first stance against the application of the Protocol may not apply. However, Lady Hale was in no doubt in her Minority judgment that such dicta of the Majority relating to the contractual status of a pre-nuptial agreement was obiter to the issues of the case, in any event. In addition, the Majority had recognised that in practice such an enforceable status is nevertheless illusory in the face of the fact that whenever a party thereto seeks to challenge the terms of the agreement, the inevitable step taken will be the issue of an application for financial relief invoking the court's discretionary jurisdiction under the s 25 process as to whether it is fair to make all, part or none of the agreement into a court order.[118]

8.13 Advising the client

Notwithstanding the now published Law Commission's report and recommendations, until Parliament has the political motivation and

---

[114] [2008] EWHC 1532 (Fam).
[115] [1980] AC 546.
[116] [1999] 1 FLR 683 CA.
[117] [2007] EWCA Civ 969. But now see Baron J in *NG v KR (pre-nuptial contract)* [2008] EWHC 1532 (Fam) below.
[118] See Lord Phillips [2010] UKSC 42.

opportunity of considering legislation in regard to the primacy and weight to be given to pre-nuptial agreements upon divorce, practitioners will need to continue to be aware of both the approach of the courts before and after *Radmacher's* case.

In regard to the pre-*Radmacher* position, such pre 2010 case-law will, for now, remain important in advising a client as to the likely effect of a pre-nuptial agreement entered into before the Supreme Court's judgment upon the eventual divorce distribution. In such cases, because the parties may have been advised that such agreements were not binding and in the absence of strict compliance with 'the six safeguards'[119] that the agreement entered into may be disregarded altogether by a court, not only the weight of such an agreement upon the eventual outcome may be in issue, but also whether it was the parties' intention that the agreement itself should have any effect.

With this situation in mind, the pre-R*admacher* position could not be better summarised than by reference to the following extract from Connell J's judgment in *M v M*:[120]

> 'In my view, it matters not whether the court bears such an agreement in mind as part of the circumstances of the case (a very important factor) or as an aspect of the parties' conduct. Under either approach the court should look at any such agreement and decide in the particular circumstances what weight should, in justice, be attached to it. Given that a significant percentage of marriages these days end in divorce, it is understandable that mature adults, and in particular those who have been married before, might wish to agree what should happen in the event of a breakdown. The desire for certainty, or the wish to know where you stand, is not unusual. It is clear, of course, that the existence of such an agreement does not oust the jurisdiction of the court ... The public policy objection to such agreements, namely that they tend to diminish the importance of the marriage contract, seems to me to be of less importance now that divorce is so commonplace. However the manner in which the courts should treat such agreements will vary from case to case.'

Following the decision in *M v M*,[121] *K v K*[122] and later *NG v KR*,[123] it was no longer the case that the advice given to clients wishing to enter into a pre-nuptial agreement could properly be that such an agreement would have little or no effect on the court's decision on a subsequent application for ancillary relief.

---

[119] Labour Government's 1998 Consultation Document: *Supporting Families* (Stationery Office, October 1998).

[120] [2002] 1 FLR 654. Connell J at para [21]. Albeit, along with other cases, criticised by Lord Phillips (at para 45 of the *Radmacher* decision) for having referred to the approach adopted in *Edgar* in relation to pre-nuptial agreement cases, when the *Edgar* decision had been in the very different context of a separation post nuptial agreement.

[121] [2002] 1 FLR 654.

[122] [2003] 1 FLR 120.

[123] [2008] EWHC 1532 (Fam) – *Radmacher's* case at first instance.

It was clear that if the wife in *K v K* and the husband in *NG v KR*[124] had not entered into the pre-nuptial agreement, both would have fared better on their applications for ancillary relief. The legal advice given to the wife in K v K at the time the agreement was signed was that it would not be binding, and, particularly so, if there were children. This advice, at the specific time that it was given, cannot be criticised, but, following *K v K*, the same advice given to clients would be negligent.

Since such time and at present, if the marriage has been of short duration and the necessary formalities surrounding the pre-nuptial agreement have been complied with, the agreement is likely to be 'the magnetic factor' in the exercise. Where the marriage has subsisted for longer and there have been events that have materially altered the respective positions of the parties, then the relevance of such an agreement and its effect on the eventual court order on divorce will depend upon the extent to which the same was sufficiently generous at the outset in meeting the projected needs of the weaker party and any children or, by its review since signed, has remained sufficiently contemporaneous to the financial position of the parties prevailing at the time of the divorce. If the agreement does by either route remain relevant to the prevailing financial circumstances, then it is likely to have a significant effect upon the final order of the court on divorce.

The majority in the Supreme Court, clearly, however, remained unwilling to adopt, without statutory reform, the position where the terms of a pre-nuptial agreement and, particularly one with a nil or decidedly unfair provision, should be regarded as 'presumptively dispositive' of the financial outcome of a divorce. Indeed, Lady Hale, in her minority judgment, was prepared to reject such a notion without reservation. Accordingly, it remains, without further legislative change, the position that the agreement's provision will be only one of the features of a given case that the court will weigh in the balance in determining the fair distribution between the parties, albeit the more relevant the agreement remains to the prevailing financial circumstances upon divorce, the more compelling or 'magnetic' its effect will be by reason of the parties' autonomous choices within a marriage being regarded now as a guiding 'rationale' to the Court's approach upon divorce distribution post the *Radmacher* decision (see *V v V*, Charles J above).

However, whether pre- or post-*Radmacher*, the acknowledged underlying statutory intention that spousal 'needs' should, wherever possible, be met within the s 25 exercise remains the overarching focus of the Court's approach in this area. The Law Commission has, again, endorsed this position in its recommendations as to the 'Qualifying Nuptial Agreement' (see more below), which if adopted would still, upon such proposals, remain open to challenge where the other spouse's needs had not been provided for. This historical perspective to the 'needs' provision being the recognised basement of judicial divorce provision was, particularly, highlighted in the pre-*Radmacher* high

---

[124] [2008] EWHC 1532 (Fam).

profile and 'huge money' case of *McCartney v McCartney*,[125] in which, as Bennett J found, despite the almost meritless case presented by the wife in regard to her contribution to the creation of wealth under consideration, she still recovered millions of pounds to cover her 'reasonable needs'. In this context, it is, instructive to consider that had there been in existence a pre-nuptial agreement in that case purporting to limit the wife's entitlement to less than her eventual recovery, the impact of the same, where there was a child and where the court concluded that the 'needs' of the wife, including those as carer, were themselves to be seen as a 'magnetic' factor in the decision, would, probably, have resulted in the Bennett J being only modestly less generous in the evaluation of what those 'needs' were.

Indeed, immediately post *Radmacher*, Moor J in the case of *Z v Z* [2011] above, further emphasised this to be the position, in circumstances where, although the pre-nuptial agreement in existence there reflected an agreed 'separation of property' between the parties, the court nevertheless, whilst acknowledging the validity of the agreement signed, was unwilling to adjust the wife's recovery below her 'reasonable needs generously assessed', resulting in a modest departure from equality and the 'sharing principle' from 50 per cent to 40 per cent on a clean break. This emphasis upon meeting the 'needs' provision of the other spouse was also was the approach vividly endorsed in the *Luckwell v Limata* case above.

8.14   The honeymoon agreement

Following on from the last section, the first instance and the Court of Appeal decisions in *Radmacher's* case, in the light of the *Macleod* decision, gave rise to the trend of parties-to-be-married agreeing not only to sign up to a pre-nuptial agreement, but also, in identical terms, to another agreement shortly after the wedding ceremony. The second or *'honeymoon'* agreement, arguably under ss 34 and 35 as a 'maintenance agreement', pursuant to *Macleod*, potentially placed the greater limitation upon the court's discretionary powers as defined in those sub-sections in the event of a subsequent divorce.

In *Westmeath v Westmeath*,[126] a distinction had been drawn between those agreements which provided for the consequences of an actual separation, which had already occurred and an agreement providing for the consequences of a future separation; the latter agreement was, as already referred to earlier, null and void. Loyal to that principle, in *Brodie v Brodie*,[127] a pre-nuptial agreement which provided for the parties to live apart and which was re-signed immediately after marriage was held void. Of course, following the Supreme Court's decision, the public policy objection to a pre-nuptial agreement has now

---

[125]   [2008] EWHC 401.
[126]   (1830) 1 Dow & Cl 519.
[127]   [1917] P 271.

been removed and so a 'honeymoon' post-nuptial agreement, which mirrored the financial provision made in the pre-nuptial agreement should not now offend the rule in *Brodie*.[128]

In the light of the Supreme Court Justices' decision in *Radmacher*, however, it is now apparent that this device will not be any more effective against an attempt by one of the parties to seek to 'water down' the impact of the agreement upon divorce where fairness requires.

Clearly, the Majority decision of the Supreme Court in *Radmacher's* case has substantially reduced, if not removed entirely, any previous perception of a difference of approach by a court on divorce to the contents of a pre-nuptial agreement and a post nuptial agreement, including one signed, possibly, immediately after the wedding ceremony itself. Indeed, the Minority speech of Lady Hale appeared to accept that agreements, which were signed immediately after a wedding, may well bear little distinction from the pre-nuptial agreement signed before. Indeed, there remains deep scepticism amongst many lawyers that Lady Hale was correct in applying the provisions of ss 34 and 35 of the 1973 Act to this situation at all and Mostyn J in a number of his most recent decisions (as above) upon pre-nuptial agreements post-*Radmacher* has repeatedly asserted that the outcome of the Supreme Court's decision is that all nuptial agreements, whether made pre or post marriage, are, within the statutory exercise upon divorce, to be given effect unless shown to be unfair pursuant to the Lord Phillips test.

The essentials and practicalities of a pre-nuptial agreement

8.15   Essentials

The central focus of the Labour Government's 1998 Consultation Paper, *Supporting Families*,[129] was upon ways of strengthening the family. Amongst a number of measures canvassed, it was suggested that making pre-nuptial agreements legally binding may well be a way in which parties, about to be married, would be able to exercise more choice and responsibility in considering their future as married partners and the financial consequences before they got married. Within the process of reaching an agreement about their financial future together, it was submitted that parties may be caused to feel more secure in entering marriage as opposed to cohabitation and, with legislative protection, the rights of the weaker party and any children of the relationship could be protected. It was suggested that should any one of some six safeguards be found not to exist then a pre-nuptial agreement should be held not to be legally binding on the parties to the agreement. Accordingly, it was recommended that a pre-nuptial agreement would not be legally binding:

---

[128] See and cf [2009] CFLQ 513 1 December 2009, *Radmacher v Granatino* [2009] EWCA Civ 649: 'Upping the ante-nuptial agreement': Case Commentary Joanna Miles Trinity College, Cambridge.

[129] *Supporting Families* (Stationery Office, October 1998).

(1)   where there is a child of the family, whether or not that child was alive or a child of the family at the time the agreement was made;

(2)   where under the general law of contract, the agreement is unenforceable, including if the contract attempted to lay an obligation on a third party, who had not agreed in advance;

(3)   where one or both parties did not receive independent legal advice before entering into the agreement;

(4)   where the court considers that the enforcement of the agreement would cause significant injustice (to one or both of the parties or a child of the marriage);

(5)   where one or both of the parties have failed to give full disclosure of assets and property before the agreement was made;

(6)   where the agreement was made fewer than 21 days prior to the marriage (this would prevent a nuptial agreement being forced on people shortly before their wedding day, when they may not feel able to resist).

It was previously thought that this list, particularly in the light of its adoption, initially, at first instance, by Baron J in *Radmacher's* case, contained the essential checklist of conditions, which should be in place if a pre-nuptial agreement was to be of pivotal relevance whenever a court was exercising its distributive powers upon a divorce etc. The discussion of this checklist by the Justices of the Supreme Court in the *Radmacher* appeal and the further development of this area by the subsequent case-law, together with now the publication of the Law Commission's report, have, in reality, further narrowed the field of essential conditions required for the Court's recognition of the terms of a pre-nuptial agreement, pending statutory reform, down to ensuring that there has been independent legal advice, material disclosure, the agreement remains financially relevant, there has been no undue pressure and that the agreement is fair, including that it meets the 'needs' of the financially weaker spouse.

Clearly, upon the current law before any reform, whether or not the agreement provides for any child of the parties (safeguard (i) above) will not prevent the court from giving, upon a divorce, appropriate weight, decisive or otherwise, to the terms of a pre-nuptial agreement, if fairness dictates, whilst making express provision for the child in question. In addition, in any given case, following the Supreme Court's decision and as very much demonstrated by the facts of the *Radmacher* case itself, the issue, where any one or more of such conditions have not been met, will, nevertheless, be whether the failure to do so was 'material' rendering it unfair in the prevailing circumstances to hold the parties to the agreement.

8.16   *Independent legal advice*

The process should start by each party taking such advice and, preferably, although by no means an obligation, each should pay for the same from their own resources.[130] In *Radmacher v Granatino*,[131] there had been objectively insufficient opportunity for the husband to take independent legal advice within the time frame that had existed there of seven days from delivery of the final draft to signing and where he had had no input as to the contents of the agreement up to that point and where such explanation as he received of the terms of the document versed in a language (German), which was not his own (French), had been given by a notary paid by the wife's family and who himself had expressed dissatisfaction as to the inadequate information afforded to the husband. Nevertheless, the husband, who had a commercial background and was thereby said to be familiar with such forms of contract, realised the agreement made no provision for him under German law on divorce.

Of course, at first instance, Baron J had stated, however, that '... neither that knowledge, his background nor the information he was given are the same as understanding the full legal consequences of his decision or its later enforceability'.

By contrast, neither the Court of Appeal or the Supreme Court supported her approach on such matters and adopted what has been called 'a functional rather than formal, or de facto rather than de jure, approach to the formalities issue'.[132] In short, the approved approach, under current law before any reform, is that independent legal advice is 'necessary in most cases and desirable in all', but under the s 25 exercise, because the court must consider 'all the circumstances of the case' in seeking a fair resource division between parties, a pre-nuptial agreement, knowingly and voluntarily made by the parties, cannot be ignored by the court simply on the basis that the usual formalities, the requirements for which are not yet prescribed by statute, were not followed.

8.17 Full disclosure

Whatever the form chosen, there should be material disclosure of the nature and net value of assets, pension worth and incomes. Clearly, there is no prescribed form. Practice differs. Some practitioners present draft Forms E – others advise that all the required copy documents should be attached. However, it is suggested that a detailed list of capital net worth and pension and income resources, identifying any supporting documentation should, in the majority of cases, be sufficient, as long as the other party is expressly offered facilities for full inspection. Baron J in the first instance decision of

---

[130] [2009] Fam Law 1056 'From Pre-Nups to Post-Nups: Dealing with Marital Property Agreements' *Independent Legal Advice*: Emma Hitchings School of Law, Bristol University, in which it is suggested that in practice, where one of the parties pays for the advice, a cap on the expense may be incurred giving rise to the problem that the extent of the advice given may have been limited and its effect less effective as a result. The client paying in this instance should be advised against imposing such a limit lest in the final analysis the advice given is deemed to have been inadequate.

[131] [2010] UKSC 42.

[132] See [2009] CFLQ 513 *Radmacher v Granatino* [2009] EWCA Civ 649: 'Upping the ante-nuptial agreement' *Case Commentary* Joanna Miles, Trinity College, Cambridge.

Radmacher's case,[133] stated that where there has been inadequate disclosure, it is impossible for a party to make a fully informed decision. Despite this, Mostyn J in *BN v MA* [2013] said this at para 30:[134]

> 'What then did the Supreme Court say about how to determine whether an agreement has been freely entered into with a full appreciation of its implications? In paragraph 69 it was stated that there is no rule at all that full disclosure, or full legal advice, is a necessary pre-condition for the satisfaction of this criterion. On the contrary, the question is in the individual case whether there has been a material lack of disclosure, or a material lack of information, or a material lack of legal advice. I venture the opinion that usually – and that is in the usual run of cases and not a case when one is dealing with such a highly intelligent sophisticate as Mr. Granatino – a full appreciation of the implications will normally carry with it a requirement of having at least enough legal advice to appreciate what one is giving up... '

Of course, in *Radmacher's* case, the wife deliberately withheld disclosure from the husband, but the fact that he was well aware that she was very wealthy and irrespective of disclosure would have signed the pre-nuptial agreement anyway, meant that the wife's deliberate non disclosure was not material on the facts of that case. The position, as to the sufficiency of disclosure will be, in every case where a pre-nuptial agreement exists upon divorce etc, whether each party had all the information which was material to his or her decision to enter into the agreement. Currently, indifference to the detailed provision of information by either party at the time of entering into a pre-nuptial agreement will deny that party any defence later that inadequate disclosure was afforded.

8.18   Periodic review

There is no magic in the period to be chosen. The convention of current practice ranges from three years to a maximum of five years. However, the pre-nuptial agreement may provide for a number of significant situations each of which will trigger the need to review the terms of the agreement, whether the same be the birth of a child or the disability of either party etc. Again, in the first instance decision of *Radmacher's* case,[135] it was considered relevant to enforceability that there was no provision for a review for either party in the event of the birth of a child. Such an event, it was observed by Baron J, altered the relationships and priorities of both sexes and was in that case one reason for the husband wanting to change career so as to spend more time with his family and, of course, thereby, impacted upon his income potential. The complete absence of consideration of such an event, her Ladyship considered 'flawed' that agreement and made it, so the court found, prima facie unfair.

Once again, the Court of Appeal and the Supreme Court adopted the opposite position. The relevance of the terms of a pre-nuptial and for that matter a post-nuptial agreement (other than an *Edgar* or *Xydhias* type) would be judged

---

[133] *NG v KR* [2008] EWHC 1532 (Fam).
[134] *BN v MA* [2013] EWHC 4250 (Fam).
[135] See *NG v KR* above.

at the breakdown of the marriage irrespective of whether there had been any provision for or an actual review. It was more likely that the longer the period of time which had elapsed since the pre-nuptial agreement had been entered into without adjustment of its terms, then the less likely the predictions as to the parties' financial futures and needs made therein would remain relevant to the 'prevailing circumstances' before the court under the s 25 exercise upon divorce and, thereby, the lesser the weight, which would be ascribed to the terms of the agreement in such circumstances.

8.19　Free will

There will, invariably, be some form of pressure, even if it comes only from the fact that one of the parties holds the wealth and seeks to limit any future claim against such asset value in the event of a breakdown. The extent of this consideration of pressure is not limited to the classic contractual issue of duress, which has overborne the free will of the other, but extends to any 'unconscionable' or 'unworthy' conduct.

> 'The presence of any of the standard vitiating factors of duress, fraud or misrepresentation will negate any effect the agreement might otherwise have (para 71). Further, unconscionable conduct such as undue pressure (falling short of duress) will likely eliminate the weight to be attached to the agreement (ibid). Other unworthy conduct, such as exploitation of a dominant position to secure an unfair advantage, will reduce or eliminate the weight to be attached to the agreement (ibid). The court may take into account a party's emotional state, and what pressures he or she was under to agree, as well as their age and maturity, and whether either or both had been married or been in long-term relationships before (para 72). The court may take into account foreign elements to determine whether or not the parties intended their agreement to be effective (para 74).'[136]

It will remain pivotal in most cases, therefore, to allow sufficient time before the marriage occurs and/or the final draft agreement is signed for negotiation and discussion to take place as to the terms of the pre-nuptial proposals. The estimate of time required for this purpose is frequently under estimated by the lay parties. Whilst, the Law Commission would with legislative reform require for validation of a 'Qualifying Nuptial Agreement' that the latest time to reach agreement should be 28 days before the marriage ceremony, this has been demonstrated under the present law, as above, in *K v K*, again in *Radmacher's* case and, subsequently, in *SA v PA* [2014],[137] to be, currently, no more than best practice.

> '63. Although it is true that the agreement was entered into on the very eve of the marriage, at a time when the wife was pregnant, and where she had only the impartial but not strictly independent advice of the notary I am satisfied that the wife freely entered into it with a sufficiency of advice to enable her to appreciate its implications.' Mostyn J in *SA v PA* [2014]

---

[136] *Kremen v Agrest (No 11)* [2012] EWHC 45 (Fam) at para 11 per Mostyn J.
[137] *SA v PA* [2014] EWHC 392 (Fam), Mostyn J at para 63.

However, evidentially, the burden of proof will be different upon such an issue, dependent upon whether the agreement was signed pre- or post-*Radmacher*. For pre-*Radmacher* agreements, what the court will continue to look for within the s 25 exercise, upon any subsequent assessment of the fairness of the agreement, is that both parties had a reasonable time to consider its provisions and to take appropriate advice upon the same before agreeing to be bound to the agreement (see the Majority decision in *Radmacher*'s case[138]). This is because, in such cases, the intention of the parties to be bound by the terms of the pre-nuptial agreement will still need to be established as a primary evidential position. In contrast, in post *Radmacher* agreements, assuming no contractual vitiating factor exists, it will be natural to infer from the very existence of a pre-nuptial agreement that both parties intended to be bound by the terms of the same and it will be for the party, who is seeking to persuade the court not to rely upon the terms of a pre-nuptial agreement, to rebut such an inference.

8.20   Fairness

At all times, the fairness of what is being proposed is at the heart of the drafting exercise of a pre-nuptial agreement, whilst s 25 of the Matrimonial Causes Act 1973, as amended, in its present form, remains the law. If the provisions within the drafted agreement appear unfair, the other party will be advised against the 'deal' and/or, eventually, assuming the same have a like appearance against the prevailing circumstances upon divorce, the court will be highly unlikely, in most cases under current law and post-*Radmacher*, to restrict itself to the terms struck.

However, what appears fair at the time of the drafting of the pre-nuptial agreement before the marital union has even commenced, is unlikely, without a wide element of generosity in the agreement's original provision and/or without subsequent periodic adjustment, to be a fair measure of the needs of the financially weaker spouse some years later

This fact should be what any client hears first when seeking advice as to the merits and contents of a pre-nuptial agreement and what should be emphasised, thereafter, within any follow up client care letter.

Both pre- and post-*Radmacher*, it is clear that the existence of a pre-nuptial agreement can alter what the court would have considered fair upon the breakdown of the marriage had such an agreement not been in place.[139] Subject to this effect, it is likely that the pre-nuptial agreement will have to address, principally, the issues of the parties' predictable 'needs' and any element of

---

[138] See [2010] UKSC 42 per Lord Phillips, paras 70–73.
[139] *M v M (Prenuptial Agreement)* [2002] 1 FLR 654. Connell J pared the wife's needs down because she had signed a pre-nuptial agreement (see para 44) and in *Radmacher*'s case the existence of the pre-nuptial agreement to preserve non-matrimonial property had the effect of the Court assessing need more conservatively than would have been the case absent that factor.

'compensation',[140] where applicable, if the same is, currently, to satisfy the court, upon divorce, that its provisions are fair. It follows that it is in the sphere of the third strand of fairness, namely 'sharing' that the existence of a pre-nuptial agreement is likely to have the greatest impact.

There will be cases, however, where a nil provision within a pre-nuptial agreement will suffice, if the parties' respective financial positions, prevailing at the time of the breakdown of the marriage when set against the fact that they have chosen to enter into a pre-nuptial agreement, can be said to meet their existing and future foreseeable individual requirements. Hence, it is more likely, post-*Radmacher*, than before that provided that the parties' needs are catered for, in the right case, the 'autonomy of the parties' to determine their financial future upon divorce within such an agreement will be fully adhered to by the court.

The advice in most cases, pending any legislative reform, for the client, who wishes there to be no provision for the other party in a pre-nuptial agreement must still be that, as the law currently stands, such an absence of provision considerably increases the likelihood that the agreement, after anything but a classic short childless marriage (up to four years), remains unlikely to be accepted as making fair provision for that other party in the event of a divorce etc. Of course, the fact that the parties did actually enter into an agreement, whether deemed fair or unfair, will still be a factor in the eventual s 25 exercise balance and it may still be submitted that where such a pre-nuptial agreement is challenged as unfair in eventual ancillary relief proceedings, the fact of its existence will still permit the party seeking to rely upon it to make by 'open offer' an additional 'top up' provision, at that stage, without loss of the argument that the existence of the agreement itself evidences the parties' intention that the other party's provision should, in any event, be more limited than would have been the case had there been no agreement at all.

The Law Commission's report has, notwithstanding the above, clearly signalled that its proposals for statutory reform in this area would not be in favour of any hierarchy of 'need' levels, differentiating between 'reasonable needs' and any perceived lower form of 'basic' or 'essential' needs. Of course, the result of the referred Family Justice Council's analysis of what constitutes 'needs' under the s 25 exercise is yet awaited. However, a primary condition of the enforceability of any 'Qualifying Nuptial Agreement' as submitted in the Commission's report, remains that the same must provide, at least, for the financially weaker spouse's reasonable needs.

8.21 Checklist

A checklist for preparing and drafting a pre-nuptial agreement

(1) Provide the client with a general overview of the likely process and the time needed to reach a signed final draft and the probable costs involved.

---

[140] Albeit in *SA v PA* above, Mostyn J has sought to limit the principle of compensation to the rare and exceptional case.

(2) Obtain from Professional Insurers the required and appropriate level of professional indemnity cover and subject thereto, advise the client as to the limited level of your professional indemnity cover for the work to be undertaken and make that level the limitation of your liability as a written pre-condition of accepting instructions in the matter, after advising the client of the potential of instructing other lawyers who may undertake the work without such a limitation.

(3) Subject to the above, obtain the client's signed consent to such limitation of liability.

(4) Advise, at least, that:

   (i) the current law has been subject to the published review by the Law Commission and it has been proposed that a 'Qualifying Nuptial Agreement', subject to various minimum conditions, will, if the parties' financial needs are met, be a binding agreement and that statutory reform by Parliament introducing such agreements is, therefore, likely in this area; and

   (ii) subject to such reform, under current law, entry into a pre-nuptial agreement will give rise to a rebuttable presumption that the parties intended that the court would enforce the division of resources/ liabilities as provided for in agreement on dissolution of marriage and the agreement is likely to be reflected in the order of the court unless in the circumstances prevailing it would not be fair to hold the parties to their agreement, eg the parties' financial needs are not met; and

   (iii) it is important that each party in advance of agreement is provided with the necessary information as to the current and foreseeable extent of respective resources/incomes with, where applicable, due accountancy and tax advice; and

   (iv) it is important that each party to an agreement has the opportunity to seek and does obtain independent legal advice upon the content and natural and legal meaning of the agreement and the effect of the same upon the rights (and obligations) at law of the client; and

   (v) there must be no threat or undue pressure exerted or untruthful, dishonest or misleading information provided to get the other party to enter an agreement; and

   (vi) any agreement, once entered into, should be kept up to date and/or reviewed where there are significant changes to the parties' circumstances to ensure that should the marriage break down, the agreement deals with the prevailing financial circumstances of the parties; and

   (vii) no term in a pre-nuptial agreement can prevent the court from deciding upon divorce whether the terms of the agreement reached should be made an order of the court or whether there should be a different provision ordered; and

   (viii) no term in a pre-nuptial agreement can affect or limit the entitlement of any child of the parties or either of them; and

   (ix) no term in a pre-nuptial agreement will be sanctioned by a court of which the effect is to place the burden of maintenance of either spouse or any children of the parties onto the State where the parties hold resources otherwise sufficient to meet such an obligation; and

(x) it is likely that under current law any provision, which leaves either party with less than they reasonably require for adequate housing and reasonable income support to meet their then existing and/or foreseeable reasonable needs or which after a significant length of committed marital relationship leaves only one spouse with a significant 'surfeit' of capital or earning capacity gained by their mutual efforts in that relationship above their needs runs the risk of being seen as unfair and the agreement reached then not being followed fully or at all by a court; and

(xi) there can be no certainty at present without legislative change that a court will fully endorse the terms of a pre-nuptial agreement between the parties on a divorce, albeit that there is an increasing incidence of the Court being prepared to do so; and

(xii) in the event that either party is a foreign national, the court will nevertheless apply English law within any divorce proceedings in regard to the terms of any pre-nuptial agreement entered into between the parties notwithstanding any foreign choice of law clause within that agreement;

(xiii) should either party envisage moving abroad it is essential that they obtain appropriate legal advice from foreign lawyers as to the enforceability of a pre-nuptial agreement within that prospective jurisdiction and any additional wording to be inserted as a result, where relevant.

(5) Schedule a number of initial meetings to take details and assemble the necessary supporting documentation will be required.

(6) Issue the client with a pro-forma document in advance of the scheduled meetings to complete with details to be given in the meetings to reduce the time to be taken.

(7) Take a very detailed preliminary statement of instructions from the client which upon completion should be read, dated and then signed by the client. The statement should cover:

(i) the client's and his partner's and any of their children's full names, dates of birth, current addresses and address of their intended matrimonial home, if known; and

(ii) the client's expected date of marriage to the partner; and

(iii) the client's and his partner's previous relationship history/chronology; and

(iv) the client's and his partner's current income, capital, chattels and pension resources and liabilities detail; and

(v) the details of any third party joint holder of any resources identified together with their address/telephone/email; and

(vi) the account numbers and address/telephone/email of identified banks/building societies/insurance companies/investments/pension fund schemes/trusts and trustees/mortgagees and loans; and

(vii) details of any recent valuations of resources and any recent statement of credit/debit account balances held; and

(viii) provisional details of any suggested valuers appropriate to value resources held; and

(ix) where businesses or trusts are involved, details of the last accounts created/company search obtained and the identity and address/telephone/email of the relevant accountants to the same; and

(x) where land/property is involved, the Land Registry details etc; and

(xi) the potential taxation upon disposal of any resource held and the identity and contact details of an accountant/financial advisor to ascertain; and

(xii) the contribution to date which either the client or his partner has made to such resources/liabilities; and

(xiii) the potential for further acquisition of such resources in the foreseeable future, including the identity of any expected inheritance and/ or any beneficiary receipt under any trusts involved; and

(xiv) where trusts are involved, the history of distribution to date to the client or his partner or any children or any other beneficiary involved; and

(xv) the client's and/or his partner's reasons advanced for wanting a pre-nuptial agreement; and

(xvi) the provisional division of resources/income/pension/liabilities desired in the event of a divorce etc; and

(xvii) the extent to which the parties have already discussed/agreed to the need for and/or the content of provisions and/or the desired division of resources/income/pensions/liabilities within a pre-nuptial agreement; and

(xviii) any plans held to have/adopt children after marriage; and

(xix) any current agreement/concerns of the client's partner concerning a pre-nuptial agreement; and

(xx) the identity and address/telephone/email of any other lawyer/financial advisor/accountant already engaged; and

(xxi) the provision of a list of family law solicitors local to the client's partner's address, if required and whether it will be necessary for the client to fund the partner's instruction.

(8) Discuss with the client what it is intended should be achieved by a pre-nuptial agreement and whether there may be other ways to address the concerns highlighted before the marriage takes place such as by gift or trust etc.

(9) Consider with the client the need to have a number of preliminary meetings with an accountant or financial advisor, to look at the available alternatives and/or to secure the detail of disclosure required.

(10) Consider whether Counsel is to be instructed to draft the agreement and discuss with the client the advantages and costs of involving such Counsel at an early stage.

(11) Consider any expressed concerns of the other party and, if at that stage there are none, what is the likely reaction of that other party? Will introduction of the issue undermine the relationship and has this been fully thought through?

(12) Caution the client against not disclosing to the other party the real reason why he or she wants the pre-nuptial agreement in place, since lack of frankness at this stage upon such an issue will undermine the agreement's effect later.

(13) Caution the client of the effect on the other party and their advisor of seeking too much protection and the likely advice the other party will get from his or her own lawyer.

(14) Advise in the light of the protection desired by the client within a pre-nuptial agreement of the likely effect of the same under the current law of divorce etc and if the current proposals for reform become law. In particular:

(i) what is likely to be seen as fair in any pre-nuptial agreement in addressing the predicted future needs (refer to the Family Justice Council's report on 'Needs' when available) of the parties and of any children (and potential compensation issues) in order both to persuade the other legal advisor and, eventually, should there be a marital breakdown, a court to follow the terms reached; and

(ii) to what extent the client's canvassed plan to protect present or future resource worth is likely to fall on one side or the other of the line of fairness and, therefore, whether, realistically, the proposed pre-nuptial can fully, or in part only, meet the protection required; and

(iii) in this context and purely as a general summary following the *McFarlane/Miller*[141] cases, that there is a greater likelihood of a pre-nuptial agreement effecting protection to a party with the greater ownership of pre-marital property, the shorter the time between the initial signing or any subsequent review of the agreement's terms and the breakdown of the marriage and where otherwise the provisions of the agreement still meet the reasonable anticipated needs/ compensation issues of the other spouse on a divorce. Carefully worded, such protection can extend to where a child is already on the scene or contemplated. The longer the marriage is to last, the more generous the provision within the agreement must be to meet the needs of the other party and any relevant child and any compensation issues; and

(iv) it should be pointed out that realistically, reliance only upon a review clause within the agreement to adapt, in the future, the terms of the provision made, may be short sighted against the likelihood that the agreement will not be returned to by most parties until a breakdown occurs, maybe many years ahead; and

(v) warn the client that silence within the agreement as to any obvious area of provision, such as that sufficient to meet the other party's

---

[141] [2006] UKHL 24.

likely need for accommodation or maintenance or the possible arrival of a child, will not be viewed as neutral in effect when a court has, eventually, to determine whether the agreement overall was fair. Experience teaches that such silence in such areas emboldens the court to justify holding the agreement as unfair where the provision otherwise made appears limited.

(15) Once it is clear that a pre-nuptial agreement will be required and if Counsel is to be involved after a preliminary conference with Counsel, ascertain from the client the extent to which the other party is aware of the client's wish for a pre-nuptial agreement and ensure that the client has made that other party aware of the imminent contact to be received from a solicitor concerning such a matter.

(16) Against such knowledge write to the other party in amicable terms inviting information as to their present position and advising if not already undertaken that the other party should instruct a solicitor to be advised as to the terms of such an agreement and to supply the name and address of the solicitor concerned.

(17) Write in amicable terms to the solicitor instructed by the other party and give a broad outline, as approved by the client, of the reasons for a pre-nuptial agreement being required, indicating the desire to provide as much assistance to the other solicitor within the process as possible.

(18) Agree with the other solicitor an ample time framework to ensure that the process can be completed after the provision of the first draft of the agreement within a reasonable timescale before the marriage.

(19) Provide the first draft and invite discussion of any problems, preferably by face to face meeting, where possible, between the solicitors first and then, if need be, with clients present.

(20) Agree the extent of disclosure required and the format for dealing with reference to the same within the agreement and also the extent of any professional accountancy advice etc required.

(21) Where delays result in the terms of the agreement not being reached until shortly before the marriage date, expressly refer to the position within the agreement and the reasons for the delay occurring and confirm therein that despite that delay each party is content that the agreement reached fully reflects their individual intention that the terms thereof should determine in fairness the division of their assets/income upon a marital breakdown.

(22) Draw up and have signed and witnessed in deed form the agreed terms of the pre-nuptial agreement, which must also exhibit any signed certificate(s) by each legal and other advisor involved that the appropriate independent advices for the purposes of the pre-nuptial agreement have been given. Ensure that the language in the agreement is kept simple and avoid using over legalistic terms, wherever possible.

(23) Ensure where a 'honeymoon' agreement is to be entered into after the marriage that again before such an agreement is signed etc each party's advisor's have provided like advice to each party and signed separate certificate(s) to this effect.

(24) Ensure that the whole file on the case is maintained in tact indefinitely in the event of subsequent complaint or enquiry.

8.22 Professional liability limitation

Family lawyers in practice have failed within this jurisdiction to seriously consider the extent of their own exposure to liability in the event that the advice given to clients contemplating a pre-nuptial agreement and/or the drafting of the agreement is later shown to have been negligent. Clearly, in the general run of family work practice such considerations would be unnecessary, but in accepting pre-nuptial instructions, family lawyers are potentially exposing themselves and/or their firm to potentially huge levels of liability at some indeterminate date in the future.

The decision of the Supreme Court in *Radmacher*'s case has made it clear that to be bound to the terms of a pre-nuptial agreement under the current law a party has to have freely entered into the agreement 'with a full appreciation' of the implications. The Law Commission have in their published report (see more below) put forward that for any 'Qualifying Nuptial Agreement', if introduced, one of the pre-requisites should be that the parties to the same have received independent legal advice and that this condition should not be capable of waiver. In addition, in a number of recent decisions of the High Court, the need for there to have been independent legal advice has been seen, in all but the highly exceptional situation, as an essential requirement when considering the fairness of the terms of a pre-nuptial agreement signed by the parties.[142]

The Law Commission has suggested that the nature of such advice should be in relation to the proposed 'Qualifying Nuptial Agreement' that the client is advised as to the fact that such an agreement will, subject to financial needs being provided for, prevent a court making an order inconsistent with the Agreement and what the effects of the Agreement are likely to be on the rights of that party. If this is to be taken as an indication of the basic required standard, then applying the same to advice under the current law, there should, at least, be advice given to the client in relation to a pre-nuptial agreement, which explains the ordinary and legal meaning of its terms and its effect at law and on the rights (and obligations) of the party being advised. The Law Commission also suggested that other matters may (as opposed to must) also be covered in any such advice given to a client and these are further considered under sub para (i)–(ix) inclusive in the next section ('Qualifying Nuptial Agreements' – legal advice guidance).

---

[142] For example, *Kremen v Agrest (No 11)* [2012] EWHC 45 (Fam) and *BN v MA* [2013] EWHC 4250 (Fam) Mostyn J.

Of course, there has been a practice for some time of legal advisors signing an appropriate certificate which is then attached to the signed agreement and which confirms that the requisite advice has been provided to the party concerned. However, it should be emphasised that prior to the Law Commission's suggested ambit for such advice, the form and content of these certificates has been very much a matter of individual judgment of the advisor concerned. It is of concern that some examples of the certificates currently in use have included references to the legal advisor providing advice as to the merits 'financially or otherwise' of the party entering into the agreement – such references to financial advice plainly fall outside the expertise of the legal advisor and should not be used in such a certificate.

The Law Commission in its consultation stage highlighted the recent experience of the Australian legal profession in this area of law. The account must serve as a cautionary tale to the almost relaxed approach presently shown by the legal professions in this country to the acceptance of instructions, without more, in relation to pre-nuptial agreements.[143]

> '5.42 .... Binding Financial Agreements in Australia have already had an extraordinary legislative history, with the relevant provisions being amended several times as problems with their pre-requisites have become apparent. More relevant here is the fact that Binding Financial Agreements are regarded with great caution by lawyers where the parties have not already separated.
>
> 5.43 In other words, Binding Financial Agreements are popular and effective as substitutes for separation agreements; once finalised, no consent order is required and the Binding Financial Agreement itself has the same force as a court order. But there is great reluctance among Australian lawyers to advise clients to take the risk of entering into a binding agreement to provide for a future separation, where the circumstances are unknown. One Australian lawyer based in New South Wales has remarked to us that:
>
> > "Many solicitors refuse to even advise parties [before marriage]. It is felt that the chance of overlooking something, changes in the circumstances of the parties, changes in the law itself, changes in the values of assets and the like make the issue very problematic."'

The basic advice standard required, as suggested above, still imposes on the legal advisor a duty to explain not only the meaning of the terms of any proposed agreement, but also what, in the circumstances of the client's case, the effect of those terms may be both under the present law and any potential future changes to the law which reasonably may occur. This requires both care and studious attention to note keeping to deal with and fully record the advice given concerning potential changes which may present themselves in the client's future married life with his new partner based upon reasonable predictions from his or her known present circumstances.

---

[143] Law Commission *Marital Property Agreements: A Consultation Paper* (2011).

Of course, legal advice based upon predictions as to the future could well be ripe territory for professional liability. The client could be a budding Bill Gates or his fiancée and their modest expectations and the draft pre-nuptial agreement drawn recording the same could in a few years of married life be set against a transformation to huge wealth against which an ill termed provision or lack of provision in their pre-nuptial agreement may become the basis for a negligence action against either one or both of the lawyers involved for a not inconsiderable claim in damages. The limitation period for professional negligence of 6 years from when the loss is incurred could be longer if it is determined that 'latent' damage is present.[144]

It is, therefore, essential that practitioners in this arena should take such steps to attempt to limit their liability to such potential liability levels as is feasible. The cost of indemnity insurance enhancement can be prohibitive, especially, if, as in most practices, such pre-nuptial work is not the main source of revenue and, in any event, even with a significant enhancement of insurance level may still be below the level of claim eventually pursued.

Of course, obtaining the client's signed acceptance of a limitation to the legal advisor's liability in the form of a maximum level of damages recovery in the event of professional negligence as part of the retainer is a route which itself is beset with problems. There will need to be compliance with the requirements of fairness of any liability limiting term pursuant to the Unfair Contract Terms Act 1977 and also in certain respects the Unfair Terms in Consumer Contracts Regulations 1999 and, if the limitation, effectively, sets a maximum damages limit, then the level of that limit may itself be deemed as unfairly restrictive in the circumstances. These difficulties, however, should not dissuade the practitioner from obtaining the client's acceptance to such a limitation.

The alternatives are, of course, not to accept instructions in such work at all or simply to take the risk – albeit, the latter route is not recommended.

Statutory reform

8.23   Ambit of reform

The Law Commission announced in June 2008[145] that it was to consider nuptial agreements with the aim of drawing up draft parliamentary legislation by 2012. Subsequently, the Law Commission announced that it would issue a consultation paper in the summer of 2010 (in the event, the first was in 2011

---

[144] Up to 15 years: see s 14A and 14B Latent Damages Act 1986.

[145] [2008] June; Tenth Programme of Law Reform and now see the comprehensive Law Commission Consultation Paper No 198 entitled 'Marital Property Agreements – A Consultation Paper'. The supporting research of E Hitchings, 'From Pre-nups to Post-nups: Dealing with Marital Property Agreements' [2009] Family Law 1056 and her 2010 Supplementary Report provide the current approach and practice of the Profession when dealing with clients who require pre-nuptial agreements.

followed by a supplementary consultation paper in 2012) and consider the required time table for further steps thereafter.[146]

In 2010, in parallel, Resolution published its report 'Family Agreements: Seeking Certainty to Reduce Disputes'.[147] The Report recommended change by substantial legislation amendment. The basis of the Resolution Report suggested that the right to choice of the parties to pre-determine the division of their resources upon divorce by a pre-nuptial agreement should be the central focus of such legislative intervention.

The Resolution report proposed new subsections 25(2A) and 25(2B) of the Matrimonial Causes Act 1973 (and a new provision to the same effect in the Civil Partnership Act 2004) in these terms:

> 's 25(2A) The court shall regard any agreement in writing entered into between the parties to the marriage in contemplation of or after the marriage for the purpose of regulating their affairs on the breakdown of their marriage as binding upon the parties and shall make an order in the terms of the agreement unless:
> (a) the agreement was entered into as a result of unfair pressure or unfair influence;
> (b) one or both parties did not have a reasonable opportunity to receive independent legal advice about the terms and effect of the agreement;
> (c) one or both parties failed to provide substantially full and frank financial disclosure before the agreement was made;
> (d) the agreement was made fewer than 42 days before the marriage;
> (e) enforcing the agreement would cause substantial hardship to either party or to any minor child of the family.
>
> s 25(2B) If one or more of the factors in paragraphs (a) to (e) of subsection 25(2A) applies, the Court shall give the agreement such weight as it thinks fit taking into account:
> (a) all the facts surrounding the agreement;
> (b) the matters in section 25(1) and (2).'

Set against such amendments, Resolution further recommended that it would also be necessary to make a consequential amendment to section 25(2) of the Act, in order to add to the list of factors in that subsection to which the court is required to have regard, 'any agreement within the new section 25(2A)'.

It is suggested, however, that Resolution's approach would still fail to adequately safeguard the rights of the weaker financial party entering marriage from the manipulation of emotional pressures inherent at the start of any relationship and which often lead to an agreement. If such an agreement effectively binds the parties to its terms upon divorce, then this is likely to result, in such circumstances, in an outcome which a court under the present law's search for a fair outcome would not have otherwise sanctioned. The

---

[146] 'The Law Commission's review following *Radmacher*' Antonia Mee, 21 October 2010, Fam Law Week.
[147] 'Family Agreements: Seeking Certainty to Reduce Disputes' Resolution 2010.

phrase 'substantial hardship', which is, obviously, intended to protect in these circumstances, echoes the similar current s 25 phrase of 'undue hardship', which Parliament intended to be a check to the court's automatic dismissal of future maintenance claims, but in practice has failed to stem the tide to the adoption of a clean break approach in a significant number of divorces, with the result that Lady Hale in *McFarlane/Miller* considered it necessary to expressly remind the courts that such a result should not under the existing legislation be the automatic outcome.

Some possible areas of reform include:

(1) simply amending the current s 25(2) list of particular factors to be taken into account to include, specifically, any agreements reached between the parties as described in the proposed s 25(2A) of the Resolution amendment above. Whilst some say this is little more than formalising the current position; in fact, it would for the first time identify within the legislation, the *'parties' agreements'* as a specific factor in the s 25 exercise and would reflect the current state of the case-law by acknowledging the relevance of such agreements in the process to be undertaken, whilst also endorsing the status of the pre-nuptial agreement within the public's perception of those issues upon the 'ordinary' divorce which matter;

(2) inserting a new sub clause within section 25, to provide that, where a pre-nuptial agreement is in place then, upon divorce etc, the terms of the same are to apply, unless it would be unfair to either party or any of the children of the family to do so. (This, actually, reflects the approach of the minority in the *Judges Response* of 1998[148] and now the approach of the Supreme Court in *Radmacher*'s case);

(3) again, inserting a new sub clause within s 25, enabling the court to give first consideration, along with the existing provision as to the welfare of any relevant child of the family, to the terms of a pre-nuptial agreement.

(4) the creation of a pre-approved form of pre-nuptial agreement, the signing of which entitles the parties to avoid entering into the s 25 process altogether upon divorce as long as their 'needs' are met. As will be seen below this, in part, at least, is the route favoured by the Law Commission's report. However, the recommendations made have fallen short of suggesting that the 'principle of autonomy' should dominate the process as, in the Commission's view, the 'needs' of the financially weaker spouse should still be the bottom line condition of the spousal entitlement to being permitted to enforce the terms of any such agreement reached.

8.24 *The Law Commission report*

'In this Consultation Paper we ask . . . . Should pre-nuptial and post-nuptial agreements continue to be enforced by the courts at their discretion – governed by the principles enunciated by the Supreme Court – within ancillary relief

---

[148] N Wilson 'Ancillary Relief Reform: Response of the Judges of the Family Division to the Government Proposals (made by way of submission to the Lord Chancellor's Ancillary Relief Advisory Group)' (1999) 29 Family Law 159, 162.

proceedings? The Supreme Court's restatement of the law in *Radmacher v Granatino* arguably takes the law as far towards an enforceable status for marital property agreements as is possible within the current statutory framework. Our consultation asks whether there should be legislative reform to enable couples effectively to contract out of ancillary relief, and out of the court's discretion, by entering into an agreement in a prescribed form and subject to appropriate safeguards.'[149]

Following on from the consultation, the Commission's published report, *Matrimonial Property, Needs and Agreements*, sought to address three specific areas, being financial needs following divorce etc, marital property agreements and non-matrimonial property. The Commission's stated intention was to render the law in the area more certain and predictable, whilst not sacrificing the protection under the law afforded to those made vulnerable by the breakdown of marriage.

The current law relating to the responsibility of former spouses upon divorce to meet each other's 'financial needs', the Commission concluded, did not at this time require reform. The Commission was satisfied that in practice the approach of the courts was such that the correct balance continued to be struck in the s 25 discretionary exercise and the same tended towards a measured outcome of financial independence for divorcing couples. However, there was evidence of some inconsistency within the court system itself as well as amongst mediators and litigants in person as to application of what is understood as the parties' financial needs' and, accordingly, the Commission considered that the meaning of that phrase should be clarified by guidance from the Family Justice Council. It was the Commission's hope that in so doing this would make clearer the kind of outcome which a judge would aim for so as to achieve a realistic level of support, which recognised the needs and responsibilities that each party had for the future whilst working towards independence where that is practicable.

The Commission was of the view that the advocating of set formulae to predict the appropriate payments to be made by one spouse to another may be of assistance and recommended Government funding for the research that would be required. However, the Commission cautioned that it should be remembered that such jurisdictions where such formulae are presently employed are very different legal systems to that of England and Wales. In any event, such guidance as could be given should not be seen as an alternative the court's discretionary exercise but a discrete aid to the parties to better negotiate an informed outcome wherever possible. Such guidance should be non-statutory and present a range of outcomes within which parties could negotiate.

As to 'marital property agreements', the Commission was clear that the presence of a discretion within the court's adjudication to the application or otherwise of such agreements was contrary to the wishes of many couples who

---

[149] Paragraph 1.11 'Matrimonial Property Agreements': Law Commission Consultation Paper No 198.

wished to base their marriage on a 'shared understanding of the financial consequences of any future separation'. Accordingly, the Commission's central recommendation was that a 'Qualifying Nuptial Agreement' should be introduced. Such an agreement would be an enforceable contract between the parties, which could not subsequently be interfered with by the court, save and except where the same failed to meet the 'financial needs' of a party.[150] The availability of such agreements, the Commission considered, would assist the predictability of outcome for parties as well as strengthening their autonomy in comparison with the present system, whilst at the same time the preservation of the protection of a party's 'financial needs' would be both consistent with the European protection of 'maintenance' rights and a necessary limitation to prevent potentially very damaging consequences for the financially weaker spouse.[151]

The Commission was clear that to constitute a 'Qualifying Nuptial Agreement', some five essential conditions would have to be met. These were that:

(a) The agreement must be contractually valid (and able to withstand challenge of undue influence or misrepresentation, for example) and any variation to the same must comply with the same requirements as the original agreement.

(b) The agreement must have been made by deed and must contain a statement signed by both parties that he or she understands that the agreement is a Qualifying Nuptial Agreement that will partially remove the court's discretion to make financial orders.

(c) The agreement must not have been made within the 28 days immediately before the wedding or the celebration of civil partnership.

(d) Both parties to the agreement must have received, at the time of the making of the agreement, disclosure of *material* information about the other party's financial situation and the Commission considered that neither party should be able to waive this requirement.

(e) Both parties must have received at the time that the agreement was formed legal advice from separate lawyers, which includes advice that the agreement is a Qualifying Nuptial Agreement that will prevent the court from making financial orders inconsistent with the agreement, save so far

---

[150] The Commission rejected the proposition that there should be different considerations for spouses of certain religious beliefs as basically discriminatory – see para 1.36 of Consultation Paper.

[151] The Law Commision noted that a Green Paper, published in 2007 entitled 'Commission of the European Communities, Green Paper: On conflict of laws in matters concerning matrimonial property regimes, including the question of jurisdiction and mutual recognition', COM (2006) 400 final; envisaged a rule that determines the applicable law, which will be the same no matter where the financial consequences of divorce are determined. This involves the courts of one country applying the law of another. It was not, of course, known at this stage if the UK would opt in to such conformity if introduced. Cf also paras 4.6–4.29 of the Law Commission's Consultation Paper considering the different jurisdictional approaches of Europe and the rest of the world.

as financial needs are concerned and as to the effect of the agreement on the rights of the party being advised. Again this requirement should not be capable of waiver.

The correct approach to 'non matrimonial property' proved more controversial and elusive for the Commission. Initially, it had been hoped to address what should and should not be included as 'non matrimonial' property by statutory reform providing specifically for those areas which were still undecided or unresolved by the case-law. In the final analysis, it was not possible to achieve a consensus for statutory intervention and the recommendation of the 'Qualifying Nuptial Agreement' was seen as being the vehicle by which the parties could best provide for themselves what should be the outcome on divorce for such property, if specific statutory definitions were not to be made available.

8.25 *'Qualifying Nuptial Agreement' – some applications*[152]

The Law Commission's Report canvassed a number of non-exhaustive working examples in which a Qualifying Nuptial Agreement (QNP) may be of use, as follows:

(i) When protecting anticipated family gifts and inheritances:

Where parties are expecting future gifts and inheritances from their families and/or have pre-accrued assets which they would wish to keep separate from being shared by the other. Such receipts/possessions under the current law would be seen as 'non matrimonial' and as long as their respective needs were otherwise met in the event of a divorce, such assets would be unlikely to be shared. However, this could not be guaranteed, whereas if there was a 'QNP' in place effectively declaring that such assets were not to be shared, then subject to the issue of the needs of the other spouse and any children of the family, a court would endorse the terms of the 'QNP' and, therefore, the wishes of the parties would be secured.

(ii) When protecting specific property:

This may arise where, although both parties are content to share equally their assets on a divorce, one party already has a home which that party wishes to ensure is, in the event of divorce, retained for his or her individual use and disposal. By use of the 'QNP' in this case, again subject to needs , that provision can be secured for that party and the 'QNP' can go on to provide what would happen to the proceeds of sale of that property if disposed before any divorce and invested in another property asset. Indeed the 'QNP' could also provide for what is to happen should the needs of the parties not be met without recourse to the property or there may be a number of pre-accrued properties catered for in this way. The 'QNP' could provide for the order in which such properties are to be used to meet any spousal need.

---

[152] Paragraphs 7.12–7.33 of the Report.

(iii) When providing for a clean break between wealthy parties:

Here the parties who are independently wealthy may wish to ensure as far as possible that no claims arise from the other upon divorce because they envisage each will have more than sufficient resources. Of course, without more, upon a divorce there may be a substantial amount of asset wealth which will have been gained by the couple as a marital acquest and which without the terms of an appropriate 'QNP' signed it would have been seen fair to share equally – whereas although one party may be left with substantially less comparative wealth than the other on a subsequent divorce, the 'QNP' spelling out the reason for 'nil provision' would prevent any investigation as to the position, assuming the parties' needs were otherwise met.

(iv) When providing certainty and excluding sharing:

The parties may have substantially different levels of wealth at the outset so that it is reasonably predictable that the one will have to meet the other's needs should there be a divorce. Whilst employment of the 'QNP' could not again guarantee scrutiny by a court in that event in due course, it could in excluding in general the sharing of assets between the parties, spell out the type of provision, including rehousing and/or term and level of maintenance that the parties considered reasonable. Such terms, as long as the circumstances were not wholly different at the divorce, would be likely to dictate the level of provision to be made as long as it was seen as meeting those needs, albeit not as generously, as without the agreement, the court may have done.

8.26 'Qualifying Nuptial Agreements' – legal advice guidance[153]

The Law Commission recommended certain pre-requisites, as above, that needed to be included in any advice to ensure the validity of a 'Qualifying Nuptial Agreement'. In addition, the Report also set out some additional matters, which the Law Commission considered should, in good practice, be dealt with in any advice given, namely:

(1) The advantages and disadvantages, at the time that the advice is provided, to that party of making the agreement, including what he or she might receive on a divorce without a Qualifying Nuptial Agreement.

(2) The provision for the party's needs, out of which the parties cannot contract by using a Qualifying Nuptial Agreement (including any uncertainty as to the form, level and duration of such provision).

(3) The need for *material* disclosure from the other party.

(4) The need, if any, to make provision in the agreement about the effect of sale and replacement of any assets specifically mentioned in it, and about the consequences of one party investing in or contributing to property during the marriage or civil partnership;

---

[153] Paragraphs 7.59–7.63 of the Report.

(5)   That the agreement will hold regardless of changes over time, such as the birth of children.

(6)   If the couple, or one of them, is a foreign national or is domiciled overseas, or has property outside England and Wales, whether it would be advisable to obtain advice from a foreign lawyer with appropriate expertise. If such foreign advice has been obtained, advice should be given about its effect on, and inter-relationship with, the English advice.

(vii)   An agreement that is no longer a Qualifying Nuptial Agreement nor valid as a contract is still a marital property agreement capable of being taken into account under *Radmacher* although its effect may be limited, depending on the reason why it does not meet the requirements for a Qualifying Nuptial Agreement.

(viii) in the event that one party is paying the costs of advice for the other party, a costs ceiling imposed must not be perceived as limiting the advice reasonably required in the particular case.

(ix)   the above is not to be seen as exhaustive of the matters for which advice is to be given and the requirements in this respect of each case will differ. See generally the 'Checklist' set out in the previous section.

8.27   'Qualifying Nuptial Agreements' – an overview

There will be many who will consider the recommendations of the Law Commission as disappointing and not radical enough.[154] The concept of Qualifying Nuptial Agreements may appear to offer the prospect of removing the distribution of parties' resources upon divorce etc entirely out of the s 25 process. However, in practice, because the strength or weakness of such an agreement will depend upon whether or not the financially weaker party's needs have been met, it is debateable to what extent this proposed model will actually reduce the number of disputes before the Court where such an agreement is in place.

Whether parties have signed up to a QNA or the present pre-nuptial form of agreement, it will remain open to the spouse who regards his or her interests as unfairly prejudiced by the agreement terms to challenge the provision made upon divorce. The only difference may well be that the debate upon such disputes where a QNA is involved may, if the essential formation conditions have been met, be restricted to the level of the need provision in place, whereas with any other form of pre-nuptial agreement the dispute may, as now, be wider and not limited to the same extent to the level of need as opposed to the level of fair provision overall under the s 25 exercise.

The Law Commission was clearly unwilling to envisage a completely unlimited autonomy of choice of parties to agree terms which could result in the State effectively being burdened with the continuing support of the financially weaker spouse where the other spouse's resources were otherwise capable of

---

[154] Professor Barton 'Matrimonial Property, Needs And Agreements' [2014] Fam Law [1124].

meeting those needs. This approach was entirely consistent with the history of spousal support within this jurisdiction since the nineteenth century and may now by its rejection of a more radical solution suggest that in fact the stage currently reached by case precedent in the weight to be given to the pre-nuptial is politically and socially as far as the principle of the parties' autonomy of choice within divorce etc can be taken.

Of course, those who would argue that the pendulum within the s 25 statutory exercise has swung too far against the interests of the married woman, in any event, by the movement over the last decade or so to give greater recognition to pre-marital agreements may be relieved at this outcome. If so, it must be observed that the forces which led to the Commission's review of the weight to be attached to Marital Agreements were in the end frustrated on this occasion not by any sense of concern for the gender discrimination still present in divorce distribution but rather the potential cost to the taxpayer.

8.28   Need for reform – commentary

It is, at least, debatable whether the arguments which have been advanced for greater recognition of the parties' autonomy in this arena are truly reflective of the actual concerns of the vast majority of ordinary men and women, who, following the breakdown of their marriage, make use of the court's divorce process within this jurisdiction.[155]

It is also doubtful that Parliament's intervention by any future legislative change in this area to enhance the status and effect of a pre-nuptial agreement upon divorce will actually result in a lesser cost burden to the average petitioner or respondent in divorce proceedings, in the absence of a wholesale change in the broader approach to distribution of resources upon dissolution of marriage.

The whole promotion of pre-nuptial agreements in the modern context, of course, has been driven by those divorcing couples whose individual or family wealth was the reason for there being a pre-nuptial agreement in the first place. The demands for the greater use and recognition of pre-nuptial agreements made on behalf of this small but influential minority of individuals have been wholly out of proportion to the real priorities for change in this area of family law, especially when measured against the impact that such changes would have upon the majority of divorcees.

The introduction of a 'Qualifying Nuptial Agreement' may potentially result in many more couples feeling under pressure to engage a professional to draw up such an agreement or, at least, to confirm an overview of the parties' own completion of a standardised 'one size fits all' version as part of their marriage preparations. Thereafter, only a small number of these couples, once married, will keep the same under periodic review and the agreement document will then gather dust in some drawer in the matrimonial home alongside the marriage

---

[155] See more below.

certificate or some other such documentation. Only years later upon a marital breakdown, will that by then outdated agreement re-emerge to be used by the spouse, who insisted on the agreement in the first place, against the other to ensure a recovery based upon not what is fair after many years of marriage, but whichever is the greater of the limited provision made at the outset of the marriage or that other spouse's needs upon divorce.

It is argued that this is the just recognition of the autonomous choices of parties about to enter matrimony. Certainly, there are marriage arrangements where there will be very respectable reasons for formalising outcomes in advance by such agreements. However, there will be many more where the very idea of a limited liability agreement between a couple entering marriage speaks far more about the absence of a true mutual commitment in the relationship. However ornate the legal language used in a pre-nuptial agreement, the same is little more than a hard headed commercial agreement intended in most instances to limit one spouse's recovery to less and in many cases much less than the law would have otherwise provided. It is likely to be entered into by one of the two parties with a serious underestimate as to its likely future relevance and with little or certainly significantly less financial awareness than their partner. There is highly likely, too, to be a wholly different perception between the parties as to the pre-marriage arrangement priorities within which the signing of such an agreement has become part. Unless, the parties have been in other long term relationships previously, neither and certainly not the financially weaker spouse-to-be can properly evaluate before marriage what with maturity and experience of married life their view of fairness of division on an eventual divorce will be.

It is unlikely, therefore, that a change of the current approach of the law wherein the weight of a pre-nuptial agreement remains within the discretionary judgment of the court, by the introduction of a 'Qualifying Nuptial Agreement' as envisaged by the Law Commission will either be a reflection of the parties' true autonomous choices or provide a fairer outcome.

8.29 The future

In *Charman*,[156] the former President, Sir Mark Potter said:

> 'The difficulty of harmonising our law concerning the property consequences of marriage and divorce and the law of the Civilian Member States is exacerbated by the fact that our law has so far given little status to pre-nuptial contracts. If, unlike the rest of Europe, the property consequences of divorce are to be regulated by the principles of needs, compensation and sharing, should not the parties to the marriage, or the projected marriage, have, at the least, the opportunity to order their own affairs otherwise by a nuptial contract?'

Of course, since those remarks, there has been a Supreme Court decision and now a Law Commission report. However, as referred to previously, our current

---

[156] [2007] EWCA Civ 50.

law's position in divorce remains, at least for the time being, that of leaving the relevance and weight to be attached to a pre-nuptial agreement reached by the parties entirely to the discretion of the individual judge in any given case and such a position remains exceptional amongst our European partners and, as set out above, is an isolated position against the law applicable in many other parts of the world.

However, it remains to the purist unsatisfactory that, amongst a number of other anomalies created by the present position, the most obvious one is that had the parties to the pre-nuptial agreement not married at all, there would have been less room for judicial interference in implementing the identical terms of such a cohabitation agreement.

For better or for worse, society has moved on from when in 1929 the House of Lords considered pre-nuptial agreements to be contrary to the sanctity of marriage and when divorce was exceptional and there was no power in a divorce court to transfer capital. Today, both parties in entering a marriage will be more aware of the fact and possibility of divorce and are more readily seen as entering into a partnership of equals. There is clearly gathered evidence, no doubt the result of the greater recent publicity upon the subject, that parties about to cohabit or marry are far more interested in formalising from the outset their financial arrangements in advance of any breakdown.[157]

However, there is also increasing evidence that there exists a gender divide within the judiciary in this jurisdiction not only as to the appropriate weight to be given to the existence of a pre-nuptial agreement within the statutory exercise on divorce, but, of greater concern, also as to whether the parties can be taken as having intended that the pre-nuptial agreement should apply in the first place in the event of a later divorce. As to this, Lady Hale made her views very clear in *Radmacher's* case when she stated:

'137. Above all, perhaps, the court hearing a particular case can all too easily lose sight of the fact that, unlike a separation agreement, the object of an ante-nuptial agreement is to deny the economically weaker spouse the provision to which she – it is usually although by no means invariably she – would otherwise be entitled (see, for example, G F Brod, "Premarital Agreements and Gender Justice" (1994) 6 *Yale Journal of Law* and *Feminism* 229). This is amply borne out by the precedents available in recent text-books (see, for example, I Harris and R Spicer, *Prenuptial Agreements: A Practical Guide* (2008, Appendix D), or H Wood, D Lush, D Bishop, and A Murray, *Cohabitation: Law, Practice* and *Precedents* (2009, 4th ed, pp 583–592)). Would any self-respecting young woman sign up to an agreement which assumed that she would be the only one who might otherwise have a claim, thus placing no limit on the claims that might be made against her, and then limited her claim to a pre-determined sum for each year of marriage regardless of the circumstances, as if her wifely services were being bought by the year? Yet that

---

[157] Catherine Baksi 'Pre-nuptials booming' *Law Gazette*, 17 August 2008 (www.lawgazette.co.uk/news/pre-nuptials-booming) and 'Family Agreements: Seeking Certainty to Reduce Disputes' Resolution 2010 and Matrimonial Property Needs and Agreements: Law Commission Report [2014] Feb.

is what these precedents do. In short, there is a gender dimension to the issue which some may think ill-suited to decision by a court consisting of eight men and one woman.'

Whilst the authors of this edition have, obviously, taken note of her Ladyship's observations upon the earlier pre-nuptial precedent published in the 4th edition and, in due recognition, have made certain amendments thereto in the precedent appearing in the last and now this current 6th edition to reflect the same; the fact of the matter is that, despite her Ladyship's comments, there have been and no doubt will continue to be many individuals, who are willing to sign such one sided agreements as previously appeared. Equally, it is anticipated that her Ladyship would acknowledge that the last several editions of this work have fully and consistently advocated and supported the position in this area of the law as reflected by the concerns which she strongly expressed in both *Macleod* and later in *Radmacher*.

Those who may yet debate the course of any future statutory amendment to the current law relating to pre-nuptial agreements may be well advised to adopt as the foreword to their preliminary considerations, the following perceptive appraisal of Baron J, at first instance, in the *Radmacher* case[158] as to the state of the law concerning pre-nuptial agreements, when she said:

> '129 It is understandable that English society in general (therefore the state) regards Court supervision as a necessary safeguard. To my mind, independent scrutiny of these agreements remains as necessary in modern times as it was in the last century because of the vulnerability of parties involved at times of high emotion where inequality of bargaining power may exist between them. Although civilization has made much progress over the centuries and the roles of men and women have altered so that, in some cultures, equality has been achieved that does not mean that fundamental human nature has changed. Whilst the Court must permit of current mores and will take full account of contemporary morality, it should not be blind to human frailty and susceptibility when love and separation are involved. The need for careful safeguards to protect the weaker party and ensure fairness remains.'

These are incisive words of a much respected female judge whose own journey within a historically male dominated profession would have undoubtedly witnessed gender discrimination along the way and sensitised her to the position of other women in far less privileged positions than her own. In the event, women should remain sceptical that the increasing pressure for legislative changes to give formal recognition to pre-nuptial agreements within ancillary relief proceedings is indeed a gender benevolent movement singularly motivated by an intention to complete the circle of changes, pioneered by the Married Women's Property Act 1882, or truly intended to achieve their equal entitlement with men in this area of the law. As was said by Lady Hale in Macleod's case:[159]

---

[158] [2008] EWHC 1532 (Fam).
[159] [2008] UKPC 64.

'33. It is said that calls for the legislative recognition of ante-nuptial agreements appear to have increased with the development of more egalitarian principles of financial and property adjustment on divorce, following the decisions of the House of Lords in *White v White* ... and *Miller v Miller, McFarlane v McFarlane* ... If such calls are motivated by a perception that equality within marriage is wrong in principle, the more logical solution would be to examine the principles applicable to ascertaining the fair result of a claim for ancillary relief, rather than the pre-marital attempt to predict what the fair result will be long before the event. If such calls are motivated by a fear that people who feel threatened by what might happen in the event of divorce will not get married at all, there is a need for serious research and consideration of the extent of and reasons for the reduction in marriage rates over recent decades. It certainly cannot be demonstrated that the lack of enforceable pre-nuptial agreements in this country is depressing the marriage rate here as compared with other countries where such agreements can be made.'

As a former Law Commissioner herself, Lady Hale's consistent call has been that any development of the status and effect of nuptial agreements upon divorce should be the business of the Law Commission and Parliament and not that of the judiciary.

The issue as to the status of the pre-nuptial agreement within the discretionary exercise upon divorce etc is in truth just one part of the wider and more pressing debate required as to the need for a complete review of the Court's powers of financial remedy provision under the Matrimonial Causes Act 1973. Much in society has altered over the last 40 years since Parliament approved this legislation. The landmark cases of *White, Miller/McFarlane* and *even Radmacher v Granantino* have all been instances, in the absence of a comprehensive legislative review, of substantive re-interpretation of the law by a judiciary with a predictably narrow and limited outlook on society's values and mores. As divorce affects substantially more than one in three marriages within this jurisdiction the need for a Parliamentary re-evaluation of the current law including the status of the principle of autonomy has become paramount. Coleridge J in a recent address to the Family Law Conference put it this way:[160]

'I am convinced that the judges, at whatever level, cannot sensibly take the matter any further without making matters worse and more uncertain. Government simply has to grasp the nettle and get on with it. In the end we are of course doing the classic British thing of reform by inertia, stealth, common sense and the laws of cricket. That may in the end not be too disturbing in fact and from the point of view of the family lawyer trying to earn an honest shilling, endlessly fascinating and rewarding, in more ways than one. But it is not the way to run a railway or a modern family justice system.'

---

[160] 'Lobbing a few pebbles in the pond: the funeral of a dead parrot' [2014] Fam Law 168.

PART B　PRECEDENTS

8.30　Pre-nuptial agreement

A PRE-NUPTIAL AGREEMENT[161]

THIS DEED OF AGREEMENT is made on the [day] of [month] [year]

BETWEEN

(1) Jack Smith (hereinafter called "Jack") of [insert address].

(2) Emily Roberts (hereinafter called "Emily") of [insert address].

NOW THIS DEED WITNESSES as follows:

---

[161] This is an example of an agreement where upon a breakdown of the marriage, the parties wish, subject to the payment due to the wife under the agreement, to retain their exclusive ownership of their individual assets whenever acquired, any received inheritance, any gifts from each other and from third parties to themselves as individuals and personal belongings, whilst sharing equally assets, furniture and other chattels of both of them acquired jointly during the marriage, on the basis of a clean break. The agreement provides that the payment due to the wife is to be the lesser of either a percentage of the parties' combined Separate property/assets at the date of separation (after deduction for their Separate property value as held at the point of their marriage and as enhanced for passive inflation by the CPI) <u>or</u> an amount assessed based upon the years together with an overall cap on the amount whichever applies. This would mean that the wife would recover the outcome of this calculation together with her share of any equally held assets and any gifts received. It is imperative to appreciate that every case is different and whilst the Precedents herewith reflect the particular approach to the drafting required in the given example, the same can never be a blue print for every such case where similar approaches are adopted. Lay clients often make the mistake in believing that the solicitor is simply going to press a button on the computer and the necessary draft produced at minimum cost, whereas in most cases quite the opposite is the case, especially in the field of drafting where much is 'crystal ball gazing'. Clearly, careful instructions must be taken to ensure in each case that the particular requirements of the client are embraced in the terms of the agreement drawn and it is essential that consideration is given by the professional advisor to the terms of his professional insurance cover. The Precedent has been modestly amended from a previous version which appeared in the fourth edition in the light of the comments of Lady Hale in the *Radmacher* case that 'no self respecting' woman would sign up to such (previous) one sided ante-nuptial agreements, which evaluated her contribution to the marriage in terms of time alone. Unfortunately, the truth remains that many 'self respecting' women have and continue to sign up to these type of agreements as, indeed, in the opposite gender, did Nicholas Granatino in *Radmacher's* case. Clearly, as was expressed in previous editions, the authors have considerable sympathy with the Minority view expressed by Lady Hale as to the gender divide apparent in the current judicial approach to pre-nuptial agreements; sentiments which fully echoed many of the previous and current edition's concerns as to the present law in this area. Finally, if appropriate, the provision of advice and the drafting of the pre-nuptial agreement should, specifically, be made the subject of a written limitation of liability signed by the – a copy of one such example also being provided in these Precedents below. Whatever the reliability of this form of attempted limitation to potential liability, experience in the United States and elsewhere has shown this area to be fertile territory to professional negligence actions and it would be advisable to ensure, at the very least, that the files relating to such work are preserved indefinitely.

RECITALS:-

1 Intended marriage

(a) This Deed of Agreement is made in contemplation of, and is conditional upon, the intended marriage of Jack and Emily on [insert date] day of [insert date] or such other date as Jack and Emily agree upon.

(b) Jack and Emily have been cohabiting since [insert date] and they each agree that this period of pre-marital cohabitation and Jack's and Emily's respective present and future needs have both been taken fully into account in the provision as set out in this Deed of Agreement to be made following upon a permanent separation between them and/or a breakdown of their marital relationship and/or a divorce, nullity or judicial separation and/or a pronouncement of a decree thereon and/or in the event of the prior death of Jack. (the 'specified events').

[if desired] **Marital Agreement:**

(c) Jack and Emily are agreed and intend within 28 days [or such other period] of the date of their marriage to enter by further Deed into a marital agreement ('Deed of Marital Agreement') in the terms of the document annexed to this Deed of Agreement]].

2 Present Positions and Intention to settle financial arrangements

(a) Jack and Emily are to be married and they having in particular been advised about the principle of fairness within claims for financial remedy upon the breakdown of marriage, wish to enter into an agreement recording their wishes and intentions regarding their finances and property upon any of the specified events, whatever the circumstances, and in all jurisdictions. They declare that, whilst they intend to enter into their marital vows to each other with full commitment and solemnity, they each wish to avoid the distress and costs of any dispute as to their individual financial provision following upon any of the specified events and/or any claim/proceedings in relation to the same and to declare from the outset their agreement as to such provision for each of them as set out in this Deed of Agreement.

(b) Jack was born on [insert date] and is aged [insert age]. This is his second marriage and he has two children by his first marriage, being [insert name], who was born on [insert date] and is aged [insert number] years and is attending [insert details] School and [insert name], who was born on [insert age] and is aged [insert number] years and is attending [insert details]. Jack currently has a child care sharing arrangement with his former wife in regard to his children and he provides for their maintenance, including a school fees provision for each of his children [insert details] by way of a Consent Order dated [insert date] made by the [insert Court] County Court (Case No: [insert details]).

(c) Jack is in employment with and a [insert percentage] shareholder in [insert details] Limited. He has an option to acquire a further [insert percentage] shareholding at a preferential price. There is a present potential that the company will be sold and that Jack will receive valuable consideration for his shareholding and that he may be retained in employment by any new owner of the company. In addition, Jack has up to the date of this Deed of Agreement acquired a number of other company interests and assets, which include beneficial interests held under Trusts created by [insert name(s)] as well as his interests and entitlements in pension funds, as are set out in **Appendix A** hereto.

(d)   Emily was born on [insert date] and is aged [insert number]. This is her second marriage and she has one child [insert name], who was born on [insert date] and is aged [insert number] years and is attending [insert details] University as part of her degree course. Both Jack and Emily currently make a contribution towards [insert name] university expenses in agreement with [insert name]'s natural father. It is the mutual intention of both Jack and Emily to continue to assist in the financial support of [insert name] during her tertiary education up to first degree level. [insert name] resides at the home of Jack and Emily when not attending university and it is envisaged that this arrangement will continue.

(e)   Emily is [insert employment] and has held [insert broad previous employment experience]. Currently, she is without remunerative employment. Emily anticipates returning to some form of part time employment within the [insert sector] during [insert time frame]. Emily has up to the date of this Deed of Agreement acquired a number of assets, including her interests and entitlements in pension funds as are set out in **Appendix B** hereto.

(f)   Jack and Emily each acknowledge and agree that there is a substantial present disparity at the date of this Deed of Agreement in their respective assets, interests and other resources, including their incomes and they wish to record and confirm that:

   (i)   an important purpose of this Deed of Agreement is to protect those assets, interests (inclusive of any interests held in trust(s)) and other resources, including any accumulated income, which Jack already has, following upon any of the specified events and/or in the event of any claim/proceedings brought by Emily and/or on her behalf and/or by her estate in relation to the same against him and/or his estate, save as otherwise agreed and provided for herein; and

   (ii)   Jack's agreement to enter into their intended marriage is conditional upon the due completion and bringing into effect of this Deed of Agreement.

(g)   Jack recognises and agrees that the origin of Emily's assets, interests and other resources, including any accumulated income at the date of this Deed of Agreement as set out at **Appendix B** emanates from her activities, which pre-date their marriage and any cohabitation with him and to which he has made no contribution whatsoever.

(h)   Emily recognises and agrees that the origin of Jack's assets, interests (inclusive of any trust(s)) and other resources, including any accumulated income at the date of this Deed of Agreement as set out at **Appendix A** emanates from his activities which pre-date his marriage and any cohabitation with her and to which she has made no contribution whatsoever.

(i) Jack and Emily each wish to record his/her intention and agreement that he/she will make no claim nor commence any proceedings whatsoever against the other or that other's estate following upon any of the specified events, howsoever arising in any jurisdiction, save and except only to obtain/implement such provision as is provided for strictly within this Deed of Agreement.

(j) Jack and Emily each intend and agree that this Deed of Agreement shall fully set out his and/or her respective rights and obligations in respect of the other following upon any of the specified events and/or in the event of any claim/proceedings brought by either against the other or the other's estate in relation to the same and shall be fully binding upon each of them and/or their agents and/or receivers and/or trustees to the fullest extent permissible by law in all jurisdictions.

(k) Jack and Emily each also intend and agree that this Deed of Agreement shall fully set out his and her respective rights and obligations towards each other and/or those of their respective heirs and/or personal representatives and estates in the event of death and they intend and agree that, save where it is contrary to the law of England and Wales, this Deed of Agreement shall be fully binding on their respective heirs and/or personal representatives and estates and fully determinative of any claim/proceedings brought in relation to such rights and obligations in all jurisdictions.

(l) Jack and Emily agree that a first draft of this Deed of Agreement was sent to Emily's solicitors on [insert date] and the final form of the Deed of Agreement was agreed between Jack's and Emily's respective solicitors on [insert date], following correspondence and discussions between them from [insert date] to [insert date]. Jack and Emily each acknowledge and agree that this Deed of Agreement is being entered into prior to the date of their intended marriage ceremony, that there has been sufficient time for appropriate advice, negotiation and reflection upon the terms herein, and that they have each consequently given full consideration to the ramifications of entering into this Deed of Agreement.

3 Children

(a) Jack and Emily wish to record, acknowledge and agree that the contents of this Deed of Agreement cannot limit or otherwise adversely affect the rights and entitlement of any child or children of either of them or of any child or children born to Jack and Emily or treated by them as a child or children of their family or treated as their biological child or children by virtue of the provisions of the Human Fertilization and Embryology Act 1990 (or any successor legislation) or any child or children legally adopted by them.

(b) Jack and Emily agree that following upon any of the specified events they shall each, as a first consideration, make contribution to and provision for the reasonable needs (and/or in the event that either should pre-decease the other they shall make reasonable provision by their estate), whilst dependent, of any child or children as referred to herein as required of them by the Law of England and Wales and the provisions of this Deed of Agreement shall at all times remain subject to such contribution and provision.

4 Independent advice as to Effect and Meaning:

(a) Jack confirms that:

     (i)   he has received separate and independent legal advice in relation to the intent, meaning and effect of this Deed of Agreement and in respect of the applicable law in England and Wales arising in relation to the matters referred to in this Deed of Agreement [insert name] Solicitor of [insert address] and from [insert name] of Counsel of [insert name] Chambers, [insert address] prior to entering into this Deed of Agreement; and

     (ii) he has received separate and independent accountancy and tax advice concerning the meaning and effect and tax consequences of this Deed of Agreement from [insert name and address]

 and he further confirms he has fully understood the advice given and in consequence has signed the attached Certificate marked **Appendix C** by the legal advisor(s) and marked **Appendix D** by the accountant/tax advisor(s) concerned.

(b) Emily confirms that:

     (i)   she has received separate and independent legal advice in relation to the intent, meaning and effect of this Deed of Agreement and in respect of the applicable law in England and Wales arising in relation to the matters referred to in this Deed of Agreement [insert name] Solicitor of [insert address] and from [insert name] of Counsel of [insert name] Chambers, [insert address] prior to entering into this Deed of Agreement; and

     (ii) she has received separate and independent accountancy and tax advice concerning the meaning and effect and tax consequences of this Deed of Agreement from [insert name and address]

 and she further confirms she has fully understood the advice given and in consequence has signed the attached Certificate marked **Appendix E** by the legal advisor(s) and marked **Appendix F** by the accountant/tax advisor(s) concerned.

(c) Jack and Emily confirm and agree that each is fully aware of the rights that he or she may be respectively surrendering and/or acquiring pursuant to this Deed of Agreement, although they each surrender those rights only so far as is permitted by law.

(d) Jack and Emily confirm and agree that the terms of this Deed of Agreement are intended to make such provision for each of them and/or the needs of any child or children as referred to herein as they each consider fair and adequate in the circumstances and without discrimination against either of them and/or such child or children and, subject thereto, such terms are intended to preclude the sharing by either of the other's Separate Property as referred to and/or defined below in clause 10 of this Deed of Agreement and/or of the other's Absolute Property as referred to and/or defined at clause 12 below .

(e) Jack and Emily acknowledge and agree that each of them has read this entire Agreement and has had its meaning and legal consequences fully explained, as well as having any questions answered by his or her respective solicitors/accountant/ tax advisor. Each of them has ascertained and weighed all the facts, conditions and circumstances likely to influence their individual judgement upon the terms herein; each of them understands and is satisfied with and approves of the provisions of this Deed of Agreement and its legal/financial/tax, as well as practical, ramifications and effects.

(f) Jack and Emily agree that they are each entering into this Deed of Agreement freely and voluntarily and without any pressure or undue influence or duress and without reliance upon any collateral promise or representation whatsoever and with full knowledge of the facts stated herein and each declare that they are content to be fully bound by the terms of this Deed of Agreement.

(g) Jack and Emily each agree and intend that nothing in this Deed of Agreement should be read or interpreted as in any way limiting the jurisdiction of the Court according to the law.

5 Agreement to be legally binding

(a) Jack and Emily each respectively acknowledge that he/she has been informed that under the law of England and Wales as presently understood;

   (i) pre-marital agreements may not be contractually binding and it is not presently at the date of this Deed of Agreement possible to exclude the jurisdiction of the Court to make orders for financial provision pursuant to the Matrimonial Causes Act 1973 (as amended) nor the Inheritance (Provision for Family and Dependants) Act 1975 (as amended);

   (ii) a pre-marital agreement will be one of the factors that the court will take into account in the event of an application for a financial remedy in the event of a divorce, nullity or judicial separation, or a claim for reasonable provision in the event of the prior death of either of them, but it is not necessarily binding upon the court;

   (iii) a pre-marital agreement is more likely to be adhered to and implemented by the courts of England and Wales if the parties have freely entered into the same with each having provided the other with appropriate disclosure of his and her respective assets, incomes and liabilities and having had the benefit of independent legal advice unless in the circumstances prevailing it would not be fair to hold the parties to their agreement;

   (iv) the position in relation to the status of pre-marital and post-marital agreements has been the subject of a report by the Law Commission

(Marital Property, Needs and Agreements – Feb 2014) and that report has recommended, in particular, the introduction of Qualifying Nuptial Agreements, which, subject to the respective needs of the parties to such Agreements being met, would be binding upon the court;

(v)   therefore a change in the substantive law by Act of Parliament in relation to pre-nuptial agreements, their effect and impact is possible at some future date and, pending such changes, it is likely that decisions will continue to be made by the courts, which further interpret and develop the law in relation to the status of pre-nuptial agreements.

(b)   Jack and Emily nevertheless hereby each respectively agrees and declares, without derogating from the position at law as last stated;

(i)   that they intend this Deed of Agreement to the fullest extent permitted by the law, upon any of the specified events, to be fully binding upon each of them and/or on their respective agents, receivers and trustees and/or, should either predecease the other, upon their heirs, personal representatives and estates and/or in the event of any claim/proceedings brought in respect of the same and/or in all jurisdictions wherever they may reside or be domiciled;

(ii)   that they shall at all times each take all steps that are lawfully possible in order to give effect to this intention.

(c)   Jack and Emily have each been informed and acknowledge, that the law of England and Wales relating to the status of pre and post marital agreements may change during the currency of this Deed of Agreement. In addition, there may arise circumstances in the future where Jack and/or Emily may choose to reside and/or become domiciled in another jurisdiction. In the event of any of these occurrences, they each agree as set out in clause 14 c) below that they will without undue delay each take such steps as are required of them to ensure that this Deed of Agreement remains fully binding upon them. They have, accordingly, provided herein for review in the event of any such change so that everything lawfully possible is done to ensure the validity of and effect of this Deed of Agreement.

6 Disclosure

(a)   Jack and Emily agree that they have each disclosed their respective assets, interests (inclusive of any trust(s)) and other resources, including income to each other as at the date of this Deed of Agreement. Each acknowledging and agreeing that they have offered to provide the other with such further information as may be requested concerning the disclosure given, they further agree and acknowledge that the disclosure made is sufficient information to give each an appropriate understanding of their respective financial positions upon which to allow the intention of both parties to be carried out. Details of their respective assets, interests (inclusive of any trust(s)) and other resources, including income are to be found in the **Appendices A** and **B** annexed to this Deed of Agreement. Jack and Emily recognise that the values of investments vary from day to day according to market fluctuations and that the nature of some investments makes them inherently difficult to value. Notwithstanding this position both Jack and Emily agree and are content that the values for their respective assets, interests (inclusive of any trust(s)) and other resources and incomes given in the **Appendices A** and **B** annexed to this Deed of Agreement and the potential selling agent and legal costs and consequential taxation shown therein in the event of sale/disposal thereof, shall be adopted for the purposes of this Deed of Agreement as the actual values thereof and/or the actual costs/taxation arising in the event of sale/disposal thereof at the date of this Deed of Agreement.

(b) Jack and Emily each agree to waive the right to have the assets, interests (inclusive of any trust(s)) and other resources, including income appearing in the schedules valued/ascertained further for the purposes of this Deed of Agreement and agree and accept that the values referred to therein are to be adopted as above referred to.

7 Domicile and Residence:

(a) Jack confirms he is a national of the United Kingdom and is currently domiciled in England and Wales.

(b) Emily confirms she is a national of the United Kingdom and is currently domiciled in England and Wales.

(c) Jack and Emily confirm that they are each currently habitually resident in England and Wales but each agree and intend that the terms of this Deed of Agreement shall be binding upon them and upon their agents, receivers, trustees, heirs and personal representatives and estates not only in this jurisdiction but also elsewhere in the world, wherever they may reside or be domiciled from time to time.

IT IS THEREFORE AGREED BY THE PARTIES THAT:

8 Condition Precedent to this Deed of Agreement becoming binding

This Deed of Agreement shall become operative upon Jack and Emily celebrating a valid ceremony of marriage, whether on the date recorded above or on some other date within 12 months of the date of this Deed of Agreement, provided always that should the marriage not be celebrated within such period, this Deed of Agreement shall be deemed to be discharged unless revived by a supplemental written agreement executed by Jack and Emily.

9 Confidentiality and Publication Prohibition

Jack and Emily agree that neither of them will:

(a) reveal to any third party unconnected with this matter (excluding any person to whom it is necessary to disclose relevant parts of this Deed of Agreement for the purpose of the taking or implementation of professional advice) any of the financial particulars disclosed in the negotiations leading to the making of this Deed of Agreement, nor the terms of this Deed of Agreement nor any annexes thereto;

(b)   cause or permit publication by the Press or other media of the said terms or particulars;

(c)   take any steps as a result of which these terms or particulars are likely to become public knowledge or in regard to which it is reasonably foreseeable would be likely to lead to the same becoming public knowledge;

(d)   Fail to take any steps which either of them may reasonably be expected to take to prevent the said terms or particulars from becoming public knowledge in circumstances where it is likely they would otherwise do so.

10 Separate Property

Jack and Emily agree that:

(a)   'Separate Property' as referred to in this Deed of Agreement is defined as all assets, interests (inclusive of any, where of immediate realisable value, held in trust(s)) and other capital resources (including any accumulated income), not being Absolute Property as referred to below at clause 12, as held upon any of the specified events by Jack and Emily in his or her respective sole legal and beneficial or sole beneficial ownership and including for the avoidance of any doubt those where they continue to be so held as set out in the **Appendices A at A (i)** and **B at B (i)** annexed hereto;

(b)   subject to sub-clause c. below and/or the provisions made in this Deed of Agreement for either of them or for any child as referred to, it is their wish and intention for each of them to retain sole absolute entitlement of their respective Separate Property as above, following their intended marriage and/or following upon any of the specified events.

(c)   they shall be at liberty by an express declaration in writing made between them for either to hold the beneficial interest of any Separate Property as above absolutely for the other in which event that Separate Property shall thereafter and following upon any specified event be regarded as held absolutely for that other and such declaration shall be binding upon them, their agents, receivers, trustees, heirs and personal representatives and estates in all jurisdictions and that other shall be entitled at all times to call for the transfer to him/herself absolutely of the legal title of that Separate Property.

(d)   subject to sub-clause c above, neither of them shall make any claim/take any proceedings during the intended marriage or upon any of the specified events in respect of the other's Separate Property as above whatever the circumstances in any jurisdiction, save and except only to obtain/ implement such provision as is provided for strictly within this Deed of Agreement and both Jack and Emily agree to release all rights and/or not to pursue claims in respect of any rights which either may otherwise acquire by reason of the intended marriage over the Separate Property of the other.

11 Jointly Held Assets/Interests/Resources/Chattels

Jack and Emily agree that

(a) subject to sub-clause c) ii) and clause 15 b) below, forthwith (or after such period as they may agree otherwise in writing) following upon any specified event and subject to sub clause b) below, any assets and/or interests and/or other capital resources and/or chattels held in the joint names of the parties ('asset etc' or 'asset(s) etc') shall accordingly be distributed between Jack and Emily in equal shares unless they have expressly declared in writing beforehand that, whilst held in joint names, the asset(s) etc is/are to be regarded as held absolutely by either of them or otherwise by them in disproportionate shares, in which case that declaration shall be binding upon them, their agents, receivers, trustees, heirs and personal representatives and estates in all jurisdictions and for the purposes of such distribution.

(b) subject to sub-clause c) ii) and clause 15 b) below, the method of distribution to effect the intention reflected by sub-clause a) above, where the asset(s) etc in question is/are held in other than an account and/or money form and other than absolutely by either Jack or Emily by their written declaration, shall be by agreement within 28 days of the first of any specified event (or any other period agreed in writing between the parties) and in default of agreement within such period shall forthwith thereafter be sold upon joint instruction by auction and the net proceeds of sale after discharge/account is made for any consequential disbursements, being selling agents and legal costs of sale, consequential commission and tax arising and the redemption of any secured charge (inclusive of any mortgage) as appropriate, shall be distributed between the parties in equal or such other declared shares as provided for in sub-clause a) above.

(c) for the avoidance of any doubt:-
   (i)   subject to c) ii) below and clause 15 b), in the event of an auction being effected as above, either party shall have the right to bid at such auction for the asset(s) etc in question.
   (ii) subject to clause 15 b), where the jointly held asset in question is the sole respective residence of either Jack or Emily, that party shall have the right to exercise the option, in the absence of prior agreement and before the asset is entered for any auction as above, to forthwith buy out the equal or other declared share of the other as above at a value agreed between them less any consequential (notional or actual) disbursements as above or in default as determined on the basis of the value of the asset in question (less such consequential disbursements) ascertained by the average of at least two jointly

instructed valuations from chartered surveyors engaged for the purpose; the cost of such instruction being borne by the party in sole residence of the asset.

12 Gifts

Jack and Emily each respectively acknowledge and agree:

(i) that nothing in this Deed of Agreement shall prevent either party from time to time voluntarily making gifts to the other or provision solely for the other by will or by trust. Such gifts or provision, if made, shall not otherwise be treated as varying the meaning and effect of this Deed of Agreement and/or be construed as a waiver of any provision of this Deed of Agreement, nor as evidence that there is or was any agreement or understanding between Jack and Emily otherwise than is specifically contained in this Deed of Agreement.

(ii) that the other may from time to time solely receive gifts, including of money or property, from friends or family members.

Each agrees that such gifts and/or provision as above and/or any chattel purchased solely by either of them during their marriage shall be their respective Absolute Property and neither of them will make a claim/take proceedings against the other in respect of the same either during the intended marriage or following upon any specified event, howsoever arising in any jurisdiction, save and except only to obtain/implement such provision as is provided for at i) and/or ii) or recover such gift/provision/chattel as above strictly in accordance with this Deed of Agreement.

13 Debts

Jack and Emily agree that all debts incurred:

(i) solely by either of them before and/or during the intended marriage or following upon any specified event, shall be the separate and sole obligation of the party who incurred the debt; and

(ii) by them jointly before and/or during the intended marriage or following upon any specified event, shall be the obligation of each party in equal shares and each shall, in so far as the same is necessary, keep the other indemnified in respect of their respective liability therefor.

14 Commencement of Proceedings and Jurisdiction:

Jack and Emily agree that:

(a) This Deed of Agreement shall be governed by and construed in accordance with the law of England and Wales and where the courts of any other legal jurisdiction shall also have jurisdiction, the parties agree that they each intend that the courts of England and Wales shall deal exclusively with any such application or claim.

(b) In the event of any specified event and unless otherwise expressly agreed in writing, no proceedings in connection with the termination of the marriage (or the deceased's estate) and/or this Deed of Agreement shall be commenced by either of them other than in the jurisdiction of England and Wales, provided that a court of England and Wales has the power to be seized of the proceedings. In any event, the parties hereby expressly agree and declare that each will be bound by the terms of this Deed of Agreement, to the maximum extent permitted by law, even if either of them should be forced to bring such proceedings in another jurisdiction in circumstances where England and Wales does not have jurisdiction.

(c) Moreover, in the event that Jack and Emily shall reside and/or become domiciled in a jurisdiction other than England and Wales, they each agree to take independent legal advice without delay from appropriately qualified lawyers in that other jurisdiction and to take all such steps as each/they may be advised to take to ensure that this Deed of Agreement is effective in that jurisdiction, including, if necessary, entering into a fresh agreement.

15 Family home

Jack and Emily agree that:

(a) they plan to live, in the first instance, at least, at the property owned by them jointly known as [insert address] (the 'family home'); and

(b) in the event that Jack and Emily should sell/dispose of the family home and subject to an agreement in writing between them or the property transfer declaring the beneficial interests otherwise, the beneficial interest which each shall respectively hold in any future family home shall upon any specified event be determined strictly and:
  (i) each respectively shall have contributed towards any deposit paid towards the purchase price; and
  (ii) of the liability which each respectively shall have undertaken in respect any mortgage/borrowing required to purchase of the property;

and, where, after purchase any structural works have been carried out to such property which have effected an increase in value of the property above the price paid on acquisition, the proportions each shall have respectively contributed directly towards the costs of those works and, where in part or in whole funded by mortgage/borrowing, the proportions of that liability each shall have undertaken in effecting that increase in value.

16 Provision upon divorce, nullity or judicial separation

Jack and Emily agree that following upon any specified event, each will have family responsibilities to meet in respect of their natural children and/or any grandchildren therefrom and that the agreed provision between them in this Deed of Agreement is intended to include each party following upon the first of any specified event being responsible for their own needs and those of their natural child or children (subject always to the obligations upon Jack and/or Emily in relation to any such children otherwise required by the law). The agreed provision therefore shall be:

A.   Subject to B, C and D below, following the first of any specified event, Jack will make payment of a lump sum and/or as otherwise agreed between them transfer any asset/resource/interest value to Emily within [insert period] of a final decree of divorce or nullity or a decree of judicial separation, whichever shall first occur, <u>equivalent to the **LESSER** of either:</u>

a.   [eg 25%] of the following calculation, being:

(i)   'the net value' (defined for all purposes within this Deed of Agreement, unless otherwise stated and including a reference to 'notional' in the event that no sale/disposal occurs, as 'the actual or notional gross value less any actual or notional selling agent's and/or legal costs of sale/disposal and/or any actual or notional taxation consequent upon such sale/disposal and/or any secured mortgage(s)/charge(s)') of the Separate Property at the date of the first of the specified events;

(ii)   **Less** the net value of the combination of:

(a)   the assets etc at **Appendices A (i)** and **B (i)** annexed to this Deed of Agreement as adjusted, between the date of this Deed of Agreement and the date of the first of the specified events by the rate(s) applicable during such period of the Consumer Prices Index;

(iii)   **AND** for the avoidance of any doubt, without any account being taken of any debts which either Jack and Emily may be liable for within the meaning of clause 13 above.

(iv)   **BUT WITH** full credit being given to Jack against any such lump sum /transfer of value to be made by him to Emily as above for the following calculation of value, being:

(a)   the net value of Emily's Separate Property at the date of the first specified event;

(b)   **Less** the net value of her assets etc at **Appendix B (i)** annexed to this Deed of Agreement as adjusted, between the date of this Deed of Agreement and the date of the first of the specified events by the rate(s) applicable during such period of the Consumer Prices Index.   ·

Or

b.   a sum calculated on the following basis, namely:

(i)   where prior to the date of the first specified event there has been a period of continuous cohabitation between Emily and Jack of, at least, [eg 12 months] ('the initial marital period') from the date of the intended marriage to the date of first specified event, a lump sum of £[insert amount] (the 'initial amount');

(ii)   AND for each subsequent 12 months of continuous cohabitation between the parties following the initial marital period, the initial amount shall be increased by additional sums of £[insert amount] (the 'additional amounts') for each such completed period up to a maximum lump sum in total (being the initial amount plus any additional amounts) of no more than £[insert amount].

B. It is agreed between Jack and Emily, for the avoidance of any doubt, that:

(i) no lump sum/transfer of value as referred to at A above whatsoever is payable to Emily in the event that there has not been the 'initial marital period' between them as referred to in A b. above.

(ii) in the event that such initial marital period has not occurred, then neither Jack and Emily will have any claim against the other whatsoever within any jurisdiction and Emily will be entitled only to her Separate and Absolute Property, her due share of any Jointly Acquired Property as provided for in this Deed of Agreement and her personal possessions.

(iii) in the event that the payment of the lump sum/transfer of value as referred to at A above:

(a) (subject to (b) below) requires Jack to liquidate any asset etc which would result in a more than nominal loss of value to him in consequence of the timing of the liquidation of that asset etc, he shall be permitted to defer that part of the payment of the lump sum/ transfer of value referred to for a period of up to 12 months or such other period as agreed in writing between the parties subject to the payment of interest payable to Emily upon that deferred payment equivalent to the base lending rate of the Bank of England applicable from year to year until full payment is made;

(b) requires Jack to secure payment from any loan note(s) held by him then he shall be permitted to defer that part of the payment of the lump sum/ transfer of value referred to for a period equivalent to that necessary in accordance with the terms of his holding of the loan notes in question to secure sufficient realisation of the same to meet his obligation hereunder or such other period as agreed in writing between the parties, subject to the payment of interest payable to Emily upon that deferred payment equivalent to the base lending rate of the Bank of England applicable from year to year until full payment is made.

C. It is further agreed by Jack or Emily that it is intended that within this Deed of Agreement that where the first of any specified events is the date of the parties' 'permanent separation' then such phrase shall mean the earliest of the following, namely:

(i) such date upon which either Jack and/or Emily move out of their marital home to permanently live separate and apart from the other; or

(ii) such date upon which Jack and/or Emily , notwithstanding that they may continue to live in the marital home, set(s) up a separate household therein from the other; or

(iii) such date upon which either Jack or Emily delivers to the other a declaration in writing of his or her decision to live separate and apart from the other; or

(iv)   such date, upon which either Jack or Emily issues a Petition seeking the annulment or dissolution of the intended marriage or an application for Judicial Separation.

D.   It is further agreed between Jack or Emily that the terms as above of 'value', 'net value', 'gross value', 'selling agent's costs', 'legal costs' and 'taxation' in so far as they refer to the same at the date of a 'permanent separation' and, where not otherwise identified/defined within this Deed of Agreement, shall mean such amount(s) as may be agreed between Jack or Emily or in the absence of agreement, as determined by a jointly appointed RICS qualified surveyor or jointly appointed valuer (as appropriate) based on a sale between a willing buyer and willing seller negotiating at arm's length or by a jointly appointed accountant.

17 Clean Break Agreement

(a)   Both Jack and Emily agree and declare that this Deed of Agreement resolves his and her respective rights and obligations in respect of each other regarding all forms of financial provision in any jurisdiction whatsoever and howsoever arising, including lump sum provision, property transfer order, pension orders and spousal support/periodical payments secured or unsecured, in the event of a decree of divorce, nullity or judicial separation and, as provided for below, should either pre-decease the other.

(b)   Save as expressly provided herein, Jack and Emily each waive his and her respective rights to seek and obtain orders for financial provision from the other, whether of an income or capital or pension nature, and he and she hereby expressly declares and agrees that he and she shall, in the event of a permanent separation, decree of divorce, nullity or judicial separation, take all necessary steps to secure an order from the court in accordance with this Deed of Agreement determining by a 'clean break' all of their rights to make an application for financial provision pursuant to the Matrimonial Causes Act 1973 (as amended), the Married Women's Property Act 1882 (as amended), the Law of Property Act 1925 and the Trusts of Land and Appointment of Trustees Act 1996 or any legislation of like purpose that may replace it, to the fullest extent permitted by law.

18 Provision on death

Jack and Emily agree that:

(a)   The provision set out in this Deed of Agreement for Emily and/or any child is a reasonable provision and shall also apply in the event of Jack predeceasing Emily during the subsistence of their marriage or after a decree of divorce, nullity or a decree of judicial separation and Jack agrees he will make a Will reflecting such provision as is set out in this Deed of Agreement and neither Jack and Emily will as is previously referred to make any claim upon the estate of the other under the Inheritance (Provision for Family and Dependants) Act 1975 or any legislation of like purpose which replaces it.

(b) Jack and Emily hereby expressly declare that he and she will, in the event of a permanent separation, decree of divorce, nullity or judicial separation, seek in accordance with this Deed of Agreement a 'clean break' order from the court determining the right of either party to make an application for provision for themselves pursuant to the Inheritance (Provision for Family and Dependants) Act 1975, or any legislation of like purpose that may replace it, to the fullest extent permissible by law.

19 Severance and Duration of Agreement

Jack and Emily agree that:

(a) The invalidity or unenforceability of any provision of this Deed of Agreement will not affect the validity or enforceability of any other provision and any invalid or unenforceable provision will be severable.

(b) The terms of this Deed of Agreement will continue in force notwithstanding the dissolution or annulment of the marriage or the separation of Jack and Emily.

(c) In the event that either Jack and Emily do not vary or review, as below, the terms of this Deed of Agreement or cannot agree upon alternative arrangements for review, then, for the avoidance of any doubt, the terms of this Deed of Agreement will continue in their present form.

20 Review

Jack and Emily each acknowledges and agrees that if, in the event of a change in law or practice or a change of marital significance, something needs to be done by one or both of them to make it more likely that this Deed of Agreement will be binding, they shall each without delay take such steps as are reasonably required of them including the taking of independent advice to give effect to this. In particular, they have each been advised that the Law Commission for England and Wales has reported to the Government on the issue of marital agreements and accordingly they each appreciate that a change in law or practice is likely, in which event they shall each take such steps as can be taken to ensure that this Deed of Agreement is enforceable under the law of England and Wales including, if necessary, executing a further Deed of Agreement or amendment to this Deed of Agreement.

21 Entire Agreement

Jack and Emily agree that:

This Deed of Agreement, with its Appendices, constitutes the Entire Agreement and understanding between the parties. There are no representations, promises, covenants or undertakings, whether written or oral, other than those expressly set out herein.

22 Applicable Law

Jack and Emily agree that this Deed of Agreement shall be governed by and construed in accordance with the law of England and Wales.

23 Costs

Jack and Emily agree that the costs arising in relation and incidental to this Deed of Agreement shall be borne by the party incurring the same save and except that Jack will make a contribution to such costs as are incurred by Emily up to a maximum of £[insert amount]. The making of such contribution by Jack is not to be construed that he has sought thereby or otherwise to influence Emily's advisers or the way in which they have advised her.

NOTICE TO JACK SMITH AND EMILY ROBERTS

THIS DOCUMENT ONCE SIGNED IS INTENDED TO CREATE LEGAL RELATIONS AND TO BE LEGALLY BINDING UPON YOU AND TO DETERMINE THE OWNERSHIP AND DISTRIBUTION BETWEEN YOU OF THE CAPITAL, PENSIONS AND INCOME REFERRED TO WITHIN ITS TERMS IN THE EVENT OF ANY OF THE SPECIFIED EVENTS REFERRED TO

YOU SHOULD NOT SIGN THIS DOCUMENT UNLESS YOU HAVE EACH HAD LEGAL ADVICE UPON ITS CONTENTS AND EFFECT AND YOU HAVE FULLY UNDERSTOOD THE SAME AND ARE FULLY SATISFIED YOU HAVE BEEN GIVEN ADEQUATE INFORMATION ABOUT EACH OTHER'S FINANCIAL CIRCUMSTANCES AND PLANS AND HAD SUFFICIENT OPPORTUNITY TO CONSIDER THE POSITION.

IN WITNESS whereof the parties hereto have executed this instrument on the date first before written,

SIGNED by
JACK SMITH
In the presence of
Witness signature
Witness name
Witness address
Witness occupation

SIGNED by
EMILY ROBERTS
In the presence of
Witness signature
Witness name
Witness address
Witness occupation

[The reader should attach the Appendices A to F (Precedents of which appear below) as applicable].

[Also – *if desired* – ATTACHED MARITAL AGREEMENT:

THIS DEED OF MARITAL AGREEMENT is made on the [day] of [month] [year]

BETWEEN
(1)   Jack Smith of [insert address] ('Jack') and
(2)   Emily Roberts of [insert address] ('Emily')

Introduction:
1.   This Deed of Marital Agreement is made further to the marriage of Jack (who was born on [insert date] and Emily (who was born on [insert date] ('the Marriage') and the Deed of Agreement between the same parties dated [insert date].

[The reader should then repeat the contents of the Deed of Agreement above with the appropriate exclusions and amendments to the paragraph numbering].

Appendix A

JACK SMITH Financial Disclosure

A (i)

Sole Legal and Beneficial and Sole Beneficial Assets (gross and net values):

Property:
Bank Accounts:
Investments:
Company Shareholdings:
Interests in Trusts:
Pensions:
Furniture:
Personal / Cars/ Jewellery/ Art/ Collections

A (ii)

Joint Interests:

A (iii)

Gross and Net Income Sources:

A (iv)

Liabilities:

Appendix B

EMILY ROBERTS Financial Disclosure

B (i)

Sole Legal and Beneficial and Sole Beneficial Assets (gross and net values):

Property:
Bank Accounts:
Investments:
Company Shareholdings:
Interests in Trusts:
Pensions:
Furniture:
Personal / Cars/ Jewellery/ Art/ Collections

B (ii)

Joint Interests:

B (iii)

Gross and Net Income Sources:

B (iv)

Liabilities:

APPENDIX C (or E as appropriate)

CERTIFICATE OF LEGAL ADVISOR

I, *(solicitor's full name)* of *(firm name and address)* certify as follows:

1. I am a qualified solicitor of the Supreme Court of England and Wales.

2. Before Jack (or Emily as appropriate) (entered into this Deed of Agreement to which this certificate is annexed, I provided to him (or her as appropriate) independent advice as to the following:

(i) the current law and the anticipated changes thereto following the Law Commissions Report on Marital Agreements (Feb 2014);

(ii) the effect of the agreement on his (or her as appropriate) rights and entitlements;

(iii) whether, at the time my advice was given, it was to his (or her as appropriate) advantage financially or otherwise to enter into the agreement;

(iv) whether it was prudent for him (or her as appropriate) to enter into the agreement; and

(v) whether in light of such circumstances as were reasonably foreseeable, the provisions of the agreement are fair and reasonable.

(vi) the effect upon the terms of the agreement should either him (or her as appropriate) or Emily (or Jack as appropriate) during their marriage reside or become domiciled elsewhere.

SIGNED [insert solicitor's name and address]

APPENDIX D (or F as appropriate)

CERTIFICATE OF ACCOUNTANT/FINANCIAL ADVISOR

I, *(advisor's full name)* of *(firm name and address)* certify as follows:

1. I am a qualified (insert details as appropriate).

2. Before Emily (or Jack as appropriate) entered into this Deed of Agreement to which this certificate is annexed, I provided to her (or him as appropriate) independent advice as to the following:

i) [insert details as appropriate]

SIGNED [insert accountant's/ advisor's name and address]

Limitation of Counsel's Liability for all Advices and Work undertaken in relation to Pre-Nuptial Agreement Instructions

I, JACK SMITH, of   , agree to the terms of limitation as appear below in relation to all Advices and other Work undertaken by [insert name], Barrister-at-Law, of [insert address] in regard to instructions provided to him by me and/or on my behalf by my solicitors [insert name and address] in respect of a Pre-Nuptial Agreement between myself and [insert name].

I, [insert name of Solicitor], Solicitor of [insert address], agree to the terms of limitation as appear below in relation to all Advices and other Work undertaken by [insert name], Barrister-at-Law, in regard to instructions provided to him by [insert solicitor's firm name] and/or on behalf of Jack Smith in respect of a Pre-Nuptial Agreement between Mr Smith and Emily Roberts.

The Terms of Limitation are:

1. That any liability for negligence or any other default, howsoever arising, in the provision of Advices and/or other work undertaken by [insert name], Barrister-at-Law, in the relation to and/or in connection with the instructions provided to him in regard to a Pre-Nuptial Agreement between Jack Smith and Emily Roberts will at all times be strictly limited to his Professional Indemnity insurance maximum cover of [insert amount] as provided to [insert him or her] by the Bar Mutual Indemnity Fund or its successors.

2. That it is understood that the instructions to [insert name], Barrister-at-Law are only accepted by him on the basis of the strict application of the limitation of liability referred to herein.

3. That It is acknowledged by the signing of this document that the signatories are fully aware and understand the terms of the limitation which apply hereby and that should he/she/they not agree to such terms he/they should not sign this document and if he/she/they wish to obtain other counsel on different terms of instruction/liability each is at liberty to do so and to forthwith withdraw any instructions provided to [insert Counsel's name] without incurring any fee.

SIGNED

JACK SMITH

....

<u>SIGNED</u>

[insert solicitor's name and address]

....

<u>SIGNED</u>

[insert Counsel's name]

....

DATED [insert date]

CHAPTER 9

COHABITATION AND WELFARE BENEFITS

Introduction

9.1 'Living together as a married couple'

'Cohabitation' is not a term that has been officially used in modern social security law since 1977. Benefits legislation now refers instead to the status of *living together as a married couple.*[1] This is now gender-neutral. Before 13 March 2014 it was split into the two alternatives of *living together as husband and wife*[2] and *living together as if civil partners.*[3]

Nonetheless, departmental officials, judges, practitioners and claimants themselves will often use the term 'cohabitation' as shorthand for the 'living together' concepts; DWP guidance on the other hand prefers the acronym LTAMC. Either way, practitioners must understand what the concept comprises. The law on their meaning is amorphous and difficult to pin down, a difficulty recognised in many of the judgments. Mr Commissioner Howell QC in *CP/8001/1995* described it as:

> 'one of the most difficult problems of definition there could be, since it involves investigating and analysing the nature of a human relationship between two people and this is inevitably a complex and sensitive thing.'

He later observed, in the same case, that:

> 'a true relationship of cohabitation is probably easier to recognise when one comes across it than to define exhaustively in the abstract.'

This chapter addresses the status of couple, outside of marriage or civil partnership, insofar as it relates to welfare benefits and tax credits.

9.2 Welfare benefits: a very brief introduction

Before focusing on the detailed issues of how 'living together' decisions impact on entitlement and how to challenge them, it may be useful to review the range of benefits and tax credits available, so as to put in context those areas of the system where cohabitation is an issue, and to clarify where it is not.

---

[1]   Social Security Contributions and Benefits Act 1992, s 137.
[2]   Since 4 April 1977.
[3]   Since 5 December 2005.

Type of benefit	Benefit	Typical client-group and purpose	Relevance of cohabitation
Means-tested benefits: for claimants of various categories, but only if on low or zero incomes	Universal credit (see also **3.6**)	Working age people on low incomes: low-paid workers, parents, unemployed people, carers, those with limited capacity for work. Early 'Pathfinder' claims in 2014-2015 are confined to single people	Cohabitation and couple status is particularly important in all these benefits and tax credits as they are assessed differently depending on whether the claimant is single or a member of a couple.
	Income support*	Single parents with a child under 5 yrs, carers, some young people at school – who are not in 16 hours' work or more	Couples' income – including cohabiting couples' – is aggregated for the purpose of means-testing both capital and income.
	Income-based jobseeker's allowance*	For claimants who sign on at the JobCentre and are available for, and actively seeking, work – cannot be in 16 hours' work or more	Couples (including cohabitants) not eligible for universal credit at early Pathfinder phase of UC (2014-15).
	Income-related employment and support allowance*	Paid to those who satisfy the work capability assessment as having limited capability for work – cannot be in 16 hours' work or more	In the case of single parents with a young child, Income Support is *only* available if they are single; cohabitation negates this.
	Pension credit	Paid to claimants who have reached women's pensionable age	
	Housing Benefit*	Paid in respect of rent to those on low incomes whether in or out of work	
	local council tax reduction schemes	Paid in respect of council tax to those on low incomes whether in or out of work	

Type of benefit	Benefit	Typical client-group and purpose	Relevance of cohabitation
Tax credits	Child tax credit* (see also **3.6**)	Paid in respect of dependent children/young persons to those on low to middle incomes whether in or out of work	
	Working tax credit* (see also **3.6**)	Paid to those in at least 16 hours' work and on low incomes	

*for those of working age, these benefits and tax credits are only applicable in cases where Universal Credit has not yet commenced.

Type of benefit	Benefit	Typical client-group and purpose	Relevance of cohabitation
Contributory benefits	Retirement pension	Paid upon reaching pensionable age to those who have paid or been credited with enough NI contributions during their working life – or their spouse or civil partner has	Paid individually so cohabiting does not affect entitlement. But note that cohabiting couples do not have the same advantages here as married couples and civil partners. Cohabitants cannot claim Category B RP on their partner's NI contributions, nor can they inherit the benefits of a deferred claim for RP. Cohabiting with another person does not interfere with a person's right to RP based on their current, late or former spouse's or civil partner's NI contributions
	Employment and support allowance (contributory)	For people who satisfy the work capability assessment as having limited capability for work – and who have paid enough NI contributions in the 2-3 years before stopping work	This is paid on an individual basis so cohabiting does not affect entitlement. Two cohabitants could each get a full entitlement unaffected by the other's

Type of benefit	Benefit	Typical client-group and purpose	Relevance of cohabitation
	Jobseeker's allowance (contributory)	For people who sign on as jobseekers actively seeking and available for work – and who have paid enough NI contributions in the 2-3 years before becoming unemployed	This is paid on an individual basis so cohabiting does not affect entitlement. Two cohabitants could each get a full entitlement unaffected by the other's
	Bereavement allowance	Payable for one year to surviving spouses and surviving civil partners over 45 whose late spouse or civil partner paid enough NI prior to their death	These are affected by cohabitation: entitlement is suspended when a claimant cohabits. They are not available to cohabitants whose partner dies
	Widowed parent's allowance	Payable to surviving spouses and surviving civil partners who have dependent children or young persons and whose late spouse or late civil partner paid enough NI prior to their death	
	Incapacity benefit	Payable to those who satisfied the personal capability assessment as being incapable of work – for claims prior to October 2008 – most such existing claims have now switched to ESA	This is paid on an individual basis so cohabiting does not affect entitlement. Two cohabitants could each get a full entitlement unaffected by the other's
Other benefits neither means-tested nor contributory	Carer's allowance	For those who are caring regularly and substantially for a disabled person who is on Attendance Allowance, Personal Independence Payment Daily Living Component, or middle/highest rate of Disability Living Allowance Care Component	Cohabitation does not affect this; it can be claimed by a cohabitant in respect of looking after the person they are cohabiting with

Type of benefit	Benefit	Typical client-group and purpose	Relevance of cohabitation
	Personal independence payment	Paid to disabled claimants who have either significant care needs or mobility difficulties or both, and who claim before they reach age 65 (rising to 66 by 2018)	Unaffected by cohabitation. Two qualifying cohabitants could each get a full entitlement unaffected by the other's
	Disability living allowance	Paid to disabled claimants with significant care needs or mobility difficulties or both, and who claimed before age 65 and before April 2013. Still available to under-16s making a new claim	Unaffected by cohabitation. Two qualifying cohabitants could each get a full entitlement unaffected by the other's
	Attendance allowance	Paid to disabled claimants who have significant care needs, and who claim after they reach age 65 (rising to 66 by 2018)	Unaffected by cohabitation. Two qualifying cohabitants could each get a full entitlement unaffected by the other's
	Child benefit	Paid to those who live with and are responsible for a child or dependent young person	Largely unaffected by cohabitation except that only one person may claim in respect of a given child, and rules govern who has priority in certain cases where two cohabitants both qualify but only one may succeed in their CB claim
	Guardian's Allowance	Claimed by a Child Benefit claimant in addition to the CB where a child is without parents	
	Maternity allowance	Claimed during the maternity period by a woman who has recently worked but not enough to qualify for SMP	Unaffected by cohabitation: she may claim whether single or not

Type of benefit	Benefit	Typical client-group and purpose	Relevance of cohabitation
	Industrial injuries disablement benefit	Paid in respect of disablement caused by industrial injuries or a prescribed industrial disease	Unaffected by cohabitation: the claimant may claim whether single or not. Note that entitlement to a death benefit under this scheme (for deaths prior to April 1988 only) would only accrue to a late *spouse*, and not if a cohabitant's partner died
Employer-paid benefits	Statutory maternity pay	Paid during the statutory maternity period to women who have recently worked for a sufficient time for the same employer	Unaffected by cohabitation: a woman may claim whether single or not
	Statutory paternity pay	Paid to a father, or the partner of a mother, with some upbringing responsibility, during prescribed periods following a birth or following a partner's return to work from maternity leave	To qualify other than as a father, the person must be the mother's partner – whether cohabiting or married or civil partners
	Statutory adoption pay	Payable to those adopting a child, during the statutory adoption period	May be claimed whether the adopter is single or a member of a couple, and in the case of a couple, including a cohabiting couple, one partner may claim longer-term SAP and the other may claim a version of SPP, whether they are jointly adopting or only one partner is adopting

Type of benefit	Benefit	Typical client-group and purpose	Relevance of cohabitation
	Statutory sick pay	Payable as a minimum entitlement during periods when an employee is off work through inability to work caused by illness or disability	Unaffected by cohabitation: a person may claim whether single or not. Two qualifying cohabitants could each be entitled, unaffected by the other's claim
Single Payments and grants	Social fund: budgeting loans	Discretionary repayable loans to assist with one-off needs in certain circumstances	Eligibility to apply for these payments largely depends on entitlement to a qualifying benefit – mostly this means IS, ib-JSA, ir-ESA or PC Consequently the circumstances put forward as justifying the payment, eg for budgeting loans, are assessed on a couple basis where two people are cohabiting
	Social fund: Surestart maternity grant	Single non-discretionary lump sum paid at time of birth	
	Social fund: funeral grants	Single non-discretionary lump sum paid to cover some funeral costs for a person who is responsible for a funeral	
	Winter fuel payment	Single payment per Winter per household for those who have reached women's pensionable age	Only one payment is made to a couple – including cohabiting couples
	Bereavement payment	Single lump sum payable to surviving spouses and surviving civil partners upon the death of their spouse or civil partner	Not payable if the claimant is cohabiting with a person other than the spouse or civil partner at the time of the death. Later cohabitation does not disqualify however. To qualify for the payment the claimant must have been married or in a civil partnership – cohabitation will not suffice

Using this chapter

9.3   Your client

Most of this chapter assumes that you will be representing or advising a client who has encountered a problem (disqualification or reduction) in their benefits or tax credits because they are considered to be a member of a couple, and feel this has been wrongly decided. Or they may be seeking advice on how to manage their relationship in order legitimately to avoid falling foul of the living together rules.

If the latter applies, there is nothing fraudulent about avoidance manoeuvres that deliberately set up a *bona fide* non-cohabiting relationship, as long as that will be a genuine one. Needless to say, what practitioners must not do is collude with any falsification of the facts in a case. The advice in this chapter should not be seen as condoning any kind of misrepresentation of the character of your client's relationship.

Social security law tells us what a *couple* is; it does not define *single* status. Yet it is 'single' status that is often contended for by the client. Generally if a person is not a member of a couple, s/he must be assumed to be single.[4] The tactical relevance in social security cases of knowing how to define 'couple' is typically that your client will want to argue that s/he is single and *not* a member of a couple. His or her welfare benefits position will nearly always be better as a single person.

9.4   Who is your opponent?

The decision-maker who has adversely decided any living-together point against your client will most likely be an official of:

(a)   for most welfare benefits, the **Department for Work and Pensions** (DWP), which comprises the Jobcentre Plus, the Pension Service, and other sections;

(b)   for housing benefit and council tax reduction, the **local authority**; or

(c)   for tax credits, **Her Majesty's Revenue and Customs** (HMRC).

For all these, this chapter usually adopts the generic term 'the department'.

Increasingly those departments work together to collect evidence, rely on one another's evidence, and base their decisions on each other's decisions. In general this is lawful and correct. Where a fraud is suspected, the single Benefit Fraud Investigation Service will investigate. Their evidence may be produced in cohabitation cases even where no fraud is alleged.

---

[4]   The exception to this is the recognition in s 133 of SSCBA of legally-contracted polygamous marriages.

In areas where statute creates a passported entitlement from one benefit to another, the decision-maker dealing with the passported benefit is probably bound by the decision-maker who decided the qualifying benefit. Where, for example, an Income Support decision finds a claimant to be single, the decision in respect of the person's Housing Benefit should not go behind this,[5] unless there is an indication of fraud. It is submitted, however, that the position is less clear where there is no statutory link, such as where an HMRC decision on couple status dissents from a pre-existing couple status decision made by the DWP in respect of Income Support. The judgment in *R (on the application of Tilianu) v Secretary of State for Work and Pensions*[6] gives some support for the proposition that the second decision-making authority is not so bound. The position is equally unclear where, say, an Income Support decision-maker takes a different view as to couple status to a decision-maker in the Child Maintenance and Enforcement Commission.

9.5 Benefit fraud

The incursion of criminal law into the living-together realm is largely outside the scope of this chapter. But the reality is that many lone parents find themselves accused of benefit fraud, sometimes based on a living-together allegation. *CG v Secretary of State for Work and Pensions (IS)*[7] contains a sobering account of the collection of evidence in a police raid on the claimant's home, in which 'holiday receipts, family photos and letters written to the claimant by her husband from prison' were seized. The underlying law on whether there is or has been cohabitation is no different; indeed it is submitted that a proper hearing of that issue within the benefits adjudication framework should certainly precede the prosecution of a criminal case by the department. That is not always the case, nor does the law say it must be. This is unfortunate because the magistrates' court is arguably not the best forum in which to ventilate the finer points of living together.

9.6 Using social security case-law

This chapter cites a number of social security cases. These are useful not only for the precedents some of them set, but also because they illustrate examples of the judicial response to a wide variety of factual situations. For that reason the facts in quite a number of the cases are outlined here. That a decided case has similar facts to your client's scenario is no reason to expect the same outcome however. Producing cases with similar facts to your client's should be done with care, and with no suggestion that the tribunal is bound to reach the same result. An analogy between a decided case and your fact-matrix may be drawn, bearing in mind that the outcome on a given set of facts is very rarely binding, given that the subtleties of factual variation are so finely shaded.

---

[5] *R v Housing Benefits Review Board of Penwith District Council ex parte Menear* (1992) 24 HLR 115; *GB v London Borough of Hillingdon (HB)* [2010] UKUT 11 (AAC).

[6] [2010] EWHC 213 (Admin).

[7] [2011] UKUT 97 (AAC).

Most social security case-law consists of decisions of the Upper Tribunal, which hears cases on appeal on a point of law from the First-tier Tribunal. Before 3 November 2008, the equivalent arrangement was that Tribunals Service social security tribunal decisions were appealable to the Social Security and Child Support Commissioners. They were equivalent to the Upper Tribunal, and their case-law is as binding as the Upper Tribunal's is now.

- Many cases here predate 3 November 2008 and their citations follow the pattern **CIS/1234/2002** – where 'C' means Commissioners' File; 'IS' denotes the benefit – here Income Support – and a number and four-digit year is applied.

- Reported cases follow the format **R(IS)3/07** where 'R' means Reported, followed by which benefit, a number and two-digit year.

- Where the benefit in question is signified by a 'G', this stands for 'general' and covers bereavement benefits and the like.

- An intervening 'S' between the 'C' and the benefit initials means the case is a Scottish case, and equally binding in England and Wales. The Northern Ireland system used different citations, and such cases are highly persuasive in Great Britain.

- Since 3 November 2008, the citation format in Great Britain is *ZX v Secretary of State for Work and Pensions (IS) [2010] UKUT 123 (AAC)*: 'UKUT' denotes UK Upper Tribunal, and 'AAC' is the Administrative Appeals Chamber.

Useful sources for downloading decisions of the Upper Tribunal and Social Security Commissioners include:

(a)   https://www.gov.uk/administrative-appeals-tribunal

(b)   www.osscsc.gov.uk/Decisions/decisions.htm.

(c)   www.bailii.org.

(d)   www.rightsnet.org.uk.

9.7   Using departmental guidance

The Decision Makers' Guide is published at www.gov.uk/government/collections/decision-makers-guide-staff-guide and provides a very useful insight into why a decision has been made in the way it has. The guidance is carefully and moderately written, and cites useful legal authority. However, practitioners should remember at all times that it is not law. By all means quote it where it assists your client, but where it is invoked against your client's case, it should be rebutted with the correct position in law, and it should be argued that it carries no legal authority at all.

Why cohabitation is relevant in social security and tax credits law

9.8 Differences in treatment as between couples and single people

Here are five examples of situations in which a client may be affected by the cohabitation rules; in these first four cases, one will hope to argue – depending on the facts – that the client is single.

Case 1: disqualified from jobseeker's allowance (JSA): Andrea is separating from her partner Adrian. They both still live in the same property, with their children, aged 10 and 13, but have separated out their households within the home. Adrian is in full-time, well-paid work; Andrea is not. She needs to claim jobseeker's allowance and child tax credit as she is not working and is fairly sure that she will be the main childcarer. If they are treated as a couple[8] then she cannot get any Jobseeker's Allowance (she is disqualified by Adrian's full-time work[9] as well as by their aggregated joint income,[10] ie his sizeable earnings). As a member of the couple she is also ineligible for child tax credit if the joint income exceeds approximately £21,300 (two or more children).[11]

Case 2: less JSA: Bereket shares a flat with his friend Mariam; they are not married. Both are in their 30s, unemployed and claiming income-based Jobseeker's Allowance. If seen as a couple they are entitled to £114.85 per week[12] between them; if regarded as two single people they will receive £73.10 per week each – £31.35 more in total.

Case 3: access to income support: Chloe is a single parent with two children aged two and four. She claims income support, child benefit and child tax credit. Her eligibility for Income Support depends on her lone parent status. If she begins a relationship with a new partner and this relationship gradually becomes more serious, then at some point the DWP may decide she is no longer a single parent, so her eligibility for income support stops.[13] She might still be able to claim jobseeker's allowance (depending on her new partner's status and income), but getting income support *as a lone parent* is no longer an option once she is a member of a couple. Sadly, cases like this can all too readily produce fraud prosecutions. Arguing against couple status matters doubly in such cases.

Case 4: bereavement benefits: Danny claims bereavement allowance after the death of his wife Joyce. When he begins cohabiting with a new partner eight months after his bereavement, his bereavement allowance is suspended.[14]

---

8   Jobseekers Act 1995, ss 3, 4, 35; JSA Regulations 1996 (SI 1996/207), reg 1.
9   Jobseekers Act 1995, s 3(1)(e).
10 JSA Regulations 1996, reg 88.
11 Tax Credits (Income Thresholds and Determination of Rates) Regulations 2002 (SI 2002/2008), reg 8 as amended. Approximate amounts applicable in 2015-2016 tax year.
12 Weekly amounts are for 2015-2016.
13 Income Support (General) Regulations 1987 (SI 1987/1967), Sch 1B.
14 Social Security Contributions and Benefits Act 1992, s 39B(5)(b).

However, in other circumstances, admittedly rarer, it is in the client's interest for the relationship to be seen as a stronger one.

Case 5: capital value of a former shared home: Eldon moves out of the home he used to share with his partner. She remains in the home, valued at £1.2m, which they continue to own jointly. There are no children. Because DWP take the view that they are 'estranged', the value of his share in the jointly owned property starts to count as his capital 26 weeks after he moves out,[15] disqualifying him from jobseeker's allowance. Were they not 'estranged' the value of his share would be disregarded as capital indefinitely.

Cohabitation rules in the benefits system

Which benefits and tax credits are affected by the 'living together' tests?

9.9   Benefits and tax credits affected: I – for the purposes of applying a means-test

Claims for the following benefit and tax credits are made on a couple basis for cohabitees – with both partners as *joint claimants*:

(a)   Universal credit.[16]

(b)   Working tax credit.

(c)   Child tax credit.

Claims for the following means-tested benefits and support are also made on a couple basis for cohabitees – one partner being the *claimant* and the other the *partner*:

(d)   Income support.[17]

(e)   Income-based jobseeker's allowance.[18]

(d)   Income-related employment and support allowance.[19]

(f)   State pension credit.[20]

(g)   Housing benefit.

(h)   Local council tax reduction schemes.[21]

---

[15]   Jobseeker's Allowance Regulations 1996 (SI 1996/207), Sch 8 paras 4(b) and 5.
[16]   Welfare Reform Act 2012, s 39(1).
[17]   SSCBA 1992, s 124(1).
[18]   Jobseekers Act 1995, s 3(1).
[19]   Welfare Reform Act 2007, Sch 1, para 6(1).
[20]   State Pension Credit Act 2002, s 5.
[21]   Council Tax Reduction Schemes (Prescribed Requirements) (England) Regulations 2012 (SI 2012/2885), reg 4 and Council Tax Reduction Schemes and Prescribed Requirements (Wales) Regulations 2012 (SI 2012/3144 (W 316)), reg 4.

9.10 Benefits affected: II – for the purpose of disqualification where cohabitation exists

(a) Bereavement allowance.[22]

(b) Widowed parent's allowance.[23]

(c) Widow's pension.[24]

(d) Widowed mother's allowance.[25]

(e) Bereavement payment.[26]

9.11 Is the definition the same for these two lists?

According to Mr Commissioner Rice, the definition of 'living together' is the same for means-tested and widows' (now *bereavement*) benefits: *R(SB)17/81*. But Mr Commissioner Goodman entered a proviso in *CIS/317/94* at least in respect of the burden of proof:

> 'Mr Wright cited a passage at page 25 of the 1994 edition of Mesher and Wood on "Income Related Benefits: The Legislation" as follows:
>
>> "what these points come to [the criteria for determining whether a couple are living together as husband and wife] is that the so called 'objective facts' of a relationship may be capable of being interpreted either way. This, then, leaves the authority in difficulty, although it is clear that the burden of proof, since the rule operates as a disqualification, is on the DSS."
>
> However, although living together as husband and wife does operate as a disqualification for widow's benefit (SSCBA 1992, s 38(3)(c)), it does not in my view so operate for income support. What is involved here is the whole gamut of facts leading to the question of whether a particular claimant is entitled to Income Support by reason of his or her financial position and if so its amount.'

The distinction between a disqualifying factor and a determining factor is subtle but important. The stakes are evidently more stark in bereavement benefits. But for practical purposes it is submitted that practitioners may safely treat the definition as the same for the two types of benefit.

9.12 Areas where cohabitation matters

Thus cohabitation is raised specifically in rules which prescribe that:

(a) in order to claim income support as a lone parent, the client must indeed be considered single and the parent of a child under 5 years;[27]

---

[22] SSCBA 1992, s 39B.

[23] SSCBA 1992, s 39A.

[24] SSCBA 1992, s 38(3).

[25] SSCBA 1992, s 37(4)(b).

[26] SSCBA 1992, s 36(2): not payable if the claimant is cohabiting with someone other than their spouse or civil partner at the time of the spouse's or civil partner's death.

[27] Welfare Reform Act 2012, s 57.

(b)   the income and capital of a couple are aggregated for the purposes of calculating all means-tested benefits and tax credits;

(c)   for universal credit, different rules about disregarding income apply, according to whether the claim is a couple claim or a single claim;

(d)   a claimant whose partner is in full-time work is not entitled to income support, income-based JSA and income-related employment and support allowance;

(e)   bereavement benefits (bereavement allowance, widowed parent's allowance, widow's pension and widowed mother's allowance) are suspended when a widow, widower or surviving civil partner starts cohabiting with a new partner;[28]

(f)   past cohabitation can interfere[29] with current housing benefit entitlement where a claim is made for rent paid to a former partner on a property that was previously occupied by the tenant and the landlord as a couple;

(g)   that where a person from abroad, in the UK subject to a prohibition on recourse to public funds, joins their family in the UK who do not have that prohibition, the newly arrived person may inadvertently end up being deemed to have claimed on public funds if s/he cohabits with a claimant partner whose housing benefit or help from the council tax reduction scheme increases due to the arrival of the new partner. If they are not regarded as partners, and the new arrival refrains from making their own housing benefit/council tax reduction claim, there is no such problem;

(h)   a member of a couple purporting *both* to get a severe disability premium as part of their income support, income-related employment and support allowance etc, can only do so if the other member of the couple also receives a qualifying benefit or is blind;[30]

(i)   in JSA claims made by couples without children, the partner as well as the claimant must sign on at the Jobcentre Plus;

(j)   rules governing child benefit, so as to determine who has priority in competing claims from different qualifying adults, differ slightly as between married and unmarried couples;

(k)   a person – often in practice a former cohabiting partner though this is not necessary – who de facto pays maintenance in respect of a claimant's children, may because of this be treated as the children's father so as to make him a 'liable relative' in the Income Support (et al) Regulations,[31] meaning that any additional maintenance he pays not to the children but to the mother will be treated as a liable relative payment and will punitively reduce or extinguish her income support payments;

(m)   Universal credit, introduced tentatively in some areas in 2013, is due to replace other mean-tested benefits (except council tax reduction schemes)

---

28   The 'living together' criteria are the same in bereavement benefits as for means-tested benefits: *R(SB)17/81*.

29   Housing Benefit Regulations 2006 (SI 2006/216), reg 9(1)(c).

30   eg for Income Support, Income Support (General) Regulations 1987 (SI 1987/1967), Sch 2, para 13(2A). *CIS/2900/1998* dealt with such a case, though this concerned a married couple.

31   For Income Support, Income Support (General) Regulations 1987 (SI 1987/ 1967), reg 54.

and tax credits. Part 1 (ss 1-43) of the Welfare Reform Act 2012 provides that the scheme will unsurprisingly adopt the same wide approach to aggregation of income and capital in couples as previously: it is possible for clients to be treated as a couple despite the absence of a marriage or civil partnership. Moreover section 39 of the Act mirrors exactly the existing legislation's couple definitions for means-tested benefits.

9.13   When does 'couple' require marriage or civil partnership?

On the other hand, a different, more restrictive view of 'couple' obtains in other areas of the social security system. In particular, it should be noted that:

(a)   in retirement pension, entitlement to Category B state pension based on the national insurance contribution conditions of a spouse, civil partner, deceased spouse or deceased civil partner only arises where there is or was indeed a marriage or civil partnership – in other words, mere cohabitation will not suffice;

(b)   similarly there is no entitlement to bereavement benefits (bereavement allowance, widowed parent's allowance and bereavement payment) unless a spouse or civil partner (not a cohabitee) has died;

(c)   other areas of retirement pension also require there to be (or have been) a marriage or civil partnership; and

(d)   corresponding provisions apply in the war pensions and (for deaths before April 1988) industrial injuries schemes wherever the claimant is a surviving spouse or surviving civil partner.

Social security definitions of couple

9.14   Nine types of couple

Legislation prescribes a number of alternative definitions of couple status, depending on whether married/civil partners or not. The gender-mix is now less important though. The Marriage (Same Sex Couples) Act 2013 prescribed changes to many instances in social security law so that from 13 March 2014, references to 'a man and a woman' were replaced by a simpler reference to 'two people'[32]. However, some relevant couple definitions appear to have missed out on this amending process: tax credits law in particular would appear to have remained unchanged, leaving an unsatisfactory level of inconsistency.

---

[32]   Marriage (Same Sex Couples) Act 2013 (Consequential and Contrary Provisions and Scotland) Order 2014 (SI 2014/560).

Social security definitions of couple

	Married or civil partners	*Cohabiting: not married or civil partners*
New rules from 13 March 2014		
New wording: regardless of whether same-sex or opposite-sex	*benefits:* two people who are married to, or civil partners of, each other and are members of the same household[33]	*benefits:* two people who are not married to, or civil partners of, each other but are living together as a married couple[34]
	tax credits: at the time of writing, the tax credits rules have not changed so as to expressly reflect the possibility of same-sex marriage. See below for the position, pending any change.	
Existing rules before 13 March 2014		
Opposite-sex couple	*benefits:* a man and a woman who are married to each other and are members of the same household[35]	*benefits and tax credits:* a man and a woman who are not married to each other but are living together as husband and wife[36]
	tax credits: a man and a woman who are married to each other and are neither separated under a court order nor separated in circumstances in which the separation is likely to be permanent[37]	

---

[33] Marriage (Same Sex Couples) Act 2013 (Consequential and Contrary Provisions and Scotland) Order 2014 (SI 2014/560), Sch 1, para 22(8).

[34] Marriage (Same Sex Couples) Act 2013 (Consequential and Contrary Provisions and Scotland) Order 2014 (SI 2014/560), Sch 1, para 22(8).

[35] SSCBA 1992, s 137(1).

[36] SSCBA 1992, s 137(1).

[37] TCA 2002, s 3(5) and 3(6).

	Married or civil partners	Cohabiting: not married or civil partners
Same-sex couple[38]	*benefits:* two people of the same sex who are civil partners of each other and are members of the same household[39]	*benefits and tax credits:* two people of the same sex who are not civil partners of each other but are living together as if they were civil partners[40] – if, but only if, they would be regarded as living together as husband and wife were they instead two people of the opposite sex[41]
	tax credits: two people of the same sex who are civil partners of each other and are neither separated under a court order nor separated in circumstances in which the separation is likely to be permanent[42]	

9.15   Types of cohabitation in social security law

Traditionally the cohabitation test was whether two people, a man and a woman, were 'living together as husband and wife' (LTAHAW).

From 2004 that expanded to also cover same-sex couples, with 'living together as if civil partners' (LTACP) added to the legislation.

The current wording, effective from 13 March 2014, is '**living together as a married couple**' (LTAMC). Like its predecessors, it can only apply if there is no marriage or civil partnership. For decisions after 12 March 2014, there can be no test of whether two people are 'living together as if civil partners' (LTACP) except in tax credits decisions. Time will tell whether the new concept of *living together as a married couple* produces any different result than the old LTAHAW. It is submitted it is unlikely to be interpreted very differently.

Sexual orientation does not, strictly speaking, play any part. Nor, now, does gender. There should now be no need to focus on whether it is an opposite-sex couple or a same-sex couple, much less whether the parties are heterosexual or homosexual. It does not strictly matter. In the case of one or both partners being transsexual, it is reasonable to assume that the provisions of the Gender Recognition Act 2003 apply, so that a person may legally inhabit their acquired sex only once a gender recognition certificate is in place.

---

[38]   Since 5 December 2005, Civil Partnership Act 2004.
[39]   SSCBA 1992, s 137(1).
[40]   SSCBA 1992, s 137 and s 122(1A).
[41]   SSCBA 1992, s 137(1A) – added by Civil Partnership Act 2004, Sch 24(3), para 46(5).
[42]   TCA 2002, s 3(5) and 3(6).

From 2004 to 2014 the legislation sought (tortuously some might argue) to keep parity of definition as between same-sex and opposite-sex cohabiting couples. Only belatedly did some difference start to emerge in the caselaw as to the norms to be expected in a civil partnership compared to a marriage. Judge Levenson discussed some of the characteristics of civil partnership in *JP v Secretary of State for Work and Pensions (IS)*.[43] But now, for alleged cohabitants, *married couple* is the only comparator, except in tax credit cases.

The rule also presupposes that the relationship is not prohibited, unlawful or criminal.[44] In other words, for example, it cannot be said that somebody under 16 is a member of a couple, or that a relationship between siblings can constitute a couple (however couple-like it is).

9.16   Checklist: are they married or civil partners?

The first step in any case involving couple or single status is to determine whether your client and the alleged partner are married to each other or civil partners of each other:

(a)   if they are married or civil partners, the only test that then applies is whether they are members of the same household (or, for tax credits, whether they are not separated).[45]

(b)   if they are not married or civil partners, then the more complex tests described in this chapter will apply.

This distinction should be borne clearly in mind.

9.17   Applying the 'living together' test if marriage and civil partnership are discounted

In benefits cases, where two people are married or civil partners, and it is decided they share a household, then they are a 'couple'. Where two people are married or civil partners, and it is decided they *do not* share a household, then they are not a 'couple', and cannot be assessed under the LTAMC test, because they are married or are civil partners.

In tax credits cases, this can appear less clear because the criteria for being assessed as a couple for marriages and civil partnerships do not refer to 'household' in the tax credits rules. Consider a former couple, a man and a woman, still married, who consider themselves permanently separated from one another, but who have not (or not yet) moved to different accommodation. They should fall outside the tax credits married couple test in that they are 'a man and a woman who are married to each other' and are 'separated in circumstances in which the separation is likely to be permanent'. If so, they are

---

43   [2014] UKUT 0017 (AAC).

44   DMG, paras 11030-11032 and Appendices to DMG Chapter 11.

45   This is clear in the legislation but made even clearer by Miss Commissioner Fellner in *CIS/2900/1998*, paras 17-18.

home and dry in the quest to be considered single. It is not open to the HMRC to assess them as possibly living together as husband and wife (as the tax credits cohabitation test remains), *because* they are married. LTAHAW does not allow for that.

On the 'legal separation' limb of the tax credits rule concerning marriage and civil partnership, the decision by Judge Wikeley in *DG v Her Majesty's Revenue and Customs (TC)*[46] should be noted for its observation that separation here must be judged in the round on all the evidence available, and there was no absolute requirement of legal documentation.

In other cases, it may be that despite appearances, there never was a marriage. These cases may well permit application of the LTAMC rule instead. Issues can arise as to the validity of a marriage that the parties maintain is genuine. These often concern the validity in the UK of a marriage contracted outside the UK under different national rules. If a purported marriage turns out to be invalid, the couple fall to be assessed under the LTAMC rule as possible cohabitants. In *CIS/11304/1995* Mr Commissioner Goodman ruled on the validity of a marriage contracted by the claimant in the UK under Islamic rules though she was already legally married to another man. The purported marriage was invalid and so the relationship had to be assessed on the basis of the 'living together' rules. Where the validity of a marriage is questioned, it is important to hold the respondent, and the Tribunal, to a logical legal framework, in other words to make sure that it deals with validity first, and only if it finds the marriage unproven goes on to assess LTAMC. Failure to adhere to that sequence had been the error of law committed by the First-tier Tribunal in *FB v Secretary of State for Work and Pensions (IS)*.[47]

What constitutes living together as a married couple?

9.18   General approach

LTAMC is not defined in the legislation, so it is for the DWP or other benefit-paying agency initially to decide whether 'the whole relationship of two people who are not married to each other is comparable to that of a couple who are married to each other'.[48] The courts have been reluctant to impose a fixed view of what LTAHAW (and now LTAMC) comprises: Woolf J, as he then was, made this clear in an early living-together case, *Crake v Supplementary Benefits Commission; Butterworth v Supplementary Benefits Commission*:[49]

> 'I am not suggesting that it is any function of this court to try and put some gloss on the wording of the paragraph, of general application. Indeed, it would be very undesirable for this court to seek to do that.'

---

[46]   [2013] UKUT 0631 (AAC).
[47]   [2011] UKUT 335 (AAC).
[48]   *R(G)3/71*; DMG 11101. ·
[49]   [1982] 1 All ER 498 at 501.

Each case should be assessed on its merits. But there is a structure within which this can usefully be done: the authorities of the last 40 years or so have adumbrated at least two if not three structures for the assessment of 'living together' status. However, they have been equally at pains to warn against a 'checklist' approach, suggesting that there is indeed something intangible, some perhaps almost indefinable characteristic, that will often distinguish two people living together as a married couple from two people living together in some other way. It is possible to trace a strong jurisprudential counterpoint of refusal to approve any absolute test, running alongside a considerable degree of deference to Woolf J's apparent endorsement of a six-factor test; such tension as there is between these two approaches must be understood and factored in to arguments about living together.

In a widow's case, *CP/8001/1995*, Mr Commissioner Howell QC commented that:

> 'the legislation presents adjudication officers and tribunals with one of the most difficult problems of definition there could be, since it involves investigating and analysing the nature of a human relationship between two people and this is inevitably a complex and sensitive thing. An adjudication officer or tribunal faced with such a problem is unlikely to achieve a satisfactory result by simply regarding the task as ticking off items on a checklist, without also standing back and asking itself whether having looked at all the detailed evidence about individual aspects of the claimant's living arrangements in the case before them, the relationship between her and the man she is alleged to be living with can fairly and justly be described in normal parlance as that of two people living together in the manner of husband and wife.'

Mr Commissioner Jacobs, in *CIS/443/1998*, cited Neuberger J in *Re Watson (Deceased)* [1999] 1 FLR 878, at p 883, in the context of the Inheritance (Provision for Family and Dependants) Act 1975:

> 'When considering the question, the court should ask itself whether, in the opinion of a reasonable person with normal perceptions, it could be said that the two people in question were living together as husband and wife: but, when considering that question, one should not ignore the multifarious nature of marital relationships.'

It is submitted then that an unquestioning adherence to either of the two main checklists (see below) is to be avoided. Arguments against couple status can be well-served by a degree of non-compliance with any prescriptive factors.

The Departmental Guidance states some fairly unequivocal principles, helpful insofar as they set the threshold quite high:

> 'To be treated as LTAMC the relationship has to be the same as that of a married couple. Marriage is where two people join together with the intention of sharing the rest of their lives. There is no single template of what the relationship of a

married couple is. It is a stable partnership, not just based on economic dependency but also on emotional support and companionship.'[50]

But the 'no single template' view is very consonant with the key authorities.

The traditional test since *Crake & Butterworth* has been the six key factors or 'admirable signposts' (dealt with below, these comprise: household, stability, sex, children, finances, public acknowledgement) which originally appeared in the Supplementary Benefits Handbook[51] and were later endorsed by Woolf J in *Crake & Butterworth* at p 505. Many practitioners, and not a few tribunals, have been led astray by this endorsement, however, and it cannot be stressed too highly that, much as the six signposts provide a useful framework, they do not tell the whole story.

9.19 Two checklists?

Despite the sensible resistance to a mechanistic checklist approach, the case-law has also been unable to resist imposing structure to the LTAMC test. Two key tests tend to emerge, and practitioners are advised to utilise these where they favour the client's position, and to feel free to move outside the tests when they are unhelpful. It is moreover reassuring to know that the tests are to some extent regarded as interchangeable.[52]

9.20 The 3 factors

The three-part assessment looks at three areas of a relationship:

(a) sexual;

(b) financial; and

(c) general.

In *R(G)3/71* Mr Commissioner Shewan heard a case under the old pre-1977 'cohabitation' rules involving a widow whose alleged partner, her lodger, was admittedly the father of her child and had left his wife to go to live with the claimant. In deciding that this *was* cohabitation, and so disqualified the claimant from her Widowed Mother's Allowance, the Commissioner set out his test as follows:

> 'it is generally accepted that the question whether a woman is cohabiting with a man as his wife, within the meaning of the statute, requires an examination of three main matters:
> (1)   their relationship in relation to sex;
> (2)   their relationship in relation to money; and
> (3)   their general relationship.

---

[50]   DMG 11103.

[51]   Mr Commissioner Edwards-Jones in *R(SB)35/85* thought that Woolf J was using the 1979 revision of this guidance.

[52]   *R(SB)17/81*.

Although all three are as a rule relevant, no single one of them is necessarily conclusive.'

The claimant's case was then analysed according to these factors. It is significant that sex comes first here. Its importance cannot be denied. But even with that structure there is immediately a problem of the subtle shades of distinction available as to what (ie how much sex) amounts to a sexual relationship. On the facts of that case, the alleged couple had had sex once only, resulting in a child. Although registering scepticism about the 'once only' claim, the Commissioner felt obliged to combine the evidence about intercourse with evidence about the subsequent nature of their living together in order for that factor to carry weight against the claimant; held: there *was* cohabitation.

The financial factor was framed very much in terms of distinguishing between the way a husband would support his wife and the commercial nature of the landlady/lodger relationship. The fact that the alleged partner paid the claimant variable amounts of money according to his means pushed this situation closer to a husband-wife relationship – even though to some extent his contributions represented a form of maintenance to his child. Argued differently in more modern terms, the claimant might have suggested that if voluntary child maintenance was involved, that spoke of a separation rather than a cohabitation.

The general relationship factor covers issues like time spent together, mutual assistance with household tasks, shared childcare, shared socialising and intentions for the future. The degree of mutual assistance around the house and the level of social life ('If she could get someone in to look after the children she and S "had a night out"') persuaded the Commissioner that this was akin to the behaviour of a husband rather than a lodger.

The three factors do not in terms address whether there was a shared household, yet the rules then required this for cohabitation. It is somewhat presupposed – here the admitted facts of a landlady/lodger arrangement were rather assumed to fall within the definition of household. It is nowadays still sensible to regard the existence of a household almost as a prerequisite for a living together finding.

9.21 Using the three factors

Naturally, where your client truthfully denies any sexual relationship, that fact should be stressed, along with the primacy of this factor in Commissioner Shewan's judgment and later cases. Financial arrangements which differ in some way from whatever it might be said is the norm in married couples need to be emphasised. The true usefulness of these factors arguably lies in factor number 3, the 'general' relationship, which is so vague in reality that any relevant circumstances can be adduced in support of single status, and yet has been elevated to 'paramount importance'.[53]

---

[53]   By Mr Commissioner Jacobs in *CIS/443/1998*.

9.22   The six signposts

In *Crake v Supplementary Benefits Commission; Butterworth v Supplementary Benefits Commission*[54] Woolf J was referred to the Supplementary Benefits Handbook published by the then DHSS and labelled the guidance 'admirable signposts', creating a presumed doctrine in a move that has dominated – some would say burdened – the assessment of couples ever since. The 'six admirable signposts' are employed so universally as a checklist that it is easy to imagine they constitute the long and short of 'living together' law; they do not. The six factors elaborated by the Handbook were:

(a)   membership of the same household;

(b)   stability;

(c)   financial support;

(d)   sexual relationship;

(e)   children;

(f)   public acknowledgement.

Woolf J felt they could not be faulted. It is submitted that despite caveats against the need to demonstrate systematic compliance with these factors, these are still a very useful and well-understood starting point, provided it is remembered that other factors may well come into play, and that, as with the three-factor test, where the signposts do not favour the facts in your client's case, they can be summarily dropped from the argument.

The departmental attitude to the signposts has since *Crake & Butterworth* been reverential (after all, these started as mere internal guidance and then gained judicial assent). Submissions at tribunals on behalf of the Secretary of State or local authorities still typically frame the matter on the same six-part basis. For that reason alone their contents need to be unpacked and examined for their potential in arguing your client's case.

9.23   Other tests

Mr Commissioner Jacobs in *CIS/443/1998* was not the first authority to doubt the comprehensiveness of the six signposts:

> [The six signposts] 'must be considered, but they must not be considered in isolation from their context. There is more to living together as husband and wife than these cold, observable facts. This is shown by some of the characteristics to be expected of a relationship of husband and wife listed by Lord Justice Waite *in Fitzpatrick v Sterling Housing Association* [1998] 1 FLR 6 at p 19:
> * mutual love;
> * faithfulness;
> * public acknowledgement;
> * sexual relations;
> * shared surname;

---

[54]   [1982] 1 All ER 498.

- children;
- endurance;
- stability;
- interdependence; and
- devotion.

It is only when the external aspects of the relationship are viewed in the context of the more emotional and less tangible side of the relationship that their proper significance can be determined. I believe that this is what the Commissioner meant in CIS/87/1993, para 11 when he said:

> "In my view the 'admirable signposts' place a wholly inadequate emphasis on the significance of the parties' 'general relationship'. Indeed, it is arguable that it is the parties' 'general relationship' that is of paramount importance and that their sexual relationship and their financial relationship are only relevant for the light they throw upon the general relationship."

If this is what the Commissioner had in mind, I respectfully agree. Of course, this does not mean that all of these characteristics must be present and it must be remembered that a couple may be living as husband and wife even though their relationship is unsatisfactory and unhappy.'

Practitioners will see the usefulness of expanding the list along the lines of *Fitzpatrick* if only to deny such factors are present in a given case. Helpfully, the DMG cites the case[55] though observes that not all these factors need to be present for there to be a couple.

It is one of the very few instances in which *love* is mentioned in the case-law. Perhaps that goes to the elusiveness of love, where evidence is concerned – a difficulty implicitly recognised by Mr Commissioner Jacobs in *CIS/443/1998* in which he considered whether the tribunal below should have scrutinised emotions more carefully:

> 'The tribunal did not refer to the emotional side of the relationship. I have considered whether this shows that the tribunal failed to take into account a relevant consideration or applied the wrong principle. There is a limit to which it is possible to explain how a tribunal exercised its judgment to assess the overall significance of a combination of factors. There is a limit to which it is possible for the members themselves to understand the mental processes involved. It is not realistic to expect every single factor to be set out and its contribution to the decision explained. The law recognises this and does not require every process of reasoning to be set out.'

Notwithstanding the Commissioner's generosity around the Tribunal's failure to refer to emotion, it should be stressed here that the emotional dimension may well be exactly that ingredient that is somehow missing in an empirical enquiry, and there is good reason to adduce evidence (most usefully done orally) about such matters.

---

[55] DMG, para 11104.

More recently, the same Commissioner, now Judge Jacobs, has pursued the very same focus on areas outside the six signposts, citing *Fitzpatrick* again in *PP v Basildon District Council (HB)*[56] and defending its relevance despite being a Rent Act case concerning a gay couple, and notwithstanding the outcome in the House of Lords. Developing the theme further, Judge Jacobs also cited *Nutting v Southern Housing Group Ltd*[57] in which, on appeal, the two questions the recorder had posed were endorsed as entirely adequate; they were:

'(b) Is the relationship an emotional one of mutual lifetime commitment rather than simply one of convenience, friendship, companionship or the living together of lovers?

(c) Is the relationship one which has been presented to the outside world openly and unequivocally so that society considers it to be of permanent intent — the words "till death us do part" being apposite?'

Mention of *lifetime commitment* in contrast to the *living together of lovers* would seem to set the test very high for the benefit-paying agencies, usefully for appellants. Judge Jacobs' view in *PP v Basildon* was strongly endorsed soon after by Judge Levenson in *JP v Secretary of State for Work and Pensions (IS)*,[58] a case concerning whether an alleged same-sex couple met the LTACP test. Judge Levenson also cited the Court of Appeal in *Amicus Horizon Ltd v The Estate of Miss Judy Mabbott (Deceased) and Another*,[59] and found that

'denial by a party that there is an emotional relationship in itself severely undermines the notion that there is such a relationship and in my opinion it would require very strong evidence indeed (and more than just disbelieving the claimant or witness) to displace that denial'.

9.24 Using the lists of factors: standing back

In *R(SB)17/81* Mr Commissioner Rice skillfully dovetailed the *R(G)3/71* 'three factors' with the *Crake & Butterworth* 'six signposts' so as to determine that the two tests are not at odds, they do correspond, and are essentially the same criteria. Clearly, the Commissioner suggested, a *household* test is an essential requirement. Also clearly, the tests relating to *financial relationship* and *sexual relationship* correspond precisely. Of the remainder of the 'signposts', *children* goes to both *sexual* and *general relationship* in the Shewan scheme, and *stability* and *public acknowledgement* go to *general relationship*.

More recently the trend in the authorities has been to look outside of the strict criteria, or more accurately to recognise that Woolf J had never intended them to be more than a starting point. Overturning a tribunal decision in which the six signposts had been used, Mr Deputy Commissioner Wikeley judged in *CIS/4156/2006* that the tribunal 'had erred in law by relying too heavily on the

---

56 [2013] UKUT 0505 (AAC).
57 [2005] HLR 25.
58 [2014] UKUT 0017 (AAC).
59 [2012] EWCA Civ 895.

checklist of indicators'; the Deputy Commissioner drew approvingly on the decision by Mr Commissioner Goodman in *CP/8001/1995*:

> 'An adjudication officer or tribunal faced with such a problem is unlikely to achieve a satisfactory result by simply regarding the task as ticking off items on a checklist, without also standing back and asking itself whether having looked at all the detailed evidence about individual aspects of the claimant's living arrangements in the case before them, the relationship between her and the man she is alleged to be living with can fairly and justly be described in normal parlance as that of two people living together in the manner of husband and wife.'

Deputy Commissioner Wikeley essentially agreed, when it was argued before him:

> 'that the relationship between the appellant and Mr W was and is one of mutual support, being more similar to one of brother and sister than husband and wife, and that the tribunal should have looked at the totality of the relationship, rather than using the signposts as a checklist.'

There is no doubt that whichever set of factors is used as a starting point, by the practitioner or the DWP, there is ample authority for going beyond their limits. They should not be regarded as conveying the totality of a relationship. That said, if as is likely the DWP's submission is based on the six signposts, any factual or logical issues contained therein do need to be addressed in submissions for the client. And it is probably unwise to eschew the checklists altogether: note how Mr Commissioner Ward held a tribunal to have been in error of law for its failure to look at either test. In *CIS/2074/2008* he held:

> 'There are two ways by which one can approach the point, but both of them lead to the conclusion that the tribunal erred in law: either, because they failed to consider the issue of whether a sexual relationship existed, thereby failing to consider, as they should have done, a potentially relevant "admirable signpost", or because they failed to apply the test in *R(G)3/71*, at very least in order to determine what significance any sexual aspect might have for the categorisation of the general relationship.'

But it is arguably the omission of potentially relevant points that was at fault, not the mere failure to have regard to the checklist – in other words, a submission that takes into account the right factors will not be penalised for its failure to cite the checklists.

Where one or other of the checklists is deployed in argument, it is equally important to argue, where this assists, that no single factor can be overriding, and in fact it is legitimate to argue that they have equal status, where this suits the client's factual circumstances. On this point however, a proviso follows below in relation to the 'household' factor.

With that firmly in mind, practitioners are advised to adduce evidence, insofar as relevant, on all the following sections.

Members of the same household

9.25   How to approach the question

There is a hierarchy of persuasiveness as to the household factor. In order of the strength of argument they generate, possible scenarios are:

(a)   there is no such person as the alleged partner (this option is passed over here as being one unlikely to produce a realistic challenge by the department);

(b)   there does exist such a person but s/he lives elsewhere: the strongest position in the household argument (see **9.29**);

(c)   the alleged partner does stay over sometimes but still mainly lives elsewhere (see **9.31**);

(d)   the alleged partner lives at the same address but there is no shared household: harder still but not impossible to argue (see **9.33**);

(e)   there is a shared household with the alleged partner: here one must concede defeat on the household factor and move on to alternative supporting factors like the non-spousal purpose of the relationship (see **9.36**).

9.26   What the Handbook says

The Supplementary Benefit Handbook – endorsed in *Crake & Butterworth*, stated:

> '*Members of the same household.* The man must be living in the same household as the woman and will usually have no other home where he normally lives. This implies that the couple live together wholly, apart from absences necessary for the man's employment, visits to relatives etc.'

9.27   Is the household test overriding?

In applying the six signposts or any other chosen combination of factors, the household test *is* largely over-riding in the sense that if they do not share a household (and cannot be deemed to), they probably cannot be a couple. But where there is some kind of a shared household, or this is unclear, then the other factors come into play and will need to be addressed by your client.

That this is a necessary but not sufficient characteristic of the circumstances is confirmed by a number of authorities. In *R(SB)17/81* Mr Commissioner Rice held at para 11 that:

> 'it is axiomatic that the man and woman concerned must be living in the same household. This requirement is not spelt out specifically in Decision *R(G)3/71*, but only, in my judgment, because it is self-evident.'

Lest this be seen as a principle confined to the pre-1977 rules (which *were* more explicit on the point), Mr Commissioner Jacobs confirmed this more recently in *CIS/443/1998* at para 11:

'Many factors have to be considered when determining if parties are living together as husband and wife. Few are capable of being decisive on their own. One is whether the parties live in the same household.

11.1 It is only in the most unusual circumstances that parties who are not living in the same household can be living as husband and wife: see the judgment of Neuberger J in *Re Watson (Deceased)* [1999] 1 FLR 878 at page 883. So, **the fact that parties are not living in the same household is likely to be decisive.** However, temporary absences from the shared accommodation do not necessarily show that the common household has been disbanded: see Neuberger J at pages 882-882 and the decision of the Commissioner in *R(SB)19/85*, paragraph 11.' (author's emphasis)

In *CIS/7249/1999* the Secretary of State appeared to concede that a shared household is a prerequisite:

'the first step is to determine as a separate issue whether the parties are members of the same household. Only if the answer is "yes" can the tribunal go on to consider whether the parties are living together as husband and wife.'

and Miss Deputy Commissioner Ovey, hearing the case, appeared to agree, though with a reservation:

'[W]hile it seems clear that an essential element of any decision that the parties are living together as husband and wife is that that they should be living in the same household, it may not be helpful to describe that as a wholly separate issue. It is not a distinct statutory requirement and is one of the six factors set out in *R(SB)17/81*; [...].

I make [that] point because the submission points towards a completely isolated approach to the question whether the parties are living in the same household, and I am not persuaded that that is correct.'

The necessity of sharing a household was plainly accepted by Judge Williams in *VG v Secretary of State for Work and Pensions (IS)*:[60] that 'there must be a common household' had been emphasised from the start in the *Supplementary Benefits Handbook* even if not in *R(SB)17/81* which endorsed the Handbook. But the language in *R(SB)17/81* had given rise to an issue when it stated the test as being whether the couple were *wholly* living together. Here they were not wholly living together as the partner was prevented from sleeping by one of the children and as he needed his sleep because of his job, he slept elsewhere when working. *Normally* or *ordinarily* might be better qualifiers than *wholly*, thought Judge Williams; it was a question of probabilities.

---

[60] [2012] UKUT 470 (AAC).

So where the client does *not* share a household with the alleged partner it should be strenuously argued – and evidenced – that this is the case and that the issue is conclusive as to the client's single status. If decided in her favour then (ie the finding is that there is no shared household) it ought to be determinative and the other factors should drop away as irrelevant, the case won. However, they must still be addressed, just in case the tribunal or decision-maker consider the rare possibility of a cohabitation finding despite absence of a shared household.

9.28 Does the client share a household?

Unlike other factors, defining 'household' is assisted in cohabitation cases by case-law concerning married couples just as much as by those relating to unmarried couples, because the question bears heavily on married cases. The early social security cases involving marriage rely in turn on family law case-law to a great extent.

The existence of a shared household may or may not be obvious. The legislation does not define 'household': this much was clear to Mr Commissioner Powell when deciding *R(IS)1/99*, in which the issue was whether couples living in residential care homes were capable of being treated as living in the same household. The five joined cases all concerned married couples, but the issue was clear: was there in each case a household? Drawing on the judgments of Mr Commissioner Sanders in both *CIS/671/1992* and *CIS/081/1993*, Commissioner Powell held that a domestic establishment was an 'essential attribute' of a 'household', and that such a domestic establishment must 'involve a group of two or more persons living together as a unit where that group enjoys a reasonable level of independence and self-sufficiency'. Perhaps this gives more guidance where the distinction must be made within the residential care home context of that case than in situations in which the client is arguing that she alone runs her own household and the alleged partner is not part of it.

Notwithstanding housing case-law such as *Crawley Borough Council v Sawyer*,[61] a person cannot be part of two households at the same time: *R(SB)8/85*, confirmed by Mr Commissioner Rice in *CIS/11304/1995*, though in that case the alleged partner did have two households but did not occupy them at the same time (he was occupying one for half the year, the other for the other half-year).

In relation to matrimonial cases, Sachs LJ, giving judgment for the Court of Appeal in *Santos v Santos*,[62] distinguished between 'house' relating to 'something physical', and 'household', 'a word which essentially refers to people held together by a particular kind of tie', noting too that 'household' 'connotes being in the same family: *English v Western* [1940] 2 KB 156'.

---

[61] (1988) 20 HLR 98.
[62] [1972] 2 WLR 889, [1972] Fam 247.

In *Re Dix*[63] Ward LJ approved the approach taken by the Court of Appeal in *Santos v Santos*:

> 'The relevant word is "household" not "house", and "household" bears the meaning given to it by Sachs LJ. Thus they will be in the same household if they are tied by their relationship. The tie of that relationship may be made manifest by various elements, not simply their living under the same roof, but the public and private acknowledgment of their mutual society, and the mutual protection and support that binds them together. In former days one would possibly say one should look at the whole consortium vitae. For present purposes it is sufficient to ask whether either has demonstrated a settled acceptance or recognition that the relationship is in truth at an end. If the circumstances show an irretrievable breakdown of the relationship, then they no longer live in the same household and the Act is not satisfied. If, however, the interruption is transitory, serving as a pause for reflection about the future of a relationship going through difficult times but still recognised to be subsisting, then they will be living in the same household and the claim will lie. Just as the arrangements for maintenance may fluctuate, using Stephenson LJ's expression in *Jelley v Illiffe* [1981] Fam 128, 136, [...] so the steadfastness of a commitment to live together may wax and wane, but so long as it is not extinguished, it survives. These notions are succinctly encapsulated in the judge's test, which was to ask whether the relationship was merely suspended, and I see no error in his approach.'

The particular kind of tie needs to be specified by the party alleging cohabitation then, and if it is not, the client must highlight the absence of this part of the department's argument. Alternatively, s/he will need to rebut such 'ties' as are contended for by the department, or show that such an arrangement is temporary only.

9.29　The alleged partner lives at a different address

The strongest arguments against the existence of a shared household usually show that the alleged partner lives altogether elsewhere. Living together must on the whole mean that neither alleged partner has some household elsewhere at the same time where s/he normally lives. If it can be shown that your client's alleged partner has another address where he lives, that will often make the most conclusive case for the client's single status. Your client's ignorance of his address will undermine her case.

9.30　Checklist: points to adduce on alternative address

Evidence will be needed as to the reality of his living at the other address, and should be adduced in regard to whether he:

(a)　can provide an actual address;

(b)　pays rent or a mortgage on the other property (produce documentary evidence eg tenancy agreement) or is otherwise allowed to live there (eg as a non-dependent: if this applies, is the main householder there subject to

---

[63]　[2004] EWCA Civ 139, [2004] 1 WLR 1399.

non-dependent deductions from their Housing Benefit, Council Tax reduction scheme or benefit for mortgage interest?);

(c) is liable for council tax there as a resident (council tax bills will assist);

(d) receives mail there (best if examples can be produced);

(e) is based there as far as other authorities or agencies are concerned (utility bills are always useful evidence);

(f) spends time there;

(g) sleeps there (mostly);

(h) eats there;

(i) does domestic tasks like washing clothes there;

(j) is regarded as living there by friends and relatives;

(k) knows his neighbours there;

(l) receives other friends, family, relations, his children, as guests there;

(m) keeps some, most or all of his belongings there.[64]

There will be other factors that practitioners can add in as circumstances permit. An inability to produce such evidence is likely seriously to damage your client's credibility. But documents may not suffice. The tribunal below in *CIS/3655/2007* had been unconvinced that documents merely showing another address for the alleged partner (at which he was registered in respect of various agencies) amounted to proof that he was living there. Though it is not the main ratio of the case, Mr Commissioner Jacobs held that it was rational for the tribunal to have found the documents did not prove where he was living. That can cut both ways though; documents appearing to place the alleged partner clearly as living at your client's address do not inevitably establish him as living there.

9.31 The alleged partner stays over but it is not a shared household

There is a commonly-held belief in the existence of a 'three-night rule' or sometimes, a 'four-night rule'. These 'rules', though often propagated by claimants, advisers and departmental officials alike, do not actually exist, however. The gist of the belief is that if an alleged partner stays overnight with the claimant for so many nights a week, this is taken to prove the sharing of a household and hence a living together arrangement; by the same token a client will often assume that if he stays with her only two or three nights a week she is exempt from the living together rule. Though it contains a grain of truth, it must be resisted as any kind of satisfactory test: staying over may be one pertinent factor but it does not of itself prove or disprove a shared household, far less a cohabitation arrangement.

---

[64] Mr Commissioner Ward urged that the tribunal below in *CIS/2074/2008* should have asked about whether the claimant's daughter-in-law noticed 'evidence of Mr Tripp's belongings' when she visited her mother-in-law.

Evidence on this is sometimes sourced from one of the benefit fraud hotlines, and if factually wrong it must of course be corrected.

9.32 Checklist on staying over

If it is true that the alleged partner sometimes stays, the arguments must be that:

(a) the alleged partner's other address is his/her main residence;

(b) the staying-over pattern is variable;

(c) the purpose of the stay-over is:
 (i) social (TV, drinking, playing cards);
 (ii) not connected with sex;
 (iii) connected with childcare in respect of a mutual (or not) child;
 (iv) to do with support for a friend;
 (v) for company;
 (vi) for work reasons; or
 (vii) to provide overnight care in respect of a person with disabilities or illness.

(d) even if the argument as to main residence is lost (ie it is found that the number of times of staying over amounts to living there and therefore that the household is shared): that the sharing of the household is not conclusive as to cohabitation – ie the other factors come into play so as to eclipse the importance of shared household;

(e) apply *Re Dix* and *Santos v Santos*.

Some of the arguments in this list also go to the question of whether any agreed relationship actually has a different purpose from that of living like spouses or civil partners: see **9.37**.

Of some concern is Miss Commissioner Fellner's logic in *CIS/2900/1998* (a marriage case admittedly) in which the argument that the parties were not members of the same household foundered not least on the basis that the appellant received the highest rate of Disability Living Allowance Care Component; the onerous day- and night-time care conditions for this entitlement 'did not support the assertion of separate households' in the Commissioner's view. Note that this case concerned two people who were married to each other, who had separated and then the wife moved back in order to fulfil a carer role in respect of the husband. Disproving a household was all-important therefore. It is submitted that on the same facts in an unmarried case, such a claimant would have had some prospect of success.

The self-evident sexual overtones of the three-nights/four-nights allegation cannot be ignored: any such insinuation must be confronted head-on, and the department asked for a full submission on what precisely is being alleged, and the matter resisted, even in the face of scepticism, if untrue: see below at **9.41**.

They live at the same address but in separate households under the same roof

9.33 Separating the households out

The facts may be that the alleged partners do indeed live at the same address but maintain separate households under one roof. The issue is still more likely to arise outside of cohabitation territory – ie in cases where the parties are still married or civil partners, are about to divorce or dissolve the civil partnership, still live under the same roof, but are arguing they no longer share the same household. But it can still be important in alleged cohabitation cases; sometimes this will be where the alleged partners *were* married or civil partners but are now divorced or the civil partnership dissolved. Or they may have had an admitted cohabitation relationship, as in *CIS/443/1998*, which they say is now at an end, though they are still in the same dwelling. The more general arguments as to household tend to be similar, whether marriage or civil partnership is/was involved or not.

9.34 Checklist for 'same dwelling, separate household' cases

The case is stronger if your client and the alleged partner:

(a) have separate food storage areas in the kitchen, including the refrigerator;

(b) do not eat together, share meals (even at separate times) or make drinks for each other;

(c) spend leisure time in different rooms of the house;

(d) do not share family activities like outings, watching television, DIY or gardening;

(e) undertake childcare separately;

(f) separate their finances as much as possible (this is difficult given that your client is presumably on such a low income that their successful benefit claim is imperative);

(g) discontinue any sexual relationship;

(h) agree that the situation will not stay the same indefinitely: there is an intention that one of them will leave – whether before or after actual divorce/dissolution.

Sharing such things is not necessarily fatal to an argument that there is no shared household, however. In *CIS/72/1994*, as cited by Miss Commissioner Fellner in *CIS/2900/1998*:

> 'the only thing the wife was still doing for the husband was wash his shirts (in order to stop him running up electricity bills by using the washing machine for one shirt). He did his own catering, took the rest of his washing home to his mother, and sometimes at least contributed nothing to household expenses. The wife was doing everything she could to obtain separate accommodation for herself and the children.'

Such separation of households will often be investigated by a DWP visiting officer, or may be asked about in writing. If there is a home visit from the DWP, it can be important to seek the former spouse's/former civil partner's/former cohabitee's co-operation in corroborating these facts, should s/he be at home at the time of the visit. Alternatively, if s/he is likely to be unco-operative, the visit should be arranged when s/he is out. Unhelpfully for the appellant in *CTC/3864/2004* her alleged partner, in his evidence as to contributions to childcare, clearly credited himself with more involvement than did her version of the arrangements.

DWP Guidance (DMG) may assist here. One example at para 22016 of the Guidance may prove to be a useful template:

> 'Andy and Aniza are estranged and continue to live in the same house. They do not financially support each other or share domestic and social activities. One partner is reluctant to leave, until a satisfactory financial agreement has been reached with the other partner. **They each have separate households.**' (author's emphasis)

Paragraph 11054 of the DMG enjoins decision-makers to recognise that:

> 'People living in one dwelling are not necessarily living together in the same household. Examples are:
> (a) lodgers or students who necessarily share a single gas/electricity supply etc. and may have an arrangement to share costs for items such as food and cleaning materials; **or**
> (b) two people who are married to each other or who are a civil partner of each other who separate and refuse to leave the home'.

It is instructive to note the types of scenarios which, in married couple cases, have produced a finding that there was **no** shared household:
(a) living separately under the same roof but the husband financially maintaining the wife;
(b) exclusive occupation of separate rooms within the same dwelling;[65]
(c) sharing a room but living separately in other respects;[66]
(d) husband and wife with dementia sharing a room in a residential care home but unaware that they were married;[67]
(e) husband and wife sharing a double room in residential care accommodation, taking main meals in the dining room, giving mutual assistance with self-care but not living together as an independent and self-sufficient unit which would constitute a domestic establishment;[68]
(f) a 30-year attachment living together for companionship but without a sexual relationship.[69]

---

[65] *R(SB)4/83.*
[66] *CSB/463/1986.*
[67] *CIS/671/1992.*
[68] *R(IS)1/99.*
[69] *Re Watson (deceased).*

These examples may be invoked in cohabitation cases, bearing in mind that factual similarities are not binding, much less a guarantee of a similar outcome. The existence of two households under the same roof was well illustrated in *R(SB)4/83* in which the 67-year-old widower claimant was in poor health with relapsing acute bronchitis, and let out two rooms in his council house to a Mrs P partly with the purpose of her attending to him in emergencies. Mr Commissioner Mitchell took the view that

> 'a person who has, and lives in, his own separate home cannot reasonably be regarded as being a member of someone else's household. In the case under appeal, Mrs P clearly had a home of her own. She had the exclusive occupation of two rooms, which she herself had furnished. She bore her own costs in respect of lighting and heating. She bought and cooked her own food and provided for herself such other household goods as she required. **All this is quite incompatible with her having been, at the same time, a member of the claimant's household.**'
> (author's emphasis)

9.35   Sharing a degree of family life – but perhaps not as a couple

Such advice is borne out by the cautionary story in *CIS/443/1998*, in which the facts bear some detailed scrutiny in this regard.

Although the alleged partners had never been married, they had had a relationship between 1969 and 1979, during which time they had a daughter. They remained living in the same house, and had done so continuously since 1979. He had claimed Income Support in 1988 and Housing Benefit in 1995, stating on both claims that she was his partner. Their latest home was rented in joint names; they had separate bedrooms and had not had a sexual relationship since 1979. The furniture was owned by both. They ate together if they were both at home. The claimant did the decorating, small repairs and the gardening. She did the laundry and the shopping, although he sometimes came to the shops with her. They shared the housework, cooking and washing up. She paid for the food and household items, and he paid the other bills. He also said that he bought his own toiletries. Although he enjoyed painting, they watched television together and went together for a drink or to visit relatives. He said that they shared accommodation for convenience and because it was cheaper than living separately. She wished to retain her independence and her separate finances, which was one reason why their relationship had foundered in 1979.

The tribunal had found they were living together as husband and wife, and the claimant appealed.

Confining his judgment carefully to his reviewing jurisdiction (had the tribunal below erred in law in the way it undertook a balancing exercise as to the various factors?), Mr Commissioner Jacobs held in his determination that there had been no error of law; the facts which were largely agreed were capable of a living-together conclusion, and the tribunal had been entitled to reach this view. As to the absence of sex since 1979, see below under that section.

By contrast, in tax credits case *CTC/3864/2004* Mr Commissioner Mark agreed that the tribunal had erred in law in finding that the appellant was a member of a couple, and remitted the case for a fresh hearing, in the following circumstances:

The appellant and the alleged partner had also been living in the same household, since 1993, they had two children and both helped to run the household and look after the children. The evidence tended to show that they led separate lives even though, as father of the children, he had a relationship with them. There was evidence to support their leading separate lives, eg the claimant stated that he washed his own clothes, bought and cooked his own food (save for the occasional Sunday roast). There was no evidence that they represented themselves to other people as husband and wife, or that they socialized together, or had a family life together.

9.36   What if a shared household is proved though?

The argument will then shift to the other factors (which it does not where the parties are married or civil partners). Evidence on the other factors should be adduced not only to prove them in their own right, but as a means of revisiting the household issue so as to instil in the tribunal's or decision-maker's mind the possibility that the strength of the household finding at least requires some re-evaluation. As Mr Commissioner Edwards-Jones in *R(SB)35/85* observed:

> 'the existence of a common household – the fact as to which was not in dispute – was only one ingredient in the complex evaluation properly falling to be made.'

It is submitted that even a clear finding that there is a household may still disclose shades of meaning such that its importance as a factor supporting a couple finding is diminished. The closing comments of Mr Commissioner Edwards-Jones also help, where he exhorted (in vain as it happened) the then DHSS to reflect in its guidance the gist of Woolf J's view in *Crake & Butterworth* 'as to a couple "living together" being rather a starting point than a finishing point in the required evaluation, and as to what inquiry lay next'.

Miss Deputy Commissioner Ovey's decision in *CIS/7249/1999* provided an interesting matrix of facts in which the claimant lived with her former husband in his home. Since they were divorced, fortunately the full panoply of cohabitation criteria (here largely based around the 'six signposts') fell to be applied. The Deputy Commissioner found that there had been inadequate findings and remitted the case for a fresh hearing. The known facts in the case are instructive though, insofar as they illustrate the evolution of a relationship from marriage to something rather different over some 30 years. On these facts however, there *was* a household so the issue shifted to whether other factors would disclose a living together relationship.

More recently the point was freshly endorsed (if that were necessary) by Deputy Commissioner Green in *CTC/3864/2004* who held:

'The main reason given by the tribunal for reaching th[e] conclusion [that on the facts of the case there was a couple] was that they had been living in the same household since 1993, they had two children and both helped to run the household and look after the children. The tribunal have erred in seeming to equate living in the same household as living as husband and wife. Living in the same household is obviously a significant factor, but there were other matters that the tribunal should have considered.'

Underlying this finding, like those in many other judgments, then, is the salient question of whether, where two people do share a household, they do so for some reason other than pursuing a life together as if spouses or civil partners. This is discussed next.

9.37 Alternative reasons for living together

If the existence of a household shared by both the claimant and the alleged partner is proved, or indeed conceded, your argument must shift first to whether there can be an alternative explanation for the sharing of the household, preferably one that overrides any hint of a spousal or civil partnership-like couple arrangement.

9.38 Disability and care – and some general principles

Woolf J provided a useful principle in *Crake & Butterworth* before deciding favourably the case of Mrs Butterworth, a single parent with some disability following a car accident who, whilst divorcing her husband, had taken in a Mr Jones to perform household tasks and assist with looking after her:

'It is not sufficient, to establish that a man and woman are living together as husband and wife, to show that they are living in the same household. If there is the fact that they are living together in the same household, that may raise the question whether they are living together as man and wife, and, indeed, in many circumstances may be strong evidence to show that they are living together as man and wife; but in each case *it is necessary to go on and ascertain, in so far as this is possible, the manner in which and why they are living together in the same household*; and if there is an explanation which indicates that they are not there because they are living together as man and wife, then they [...] are not two persons living together as husband and wife.' (author's emphasis)

It is impossible to categorise all the explanations which would result in [a finding that they are not cohabiting] but it seems to me that if the reason for someone living in the same household as another person is to look after that person because they are ill or incapable for some other reason of managing their affairs, then that in ordinary parlance is not what one would describe as living together as husband and wife [...].

Quite clearly if that were not the position, housekeepers performing no other functions, other than those of housekeepers, could be regarded as falling within this paragraph. A couple who live together because of some blood relationship could be treated as falling within this paragraph. In my view it was not the intention of Parliament that they should.'

Practitioners are encouraged to ask clients in detail about the caring responsibilities taken on by co-householders alleged to be couples.

The approach was roundly endorsed by Mr Commissioner Edwards-Jones in *R(SB)35/85*, whose logic also went to the issue of sharing a household as a matter of expediency for a person with disabilities. In this case Mr W the alleged partner suffered from a war injury causing him pain, depression and memory lapses, and affecting his co-ordination; he went to live with the appellant and her brother as an admitted member of their household. Meals were taken together by both alleged partners; the appellant and her brother provided Mr W with help and care. The tribunal below had decided that there was cohabitation, because they were living in the same household and it was a stable and caring relationship, adding reassuringly, 'No moral judgment is being made and the tribunal hope the relationship and caring will continue'. The *moral judgment* point was well-made, if it meant they had not found that there was a sexual relationship, but ultimately the relationship was a bit too asexual for Commissioner Edwards-Jones to confirm the tribunal's conclusion as to couple status: in allowing the appeal he noted that:

> 'What one can [...] conclude with confidence is that such element of care as there was, together with elements of companionship and mutual convenience, explain why the claimant and Mr W were living together in the same household and in the context of the circumstances of the case as a whole constitute "an explanation which indicates that they are not there because they are living together as man [sic] and wife". And that, to my mind, is as far as one has to go.'

'As far as one has to go' creates a fairly untraversable line in the sand: once the non-cohabitation 'explanation' for the client's household is established, the case is won. If not, then at the very least the burden would appear to shift.

In these early cases it is hard to avoid an underlying presumption (useful to those claimants) that disability and a sexual relationship had to be mutually exclusive, and it is submitted that this partly explains the dichotomy between the favourable treatment in cases such as *Robson* (see below), *Butterworth* and *R(SB)35/85* compared with the tougher line taken in the sexually more active cases of *R(G)3/71* and the bed-sharing pair of students in *R(SB)17/81*. Underlying *that* assumption was the understated acknowledgment that in defining a 'couple', sex matters: more of which below. In practice the absence of a sexual relationship does need to be made clear; practitioners should be more careful nowadays, in the author's view, to underline the facts in scenarios where the carer relationship is a primary, but not the sole, characteristic of the relationship. Perhaps evidence such as that concerning the locks on the bedroom doors of both Mrs Butterworth and the gentleman alleged to be her partner will be decidedly helpful.

Robson v Secretary of State for Social Services[70] held to the pattern, if such it be, on facts also involving bereaved and disabled claimants:

> 'In November 1979 the appellant, a widow aged 45, and Mr Williams, a widower aged 65, moved into a two-bedroomed council flat. They were both severely disabled and each required the use of a wheelchair and invalid car. They had been long-standing friends before the deaths of their respective spouses but there had never been any kind of sexual relationship between them. Although they were free to marry each other they had no intention of doing so.'

And:

> 'It is not alleged that they are now sharing a bedroom or ever have been.'

Allowing the appeal and remitting for a fresh hearing, Webster J gave the new tribunal a strong steer:

> 'There is not, and never has been, any sort of sexual relationship; they moved into the same house, on the face of it, because they were advised so to do by a social worker for the purpose of sharing, and therefore reducing, their expenditure; they are both free to marry and have not done so; there is no suggestion that they either regarded themselves as husband and wife or that they have been regarded or treated as husband and wife; and, most importantly, they are both very severely handicapped, a fact that provides a wholly understandable motive for their wishing to live together other than as husband and wife.'

The references to intention, motive and purpose are issues to which this chapter returns below at **9.40**.

Can receipt of a disability benefit reinforce *caring* as the main reason for sharing a household so as to displace the living-together as husband and wife reason? It is submitted that in theory it could. But the limited treatment of the matter in the case-law is not that encouraging. The fact that the claimant in *CIS/087/1993*[71] received only the lowest rate of Disability Living Allowance Care Component seems to have caused Mr Commissioner Rowland to doubt the primacy of a carer/patient relationship, though in the context of a dearth of findings on sex, which might have been determinative in the re-hearing that he ordered. And Miss Commissioner Fellner's take on the receipt of highest rate DLA Care Component in *CIS/2900/1998* has already been cited above at **9.32**; it merely added weight to a shared household finding in her view (in a marriage case, however).

9.39 Other reasons for living together in the same household

The cases overall (including some married couple cases) disclose plenty of engaging obiter comment on, or just examples of, scenarios which it is

---

[70] (1982) 3 FLR 232.
[71] Also reported as *Re J (income support: cohabitation)* [1995] 1 FLR 660.

sometimes suggested Parliament could not possibly have intended to catch in the living-together net. Though not amounting to binding authority, useful examples include:

(a) saving money;[72]

(b) housekeeper;[73]

(c) lodger and landlady;

(d) patient and carer;[74]

(e) attending to a person in case of emergency connected with acute bronchitic attacks;[75]

(f) companionship – the presence of another human being in an otherwise lonely establishment;[76]

(g) elderly widow and elderly widower choosing for companionship in old age to live together, pool resources and care for each other;[77]

(h) circumstances akin to a brother and sister who happen to live together in a close and affectionate relationship;[78]

(i) mutual support;[79]

(j) grown-up students sharing a household and living expenses;[80]

(k) adult brothers and sisters living together;

(l) retired people living as friends;

(m) living with an 'old family friend'[81]

(n) living together prior to marriage and prohibited from having pre-marital sexual relationship by religious beliefs;[82]

(o) convenience and absence of other resources;[83]

(p) in order to comply with a curfew order.[84]

The assessment exercise of whether Parliament can have intended such-and-such a case to be caught by cohabitation rules is admittedly a risky one, but perhaps it translates usefully into a criterion for testing the *reasonableness* of deciding that a given pair of people are a couple on a par with a married couple or a civil partnership.

Practitioners are strongly advised to consider very carefully the evidential issues that arise in such claims. In the absence of an intrusive degree of evidence,

---

72 *Robson.*

73 *Crake & Butterworth.*

74 *CIS/087/1993.*

75 *R(SB)4/83.*

76 *R(G)3/81.*

77 *R(SB)35/85.*

78 *CP/8001/1995.*

79 *CIS/4156/2006.*

80 *CP/8001/1995.*

81 *CIS/2599/2002.*

82 *CSB/150/1985.*

83 *CIS/7249/1999.*

84 *CIS/1243/2007.*

claimants alleged to be members of a couple will be hard-pressed to show that the 'mutual support' they claim as the sole basis of the relationship is no more than that. And yet again, these issues remind us that what seems to matter more than other indicators (even if this is often disclosed only in the authorities' subtext), is sex.

9.40 Future plans, intention, motive and purpose: why living together?

Clients may find the question 'why do you live together?' strange and unnatural. But it is a question worth asking them. The replies may disclose a 'purpose' that is somewhere outside the sphere of why two people get married or enter a civil partnership, and if so that is a useful building block in contending for 'single status'.

To some extent this notion overlaps with alternative reasons for living together, discussed above at **9.37**. But it may be that a less tangible purpose exists in the relationship that, whilst hard to specify or define, is enough to displace a cohabitation finding.

Mr Commissioner Rowland in *CIS/087/93* equated the 'general aspects' of a relationship with *why* the parties live together:

'14. In any event, I accept the submissions of both the claimant and Mr Connolly [for the department] to the effect that the tribunal have erred in failing to record adequate findings in respect of the general relationship between the claimant and Mrs B. They should consider why the parties are living together.'

The question of *why* two people live together was explored in more depth by Mr Deputy Commissioner Wikeley, drawing on principles in *Robson v Secretary of State for Social Services*; in *CIS/4156/2006* the Deputy Commissioner held that:

'[The tribunal] failed adequately to address the more fundamental question identified by Mr Commissioner Howell QC in *CP/8001/1995*. That question is this – why were the two parties living together?

In *Robson* Webster J observed that:

"usually the intention of the parties is either unascertainable, or, if ascertainable, is not to be regarded as reliable. But if it is established to the satisfaction of the tribunal that the two persons concerned did not intend to live together as husband and wife and still do not intend to do so, in my judgment it would be a very strong case indeed sufficient to justify a decision that they are, or ought to be treated as if they are, husband and wife" (at p 236).

In my judgment the tribunal in this case failed to deal with the question of the parties' intentions. This was because the appellant's evidence as to the circumstances in which she and Mr W came to share the same house again was not adequately dealt with by the tribunal. The tribunal should have examined those circumstances more closely, and indeed whether matters had changed at all during the period since 1997.'

The Deputy Commissioner thus regarded the question *why* as leading inexorably to an inquiry about *intention*, and though they are not the same thing, practitioners should address both. Any evidence as to intentions may be important, though it must be said that a relationship in which a settled status quo obtains may not disclose any intention: it just subsists as it is.

But Webster J had observed in *Robson* that intention is usually either unascertainable or unreliable. Evidence is often to be deduced from the observable facts in any case. Conduct matters insofar as it throws light on intention: per Mr Commissioner Rice in *R(G)3/81*, 'regard should be paid to the conduct of the people concerned since their intention cannot be ascertained without regard to that'.

It is submitted nevertheless that intention *can* also be ascertained by hearing the clients' evidence. Adducing their own statements as to intention will make a difference.

Lack of intention (of taking the relationship further for example), however, may assist the argument, where it can be substantiated somehow: it was indeed a salient factor in *R(G)3/81*. The appellant was a widow who had moved in with a man who provided her with free accommodation in return for her services as a housekeeper; she paid only a £5 per week contribution to the bills; they did not have a sexual relationship. Mr Commissioner Rice, allowing the appeal, found both parties were:

> 'at pains to point out that the relationship was totally different from that which they had previously enjoyed with their respected [sic] spouses, and they certainly had no intention of marrying, nor did they entertain any serious thought about it.'

And the disabled widow in *Robson* also had no intention of marrying.

Perhaps 35 years ago the lack of intention to marry carried more weight than in 2015; but even then this feature did not assist another appellant whose case, *R(SB)17/81*, was determined by the same Commissioner the following day. This concerned two students at Sheffield University who had started living in a one-bedroom flat but returned to their parents during vacations, the arrangement continuing for a time after they completed their degrees. The Commissioner was not persuaded by the agreed lack of marital intention; disallowing the appeal, he held:

> 'In particular, the fact that they did not intend to marry – and I was told this was a feature of many student relationships of the kind under consideration – does not mean that they did not intend to live together as though they were married.'

It is not clear whether intentionality here relates to the future, or rather to what the intentions had been upon starting to share a household. It is submitted that the ambiguity persists to this day, though Deputy Commissioner Wikeley in *CIS/4156/2006* saw they were not identical and implied that both matter, in accordance with Webster J in *Robson*.

Practitioners are advised to address the intentions the client and the alleged partner had at the beginning of the relationship, at the beginning of the sharing of a household, and as to the future. A clear commitment to moving out and living separately will assist in proving single status. That the parties, on starting to share a household, had made some decision that they would live together as a couple, like the Sheffield students, will damage their case.

The client and alleged partner may be wholly without conscious – or any – motives. That itself should be plausible – people do drift into and out of relationships – and it may be useful to adduce their oral evidence that this is the case as a way of heading off the imputation of a marital-type intention. A client's visible bewilderment at the question '*why* are you living in the same household?' need not damage the case at all.

Intention is *not* the same as why the parties share a household, and even once a clear view of intention is formed, the question *why* may still linger. A well-worded statement from the appellant, and perhaps the alleged partner too, may convince a Tribunal Judge that the purpose of living together makes your client's relationship unlike a married couple or civil partners.

Sexual relationship

9.41   Sex does matter – but is it a determinative factor?

Ever since Mr Commissioner Shewan boldly placed sex at number one of his three-part list of factors in *R(G)3/71*, one jurisprudential faultline has been clear: between the obvious and undeniable fact that sex is a hugely important determinant of couple status in our society, and the equally powerful inhibition as to enquiring too deeply – some of the latter being mere unfounded reserve, but there being also a justified disquiet about state bureaucracies knowing what goes on between adults in the privacy of their bedroom (or elsewhere).

DWP sensitivity to accusations of intrusiveness has led to decision-makers being reluctant to even ask about this. Where your client does not have a sexual relationship with the alleged partner (and especially if s/he never has had) then this information should be volunteered, and must go into the whole equation.

Sex matters: as Miss Deputy Commissioner Ovey observed in *CIS/7249/1999*:

> 'Although the nature of the relationship between husband and wife will differ widely according to the enormous variety of circumstances in which married couples live, it seems to me undoubtedly the case that as a matter of general usage

the expression "living together as husband and wife" is used when the meaning intended is that the relationship between the parties extends to a sexual relationship, and that the general expectation is that a significant element of the relationship between a married couple will be the sexual relationship.'

9.42   What kind of sex?

It had been argued that sex was so determinative that the test should be applied first, and that only then and if there was a sexual relationship should the inquiry turn to the other five 'admirable signposts'. Miss Deputy Commissioner Ovey resisted this approach, noting that sex is not so wholly determinative as all that, and that in any case there was a need to be more nuanced about sex than to bluntly determine its existence or otherwise: the question that had to follow, if there was a sexual relationship, was whether:

> 'the sexual relationship [was] one of a committed, faithful nature such as might be thought to be traditionally expected of married couples (as may be inferred from the continued status of adultery as a fact evidencing the irretrievable breakdown of a marriage), or was it of a more casual kind, in which the parties took advantage from time to time of the opportunities which their common household offered?'

Despite the Deputy Commissioner's reservations about the delicacy of investigating this detail, she appeared, obiter, to expand the possibility that a sexual relationship of a casual kind need not automatically result in a couple finding.

Sex, then, is not determinative as such. The existence or otherwise of a sexual relationship, important though it is to the couple concept, has never been absolutely conclusive, and it should remain open to alleged partners to argue that despite occasional sex they are not a couple.

9.43   What the Handbook says

The Supplementary Benefits Handbook endorsed in *Crake & Butterworth* stated:

> '*Sexual Relationship.* A sexual relationship is a normal and important part of a marriage and therefore of living together as husband and wife. But its absence does not necessarily prove that a couple are not living as husband and wife, nor does its presence prove that they are. The Commission's officers are instructed not to question claimants upon the physical aspect of their relationship, though claimants may choose to make statements about it.'

The wisdom of departmental 'don't ask' policy in this respect has been called into question more than once, but it appears to remain in force. Whilst that hampers the tribunal's full fact-finding exercise, it is valuable for the claimant in one sense, in that it is hard for the department to argue for the existence of a sexual relationship as they will usually have no evidence, unless the claimant or the alleged partner volunteer this; moreover it is always open to the claimant to give oral evidence (if true) that there is no sexual relationship.

The judicial approach to the policy is discussed below; there is little mileage in practitioners seeking to challenge its lawfulness or arguing that it invalidates an adverse decision because it is irrational. Instead, focus should be placed on the low evidential weight of any departmental submission that relies on inference (eg 'They admit to sharing a bed') or guesswork.

9.44 The need for enquiry about sex

Mr Commissioner Shewan may have sought to avoid too much detail when he said in *R(G)3/71*:

> 'But there is no need to speculate on the extent to which intercourse took place. The fact that there was sexual intercourse [inter alia] goes a very long way, in my view, to establishing "cohabitation" within the meaning of the Act.'

Enquiring as to 'the extent to which intercourse took place' might now be considered appropriate, if not a duty. Repeated Commissioners have lamented the lacuna in the evidence that results from the 'don't ask' policy.

Most notably in *CIS/087/1993* Mr Commissioner Rowland expressed disapproval, and noted that the consequence might be tribunals paying more attention to sex in their questioning:

> 'I asked Mr Connolly how, if, as he accepted, the parties' relationship as to sex was an important consideration when determining whether they were living together as husband and wife, those charged with investigating the facts could properly be instructed not to ask about the physical aspects of the relationship. Mr Connolly said that a policy decision had been taken although he conceded that the instruction was, to use his words, "detrimental to the administration of the law". **In my view, the instruction is inappropriate in an inquisitorial system** and, where relevant – information is not volunteered, questions may have to be asked by the Department's officers and, on appeal, by tribunals.' (author's emphasis)

Eight years later the same Commissioner was lamenting in *CIS/2599/2002* how his words had gone unheeded:

> '3. On granting leave in the present case, I observed that the documents in this case showed that the instruction was still in force and that the evidence that the claimant and her friend had separate bedrooms seemed to have been regarded as irrelevant. I also asked whether, on the facts relied upon by the Secretary of State, there was anything that suggested that the claimant and her friend were living together as husband and wife, rather than just living together in the same household.

4. In an otherwise very full and helpful response, the Secretary of State's representative has skirted round the question of the instruction not to ask a claimant whether he or she has ever had a sexual relationship with a suspected partner.'

Like the DWP decision-maker, the tribunal had not addressed:

'the question whether the claimant had ever had any sexual relationship with the man in whose house she was living and whether, if not, there was any reason to regard the claimant and her friend as living together as husband and wife rather than as friends.'

Mr Commissioner Jacobs was still noting the avoidance of the topic by 2007, stating in *CIS/3655/2007*:

'Other than reciting that the [sex] factor formed one of the "admirable signposts", the tribunal avoided the topic. Even without asking questions or information being volunteered, there was material known to it (such as the categorisation of the relationship as "common law" on the finance application form) from which the tribunal might or might not have seen fit to draw inferences on this point, but it did not appear to have considered the topic.'

Mr Commissioner Ward's subtly different take on the issue was expressed in *CIS/2074/2008* [2008] UKUT 8 (AAC):

'[The new tribunal's enquiry] will include a need to address by questioning and inference from other known facts the question of whether there is or has been a sexual relationship. Such questioning generally need not be unduly intrusive and should as a minimum give Mrs Jackson the chance to indicate whether she has never had a sexual relationship with Mr Tripp.'

The Commissioner considered the necessity or otherwise of asking those questions:

'In *CIS/2599/2002* Mr Commissioner Rowland stated that questions "may" have to be asked not that they "must" be asked. I do not regard this as a point of substance. In my view, the wording is concerned with ensuring that a particular "admirable signpost" could be addressed. It would not have been appropriate to lay down a hard and fast rule applicable to every case: for instance, even if information had not been volunteered, other information might have become available from which a tribunal could draw inferences on the point, without the need to ask questions.'

The consequence of this is that practitioners are unlikely to succeed in any attempt to rule sexual issues inadmissible. Even a degree of sexual detail is fair game. However, the corollary is that your client is entitled to adduce detailed evidence on the lack of any sexual contact (if that be the case) or on the non-sexual character of the otherwise close and even apparently intimate relationship. Where a tribunal makes an adverse decision based on speculation without a full ventilation of the sexual issues, an appeal to the Upper Tribunal may well lie on that point of law, if the matter would have been material. Noted already above is the case of *CIS/2074/2008* in which Mrs Commissioner Ward found an error of law in the sense that neither the *R(G)3/71* three-part test nor the 'six signposts' had been applied.

> 'There are two ways by which one can approach the point, but both of them lead to the conclusion that the tribunal erred in law: either, because they failed to consider the issue of whether a sexual relationship existed, thereby failing to consider, as they should have done, a potentially relevant "admirable signpost", or because they failed to apply the test in *R(G)3/71*, at very least in order to determine what significance any sexual aspect might have for the categorisation of the general relationship.'

Hence the problem, for the Commissioner, was that sex had been ignored, as had its relevance within the wider test of 'general relationship'.

Claimant and alleged partner have never had sex

9.45 No sex ever – yet cohabitation a possibility

The fact that the client and the alleged partner have never had sex is in practice a strong argument that they are not a couple. But the authorities take pains to point out that it is not determinative: thus Mr Commissioner Rowland held in *CIS/87/1993* that:

> '18. It will also be relevant for the tribunal to ask whether the claimant and Mrs B have *ever* had a sexual relationship. However, even if the tribunal finds that the claimant has never had a sexual relationship with Mrs B, this may be one of those cases where the absence of such a relationship is not fatal to the adjudication officer's case.'

That proviso was connected with the sleeping arrangements: see below.

9.46 No sex ever – appeals allowed

Mr Commissioner Howell QC found in *CP/8001/1995* there had been no 'living together as husband and wife' – or at least not sufficiently that the claimant had any duty to report her living arrangements, in circumstances in which she, a policeman's widow, had let a room in her council house to a male lodger either 13 or 22 years younger than her (it is not clear), who had recently separated from his wife; they had met playing darts, he had moved in, and now they had a settled relationship. The word 'stable' is not used but it could well have described the scenario. They 'did not share finances', although interestingly he had allowed her, 'for convenience', to draw cheques on the account into which his wages were paid. By 1993, 13 years into this arrangement, they were going on holiday, took meals and watched TV together. There was no sexual relationship between them. It was in this case that the tribunal had:

'failed to "stand back" and consider whether the evidence really did show a relationship of the kind that exists between a husband and wife, over the whole or any part of the period at issue, or whether the arrangement might be equally explainable in some other terms such as that between a brother and sister.'

However, it seems to have been assumed by the tribunal (perhaps because the department had not really disputed it) – and this was not doubted by the Commissioner – that there had never been a sexual relationship; this does seem to have influenced the judgment.

More explicitly, there was not, and never had been, any sort of sexual relationship in *Robson*, in which the alleged couple were both severely disabled, lived together partly for cost reasons but to provide mutual care as well, and it was this inter alia that led Webster J to such an unequivocal conclusion as to the intention of the parties in moving in together: there was no cohabitation.

And in *R(G)3/81* Mr Commissioner Rice made abundantly clear how determinative the sex question was in circumstances in which the 61-year-old widowed claimant had moved in with a man in what seems even by 1981 standards to have been a very 'proper' relationship. He was anxious to have companionship, it is true; but broadly she was his housekeeper in return for free accommodation:

> 'The relations between the claimant and Mr H seemed to have been somewhat formal, in that normally they would refer to each other by their respective surnames prefixed by "Mr" or "Mrs", as the case might be. Nearly every Saturday morning the claimant went to stay with her son or daughter until Sunday evening, and she had no dealings other than of a purely formal nature with Mr H's two daughters. Furthermore, Mr H had never visited the homes of the claimant's daughter or son.'

But even more to the point,

> 'Mr De Freitas [for the claimant] submitted that on the facts of the case the claimant and Mr H did not satisfy the criteria for concluding that they were living together as man and wife. **He pointed out that there was no sexual relationship whatsoever. Indeed, they did not even kiss or hold hands, and on his putting the suggestion to them in turn when they came to give evidence, they rejected the suggestion with something approaching abhorrence.** I am fully satisfied that there was no sexual relationship whatsoever.' (author's emphasis)

The appeal was allowed. Sex had been addressed head-on, even at the risk of causing abhorrence. This was right and proper: it mattered. Practitioners will note the value of 'something approaching abhorrence' in the course of oral evidence on this point; the facial language was no doubt persuasive and does seem to have carried the day.

9.47   Engaged to be married – but no sex yet

Clients refraining from sex prior to getting married, even though their pre-marital shared household resembles in most other respects the household they hope to maintain once married, may derive a degree of protection from the judgment in *CSB/150/1985*[85] which concerned an engaged couple sharing a household who did not have, and had never so far had, sex. They were prohibited from having a pre-marital sexual relationship by their shared religious beliefs. In those circumstances the judgment was that they were not living together as husband and wife, the logic being that the pre-marital relationship was being differentiated from the forthcoming marriage very unequivocally by their behaviour. The words 'as husband and wife' assumed even greater significance in such circumstances.

9.48   No sex ever – failure to investigate

Clients should be advised to distinguish carefully between different meanings of the word 'partner' in their dealings with the department. In a Pension Credit case, *CPC/3891/2004*, Mr Commissioner Mesher berated the department for its misunderstanding or falsification in relation to circumstances where:

> 'On the claim form [the claimant] said that he lived rent-free at R Boarding Kennels in return for assistance with the work of the kennels. He declared capital of £5,222.04 and stated that he did not have a partner. It appears that the Department already had some information that the claimant had ceased self-employment on selling a public house in 2002, so that a visit was carried out on 18 March 2004 to check the proceeds of sale and what had happened to the money. On the visit, an officer was informed by an employee of the owner of the kennels that the claimant and "his partner", the owner Mrs G, had had to go to America suddenly to deal with a family matter. A note was made for further investigation of whether they were business partners or partners in the sense of an unmarried couple.'

Despite an apparently inadequate investigation of what he might have meant by 'partner', the facts eventually emerged that there had never been a sexual relationship and that there was a credible explanation of the sharing of a household other than that the claimant and Mrs G were living together as husband and wife.

9.49   No sex now? No sex ever?: the evolution of the Handbook

In *R(SB)35/85* Mr Commissioner Edwards-Jones undertook a brief historical analysis of the changes made to the Supplementary Benefits Handbook through the early 1980s. He suggested that the version that Woolf J had had in mind in *Crake & Butterworth* when endorsing the 'six signposts' was that of 1979 as cited above, and including the sentence:

---

[85]   Cited in *CIS/7249/1999*.

'But [the] absence [of a sexual relationship] does not necessarily prove that a couple are not living as husband and wife, nor does its presence prove that they are.'

It is submitted that this version must be the one that is taken to be approved. But as the Commissioner noted, the revisions are of interest: by 1982 that sentence was supplemented by another that said:

'However, if a couple have *never* had such a relationship it is most unlikely that they should be regarded as living together as husband and wife.'

By 1983 this read:

'If a couple have never had such a relationship it may be wrong to regard them as living together as husband and wife.'

In 1984 the point was omitted altogether.

Mr Commissioner Edwards-Jones acknowledged that he had no judicial authority over the contents of the Handbook, but suggested it ought to reflect the real flavour of Woolf J's endorsement, that the 'signposts' were a starting point only. However his analysis of the amendments also reflected the Handbook's real engagement with how to deal with relationships that are and always have been non-sexual.

The publication of the Handbook expired altogether with the abolition of Supplementary Benefit in 1988, so the Handbook may seem to be history of a very dull kind now, but the very present potency of the 'six signposts' does mean its content still attracts regular scrutiny. Mr Commissioner Rowland was still grappling with its 'sex' advice in *CIS/087/1993*:

'It is arguable that the 1983 Edition of the Supplementary Benefits Handbook more accurately reflected what Woolf J actually said than the 1982 Edition did. Nevertheless, it does seem to me **that there must be strong alternative grounds for holding a relationship to be akin to be that of a husband and wife when there has <u>never</u> been a sexual relationship,** because the absence of such a relationship in the past does suggest that the parties may be living together for reasons other than a particularly strong personal relationship.' (author's emphasis)

And Ms Deputy Commissioner Green adopted the Handbook's approach directly, without any reference to *Crake & Butterworth* when she decided the tax credits case *CTC/3864/2004*:

'It seems that [the tribunal] did consider the sort of criteria [...] identified in the Supplementary Benefits Handbook, which although not of legal force, have been found helpful when considering whether people are living as man [sic] and wife in the social security field [...]. They may provide a useful starting point when considering this issue in the tax credits field.'

9.50   No sex at the material time – could they still be a couple?

Essentially, the answer is yes. Mr Deputy Commissioner Wikeley considered the matter at length in *CIS/4156/2006* in which it had been contended that a finding of no sexual relationship must be determinative. However, the Deputy Commissioner held:

> 'A finding that there was a sexual relationship at the material time **is not an essential stepping-stone** to a finding that two people were living together as husband and wife. It is, however, an important feature of such a relationship and this tribunal did not explain why it had discounted other highly relevant evidence on this point.' (author's emphasis).

This was consonant with Woolf J's opinion in *Crake & Butterworth* as to the essentiality of sex for a 'couple' finding:

> 'I should also make it clear that [the cohabitation finding] does not involve a finding that Mr Watts and Mrs Crake are having sexual relations. Neither counsel have suggested, for the purposes of the paragraph, that that is necessary and the tribunal in no way indicated that that was the conclusion which they had come to, and I certainly do not draw any inference as to that.'

9.51   Sleeping arrangements

Traditionally the sharing of a bed was, and perhaps still is, a proxy test for whether there is a sexual relationship; and 'sleeping together' of course has both a literal meaning and a euphemistic one. In *R(SB)17/81*, for example, the claimant and Miss G had moved into a 1-bedroom flat, and it was not in dispute that from that point on they had been 'sleeping together'. They were found to be living together as husband and wife.

9.52   Sharing a bed but no sex ever

But clients who admittedly sleep in the same bed but never together, will not necessarily escape a 'couple' finding. It is axiomatic anyway that absence of sex does not necessarily indicate the parties are not living together as husband and wife (see, below, the discussion of *CIS/4156/2006* for example). In *CIS/087/1993* Commissioner Rowland recorded the findings of the tribunal below, that:

> "[The claimant] volunteered the information that they had no intimate sexual relationship. He accepted that they slept in the same bed. However, he said that Mrs [B] goes early to bed and he then goes to bed at about 3am. When he goes to bed she gets up and sleeps in the living room.'

Taking no view on the plausibility of this account, the Commissioner continued:

'The claimant has not disputed the accuracy of that note. He tells me that he and Mrs B had been trying to move to a two bedroomed accommodation but only since shortly before the tribunal hearing. It seems to me that, in this day and age, **sharing a bed even at different times, does suggest a degree of intimacy or a surrender of dignity that could, when taken with other evidence, properly be regarded as connoting a relationship akin to that of husband and wife.** Obviously, the sharing of a bed as a very short term expedient might be viewed differently, but this was an arrangement that had been going on for years. It is the sort of situation that might give rise to the "unlikely" finding that a couple are living together as husband and wife despite never having had a sexual relationship. That would be a matter for the tribunal to consider when they have heard any explanation offered by the claimant.'

9.53   Separate bedrooms

If your client can truthfully claim to be sleeping in a different bedroom that is useful evidence to adduce. It goes to 'sexual relationship' but also to the intimacy alluded to by Mr Commissioner Rowland in *CIS/087/1993*. 'Separate bedrooms' occupy an important place in the range of factors militating towards single status.

Practitioners will recall Mrs Butterworth, in *Crake & Butterworth*, who had given evidence that:

'by arrangement with her daughter-in-law, Mr Jones moved into her home in about January 1979. She said that that gentleman **had his own bedroom with a lock on the door**; she had her bedroom also with a lock on its door.'

Similarly, though we are not told about locks, Mr W in *R(SB)35/85* 'had his own separate bedroom in the bungalow, and some of his own furniture there'. So too did the claimants and alleged partners in *CIS/2599/2002* (in which the single parent claimant had moved in rent-free with a man) and *Robson*. In none of those cases there was a 'living together as husband and wife' finding.

However, the claimant in *R(G)3/71* had less success in persuading Mr Commissioner Shewan that separate sleeping arrangements obtained, or, that if they did, this meant the parties must be single:

'The claimant said S slept on a couch in the living room. Whether one accepts the claimant's evidence as to the sleeping arrangements or not, it is obvious that sexual intercourse took place between the claimant and S; because on 10th July 1970 the claimant gave birth to a child of which S was admittedly the father.'

The Commissioner's robust scepticism did not serve the claimant well, and it is noteworthy that the possibility of sex outside the bedroom could be envisaged as early as 1971.

Previous sexual relationship, now ceased

9.54 One single intercourse only

The case cited immediately above, *R(G)3/71*, is a cautionary example of why clients should not expect to rely on a once-active sexual relationship having diminished to sexual inactivity. That a single instance of intercourse might suffice to then colour the whole tenor of the subsequent relationship, is salutary. But Mr Commissioner Shewan's analysis bears scrutiny:

> '6. The claimant asserts that the birth of the child Elizabeth, of whom S is the father, resulted from an isolated act of intercourse. This may be thought improbable, in view of the fact that the overt association between her and S continued, apparently unchanged, after that admitted act took place. But there is no need to speculate on the extent to which intercourse took place. The fact that there was sexual intercourse, which must have taken place just about the time when S came to live at the claimant's address, and that he thereafter continued to live at that address and to associate with the claimant in the manner hereafter to be described, goes a very long way, in my view, to establishing "cohabitation" within the meaning of the Act.'

Of course, the Commissioner struggled with the witnesses' credibility here – and that too remains instructive today. But even accepting the parties' account at its highest, his logic suggested it was not just the single act of intercourse that defeated the 'single status' claim; it was the way this fact acted upon the subsequent living-together arrangements. Even applying the Commissioner's own three-part test, two of the indicators ('sex' and 'general relationship') appeared to be capable of intertwining.

So where clients' evidence is that a previously sexually active relationship is now sexually dormant, such accounts must be handled with some care so as to avoid merely creating an impression that the relationship is similar to a sexually quiescent marriage. The unspoken question is whether it would be usual for a married couple to have allowed their sexual activity to diminish to the same degree.

9.55 No sex for 20 years

The same advice is indicated by another case where there had been a previous sexual relationship. In *CIS/443/1998*, the facts were that:

> 'The couple had lived together continuously since 1979, despite having moved house. The claimant had described the lady as his partner when he claimed Income Support in 1988 and when he claimed Housing Benefit in 1995. In 1995 he had also told the Department of Social Security that she had ceased work and had no income. Their latest home was rented in joint names. They had separate bedrooms and had not had a sexual relationship since 1979.'

Mr Commissioner Jacobs held that the tribunal below had not been in error when it found that they were living together as husband and wife.

9.56   No sex for 10 years

However, the shorter period (10 years) over which sexual activity had been discontinued (or at least 'not enjoyed': one assumes this is not a qualitative assessment) by the unmarried couple in *Re Watson (Deceased)*,[86] was not enough, in Neuberger J's view, to cancel the existence of a cohabiting relationship – though that case concerned inheritance provision not social security and the claimant G had sought to argue that there *had* been cohabitation.

9.57   No sex since accident

In *Crake & Butterworth* the facts giving rise to Woolf J's finding that Mrs Butterworth was not cohabiting with her alleged partner Mr Jones may be distinguished from both the foregoing unsuccessful appeals, *R(G)3/71* and *CIS/443/1998*. The evidence implied, rather than made wholly clear, that there had been a sexual relationship, but that following her car accident Mrs Butterworth:

'had suffered from amnesia and that she did not recognise Mr Jones when he moved into the house, and she says that there has been no sexual relationship whatsoever since that time.'

The basis of any pre-existing relationship had changed: this is an important qualifier, and clients arguing the diminution of a previous sexually active relationship should be advised to consider whether any factual circumstances have had a bearing on the level of sexual activity.

9.58   Previous sexual relationship now ceased: loss of libido

It is therefore not just a question of how long the sexual element of a relationship has lain dormant. It is a question of *why*. Practitioners will need to enquire of clients why a sexual relationship became non-sexual, if that is what has happened. Mr Deputy Commissioner Wikeley addressed in detail the factually difficult case of *CIS/4156/2006*. The alleged couple in that case had never married but they had admittedly cohabited previously. The relationship had changed however. The facts superficially appeared to ground a strong case for a cohabitation finding:

'[T]he appellant and Mr W have known each other for over 30 years. They lived together as cohabitants between 1975 and 1983. Mr W stayed intermittently with the appellant between 1995 and 1997. In 1997 Mr W moved in permanently to the appellant's house (a different property to the one they had jointly occupied between 1975 and 1983). Mr W has been in full-time employment throughout this

---

86   [1999] 1 FLR 878, [1999] 3 FCR 595.

period while the appellant has been receiving income support. In September 2005 the appellant bought her house from the local authority, under the "right to buy" scheme, using funds supplied by Mr W.'

That funding of the house looked almost conclusive. As the departmental submission writer had argued:

'How many carers would purchase a property for the person they are caring for? The mutual support and trust displayed by this action is more akin to a couple than to carers or friends.'

The pattern of facts was nuanced but not unusual in that:

'Mr W had assisted the appellant financially, had done DIY, bought furniture and shared bills 50:50, trusting her to tell him what his contribution is. He had helped her physically as her medical condition had required. Although he slept in a separate bedroom, he also used the kitchen, toilet and lounge. Mr W's work commitments and their different interests meant that they were not together continuously when in the house. They went out socially and Mr W "occasionally" went shopping with the appellant. The fact that they did not watch TV together or always eat their meals together was accounted for by their different interests and was not inconsistent with living together as husband and wife. The appellant helped him with his paperwork and cooked for him.'

It was also salient that 'The tribunal also found that Mr W "sleeps separately in a bedroom on the top floor of the house"', that Mr W had said 'that the fact that they don't now sleep together is the only difference from the relationship they had had when they previously lived together between 1975 and 1983', and that she had said 'since their cohabitation ended in 1983 "we never slept together except once in 1986" [...] but 'that she had "not had much sexual feeling" since a hysterectomy in 1987'.

Confirming the tribunal's view that 'a finding of a sexual relationship was not an *essential* prerequisite for a conclusion that a couple were living together as husband and wife', the Deputy Commissioner nevertheless considered that inadequate findings had been made, and other evidence before it had been given too little – or no – weight; there was a positive finding that:

'Mr W had "stayed the odd night with the appellant" after his aunt died in 1994 and for a fortnight after the appellant had been admitted to hospital in 1995, followed by "occasional nights" until 1997',

but the tribunal failed to address the *capacity* in which he stayed. This was material; it went to the issue of:

'whether a previous sexual relationship evolved into one of abstinence or whether the parties embarked on an entirely different type of relationship after a gap of over a decade.'

The absence of sex following a period in which there had been a sexual element to the relationship needs explaining. The suggestion is that embarking on a completely different type of (non-sexual) relationship would give greater credence to a claimant's single status than the evolution into abstinence which could justifiably still be seen as living together as husband and wife. Mr Deputy Commissioner Wikeley drew in part on the reasoning, cited with approval, in the commentary in *Social Security Legislation 2006, Vol I: Non means tested benefits* at p 79 where it states that the current departmental guidance on living together:

> 'is correct in asserting that the absence of a sexual relationship at any particular time does not prove that the parties are not cohabiting – a 'common law marriage' may evolve into a state of abstinence from sexual relations just as easily as a marriage may, and the parties will not thereby cease to live together as man and wife ... It should be repeated that the question is whether the parties' relationship sufficiently approximates to marriage, and in that the possibility of, or a history of, a sexual relationship is important.'

'Evolution into abstinence' then is a concept that must be dealt with: there is a potential pitfall here. Such a diminution in sexual activity, over the years, is arguably considered too close to what can happen in a marriage for the parties to be able to argue otherwise. But where it can be argued that your client and the alleged partner have indeed embarked on an entirely new kind of relationship, the scope for demonstrating a convincing single status is greater.

Once again the criticism the claimant sought to make of the way the tribunal below had handled the case was based inter alia on their failure to investigate.

9.59   Faithfulness – other sex partners

The concept of faithfulness was raised though not analysed by Mr Commissioner Jacobs when he cited the *Fitzpatrick v Sterling Housing Association*[87] test. Presumably it means refraining from sexual relations with somebody other than the other member of the couple, also known as adultery, whether secretly or openly. It is submitted that this must matter.

Little attention has been paid in the case-law to the effect on the living together analysis where the alleged partner has a sexual relationship with another person, not the claimant. It will be hard to corroborate, unless the third party partner is called to give evidence. In practice, where the evidence on this is persuasive then this creates a very strong argument against couple status (as between the claimant and the alleged partner).

Mr Deputy Commissioner Wikeley suggested a clear approach to this in *CIS/4156/2006*, in which the appellant's evidence had been:

---

[87]   In *CIS/443/1998*.

'that "he's been out with a few other females but he's not brought them back as far as I'm aware. I told him to be discreet as it's right above my bedroom". If an accurate account, and it does not appear to have been put to Mr W, the only relationship this is akin to is a so-called open marriage. Adultery and a lack of faithfulness between partners may be facts of married and unmarried life, and the statutory expression "living together as husband and wife" may be an elastic term, but I do not think that it can be stretched that far.'

'Committed' and 'faithful' were characteristics accorded to a traditional couple relationship by Miss Deputy Commissioner Ovey in *CIS/7249/1999*.

The existence of another relationship, between the alleged partner and another, must be useful evidence to undermine a couple finding in relation to the claimant. Evidence on this – notably a statement from the third person – will be needed where the argument is run, and it is submitted that the other relationship must be in some way serious rather than a fleeting infidelity which might not suffice to undermine couple status.

Stability of the relationship

9.60   *What the Handbook says*

Stability. Living together as a married couple clearly implies more than an occasional or very brief association. When a couple first live together, it may be clear from the start that the relationship is similar to that of a married couple, eg the woman has taken the man's name and has borne his child.

9.61   *What does stability mean?*

It is sometimes hard to know what precisely is meant by the word 'stability' – one can legitimately read it as meaning:

(a)   long-term, established, settled, changeless or constant etc, or alternatively as suggesting in some way:

(b)   harmonious, congenial, like-minded etc.

If so, the arguments against 'stability' would tend to major either on features like brevity, transience, the uncommitted nature of an involvement, or on the degree of disagreement, argument and friction that exists between the alleged partners.

The original Handbook entry suggests that the notion is meant to exclude occasional, brief or fleeting relationships. That is useful, where it fits your client's fact-pattern. But it will not necessarily exclude relationships that are brand new yet with a clear intention, eg marriage.

It is submitted that the concept is a very loose one, and if used in a way that is unfavourable to your client, it may be worth querying the premise, ie suggesting that the meaning of 'stability' is not established beyond doubt, and may inadvertently import a number of value judgements, which should be removed from the equation.

But it may be that the presence of other factors over time can embed the notion of stability: that was an obiter view suggested in *NA v Secretary of State for Work and Pensions (IS)*,[88] as regards an extended period of living together and a sexual relationship.

Arguments might follow the logical pattern that if the clients truly were in a stable relationship as contended by the department, then one would not see evidence such as is adduced, eg, of:

(a)   disharmony;

(b)   lack of commitment;

(c)   frequently changing intentions;

(d)   arguing;

(e)   intercalation of other relationships;

and there *would* by contrast be some evidence of:

(f)   commitment;

(g)   unanimity;

(h)   faithfulness;

(i)   endurance;

(j)   mutual promises.

9.62   How is time spent together?

The DMG seems to prefer a different interpretation of the word 'stability', instructing decision-makers at para 11113, in order to ascertain the degree of stability, to have regard to 'the important signs' of:

> 'the way in which two people spend their time together and the way that this has changed while they have been together.'

The Guidance then goes on to address,[89] under the *Stability* heading, issues as to whether the two people do certain 'activities together or for one another: providing meals and shopping; cleaning and laundry; caring for the members of the household during sickness; decorating; gardening; caring for children; [...] DMs should also consider the way in which two people spend their leisure time and whether they take their holidays together'.

It is submitted that this advice is logically deficient and is possibly under the wrong heading ('General relationship' might have been a better section for it) in

---

[88]   [2012] UKUT 299 (AAC).

[89]   At para 11114.

that there is no sensible connection between those activities and the degree of stability. They may well be proxy indicators of a relationship akin to marriage or civil partnership who live together, but they certainly do not suggest, even at a merely indicative level, stability as such.

Practitioners should therefore be ready to counter any suggestion by the department that such activities either necessarily or probably denote stability. Instability in a relationship may co-exist with decorating, gardening, childcare etc done on a mutual basis. The activities listed suggest a degree of interest in the home and in living together, but in reality they get us no closer to the core of what a couple is.

9.63   Impermanence

The impermanence of the student relationship in *R(SB)17/81* was no bar to a 'stability' finding by Mr Commissioner Rice:

'Account may be taken of the stability of the relationship but the absence of an intention to marry does not mean that the couple have no intention to live together as though they are married.'

He noted too the submission that 'in particular there had never been anything permanent about the relationship'. Nevertheless, this did not avail the claimant:

'having heard the evidence including the claimant's statement to the above effect the tribunal took the view that the claimant and Miss G were living together within the meaning of the relevant statutory provisions. I am satisfied on the evidence that the tribunal could properly have come to that conclusion. In particular, the fact that they did not intend to marry – and I was told that this was a feature of many student relationships of the kind under consideration – does not mean that they did not intend to live together as though they were married.'

Addressing, it is submitted much more pertinently than para 11114 (above), the temporal interpretation of Stability, the Guidance suggests at para 11116 that:

'It is for DMs to determine at what point a relationship should be regarded as LTAMC. The length of time two people have been together is not proof of the stability of a relationship. There is no specified time limit in determining the stability of the relationship and DMs should consider the following questions: (1) is there strong evidence that they have been LTAMC from the time they began living together, that would enable DMs to determine that LTAMC existed from the outset?; (2) are they living together as a temporary arrangement without commitment on either side? If so, DMs might determine they are not LTAMC; and (3) to what extent do they both take responsibility for the activities listed at DMG 11114? Where there is doubt about the stability, DMs might determine two people were not LTAMC.'

And at 11117:

> 'DMs should not assume a stable relationship exists just because two people have been LTAMC on a previous occasion.'

Here, the DMG advice is appropriate, and as has already been seen, relationships may evolve from something akin to marriage or to civil partnership into something else, remaining ostensibly 'stable' the whole time, yet further enquiry into the facts in such cases may reveal some erosion of the claimed stability taking place.

9.64 A settled relationship

R(SB)35/85 is one of the few other cases to address stability, at least in passing. The context was one in which the disabled Mr W had come to live with the claimant, a widow, and her brother, contributing in cash and kind to the running expenses of the household, occupying his own separate bedroom with his own furniture. They ate together; she cared for him. Notably the arrangement had subsisted for ten years at the time of the appeal.

> 'The claimant's case being that she and Mr W who though living in a common household and having a stable relationship were *not* living together as husband and wife, the tribunal needed to concentrate closely both in arriving at and in expressing reasons for decision upon what constituted as [sic] living together as husband and wife.'

And evidence accepted by the tribunal had included that:

> 'It is a stable and caring relationship.'

The degree of 'stability' here was still not enough on its own to persuade the Commissioner that the claimant and Mr W were living together as husband and wife (even though it was a perfectly sustainable argument to say that a married relationship might eventually look identical).

9.65 Relationship long-term but evolving?

That stability and longevity in a relationship are not necessarily the same is shown in the tax credits case *CTC/3864/2004* in which Ms Deputy Commissioner Green sought to mark out a distinction:

> 'The tribunal's reasoning that "*clearly they have a stable and longstanding relationship*" was flawed in that they seemed to place undue weight on the length of time they had shared a house, but failed to give adequate weight to the evidence that the relationship had changed from about six years earlier when they ceased having a sexual relationship and started sleeping in separate rooms.'

The degree of stability, if it is prayed in aid of a couple finding by the department, can perhaps only carry weight insofar as the other living-together characteristics evince stability; it is of far less – if any – consequence if stability, however solid, attaches only to a non-LTAMC period during the relationship.

Somewhat circular though this logic may be, practitioners are encouraged to argue that stability is not a feature that can usefully be imputed to any portion of time in which the relationship is claimed to have evolved into something less than a cohabiting one.

In *CIS/4156/2006*, one of the factors that might have influenced the tribunal below was the finding confirming the 'stability of the relationship since 1997 and the mutual support, which was "much more than simply mutual carers"'; in this case the tribunal had been less than balanced in its findings (for many other reasons besides the stability point though) and Mr Deputy Commissioner Wikeley remitted the case for re-hearing.

9.66 Endurance

This is one of the factors listed by Lord Justice Waite in *Fitzpatrick v Sterling Housing Association* [1998] 1 FLR 6 and approved for the living together test by Mr Commissioner Jacobs in *CIS/443/1998*. It is not addressed directly by either authority, but it is submitted here that the quality of endurance is not only a measure of time elapsed (which would better be described as 'duration') but rather it connotes some moral quality of stability and even a stolid toleration of an adverse conjugal situation. That is not a happy concept in the context of a relationship, but once again, the argument adopted for your client may be that this is indeed lacking: if the relationship has not broken down yet, then it will, 'endurance' being missing from both the client's and the alleged partner's attitude to each other and the situation.

9.67 Arguing stability points

Stability is never the sole determinant and is unlikely even to be particularly significant. The key is to argue whatever nuance suits the case best. In a relationship that has lasted a long time one might be saying that it is so unsettled and stormy that the stability factor is not satisfied. Or the argument may be run that such stability as can be discerned is to be disregarded, being stability of the 'wrong kind' – ie stability in a carer/patient, householder/ housekeeper relationship, or that which is necessary where ex-partners still share childcare in the interests of their child(ren).

Alternatively a noticeably harmonious relationship that nevertheless began only recently could equally be argued to fall outside the definition of 'stable' due to its short duration. This will chime comfortably with question 2 that is urged upon decision-makers in para 11116 (see **9.63** above) of their Guidance, especially where linked evidence can be shown of lack of any intention to marry, enter a civil partnership, stay together or live together as a married couple.

9.68   Financial support

This is a problematic test, because traditionally the DWP have tried to argue both corners: substantial support means they're a couple; lack of support means it's a couple because it's not solely a financial relationship. On the whole though, a lack of financial support is marginally advantageous when arguing for single status. But it produces a catch-22 position in which caution must be exercised if you argue that she is financially independent of him: remember that she is trying to claim means-tested benefit or tax credits on the basis of low income.

9.69   *What the Handbook says*

Financial Support. In most married couple relationships one would expect to find financial support of one party by the other, or sharing of household expenses, but the absence of any such arrangements is not conclusive.

9.70   *What the Guidance says*

DMG poses some pertinent questions which can be usefully asked of the client, as a starting point. They are:[90]

(1)   Is one person supported by the other?

(2)   How is the household income shared or used?

(3)   Are their resources pooled in a common fund? Is this all their income or only the money for eg shopping or bills?

(4)   Is one person bearing the major share of the household expenses, for example mortgage, rent, gas, electricity? Whose name is on the bills?

(5)   Is there a joint purchase of the property or other mortgage arrangements?

(6)   Have these financial arrangements always been the same or have they changed? If so how and when?

(7)   If there are no financial arrangements why not?

> 'If any of the above applies over the long term, it could be an indication of LTAMC. However, two people may be LTAMC even if they keep their finances completely separate. The relationship of two people concerning money has to be looked at in the context of the whole relationship.'

9.71   *Does either alleged partner maintain the other?*

Support or maintenance is certainly an indicator. That money changes hands is not enough to prove that it is maintenance, however, and practitioners are advised to take note of the need to distinguish support from something more commercial.

---

[90]   DMG para 11109.

Unsurprisingly in the earlier widow and lodger cases like *R(G)3/81* and *R(G)3/71* the distinction was rather critical. It assisted the appellant's case in *R(G)3/81* that as regards their financial relations:

> 'their evidence showed that they divided the cost of food equally, and that as regards other bills they provided a box, into which the claimant put £5 a week and Mr H somewhat more. In the event Mr H discharged all the bills with the exception of the telephone account, for which the claimant assumed sole responsibility – she had had the telephone installed in her bedroom on her arrival at the bungalow-and, to the extent that the claimant's contribution to these bills was inadequate, the shortfall was made up by Mr H.'

This rather informal arrangement was not so relaxed as to damage the case for singe status. By contrast the appellant in *R(G)3/71* failed to make a strong enough case that the lack of maintenance by the alleged partner took them outside the cohabitation definition. In discussing the point, in the context of the second point in his three-part test, Mr Commissioner Shewan had regard to the married norms as he then saw them, acknowledging they could be wide-ranging and various:

> 'The claimant strongly contends that she was not cohabiting with S because he was not maintaining the household as a husband does. In relying so strongly on this matter, the claimant in my view unduly stresses only one aspect of the situation: whereas the situation must be considered in a number of aspects. There are great variations in the way husbands maintain their households. In some cases they do not maintain them at all. If there is any generalisation that can be ventured, it is probably that as a rule husbands maintain their households to the extent that they – with or without consultation with their wives – consider they can reasonably afford. This was very much the basis of S's contributions in the present case. To start with, he paid nothing: because apparently he satisfied the claimant that in view of his obligations to his own wife he could not afford anything. Later he paid £5 a week, plus (as a rule) some 30 or 40 shillings [£1.50 to £2] a week; the fact that the 30s or 40s was not always paid indicates that what he paid was being represented as the limit which he could afford. This is not indicative of the status of a lodger. What a lodger pays is generally determined on a commercial basis, as a reasonable counterpart to what he is to receive by way of accommodation, meals and services. A person who cannot afford to pay the stipulated charge does not become a lodger. If on the other hand he has ample means and could well afford to pay more, that is no concern of the landlady; it does not determine what the charge is to be. On the admissions of the claimant and S, their financial relationship was much more indicative of that of husband and wife than that of land lady and lodger.'

The voluntary quality of the contributions struck the Commissioner as characteristic of a non-commercial relationship.

In *R(SB)17/81* the fact that Sheffield students:

> 'had shared the expenses, although Miss G had to lend the claimant something like £10 a week in order to enable him to meet his proper share.'

did not assist their case. And for Mrs Crake (the unsuccessful of the two claimants in *Crake & Butterworth*), who had left her husband to go and live with Mr Watts, evidence was adduced, with a view to establishing some commerciality to the relationship, that:

> 'Mr Watts could not keep her; that they led completely separate lives [...]; the representative repeated that she was a housekeeper and got her board and money for some meals; and that she was being paid in kind for the services which she performed.' (author's emphasis).

The inability of the alleged partner to maintain the claimant did not avail her then.

To suggest that one partner needs to be shown to be categorically supporting the other would be inaccurate though. In *NA v Secretary of State for Work and Pensions (IS)*[91] Judge Ward noted the tribunal below had found relevant evidence of the alleged partner participating in the financial life of the household via payment of insurance bills, phone bills, the Sky subscription and the TV licence.

9.72   Shared or separated money

In another key widow case, *CP/8001/1995* (the darts-playing widow of a policeman: appeal allowed), Mr Commissioner Goodman took a very relaxed view even of the claimant's free access to the alleged partner's bank account, noting that:

> 'He paid her a rent and a contribution to expenses; and although for convenience she was given the right to draw cheques on the bank account his wages were paid into, they did not in any sense pool their resources or have joint finances of the kind that married people commonly do.'

The Commissioner noted the general importance of money in arriving at an overall view of the relationship:

> '[the] complex problem of identifying when a whole concatenation of basic facts, such as who sleeps where, who does the housework and whose money is used for expenses, together come to add up to a state of affairs.' (author's emphasis)

It will be recalled that *CIS/443/1998* concerned a former cohabiting couple who now argued their relationship had changed into one of non-cohabitation. The evidence they adduced in support of this included that:

> 'Their latest home was rented in joint names.'

> 'She paid for the food and household items, and he paid the other bills. He also said that he bought his own toiletries.'

---

91   [2012] UKUT 299 (AAC).

'He said that they shared accommodation for convenience and because it was cheaper than living separately. She wished to retain her independence and her separate finances, which was one reason why their relationship had foundered in 1979.'

That too failed to persuade the Commissioner that they were not living together as husband and wife.

9.73 Property purchase

The purchase of a property in *CIS/4156/2006* struck Mr Deputy Commissioner Wikeley as strongly suggestive prima facie of a cohabiting relationship: the tribunal below had:

'accepted the presenting officer's submission to the effect that Mr W's investment in the purchase of the property was "striking ... It's a financial commitment + more friendship than a caring relationship. Not been a significant diversion from the old relationship other than sexual point of view."'

But the Deputy Commissioner was careful to ensure that this was not seen as conclusive.

9.74 Child maintenance

Properly dealt with under the head of 'Children' (see **9.76** below), the question of maintaining children is important. If it is a case of a cohabitee who pays money towards the children under some kind of duty (whether court-ordered, or arising under the liable relative rules, as a parent, or deemed liable relative who was formerly the partner of the parent/claimant and took on that responsibility by virtue of time previously spent living with and raising them) this should be explained and should not undermine a 'single status' argument. After all, the payment of maintenance – identified as such – as between ex-spouses is far from being a sign of the relationship's strength; rather it is an indication that the marriage is over.

But where maintenance payments are genuinely voluntary in the sense that the payer has undertaken, in the absence of any duty, moral or legal, whatsoever to pay maintenance to the children, that might well add up with other factors to indicate a cohabiting relationship. Where a lone parent client is accused of having a new relationship, the new alleged partner's relations with the child(ren) need to be assessed generally, but if he is supporting them financially, the single status argument is severely weakened.

9.75   *Questions to ask*

It is hard to discern any really firm principle threading the authorities together as regards financial affairs. But the distinctive, always unique textures of the way two people handle their money affairs in relation to each other is clearly very relevant.

The DMG questions are a good starting point, but the reasoning behind a given arrangement also matters. If the 'rent' in payment is unduly low, is there a reason for that? If one party subsidises the other as to living expenses, education costs, childcare, why has that arrangement come about? Would the level and type of subsidy between the alleged partners be out of place in a non-couple relationship or would it normally only arise in a marriage type of relationship?

Children

9.76   *What the Handbook says*

Children. When a couple are caring for a child or children of their union, there is a strong presumption that they are living as a married couple.

9.77   *What the guidance says*

At para 11118, the DMG majors on children who are *not* those of both the two alleged partners. It suggests that

> 'When two people are caring for a child they have had together, there is strong evidence that they are LTAMC. DMs can also consider:
> (1)   a man acting as father to a woman's children; or
> (2)   the woman acting as mother to the man's children; or
> (3)   one of two people of the same sex caring for the other person's children; or
> (4)   two people of the same sex caring for a child(ren) under a court order that gives them parental responsibility
>
> as evidence that they are LTAMC.'

And in previous DMG editions mention was made of situations where two people of the same sex were caring for a child they had adopted together.

9.78   *Children as proof of sexual relationship*

The first point is that this goes straightaway to another of the factors, sex, and has often been inseparable from that in the thinking of the judiciary. We have already seen the view taken by Mr Commissioner Shewan in *R(G)3/71* in relation to there having been one single instance of intercourse, in which the child was conceived. The child was proof of sex:

'it is obvious that sexual intercourse took place between the claimant and S; because on 10th July 1970 the claimant gave birth to a child of which S was admittedly the father.'

Mr Commissioner Rice takes us through the same logic in R(G)3/81 in relation to reconciling the two tests (three-part and six signposts) relevance to the tests:

'The existence of children is indicative of a sexual relationship and/or the general relationship of the man and woman.'

9.79 *Whose children are they?*

This rule has tended to work most adversely where any children are the offspring of both members of the alleged couple. That is not possible in same-sex couples of course. However, even where this is the case in a heterosexual alleged couple, common sense should remind the DWP that having once been a couple does not mean the two parents still are. Far from it. It is even harder for DWP to build a case on this point where the child is biologically or adoptively of only one of the alleged partners. On the whole then this factor must fail if applied adversely in isolation from the other five factors.

However, given the disproportionate deployment of the living together rule against lone parents, it is the four co-parenting scenarios in DMG 11118 above that create real pitfalls.

9.80 *Childcare*

It was salient in *R(G)3/71* that:

'[The claimant] thought of him as the man she was to marry as soon as he was free to marry. When he came back to stay with her after the birth of the child Elizabeth, he did so at her request because "there was nobody else she could think of who could look after and control the children" (ie **her** children, not simply **his** child Elizabeth).'

Thus the caring responsibilities taken on by an alleged partner may also play a part in the analysis. In *CTC/3864/2004* it was nevertheless his own children that the alleged partner was (in his evidence) looking after:

'The claimant made a single parent claim for tax credits on 4 December 2002 on behalf of herself and her two dependent children. [...] It came to light that the father of the claimant's children was also living in her home.

The main reason given by the tribunal for reaching [the] conclusion [that they were a couple] was that they had been living in the same household since 1993, they had two children and both helped to run the household and look after the children. [...] They led separate lives even though, as father of the children, he had a relationship with them. [...] The tribunal stated that they both helped to run the household and look after the children. However, the claimant's evidence was that, despite the fact that he was unemployed, she paid a child minder to look after the children after school.'

Remitting the case for re-hearing, Ms Deputy Commissioner Green clearly did not find the pre-existence of couple status and the bearing of joint offspring to be determinative in the slightest, if subsequent developments in the relationship meant that the couple relationship had changed, even if there was strong evidence that some shared childcare was undertaken.

The claimant in *CG v Secretary of State for Work and Pensions (IS)*[92] contended that her alleged partner had not behaved competently in relation to the childcare that he was being alleged to share with her; this informed her:

'account of the reason for her accompanying her husband on holiday (namely that on one occasion, while under the influence of alcohol, he had managed to lose their disabled son when abroad).'

It seems sensible to adduce such evidence where the department's evidence is that shared childcare evidences living together.

9.81   Regarding the alleged partner as a (step-)parent

In a Scottish case[93] in which the main ratio was not central to the present topic (it was chiefly concerned with the existence or otherwise of a marriage by cohabitation with habit and repute under Scots law), it is submitted that one part of the test applied by Deputy Commissioner Sir Crispin Agnew of Lochnaw BT QC could arguably be deployed in a living-together case:

'[H] and [the claimant] both had children who knew that they were not legally married but [the claimant's] daughters referred to [H] as dad and treated [H] and [the claimant] for all purposes as if they were a married couple.'

That point too goes to public acknowledgment (see below).

9.82   The birth certificate

This may be material, especially in terms of findings as to who is the father. However, even there, appearances may be deceptive. A claim made by the respondent single parent in *Secretary of State for Work and Pensions v AM (IS)*[94] which 'stretched credulity' concerned:

'the circumstances surrounding the registrations (and re-registrations) of the births of the older two of her four children (the younger two had no father registered). The older two children were both originally registered by the claimant alone. In May 1999, however, the claimant and Mr S re-registered the details of both

---

[92]   [2011] UKUT 97 (AAC).
[93]   *CSG/681/2003*.
[94]   [2010] UKUT 428 (AAC) (CIS/0384/2010).

children identifying Mr S as the father of both children. The DWP, unsurprisingly, relied on this as a factor showing that they were living together as husband and wife.'

However, the tribunal below had found in the single parent's favour, and in the light of her explanation involving protecting herself from domestic violence from another former partner, Judge Wikeley saw no reason to disturb that conclusion. But it is another cautionary tale in that an explicit move like registration which asserts paternity, combined with other living together features, is bound to cause difficulties when and if the relationship changes. The tribunal had been entitled not to regard the claimant's admitted deception of the Registrar of Births as undermining her evidence.

In *CIS/1243/2007*, the birth certificates of the children appeared to assist the case, in that they had disclosed different addresses for the two parents.

The facts in *R(IS)13/05* also illustrate a scenario in which a lone parent was alleged to be living with the admitted father of her children.

9.83 Inaction by the Child Support Agency or Child Maintenance Service

In the same case, *CIS/1243/2007*, Miss Deputy Commissioner Ovey found that the tribunal below had erred in its couple finding when the principle plank of its reasoning had been that the Child Support Agency had written to the father of the child (ie the alleged partner) at the mother's (ie the claimant's) address; moreover since it had not followed up this letter by way of further action to recover Chid Support, it had been inferred that the likely explanation for this was that he had moved in with her (and so was no longer a non-resident parent liable to pay Child Support). Yet the tribunal had no evidence as to why the CSA had failed to follow the case up. In those circumstances it was:

> 'in the absence of further reasoning, a step too far to conclude from the absence of further signs of activity by the Child Support Agency that the father moved in with the mother by 1 July 2002 and that for some reason which is not spelt out in terms that led the Child Support Agency not to pursue the maintenance claim. In this respect, then, I decide that the tribunal erred in law.'

This must amount to a useful line of argument, or at least a caution that the department is not entitled to rely on such non-sequiturs as informed it here.

9.84 Stages of children growing up

Whilst the child in *CIS/443/1998* had now grown up and by the time of the appeal was adult, her effect lingered insofar as Mr Commissioner Jacobs did allude to the stages in a couple relationship as they adjust to parenting growing children:

'Relationships are not static. All relationships have a beginning. Some have an end. Most that last for any length of time go through stages of development. The significance of a particular factor may vary according to the stage which the relationship has reached. For example: the financial contribution of the parties to the household may vary as children are born, go to school, grow up and eventually leave home. It is necessary to take account of how the relationship has developed to the stage that it has reached and how it appears to be developing. A change from one stage of a relationship to another does not necessarily involve that relationship ceasing to be equivalent to that of husband and wife.'

The point being made was a general one, but clearly there is a need for practitioners to be ready to counter arguments by the department that the diminution in given aspects of the relationship (here it will be recalled that the alleged partners had not had sex since 1979) is a factor of the stages in the child(ren)'s development.

9.85   Public acknowledgement

This vague and subjective test is hard to pinpoint. It concerns the way the alleged partners present themselves publicly, as evidenced – according to the DWP in DMG para 11119 – by representations they may have made:

(a)   on the electoral register;

(b)   in claiming benefits;

(c)   in obtaining accommodation;

(d)   if their friends and neighbours accept them as a married couple or civil partners;

(e)   if one person has assumed the other person's surname.

Previously the now-expunged para 11060 cited a wider range of matters, like whether they

(a)   use the same surname and titling themselves Mr and Mrs;

(b)   [sic] spend major festivals like Christmas together;

(c)   go on holiday;

(d)   socialise together;

(e)   go shopping together.

In the end, it is difficult to identify what it is 'normal' for couples to do by way of showing that they are a couple. But all such allegations are often capable of a strong rebuttal, and once again no single piece of evidence as to public presentation will alone be enough to make the DWP case.

A recurring ambiguity, still unresolved, is whether the acknowledgement in question is:

(a)   acknowledgement *by the public* of the relationship (do people think they are a couple, no matter what the parties say about it?); or

(b)   the acknowledgement *by the couple* of their relationship before the eyes the public (do they hold themselves out to be a couple, no matter what people end up thinking about it?).

Both perspectives arise equally.

9.86   What the Handbook says

Like the DMG, the Handbook favours the 'holding out' perspective:

> '*Public Acknowledgement.* Whether the couple have represented themselves to other parties as husband and wife is relevant, but many couples living together do not wish to pretend that they are actually married, and the fact that they retain their identity publicly as unmarried persons does not mean they cannot be regarded as living together as husband and wife.'

Arguably that is the approach to take then; and factors relating to how they are seen by others relegated to secondary importance. If so, that may well be useful where the department adduces evidence from neighbours and even acquaintances that the parties are 'considered' to be a couple.

9.87   Claimant's own description

In *CIS/443/1998* it was material that:

> 'the claimant had described the lady as his partner when he claimed Income Support in 1988 and when he claimed Housing Benefit in 1995.'

He had also:

> 'completed the Income Support claim form identifying the lady as his partner without being forced to do so and despite the clear definition of that word on the form. The tribunal was entitled to reject his evidence [that he had always maintained "that we do not live as man and wife"].'

Thus it is possible for the description a claimant applies to the relationship in the course of their benefit claim to be later held against them; clients should be warned that when they describe someone as a partner in any official capacity it may be hard later on to disavow that label.

The appellant in *Robson* had created similar difficulties for herself:

> 'evidence [was] adduced by, or on behalf of, the Commission, namely that at one time, specifically on 31 October 1979, the appellant said "Mr Williams is my common-law husband".'

On that point alone Webster J remained neutral, preferring to allow the freshly convened tribunal to make findings on that point. So it was not determinative, there being a possibility, it seemed in *Robson*, that such a self-description need not be fatal to her case.

9.88 Acknowledging themselves as a couple

There was certainly no public acknowledgement of any relationship as a married couple as between Mr H and the claimant in *R(G)3/81* and this had to go in their favour; and, in *Robson*, despite Mrs Robson's slip of the tongue in describing Mr Williams as her common-law husband, the:

'fact is that there was no suggestion before the tribunal either that they acknowledged themselves publicly as man and wife or that anyone in the community thought of them as man and wife.'

However, the students in *R(SB)17/81* had also 'not acknowledged themselves as husband and wife' (and incidentally 'visited parents separately') but were held to be a couple despite that.

More recently, Judge Levenson considered the public acknowledgment test in a case, *JP v Secretary of State for Work and Pensions (IS)*,[95] that concerned an alleged same-sex couple who denied they were a couple – an unacknowledged relationship, as he put it. Applying the then-current LTACP test, it seemed to the Judge that if the relationship were truly denied, then that ran counter to the key characteristic of marriage and civil partnership – these were in their very nature a 'public acknowledgement of an emotional relationship'. Mr Justice Lewison had held in *Baynes v Hedger and Others*,[96] a case concerning inheritance provisions, that such a 'relationship must be openly and unequivocally displayed to the outside world'.

9.89 Surnames

This may traditionally have been something of an indicator, but it probably mattered more in the past than now.

It can have done the parties no harm in *R(SB)35/85* that:

'In public they were known respectively by his name of Mr W and her married name of Mrs T.'

Similarly the claimant's case was helped in *R(G)3/81* by the finding that:

'normally they would refer to each other by their respective surnames prefixed by "Mr" or "Mrs", as the case might be.'

---

95 [2014] UKUT 0017 (AAC).
96 [2008] EWHC 1587 (Ch).

Presumably others did the same when speaking to them.

However, it must be accepted that nowadays using different surnames comes nowhere near a safeguard as regards the public acknowledgement factor.

9.90 Socialising

Again the social meaning of sharing a social life has changed. In this respect the change may be helpful, in that a shared social life may indicate far less conclusively that two people are a couple.

The living together finding in *R(G)3/71* was not uninfluenced by the evidence that:

> 'If [the claimant] could get someone in to look after the children she and S "had a night out".'

And once again the widow who did not socialise with the alleged partner in *R(G)3/81* already had a strong case. We have already seen how Mrs Crake (the live-in housekeeper) claimed (contradictorily?) that she and her alleged partner:

> 'led completely separate lives; [...] the only time they could go out together was on a Sunday night'

and Woolf J in her case found there was cohabitation.

We have also seen though that the social life factor could be elastic, as in *CP/8001/1995* in which Mr Commissioner Goodman held that:

> '18. In the present case, although there was evidence that the claimant and her lodger engaged in social activities together, and once or twice went halves on a twin bedded room when staying at a hotel in a group of friends, these factors together with the other aspects of the living arrangements and their friendship as it developed over the years fall short of showing with sufficient clarity that [...] their relationship had deepened into that of a cohabiting couple.'

Needless to say, the *R(SB)17/81* students 'socialised together'.

9.91 Wider factors

Being on record as a contact person in relation to the children's schooling was noted, obiter, by Judge Ward as indicating a degree of public acknowledgement in *NA v Secretary of State for Work and Pensions (IS)*.[97]

---

[97] [2012] UKUT 299 (AAC).

Living together in same-sex cases

9.92　*Provisions of the Civil Partnership Act 2004*

Until 5 December 1995 it was not possible for two people of the same sex to be treated as a couple in social security law: even if they *were* clearly a couple, they would be regarded as two single people. The Civil Partnership Act 2004 changed this, by inserting new definitions, as in the table at **9.14**, for same-sex couples, into SSCBA 1992, Tax Credits Act 2002 and Jobseekers Act 1995. The Civil Partnership Act also required that the LTACP ('living together as if civil partners') concept be defined by going back to the (now also obsolete except for tax credits) *living together as husband and wife* test after all. It added a further gloss ostensibly to assist in defining LTACP:[98]

> 'For the purposes of this paragraph, two adults of the same sex are to be regarded as living together in the same household as if they were civil partners if, but only if, they would be regarded as living together as husband and wife were they instead two adults of the opposite sex.'

That strange subsection has now disappeared, at least for benefits, as opposed to tax credits, since the coming into force of the Marriage (Same Sex Couples) Act 2013, because all couples who are not married or civil partners must be compared now to the gender-neutral 'married couple' comparator, carrying, as it now does, no assumptions as to whether such a couple is a man and a woman, two men or two women.

So the need to pretend, per s 137(1A), that one member of a same-sex couple has temporarily switched gender – surely an inelegant approach that at worst could cause offence – is now obviated.

There is no escaping the fact that in each case of alleged same-sex cohabitation, the decision-maker must first determine the 'living together as a married couple' definition whilst bearing clearly in mind the nature of marriage.

With the Civil Partnership Act 2004, clearly Parliament had gone out of its way to head off the risk that case-law on couple status should develop two separate lines of jurisprudence, one for heterosexual couples and another in same-sex cases. That is now easier to achieve, by referring only to that gender-neutral 'married couple'.

9.93　*Arguing for single status in alleged same-sex couple cases*

Despite the legislation's adoption of a clear gender-agnostic 'living together as a married couple' test, and the very clear steer given to decision-makers that they must be totally even-handed, it is entirely possible that for same-sex couples different standards will continue to develop as to the application of some of the

---

[98]　For example at SSCBA 1992, s 122(1A) (bereavement benefits) and s 137(1A) (means-tested benefits); also Tax Credits Act 2002, s 48(2).

key indicative factors. It may be said that the weight of a historically ingrained culture of opposite-sex marriage has created a very different set of assumptions to any that are brought to the brand new concept of same-sex marriage, which will be writing its own 'definition' for years to come. In a same-sex case, can it be argued that the married couple comparator ought only to be that in a same-sex marriage? Or must one look at all types and genders of marriage to see whether the one in question matches up to some 'average' married couple? Probably the latter must be the correct approach, and some same-sex couples may rightly baulk at a suggestion their relationship is like an average married couple.

9.94 *Members of the same household*

Can it be argued that any different factors should apply in same-sex cases? In other words is there anything fundamentally different about sharing a household in a same-sex marriage as compared with an opposite-sex marriage? The question may need to be put, and differences highlighted if the same-sex relationship your clients have differs fundamentally, and will benefit from the comparison.

9.95 *Sexual relationship*

DWP sensitivity to accusations of intrusiveness has led to decision-makers being doubly reluctant to ask about this in same-sex cases in the decade so far when it has mattered. Where your client does not have a sexual relationship with the alleged partner (and especially if s/he has never had) then this information should be volunteered, and must go into the whole equation. But as with heterosexual cases, important though it is to the couple concept, sex is not absolutely determinative, and it should remain open to same-sex alleged partners to argue that despite occasional sex they are not a couple.

9.96 *Children*

Given that it is impossible[99] for a child to be biologically the offspring of both members of a same-sex couple, this factor must surely have a reduced impact in same-sex cases, since traditionally in heterosexual cases it has tended to work most adversely where any children are biologically of both members of the alleged couple. Nevertheless, the existence of a resident child adopted by both members of an alleged same-sex couple will be a factor suggesting couple status.

9.97 *Public acknowledgement*

This vague and subjective test may be even harder to apply in same-sex cases than in heterosexual ones. What is 'normal' for couples to do by way of showing that they are a couple, is difficult to identify, and in a still-homophobic

---

[99] Except in cases where one has had a gender change.

society it may be said that a greater reticence is necessary for many same-sex couples than for heterosexual couples. This could have an adverse effect on the adjudication of same-sex cases.

That an alleged same-sex couple have not married or entered a civil partnership, and deny the relationship anyway, may be strongly suggestive that whatever their relationship is *like*, it is *unlike* that of a married couple: *JP v Secretary of State for Work and Pensions (IS)*.[100]

9.98 Temporary separations

Notwithstanding the SSCBA definitions of couple, regulations[101] deem there still to be a couple even though one member is 'temporarily living away from the other members of his family'. Situations where one has moved out and the other – your client – remains in the cohabitation home not quite knowing what will happen next can be caught by this, where the department decide to invoke it adversely. Framed in terms of exceptions, the deeming will, however, not bite where:

(a)   the alleged partner 'does not intend to resume living with' the client; or

(b)   his absence is likely to exceed 52 weeks.

In the tax credits legislation, it is necessary in the case of married couples or civil partnerships to show that any separation is 'likely to be permanent', but there is no formal deeming provision.

9.99   DMG guidance on the temporary absence of one party

DMG[102] suggests that:

> 'A couple should not automatically be regarded as having stopped LTAMC just because of the temporary absence of one of the parties. When DMs determine whether LTAMC[103] continues during a temporary absence, the reason for the absence is an important factor. Absences for the following reasons would not normally mean that the couple have stopped LTAMC:
> (a)   work;
> (b)   a period as a hospital in-patient;
> (c)   holiday;
> (d)   a visit to a relative(s);
> (e)   higher education.'[104]

---

[100] [2014] UKUT 0017 (AAC).
[101] Regulation 16(1)–(3), IS (General) Regulations 1987 (SI 1987/1967); the other means-tested benefits have similar equivalents.
[102] At para 11151.
[103] R(G)11/59; R(SB)19/85.
[104] R(SB)30/83.

9.100 He might come back

In the light of the deeming provisions, the impression your client gives about a former partner who 'has left', and the circumstances in which he or she left, can make a crucial difference to the success of her benefit claim. For tax credits, the following points may help to establish 'permanence'. In cases involving both benefits and tax credits, it will assist your client's case for being regarded as single if:

(a) the departing party said that – or your client was given to understand that – he would not come back;

(b) she does not wish him to return;

(c) she told him or asked him not to come back;

(d) there is agreement between them that the relationship is over;

(e) they were married but are now divorced;

(f) they were civil partners but the civil partnership is now dissolved;

(g) she can separate out her hopes (eg *I'm hoping he'll be back one day soon*) from the reality (ie, he is simply not coming back);

(h) there are no previous examples of his having 'left' and then returned some time later – a history of splits and reconciliations is decidedly unhelpful;

(i) he has gone on to some different situation (perhaps a new relationship) which appears permanent as far as can be ascertained;

(j) there are no other strong reasons why he has left (eg work, a holiday, visiting relatives, undertaking higher education).[105]

Naturally, where the client is upset by his leaving and would like to repair and resume the relationship, it can be extremely painful for her to point out these factors. Briefing her therefore as to what to say and how to make her case needs to be done with great sensitivity.

DWP should only investigate these cases where there is a prima facie reason for doubt, in accordance with their own guidance.[106] If they appear to be investigating in detail on a routine fishing basis, they should be asked if they will discontinue such investigation. As for tax credits, it is less likely that there would be a detailed investigation of these circumstances.

Where your client is in an admitted cohabitation relationship, then she must be careful in relation to claiming benefit if it is only temporary (eg a female partner claiming Income Support as a lone parent whilst her male partner spends a year working in the family business abroad in the country of origin). In such circumstances her claim will of course be tested as to its permanence and as to its falling outwith the deeming provisions, by the department, but it is still wise to ensure the client does not put herself in a position where the claim could later be viewed to have been fraudulent.

---

[105] DMG, para 11151.
[106] DMG, para 11152.

9.101 Multi-partner scenarios

In social security law the following rules are applied:

(a) marriage is usually only between *two* spouses; polygamy is the exception;

(b) civil partnership is always between only two civil partners;

(c) living together as a married couple always applies to only two partners.

Polygamous marriages (a husband with more than one wife) are provided for – but only if such a marriage was legally contracted in a country where polygamous marriages are available.[107] In a case where a man claims to be married to more than one woman, but the finding on the facts is that he is actually married to only one of them, he cannot be held in social security law to be living together as a married couple with his subsequent alleged wife or wives. If he is found to be married to none of them, any finding of living together as a married couple can only be made in relation to one of them. In other words there is no polygamous version of the LTAMC concept.

There is also no equivalent provision for polyandrous marriages (one wife with more than one husband). A finding of marriage could be made in respect of one of the husbands, or of living together as a married couple with one of them.

9.102 Unlawful or prohibited relationships

When are two people treated as **not** being a couple?

Despite any evidence that would otherwise point to a LTAMC relationship, two people cannot be treated as 'living together'[108] if:

(a) their relationship would be a prohibited one for marriage or civil partnership purposes; or

(b) it would be illegal for them to have sexual intercourse (ie one or both would be committing a crime).

The full list supplied by DMG at Appendix 1 to para 11082 is:

(1) adoptive child

(2) adoptive parent

(3) child

(4) former adoptive child

(5) former adoptive parent

---

[107] See definitions of 'partner' and 'polygamous marriage' in Income Support (General) Regulations 1987 (SI 1987/1967) reg 2(1); Jobseeker's Allowance Regulations 1996 (SI 1996/207), reg 1(3); Employment and Support Allowance Regulations 2008 (SI 2008/794), reg 2(1); State Pension Credit Act 2002, s 12; Housing Benefit Regulations 2006 (SI 2006/213), reg 2(1); Housing Benefit (Persons who have attained the qualifying age for State Pension Credit) Regulations 2006 (SI 2006/214), reg 2(1); for Council Tax Benefit, see SSCBA 1992, s 133.

[108] DMG 11031-11032 and Appendices 1 and 2 to DMG, Chapter 11.

(6) grandparent

(7) grandchild

(8) parent

(9) parent's sibling

(10) sibling

(11) sibling's child

(12) child of former civil partner

(13) child of former spouse

(14) former civil partner of grandparent

(15) former civil partner of parent

(16) former spouse of grandparent

(17) former spouse of parent

(18) grandchild of former civil partner

(19) grandchild of former spouse.

'Sibling' includes half-siblings. No living together finding can be made where there is such a relationship. Whilst 'child' and 'grandchild' in this list go wider than the social security definition (ie a person under 16), it should be made clear too that all children under 16 are outside the reach of the living together rules; they cannot be partners.

Running a cohabitation case against the DWP, HMRC or a local authority

9.103 *How the DWP, HMRC and local authorities make adverse cohabitation decisions*

The departments concerned increasingly try to pool resources as to investigation using the Benefit Fraud Investigation Service, but in theory it is possible for any one of the DWP, the local authority or HMRC to undertake investigations of alleged couple status. Sometimes investigations relate to suspected fraud;[109] here it is assumed that the investigation of your client seeks to show a couple relationship exists so as to stop or reduce benefit payment.

9.104 *Pressure to withdraw*

Investigations may include interviews under caution and if so your client will need your (or another practitioner's) advice from a criminal law perspective, including application of the PACE 1984 rules. Sometimes an investigation will result in the client being told there is evidence of fraud and that if they withdraw their claim and repay any overpayment to date, there will be no prosecution. That degree of pressure can escalate to the 'offer' of paying an

---

[109] There will soon be a Single Fraud Investigation Service which will take over all such work on behalf of benefit-paying agencies.

administrative penalty to ward off a prosecution. Your advice in those circumstances needs to be preceded by very careful scrutiny of the case against the client to see if it has substance. If it appears unfounded, pressure to withdraw the claim should be resisted, and an appeal lodged against a subsequent decision to stop benefit, but the client is likely to want a high degree of confidence in your view that the allegation can be defended.

9.105 Types of evidence gathered by the departments

Evidence is gathered through:

(a) witness and neighbour reports;

(b) undercover observation;

(c) questioning neighbours;

(d) the benefit fraud hotlines;

(e) interviews under caution.

The validity of such evidence must be treated with caution insofar that there is scope for hearsay which, while arguably admissible at a tribunal, should not carry any significant weight. The unreliability of unhelpful evidence does need to be stressed to the tribunal. Where observations have been done by investigators sitting in a car near the claimant's home for example, it is important to see the original record of those observations and to assess their shortcomings.

Visiting officers will record the claimant's answers to questions and will also ask to see the premises. Claimants do not have to accede to this, but if a glance at the bedroom arrangements will be enough to demonstrate separate bedrooms that is always a useful line of argument and the evidence of being shown the bedrooms can be conclusively favourable to the point that the department concedes without further ado.

Assuming that the matter is not so easily won, clients need to be advised to be careful with the personal and sometimes intimate information that they may be asked about. Helping clients to understand the admittedly quite opaque rules on living together is one way to ensure that they avoid giving a misleading impression about the relationship, or refrain from giving too much detail where they are unsure if it helps. Naturally they must also be advised that deliberately misleading the department would be wrong and perhaps fraudulent.

Practical issues to address

9.106 Checklist: what to do if your client's benefit/tax credits are stopped

(a) Challenge the decision via revision or appeal – within one month.

(b) Re-apply for benefit if circumstances change (eg contact with the alleged partner breaks down in some way) – even pending appeal.

(c)   Apply for other benefits that might be payable instead – eg where Income Support entitlement has been stopped, the client could nevertheless make or amend a claim for Housing Benefit despite the DWP's couple finding.

(d)   Prepare the appeal/revision request.

(e)   Is there a fraud charge as well? Advise on, or refer, the criminal aspects of the case.

9.107   What is the allegation?

The department must be clear about what is alleged. However, often the detail of the evidence on which they base their decision is hard to determine from the bald wording of the refusal letter. It is possible to ask for reasons for the decision, and this can be a useful first step in formulating the challenge.

However, it is often advisable to seek a reconsideration anyway, as the grounds do not need to be spelt out exhaustively at the point of making that application.

9.108   Burden of proof

The department seeking to close or end an existing claim has the burden of showing that circumstances have changed so as to end the entitlement. On a first claim though, it is open to the department to refuse it because the claimant has failed to discharge their burden of showing that they are entitled.

9.109   Is it also an overpayment case?

Very often, the context in which the cohabitation question is aired is when the client has been told they must repay overpaid benefit that they received whilst claiming as a single person when in fact they were a member of a couple.

Overpayment cases have two distinct aspects:
•   was the person overpaid? and
•   if they were, is the overpayment recoverable by the benefit-paying agency?

It is the first of these questions that will raise the issue of whether they were living together. The legal burden, in an overpayment recovery case, is on the benefit-paying department to make out all aspects of their case. You should put them to proof as to the allegations they make; all the more since their case may consist in part of insinuations and vague assertions. The department must be clear about what is alleged. However, the detail of the evidence on which they base their accusations may be sketchy, under scrutiny.

9.110   Is it also a benefit fraud case?

An indication that the benefit-paying department suspects a cohabitation fraud (ie they think that couple status is deliberately being concealed, perhaps so as to allow a lone-parent Income Support claim) is where the Benefit Fraud

Investigation Service ask the claimant, and often the alleged partner too, to attend, separately, an interview under caution. These are subject to the same protections and safeguards as police interviews, under the interview codes to the Police and Criminal Evidence Act 1984. The interviewee may have their legal adviser present, for example, and may ask for breaks as needed. If your client is invited to attend such an interview, your, or a colleague's, knowledge of criminal law will form part of the advice they may need.

9.111 Penalties

One area that sits somewhere between criminal law and the administrative law of benefit entitlement is that of civil and administrative penalties. Your client may face one or both of these two charges.

He or she may find that in addition to being asked to repay an overpayment following a living together allegation, they are also required to pay a one-off £50 civil penalty.[110] It is only chargeable if there was indeed an overpayment – ie the living together arguments have been lost – and then only if they acted negligently or they failed without excuse to supply information or report a change. If you lose the living together argument on behalf of a client, consider whether it was nevertheless a scenario in which there was enough doubt about what kind of relationship they were in, that their failure or alleged negligence was justifiable. The imposition of the civil penalty is discretionary, and a key factor informing that discretion is the degree of blameworthiness; arguments should be focused on that.

Separately, the option of paying an administrative penalty can be 'offered' by the investigating benefit-paying agency as an alternative to prosecution.[111] These can be up to £2000, and all too often a claimant who is in the middle of a living together case, already overwhelmed by the prospect of losing their appeal, will seize upon the penalty as a way of avoiding the further calumny of a fraud prosecution. Clearly, it should only be considered as an option in cases where the department has evidence likely to achieve a conviction. That is a matter to which your (or a colleague's) expertise in criminal law must be applied. It is not unknown for administrative penalties to be sought from, and duly paid by, claimants against whom the available evidence would have been unlikely to secure a conviction.

9.112 Decisions susceptible to challenge

It is now well-established that 'outcome decisions' attract an appeal right.[112] A decision whether a person is single or a member of a couple is of itself only one

---

[110] Social Security Administration Act 1992, ss 115C-115D.

[111] Social Security Administration Act 1992, s 115A.

[112] The question of the tribunal's jurisdiction and the triggering, or not, of appeal rights in this respect is dealt with at length in decisions *CPC/3891/2004*, *CIS/1720/2004* and *CIS/3655/2007*, but practitioners will only rarely need to refer to these authorities. See also the application of these principles by Judge Wikeley in *Secretary of State for Work and Pensions v AM (IS)* [2010] 428 (AAC).

of the 'building block decisions' that go towards the outcome decision of whether the client is entitled and if so to how much. A 'building block' gives rise to appeal rights once it becomes part of the outcome. An outcome decision will broadly read something like 'Mr G is not entitled to Income Support as a lone parent from 1.1.2011 on the basis that he has been living together as a married couple with Ms F and is therefore a member of a couple.' Such a decision may be appealed.

Decisions as to entitlement further divide into those made on an initial claim, where the claimant has claimed benefit and not yet had any previous decision in the current circumstances, and those in which an on-going claim is stopped (this is usually a department-instigated supersession) because the department now take a different view on the cohabitation point. Either type of decision is appealable but it is fairly clear that the burden of establishing single status falls on the claimant upon lodging their claim, but the burden is on the department when it wishes to stop or reduce an existing live claim.[113]

Another context in which decisions may need to be challenged though is where the client has received benefit in the past, but the department in question now seeks to recover that benefit on the basis that it was overpaid because it has supposedly come to light that the claimant was living together as a married couple with another person. Here the client may be arguing that they were not living together as a married couple – and therefore benefit was not overpaid – in order to resist recovery of the benefit.

9.113   Challenging the decision

The following is only a brief guide to the complex rules on decisions and appeals. It is governed by the Tribunals, Courts and Enforcement Act 2007 and the Social Security Act 1998; the finer detail is covered by the Social Security and Child Support (Decisions and Appeals) Regulations 1999 (SI 1999/991).[114]

The starting point is that the client receives a decision capable of challenge, ie:

(a)   an outcome decision as to entitlement; or

(b)   a decision to recover an overpayment.

Action should be taken as soon as possible; the deadline is:

(a)   one month (for benefits); or

(b)   30 days (for tax credits)

---

[113] *CIS/317/1994*; *CIS/4156/2006*.

[114] For tax credits, see relevant sections of the Tax Credits Act 2002, the Tax Credits (Claims and Notifications) Regulations 2002 (SI 2002/2014) and the Tax Credits (Appeals) (No 2) Regulations 2002 (SI 2002/3196). For housing benefit, see Sch 7 to the Child Support, Pensions and Social Security Act 2000 and the Housing Benefit and Council Tax Benefit (Decisions and Appeals) Regulations 2001 (SI 2001/1002). For universal credit see the Universal Credit, Personal Independence Payment, Jobseeker's Allowance and Employment and Support Allowance (Decisions and Appeals) Regulations 2013 (SI 2013/380).

from the date of the decision under challenge. This means the date of the letter or the postmark. Within one month (30 days for tax credits) the claimant must seek a **mandatory reconsideration**: this means asking the department to look again at their decision and to revise it in the client's favour.

If the outcome of the mandatory reconsideration is adverse, then the claimant may lodge an **appeal**. They have a further month (30 days for tax credits) to do this from the date of the outcome of the mandatory reconsideration.

Rules for Housing Benefit reconsiderations and appeals are slightly different but the pattern is similar.

The relevant action must be taken so that the request or appeal *arrives* at the relevant destination address within the one-month (30 days for tax credits) period. Merely posting it within the one month will not suffice.

Where the decision is favourably revised upon revision or appeal, then any backdating of benefit will go back usually to the date of the decision that has been challenged – or in the case of recovery of an overpayment, the overpayment is waived.

Decisions may be challenged outside the one month deadline by way of:

(a)   late appeal or late revision request – where there are compelling good reasons for the delay – up to a maximum time-limit overall of 13 months;

(b)   in a narrow range of cases involving mistake or error, the 'any time revision' route; or

(c)   at any time at all, seeking a supersession: this means asking the department to reconsider outside the time limit but on the basis that if the decision is favourably revised, then any backdated benefit is only paid back to the date when the supersession was sought.

Appeals procedure in 'living together' cases

9.114   Lodging the appeal

The appeal should normally be lodged on the official form SSCS1 and usually should be sent to HMCTS. This is called direct lodgement. The appeal needs to state grounds. However, these do not have to be exhaustively set out at the initial stage. It is acceptable to add further arguments and amend or elaborate the grounds later in the process without formality or making any application. On the other hand, it assists the process if the grounds are set out as fully as the time-limit permits.

9.115   The appeal hearing

Living-together matters in welfare benefits and tax credits cases are heard by a single Judge sitting in the Social Entitlement Chamber of the First-tier Tribunal.

He or she will be a qualified lawyer or other person with equivalent legal experience. The hearing is usually fairly informal. Often there is nobody present from the decision-making department. But where there have been extensive investigations and/or an interview under caution it is common for the department to send a presenting officer, and sometimes an investigating officer as a witness. Appellants often appear unrepresented; the current ungenerous Legal Help climate does not ameliorate this situation. But for that reason, the proceedings are relatively informal and conducted in an inquisitorial style. There is often no formal examination and cross-examination of witnesses; the appellant may be the only witness.

Proceedings are governed by the Tribunal Procedure (First-tier Tribunal) (Social Entitlement Chamber) Rules 2008 (SI 2008/2685) which give considerable leeway to Judges as to how to manage the hearing. A typical living together hearing might last 30-90 minutes.

If the client is to appear unrepresented, consideration should be given to how they will present their case – or whether they will merely respond to the Judge's questions, and if so, advice on predicting likely questions and responses is useful. Clients may be advised that they will not have to stand up or make any formal submissions or speech. It is unlikely but not impossible that they will have to take an oath.

9.116   Witness evidence at the tribunal

Oral evidence from your client does not need to be accompanied by a written witness statement – this is not required though it can sometimes help. Clients may ask if they can refer to such a statement while they give evidence. If other witnesses such as the alleged partner cannot attend, a signed witness statement (even of the most informal kind) is acceptable. But attendance in person by the witness, if only to adopt and confirm the content of their statement, must inevitably add some weight. Other supporting letters eg from friends and family are perfectly admissible, but clients should not over-estimate the weight that will be placed on them.

Living together cases are a rare instance in social security matters when it is useful to call other witnesses; practitioners are advised to consider this, so that where helpful the alleged partner can appear, or sometimes the actual partner of the alleged partner (so as to vitiate the charge of couple status against your client). Witness orders are very rare but still possible in this jurisdiction. You can make an application to the Tribunal for a witness summons (eg in relation to the alleged partner) if you think this could help your client's case.[115]

If you do not represent your client at the hearing because legal help will not cover this, or for any reason, remember that there will be no formal examination in chief; rather the Tribunal Judge is likely to ask the questions, and whilst these will not be strongly leading questions, they may be slightly

---

[115] Tribunal Procedure (First-tier Tribunal) (Social Entitlement Chamber) Rules 2008, r 16.

more so than those that you might have asked. There is still a chance, in cases where the department investigated forensically, that a departmental presenting officer may attend, and s/he may cross-examine the client. You should advise your client as to the type of questions that could be asked, based on your own analysis of how the department might be expected to present their case.

Where investigating officers attend as witnesses for the benefit-paying department, you should try to ensure they are not allowed to make submissions as well. You may wish to prepare questions with which to cross-examine them too, especially if you think you can throw doubt on, for example, the reliability of covert observations.

9.117   Credibility of the evidence

It is necessary to be very rigorous as to what meaning is imputed to agreed evidence. In remitting case *CG v Secretary of State for Work and Pensions (IS)*[116] for rehearing Judge Wikeley advises prudence and care:

> '44. The tribunal should take particular care in making findings about the period over which there were incidents of domestic violence. If the tribunal takes the view that the documentary evidence on file is broadly accurate – namely that the police were involved in two such incidents in 2001 and 2002 and then again repeatedly from March 2008 – then that may well indicate that the couple were maintaining a common household throughout the relevant period (at least until late 2007 in any event). However, it is by no means conclusive. The tribunal must consider all the relevant evidence in the light of all the factors that go to the issue of sharing a common household.

> '45. So, for example, the tribunal will need to make findings about holidays. Do the photos seized by the DWP indicate shared and happy family holidays? Or does the tribunal believe the claimant's account of the reason for her accompanying her husband on holiday (namely that on one occasion, while under the influence of alcohol, he had managed to lose their disabled son when abroad)? These issues may not be straightforward. The tribunal might note that the receipt for the Ryanair flights booked in 2005 gives a contact address for the husband which is different from the claimant's. The tribunal might also note that the claimant was on holiday without her husband at the time of the police raid in 2007.

> '46. Likewise the tribunal will need to decide what weight to attach to the letters sent by the claimant's husband when he was in prison. Do they show, as the DWP argue, that the couple were sharing a common household because of the nature of some of the issues being discussed (eg advice about works on the property?). Or, as the claimant's representative argues, do they demonstrate the manipulative nature of the claimant's husband? I simply observe that the representative's point that all the letters were from the claimant's husband to her, rather than vice versa, may not carry much weight, as it is plain from the letters that this was a two-way correspondence (eg "I got your letter ..."). However, the evaluation of such evidence is a matter for the new tribunal.'

---

[116] [2011] UKUT 97 (AAC).

It is Mr Deputy Commissioner Wikeley (as he then was) too who elaborated what must be considered a definitive approach to claimant credibility, in *CIS/4022/2007*, which he later cited with approval specifically in the living-together context in *Secretary of State for Work and Pensions v AM (IS)*:[117]

'52. In my assessment the fundamental principles to be derived from these cases and to be applied by tribunals where credibility is in issue may be summarised as follows:

(1) there is no formal requirement that a claimant's evidence be corroborated – but, although it is not a prerequisite, corroborative evidence may well reinforce the claimant's evidence;

(2) equally, there is no obligation on a tribunal simply to accept a claimant's evidence as credible;

(3) the decision on credibility is a decision for the tribunal in the exercise of its judgment, weighing and taking into account all relevant considerations (e.g. the person's reliability, the internal consistency of their account, its consistency with other evidence, its inherent plausibility, etc, whilst bearing in mind that the bare-faced liar may appear wholly consistent and the truthful witness's account may have gaps and discrepancies, not least due to forgetfulness or mental health problems);

(4) subject to the requirements of natural justice, there is no obligation on a tribunal to put a finding as to credibility to a party for comment before reaching a decision;

(5) having arrived at its decision, there is no universal obligation on tribunals to explain assessments of credibility in every instance;

(6) there is, however, an obligation on a tribunal to give adequate reasons for its decision, which may, depending on the circumstances, include a brief explanation as to why a particular piece of evidence has not been accepted. As the Northern Ireland Tribunal of Commissioners explained in *R3/01(IB)(T)*, ultimately "the only rule is that the reasons for the decision must make the decision comprehensible to a reasonable person reading it".'

Credibility of the claimant's (your client's) evidence and to a large degree that of the alleged partner, if available, will be critical. There will be details which no third party or documentary evidence can corroborate. Ask how plausible your client's account would be, to a reasonable but reasonably sceptical observer. Remember that credibility will be judged against the obvious backdrop of the financial motivation to lie, that a claimant might be susceptible to. Judge Jacobs entered a reminder about that possibility in *PP v Basildon District Council (HB)*.[118] The emphasis in social security law was, he warned, 'on the protection of public funds in a context where the parties have an incentive to conceal their true relationship'. That does not (and must not) amount to a presumption of course, but it can quite properly result in a Tribunal Judge's scepticism and may trigger[119] the Judge's inclination to test it rigorously.

---

[117] [2010] UKUT 428 (AAC).
[118] [2013] UKUT 0505 (AAC).
[119] *CJSA/2034/2005*.

9.118   Representing your client at the hearing

If you represent the client be aware that the proceedings are less formal than most courts. You do not need to stand, nor should you present too formally. It is wise though to keep some separation between your examination in chief and your submissions, and to avoid giving evidence yourself. That said, lawyers are sometimes surprised at the extent to which the hearing of evidence can apparently intermingle with the making of submissions even at the Judge's behest, and you should not be troubled by this, nor believe that it means there is no structure.

9.119   If you cannot represent

In these circumstances you should consider preparing a skeleton argument of no more than 4-6 pages, in support of your client's case. This can be done in much the same way as you would write it for any other court, but bearing in mind that it must substitute for your attendance in person, not supplement it.

9.120   Case-law arguments

Even if (as is likely) none of the case-law supports precisely your client's circumstances, consider nevertheless producing cases in which the appellant succeeded on facts which bear some resemblance to your client's case. But do not make the mistake of arguing that the Tribunal Judge is bound by a given case where the facts are merely *similar*. S/he is patently not. Where judgments have produced an adverse result for the claimant in question, consider using those cases by distinguishing them convincingly. You should produce copies of the cases you wish to rely on, either in advance or on the day if they are few in number. Do not produce more than 3 or 4 judgments in any case. Most of the cases in this chapter can be found on one or other of the websites listed above at **9.6** above.

9.121   Checklist of issues to address in preparing the appeal

(a)   What is the DWP's/local authority's evidence?

(b)   Can its reliability be attacked?

(c)   What is the prima facie account of your client and of the alleged partner (and any other third parties)?

(d)   If proven, will this win the case?

(e)   Or are there points of law to be won as well?

(f)   How credible is your client's account?

(g)   What are its strengths and weaknesses?

(h)   Does it disclose internal inconsistencies?

(i)   Is it implausible? – examples include: sharing a bed at different times, never together; 'only one single instance of intercourse took place'; previous cohabitation has now changed completely though a single household is still shared. Address the implausibility.

(j) Are the client's and the alleged partner's accounts consistent with one another?

(k) Can the alleged partner assist? The importance of his/her witness evidence cannot be overstated. Very often this will be determinative.

(l) Was there an interview under caution? If so is its accuracy disputed at all by the interviewee (your client or the alleged partner)? What did your client concede in the interview?

(m) Can oral or witness statement evidence be corroborated with documentary evidence? Review for example Judge Wikeley's advice at para 43 et seq (cited above) of *CG v Secretary of State for Work and Pensions (IS)* [2011] UKUT 97 (AAC)?

(n) Have DWP and local authority collaborated on the investigation? If so is there inconsistency between either their arguments or their evidence?

9.122 Checklist of areas to cover in your arguments

Whether you are appearing in person for the client or not, you should make sure that the key areas of cohabitation law are addressed:

(i) The general relationship: describe its general 'flavour'.

(ii) Is there a shared household? Be clear as to where you stand on this but if arguing there is no shared household, prepare arguments in the alternative, which include minimising the household's importance.

(iii) Is there some reason (other than LTAMC) to explain the living together arrangement? Is anyone disabled, ill, mentally ill, vulnerable or dependent in some other way?

(iv) Does the claimant have any purpose, intention or motive as to the shared household that will help the case?

(v) Is there a sexual relationship? If not, what evidence can you adduce? If there is, how can you minimise its significance?

(vi) How stable is the relationship? How are you going to seek to define 'stability' for best advantage?

(vii) Are there children? What circumstances will diminish the adverse effect of this fact? Are the children the only reason the claimant and the alleged partner share a household?

(viii) What are the money arrangements in the relationship?

(ix) What evidence can the client give as to love, commitment, common purpose – or lack thereof?

(x) How do the claimant and the alleged partner lead separate lives?

(xi) If the relationship used to be one of cohabitation, marriage or civil partnership, why and how did it change?

CHAPTER 10

MISCELLANEOUS

PART A   LAW AND PRACTICE

10.1   Change of name[1]

A person can be called by whatever name he or she chooses.[2] No formalities are necessary, and a name can be acquired simply by habit and repute.[3] At some stage somebody is likely to require evidence of the change of name, and so it is usual practice to document a change of name by means of one of the more formal procedures, such as executing a deed or making a statutory declaration.[4] As far as children are concerned, where a residence order[5] or care order[6] is in force, nobody can cause the child to be known by a new surname without the leave of the court or the written consent of every person who has parental responsibility for the child.[7] Where a change of name deed is to be enrolled in the Central Office of the Supreme Court, the enrolment regulations distinguish between children who have attained the age of 16, and those who have not.[8] A child of 16 or over can either execute the deed poll himself or endorse his consent on the deed executed by his parent or guardian on his behalf.[9] Where a child is under 16 the deed poll must be executed by his parent or guardian, and the application for enrolment must be supported by an affidavit showing that the change of name is for the child's benefit.[10]

10.2   Contractual licence

A contractual licence is permission granted by the owner of property allowing another person to be on or in the property. The licence need not assume any particular form, and can be written or oral, but there must be an intention to

---

[1]   See, generally, Nasreen Pearce *Name-changing: A Practical Guide* (Fourmat Publishing, 1990).

[2]   Provided he does not do so for any fraudulent purpose or in order to deceive and inflict economic loss on another (*Du Boulay v Du Boulay* (1869) LR 2 PC 430; *Cowley v Cowley* [1901] AC 450).

[3]   *Dancer v Dancer* [1949] P 147.

[4]   Other methods include Notarial Instrument, Royal Licence, and even a private Act of Parliament.

[5]   Defined in CA 1989, s 8(1).

[6]   Defined in CA 1989, ss 31(11) and 105(1).

[7]   CA 1989, ss 13(1) and 33(7). And see **5.19**.

[8]   Enrolment of Deeds (Change of Name) Regulations 1983 (SI 1983/680), reg 8.

[9]   Ibid, reg 8(3).

[10]   Ibid, reg 8(5). See also *Practice Direction of 24 May 1976* [1977] 1 WLR 1065.

create legal relations, and there must also be consideration.[11] For several years, landlords used the device of the contractual licence as a means of circumventing the operation of the Rent Acts. This contrivance was defeated by the decision of the House of Lords in *Street v Mountford*.[12] At the end of his judgment in that case Lord Templeman stated[13] that: 'henceforth the courts which deal with these problems will, save in exceptional circumstances, only be concerned to inquire whether as a result of an agreement relating to residential accommodation the occupier is a lodger or a tenant'.

It is submitted that a cohabitant sharing residential accommodation with his or her partner is usually neither a lodger nor a tenant, and would presumably fall within that residual category of 'exceptional circumstances'. Where a licensee shares accommodation with the licensor in his or her only or principal home, the licence is an excluded licence for the purposes of the Protection from Eviction Act 1977.[14]

---

11   *Horrocks v Forray* [1976] 1 WLR 230 at 236.
12   [1985] AC 809.
13   Ibid at 827E.
14   Protection from Eviction Act 1977, s 3A(2) (inserted by the Housing Act 1988, s 31).

PART B   PRECEDENTS

10.3   Change of name deed: not intended for enrolment[15]

THIS CHANGE OF NAME DEED made on (*date*)

BY me (*forename(s) and new surname*) of (*address*) formerly known as (*forename(s) and old surname*)

WITNESS that:

1   I now completely renounce and abandon the use of my former surname (*old surname*).

2   I now adopt and assume the surname (*new surname*).

3   I ask and authorise all persons at all times to address, describe and identify me by using the surname (*new surname*).

4   From now onwards I will use and sign the name (*forename(s) and new surname*):
    (a)   in all deeds, documents, forms, records and other written instruments;
    (b)   in all actions and proceedings;
    (c)   in all dealings and transactions; and
    (d)   on all occasions.

SIGNED as a Deed by (*forename(s) and old surname*) in the presence of:

10.4   Contractual licence[16]

THIS LICENCE is made on (*date*)

BETWEEN 'the parties' (1) (*name 1*) of (*address*) ('*name 1*') and (2) (*name 2*) (also) of (*address*) ('*name 2*').

IT IS AGREED that:

1 Recitals

1.1   The parties (intend to) live together at (*address*) ('the property').

---

[15]   See, generally, Nasreen Pearce *Name-changing: A Practical Guide* (Fourmat Publishing, 1990). For enrolment in the Central Office of the Supreme Court, see the Enrolment of Deeds (Change of Name) Regulations 1983 (SI 1983/680).
A change of name deed is commonly referred to as a 'deed poll'. Historically, a deed was either 'indented' or 'poll'. A deed indented was made by more than one party; more than one copy was made; each copy was cut or indented so that its indentations corresponded with the indentations in the other copy or copies. A deed poll was made by only one party, and was 'polled' or cut evenly without any indentations. For a change of name deed made by a mother on behalf of her child, see **5.86** above.

[16]   See, generally, Jean Warburton *Sharing Residential Property* (Sweet & Maxwell, 1990) at pp 24—35.

1.2 The property is owned by (*name 1*) (and is mortgaged to (*lender*)).[17]

1.3 The parties intend that this licence will be legally binding on them.[18]

1.4 This licence is made in consideration of the mutual concessions it contains and for other good and valuable consideration, the sufficiency of which each of the parties acknowledges.[19]

2 Licence

(Name 1) allows (name 2) to:

2.1 live with (him)/(her) in the property; and

2.2 use (his)/(her) furniture and fittings in the property; and

2.3 use the garage, parking space and garden belonging to the property.

3 Payment

On the first day of each month (*name 2*) will pay to (*name 1*) the sum of £   , or such other sum as the parties may from time to time agree, as a contribution towards (his)/(her) living and accommodation expenses.

4 Terms and conditions

(Name 2) will:

4.1 keep the property reasonably clean and tidy;

4.2 not intentionally damage the property or any part of it or any furniture and fittings in it;

4.3 not remove any of the furniture and fittings from the property;

4.4 not allow anyone else to stay overnight in the property without first obtaining the consent of (*name 1*);

4.5 consent to the sale of the property by (*name 1*), (his)/(her) personal representatives, trustee in bankruptcy or mortgagee, and vacate the property before completion of the sale;

4.6 not do anything that may annoy or cause a nuisance to (*name 1*) or the owners or occupiers of the premises nearby; and

4.7 not do anything that could render the insurance on the property void or voidable or could result in an increase in the insurance premium.

5 Licence revocable without notice

(*Name 1*) can revoke this licence at any time without having to give notice to (*name 2*) in advance if (*name 2*):

---

[17] The mortgagee will probably require the licensee to execute a deed postponing his or her rights in the property and undertaking not to assert an overriding interest against the mortgagee (*Williams & Glyn's Bank v Boland* [1981] AC 487).

[18] *Horrocks v Forray* [1976] 1 WLR 230 at 236, per Megaw LJ.

[19] Ibid.

5.1 fails to pay (his)/(her) contribution towards (his)/(her) living and accommodation expenses when it is due; or

5.2 fails to comply with any of the terms and conditions of this licence.

6 Termination of licence

Subject to the above, this licence will come to an end when the first of the following events occurs:

6.1 the expiration of (one month's) written notice given by either party to the other; or

6.2 (*name 2*) vacates the property with the intention of never resuming residence in it; or

6.3 (two months) after (*name 1's*) death; or

6.4 when the property is sold.

7 The nature of this licence

(*Name 2*) acknowledges that:

7.1 this licence is not a lease;

7.2 this licence does not create any kind of tenancy;[20]

7.3 (he)/(she) has no exclusive right to occupy the property or any part of it;

7.4 (his)/(her) occupation of the property and use of its furniture and fittings will not give rise to joint ownership of the property or its furniture and fittings;

7.5 regardless of the contributions (he)/(she) makes towards (his)/(her) living and accommodation expenses (he)/(she) will not acquire any legal estate or beneficial interest in the property;

7.6 this licence is personal to (him)/(her) and cannot be transferred to anyone else; and

7.7 (he)/(she) understands the nature and effect of this licence and is entering into it freely and voluntarily after receiving legal advice on its provisions and implications.

SIGNED as a Deed by (*name 1*) in the presence of:

SIGNED as a Deed by (*name 2*) in the presence of:

10.5   Separation agreement

THIS SEPARATION AGREEMENT is made on (*date*)

---

[20] 'To consolidate a tenancy the occupier must be granted exclusive possession for a fixed periodic term certain in consideration of a premium or periodical payments' (*Street v Mountford* [1985] AC 809 at 818E, per Lord Templeman).

BETWEEN 'the parties' (1) (*name 1*) of (*address*) ('*name 1*') and (2) (*name 2*) of (*address*) ('*name 2*').

IT IS AGREED that:

1 Recitals

1.1 The parties lived together from (*date*) to (*date*).

1.2 The parties are now living apart.

1.3 The parties have (two) children, namely (*name 3*) who was born on (*date*) and (*name 4*) who was born on (*date*) ('the children').

1.4 Both of the parties have parental responsibility for the children.

1.5 The parties wish to effect an agreement which will dispose of any financial claims that either of them may have against the other and which will make provision for the future welfare and support of the children.

1.6 Each party has fully disclosed his or her financial situation to the other and each party is generally aware of the other's financial situation.

1.7 Each party is entering into this Agreement freely and voluntarily after receiving independent legal advice on its provisions and implications.

1.8 The parties intend that this Agreement will be legally binding on them.

2 Separation

The parties will (continue to) live separately and apart from each other.

3 Non-interference

Neither party will annoy or interfere with the other or his or her relatives, friends, colleagues or business contacts.

4 Confidentiality

Neither party will disclose, divulge or use to the detriment or disadvantage of the other any confidential information about the other's private life, family life, financial affairs or business interests which may have come to his or her knowledge during the course of their relationship, unless such disclosure is required in legal proceedings or for the purpose of making a maintenance assessment under the Child Support Act 1991 ('a maintenance assessment').

5 Children

5.1 The provisions of this Clause will at all times be subject to the ascertainable wishes and feelings of the children themselves, considered in the light of their respective ages and understanding.

5.2 The children will live with (*name 2*).

5.3 The children will be entitled to spend at least (two weekends) with (*name 1*) each month.

5.4 The children will be entitled to spend at least (two weeks) with (*name 1*) during the summer holidays each year.

5.5 The children will be entitled to spend Christmas Eve, Christmas Day and Boxing Day with (*name 1*) each alternate year.

5.6 The children will be entitled to maintain contact with (*name 1's*) parents, brothers and sisters.

5.7 All major decisions affecting the children's education, upbringing, health, welfare and the administration of their property will be made by the parties jointly.

5.8 Neither party will cause or allow the children to be known by a new surname or removed from the United Kingdom without the consent of the other party or the leave of the court.

5.9 Each party is responsible for maintaining the children.

5.10 From the date of this Agreement (*name 1*) will pay to (*name 2*) for the benefit of both of the children the sum of £   a month or such other sum as the parties may from time to time agree.

5.11 (*Name 1*) will continue to pay maintenance to (*name 2*) for the children's benefit in accordance with the terms of this Clause until a maintenance assessment takes effect or until such time as a maintenance assessment, if it had been made, would cease to have effect.

5.12 Regardless of the terms of this Clause, either party can at any time apply to the Child Support Agency for a maintenance assessment to be made in respect of either or both of the children.

6 Property

6.1 Within a period of (4) weeks from the date of this Agreement (*name 1*) will transfer to (*name 2*) (his)/(her) legal estate and beneficial interest in the property known as (*address*) ('the property') subject to the mortgage in favour of (*lender*).

6.2 (*Name 2*) will be responsible for the payment of the mortgage and all the other outgoings on the property.

6.3 (*Name 2*) will ensure that all future accounts relating to the outgoings are addressed to (him)/(her).

7 Personal chattels

7.1 The parties have already divided between them all of the personal chattels which formerly belonged to them jointly.

7.2 Each party is now the absolute owner of the personal chattels in his or her possession free from any claim, right or title of the other.

8 Debts

8.1 The parties have divided between them all the debts for which they are jointly and severally liable.

8.2 (*Name 1*) has assumed responsibility for the payment of the following debts:

(name and address of creditor)   (amount outstanding).

8.3 (*Name 2*) has assumed responsibility for the payment of the following debts:

(name and address of creditor)   (amount outstanding).

8.4 Each party promises to pay the debts for which he or she has assumed responsibility and will indemnify the other against all costs, claims, proceedings and demands arising in respect of those debts.

9 Conciliation

Any difference, disagreement or dispute arising out of or in connection with this Agreement will be referred in the first instance to the Family Conciliation Service without prejudice to the right of either party subsequently to apply to the court for adjudication or to the Child Support Agency for a maintenance assessment to be made or reviewed.

10 Variation

This Agreement can only be varied by an instrument in writing executed as a Deed by both parties.

SIGNED as a Deed by (*name 1*) in the presence of:

SIGNED as a Deed by (*name 2*) in the presence of:

10.6   Family Law Protocol: Part 12 Cohabitation

[The kind permission of the Law Society to reproduce the following material is gratefully acknowledged.]

> *Solicitors should keep under review at all times the availability of public funding and the need to provide clients with costs information at the outset and on a regular basis.*

12.1   Scope

12.1.1 English law does not yet recognise cohabitation as a defined legal status and so very few specific rights exist for cohabitants. This position is becoming untenable as increasing numbers of the population (1 in 6 of all couples according to the 2001 census) live together without marrying or, if same-sex, entering into a civil partnership. The problems they face on relationship breakdown are similar to those faced by couples who have married or who are civil partners.

12.1.2 The lack of a single statute to deal with cohabitants can make the task of resolving their problems particularly complex. The Law Commission has acknowledged this and proposed reform of this area of law in 2007

(*Cohabitation: The Financial Consequences of Relationship Breakdown* (Cm 7182)). However, the government announced that it would postpone action until it had studied research findings following the implementation of the earlier Family Law (Scotland) Act 2006, which had introduced some specific remedies for cohabitants in that jurisdiction, and so failed to support Lord Lester's Cohabitation Bill in the House of Lords in 2009. Meanwhile, a bill has been introduced in Eire which would, inter alia, have the effect of introducing similar remedies for cohabitants in that country (the Civil Partnership Bill 2009). There are, of course, remedies for cohabitants in many other jurisdictions. Solicitors should be alert to prospective changes to the law and the need to advise clients accordingly.

12.1.3 Much of the Protocol applies equally to cohabiting couples as to married couples or civil partners. See in particular, the approach contained in the Main Protocol (see Part 1) and also Parts 5 and 6 (relating to children), Part 4 (domestic abuse) and Part 2 (mediation/alternative dispute resolution).

12.1.4 It is primarily in the area of finances that the options available to cohabitants on relationship breakdown differ greatly from those available to spouses or civil partners. This section of the Protocol deals mainly with those financial claims which arise on cohabitation breakdown. The key point for solicitors to remember in this area is that there is usually no discretion for the court to adjust the interests of the parties in order to achieve a fair outcome. The most that the court can do is to declare and enforce their existing interests, applying established principles of trust and property law.

12.1.5 Solicitors must be aware that same-sex couples who register their relationship under the Civil Partnership Act 2004 acquire rights equivalent to those of married couples and should not be treated as cohabitants.

12.1.6 Solicitors should bear in mind that it may occasionally be necessary to ascertain the beneficial interests in property in the case of even a married couple or civil partners where there is a third-party claim against the interest of one of them, eg following bankruptcy or the making of a charging order, and that in such circumstances the procedure outlined in 12.4—12.5 would apply.

12.2 Advice at the commencement of or during cohabitation

12.2.1 Experience shows that most clients are completely unaware of their legal position when they cohabit and that they usually have misconceptions as to their rights. Clients may consult solicitors either at the start of their relationship or during it and solicitors should use such opportunities to explain to clients their legal position.

12.2.2 Clients may seek advice at the commencement of a relationship. If so, they should be encouraged to consider entering into a formal cohabitation agreement, if such an agreement would be beneficial to them. Solicitors should have access to appropriate precedents for cohabitation agreements at all times (model cohabitation agreements can be obtained from Resolution and from a number of other sources (see Appendix Aj).

Solicitors must advise clients that they can only act for one of the parties in drawing up such an agreement and that the other party must be separately represented.

12.2.3 Clients should be referred to the Advice Now website (see www.advicenow.org.uk/living-together) which is funded by the Ministry of Justice as part of its Living Together campaign. They may also wish to consider the 'Living Together Agreement' which is published on that website.

12.2.4 Clients will often consult solicitors when they are intending to purchase a property together. In such circumstances, careful consideration needs to be given as to how the property is to be held. Particular care is needed where the property is to be held in the name of only one of them or where they have made or are intending to make unequal contributions towards the purchase price. If legal title is to be held in their joint names, solicitors must discuss with them the implications of owning the property either as beneficial joint tenants or tenants in common and ascertain whether a declaration of trust is desirable and/or whether they wish to enter into a cohabitation agreement. To fail to give and record such advice in an appropriate case can lead to a claim for negligence.

12.2.5 Where cohabitants decide to prepare a declaration of trust at the time of purchase of a property, solicitors can act for both cohabitants in preparing the declaration only if it is clear that there is complete agreement from the outset as to all the terms of the declaration and there is no conflict of interest.

12.2.6 At all relevant times, solicitors should advise cohabitants about the importance of making wills, making pension and death-in-service benefit nominations, considering life assurance policies and the benefits of parental responsibility agreements. Solicitors should also advise as to what might occur in the event that these matters are not dealt with. Such advice should be recorded in writing.

12.2.7 Cohabitants should be warned that there is no equivalent to the spouse exemption for them on inheritance tax (IHT) and therefore that gifts made within seven years of death will attract IHT. At the time of the making of a will, estate planning should be discussed. Practitioners should advise clients of the effect of the ruling in *Holland v IRC* [2003] WTLR 207 which confirmed that the lack of spouse exemption from IHT for cohabitants is not in breach of the Human Rights Act 1998. Unless there is a change in the law there will be no tax relief on any gifts between cohabitants other than in the normal way. Note that since the Civil Partnership Act 2004, there has been a tax exemption for registered civil partners equivalent to the spouse exemption for married couples.

12.2.8 Solicitors are reminded that they may need to liaise with conveyancing practitioners or third parties who are involved in any existing wills, trusts or settlements. They should obtain letters of authority from their client where appropriate. Solicitors must avoid giving investment advice unless authorised to do so.

12.3 Advice following relationship breakdown

12.3.1 At the first meeting or early on in the case, solicitors should consider and advise, where appropriate, on all the matters referred to in Part 1. The sections relating to reconciliation and other support services apply equally to cohabitation.

12.3.2 The paragraphs relating to family dispute resolution, mediation and collaborative law in Part 2 are also equally applicable in cohabitation cases. Accordingly, solicitors must, at an early stage, unless it is clearly inappropriate to do so, explain the mediation process and advise clients on the benefits and/or limitations of mediation and/or collaborative law in their particular case as well as the role of solicitors in supporting the mediation process. The suitability of mediation should be kept under review throughout the case and clients should be referred to mediation when and where appropriate.

12.3.3 The rest of Part 1 will apply equally to cohabitation cases and should be referred to. It is important that solicitors screen appropriately for domestic abuse and consider whether there are any urgent issues to be dealt with.

12.3.4 Solicitors should check whether a client has made a will and, if so, consider with them whether it is still appropriate in the circumstances.

12.3.5 Solicitors should check how the property is held by obtaining office copies of the Land Registry title documentation. They should also consider obtaining a copy of the original conveyancing file relating to the property in question if, for example, there is likely to be any dispute as to original contributions or intentions at the date of purchase.

12.3.6 If the property is held as a joint tenancy, then consideration should be given to severing the joint tenancy and an appropriate notice prepared, signed by the client and served on the other property owner.

12.3.7 Solicitors should consider whether it is necessary to register a restriction at the Land Registry to protect a client's interest in a property. This is done by completion of Form RXI with a request for entry of a standard-form restriction, usually in Form A of Schedule A to the Land Registration Rules 2003, SI 2003/1417. Reference may be had to Land Registry Practice Guide 24: Private Trusts of Land (2009) (at www.landregistry.gov.uk). Provided that the application is clearly worded and shows how and why the client's beneficial interest arose, this will be accepted by the Land Registry as evidence that the client has 'sufficient interest'. It should be noted that the Land Registry will give the (other) registered owner of the land notice of the application and an opportunity to object. If a dispute is identified at this stage, the matter may be referred to the Land Registry Adjudicator for determination, although in practice the adjudicator will usually direct one or other of the parties to commence court proceedings within a specified time-frame.

12.3.8 Solicitors should consider whether to advise a client to contact the mortgage company to place a dispute indicator on their records in order to prevent one party from drawing down on the mortgage if there is any flexibility to do so.

12.3.9 In certain cases it may be appropriate to write and request that the other side consent to the mortgage being converted to interest-only whilst the issues are sorted out, or if one person is paying a lot more, write and put them on notice that they may expect credit by way of equitable accounting. For example, an application under the Children Act (CA) 1989, Schedule 1 would not provide for anything other than an interest-only mortgage, but if the father is meeting the mortgage on a repayment basis he is in effect adding to the mother's capital which is not permitted by Schedule 1.

12.3.10 Matters relating to children and the provision of information are equally applicable to cohabitation cases, although it is acknowledged that the availability of standard information for cohabitants is not as wide as for other family matters.

12.3.11 Under 1.5 of Part 1 it is important that solicitors should, at the end of the first meeting or at an early stage, outline the possible remedies that are available and the possible outcomes, as far as this is practical with the information available. It is important that clients are not given unrealistic expectations either of what can be achieved or of the time the matter may take to resolve.

12.3.12 Solicitors should advise clients that they might have claims in both property law and family law. Property law claims may be claims for a beneficial interest in a property by way of a resulting or constructive trust dealt with under the Trusts of Land and Appointment of Trustees Act (TLATA) 1996, or proprietary estoppel and/or equitable accounting. If a couple has children, a client may also have claims under CA 1989, Schedule 1 and the Child Support Act 1991 (as amended). In exceptional cases these can extend effectively to support of the parent as well as the child.

12.3.13 Solicitors need to bear in mind that practice and procedure for property law and family law claims are very different, the former being governed by the Civil Procedure Rules 1998 (CPR) as amended, the latter by the Family Proceedings Rules (FPR) 1991, SI 1991/1247 and the Family Proceedings Courts (Children Act 1989) Rules (FPCR) 1991, SI 1991/ 1395 as amended. This is a developing area of law (see for example the cases of *Stack v Dowden* [2007] UKHL 17 and *Kernott v Jones* [2010] EWCA Civ 578) and solicitors must ensure that they are aware of the latest case-law and confident in their knowledge before offering advice in this area.

12.3.14 When dealing with property claims of cohabiting couples, solicitors should also check to see if they were engaged. Provided that less than three years has elapsed since any engagement was broken off, an application could also be made under the Married Women's Property Act (MWPA) 1882 for a declaration in respect of property (which would include chattels).

12.3.15 Although in general, engaged couples are treated in the same way as unmarried couples, solicitors should be aware of the Law Reform (Miscellaneous Provisions) Act (LR(MP)A) 1970, s 3(1) relating to gifts between engaged couples and also the Matrimonial Proceedings and Property Act (MPPA) 1970, s 37 allowing an entitled applicant to argue that he has a share, or an increased share, in property by virtue of substantial contributions to the improvement of that property. In practice, MPPA 1970, s 37 is rarely relied upon because such works would usually now form the basis of a constructive trust or proprietary estoppel claim. They would, however, be family proceedings and FPR 1991 would apply.

12.3.16 There are similar provisions relating to those who were in an agreement to enter into a civil partnership which has been terminated within the last three years (Civil Partnership Act 2004, s 74) – see s 65 for the equivalent to MPPA 1970, s 37; s 66 for MWPA 1882; and s 74(5) for LR(MP)A 1970.

12.3.17 The above provisions are particularly useful in relation to property other than real property. Claims concerning real property are better dealt with under the TLATA 1996 as the court has a wider discretion and can, for example, delay sale.

12.3.18 Requirements for solicitors to provide costs information as outlined in the Main Protocol (see 1.8) apply equally to cohabitation cases. Clients should be advised realistically as to likely costs and solicitors should be aware that contested applications are significantly more expensive than, for example, comparable ancillary relief proceedings. In addition, significant civil court fees are payable on issue, on allocation, on listing and for trial.

12.3.19 Public funding may be available where the proceedings relate to the ownership or possession of the client's home (Legal Services Commission Manual, para.3C-014). Applications under TLATA 1996 are not 'family proceedings' within the meaning of the Courts and Legal Services Act 1990 and so they can be funded under a conditional fee agreement. If so, an appropriate funding notice must be served on the other party as any success fee would otherwise be unrecoverable under CPR, rule 44.3B(I)(c).

12.3.20 Clients should be advised that, unlike most other 'family' proceedings, the court is likely to make a costs order in favour of whichever party is considered to have 'won' the case – since under CPR, rule 44.3(2)(a) the general rule is that costs will follow the event.

12.3.21 The provisions within the Main Protocol as to communications with the other party (see 1.9) and the giving of notice of issue of proceedings (see 1.11) are both applicable to cohabitation cases.

12.3.22 Clients should be reminded at this early stage that cohabitation cases depend heavily on evidence. Consideration should be given as to how the case is to be pleaded and the evidence that will be necessary in order to prove that case. Witness statements should be taken from the client and any likely witnesses and clients should be advised of the necessity of keeping and producing relevant documentary evidence (eg bank statements, receipts and the like) as the case proceeds. Solicitors should seek to establish the strength of the client's case at this early stage and advise appropriately.

12.4   Prior to issuing proceedings for financial matters

Voluntary disclosure and ADR

12.4.1 Solicitors must consider and discuss the following with clients:
(1)   The importance of pre-application disclosure and negotiation. An application must not be issued when settlement is a reasonable prospect. Solicitors are referred to the Pre-Application Protocol for Ancillary Relief (see 11.5). Making an application to the court should not be regarded as a hostile step or a last resort but rather as a way of starting the court timetable, controlling disclosure and endeavouring to avoid the cost of final hearing.
(2)   The most appropriate form of dispute resolution for the case, based on clients' needs and individual circumstances, at an early stage. Solicitors must discuss alternative dispute resolution (ADR) with clients, except where it is inappropriate to do so, and advise on whether it is likely to be suitable to their case and, where appropriate, refer them to an appropriate individual (see Part 2).

Identifying the issues

12.4.2 Solicitors must seek to clarify the parties' claims and identify the issues between them as soon as possible. To achieve this the parties must provide, as soon as possible, a full, frank and clear disclosure of facts, information and documents which are material and sufficiently accurate to enable proper negotiations to take place in order to settle their differences. Openness in all dealings is essential.

Pre-action protocol

Civil Procedure Rules 1998, SI 1998/3132

12.4.3 Although there is no protocol specific to TLATA 1996 cases, solicitors (or parties where unrepresented) will be expected to comply with Annex A of the Practice Direction (Pre-Action Conduct) which applies to all types of civil cases and therefore to cohabitants in proceedings under TLATA 1996.

12.4.4 The common objectives of all the pre-action protocols are as follows:
(a)   to encourage the early and full exchange of information between the parties about any dispute between them which might need resolution by a court;
(b)   to enable the parties to avoid proceedings by agreeing a settlement of the claim before commencement of proceedings, either through

negotiation directly between them, with or without the assistance of a mediator if appropriate, or negotiation between the solicitors; and

(c)   to support the efficient management of proceedings where litigation cannot be avoided.

12.4.5   Under para A.2 of the Practice Direction, the court will expect the parties and their legal advisers to act reasonably in exchanging information and documents relevant to the claim and generally in trying to avoid the necessity for the commencement of proceedings (in accordance with the overriding objective and the matters referred to in CPR, rule 1.1(2)). In view of the nature of family proceedings, the parties and their representatives should act in a conciliatory and constructive manner at all times.

Pre-action procedure for Trusts of Land and Appointment of Trustees Act 1996 claims

12.4.6   For TLATA 1996 claims, solicitors (or unrepresented parties) should comply with the following key elements of pre-action procedure, if appropriate, unless there are very good reasons for not doing so. They should:

(1)   Send an initial letter (referred to in the CPR as a 'letter of claim') setting out the following information in concise form:
   (a)   a clear summary of uncontroversial facts;
   (b)   the main allegations of fact including, where appropriate, a summary of what was said by the parties at the time;
   (c)   an indication of the exact financial claim;
   (d)   indications as to witnesses and a summary of their evidence;
   (e)   disclosure of any relevant documents supporting the claim.
   Care should be exercised to ensure that the tone of the letter is non-threatening and sets out facts in a non-aggressive way. If addressed to a party who is not represented the letter must advise the party to seek legal advice and should enclose a second copy of the letter to facilitate this.

(2)   If possible and appropriate, refrain from issuing proceedings for six weeks, during which time full disclosure should be given and negotiations commenced.

(3)   If responding, give a preliminary reply within two weeks of receiving the initial letter of claim.

(4)   If responding, give a full reply within four weeks of receiving the letter of claim.

12.4.7   Preparation of the initial letter of claim will involve a substantial financial commitment from clients. Solicitors must give proper advice to ensure that the claim is framed in the correct way bearing in mind that the court will impose penalties if the case is later presented on a different basis.

12.4.8   Solicitors must consider and discuss with clients the fact that failure to comply with the pre-action protocol may lead to an order for indemnity costs and other financial penalties. CPR, rule 43.3(5)(a) requires the court to consider the conduct of the parties before, as well as during, the proceedings and in particular the extent to which the party has followed the relevant protocol. If no letter is sent, then this will usually be regarded as unreasonable conduct and indemnity costs will be awarded against the claimant.

12.4.9 Solicitors must consider with clients whether the immediate issue of proceedings is required in order to obtain protection of assets. An injunction can be sought to restrain the disposal of an asset pending final hearing. Reference should be made to CPR, Part 25.

12.4.10 If matters between the parties are concluded without the issue of court proceedings, the outcome should be recorded in a formal deed.

12.5 Issue and conduct of proceedings

12.5.1 Applications for an order under TLATA 1996, s.14 (usually brought under CPR, Part 8) will be issued on Form N208 with a claim form, a signed statement of truth and a witness statement from the claimant. They attract a court issue fee. The defendant has 14 days from receipt of the claim in which to file an acknowledgement of service and witness statement. In practice, 14 days will seldom be long enough and it would be usual to agree a voluntary extension.

12.5.2 Solicitors will be aware that the proceedings will offer only a declaration of an equitable interest in a property and a consequential order, for example an order for sale.

12.5.3 Solicitors should note that if there is to be a substantial question of fact or law raised within a case, eg a dispute as to whether a claimant has any beneficial interest in the property at all or as to the extent of that interest, it will be more appropriate to issue the proceedings under the CPR, Part 7 procedure with a claim in Form N201 supported by formal particulars of claim containing full details of the legal basis of the claim and remedies sought. Although a strict reading of CPR, rule 64.3 and PD 64A, para l(1)(a)(iii) suggests that Part 8 should be used for these applications, the court is unlikely in practice to raise any issue if the Part 7 procedure is used, particularly if the parties have agreed to its use. Claims commenced under Part 8 can be transferred to Part 7 at an early stage under CPR, rule 8.8 if the other party objects, or by the court itself under rule 8.1(3).

12.5.4 It should be noted that there are specific requirements for the contents of particulars of claim and reference should be made to CPR, rule 16.4 and para 7 of the accompanying Practice Direction.

12.5.5 In all cases, further consideration should be given to mediation as the court will agree to stay the proceedings for a fixed period to enable the parties to attempt to settle the action either by negotiation or another form of ADR.

12.5.6 Most applications under Part 7 will be allocated to the multi-track because they have a value of over £25,000 and/or the court considers that the trial will last longer than one day, as will usually be the case. Applications under Part 8 are automatically treated as allocated to the multi-track, although a specific allocation is usually sought if the parties wish to ensure that the route of appeal is to the Court of Appeal (which is not available if the case is merely 'treated as' allocated to that track).

12.5.7 Solicitors should be aware that most interlocutory hearings in civil cases take the form of a telephone hearing, and that it is usually the responsibility of the applicant/claimant to arrange these. BT Legal Conferencing can be contacted on 0800 028 4194 in order to arrange such a hearing.

12.5.8 Although FPR 1991 do not apply to these claims, many courts are prepared to direct that a case management conference be conducted as if it were a financial dispute resolution (FDR) appointment in an ancillary relief application and an appropriate direction should be sought at allocation stage.

12.6 Directions

12.6.1 Directions which the court might be asked to make are:

(a) that the case be listed for a directions appointment for the purpose of assessing the parties' positions and for the purpose of discussion and negotiation;

(b) that the parties serve signed witness statements in advance;

(c) that the parties file:

(1) details of all offers;

(2) a position statement;

(3) an agreed statement of issues;

(d) that the parties shall attend personally;

(e) that the appointment shall be conducted on a without prejudice basis;

(f) in the event that the proceedings are not settled at the hearing the district judge hearing the appointment should not make any orders or directions that the case shall be listed for a case management conference.

12.6.2 Note that the court should be asked to list the appointment with a realistic time estimate (at least one hour) and the parties asked to attend one hour prior to narrow the issues.

12.6.3 Clients should be encouraged to make a reasonable offer of settlement and in most cases the procedure under CPR, Part 36 should be followed. The recipient has 21 days in which to accept the offer. If the claimant fails to beat a Part 36 offer, then there are costs consequences.

12.6.4 Clients should be reminded that the trial of an application under TLATA 1996 takes place in open court, to which the public are admitted. Advocates will usually be robed.

12.6.5 Solicitors are advised to carefully consider the provisions of the CPR when undertaking an application under TLATA 1996, and if they feel that they are not sufficiently proficient in this area, should consider taking advice from a more experienced civil practitioner or transferring the file to another solicitor. Failure to comply with the CPR can lead to sanctions, including the automatic striking out of claims or defences at very short notice, if procedural steps are not taken in a timely fashion.

12.7 Claims under the Inheritance (Provision for Family and Dependants) Act 1975

12.7.1 Most firms distinguish between contentious probate work and claims under the Inheritance (Provision for Family and Dependants) Act (I(PFD)A) 1975. In some firms, I(PFD)A 1975 cases are dealt with by family lawyers.

12.7.2 Solicitors should not undertake without supervision any work which they know to be outside their area of expertise.

12.7.3 If a case appears complex or beyond the expertise of a practitioner they should consider whether the case should be passed to a member of the Association of Contentious Trust and Probate Specialists (ACTAPS). Solicitors are referred to the ACTAPS Practice Guidance Notes and Code of Conduct which can be found on the Association's website at www.actaps.com. Best practice pre-action procedures are contained in their Draft Pre-Action Protocol for the Resolution of Probate and Trust Disputes and failure to follow this Protocol can lead to costs penalties.

12.7.4 Solicitors must understand that claims brought under I(PFD)A 1975 are also governed by the CPR. In particular, CPR, rule 57.16 clearly requires that claims under I(PFD)A, s 1 be issued under CPR, Part 8, even though the Part 8 procedure is probably not appropriate if there are substantial disputed facts and the case is likely to be dealt with under Part 7.

12.7.5 Particular care needs to be taken as to the persons who are to be parties to the proceedings as it would be usual to have the personal representatives and the beneficiaries of the estate as separate defendants. Solicitors should note that personal representatives have no power to compromise a claim under the I(PFD)A 1975 unless the beneficiaries instruct them to settle the claim. Note also that if any beneficiary is a minor, then the approval of the court will be needed for any settlement.

12.7.6 Solicitors must note that the time limit for issuing a claim is six months from the date of the issue of the grant of representation, for example the date of the grant of probate.

12.7.7 In the case of *Re Parnall (Deceased)* [2003] All ER (D) 40 the court confirmed that it was not appropriate in I(PFD)A 1975 cases to seek to prevent a grant from being issued while negotiating a claim by entering caveat.

12.7.8 Instead, to be put on notice of the issuing of a grant in an estate a request should be made to the Probate Registry for a standing search. The fee is currently £5.00 and covers a period of six months. Successive periods can be covered by making additional applications. If in that period a grant is issued the Registry will send notification of the person who has extracted the grant and solicitors can obtain a copy of the grant. It will therefore be possible to issue a claim within the time limits of the grant.

12.7.9 In view of the time limit for issuing a claim, pre-issue negotiation is necessarily limited, but this may serve to focus the minds of those involved.

12.7.10 It is helpful to agree, wherever possible, that a directions hearing in an I(PFD)A 1975 case be treated similarly to an FDR hearing so that the judge gives an indication of his or her view of a case and an indication to the parties of the costs implications of continuing to a final hearing.

12.7.11 Solicitors requiring information on the subject of probate are referred to the Probate Practitioner's Handbook (6th edn, Law Society, 2010) which deals with both contentious probate and I(PFD)A 1975 claims.

12.7.12 Solicitors are reminded that the same civil costs rules apply to claims under I(PFD)A 1975 as to those under TLATA 1996.

12.8 Financial issues relating to children

12.8.1 Solicitors are referred to Part 5 for guidance on acting in private children law cases, Part 9 for claims under CA 1989, Sch 1 and Part S for general child support issues (i.e. the Child Maintenance and Enforcement Commission (CMEC)).

12.9 Jurisdiction and in which court to commence proceedings

12.9.1 Before proceedings relating to disputes about property, money, other belongings and children are issued, solicitors must consider carefully where they should issue the application. Where proceedings about different issues are being conducted in relation to the same couple, all proceedings must, where possible, be heard in the same court. If there are applications under TLATA 1996 and under CA 1989 they should be consolidated and heard together (*W v W (Joinder of Trusts of Land Act and Children Act Applications)* [2004] 2 FLR 321).

12.9.2 The county court has unlimited jurisdiction under TLATA 1996 although the application must be issued in the appropriate court for the area in which the defendant resides or in which the property is situated. The Principal Registry of the Family Division, which sits as a county court, has full jurisdiction to deal with applications under TLATA 1996, s 14 and such claims can be issued out of the Principal Registry (see CPR, PD 2B, para 3.2 and *Practice Direction (Family Division: Allocation of Cases: Costs)* [1999] 3 All ER 192).

12.9.3 Claims can be issued out of any District Registry of the High Court. Solicitors should be aware that proceedings may not be started in the High Court unless the value of the claim is more than £25,000 (CPR, PD 7A, para 2.1). Subject to that limitation, if the financial value of the claim, the amount in dispute and/or the complexity of the facts, legal issues, remedies or procedures involved and/or the importance of the outcome of the claim to the public in general are such that solicitors believe that the claim ought to be dealt with by a High Court judge, then the case should be issued in the High Court. In any event, a claim with a value of less than £50,000 will generally be transferred to the county court (CPR, PD 29, para 2.2).

12.9.4 Claims may be issued in either the Family Division or Chancery. The Family Division is likely to be the more appropriate where the parties were living together as a family unit, particularly if they have children or if there are to be linked family claims. The latter may be more appropriate if their relationship was more business-like.

INDEX

References are to paragraph numbers.